A NEW LOOK AT
SEGOVIA
HIS LIFE ◆ HIS MUSIC

A CD recording is available which serves to demonstrate the technical and interpretive solutions discussed throughout the analysis section of this book. It also serves to demonstrate the modern editions presented in Appendix B. The publisher strongly recommends the use of this recording along with the text to insure accuracy and ease of learning.

by *Graham Wade & Gerard Garno*

VOLUME ONE
A Biography of the Years 1893-1957
Segovia's Classical Guitar Masterpieces by Narváez, Frescobaldi, Bach, Scarlatti and Sor

TABLE OF CONTENTS

PART II: A New Look at the Segovia Repertoire—An Analysis of Segovia's Narváez, Fescobaldi, Bach, Scarlatti and Sor Editions, by Gerard Garno 195

This book is dedicated to the memory of the most outstanding classical guitarist of the 20th century:

ANDRÉS SEGOVIA

(1893-1987)

PREFACE

The two volumes in this series were written to explore and evaluate the achievements of Andrés Segovia (1893-1987). Thus each book presents itself in two parts—1.) a new look at Segovia's life seen through a musical biography chronicling the guitarist's career as recitalist, recording artist, editor, and teacher, and 2.) a new look at Segovia's repertoire as seen through an analysis which documents his editorial procedures and interpretive concepts.

Writing about Segovia is never easy. His giant personality dominated the lives of all classical guitarists for so many years, and during that time concert performers and teachers fixed their attention constantly on Segovia's musical and technical prowess, his editions, and his recordings. He was the founding father of the guitar in the twentieth century, bringing together all previous traditions, creating a new technique and a new sound quality. For decades Segovia set the standards and the pace. How do we come to terms with such achievements?

What seemed essential in the musical biography section was the chronicling of the most significant information about his amazing career. The younger generation (and even some of those not so young), may not be aware how enormous and prolonged his contribution was. It is time to remind ourselves of the facts of his progress over the years of this century.

At the same time that we survey the broad scope of Segovia's activities, we have tried to provide a close look at the stylistic features of his artistry. This has been accomplished through an analysis of some of Segovia's favorite works that still appear to be in great demand. In the second section of each book we will take a new look at the Segovia repertoire, first offered to the public many decades ago. By analyzing Segovia's editions and comparing them to the original scores, as well as present day concepts of scholarship and performance practice, it is hoped that fresh insights can be offered to new generations of guitarists.

We would like to thank William Bay, Vice President of Mel Bay Publications, for his patience and forbearance during the writing of these books, as well as for his unflagging enthusiasm and support at all stages. Without his invaluable help and advice this project would not have been possible.

Graham Wade
Gerard Garno

April, 1996

ABOUT THE AUTHORS

Graham Wade

Graham Wade is Head of the School of Strings and Professor of Classical Guitar at the City of Leeds College of Music, England and Guitar Tutor for the Universities of Leeds and York. He has been guest lecturer at Summer Schools all over the world including the Segovia Master Course at the University of Southern California in 1986.

His previous books include: *Traditions of the Classical Guitar; Segovia—A Celebration of the Man and His Music; Maestro Segovia; Joaquín Rodrigo—Concierto de Aranjuez; The Guitarist's Guide to Bach; Your Book of the Guitar; The Shape of Music; A Guitar Method* in Two Volumes. From 1990 to 1994 he was Editor of the European Guitar Teachers' Association (UK) *Guitar Journal.* He is a contributor to *The New Grove Dictionary of Music and Musicians.* Over the years he has written for a variety of periodicals including *Soundboard, Guitar Review, Classical Guitar, Guitar International, BMG, Guitar News, The Strad, Musical Times, The Times,* etc. He has prepared program notes for concert tours of eminent guitarists such as Andrés Segovia and Julian Bream and liner notes for a number of recording artists.

He has given recitals in various countries including Spain, Canada, Holland, Norway, Sweden, Kuwait, Hong Kong and New Zealand. Several original guitar works have been dedicated to him including four Guitar Concertos which he has premiered. His travels and researches have taken him to China, India, Mongolia, Cuba, Russia, Siberia, the USA, North Africa, the Middle East and Australia, as well as to many European countries.

Graham Wade

Graham Wade, Andrés Segovia and his son, Andrés Jr. at the Westbury Hotel, London, 1985.

Gerard Garno

Gerard Garno began serious study of the guitar at age 11. Shortly thereafter, he heard the recordings of Andrés Segovia and was inspired to pursue exclusive study of the classical guitar. He studied with Segovia disciple Ken Hummer until he began his university training at the age of 18.

Gerard received his college education at the Cincinnati Conservatory of Music with Professor Clare Callahan, a student of Segovia. He graduated from that institution *Magna Cum Laude* in 1988.

During his college years, Garno continued to develop his appreciation of the Segovia heritage as he studied with Oscar Ghiglia and Eliot Fisk, also students of Segovia, during Summer courses at the Aspen Music School.

In 1983 Gerard was accepted to study with one of Segovia's most successful students, Christopher Parkening, at a three day master class held at Messiah College in Grantham, Pennsylvania. This was to be the first of several master classes that Garno participated in with Parkening over the next few years. He was selected to be a part of a group of students from that class who performed a special recital. After the concert, master class organizer David Stafford wrote that Gerard's performance "...really turned the audience on and helped make it possibly the best student recital that Chris has had in a master class." Parkening issued a promotional statement on Gerard's behalf in 1988 which said that Garno was a "...gifted young player."

Gerard Garno

Garno is the first-prize winner of the 1981 Society of American Musicians National Competition, a prize winner in the 1983 Music Teachers National Association Competition, first-prize winner of the 1984 Society of American Musicians National Competition, first-prize winner of the 1986 American String Teachers Association National Competition, and was a finalist in the 1987 Toronto International Guitar Competition.

Since the time of his graduation from the Cincinnati Conservatory in 1988, he has made his living as a full time concert artist, touring extensively in the United States and Canada. Garno resides in Toledo, Ohio, with his wife and six children. In addition to his work in the field of music, he is currently pursuing a career in law. He has written several books for Mel Bay Publications and has also made over a dozen recordings, including the following CD's demonstrating the modern editions of the Segovia repertoire presented here in Appendix B of Volume One and Two (available through Mel Bay Publications):

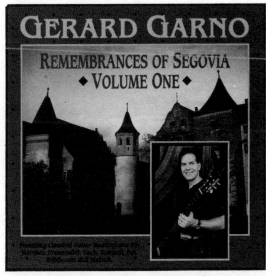

Featuring Classical Guitar Masterpieces by: Narváez, Frescobaldi, Bach, Scarlatti, Sor, Beethoven and Malotte.

Featuring Spanish Guitar Masterpieces by: Tárrega, Alard, Malats, Albéniz, Granados, Llobet, Ponce, Barrios and Villa-Lobos.

ACKNOWLEDGEMENTS

Graham Wade

My first debt is to Andrés Segovia, who encouraged me in the writing of two previous books about him and offered guidance and friendship in unstinting measure.

My second debt is to Alberto López Poveda of the Segovia Museo, Linares, Spain, for his great generosity in providing information from his vast archives and unique knowledge of Segovia's life.

In researching the early decades Andrés Segovia's autobiography is one of the central texts. But for the period between 1923 and 1948, the primary published source for information is Miguel Alcázar's edition of The Segovia-Ponce Letters (trans. Peter Segal), published by Editions Orphée, Inc., Columbus. All guitarists wishing to understand Segovia's progress during these years should give this book their closest attention. In this context I am also indebted to Matanya Ophee, publisher of The Segovia-Ponce Letters, who has in the past pointed out my more blatant errors and helped me some way towards a more rigorous awareness of guitar history.

The researches of Corazón Otero on Castelnuovo-Tedesco and Ponce, and Richard Stover on Barrios, have proved invaluable and to their scholarship this book is deeply indebted.

Special thanks to Maurice Summerfield and Colin Cooper of Classical Guitar, Ashley Mark Publishing Company, Newcastle-upon-Tyne, England. From February, 1993, until July 1994, I contributed an article each month to Classical Guitar, about Segovia's career, and through this series the invitation came from William Bay to write a book in co-authorship with Gerard Garno.

I must express profound gratitude to Julian Bream, for his invaluable wisdom on Segovia matters over the years, and for specific information such as details of the Guitar Competition of 1956.

To John W. Duarte, a particular vote of thanks. His long friendship with Segovia between 1947 and 1987 established him as a unique source of information on all aspects of Segovia's career. Over the decades his prolific writings formulated a vital critical response to the Maestro's art and to such a perceptive and sustained oeuvre we acknowledge a great debt.

Catherine Dickinson and Andrew Liepins of the Spanish Guitar Centre, Nottingham, have provided innumerable editions, as well as information and access to their own archives, and, as always, helped in the acquisition of various texts. I thank them with deep appreciation.

I would like to thank John Mills, whose perennial enthusiasm for Segovian ideals and repertoire has been so precious and supportive over many years.

My gratitude is due to Professor Wolfgang Jungwirth, of the Brucknerkonservatorium, Linz, Austria, for providing some remarkable historic programs from the archives of Robert Treml.

I must thank Peter Houghton for the gift, almost thirty years ago, of his invaluable collection of Guitar News, Harvey Turnbull for providing me with a complete set of Soundboard, and Alec Warman for permitting me to acquire a fine run of B.M.G. magazines covering essential decades.

Many other people have helped with obtaining all kinds of published material about Segovia, as well as offering advice, guidance, information and inspiration. My sincere gratitude to the following who have contributed in some essential way to the writing of this book and my apologies to any unintentionally omitted: Carlos Bonell, Arnie Brown, Manuel Orozco Diaz, Oscar Ghiglia, Ian Gibson, Angelo Gilardino, Ivor Mairants, Jorge Morel, Eusebio Rioja, José Romanillos, Turibio Santos, James Smith, Pieter van der Staak, and Gerta Zelt.

I would like to express my gratitude to Anna Eker, my mother-in-law, for her translations of various passages from German texts.

For the use of copyright material I gratefully acknowledge the courteous permission of the following: Bold Strummer, Westport; Bolton Evening News; Marion Boyars Ltd., London; John Calder Publications Ltd., London; Cambridge Evening News; Chanterelle, Heidelberg; Chicago Sun-Times; Chicago Tribune; Classical Guitar, Newcastle-upon-Tyne; Daily Express, London; Daily Telegraph, London; Dover Publications, Mineola, NY; EGTA (UK) Guitar Journal; Faber, London; Victor Gollancz/Cassell, London; The Guardian, London; Gloucestershire Echo, Cheltenham; The Gramophone, Harrow; Guitar Solo Publications, San Francisco; Guitar Review, New York; Harper Collins, London; Little, Brown & Co., Boston & London; Latin American Literary Review Press, Pittsburgh; Louisiana State University Press; Macmillan, London; The Observer, London; Oxford University Press; Penguin, Middlesex; Seattle Post-Intelligencer; Simon & Schuster, New York; Soundboard; The Times, London; Walker & Co., New York; Yorkshire Post, Leeds.

Any copyrighted source inadvertently omitted from these acknowledgements will of course be included in future editions.

I would like to express my sincere thanks to William Bay for making this project possible, and to my co-author, Gerard Garno, for inviting me to participate in the book.

Finally, I must express my deepest gratitude to my wife, Elizabeth, who has worked many hours in arduous editorial duties and provided her whole-hearted support in every way.

Gerard Garno

I would like to say thank you to the following people who contributed significantly to this project. These people responded enthusiastically to my requests for help by sending valuable information, scores and photographs. Some of them knew and/or studied with Segovia and possess an intimate knowledge of his repertoire. Their help was especially critical to the success of this project: Emilita Segovia, Christopher Parkening, Eliot Fisk, Michael Lorimer, Carlos Bonell, Miguel Alcazár, Corazon Otero, Ron Purcell, David Grimes, Michael MacMeeken, Brian Jeffery, Manuel López Ramos, Patrick Russ, Maria Cerda, Juan Helguera, Dr. William Paden and Dr. Marielle McNamara.

I would also like to thank the following librarians: Rebecca Willingham, Librarian at the University of Cincinnati Music Library and Mr. Calvin Eliker, Librarian at the University of Michigan Music Library. Also, a special thank you to the inter-library loan staff at the University of Cincinnati.

A very special thank you goes to the following people:

To Mr. William Bay. It was his initiative and subsequent support that made these books possible.

To Ken Hummer, my first classical guitar teacher. Ken is currently the guitar instructor at Lourdes College in Sylvania, Ohio. As well as being an excellent guitarist, teacher, composer and arranger, he is also fluent in Spanish and was able to help greatly with the many Spanish translations that are included throughout Part II and the appendices of these two volumes. I also thank him for helping with the final proof reading.

To Clare Callahan, who introduced me to much of the information that was used in the preparation of these books through her classical guitar program at the University of Cincinnati. She helped me to learn the guitar skills necessary for this project. Under her expert guidance I was also taught to love and appreciate scholarship. Clare spent a significant amount of time proofing and editing these manuscripts and gave much valuable advice. For this I am truly grateful.

To Graham Wade, co-author of these books. Graham was a tremendous help and support throughout the time that it took to complete this project. His great wisdom and experience proved invaluable, and it was an honor to work with such a fine scholar.

To Elizabeth Wade, Graham Wade's wife. She spent considerable time scrutinizing these books, thoroughly proofing the text manuscript.

To Mr. Russel Brazzel, who did the proofing of the text and musical manuscript for both volumes. Russel is a guitar teacher on the faculty of Millikin University in Decatur, Illinois, and has an excellent knowledge of Segovia and his repertoire. As well as being responsible for the quality control of these books, he was able to offer much constructive criticism as the project developed.

To Mr. Matanya Ophee, president of Editions Orphée in Columbus, Ohio. While not endorsing this project, Mr. Ophee was helpful in allowing me to cite and use materials he has written and collected over the years. I also thank him for all of his input and constructive criticism.

To Laurie Watermann and the rest of the production department at Mel Bay Publications. Many months of arduous effort were required from these people to produce the two large volumes in this series. I thank them for all of their patient hard work.

To the copyright and photograph departments at the Library of Congress in Washington, D.C. Much needed material and information was provided by this national archive, and I especially thank these departments for their kind cooperation.

To Dr. Clifford Davidson, a classical guitar enthusiast that I met while on tour. Dr. Davidson made a generous contribution that helped make these books possible. I also appreciate the helpful suggestions he was able to offer after reading the text.

To my wife Laura, for her help with the design, layout and proofing of these books. Her constant love and support was critical during the long and difficult time of writing and preparation that this project required.

I would also like to thank God for providing the grace, inspiration and strength necessary to complete this project on top of my already strenuous activities as a husband, father and full-time concert artist.

I would like to thank and acknowledge the following for the use of copyrighted material as it appears in citations throughout these books: Editions Orphée, Columbus; Tecla Editions, Penderyn; Editorial Nañduti, Asunción; Chanterelle Editions Ltd., Heidelberg; The Toledo Blade; Detroit Free Press; USA Today; Chicago Maroon; Journal of Commerce; Guitar Review, New York; Classical Guitar Magazine, Newcastle-upon-Tyne; W.W. Norton & Company, New York; The Belknap Press of Harvard University Press, Cambridge; Schirmer Books, New York; Early Music, Oxford; René Kister, Geneva; MCA Records, Universal City; Valparaiso University Press, Valparaiso; Summy-Birchard Music, Secaucus; Hutchinson & Co. Ltd., Portsmouth; Princeton University Press, Princeton; Faber and Faber Limited, Winchester; Novello and Co., Ltd., London; American Music Teacher; The Macmillan Co., New York; Harwood Academic Publishers, Newark; Gerald Duckworth & Co., Ltd., London; William Morrow and Company, New York; American String Teacher, Cincinnati; Musical New Services Limited, Denmark; Peter E. Segal, University Microfilms, Ann Arbor; Ediciones Musicales Yolotl, Mexico City; Fingerstyle Guitar, Colorado Springs; Cassell and Company Ltd, London and King's Crown Press, New York.

COPYRIGHT & PHOTO ACKNOWLEDGEMENTS

COPYRIGHTED MUSIC

Copyrighted music appears in this volume from the following sources by kind permission of the publishers:

Frescobaldi: ***Aria con Variazione detta "La Frescobalda."***
> Transcription by Andrés Segovia. Copyright B. Schott's Soehne, Mainz, 1939. Copyright renewed. All rights reserved. Used by permission of European American Music Distributors Corporation, sole U.S. and Canadian agent for B. Schott's Soehne, Mainz.

J. S. Bach: ***Andante-Bourrée-Double,*** Volume III.
> Transcription by Andrés Segovia. Copyright B. Schott's Soehne, Mainz, 1928. Copyright renewed. All rights reserved. Used by permission of European American Music Distributors Corporation, sole U.S. and Canadian agent for B. Schott's Soehne, Mainz.

J. S. Bach: ***Prelude.***
> Transcription by Andrés Segovia. Copyright B. Schott's Soehne, Mainz, 1928. Copyright renewed. All rights reserved. Used by permission of European American Music Distributors Corporation, sole U.S. and Canadian agent for B. Schott's Soehne, Mainz.

J. S. Bach: ***Sarabande.***
> Transcription by Andrés Segovia. Copyright by Union Musical Española, 1930. All rights reserved. Reprinted by permission of Music Sales Corporation on behalf of Union Musical Ediciones.

Scarlatti: ***Sonata*** e-moll.
> Transcription by Andrés Segovia. Copyright B. Schott's Soehne, Mainz, 1954. Copyright renewed. All rights reserved. Used by permission of European American Music Distributors Corporation, sole U.S. and Canadian agent for B. Schott's Soehne, Mainz.

Sor: ***Variations on a Theme from "The Magic Flute."***
> Fingering by Andrés Segovia. Copyright B. Schott's Soehne, Mainz, 1931. Copyright renewed. All rights reserved. Used by permission of European American Music Distributors Corporation, sole U.S. and Canadian agent for B. Schott's Soehne, Mainz.

PHOTO CREDITS:

Courtesy of Graham Wade: 94, 222, 232, 264, 268, 281, 312, 321, 329, 351, 360, 363.

Courtesy of EMI: cover.

Courtesy of Christopher Parkening: 213, 245, 273, 289, 385.

Courtesy of Clare Callahan: 30, 161, 298, 338, 377.

Courtesy of Ibbs and Tillet Ltd.: 1.

Courtesy of Library of Congress: 123, 260, 334, 349, 369.

Courtesy of White House Photo Office: 202.

INTRODUCTION

by Gerard Garno

In 1992 I proposed to Mr. William Bay, Vice President of Mel Bay Publications, the idea of a scholarly musicological work that would examine the life, style and editions of Andrés Segovia. My idea was to make use of the tremendous advances that have been made in the areas of technology and musicology to analyze, critique and preserve for future generations the important aspects of Segovia's life and work. It was also my goal to illuminate Segovia's editorial thought process as well as his artistic identity. Mr. Bay received the idea with enthusiasm and asked me to start on the project immediately.

Both Mr. Bay and I were aware of the efforts of the brilliant scholar from England, Graham Wade. His books and articles on Segovia, as well as the maestro's choice of him as writer uniquely qualified him to join in this project. We contacted him and he graciously agreed to contribute the musical biography section of this book. While Segovia was alive, he had asked Graham *not* to write his biography because he had intended to write his own complete autobiography eventually (Segovia published an autobiography of the years 1893-1920 in 1976).[1] Unfortunately, Segovia died before he was able to achieve this goal. Graham Wade fills a void for us by providing an insightful *new look* at the life of this important guitar master.

Bill Bay, Graham Wade and I were all in agreement that it was time for the production of a scholarly modern edition of those pieces that had become the most beloved to Segovia and, indeed, to the rest of the world through his worldwide concert career that spanned an amazing 78 years (1909-1987). These have been prepared with the information presented in our analysis and appear in Appendix B.

These two volumes strive to present a comprehensive and authoritative analysis of a major portion of the Segovia repertoire. The pieces being examined were the favorite works of Andrés Segovia as shown by his constant references and continual selection of them as concert solos. They are also the pieces that have become favorites of other guitarists, as well as the general public, and comprise a "greatest hits of the classical guitar" list. They will, no doubt, continue to be a significant part of the standard guitar repertoire. All serious students of the classical guitar will probably want to study and perform these works to one degree or another. This fact emphasizes the importance of having an extensive analysis of Segovia's treatment, as well as the suggestion of alternatives based on the most current scholarship. All this is given here along with many relevant sources which are cited throughout, and an attempt is made to arrive at valid conclusions. A copy of the composers' original scores are provided in Appendix A and a set of modern editions forming a conclusion to our study are presented in Appendix B. The practical value of including all of these materials is that, along with the analysis, they may serve to provide a foundation for guitarists to use when preparing their own editions for performance. They are intended to supplement the study of Segovia in a historical context.[2]

Segovia's editions are masterful records of an artist's response to the scores available as well as the aesthetic spirit prevailing during much of his career. They stand as unique historical works just as those of Kreisler and Busoni do. They represent the *Zeitgeist* of the late Romantic era that was dominated by figures such as Pablo de Sarasate, Mischa Elman and Fritz Kreisler on the violin, Pablo Casals on the cello, Enrico Caruso and Nellie Melba with their voices, Leopold Godowsky and Enrique Granados on the piano and Francisco Tárrega and Miguel Llobet on the guitar.[3] His editions are not to be improved upon, but the compositions themselves can be looked at in different ways. Musicology has unearthed

1. Andrés Segovia, *Segovia: An Autobiography of the Years 1893-1920,* New York, Macmillan Publishers, 1976.

2. In other words, all of the information given in this book, including the appendixes, are included to be a service to guitarists in the pursuit of their own scholarship and creativity. Segovia's fingerings and interpretations are documented and guitarists can use these exclusively if they choose to. Or, guitarists may choose to use only the scores given in Appendix A and B. However, all are encouraged to use the available resources as tools to help express their individual convictions. This is exactly what Segovia did, including those times when he played editions made by other guitarists (those by Tárrega and Llobet, for example).

3. Segovia is a great product of the Romantic Era. His interpretations of nationalistic Spanish/Romantic pieces are prime examples for guitarists to look to.

new information about many of these works and it would be fascinating to see what Segovia would do with all of this.[4] All we can do is provide it and let the reader make choices.

In doing this analysis the intent was not to reject everything that Segovia did. It was, rather, to understand, learn from and appreciate what he did while providing other relevant information. The editorial view taken here is this: Segovia's way of fingering, quality of sound, general approach to interpretation, choice of repertoire and approach to editing all set standards for excellence on the modern classical guitar. However, there is always room for differences in the *application* of standards to specific details, based on new historical scholarship and personal preference. The second section of this book is an effort to take a *new look* at the Segovia repertoire with these considerations in mind. My intention in writing this section of the book was to honor the work of the maestro and the composers while seeking a practical modern approach to these compositions that Segovia made popular.[5]

The scope of this project is enormous, and therefore it was decided that two volumes would be necessary to properly present the material. The first volume is devoted to the years 1893-1957 and to Segovia's Renaissance, Baroque and Classical masterpieces by Narváez, Frescobaldi, Bach, Scarlatti and Sor.[6] The second is devoted the years 1958-1987 and to his Spanish/Romantic and Contemporary/Neo-Classical masterpieces by Tárrega, Albéniz, Granados, Llobet and Ponce.[7]

THE SEGOVIA STYLE

Throughout the second section of this book we will closely examine the Segovia style. It is obvious that Segovia played everything in a way that left the music stamped with his own individuality. What are the elements that most characterized this style? After scrutinizing Segovia's published and recorded work, it has been determined that there are eight essential elements.[8] They are:

1. A horizontal approach to fingering. In the mid-nineteenth century, the luthier Antonio Torres (1817-1892) developed some of the major structural characteristics of the modern classical guitar. He emphasized the soundboard or front of the guitar as one of the most important factors in tone production. This helped him to perfect the use of fan-bracing underneath the top. He also established the fingerboard width at a minimum of five centimeters and standardized the vibrating string length at sixty-five centimeters. All of his innovations allowed the guitar to produce a richer sound, greater volume and a more balanced tonal response.[9] Thus, the expressive potential of the guitar was very much increased, and this new reservoir seems to have been first tapped by Francisco Tárrega (1852-1909). He greatly exploited the higher positions of this improved form of guitar with its expanded vibrating string length. This led to what we may call a horizontal approach to fingering. The name is appropriate because what results is a tendency toward movement up and down individual strings to use higher positions as opposed to vertical movement across all strings within a given position. Overall, he emphasized a type of fingering which is sensitive to the coloristic capacity and vibrato potential of each string.

---

4. Obviously some of this information was available during Segovia's lifetime. Still, much of it was *not* available during the years when he was maturing as an artist and preparing most of his editions.

5. Respected concert artist Eliot Fisk stresses the importance of understanding Segovia's approach when studying pieces from his repertoire: "We don't have to copy everything that Segovia did, but understanding his approach does give us an invaluable insight..." (Eliot Fisk, "A Problem in Perspective," presented in *Guitar Review,* Fall 1987, pp. 9-11).

6. For the sake of simplicity, we have grouped these under the broad general category of "Classical" on our title pages.

7. For our title pages these will simply be grouped under the broad general category of "Spanish." This title is certainly appropriate for Tárrega, Albéniz and Llobet. Regarding Ponce, it should be pointed out that while he is not actually from Spain, he is from Mexico, the country that the respected Latin American musicologist Gerard Béhague calls "New Spain." Ponce's primary interest was the obviously Hispanic Mexican folk music, and his motivic ideas, even in his contemporary and neo-classical works were influenced by this. Therefore, he is being included in the Spanish category as well. See: Gerard Béhague, *Music in Latin America,* Englewood Cliffs, New Jersey, Prentice-Hall, Inc., 1979, pp. 124-129.

8. For an excellent and much more detailed examination of the Segovia style see: Charles Duncan, *The Art of Classical Guitar Playing,* Princeton, N.J., Summy-Birchard Music, 1980. While this book is very comprehensive, there is a conspicuous silence regarding the *glissando,* which is a major element in the Segovia style. It is also somewhat dated. For example, it advocates the use of the footstool only, whereas many other inventions (such as the popular A-Frame support) are now in use that accomplish the same thing while leaving the body in a more natural posture.

9. Harvey Turnbull, *The Guitar from the Renaissance to the Present Day,* New York, Charles Scribner's Sons, 1974, pp. 77-79. The view that all of the innovations of the modern guitar can all be attributed to Torres has been refuted by Matanya Ophee. He presents some interesting evidence and suggests that Torres "...simply made a better guitar, by using the best ideas that he could garner from his predecessors." See: Matanya Ophee, "Historical Research, A Guest Essay," presented in *Guitarra* magazine, July-August 1980, Issue No. 39, pp. 13-15.

Segovia developed this approach into a refined art form. His fingerings represent a unique aspect of guitar orchestration and expression. This approach is respected and maintained here as much as possible.

2. Vibrato. Vibrato appears to have originated as a vocal technique. Indeed, it seems to be such an innate part of the singing voice that an effort is required from vocalists who try to sing without it.[10] Vocalists describe it as "a tonal oscillation above and below a mean pitch that imparts vitality, buoyancy and harmonic richness to vocalized sounds."[11] It is often stated that instrumentalists have the singing voice as their melodic ideal. Segovia was a strict follower of this philosophy, and he advocated the singing of the music that guitarists play to get the feel for the natural quality of the line.[12] It is therefore understandable that vibrato should be one of the basic elements of the Segovia style. While there do not exist many specific references in historical treatises before the Baroque period to the technique of vibrato, it is possible that it was *always* in existence as a natural aspect of vocal technique. Instrumentalists who had the potential for imitation of the voice, and this most certainly includes string players, naturally followed the vocal ideal in the application of this device.

In the quest for "authenticity," it has been suggested in recent years that the vibrato be banned from some early music. Such admonitions may go too far, since the effect seems to have always been present, although the exact degree is not certain.[13] The application of this expressive effect is said by scholars to be limited to the point at which the vibrato draws attention to itself.[14] Segovia, while sometimes accused of excess, has not been the subject of intense criticism in this area. It seems that his manner of imitating the voice was a true gauge for him of the amount of vibrato that would please the ear and lend a singing, natural quality to his music. However, at times it may be more suitable to the music to apply different standards than the one that seemed to be applied universally by Segovia.[15] We will examine the relevant evidence to try to suggest a description of the amount and type of application of this effect that is appropriate in each composition.

3. Rubato. This term is an Italian word which literally means "robbed." As applied to music it is defined as the practice of some notes robbing time from the rhythmic pulse of a piece that they were not originally given. There are two types of rubato, and both have always existed in music performance:

a.) Non-free rubato. This is also called early rubato because it was the primary form used in the early part of documentable music history and was also the first form to be actually called rubato. In this form, the pulse is not disrupted. If time is stolen from the beat by a note or group of notes, the beat is paid back by a compensating acceleration of other notes. The performer is not free to steal time without paying it back. This rubato may also take the form of the accompaniment remaining steady while the melody is flexible. Strictly speaking, ornamentation falls under this category. This is because ornaments are created by stealing time from either the preceding or the following note. Ornamentation forms of non-free rubato that are applied to *whole pieces* are called, in English: *division, diminution, variation, embellishment* or simply *ornamentation.* In Spanish: *diferencia* or *glosa.* In Italian: *coloratura, fioritura* or *passaggio.* In German: *koloratur.* Non-free ornamentation rubato that is applied to single notes is called *agrément* in French or *grace*

---

10. Cornelius L. Reid, *A Dictionary of Vocal Terminology,* New York, Music House Ltd, 1983, pp. 394-398.

11. *Ibid,* p. 394.

12. Constance McKenna, "A Segovia Masterclass," presented in *Guitar Review,* Fall 1986, pp. 1-10. Even at the age of 93 Segovia was still showing his emphasis on singing. In this masterclass he constantly sang the music being performed in an effort to encourage the students to imitate the voice.

13. Frederick Neumann, *New Essays in Performance Practice,* Ann Arbor/London, UMI Research Press, 1989 pp.171-173. "The ability of vibrato to enliven and enrich the musical sound has been known throughout the ages, and vibrato has quite certainly been used on instruments in imitation of the voice... String vibrato was not as all-pervasive as it is today but was used selectively and with discrimination. In particular the over-rich, voluptuous variety practiced by many of today's virtuosi is inappropriate for eighteenth-century music."

14. Frederick Neumann mentions as an example the time that W.A. Mozart wrote a letter to his father in 1778 in which he said concerning the vibrato: "The human voice vibrates by itself, but in a way and to a degree that is beautiful—this is the nature of the voice, and one imitates it not only in wind instruments, but also on strings, and even on the clavichord, but as soon as one carries it too far, it ceases to be beautiful, because it is unnatural." (Frederick Neumann, *New Essays on Performance Practice,* Ann Arbor/ London, UMI Research Press, 1989, p.172) See also: Charles Duncan, *The Art of Classical Guitar Playing,* Princeton, New Jersey, Summy-Birchard Music, 1980, p. 90. "With few exceptions, if the listener is actually aware of vibrato, then there is too much."

15. Cornelius L. Reid, *A Dictionary of Vocal Terminology,* New York, Music House Ltd., 1983, p. 398. Even in vocal music we find that there are exceptions to the rule. For example, there are certain times in vocal music when it is *desirable* to try to sing without vibrato. Reid mentions the times when, for interpretative reasons, the music is to convey despair, innuendo, hate, world weariness, as well as when women are attempting to imitate boy sopranos.

or *ornament* in English. Throughout the second section of this book, examples are given to suggest how this type of rubato may best be applied.

b.) Free rubato. This is also called late rubato because it became prominent later in music history, and especially during the late 19th/early 20th century Romantic period. Also, it was first referred to as rubato at a point in music history later than the early form. In this form the time that is stolen is not paid back, resulting in either a disruption of the regularity of the pulse or, in music without a regular rhythm, a change in those rhythms originally indicated. Free rubato is indicated by the following terms: *rubato, rubato ad libitum, espressivo, ritardando, allargando, ritenuto, tenuto, accelerando* and any others that indicate a change in the steady pulse. Segovia, as will be shown in the introduction to Chapter One of Part II, Volume Two, was a product of the 19th century Romantic movement. He did not make it his concern to use a type of rubato that was most characteristic of the composer and the style period. He chose to apply free rubato most often, and this in all types of music. As stated earlier, free rubato existed throughout music history. Its exact application, however, seems to be more limited in the periods prior to the 19th century, although it definitely was used. Some degree of rubato appears to have always been used, for example, at cadences. In contrast, Segovia's free rubato was true to the ethics of the 19th century. It is many times characterized by holding a note or group of notes (*tenuto*). The regular pulse is disrupted and the stolen time not paid back. This approach is described as subjective and individualistic because it apparently was employed at any point that the performer desired for expressive purposes regardless of any historical or stylistic considerations. This *ad libitum* form of free rubato is really only historically appropriate in certain forms of music.[16]

As we examine Segovia's use of this rhythmic device it is important to say that it is not being recommended that guitarists should play in a mechanical way. Studies show that the trend in this century has been towards permitting very little rhythmic flexibility at all, even in music where this device should be an integral part of the style.[17] Happily, there are signs of renewed interest in free rubato, even causing some to speculate about the possibility of a new Romantic period.[18] A certain amount of flexibility is actually necessary in all music, and the issue is really just one of degree. What is being pointed out here is some documentation as to what degree as well as what *type* of rubato is appropriate in each piece of music. Many guitarists have been conditioned, partly through Segovia's influence no doubt, to use either free rubato or none at all (although there has been increased emphasis on ornamentation forms of non-free rubato by professionals in recent years). It is hoped that *A New Look at Segovia* can promote more thought concerning this critical musical element.

4. Glissando. This is defined as a slide from one note to another. The term is an Italian version of the French word *glisser,* which means "to slide." Some confusion has been generated by the term *portamento* (Italian, literally means "to carry") which also means to slide from one note to another. The difference between the glissando and the portamento is slight but significant. The portamento generally refers to a consecutive slide in which the pitch moves up the chromatic scale without any intervals. Therefore, a portamento is only really possible with the voice or on stringed instruments such as the violin or on brass instruments such as the trombone. A glissando moves by intervals. Thus, a piano or a harp can play a glissando but not a portamento, since only half and whole steps are possible.[19] On the guitar, we can slide chromatically, but this is still an intervalic slide. A portamento, strictly speaking, is not possible on the guitar. The term is most often connected with vocal usage and will not be used here. However, both terms have been used interchangeably by some musicians throughout music history. Segovia tended to use the term portamento when referring to the slide, and this may indicate that he was thinking in terms of the imitation of the voice.

We do have evidence that the portamento was used in vocal music as far back as the early eighteenth century. It appears to have initially been used as a specific ornament.[20] This effect in vocal music has continued to be used in an ornamental fashion, and the slide is many times specifically indicated by the composer by a line between the first and

---

16. Credit goes to Richard Hudson for developing the free/non-free, early/late rubato distinction and for the most comprehensive scholarly book on this subject to date. His book has provided much of the basis for our discussion of this particular rhythmic consideration: *Stolen Time: The History of Tempo Rubato,* Oxford, Clarendon Press, 1994.

17. *Ibid.,* Ch. 10, "The Modern Rubato," p. 356.

18. *Ibid.,* Ch. 11, "The Future of Rubato," pp. 436-442.

19. Most, but not all, music dictionaries point out this distinction.

20. This is mentioned by Pier Francesco Tosi in his 1723 *Opinioni,* pp. 59-60. The use of this and other effects in vocal music were apparently much in use at this time, and Tosi calls for moderation. For a discussion of this see: Frederick Neumann, *Ornamentation in Baroque and Post-Baroque Music, With Special Emphasis on J. S. Bach,* Princeton, New Jersey, Princeton University Press, 1978, pp. 553-555.

second notes.[21] It may be used as a manner of expression.[22] It can be used to communicate emotion. This type of portamento is called the *portamento di voce*.[23] There is a slightly different and more general use of the portamento that has always existed in singing. This type of slide is referred to here as the *subtle portamento* because it should not be executed in a deliberate manner that calls attention to itself.[24] It is closely associated with the *legato style*.[25] In this context the portamento is not specifically indicated as an effect or ornament, but is used throughout as a matter of articulation,[26] and especially at slow tempos.[27] As such, it does not stand out but is almost imperceptible, lending to the overall connection of the notes, as opposed to staccato, where the notes are deliberately detached.[28] The prudent use of this kind of slide is a vital part of all masterful performing in any medium where it is possible, for it involves the matter of the two fundamental ways of articulating notes: *staccato* and *legato*.[29] So we see that in vocal music there are really two types of slides. The first type, the *blatant portamento,* is a specific ornament or effect and is to be used only rarely, such as in style periods where it was an understood part of historical performance practice or when it was indicated by the composer.[30] The second type is the *subtle portamento* and this is to be used freely as a matter of articulation.

In the late 19th and early 20th century Romantic period the use of the blatant portamento in music, and especially violin music, became an integral part of performance practice.[31] Segovia, a man of his time, was no doubt influenced by this, and developed a somewhat arbitrary approach to the use of the slide.

---

21. See examples in: *The New College Encyclopedia of Music,* New York, W. W. Norton & Co, 1960, p. 510.

22. The 19th century musicologist, Corri, writing in 1811 said: "Portamento di voce is the perfection of vocal music, it consists in the swell and dying of the voice, the sliding and blending of one note into another with delicacy and expression." (quoted by Brent Jeffrey Monahan, *The Art of Singing,* Metuchen, N.J. & London, The Scarecrow Press, Inc., 1978, p. 215).

23. Joseph Smith, *Voice and Song, A Practical Method for the Study of Singing,* New York, G. Schirmer, 1907, p. 113: "...*Portamento di voce* (carrying the voice); that is, in passing from one note to the other of the interval the voice *perceptibly glides* and anticipates the second note."

24. *Idem.,* "In *legato* the glide [portamento] is present but *not* perceptible..."

25. Brent Jeffrey Monahan, *The Art of Singing,* Metuchen, N.J. & London, The Scarecrow Press, Inc., 1978, p. 215: "Some of the early sources use the terms 'legato' and 'portamento' interchangeably. To be certain, there is a fine shade of meaning between 'smooth and connected, with no breaks between the successive notes' (legato) and 'a gliding or passing continuously from one pitch to another' (portamento)"

26. Charles Kennedy Scott, *The Fundamentals of Singing,* London, Cassell and Company Ltd., 1954, p. 344: "The art of legato consists in a 'run through' of sound, representing the continuity of an idea; *portamento,* too is almost bound to be involved, if there are to be no holes or hiatuses."

27. *Ibid.,* p. 70. "With relatively slow movement a tendency to blur the edges of notes and intervals by portamento will occur, just, as at twilight, forms are less distinct, presenting a more romantic aspect; it will also make for less keen articulation, less thrusting, brilliant tone than is required by quick movement. Portamento implies a dragging, but not a 'dawdling'; as if there were a weight to be moved that is almost, but not quite, beyond the power of the mover. This is a very important element in expressive performance. It is what determines contact between the performer and what is performed."

28. Victor Alexander Fields, *Training the Singing Voice,* New York, King's Crown Press, 1947, p.121: "Deviations in attack are said to occur, even in artistic performances. Scientific instruments can now measure irregularities of performance that escape the naked ear. Seashore's experimental analyses of the vocal performances of a group of great singers reveals the fact that about 25 percent of the tonal attacks were not direct hits but were accomplished by gliding (imperceptibly) into the tone desired. Furthermore about 40 per cent of the transitions from tone to tone were accomplished by inaudible portamentos or gliding intonations that connected the tones."

29. *Ibid.,* pp. 231-232: "The melodious inflection of the singing voice as it moves from tone to tone therefore involves a technique of note connection that is related to the process of interpretation. Two fundamental types of note connection are emphasized. They are: a) the *legato* of smoothly connected type, in which a tenuous but imperceptible gliding intonation is maintained, without breaks, between successive tones. When the gliding connection between two tones is perceptible to the ear it is called a *portamento connection...* b) the *staccato* or disconnected type, in which notes are cut short or apart by minute gaps of silence. Other types of note connection are employed in singing and instrumental performance, involving variations and gradations of these two fundamental forms in various rhythms and intensities."

30. Joseph Smith, *Voice and Song, A Practical Method for the Study of Singing,* New York, G. Schirmer, 1907, p. 113: "As an exercise the portamento is exceedingly valuable, and should be practiced assiduously; but as an ornament it should be used only rarely and with great discrimination."

31. *The New Grove Dictionary of Music and Musicians,* Stanley Sadie, editor, London, Macmillan Publishers Limited, 1980, vol. 15, p. 134: "Portamento in the voice or in string playing is a legitimate effect but one whose use is easily subject to abuse. In modern string playing, an audible portamento in shifting from one position to another is generally avoided, but it was a common means of expression in the 19th century." vol. 17, p. 380: "The use of the slide became a recognized part of violin technique with Viotti and others in the early 19th century, and it was much cultivated in the late 19th and early 20th. It has since been used more discriminately, but slides are unavoidable in many passages of double stopping that are

In guitar performance practice, as mentioned previously, the slide is really a *glissando* and not a *portamento,* although their melodic function is essentially the same with respect to the guitar and voice. A subtle amount of sliding is necessary on the guitar for the maintenance of legato playing, as well as for expression of the line. Segovia, quite appropriately, used this form of the slide in all his music to a certain degree. Again, the *subtle* use of the slide cannot be objected to because on the guitar it is a part of legato playing. The point at which this effect becomes *blatant* is the point at which we are questioning its use. Thus, when we talk about a glissando in this book it generally refers to a *blatant glissando.* It is *not* being suggested here that everything be played in a detached manner. Additionally, what is most often referred to in this book when we talk about Segovia playing a glissando is the form where the first note is plucked. Then, the slide proceeds in a deliberate manner to the note of arrival without giving any additional attack. In other words, the second note of the glissando is not plucked. This form calls attention to itself, and is appropriate only in certain types of music.

5. Slurs. This is a term used to describe the practice of grouping together notes of different pitches as indicated by a curved line, and playing them *legato* (in a smooth and connected manner). In music for bowed instruments the slur indicates that the group of notes should be played with one bow stroke. The guitar, while being a string instrument, differs in that it is plucked, and therefore relies on a percussive attack to initiate the string vibration that produces the sound. To ensure a legato connection, therefore, the guitarist relies on the left hand to make the sound from the slurred note or notes. While the left hand hammer-on or pull-off does create a legato connection, another inevitable consequence is an accent on the plucked note that initiates the slur. This means that careful and intelligent thought has to be given to the exact placement of slurs by every guitar editor, since the shaping and articulation of the line is directly affected. With the advent of the improved modern guitar came a style of playing that could be accused of editorial overslurring. The editions of Francisco Tárrega show that he promoted a slur style that was in contrast to that of his Spanish predecessors Sor and Aguado. He used generous amounts of slurs.[32] Segovia initially followed his example, although later in his life he seems to have used them to a lesser degree. The ease with which the modern guitar plays slurs may have contributed to Segovia's style that incorporated them very frequently, especially in works that are highly melodic, such as those of Bach.[33] At times it seems that Segovia's idea of slur application may have been arbitrary, leading to their overuse.[34] His approach has been examined and retained here insofar as specific musical and technical situations were found to provide ample justification.[35]

6. A full round sound with plenty of variety. Much has been said about the "Segovia sound."[36] For the last few decades of the 20th century guitarists have continued to affirm the pleasant and attractive quality of Segovia's sound.[37] Major guitar careers have been inspired by it.[38] This sound, or tone, has been analyzed with scientific detail.[39]

---

to be played legato." It has been pointed out to me by Matanya Ophee that we can document an emphasis on *glissandi* in guitar music as early as 1817 in the works of Russian guitarist Andrei Osipovich Sychra. See Matanya Ophee's preface to: *Andrei Sychra, Four Concert Etudes, The Russian Collection Volume II,* Columbus, Editions Orpheé, 1992.

32. Francisco Tárrega, *The Collected Guitar Works,* edited by Rafael Andía and Javier Quevedo, Heidelberg, Chanterelle Verlag, 1992.

33. For example; see Segovia's 1934 edition of the famous Bach *Chaconne,* published by Schott.

34. Charles Duncan, *The Art of Classical Guitar Playing,* Princeton, New Jersey, Summy-Birchard Music, 1980, p. 89. "Editorial overslurring is not as common as in the past, but one should watch it, especially in the older Bach editions." Professor Ron Purcell has pointed out in the article by Constance McKenna called "A Segovia Masterclass" (*Guitar Review,* Fall 1989, p. 5) that some of Segovia's earlier editions, and specifically the *Chaconne,* contain the addition of so many slurs because Segovia was playing on gut strings. Apparently Segovia held the opinion that gut strings, with their different sound and feel, did not give the impression of overslurring.

35. *Idem.* "Musically valid slurring always enhances either fluency, rhythmic accent, or melodic contour, sometimes all at the same time. By contrast, slurs that detract from any of these should not be used, even if they are written in the score."

36. Charles Duncan, "The Segovia Sound, What is it?," presented in *Guitar Review,* Fall 1977, pp. 25-31.

37. Frederick Noad said: "When I first heard Segovia it seemed to me impossible that such richly varied and evocative sound could come from a guitar, like the first taste of a truly great vintage wine. It was this elusive *magic* that turned me on to the guitar in the first place. It is this sound that I'm always looking for..." (quoted in *Guitarra* magazine, Vol. 12, Issue No. 68, 1986, p. 17). Larry Snitzler gives us his impressions: "I remember with absolute clarity the first moment of the sound of Segovia playing the guitar," says Snitzler. "I knew then that I would devote the rest of my life to trying in some way to produce a sound as similar to that as possible. In fact, for me the sound that Segovia makes *is* the sound of the guitar." (quoted in *Guitar Review,* Fall 1986, p. 4.)

38. Christopher Parkening, "Of Gift and Discipline," an interview by John Schroeter, presented in *Fingerstyle Guitar* magazine, Sept./Oct. 1995, No. 11, p. 19. Chris Parkening is, no doubt, one of the most respected concert classical guitarists alive today. He continues to give credit to Segovia for inspiring his pursuit of the guitar. He gives particular emphasis to Segovia's sound: "...Segovia's sound was so beautiful and so varied. It was something that I wanted to analyze and study. ...I happen to love Segovia's sound. It was the model for me." Likewise, John Williams (whom no one

It has been determined that the full round quality of Segovia's sound is achieved by the following techniques:[40]

   a.) *The use of the fingernails, padded by the flesh of the fingertip, to engage the string.* The string is activated by the nail which acts as a ramp, and the flesh pads and secures the string. This is the foundation upon which Segovia built his basic full, round sound.[41] He achieved *variety (tone colors)* in this sound by varying the angle of the nail to the string, the amount of nail used versus the amount of flesh, the place that he chose to engage the string with the right hand in relation to the bridge, whether he activated the string by a downward stroke or by plucking the string upward, and by using different strings to play each note.

   b.) *The use of rest stroke and free stroke.* The dimensions of the sound achieved as well as the color were, to a large part, determined by whether Segovia chose to activate the string with a stroke that ended by resting against the adjacent string, or one that cleared it. Obviously, most classical guitar playing requires that the free stroke be used so as not to disturb any notes that are to be sounding on the other strings. However, the careful use of the two types is an important factor in the overall sound production. These two types of strokes are used in right hand plucking, as well as in the left hand hammer-on or pull-offs that are essential for slurring.

   c.) *The use of the touch preparation sequence when activating the strings.* The analogy of the bow and arrow has been used to illustrate this important concept that is responsible for the control necessary to activate the strings firmly at all times. The analogy is this: in preparing to shoot an arrow from a bow, one must first engage the string, then draw the string, and then release it. Any attempt to draw the string without a definite preparation and engagement of the hand will result in a clumsy, inaccurate and uncontrolled stab. The same is true when engaging the strings of the guitar with the fingertips. There should always be a "touch and play" sequence of events. This may be developed consciously and slowly at first, and eventually it may not be conscious at all, but will still be there regardless, even in very fast playing. This applies to strokes executed with the fingers of both hands.

   d.) *Degree of attack.* The guitar possesses very little dynamic range when compared with, for example, a violin. Some degree of dynamics can be achieved by the amount of force that is used to engage the strings. Beyond a certain point, however, diminishing returns are yielded.[42] The quality of sound and its resulting pleasantness depend to a large degree on the ability of the performer to activate the string within its realm of potential, limited by considerations of taste. Segovia seemed to have had an ear for the point at which tones appeared the most full and round. He kept this point as his standard, and for variety would diminish or increase the attack. This principle is applied to either right hand or left hand[43] activations of the string.

   e.) *Control and suppression of extraneous non-musical sounds.* To produce a pleasant tone when playing with fingernails, it is necessary to develop a touch that minimizes nail clicks. Such can only be achieved by real sensitivity to using the flesh of the fingertip for a pad. Other factors include the condition of the nails, their smoothness, length and shape. Segovia worked daily to ensure that his nails were in the right condition.[44] A firm grasp on the technique of the

---

disputes is one of the greatest classical guitarists) gives credit to the inspirational effect of Segovia's tone production: "The first important influence of Segovia (I was about twelve when I started seeing him in Siena and in London) was his sound and the way he produced it. I had a good sound myself because I had good nails and I'd been taught properly, but it was the idea of producing and expressing a nice sound. My father had been impressed with Segovia's sound when he first heard him in London in the thirties, so naturally, being close to all that and the 'Segovia Right Hand' was a terrific influence." (quoted in *Andrés Segovia, An Appreciation,* George Clinton, editor, London, Musical New Services Ltd., 1978, p. 69).

   39. Charles Duncan, *The Art of Classical Guitar Playing,* Princeton, New Jersey, Summy-Birchard Music, 1980.

   40. Obviously, the exact way that Segovia made his sound cannot be notated, since this depends on many personal subjective aspects. We speak here in terms of generalities that can be documented.

   41. Segovia credited Aguado's method book with describing this stroke and referred students to it. See: Dionisio Aguado, *New Guitar Method,* edited by Brian Jeffery, translated into English from the original Spanish, London Tecla Editions, 1981.

   42. Harvey Turnbull, *The Guitar from the Renaissance to the Present Day,* New York, Charles Scribner's Sons, 1974, pp. 97-98. Turnbull quotes an article entitled "On the Public Performance of the Guitar" that appeared in the 19th century guitar periodical *The Giulianiad.* This article criticized those who try to force too much volume out of the guitar: "Playing generally in a large room, they naturally wish that every part of the audience should hear, and in doing this they wholly mistake the manner in which it can be successfully effected. They pull the strings with so much force, for the purpose of producing a *loud* tone, that, although they produce more noise, they in fact lessen the real tone of the instrument. Their want of knowledge in acoustics is here verified. It is not the *largeness* of tone that travels furthest and quickest, it is the *quality* of it. A mere whisper, if the tone be sweet and compact, will find its way to every corner of a large theatre, while an overstrained string will produce a tone which will fall, so to speak, dead and lifeless." As far as I know, this kind of criticism has never been aimed at Segovia.

   43. Left hand activations refers to slurs.

   44. Vladimir Bobri, *The Segovia Technique,* New York, Macmillan Publishing Co., 1972, pp. 48-49.

use of the hands for the *damping* of any ringing strings is also necessary for a clean sound. This simply means that the notes do not all ring out arbitrarily, the fingers are used to stop them when necessary. This is done to protect the performance from notes that are not rhythmically precise, or are unnecessarily dissonant to the music.

These are the primary aspects of sound production that produced what is known as the "Segovia sound."[45] As mentioned above, Segovia varied the sound in terms of its coloristic quality or its dynamic level. His example is analyzed throughout our study and imitated in the modern editions presented in Appendix B by way of the many suggested musical indications. The dynamic levels suggested, from *pianissimo* to *fortissimo,* are significant because dynamics are an important musical element, even in early music.[46] However, because the guitar has a somewhat limited dynamic range, it would be wise for guitarists to take advantage of the real strength of the guitar, namely, its capacity for color. The ways that Segovia achieved various tone colors has already been discussed above. The term *naturale* is used here to designate the general full round sound, *ponticello* to indicate a bright or metallic sound, and *dolce* to indicate a dark or sweet sound. Of course these terms are somewhat limited in that they do not give one precise measurement of all the degrees of shadings between the two extremes, and guitarists should feel free to experiment. Segovia's example shows us that many nuances of shading are possible, and a simplistic "ponticello" to "dolce" description really does not do justice to the many artistic applications of color.

7. The use of broken or rolled chords. The rolled chord is also properly called an *arpeggiation.* Because this term is now understood by guitarists to mean a written-out separation of the notes of a chord in a definite rhythm, the technique will simply be referred to here as the *rolled chord.* This is an aspect of the Segovia style that is seldom mentioned, but is nevertheless quite important. In fact, a significant percentage of the chords within any given piece were played as rolled chords by Segovia. This is usually not indicated in his editions, nor any other guitar editions for that matter. A wavy line to the left of the chord is used here to indicate that it is to be rolled. As in the case of dynamic and color indications, these markings are somewhat limited in their ability to communicate. The performer must still decide upon various elements such as the speed of the roll, the direction, the intensity, the rhythmic placement (on the beat, before the beat). The point here is simply to indicate an element that has existed historically and that most guitarists take for granted, yet to which little conscious thought is given.[47] Guitarists should feel free to experiment with this effect.

The history of the rolled chord probably goes as far back as harmony. Ancient instruments such as the lute, harp and lyre all lend themselves to the technique of rolled chords. It would be hard to imagine a performance in one of these mediums with only block harmonies. Early preludial forms for the lute were free improvisational pieces that allowed the soloist an opportunity to warm up and check his tuning.[48] In these forms rolled chords played a part by acting as a type of ornament.[49] By about 1630 we can find indications in music for lute, viol and clavecin for the rolling of chords, played with a rubato approach of rhythmic freedom.[50] Throughout the Baroque, the roll (arpeggiation) was performed in a

---

45. It should be pointed out here that these elements that produce the "Segovia sound" can only be developed through patient and consistent practice. According to Segovia student Professor Clare Callahan (Cincinnati Conservatory) the maestro always told students that three basic areas of guitar technique need to be worked on daily throughout a guitarist's life. These are: 1.) scales 2.) slurs, and 3.) arpeggios. The study of these three critical areas is not only important for developing a secure technical foundation but is also necessary for the development and maintenance of a good sound. When practicing these, guitarists will benefit by concentrating on the elements of tone production mentioned above.

46. Robert Donington, *The Interpretation of Early Music,* London, Faber and Faber, 1979, Part Five, "Dynamics," p. 482.

47. There is a fine exception to this. Matanya Ophee has written some excellent articles on this subject in *Classical Guitar* magazine, October and December 1986, in his series entitled "Considerations of 19th Century Guitar Music." Of interest as well is Erik Stenstadvold's response to Ophee in the May 1987 issue of *Classical Guitar* titled "The Bother over Broken Chords, Another Historical Perspective," and Ophee's response to Stenstadvold in *Classical Guitar,* September 1987 called "Response to the Offensive."

48. Robert Donington, *The Interpretation of Early Music,* New York, St. Martin's Press, p. 61.

49. Roy Petschauer, "Denis Gaultier and the Unmeasured Prelude," presented in *Guitar Review,* No. 36, 1972, p. 12-14. Gaultier (1600-1672) had a specific sign that indicated an ornamental arpeggiation (roll). It is interesting that he quite often indicated a roll on a two note harmony, while his music has chord rolls written into it throughout, interspersed between melodic elements. This latter type is obviously a forerunner of the *style brisé,* or broken chord style. The difference is that the *style brisé* came to be associated with forms, such as Bach's lute preludes, that existed in the context of time and measure. Gaultier's preludes, in contrast, were free improvisational forms.

50. Richard Hudson, *Stolen Time: The History of Tempo Rubato,* Oxford, Clarendon Press, 1994, p. 10.

variety of ways. It could start from the bottom or top. It could start on the beat or before it.[51] The exact speed of its execution seems to have been left up to the performer. After the Baroque period the rolled chord continued to be used as an important expressive effect.[52]

The only form of the chord roll that seems to have continued in use after the Baroque period is the type that starts from the bottom note and is rolled to the top, starting either on or before the beat. It inevitably involves a certain degree of rubato, since the performer is spreading the notes of the chord out rhythmically according to his or her own discretion.[53] It is this form of the chord roll, starting from bottom to top, that was so often employed by Segovia for expressive effect. As we have seen, these rolls have a rich history in plucked string music, and are most certainly appropriate. We do not have to limit ourselves to the same *type* of roll, however.[54] In the chord rolls suggested here, the wavy line simply indicates a roll. Decisions about direction, manner of execution (thumb alone, thumb and fingers, index finger, all nail or nail and flesh, etc.), speed and exact placement of the roll are all left up to the performer.

8. Highly subjective individualistic interpretations. As is described in the detailed explanation of the Romantic style in Chapter One of Part II, Volume Two, this is the way performers in the Romantic period, of which Segovia was a product, approached the music. The performers and the composers of this period primarily took the approach that music was to convey feelings. In regard to performance, this obviously meant a highly subjective approach since, how many performers feel a piece of music in exactly the same way? Freedoms of all types, harmonic, melodic and rhythmic were indulged in by the performers of this period,[55] and *rubato ad libitum* was the rule of the day.[56] The performer was king. The music was only a vehicle to express one's individuality.[57] This approach lasted through the early part of the 20th century, and then a dramatic shift toward objectivity and fidelity to the composer occurred. The Romantic style fell out of favor, and unfortunately, so did some of the performers who held on to that approach.[58]

Some may wonder why the 20th century brought with it an attitude that rejected the Romantic style. For the answer we only need to look at the history of the last 100 years. It is a century that went from horses and buggies to automobiles, from having no air travel at all to massive commercial jet liners, from the newspaper as one of the few forms of media to the explosion of all forms of high tech communications. The rapid technological advances that have occurred in this century have brought about the age of information. With this new potential for acquiring data came a predictable emphasis on scholarship. Now, everything could and should be explained, and the explanation was to be documented. The result was a certain objectivity. It was in this climate that the Romantic style could no longer flourish. Segovia survived because he was a pioneer, and his achievements made him a legend. His interpretive approach, however, came to be viewed more and more as an outdated example of days gone by, of a subjective style that could no longer be termed "correct." Students of the guitar were finding themselves increasingly at odds with the maestro, and he viewed those that did not emulate his approach sufficiently as lacking in expression.[59]

---

51. Robert Donington takes a view that favors on-beat chord rolls in Baroque music (*New Grove Dictionary of Music and Musicians,* vol 8, p. 853) He is challenged by Frederick Neumann, who allows for a before the beat approach (*Ornamentation in Baroque and Post-Baroque Music, With Special Emphasis on J.S. Bach,* Princeton, New Jersey, Princeton University Press, 1978, p. 492)

52. *Ibid.,* p. 23.

53. Richard Hudson, *Stolen Time: The History of Tempo Rubato,* Oxford, Clarendon Press, 1994, p. 23.

54. Segovia seemed to prefer one type of roll, from bottom to top. His rhythmic placement, however, involved some variety.

55. Segovia expressed his views on interpretation when he said "Interpretation should be like life — an explosion of freedom..." (Andrés Segovia and George Mendoza, *Segovia, My Book of the Guitar,* Cleveland/New York, William Collier Publishers Inc., 1979, p. 21)

56. Richard Hudson, *Stolen Time: The History of Tempo Rubato,* Oxford, Clarendon Press, 1994, p. 301. "The second half of the nineteenth century and the early years of the twentieth represent a high point of freedom for the performer. Pianists and conductors especially — but, indeed, all performers in general — felt they had a right, if not a duty, to apply all manner of rhythmic flexibilities, and even to alter the composer's score on occasion, in order to achieve their own personal concept of expression."

57. A statement by Franz Liszt made in 1837 shows us that even in the early Romantic period liberties could be taken quite far: "I frequently played the works of Beethoven, Weber, and Hummel... and I confess to my shame [that] in order to extract bravos from a public ever slow to perceive things of beauty, I had no scruples about changing the tempo and the composer's intentions. I even arrogantly went so far as to add a lot of brilliant passages and cadenzas..." (quoted by Richard Hudson, *Stolen Time: The History of Tempo Rubato,* Oxford, Clarendon Press, 1994, p. 258)

58. Allan Kozinn, *Mischa Elman and the Romantic Style,* London/New York, Harwood Academic Publishers, 1990.

59. Constance McKenna, "A Segovia Masterclass," presented in *Guitar Review,* Fall 1986, p. 6. "So frequent were Segovia's pleas for 'expression' that it became a litany as the master class wore on."

Students should be applauded for seeking technical proficiency and stylistic correctness. Long hours put in to achieve any level of mastery should be encouraged and never downplayed, as some may feel that Segovia was in the habit of doing.[60] Still, we are individuals, and there is no denying that individuality even in the performance of music, because to play with an interpretation implies at least a certain amount of individual subjectivity. To play without an interpretation is to express nothing but a cold, lifeless and mechanical approach that, while possibly more stylistically correct, gives little aesthetic pleasure. Segovia's priorities were on the performer expressing his individuality, on the expression of the music and the performer's love for it.[61] He maintained the view that the performer was to be an equal partner with the composer.[62] The composer creates the notes. The performer creates the interpretation. Both are viewed as works of art.[63]

What is being proposed here is a balance between two extremes: the one where the performer is king, and the other where individuality is excluded in favor of objectivity and fidelity to the composer. We *should* take advantage of the tremendous advances in musicological scholarship to inform us; to do anything less is irresponsible. Nevertheless, we are still human beings and can interpret the music with a degree of individuality, and most of all expression. The fact is, there is much that is still not known about a lot of historic music, and may never be known. New information is being put forth every day. It is not always possible to tell what specific details of interpretation the composer wanted or are called for by the style period.[64] We cannot always give an objective answer for every question and indeed, a certain degree of creativity and even spontaneity at the time of the performance itself is still desirable. The performer ultimately must take a position on how to play a piece even at the risk of being called "incorrect." In the final analysis, a judgement will be made by the audiences as to how well he or she communicated.[65] The few academics that may listen will certainly evaluate modern performers by the extent that they follow the most recent revelations in scholarship. They too, however, when they are in the privacy of their own homes, most certainly listen to the music that they *like* most, that makes them *feel* the best, that they *enjoy,* regardless of its correctness. This realm, that of the subjective, the individualistic, the emotional, this is the realm of Segovia. It is also the realm of our own *humanness.* It need not be completely jettisoned by modern guitarists.

---

60. In an interview that appeared in the *GFA Soundboard,* Fall 1993, the world renowned guitarist William Kanengeiser tells the story of how he was harshly criticized by Segovia in a masterclass for using a style different from that of the maestro, despite obvious technical mastery.

61. It is interesting to note that Segovia sometimes contradicted his romantic ethics as shown by the fact that he did not always extend the liberty to express individuality to his students. He could display an intolerance for those that didn't do things the way that he liked, even though they may have been phenomenal guitarists and musicians. In a recent interview ("A Conversation with John Williams," presented in *Guitar Review,* Winter 1992, pp. 24-25), concert guitarist John Williams described Segovia's teaching approach as "authoritarian," and said that the degree of the maestro's approval corresponded with the degree to which one copied what he did: "Every example that I can remember, in class or individually, came down to isolated bits of rubato, bits of fingering, and implications that the more you copied his style the more he would smile and feel happy... He did not encourage you to expand and develop yourself, and therefore you were increasingly inhibited from expressing what you felt—because it might be different from what he would do himself. This cannot be good in a teacher..."

62. Constance McKenna, "A Segovia Masterclass," presented in *Guitar Review,* Fall 1986, pp. 1-10. Segovia's views are stated quite clearly throughout this masterclass.

63. In a personal letter to me dated October 15, 1995, concert guitarist Eliot Fisk commented on Segovia's approach to interpretation. He said that Segovia made a comparison using the biblical story of Lazurus who is raised from the dead by Jesus: "Segovia's great allegory for musical interpretation was 'The score is like Lazurus, dead in his tomb. The interpreter comes and says *arise and walk!'* This indeed was one aspect of his phenomenal gift. He really did bring the music of five centuries to life—in a brilliant and emotionally stirring act of musical mis-prison that will remain forever embedded in the souls of those who heard him."

64. The desire to restore music to its original context has given rise to the "authenticity" movement. The goal of this movement is surely legitimate and admirable. However, one need not allow dogmatism to supplant liberty, especially in areas that are not sufficiently objective. For example, I have been told of one guitar teacher that will not allow lute music to be played on the guitar, it must be played on the lute if at all. Obviously, the composer wrote the pieces specifically for this instrument, but how do we know that he would be opposed to hearing his works in another medium, especially when we know of intabulated vocal works? The problem is that there is so much that cannot be known for certain. Many things have to be left in the realm of the subjective, and it is in this area that the taste and skill of the performer are critical. Scholars are beginning to question various aspects of the authenticity movement, and especially those that would lead to dullness and boredom: "The performance of 'early music' by organizations exclusively devoted to this specialty has in the last decades more and more assumed the nature of a cultist ritual. Under the banner of authenticity members of the cult present us with performances that are occasionally boring and dull because their aim is not, or at least not primarily, to give aesthetic pleasure, to elate and enchant, but to demonstrate, educate, and provide spiritual purification. For the audience it is an ascetic exercise in moral uplift comparable to the dutiful absorption of a long, uninspiring sermon." Frederick Neumann, *New Essays on Performance Practice,* Ann Arbor/London, UMI Research Press, 1989, p. 169. For additional discussion of this issue see: *Authenticity and Early Music,* a symposium, edited by Nicholas Kenyon, Oxford, Oxford University Press, 1988. See also: *Authenticity in Music* by Raymond Leppard, Portland, OR, Amadeus Press, 1988.

65. This was a part of Segovia's strength. He took a position and persuasively communicated it to his audiences.

The composer's intentions and the styles of the historical period he lived in will be examined here along with our analysis of Segovia in an effort to help form a more objective understanding of each piece. However, guitarists are encouraged to use this information as a point of departure for their own interpretations.

NECESSARY DEFINITIONS

Before going on, it is necessary to define some important terms as they relate to our study. First, Segovia's treatment of each of these works, as well as the new treatment presented in Appendix B, are called *editions*. It is even more correct to refer to these works that are prepared for performance as *performance editions*. For the sake of brevity *edition* will be used, but as it appears in this book, it most often refers specifically to a *performance edition*. This is defined as a version that adapts the original text. It provides technical and musical solutions for the performer while considering the capabilities and limitations of a particular instrument. Therefore, the one who prepared the edition is referred to as the *editor*. The process of preparing the edition is called *editing*.

When referring specifically to the adaptation (sometimes called arrangement) of a work originally written for another instrument to the guitar the term *transcription* will also be used. This term is a common one, and has been used to describe instrumental music adaptations for centuries. It is the one used by Andrés Segovia and most guitarists in general.

APPROACH TO ORNAMENTATION

The subject of ornamentation in early music is very controversial, and may continue to be since there is much that is yet unknown. More information will undoubtedly be discovered with the passing of time. The editorial approach taken in this book is that early music *should* be ornamented. The bulk of present scholarly evidence clearly points in this direction, so it seems unwise not to follow it (the reasons for ornamenting versus not ornamenting will be examined in detail in Chapter Three of Part II, Volume One). This burgeoning documentation is a late 20th century phenomenon unavailable and/or a minority opinion to performers in Segovia's generation. In examining the Segovia repertoire it seemed prudent to apply the most recent and relevant documentation on this unique musicological matter.

The subject of the trill is a fascinating, evolving debate because of the constant unearthing of new sources. For Renaissance music, most scholars seem to agree that the main note trill predominated. The issue of how to play this ornament in Baroque music, however, has become quite polemical. The work of the respected early music scholar Robert Donington has shown that the 19th century approach (used most often by Segovia) of playing the trill by starting from the main note was not the common practice during the Baroque Period.[66] Even though Donington's view is shared by most scholars, he was countered on this point by another respected musicologist, Frederick Neumann.[67] After studying the works of both of these excellent authorities the following conclusions have been formed:

> a.) It is impossible to be dogmatic in this very important area. There is too much that we cannot say for certain.[68]

> b.) It appears that Neumann has proved that the main note trill did not entirely disappear. It continued in use to some degree throughout the Baroque period. A good point to meditate on is that composers and musicians throughout the 17th and 18th centuries probably never planned or announced any different "periods." The designations of "Renaissance" and "Baroque" are historical classifications that cannot be applied rigidly. There was probably no radical discontinuity with the practices of the past, rather a gradual evolution as new ideas and styles were introduced and accepted. Formulas such as "in the Renaissance they played the trill from the main note, in the Baroque it was from the upper note" may be an oversimplification of the issues at hand. Complex historical and cultural forces were at work in each of the countries of Europe at that time. A study of

---

66. Robert Donington, *The Interpretation of Early Music,* London, Faber and Faber, 1977, and *Baroque Music: Style and Performance,* London, Faber & Faber, 1982. Also see Donington's entry on ornamentation in *The New Grove Dictionary of Music and Musicians,* vol. 8, pp. 838-846.

67. Frederick Neumann, *Ornamentation in Baroque and Post-Baroque Music, With Special Emphasis on J. S. Bach,* Princeton, New Jersey, Princeton University Press, 1978, *Essays in Performance Practice,* Ann Arbor, UMI Research Press, 1982, *New Essays in Performance Practice,* Ann Arbor/ London, UMI Research Press, 1989.

68. This point is emphasized by the great musicological polemicist Frederick Neumann in *Performance Practices of the Seventeenth and Eighteenth Centuries* (New York, Schirmer Books, 1993): "The present attempt at a broad and summary view of 17th- and 18th-century performance practices can make no claim to having all the answers. Nobody has and nobody will ever have them."

the relevant data shows that things were changing at a different rate and in a different way depending upon the geographical area.

c.) The Italian practice of playing main note trills apparently continued for a much longer time than was previously thought. It was in predominance throughout the period of 1590-1710. This form of the trill had an influence on German musicians and was still widely practiced in Germany in the period of 1615-1715. It continued in usage somewhat throughout the later Baroque. Therefore, it was probably still an option for J. S. Bach. The conclusion here is that main note trills may be used in Bach.

d.) The French developed a trill that began with the upper auxiliary note in the period of 1630-1715. This trill appears to have predominated, and its influence may have eventually obscured all others in the Baroque, especially towards the later Baroque, and thus, in Bach's time. Therefore, Baroque ornamentation should *favor* the trill that starts with the upper auxiliary which starts on the beat. This should be especially true at cadences, where the dissonance of the appoggiatura and its harmonic resolution is most pronounced.[69] The upper note trill need not *always* start on the beat, but it should favor the beat. The grace note form of the trill may be used occasionally.[70] The best way to determine the tasteful application of these options is to test each trill location and see what fits comfortably.[71]

The conclusion here is that Frederick Neumann has not been able to dismiss the evidence that shows that the trill most *commonly* began with the upper auxiliary note (on the beat) in the Baroque, especially in certain cases.[72] However, early Baroque music, particularly if it is Italian, may still favor the main note trill. We can see this in the music of Frescobaldi (his piece called *La Frescobalda* will be examined in Chapter Two of Part II, Volume One).[73] Therefore, the main note trill is the dominant one used here in the ornamentation of the music of Frescobaldi. Bach appears to have incorporated various kinds of trills. The Italian influence seems to have lived on so that the main note trill would have still been used by Bach, although he probably favored the appoggiatura trill. Therefore, the music of Bach has been ornamented here by using both types of trills, with the upper note trill favored, especially at cadences. The great Scarlatti scholar, Ralph Kirkpatrick, has said that the evidence shows that the trills in Scarlatti's music must be played from the upper note.[74] This is an assertion that Neumann has not disproved. He says that the appoggiatura trill was probably the *best* one being used by Italian composers during the period of 1710-1760 and that it enjoyed its most frequent use in the mid to late 18th century.[75] Scarlatti, being Italian and having written most of his 500 Sonatas during the middle part of this century, would therefore probably have used the appoggiatura or upper note trill.[76] An impressive bit of evidence in favor of the upper note trill in these pieces by Scarlatti is that there are appoggiaturas

---

69. Robert Donington, *Baroque Music: Style and Performance,* London, Faber & Faber, 1982, pp. 125-126.

70. Neumann describes the grace note trill as one that resembles the common upper note trill. The difference is in the *rhythmic placement*. The upper auxiliary occurs before the beat, creating a grace note. It proceeds to the main note which would occur on the beat, and the trill commences. In other words, the upper note functions as a *grace note anticipation* to the trill. See *Ornamentation in Baroque and Post-Baroque Music, With Special Emphasis on J. S. Bach,* p. 242.

71. On page 343 of his book *Ornamentation in Baroque and Post-Baroque Music, With Special Emphasis on J. S. Bach,* Neumann gives us some helpful hints on how to determine ornamentation that is proper and workable. The advice is that one should generally use the upper note, on the beat, appoggiatura type trill whenever an appoggiatura makes sense in that particular spot. If a long appoggiatura works, then use a long upper note trill. If a shorter one seems better, then use a short upper note trill. Where a main note trill is the most desirable, then this should be used. There are some cases where we can say with certainty that the main note trill is preferable. They are: 1.) When the trill's note of resolution is already dissonant with the bass or harmony 2.) When the use of the appoggiatura (upper note) trill would create parallel octaves or fifths 3.) Whenever the harmonic logic calls for the entrance of the main note exactly on the beat.

72. For example, see: Frederick Neumann, *Ornamentation in Baroque and Post-Baroque Music, With Special Emphasis on J. S. Bach,* Princeton, New Jersey, Princeton University Press, 1978, p. 262. French keyboard music definitely favored the upper note trill on the beat.

73. Frescobaldi even wrote out many of the trills, proving that he favored the main note. See the original score, p. 400.

74. Ralph Kirkpatrick, *Domenico Scarlatti,* Princeton, New Jersey, Princeton University Press, 1953, p. 381.

75. Frederick Neumann, *Ornamentation in Baroque and Post-Baroque Music, With Special Emphasis on J. S. Bach,* Princeton, New Jersey, Princeton University Press, 1978, p. 363.

76. Ralph Kirkpatrick, *Domenico Scarlatti,* Princeton, New Jersey, Princeton University Press, 1953, pp. 154-174. According to Kirkpatrick, the sonatas were written between 1738 and 1754.

indicated in the original score of the *Sonata in A Major, K. 322* which is presented in Vol. I.[77] Kirkpatrick emphatically states that no mixing of upper note and main note trills is acceptable in Scarlatti.[78] Therefore, the music of Scarlatti has been ornamented here with upper note trills.

All are encouraged to examine the evidence and, if there is disagreement, the original scores are provided to be used as a basis for one's own ornamentation (that is, if one determines that this music is even to be ornamented at all!)

EDITORIAL STANDARDS USED FOR THIS BOOK

In February of 1981 an article by Brian Jeffery appeared in the newsletter of the Boston Classical Guitar Society. It apparently generated considerable interest, for it was reprinted a few months later in the national guitar magazine *Soundboard*. In this article Brian Jeffery criticized Andrés Segovia for publishing his famous *20 Sor Studies* without telling the readers what Sor originally wrote. He then provided documentation which showed that the Segovia editions contained many changes from Sor's originally published scores. His criticism was blunt and to the point: *people have a right to know exactly what the composer wrote, they have a right to know the truth. Segovia did not truthfully represent what the composer wrote.* In the Summer 1984 issue of *Soundboard* an article was published by Erik Stenstadvold that showed that it was not Segovia who made all the changes. The article proved that Segovia was working from an edition by Sor's student, Napoleon Coste. Many, but not all, of the changes were present in the Coste edition that Segovia used as his source.[79] Still, Jeffery's article was good in that it caused much attention in the guitar world to become focused on this issue of fidelity. He did a service, not only to the integrity of the field of serious classical guitar, but ultimately, to Segovia himself. After all, it was Segovia's first goal to bring the status of the guitar to parity with that of other concert instruments.[80] Other instruments followed professional standards of editing since the early part of the 20th century. If the guitar is to be respected and occupy a place in the serious music world, then editors for the guitar need to follow these standards as well.

Just what are these standards? An article called *What is a Good Edition?* by Walter S. Collins, Chairman of the Choral Editing Standards Committee appeared in the November 1971 issue of *The Choral Journal*. In it he described the formation of precise guidelines for editors. This article is important in that it documents the standards that are acceptable today in the world of serious music.[81] They are:

1. The source used in the preparation of the edition is to be identified.

The editor should identify the source that he used in preparing his edition so that the authenticity of his own arrangement can be evaluated more accurately. There are editions that appear on the surface to be based on the composer's writing but are in fact made from another edition. These therefore perpetuate the errors or editorial changes of the previous manuscript. Over time as more editions are made from editions, the damage to the intent of the composers is compounded. The case given above regarding Segovia's *20 Sor Studies* is a good example. Segovia worked from the revised scores of Coste, yet did not identify his source, leading to confusion and misrepresentation of the intent of the composer.

2. All original material, including the original composer, title, opus number and original instrumentation should be supplied.

People have a right to know the truth about a piece of music they buy. Likewise, a performer has a right to know in which way the music was indicated to be played by the composer. Performance editions are notorious for changing markings and obscuring the composer's original intent. It is very helpful to know how a performer thinks about a piece,

---

77. See the facsimile, measures 3, 5, 24, and 42, p. 408.

78. Ralph Kirkpatrick, *Domenico Scarlatti,* Princeton, New Jersey, Princeton University Press, 1953, p. 379.

79. Matanya Ophee has pointed out that the manuscript by Coste of the revised Sor studies that Segovia apparently worked from bears the inscription: *Par Ferdinand Sor. Revues, classées et doigtées d'agrès les traditions de l'auteur par N. Coste* (By Fernando Sor. Revised according to the traditions of the author by N. Coste). Mr. Ophee told me that this is interpreted to mean that Coste got these changes from oral tradition, from Sor himself. Nevertheless, this does not mean that all of the changes can be attributed to Sor, for Segovia added further alterations to those of Coste. These include fingerings, expression marks and even tempo indications. It should also be pointed out that Segovia incorporated several studies (#11,14,16 and 17) that were not in Coste's collection.

80. Graham Wade, *Segovia, A Celebration of the Man and his Music,* London/New York, Allison & Busby, 1983, p. 114.

81. The article mentions that high standards were already in place for piano and orchestral music. The Executive Board of the American Choral Directors Association met in 1968 and voted to adopt the standards that are described here.

but we should also know how the composer published it. Both views are important. The Segovia *Sor Studies* were given different right hand fingerings and tempo indications by Segovia and it was assumed for many years that these were the intentions of the composer. Only with the publication of the original scores did the truth become known. There are also examples throughout the Segovia repertoire where people were not even supplied with the real composer's name! Rather, we were given a spurious attribution to another composer. The most extreme cases will be described in the chapter on Ponce. The simplest way to solve this problem is to locate the source that is the closest to the original that we have. Then the editor should print the source that the edition is made from and identify it. At the very least the source and its real composer should be identified. The modern editions presented in Appendix B are all accompanied by either: a.) a copy of the composer's manuscript, b.) a facsimile of the earliest and most reliable hand copied or engraved (usually for publication) version, or c.) an *urtext* (original text) edition based on the most reliable available sources. These items all appear in Appendix A.

3. If a text accompanies the music, its original form should be provided, as well as any translations or adaptations. The author, translator, source and use of the text (liturgical, etc.) should be identified whenever possible.

How many times have guitarists played music that was conceived with a text, and yet have totally *neglected* that text! The text not only gives us the story behind the music, it is often descriptive of how the music is to be interpreted. Many of the pieces from the Segovia repertoire were composed with text, and yet some of these texts have seldom been acknowledged. The texts and translations are presented here.

4. The composer's dates and the date of the composition should be given if known. Musical and historical information about the piece and its performance should be given if possible. Biographical information on the composer may be given but is not as important, since this information is easily obtained elsewhere.

In the world of guitar this point has been neglected until recently, much to our loss. Even a very brief amount of information about a piece can help the performer as well as enlighten the audience. Segovia was not one to follow this principle. As we shall see in the chapter on Ponce (Volume II), he deliberately remained silent about the origin of some pieces because he did not want the true story of the composition or the composer to become known. In other cases, the obscurity of the story behind the music may have come as a result of Segovia's ignorance. This left certain interesting and controversial details hidden to many, as will be discussed in the section on *La Maja de Goya* (Volume Two). Significant information about both the composition and the composer have been included here.

5. Measure numbers or rehearsal letters should be provided.

It is extremely helpful to the study of a piece of music to have measure numbers. The guitar world was quite lax in this area until very recently. Most editions now include them, thanks to the ease with which this can be accomplished using the current computer technology. Measure numbers have been given at the beginning of almost every staff throughout this book.

6. All editorial changes in and additions to the original sources should be clearly identified.

This point cannot be emphasized enough. Fortunately, it is becoming more common in our century to document editorial changes. For performers of the late 19th early 20th century generation, this was not a priority. Therefore, it is not hard to understand why Segovia did not make this his concern. His 19th century approach, however, can lead to certain problems. For example, because there was no indication in his editions showing what was editorial and what was original, whole generations of guitarists were playing music that was part Segovia's and part the original composer's without even realizing it. In the case of the Segovia *Sor Studies*, how many thousands of students thought that they were playing exactly what Sor wrote?[82] The truth is now known that Sor's original intentions differed, to various degrees,[83] from what Segovia presented.[84] Again, this problem is dealt with here by providing, along with the analysis and the modern editions in Appendix B, either: a.) a copy of the composer's manuscript, b.) a facsimile of the earliest and most reliable hand copied or engraved version, or c.) an *urtext* edition based on the most reliable available sources.

---

82. There have always been those who knew about Segovia's manner of changing the music, and this is especially true of his students. However, my point here is that there are *many* who never had the opportunity to know that Segovia's editions were changed as compared with the writing of the composer. As a student in my teenage years, I was in this category. Also, even if one was aware of Segovia's editorial procedures, the knowledge of what the composer actually wrote was still obscured until a facsimile edition became widely available.

83. See footnote #79.

84. This is not to imply that having the Segovia edition was less important that having the original. Segovia's editions are certainly more playable, in some cases, that the original. However, today it is very possible to see what the composer wrote *and* what Segovia played, which gives us two very important opinions.

7. The piece should be presented in modern notation.

Especially when working with very old music there are advances in notation practices that could help the performer. It has been pointed out by the guitar scholar Thomas P. Heck that in early forms of guitar notation the duration of the pitches was not even precisely shown.[85] There are many elements that could be updated. The common tendency today of presenting a facsimile of an early edition, while helpful, is not the perfect solution to the problems faced by guitarists when preparing a piece for performance. In the editions presented in Appendix B, all notation has been modernized in keeping with the most current standards.

These are the professional standards of editing. They have been increasingly adopted as the standard in the field of serious music. *It is suggested that the world of guitar adopt these standards as part of a universal standard.* If the guitar is to compete with other serious instruments, then the same professional standards should be followed.

Even if guitarists successfully follow the professional standards for editing, does this mean that they will be excellent editors? For example, does this mean that if Segovia would have simply told us what he was changing (editorial principle #6) that he would have been a perfect editor? The answer to this question is not simple for, as will be shown throughout this book, Segovia changed many passages. It appears that some of the changes were made simply because Segovia preferred his own way of doing things over that of the composer. Whether this is right or wrong is a sensitive matter of musical ethics that is beyond the scope of this project. What can be said with certainty is that Segovia's approach is representative of an individualistic, subjective, Romantic *Zeitgeist* of yesterday, one that is no longer respected in serious music circles. Fidelity to the composer is a part of the *Zeitgeist* of today. Therefore, besides the list of universal standards of editing mentioned above, the following standards are suggested. It is felt that these guidelines are necessary, as a matter of integrity, to avoid distortion of the basic qualities of each piece of music:

8. The composer's melodic, harmonic and rhythmic material must be left intact and may not be changed according to the editor's preference.

The only two exceptions to this are: a.) when, in extreme cases, a change is necessary for technical reasons, b.) when permission is obtained from the composer. Out of respect for Segovia, we must acknowledge that he may have, in many cases, obtained permission from the composer to make a change. Whatever the reason is, it should be identified.

9. Filling out and/or re-voicing chords, repeating non-melodic tones (bass notes or harmonic tones), octave transpositions, adding or subtracting ornamentation and occasionally repeating some of the composer's own material is permissible.

These kinds of changes do not alter the important melodic, harmonic or rhythmic elements except in situations where such procedures are permissible, as in the case of ornamentation. They may be used for strong technical and musical reasons. The reasons should be identified.

10. Every effort should be made to document the way that the composer and the style period call for the music to be interpreted.

In the Romantic style that Segovia espoused, the highest ethic was to perform the music in the way one *felt* it should be played (this is discussed in the introduction to Chapter One of Part II, Volume Two). The ideal of feeling the music should still be *highly regarded.* The danger in our technological, mechanized age is that we will start to lose all feeling and play too much like machines. Segovia's example beckons us in the other direction. Still, our responsibility to the composer and the concern for historical authenticity compels us to submit our hearts to our heads in this matter, and request that the feelings be expressed, but in the proper context, based on the proper knowledge. Extensive documentation is given in each chapter which provides a foundation for the editorial elements that are suggested regarding interpretation.

11. Interpretive elements may be added which did not exist in the mind of the composer or in the style period because of technical limitations.

In other words, we should not automatically disregard something that was not done by the players of the instrument for which the music was written. Performance practice often involves the limitations of the medium for which the piece was originally conceived. A good example of this is the use of slurs in vihuela music. They appear to have been unworkable on the vihuela for technical reasons. Therefore, we cannot exclude them based on only historical reasons in our present medium (the modern classical guitar) where they *are* workable.

---

85. Thomas P. Heck, *The Birth of the Classic Guitar and its Cultivation in Vienna, Reflected in the Career and Compositions of Mauro Giuliani,* Chapter III, "Mensural Notation and the Guitar," Dissertation, Yale University, New Haven, Connecticut, 1970, pp. 149-170.

12. Fingerings should be added in a precise manner. They should be added only in so far as they are deemed necessary for the technical and musical goals being suggested.

It has been pointed out by the guitar scholar Matanya Ophee that guitar editions have suffered from an excessive amount of fingering since the time of Tárrega. Trying to be sensitive to this issue, a conservative approach is suggested here, mostly regarding the right hand. Left hand fingerings, as exemplified by the Segovia editions, are extremely important for realizing the expressive quality of the edition on the modern classical guitar. They are essential to orchestration and the technical ease necessary for an excellent performance. Therefore, it is critical that these be specifically indicated. On the contrary, right hand fingerings are intensely personal. Their specific application will differ greatly according to each guitarist's size and shape of hand and fingernails, finger coordination and concepts of string crossing. Segovia seemed to have the right balance in this matter. He gave extensive left hand fingerings and gave right hand fingerings only when necessary to illustrate an objective solution.[86]

The barring approach taken here is one of more precision than that which is commonly seen in guitar editions. Each bar is represented by a Roman numeral and a fraction that indicates exactly how many of the six strings are to be barred, and for how long.[87] If the bar is to extend over all six strings, no fraction is given. The *glissando* is indicated with right hand fingering on the starting and ending note when both these notes are to be plucked. When the *glissando* is to slide to its note of arrival with no attack on this last note, the right hand fingering is omitted.

These then, are the standards that have been used in the preparation of this book. It is Segovia's inspiration that drives us on to dignify the instrument and its repertoire. Every effort has been made to ensure that the presentation is one of quality and fidelity. We apologize in advance for any accidental oversights or omissions and will commit to making any necessary corrections in future printings.

Now, without any further ado, let's take *A New Look at Segovia*.

Gerard Garno
Toledo, Ohio, 1996.

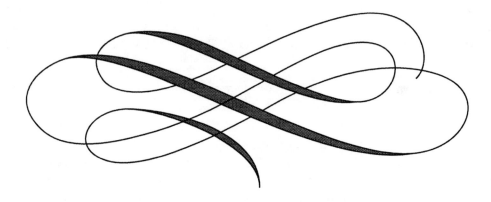

---

86. This does not mean to imply that specific right hand fingerings should not be used throughout. Indeed, it is suggested that each guitarist work out logical right hand fingerings for each piece before committing the work to memory (it is helpful to write them into the score from beginning to end). The point is that these are going to vary with each individual.

87. The exception to this is when a citation is being presented from another edition. For example, when citing a Segovia edition the barring indication as appears in the original will be used. In consideration of the fact that most guitarists use the six string guitar the denominator has been set at six. If one happens to play a guitar with a different number of strings, the denominator should be adjusted accordingly.

PART I

*A New Look at
Segovia's Life:
A Musical Biography of
the Years 1893-1957*

By Graham Wade

1. THE EARLY YEARS

Andrés Segovia's autobiography tells us something, if not the whole story, about his early years.[1] He was born in 1893 in Linares, in the province of Jaén, Andalusia, a region famous for mining and agricultural products. The exact day of his birth is not documented and this has led to the proliferation of enquiries in various publications concerning the precise birth date ever since people began writing about Segovia.

Of particular interest here is Domingo Prat's entry in his *Diccionario de Guitarristas*[2] where the text of Segovia's baptismal certificate was included:

Don Francisco Morales Aballes, Cura Párroco de la de San Pedro de esta capital - Certifica: Que al folio sesenta y seis, vuelta del libro veintiuno de Bautismos de este Archivo Parroquial aparece la siguiente - Partida: En la Ciudad de Jaén, a veinte y cuatro de Marzo del mil ochocientos noventa y tres: Yo Don Juan Garrido y Quesada, Cura Coadjutor de esta de San Pedro, con licencia del Párroco de la misma, bauticé solemnemente a un niño, que, según declaración prestada en debida forma ante mi y los testigos que también lo fueron en ésta José Carpio y Miguel Moya, dependiente de esta Iglesia; por la que dijo ser y llamarse Rosa Torres Cruz, madre del bautizado, nació el día diez y siete de los corrientes a las seis y media de la tarde en la Corredera N° 94 de la Ciudad de Linares, y residiendo en ésta accidentalmente, hijo - de Bonifacio Segobia y Montoro, y de Rosa Torres Cruz: Abuelos paternos Andrés y María Francisca: naturales, el padre y abuelos paternos, de esta Ciudad; la madre y abuela materna, de Málaga; el materno, de Churriana. Le puse el nombre Andrés: fué su madrina Teresa Granadino, de estado soltera, a quien advertí el parentesco espiritual y sus obligaciones. Y para que conste lo firmo con el Rdo. Cura Párroco. Juan Garrido, rubricado. Dn. Romero - rubricado. Es copia literal del original a que me remito. Jaén a treinta y uno de Diciembre de mil novecientos treinta. Hay un timbre de la Iglesia de San Pedro de Jaén.

(Don Francisco Morales Aballes, parish priest of San Pedro in this capital, certifies: that on folio sixty six of the twenty-first book of baptisms of this Parochial Archive appears the following — Item: In the city of Jaén, on the twenty-fourth of March, one thousand eight hundred and ninety three: I Don Juan Garrido y Quesada, Assistant Priest of this parish of San Pedro, with licence from the priest of the same parish, solemnly baptised a boy, who, according to the declaration made in due form before me and the witnesses also assembled José Carpio and Miguel Moya, officiaries of this church, by one claiming to be and to be called Rosa Torres Cruz, mother of the baptised, born on the seventeenth day of the current month at six thirty p.m. at No. 94, La Corredera, city of Linares, and residing there by chance, son of Bonifacio Segobia y Montoro and Rosa Torres Cruz: paternal grandparents, Andrés and María Francisca; inhabitants, the father and paternal grandparents, of this City; mother and maternal grandmother of Málaga; maternal grandfather of Churriana. I have given him the name Andrés. His godmother was Teresa Granadino, spinster, to whom I have advised the spiritual relationship and its responsibilities. In confirmation thereof I sign together with the Parochial Reverend Priest.

Signed: Juan Garrido... Signed: Dn Romero. This is a literal copy of the original to which I have made reference. Jaén, thirty-first of December, 1930. Bearing the seal of the Church of San Pedro of Jaén.)

According to the baptismal certificate, Segovia was born on 17 March, 1893 but this date seems not to have been accepted by the central figure himself. Segovia made the following comment in a book published in 1979:

In several dictionaries you may read different dates concerning where and when I was born. However, I suppose that no musical archeologist will ever fight with another in order to establish the exactness of that point. The truth is that I came to this world the 21st day of February in the year 1893 in Linares, a small and charming village belonging to the Andalusian province of Jaén.[3]

According to Segovia's autobiography, his parents left him in the care of his Uncle Eduardo and Aunt María, who had no children of their own. To comfort the desolate child, removed from his parents, Uncle Eduardo pretended to strum a guitar, sang a song, and taking the infant's arm, helped the boy beat the rhythm:

This was the first musical seed to be cast in my soul and it was to develop, as time passed, into the strongest and most rewarding constant in my life.[4]

No doubt child psychologists could weave a labyrinth of connections between the child's deprivation at this moment in his young life and the comforting security of the guitar, imagined or real. Though Segovia also had brothers and sisters, these are not mentioned in his autobiography except in passing. The circumstances of his adoption by an uncle and aunt,

the reasons behind this, and the emotional ramifications of such an event, are not traced or analysed. Throughout the autobiography Segovia presents the image of himself as a boy and a young man essentially alone with a guitar and music, but without the sustaining presence of a close family. The reality was undoubtedly more complex.

At the front of the autobiography there is a sketch by Vladimir Bobri of Segovia at the age of ten, the sketch being modelled on a photograph published by Bobri in a later book.[4] However, perusal of the original photograph reveals that Segovia was accompanied in the sitting by his sister and his Aunt Maria. That there is no mention of the younger sister, Emilina, in the autobiography, is tantalising, if only because the photograph may indicate closer familial bonds for the young Segovia than the autobiography, written many years later, leads us to imagine. The autobiography remains strangely secretive about the roots of Segovia's upbringing, occasionally raising more questions than it answers. Segovia's childhood is haunted by the absence of his father and mother as far as the autobiography is concerned and no attempt is made to solve the various mysteries implicit in the first chapter of the book.

Equally mysterious in the opening pages is Segovia's relationship with the indigenous flamenco music of Andalusia. His encounter with a flamenco guitarist in the autobiography produces an emotional reaction as the variations of the *soleares* "penetrated through every pore of my body."[5] But a few pages later a meeting with Gabriel Ruiz de Almodóvar, who played both flamenco and classical music induces a "sudden wave of disgust for the folk pieces I had been playing."[6] Through the medium of the autobiography, Segovia, writing many decades after the events described, clearly found it necessary to

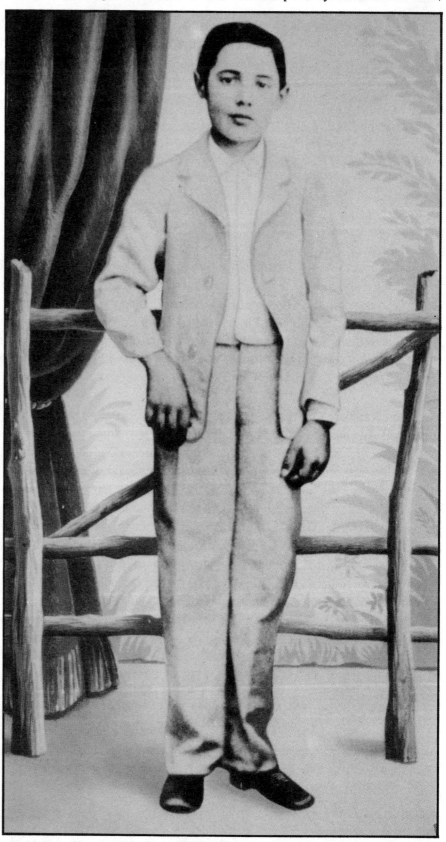

Segovia in 1903.

establish a considerable distance from the art of flamenco, by emphasising that he had experienced an innate antipathy from early childhood to the crude folk music around him.

When Segovia was about ten years old, his uncle and aunt moved to Granada in search of a formal education for the young boy. Before this they lived in the tiny village of Villacarillo, on a street called De las Barandas. This move from a rural backwater to a provincial centre was undoubtedly one of the most formative developments of Segovia's childhood. It was in Granada that Segovia's friend, Miguel Cerón, introduced him to the guitar workshop of Benito Ferrer. In the Albaicín, the gypsy quarter of Granada, he met Gabriel Ruiz de Almodóvar, who played Tárrega's *Preludes* and knew that they were in print.[7] From this point of information Segovia and his friends searched for music, discovering compositions by Arcas, Sor and Giuliani, and beginning the journey of translating the notes on the page into sounds on the guitar.

After the death of Uncle Eduardo, Segovia tells us that "my grandmother, my aunt and I," moved to another house not far from the Plaza de San Nicolás, where the window of Segovia's room faced the Alhambra and part of the city of Granada could be seen.[8] Here Segovia becomes lyrical about the beauty of the city:

Granada! If in Linares I had been born into this world, it was in Granada that my eyes were opened to the beauty of life and art... Many were the hours I spent in my youth in dreamy meditation, hearing the murmur of the streams of the Alhambra in harmony with the trees of El Bosque and the passionate song of the nightingales. [9]

This romantic view of the city contrasts with impressions recorded by a foreign visitor to Granada. J. B. Stone, a nineteenth century traveller, offers a more sober vision of its living conditions:

Granada is the poorest of all the poor cities of Spain... All the troubles and fated misery which are the unfortunate inheritance of the lower classes of Spain are concentrated in tenfold force upon the pitiable inhabitants of the city of Granada... How natural it is that a race of people, shut up as it were within a charmed area, should treasure the remembrance of former greatness... What wonder is there that such untutored people should believe in enchantments hanging about the hills and valleys around them, and be tempted to neglect the weary duties of an anxious life to search for the hidden treasure, which tradition says was concealed to a fabulous extent by the conquered Moors, after they finally quitted Granada. This pining after the shadow of the past, with the want of a healthy activity of mind and body, has naturally a baneful effect upon the place and the people. [10]

J. B. Stone adds a further twist to his vision of the Third World nature of Andalusia at this time:

....There exists in Granada a colony of people whose wretchedness, poverty and misery, far exceed the lamentable condition as of the lowest of Spaniards. These people are the Gitanos or gypsies... No district in Spain has offered greater attractions to the gypsies than the wild and secluded hills and valleys of Granada... So numerous and so lawless have these bands been at times that special codes of law have been framed to curb their actions, and attempts have been made to drive them out of the country, and even to exterminate them... the whole region is a perpetual anxiety to the Government. [11]

But another tourist and writer, Maud Howe, an American, travelling through Spain in the period when Segovia was young in Granada, while making no extreme references to the city's poverty, does emphasise the extraordinary beauty of the Alhambra:

A long straight path of gold sand between two lines of tall, black cypresses leads to the old Moorish garden of the Generalife, near the Alhambra. Every other tree is clipped square at the top, the alternate one towering to a pointed spire. There is always a sound of gliding waters: in the early morning and evening, when the birds' matins and lauds are sung, you can hear the nightingales and the merles. In the patio of the cypresses, under the shade of immemorial trees, is a great sheet of still green water like a vast chrysophrase, where you can study the cloud shadows, or your own reflection — if you are handsome — like Narcissus, or watch the greedy gudgeon and goldfish devour the bread you throw them. We passed through a long flower-bordered path with a thicket of laurel, aloes and pomegranate for a background. A hundred tiny jets of water, like white aigrettes, waved among the green, and lost themselves in the shrubbery. We climbed the long Stairway of the Cascades, cheered by the babble of the little streams of water that run down the tops of the balustrade on either side. In the mirador at the top we rested, and looked down on the wonderful garden with its terraces, cedars, clipped myrtle hedges, thousand and one fountains. [12]

Maud Howe also attended a flamenco performance in the caves of the Albaicín, in the presence of the King of the Gypsies and his son:

> *The musicians, the King's son and another youth with oiled hair and clean new jackets, took their places, twanged their guitars, and the* fiesta flamenca *began. First, a dance by two women, while the others sat by, clapping their hands, tapping with their feet, keeping time to the music.*
>
> *"More power!" cried the King.*
>
> *"Dalé, dalé," droned the chorus. The guitars twanged louder, the handclapping redoubled. Little by little the dancers woke up. The youngest woman was sixty, the oldest girl ten... The children were evidently students being carefully trained; the old women were all good artists, and intent on preserving and handing down the traditions of their art, — but the thing was somehow curiously academic! The old mother took a tambourine from the wall and shook out the music from it in fine style... A woman with a bad face gave us Jaleo, a gross, wriggling dance with unpleasant contortions of the body, wonderful as an exhibition of skill and strength, but not quite decent, and lacking the grace, the beauty, and the dignity of the old woman's performance.* [13]

It was doubtless from this kind of occasion that Segovia later recoiled in reticence and instinctive distrust. The patronising attitude to the indigenous music of Spain subtly apparent here infiltrates many accounts of travels by foreigners in the land of flamenco, perhaps even to the present time, and it was from condescension that the guitar would have to be redeemed in the end. The pioneering formulations of the rescue of the guitar from disdain and neglect are discernible in the early pages of Segovia's autobiography.

2. TOWARDS A DEBUT

Segovia's journey towards mastery of the guitar and international renown was undertaken step by step and the beginning of the ascent, when the way forward was uncharted and obscure, was perhaps as tortuous as any part of the task.

The first stage of Segovia's career was accomplished at the Centro Artístico in Granada in 1909 when he gave his public debut at the age of sixteen. By this time, slowly and very much by his own efforts, Segovia had acquired a repertoire culled from various sources, and a good measure of that inner vision necessary to sustain his quest for the guitar's hidden identity. His grounding in music had involved a rejection, instinctive and final, of formally accepted instruments such as violin, cello or piano, as far as personal study was concerned.[1] But as time went on and he discovered friends who were competent players of such instruments, he learned certain principles from them that he applied to his own study of the guitar.[2] Thus the young man concentrated all his faculties and enthusiasm on solving the problems of the guitar from an early age.

The first piece that Segovia mentions in terms of performance in his autobiography is *Capricho Arabe* by Francisco Tárrega, "at that time the *pièce de résistance* of my repertoire."[2] The young man had already experienced two romantic passions by the end of the first chapter with two girls older than himself named Eloisa and Encarnación, and his performance of *Capricho Arabe* helped to further his attachment to the latter. But Encarnación married another, more prosperous, admirer, and perhaps because of this, though it is not explicitly stated, Segovia left Granada and went to live at his mother's home in Córdoba.[3] This turned out to be unsatisfactory in terms of family relationships as Segovia was unable to get along with his brother. (How interesting it would have been if the autobiography had contained more details of his mother, brother, sisters, etc. But this was not Segovia's intention in writing the book.) As a consequence of his inability to live with his family, Segovia rented a small room on the Plaza Mayor. Fermín Garrido, a doctor from Granada, became Segovia's friend and enabled him to acquire "a fine collection of manuscripts, editions of Tárrega and other composers."[4]

Segovia was now able to enlarge his repertoire and, discovering his technical limitations, began also finding ways to overcome problems of technique:

> *From each difficult passage I would extract a new study and broaden its scope to create an improved exercise. This in turn helped me to overcome more generalized problems.*[5]

In Córdoba he encountered the Montserrat family, with three attractive daughters. One of these, Laura, was studying the piano, and Segovia seems to have learned much by observation of the disciplines needed to achieve any kind of success with the complexities of the keyboard. Most significantly he mentions how at this time he worked out the fingering of diatonic scales on the guitar, never having to change or modify them for the rest of his life.[6] From Laura he heard performances of Beethoven, Schumann, Chopin, Brahms and Mendelssohn. Segovia studied from what he calls the *Método de Armonía* by the Spanish master, Hilaríon Eslava (1807 - 1878), thereby establishing concepts of the theoretical basis of music. Eslava published a *Método Completo de Solfeo* (1846) and *Escuela de Armonía y Composición* (1861) and it is of course possible, given the apparent confusion of titles, that Segovia studied both of these texts during his formative years.

From another friend in Cordoba, Luis Serrano, a pianist and organist, Segovia was able to learn more about the music of J. S. Bach and to ponder the limitations of the guitar, whether in technique or repertoire.[7] At Serrano's home, Segovia was introduced to Rafael de Montis, a young aristocrat from Seville, who had studied pianoforte in Germany with Eugèn d'Albert.[8] Segovia played a number of pieces to de Montis, including Fernando Sor's *Study in B minor*, and a prelude and arpeggio study by Francisco Tárrega.[9] On being invited to play more, Segovia obliged with Tárrega's transcription of Bach's *Bourrée* in B minor from the second sonata for solo violin. On the strength of a sympathetic judgement from de Montis, Segovia explained that he was preparing for a recital at the Centro Artístico in Granada.

In the autobiography, Segovia passes over the debut in Granada on "a date toward the end of 1909," with remarkable brevity, mentioning only that the concert was arranged by Miguel Cerón[10] and that a favorable review appeared in the *Noticiero Granadino*.[11] (In *The Guitar Review, Vol. 1, No. 4*, 1947, p. 82, the date of the debut is given as 1910.)

Disappointingly, no details are given of the program contents. However, Alberto López Poveda, Segovia's official biographer and founder and curator of the Segovia Museo in Linares has researched the area as far as it is possible to do so and suggests the following:

FIRST CONCERT

Granada c.1910: Possible works performed:

Capricho Arabe	Tárrega
Estudio Brillante	
Preludio	
Estudio in B minor	Sor
Serenata	Malats
Mazurka	Chopin
Granada	Albéniz
Three Preludes	Segovia
Tonadilla	

After the recital Segovia returned first to Córdoba and then moved to Seville, following up the possibilities offered by Rafael de Montis. The opportunities of widening his circle of friends, admirers and potential patrons were now very good indeed and Segovia played at *soirées* to some of the "cream of Seville's musical world."[12] As well as musicians he also encountered a number of painters, (including Miguel Angel del Pino who, in the 1920's, did a fine portrait of Segovia), and poets, such as Juan Ramón Jiménez, destined to be a Nobel Prize winner. A romantic attachment to Rafael de Montis' sister, María, prolonged Segovia's sojourn in Seville for over a year.[13] The crown of his artistic development during this time was to perform at the Ateneo in Seville, and to give a number of other recitals, both at public venues and in private homes.

Segovia then travelled to other cities of Andalusia, giving concerts in Huelva, Cádiz, and Jerez. After painfully bidding farewell to María de Montis, Segovia set out for Madrid and the wide world.[14] Pausing for a while en route in Córdoba, he attended a pianoforte recital by Alfred Cortot[15] which he describes as "my first religious experience with music as a member of an audience."[16] His final departure from Córdoba was celebrated in a flamenco evening with friends.

The autobiography at first gives us few impressions of the city of Madrid in the early years of the twentieth century, leaving this to a later chapter. The most important incident that occurred to Segovia concerns the much related story of an experience in the workshops of Manuel Ramírez.[17] Segovia, up to this time, possessed only an inferior guitar and desired to acquire a better. He decided to ask Ramírez if he could hire one for a recital, in the same way as you could hire a piano. Segovia, on making this request, was handed an instrument actually made by Santos Hernández, one of the greatest of all luthiers.[18] Manuel Ramírez[19] was so impressed by Segovia's performance on this guitar that he gave him the instrument forthwith.[20] It is a charming story retold by Segovia over the years in many broadcasts, interviews and even on a recording.[21] The benediction of the gift assumes an almost mystical significance in the overall pattern of Segovia's life.

Since the autobiography was published in 1976, further information about the gift of the guitar has come to light. José Romanillos describes Manuel Ramírez as "a sensitive, thoughtful and imaginative craftsman," whose gift of a guitar to Segovia, "says a great deal about his generosity and about his business instincts too!" Romanillos points out that the guitar in question "was made for Giménez Manjón in 1912 but was in fact, presented to Andrés Segovia."[22]

José Ramírez III also gives an account of the episode from the point of view of Manuel Ramírez.[23] Manjón, "a notable guitarist at that time," asked Ramírez to make a classical guitar for him. The resulting instrument was excellent but Manjón "pointed out non-existent defects in the guitar." During the period of these negotiations, Segovia arrived at the workshop. Because of Segovia's somewhat flamboyant appearance, Manuel Ramírez did not take the young man seriously at first and offered him the first guitar that came to hand to see what would happen. (The Professor of Violin at the Royal Madrid Conservatory was also in the shop at the time in Segovia's account.) However when Segovia began to play, Ramírez's attitude and manner changed, and remarking, "This guitar is not for you," took back the first instrument and handed him the one made for Manjón. Manuel Ramírez's comment was:

Desde luego no le voy a alquilar ninguna guitarra, pero puede Vd. llevarse esa y pasearla por todo el mundo.
(Of course I am not going to hire out a guitar, but you may take this one and go with it throughout the world.)[24]

This much quoted saying may be fruitfully compared with the earlier version of Segovia's autobiographical text, first published in 1947 in the original Spanish in *The Guitar Review.* In the later text, published in book form, Segovia does not mention Manjón, but the miscreant complainer is quoted by Ramírez in fairly vivid colours in the original, berating the precious guitar for its lack of essential qualities.

More significantly, Segovia's Spanish gives us Ramírez's original words in their most poetic rendering at the moment the guitar is handed over to the young artist:

Tuya es la guitarra, jóven... Llévala contigo, mundo adelante, y que lo trabajo la haga fértil... Por lo demás no te apures... Págamela sin dinero.[25]

(The guitar is yours, young man... Take it with you through the world, and may your work make it fertile... For the rest, don't worry... Pay me for it without money.)

Segovia describes Ramírez's generosity as "one of those actions that has value but no price," a comment lost in his autobiography in its full measure. Segovia played the instrument for a quarter of a century and the guitar has entered the realm of legend in terms of its origins and qualities. (It can be heard on the early recordings from 1927 onwards.)

(A further mysterious story garlands the history of Segovia's first concert guitar. Gregor Piatigorsky relates that Segovia was playing a recital when just before the end of the concert there was a loud cracking sound as the guitar split. Segovia went into the dressing room where he repeated sadly to himself, "My guitar, my guitar," many times. According to the anecdote, Segovia discovered later that the moment the guitar cracked was when Manuel Ramírez died.)[26]

3. THE EARLY REPERTOIRE

Segovia's recital at the Ateneo of Madrid in 1912 was naturally one of the great events of his career and the gateway to other concerts throughout Spain. But at the time it seemed discouraging, mainly because it showed no "immediate result."[1] According to the *Autobiography*, however, Manuel Ramírez saved the day by praising the recital for its power and passion, and (more significantly) by offering a private recital to the young artist in the home of the director of a foreign bank.[2]

The program of the Ateneo concert is not given in the *Autobiography,* though one of the quoted letters (written to Turina) mentions "some fine little pieces by Tárrega and mostly transcriptions of minor classic and romantic works."[3] At all stages of the early career, the problem of repertoire when compared with the rich treasuries of other instruments, seems to have been an insistent and troubling issue, and it would be some years before this was adequately resolved. In the meantime it is remarkable how Segovia climbed further and further into the esteem of all who attended his concerts with very little repertoire indeed. A program of a concert in Cadiz played two years after the Madrid debut provides an interesting example of the mixture of "fine little pieces" and transcriptions:

ROYAL ACADEMY OF SAINT CECILIA

Cadiz, 19th May, 1914

I

Gavotte in D minor	Tárrega
Estudio in D, No. 24	Coste
Capricho Arabe	Tárrega

II

Bourrée	Bach
Sonata Op. 13, Adagio	Beethoven
Nocturno	Chopin

III

Granada, serenata	Albéniz
Cádiz, saeta	
Sevilla	

At one time in the perception of how guitar history developed in the twentieth century, it was firmly believed that Andrés Segovia won the battle for the solo guitar as a legitimate recital instrument single handedly and that there were no other contenders worth considering. The opening up of various areas of the developments of this century, through research and the publication of a number of biographies, has shown that Segovia was not alone, even during the period from 1912 and the establishment of his recital programs.

The kind of repertoire Segovia performed during the first part of his career was along the lines of the traditional material inherited from the era of Francisco Tárrega. Many years later in the 1940's, when Segovia was writing his autobiographical material, he chafed against the limitations of the repertoire as a horse might chafe against the restraining bit. But it may well be that in the context of guitar music as it existed during his apprenticeship years that Segovia was less displeased with the characteristic sounds of the guitar's available repertoire than he professed to be over thirty years later. The reason this view may be advanced with some confidence is that so much of the early material was retained throughout his entire career, providing evidence that Segovia was at ease and at one with the legacy of Tárrega.

What he became more aware of as time passed and his musical horizons broadened was that the boundaries of the guitar repertoire were in drastic need of expansion. Segovia's career ultimately achieved an enormous and unprecedented increase in the available repertoire, but much of the incoming new material was akin in substance and essence to the spirit of the old. In this sense Segovia maintained continuity with the traditional values of the guitar rather than any total displacement or destruction of the greatly loved pieces of the early decades of this century.

As is well known, Segovia was always eager to preserve the supremacy of melody and tonality characteristic of the world of his youth and made no concessions at any time in his life to the progressive and experimental dissonances of the European avant-garde.

It is fruitful therefore to examine the roots of the repertoire at this time, to see what was being done in terms of performance programs and practice, rather than simply dismissing the available material of the guitar as not worthy of any consideration. Out of these foundations the twentieth century repertoire was to grow and with this period the heritage of Tárrega found its fulfilment.

On 7 February,1903, Francisco Tárrega had given a recital at the Palacio Corea, Rome, Italy, performing the following:[4]

Part I

Melodia	Verdi
Barcarola	Mendelssohn
Serenata, Granada	Albéniz
Seguidillas	Chueca
Rapsodia Andaluza	Albéniz
Fantasía española	Tárrega

Part II

Trémolo	Tárrega
Motivo español	Chueca
Momento musica	Schubert
Tema con variaciones (La Pastoral)	Mozart
Nocturne in E minor	Chopin
Variaciones sobre un tema de Paganini	Tárrega

One of the most significant aspects of this concert for our purposes is surely the fact that a few of these compositions remained as perennials, including of course some of the pieces by Tárrega, Albéniz and Mendelssohn.[5] The classical transcriptions in this instance, that valiant attempt by Tárrega to give the repertoire weight and historical force, ultimately dropped out of favour. Verdi, Chueca and Chopin would become unacceptable in terms of transcribed items while Schubert and Mozart have retained a niche of some interest.[6] Also of relevance here is that Tárrega continued the long tradition of composer/performer, playing his own pieces within recitals, an aspect which Segovia eventually decided not to pursue.

Just over a decade later, in 1914 (no other date given), Tárrega's pupil, Miguel Llobet, performed the following recital in Munich, Bavaria, in southern Germany.[7]

Minuet in E minor, Op.11	Sor
Capricho Arabe	Tárrega
Romanza (transc. Llobet)	Rubinstein
Two Studies , Op. 38	Coste

Bourrée (transcr. Llobet)	J.S.Bach
Sevilla (transcr. Llobet)	Albéniz
Mazurka — Minuetto	Tárrega
Variations on a Theme by Sor	Llobet

The constant presence of the music of Sor, Tárrega, Bach, and Albéniz, as well as Llobet's own *Variations on a Theme of Sor, Op.15* (written in 1908),[8] reveals that the early recitalists of this century were performing music that would always be both at the heart of the repertoire and also popular as part of the pedagogic methods. The core works are identifiable through a host of concerts during these early years and it is impossible to believe that guitarists did not cherish and enjoy these pieces profoundly. In relative terms, compared particularly with the vast library written for pianoforte, such material may offer less than a banquet. But for the guitarists, then and now, many of these selected works provide virtuosic material and enough substance and challenge to offer a true musical experience entirely appropriate to the nature of the guitar. To the audiences of the early twentieth century such music must have seemed utterly delightful, representing skill, technical mastery, and expressive melodic lines played with passion and integrity.

On 17th January, 1916, Miguel Llobet performed a program at the Princess Theatre in New York in company with the pianist, Paquita Madriguera (protégée of Enrique Granados and later (1938) the second wife of Andrés Segovia) and Giovanni Martino, who sang some operatic arias.[9] Llobet was billed as "The World's Greatest Guitarist" for this event. The occasion shows that the cause of the guitar was not quite as neglected as we might sometimes believe and that in capable hands, the instrument received the respect and admiration of other musicians and the public. For his part Llobet performed *Minuet* (Sor), *Capricho Arabe* (Tárrega), *Bourrée* (Bach), *Danza española* (Granados) and *Fantaisie Espagnole* (Arcas),[10] apparently being given the honour of ending the concert. The sixteen year old Madriguera played several virtuosic pieces including *Allegro de Concierto* (Granados), *Aragón* (Albéniz) and *La Campanella* (Liszt).

On 1 August, 1916, many thousands of miles from Europe and the USA, Agustín Barrios performed a program in Rio de Janeiro which once again shows the possible scope of the early twentieth century guitar:[11]

First Part		Second Part	
Marche Heroica	Giuliani	*Nocturno, Op. 9, No. 2*	Chopin
Chanson de Printemps	Mendelssohn	*Phantasia sobre motivos de Traviata*	Verdi
Recuerdo del Pacífico	Barrios	*Andante y Estudio*	Coste
Rondo brillante	Aguado	*Chant du Paysan*	Grieg
Sarabande	Bach	*Biche Feio—Tango humorístico*	Barrios
Meditaçao	Tolsa	*Rapsodia Americana*	Barrios
Concerto in D minor	Arcas	*Jota Aragonesa, variations*	Barrios

The ingredients of the program here follow the contours of a characteristic Tárrega recital in various ways. There are pieces from the nineteenth century guitarists, Giuliani, Aguado, Arcas and Coste, transcriptions from the masters in the Tárrega tradition, such as Mendelssohn, Chopin and Grieg, (with a fairly short exposure to the music of Bach), and a

Segovia in Madrid, 1916.

substantial input from the composer/performer himself. Chopin's *Nocturne Op. 9, No. 2,* transcribed by Tárrega (transposed from the key of Eb to E), seems to have been a favourite among recitalists in the early twentieth century. Miguel Llobet played this in his first recital outside Spain in Paris in 1904. Janie Villiers-Wardell commented in her book, *Spain of the Spanish*:

> *Miguel Llobet is a notable guitarist... It was in Paris that I first had the pleasure of making this musician's acquaintance, and I confess to a feeling of intense surprise when I heard him playing the opening notes of one of Chopin's most exquisite Nocturnes. I had never thought of associating the guitar with serious music, but in the hands of Miguel Llobet it gave us Bach and Mendelssohn, Chopin and Beethoven.*[12]

With the drastic changes in musical taste and fashion that have occurred this century, and in an age when the medium is believed to be the message, few critics or members of the public would nowadays consider the playing of a Chopin *Nocturne* by any other than a pianist to be an indication of "serious music." But on this occasion Miguel Llobet received admiration for the content of his program and it is clear that the instrument did gain credibility from these transcriptions.

What is also worthy of emphasis is the fact that the guitar repertoire was undoubtedly developing during the early decades of the century in substantial terms. It would be an error to regard the repertoire as merely being in a passive state awaiting the arrival of a supremely dominant figure when a number of formidable performers were applying their minds to the problem of what to present to their international audiences. As well as attempting to modify the structure of a recital, Segovia was also in the process of discovery, learning from the examples of others as well as from his own experience.

One very important event in Segovia's career at this stage, was his meeting with Miguel Llobet. Ronald Purcell dates the meeting at about 1915, when Segovia at the age of twenty-two posed with Llobet and some other distinguished *aficionados,* for a famous photograph.[13] Segovia's account of his meeting and studies with Llobet in the autobiography relates how a number of vital pieces were added to his repertoire,[14] including two *Danzas españolas* by Granados and the Catalan Folk Song, *El Mestre.*[15] As Llobet had not yet written the pieces down, Segovia learned them directly from him rather in the way that flamenco is taught, not by notation but by imitation. Within ten days, despite the presence of various onlookers and other guitarists, Segovia had memorized a number of such treasures of the repertoire including the beautiful *Tonadilla, La Maja de Goya* by Granados. Presumably Segovia might have learned other Catalan Folk Songs arranged by Llobet about this time and whatever was absorbed would eventually be used in recitals.

The fruits of these consultations with Miguel Llobet provide an enrichment of Segovia's recitals and recordings throughout his life. It is difficult to imagine Segovia's repertoire without these central items somewhere at the heart of his favorite compositions. The immediate benefits of the new pieces can be discerned in a concert given at the Galerías Layetanas in Barcelona on 28 January, 1916:

I

Song without Words	Mendelssohn
Melody—The Happy Peasant	Schumann
Waltz—Nocturne	Chopin

II

Allegro in A	Coste
El Mestre	Llobet
Granada	Albéniz
Capricho Arabe	Tárrega

III

Andalucía	Segovia
La Maja de Goya	Granados
Spanish Dance in E	Granados
Spanish Dance in G	Granados

This particular set of pieces included no less than four items from the Llobet repertoire, as well as one of Segovia's own compositions (now believed lost). Of the total progam, seven items would remain perennial through Segovia's entire career, an extraordinary testimony to the strength and durable appeal of so many of these foundation works of the early twentieth century concert literature.

Don Alberto López Poveda, founder of the Segovia Museo in Linares, has provided a facsimile reprint of two recitals given by Segovia at the Alhambra Palace Hotel, Granada on 17 and 19 June, 1917. The details of the program reveal the significant extension of recital capability since Segovia's Cádiz concert, cited at the beginning of this chapter. The two programs performed by Segovia in Granada in 1917 are powerful evidence of the new horizons he was now exploring, the guitar repertoire providing a more vivid spectacle of technique and colorful musicality than ever before.

Alhambra Palace Hotel, Granada, 17 June and 19 June, 1917:

FIRST CONCERT

I

Minueto en mi	Sor
Tema con Varacione	Sor
Serenata	Malats
Scherzo—Gavota	Tárrega
Capricho Arabe	

II

Loure	Bach
Claro de Luna	Beethoven
Berceuse	Schumann
Vals	Chopin
Nocturno	Chopin

III

Lo Mestre	Llobet
L'Heureu Riera	Llobet
Granada	Albéniz
Cádiz	Albéniz
Danza	Granados

SECOND CONCERT

I

Minueto en la	Sor
Allegretto	Sor
Final	Sor
Allegro en la	Coste
Estudio	Tárrega

II

Bourrée	Bach
Sonata Patética—Andante	Beethoven
Au Soir	Schumann
Romanza	Schumann
Canzonetta	Mendelssohn

III

Allegro en la	Vieuxtemps
Mazurka	Tchaikovsky
Danza	Granados
La Maja de Goya	Granados
Sevilla	Albéniz

With the clear exception of pieces by Beethoven, Schumann, Chopin, and Vieuxtemps, much of this repertoire has retained its appeal for players and audiences alike right up to the present decade. Many of the pieces have been recorded over recent years by leading contemporary guitarists such as Julian Bream, John Williams, Narciso Yepes, Alirio Díaz, Sharon Isbin, Manuel Barrueco, Eduardo Fernández, etc. By 1917 Segovia was presenting programs which ideally represented the best of the Tárrega tradition both of transcriptions and also of original works, spiced with further excellent material gleaned from Miguel Llobet. The core of the repertoire was solid, and many of the pieces would remain at the center of Segovia's recitals for the next seventy years, especially the compositions by Albéniz and Granados. The tripartite structure, borrowed from the example of Tárrega, was also preserved in Segovia's concerts throughout his life.

A recital given by Emilio Pujol the following year on 8th June, 1918 in the Orfeó Gracienc, Barcelona, demonstrates how a recognisable identity was formulating within the program structure:[16]

1st Part

Minuet	Sor
Canço de Bressol	Pujol
Vals Intim	Pujol
Recuerdos de la Alhambra	Tárrega
Danza Moresca	Tárrega

2nd Part

Adagio	Haydn
Loure	Bach
Minuet	Bach
Moment Musical	Schubert

3rd Part

El Mestre	Llobet
El Testament d'Amelia	Llobet
Serenata española	Malats
Granada	Albéniz
Danza	Granados

The developments in the establishment of a repertoire between 1900 and 1910 have been among the well kept secrets of the guitar. So much attention has been focused on the dawning of the new repertoire of the 1920's that little emphasis has been placed on the way guitarists came to grips during the previous decade with traditional material. When in the 1950's a new age began to assert itself again with the presence of Julian Bream and John Williams, distinguished performers such as these would also come to terms with the music characteristic of Segovia's recitals before making true advances into their own individual territory. In like manner Segovia did justice to the brightest and best of his era, being very much a man of his time and developing to artistic maturity steadily in keeping with the example of fellow guitarists of his period such as Llobet and Pujol.

Llobet and Pujol were, of course, students of Francisco Tárrega. That Segovia had not studied with Tárrega or with one of the master's pupils marked him out from his fellow guitarists of distinction. In 1902 Tárrega had changed his technique from using his finger nails to the use of the fleshy tips of the fingers, the nails being cut short.[17] Llobet had ended his lessons with Tárrega before this occurred and continued to play with the combination of nail and flesh first put forward in a pedagogic Method by Dionisio Aguado in the early nineteenth century. Segovia followed Llobet's technique and continued to refine the nail and flesh approach. But many of the existing followers of Tárrega believed fervently that the way to play the guitar was with the tips of the fingers. Most noticeable among their number was Emilio Pujol whose book on this disputatious subject was first published in 1930 revealing how long the rancorous debate lingered on.[18]

What did undoubtedly occur, as Segovia travelled intensively round Spain after his 1912 debut in Madrid, was a certain antagonism towards him on the part of those who still followed the teachings of Tárrega as they understood them. The autobiography devotes a considerable amount of venom towards the perpetrators of a kind of musical snobbishness which engulfed the guitar and threatened to render it paralysed in an unprogressive and somewhat incestuous parochialism. Segovia directs his most bitter comments to the amateurish disciples of Tárrega who wished to preserve the guitar against further developments not in keeping with the assumed messages transmitted by the master to his closest disciples.

His enemies included Daniel Fortea, (1878 -1953), "one of Tárrega's last pupils," who refused to open up his collection of pieces for Segovia's inspection:[19]

> *...I was more convinced than ever that I had to free the guitar from such jailers by creating a repertoire, open to all, which would end once and for all the exclusivity of those "inherited jewels." I thought of going to Joaquín Turina and Manuel de Falla — they were already known — and to other composers... I would act as their guide through the labyrinth of the guitar's technique. I would see to it that their musical ideas came to life in the instrument.*[20]

Ironically, this "jailer" of the repertoire, Fortea, later founded the publishing firm of Biblioteca Fortea, issuing over six hundred compositions for the guitar.[21] These compositions included many of Fortea's own compositions but also a wide selection of nineteenth century guitar music from Carcassi, Sor, Coste, and especially the works of Tárrega as well as a number of transcriptions by Fortea, flamenco music, guitar duets, Bach collections, etc.

The sense of rejection and insult which Segovia received from both Fortea and the amateur followers of Tárrega may have provided one of the most significant incentives which impelled him towards contemplation of a repertoire far in excess of what was then available. The somewhat scornful response of Tárrega's supporters in Valencia to Segovia's playing, related in the autobiography, merely added fuel to the flames of indignation.[22] Fortea gave a recital in his home town of Castellón de la Plana on 30th October, 1912, and later performed in Madrid, Barcelona and Valencia.[23] His *Método de Guitarra,* appeared in 1921. Though the aims of Tárrega's supporters and Segovia had so much in common, and were united in a single love of the guitar and a desire to propagate its music, the complex politics of the twentieth century guitar, with its multiple alliances and competitive elements were already active. Many of the arguments, in one form or another, would rumble on for decades, and Segovia's ultimate disenchantment with the guitar tradition represented by Tárrega and his aftermath, can still provoke an adverse or dismissive response in certain parts of Iberia.

Awareness of the fact that from 1910 Segovia was one of a number of guitarists presenting similar repertoire to limited audiences, should perhaps make us hesitate about accepting the autobiography as a totally reliable source. It is preferable to read the autobiography as Segovia's interpretation of his early years from the standpoint of middle age, and as such the document seems vulnerable to its author's sometimes acrid re-interpretation of the years of his struggle towards international esteem. Moreover Segovia is never too scrupulous about dates or chronology, and an anecdotal approach ensures that various of the central episodes were retold and re-shaped to show the author in the best light.

The primary questions of this chapter concern the nature of the guitar repertoire around 1910. From the evidence a number of conclusions can be suggested:

1) The recital programs from 1903 onwards of Francisco Tárrega, Miguel Llobet, Agustín Barrios, and Emilio Pujol (as well as those of Andrés Segovia after 1909), suggest that the structure of guitar recitals was well established and in a condition of development.

2) As the decade progressed Segovia became increasingly aware of the work of other guitarists such as Llobet and his own repertoire developed accordingly.

3) Initially Segovia's recitals were in the apprenticeship stage as he toured Spain, encountering both admiration and some measure of antagonism whether from non-guitarists who found it difficult to believe in the guitar as a credible concert medium or players who followed Tárrega's concepts of technique and repertoire.

4) Segovia's recitals became increasingly more heavyweight according to the ideas of the day. It is difficult to judge objectively if Segovia felt as strongly about the limits of the repertoire as he did in later decades. Certainly many of the pieces he played at this time were retained in his concerts for the rest of his life.

5) As we shall see, it was in the 1920's, after his tours abroad, that radical extensions to the repertoire were achieved.

4. THE WIDER HORIZONS

Segovia's autobiography becomes vaguer on specific dates and events as it reaches the end of its alleged span of the years 1893 -1920. One reason for this is that the dates set out on the title of the autobiography are not accurate or well documented and should probably have been 1893-1918. The evidence for this is that Segovia's first son, Andrés, was born in Argentina in 1919. Yet the autobiography makes no mention of Segovia's marriage to Adelaida Portillo or the birth of Andrés. All that we have in the autobiography is an impassioned sense of the pains of parting from his fiancée:

> *I cannot describe the emotions of that farewell, the sorrow of having to leave my beloved behind, the uncertainty of what could await me across the ocean that was to separate me from my country, the thought of my mother's precarious future if my tour were to fail, the idea of arriving in a new land, after seventeen days at sea, without loved ones to meet...*[1]

This is also the first mention in the autobiography of his mother's financial dependency on her son, an area kept carefully hidden from our gaze throughout the book. Yet other incidents are also not mentioned in the autobiography. One such incident concerns Segovia's friendship with the family of Federico García Lorca, the great Spanish poet. Ian Gibson has given us a fascinating insight into the high esteem in which Lorca's family, and in particular the poet's father, Federico García Rodríguez, regarded Segovia.[2] When Lorca's first book was to be printed, at his father's expense, it was to Segovia, among others, that the family turned for advice:

> *Don Federico García Rodríguez was perplexed and disturbed by the sudden flowering of his eldest son's literary vocation. Moreover, it was clear that he was going to be expected to foot the printer's bill for* Impressions and Landscapes, *which was ready to go to press in early 1918. Did the book deserve to be published? Was its prose any good? The landowner decided to consult various people qualified to pass judgement, among them Luis Seco de Lucena, editor of* El defensor de Granada; *a cultured businessman, Miguel Cerón Rubio,[3] who admired Federico, and Andrés Segovia, then twenty-three and already a much respected figure in the town. After a careful perusal of the manuscript the three were unanimous that the book should be allowed to appear. "We liked it," Andrés Segovia recalled many years later. "We spoke to Don Federico at once and told him that, in our view, his son had a great talent as a writer and a splendid future." Federico García Rodríguez accepted the ruling of the triumvirate, and generously undertook to finance the book...*[4]

Though Segovia mentions several writers who crossed his path during the years covered in the autobiography, there is unfortunately no comment concerning Federico García Lorca or the friendship with the poet's family.

The autobiography concludes with Segovia on the deck of a ship setting out for the challenge of South America. While gazing longingly at the Spanish coast, he was tapped on the shoulder by "an aging gentleman, friendly and dignified at the same time."[5] The gentleman introduced himself as Juan Martínez Roig, from Tucumán, Northern Argentina, a "retired successful businessman." Thus the book form of the autobiography ends on a positive note of continuity and hope. It seems clear from this ending that Segovia wished to continue the autobiography at a later date.

In the summer of 1985, Andrés Segovia gave the present author a copy of a later fragment of an autobiography, picking up at the point where the young man encountered Señor Martínez Roig. This was a typed photocopy, with emendations in Segovia's handwriting, but unfortunately only fifty-five pages long. (In a letter, dated 11 May, 1986, to the English editor and agent for the publisher, Bill Swainson, Segovia announced his intention to add three more volumes of autobiography.)

This document does however shed some light on his first trip to South America. From these pages we learn that his ship, after a rough crossing, first docked in Rio de Janeiro, where Segovia, in the company of Señor Martínez Roig, was able to have a trip ashore. Eight days later the ship arrived at Montevideo, where many years later Segovia was to set up home. For various reasons no recital took place here, and Segovia's first concert on the South American tour took place at the Sala Argentina, Buenos Aires. It was a great success and after the concert Segovia was able to meet the composer, Julian Aguirre (1868 -1924).[6] Segovia also encountered Martín Gil, from the Argentinian province of Córdoba, amateur guitarist, astronomer, physicist, philosopher, writer, etc, and a most useful ally to have at the outset of a tour of a new continent.[7]

At all stages of his career the charismatic personality of Segovia attracted influential individuals towards him and inspired many friendships of a deep and lasting kind. To people unfortunate enough to offend him, Segovia was capable of unrelenting antagonism but to his supporters, helpers and friends Segovia offered deep loyalty. According to the account given in the pages of unpublished autobiography, Segovia was quite harshly subjected throughout this trip to various kinds of annoyance from those who did not understand or like the guitar and the prejudices of various critics. These hurdles had to be overcome by a mixture of diplomatic cunning in his dealings with such problems and excellent performances in recital.

According to an interview with Segovia many years later, he performed his first concerts in Montevideo and Buenos Aires in 1919 or 1920.[8] Richard D. Stover gives the dates of 11 and 27 June, 4 and 25 July (the concerts taking place at the Teatro Solís), 1920, for a series of recitals in Montevideo, Uruguay, Segovia's visit coinciding with three concerts by Agustín Barrios (19 June, 3 July and 6 July, at the Verdi Institute).[9] Richard Pinnell offers the dates of two "conciertos de la semana" advertised in the columns of La Nación in Buenos Aires, Argentina, as 16 June (Salon "La Argentina") and 19 June (Teatro Odeón), 1920.[10]

Richard Stover gives us the program of the concert of 25 July at the Teatro Solís, Montevideo, and points out that Barrios and Segovia did not meet at this time.[10] The program for Segovia's recital is an interesting example of the choice of repertoire before Segovia's own composers entered the scene:

First Part

Sonata	Sor
Andante - Allegretto -	
Minuet - Rondo	
Capricho Arabe	Tárrega

Second Part

Gavotte	Bach
Andante	Haydn
Popular Song - Petite Study	Schumann
Prelude No. 15	Chopin

Third Part

Prelude - Andantino -	Tárrega
Prelude - Allegro	
Study	Vieuxtemps
Mazurka	Tchaikowsky
Sevilla	Albéniz

Richard Stover comments that "Segovia shortly thereafter departed for Buenos Aires,"[11] but if Richard Pinnell's dates from La Nación are correct, then Segovia was already commuting between Montevideo and the Argentinian capital in order to play recitals.

Segovia's published autobiography concludes "in the days preceding my departure from Spain," with a message of hope concerning the writing of new works for the guitar:

Then there was a 'first' in the field of the guitar: for the first time, a composer who was not a guitarist wrote a piece for the guitar. It was Federico Moreno Torroba, whose musical poem had just been premiered by the National Symphony under the direction of Maestro Arbós. Moreno Torroba had been introduced to me by the orchestra's first violin, Señor Francés. It did not take us long to become friends, nor for him to accede to my suggestion: Would he compose something for the guitar? In a few weeks he came up with a slight but truly beautiful Dance in E major.[12]

The precise date of the composition of this *Danza*, destined to appear in the fullness of time as the third movement of the *Suite Castellana*, cannot be pinpointed. But Segovia makes the questionable comment that the success of *Dance in E major* "prompted Manuel de Falla to compose his very beautiful *Homage,* and Joaquín Turina his splendid *Sevillana.* "[13]

Homenaje, "Le Tombeau de Claude Debussy" by Falla was composed in 1920, so it seems likely, if Segovia's comments were at all accurate, that *Dance in E major* was written about 1919. Ronald Crichton gives the premiere of *Homenaje* as being performed by Emilio Pujol in the Salle du Conservatoire on 22 December, 1922.[14] But Manuel Orozco comments that the piece was first played by Segovia at the Alhambra Palace Hotel during the Concurso de Cante Jondo in Granada earlier that year.[15]

In a maze of contradictory statements of this kind, it may however be simply affirmed that the new concepts of establishing a different kind of guitar repertoire, from the traditional pieces composed by guitarists to a choice including a high proportion of music written by non-guitarists, would develop from this time onwards. The search was on for a new world, though in 1919/1920 it is unlikely that even Segovia was totally aware that such a movement was to constitute one of the central features of his entire approach to the guitar. But in a few years the trickle of new compositions would become a flood, and the desire for a new range of pieces to play a compelling obsession.

5. CONCURSO DE CANTE JONDO, GRANADA, 1922

With the Concurso de Cante Jondo of 1922 held in Granada, we now move out of the gravitational pull of the autobiography towards one of the most intense periods of Segovia's artistic development. In the 1920's many of his primary aims became fully established, especially with regard to the nature of the repertoire he wished to develop for recitals.

The Concurso of 1922 represented a turning point in Segovia's career, a juncture where decisions were formulated which would hold good for his entire life. The Concurso also reveals the centrality of Segovia's presence in Spanish cultural life during this era. For the events in Granada in 1922 brought together all kinds of artists in a glorious celebration of traditional Spanish values. Never again would such a celebration take place in quite this way despite the hopes of the organisers to create an annual festival.

The Concurso of 1922 is by now a massively documented occasion, with many accounts of its events available in a wide range of scholarly publications. The essential background was prepared by Manuel de Falla's return to Granada (in September, 1920), where he moved into a *carmen* (villa with a garden), at 11, Calle de Antequeruela Alta. In the next few months Manuel de Falla and Federico García Lorca became good friends. The decline of the art of flamenco in its true authenticity was something which troubled them. It has been said that Miguel Cerón Rubio first thought of the idea of a competition in which the best artists of *cante jondo* would appear.[1]

In November, 1921, Lorca began writing poems inspired by *cante jondo,* and on 19 February, 1922, gave a lecture at the Centro Artístico in Granada with the title, *Cante Jondo, Primitive Andalusian Song*. His opening paragraphs laid the foundation of his concerns:

The intellectuals and enthusiastic friends backing the idea of this festival are only sounding an alarm. Gentlemen, the musical soul of our people is in great danger! The artistic treasure of an entire race is passing into oblivion. Each day another leaf falls from the admirable tree of Andalusian lyrics, old men carry off to the grave priceless treasures of past generations, and a gross, stupid avalanche of cheap music clouds the delicious folk atmosphere of all Spain.... [2]

In the lecture Lorca defines *cante jondo* (deep song), as the name "given to a group of Andalusian songs whose genuine, perfect prototype is the Gypsy *siguiriya*." The difference between *cante jondo* and flamenco is that "the origins of the former must be sought in the primitive musical systems of India... while flamenco, a consequence of deep song, did not acquire its definitive form until the eighteenth century." The distinctions between *cante jondo* and flamenco are therefore afforded fine shades of subtlety especially as the roots of either art were transmitted aurally rather than by notation or literary means. But there is always fervent discussion concerning the nature of authentic or true flamenco and the point at which the art's natural development changes its essence so much that new manifestations no longer deserve the revered epithet of "flamenco."

It is not difficult to conjecture that Lorca's impassioned testimony to the values of the music of old Andalucía would have greatly appealed to Segovia's romantic conservatism. The central mission of Segovia's life was to be the restoration of the guitar to an imagined glory that the instrument may never have enjoyed throughout its history. A similar process enfolded the ideals of the Concurso — preservation of an ancient art form if possible, a new life for *cante jondo,* if such a resurrection could be achieved.

Thus Andrés Segovia joined Manuel de Falla and Federico García Lorca among the organizers, along with Miguel Cerón and Manuel Jofré (flamenco guitarist). According to Manuel Orozco, Segovia and Jofré eventually developed an antagonism towards each other, a sentiment which Orozco blames more on Segovia:

All the members of the Rinconcillo were great aficionados *of the* cante *and gypsy dancing. Among these were Manuel Jofré, an extrordinary guitarist and the maestro who taught flamenco dances to Andrés Segovia, before the hostility which he showed, inexplicably to that kind lover of the guitar. The desertion by Segovia as he moved towards a cult of the guitar which escaped from the popular, created a certain suspicion (more than was justified), towards him among the group.* [3]

There were other tensions in the process of organising the Concurso. The City Council of Granada, for example, were not entirely helpful in that they refused to sponsor the attendance of Maurice Ravel and Igor Stravinsky at the Concurso.[4] But despite all such problems the event took place during the month of June, 1922, in a celebration of Spanish culture of remarkable significance.

Antonio Gallego Burín gave a reading at the Alhambra Palace Hotel from Manuel de Falla's essay *El "Cante Jondo" (Canto Primitivo Andaluz): Sus Origenes, Sus Valores Musicales, Su Influencia en el Arte Musical Europeo,* published anonymously by the Centro Artístico of Granada, 13 and 14 June, 1922. As well as setting out the composer's views on *cante jondo,* this document offered some words on the nature of the Spanish guitar:

The uses of the guitar made by the people represents two clearly determined musical values:the rhythmic value, external and immediately perceptible, and the purely tonal — harmonic value.

The first of these, together with some cadential phrases of easy assimilation, was the only one to be used over a long period by more or less artistic music, whereas the importance of the second, the purely tonal-harmonic value, was hardly recognized until relatively recently; the only exception being Domenico Scarlatti.

...The harmonic effects that our guitar players unintentionally achieve are one of the marvels of our natural art. Even more we believe that our fifteenth-century instrumentalists were probably the first to add a harmonic accompaniment (with chords) to the vocal or instrumental melody.[5]

In line with this endorsement of the historical development of harmony through the guitar, are the rules of the *Cante Jondo* Competition which shed considerable light on the definitions of the art as perceived by the organisers:

For the purposes of the competition, cante jondo *will be considered to be the group of Andalusian songs, the generic type of which we believe to be the so-called* siguirilla gitana. *This is the origin of other songs still kept up by the people, like the* polos, *the* martinetes, *the* soleares, *which thanks to their very high qualities, distinguish themselves within the great group of songs commonly called* flamenco. *Strictly speaking, though, this last name should be applied only to the modern group formed by the* malagueñas, *the* granadinas, *(and their common stock, the* rondeñas), *to the* sevillanas, *the* peteneras, *etc, all of which can only be considered as derivatives of those we formerly named, and will therefore be excluded from the competition.*[6]

Eusebio Rioja, Spanish scholar of the guitar and *aficionado* of both classical and flamenco, sees these distinctions, along with Lorca's division between *cante jondo* and *flamenco,* as somewhat spurious and historically unreliable. However it was these definitions which Segovia accepted and which moulded his view of flamenco for the rest of his life:

As one can appreciate, this deals with a concept so remote and restrained, both in relation to the cante *and to guitar playing, that both are reduced to a mere structural scheme... This would be the concept which the jury followed in its criteria.*

... These principles would claim the resurrection of an anachronistic flamenco, not existing in the actual flamenco of 1922, if it ever existed, and is thus a mere pipe dream. Perhaps because of this we can explain the poor artistic outcome of the Concurso and the frustration of its architects that they did not manage to encounter the dream they were seeking.

And this was the concept of the flamenco guitar that Segovia maintained and defended all his life and in which he remained deadlocked.[7]

Felix Grande refers to Segovia's playing of four recitals at the Concurso, and comments that on 7 June, Segovia performed a *solea,* Jofré played a *petenera* and *siguiriya,* and Lorca read part of his *Poema del Cante Jondo.*[8] Segovia eventually wrote his own account of the *Concurso:*

Back in 1922 the great composer, Manuel de Falla, organized a competition of cante jondo *(deep singing) in Granada, in collaboration with personalities of that divine city, and with young artists of the pen, the brush and music, among whom they included me, Fernando de los Ríos, the painter Ignacio Zuloága, and the poet Federico García Lorca. Lorca was too young to undertake any active responsibility in the complicated organisation of this fiesta. The rest of us simply enjoyed his animated gaiety and his poetic nature which frequently gave sudden flashes of genius.*

Nevertheless I think it opportune to recall that we joined together, he and I, to overcome the lack of official economic aid in a project of such merit as to invite the great French composer Maurice Ravel, who loved Spain very much, to be present at the concurso. *The mayor of Granada was unable to provide more than one thousand pesetas, specifying them as prize money for the best contestant. Federico and I announced a joint program, consisting of recitation on his part and playing the guitar on mine...*

This gathering took place one evening in the little theater of the Alhambra Palace Hotel. First Federico recited his poem dedicated to Silverio (a true master, already disappeared from the cante *jondo), and then I began to strum the guitar,* rasgueando a soleares *with* farsetas[9] *composed by me for this occasion, and with others of Paco Lucena. The little theater was full of people. We were showered with bravos, shouts, wisecracks and teasings, and the concert was transformed into an unceremonious* juerga, *since the public was composed of friends and acquaintances.*[10]

Segovia's account presents his participation in the Concurso as a reasonably light-hearted affair, and not as a concert in which he played flamenco self-consciously and formally. Whether the riotous reception accorded to the occasion was the result of the good humour that sometimes occurs when an established player of classical music momentarily relaxes and strays over into more popular musical genres is not clear. But not too much should be made of the fact that Segovia played a few measures of flamenco at this gathering, though it seems clear that this was the last recorded instance of Segovia allowing an incident of this kind.

The central focus of the Concurso was the competition for the singing prize and Ian Gibson gives a good account of this:

The great surprise of the competition was the performance of Diego Bermúdez Cañete, 'El Tenazas' ('Pincers'), an old cantaor, *almost forgotten, who, so it was said, had walked to Granada all the way from Puente Genil, in the province of Cordova, a cross-country hike of some eighty miles. Bermúdez sang the first night with powerful* duende *and carried all before him. The second evening, however, after a day's tippling (sponsored some averred, by his rivals), 'El Tenazas' was not in such inspired form. None the less he was awarded a thousand pesetas for his first night's achievement.*[11]

In his account of the Concurso Segovia recounts the following anecdote:

I was among the judges of the contest. We had the preliminary evaluation of contestants in the small theater of the Alhambra Palace Hotel. While we were waiting at the door for all the members of the jury and other persons to arrive, a very old, short and frail man came to me and said, "Andresito," exactly as if I were still a young boy, "Don't you remember me?" I looked at him, made a strenuous effort of memory and answered, "No, I don't remember you." He insisted, "Don't you remember Diego, your servant?" Then I screamed and embraced him, saying, "Diego, what are you doing here?" He replied ,"I was told that if anybody knows the old cante *jondo, he may have a prize of several hundred pesetas. And as I am so old, and don't you remember - I used to sing very well - maybe the prize could fall to me."*

... The name of this man was Diego Bermúdez, an Andalucian. He had been a servant in the household of my uncle and was with the family for about 12 or 15 years...[12]

This certainly puts Segovia's relationship to the art of flamenco into a different perspective. Segovia, as a young man, was apparently in a house for a decade with one of the best flamenco singers of Spain. His knowledge of *cante jondo* was therefore not arbitrary but the result of close listening to some of the finest examples of the art available.

In an article in 1973, Segovia outlined his later views on flamenco, emphasising that his dislike of current flamenco trends was primarily a matter of definition:

When asked for a pronunciamento *on the new wave of flamenco guitarists — Serranito, Manolo Sanlúcar, Paco de Lucia,— who currently dominate the* tablao *scene, Segovia replied: "We have never before had such a magnificent assortment of flamenco guitarists. They are marvellous every one of them. The problem is that none of them plays flamenco. How can you expect them to play flamenco? Who understands flamenco? This art is felt and understood by a tiny group of Andalusians — not even by the average Spaniard, mind you — and foreign audiences certainly have no idea of what flamenco means.*[13]

With this kind of argument, reminiscent of similar discussions in other contexts of the meaning of "jazz," nobody wins. Segovia is perceived as a reactionary who believes that few, if any, of the artists who perform flamenco know what the music should be. Any subsequent developments or extensions of flamenco tradition are therefore ruled invalid, a most unsatisfactory state of affairs for all concerned.

Did this critical impasse originate through the events of 1922? Perhaps not, yet it is surely clear beyond doubt that the Concurso in Granada changed the direction of Spanish music in subtle ways. Manuel de Falla, for example, would no longer pursue the Holy Grail of Andalusian folk music:

The festival over, Manuel de Falla returned with relief to the seclusion of his carmen. *"You could not imagine,' he wrote to Trend on 7 July, 1922, "the extent to which my work and other things put off till later piled up during the long and laborious preparations for the competition." Falla was scandalized by the fact that the competition left in its aftermath an ugly discussion about what should be done with the profits that had accrued as a result of the venture's undoubted success. The punctilious composer decided that he had had enough, and henceforth largely avoided the Arts Club. From this moment, too, the Andalusian elements in his work were drastically reduced.*[14]

Segovia's attitudes too were no doubt deeply affected by the events in Granada. From now on Segovia's career would become ever more international, departing from the more parochial or inward looking aspects of Andalusian culture into a wider world. Perhaps he realised at this point the virtues of a totally purist approach, leaving the art of flamenco in the hands of such luminaries of the Concurso as Ramón Montoya and La Niña de los Peines, while he pursued a path which implicitly led by slow steps away from the Spanish cultural habitat towards the broad uplands of the international concert hall.

6. THE NEW REPERTOIRE

If Segovia took stock of the development of his career shortly after the Concurso of 1922, he could already have been reasonably satisfied with progress achieved. Following the Granada debut in 1909, he had given concerts throughout Spain, made tours to South America, had a wife and child, various works were already dedicated to him, and at the Concurso he was respected, in the company of Falla and Lorca as one of the most significant of Spanish artists. An apprenticeship had been worked, a repertoire established, and Segovia had acquired an audience for the kind of recital he was interested in giving. In 1922 he stood shoulder to shoulder, as it were, with Pujol and Llobet, whose concert careers and other achievements, such as scholarship, editing and arranging, provided an example of opportunities that could be explored.

The decade of the 1920's was to be full of triumphs and surprises, as Segovia looked for ways of raising his career to new heights. From 1923, when Segovia was thirty, a multitude of doors began to open. At one time this period of Segovia's life was often obscure in its details. But the publication of letters from Segovia to Manuel Ponce between 1923 and 1947 has provided us with an unexpected and unprecedented fund of information about the circumstances of Segovia's life and inner thoughts during these crucial years.[1]

Andrés Segovia made his debut in Mexico in 1923. Manuel Ponce attended the recital and wrote a eulogistic article in *El Universal* on 6 May, mentioning also Segovia's work in persuading "young Spanish musicians" to write for the guitar.[2] Part of his review commented on Moreno Torroba's *Sonatina* which Ponce regarded as "the most important work of the program." Segovia invited Ponce to write for him,[3] and later that year in an undated letter informed the composer that he had played his Sonata in Madrid, the piece in question presumably being *Sonata Mexicana*.[4]

In the same letter Segovia tells of his happiness that composers were actively interested in the guitar.[5] In his list of composers fulfilling this task are Albert Roussel, who had already given him a work entitled *Segovia,* while promises had been given by Ravel, with some possibilities from the direction of Volmer Andreas, Suter, Schoenberg, Weles, Grovlez, Turina, Torroba and Falla. Roussel wished to extend his piece by two more movements and Torroba was working on a Sonata, and a Suite.[5]

Thus Segovia had many irons in the fire at this stage and yet so few of these names in the end contributed anything to Segovia's repertoire. The loss of Ravel in this missionary work of recruiting composers for the guitar is a sad one for all lovers of the instrument. The name of Schoenberg in the list may raise eyebrows but in 1923 this composer contributed his *Serenade Op. 24,* for ensemble (clarinet, bass clarinet, violin, viola, cello, mandolin, guitar, and baritone voice). If Segovia ever came into contact with this work (and its guitar part) he has not told us about it, though his hatred of avant-garde dissonance and the whole movement it represented may well have originated in this kind of composition and from this era. Nowadays such a work has been absorbed into the blood stream of twentieth century musicians and can be regarded as a congenial work with a certain humour:

In this opus 24, which is linked to the light-hearted Viennese tradition, Schoenberg tries to apply the new compositional techniques to a range of older forms like the minuet and the march. In the whole work it becomes clear that Schoenberg desires to carry over twelve-note principles into every aspect of composition including the vertical one, i.e. into chords and accompanying figures...

The Serenade *is peculiar in that its complexity from the point of view of compositional technique never consciously strikes the listener. He is diverted in this witty gay work by its fire-engine noises (in the dance scene), its potpourri-like improvisation (in the final march), and its Mediterranean chirping sounds evoked by guitar and mandolin. It is not until the score is examined that the amount of artistic craftsmanship and sovereign technique employed becomes apparent.*[6]

Such exuberance as "fire-engine noises" and "Mediterranean chirping sounds" would not have been appreciated by Segovia at any time in his career. Yet in the early 1920's such atonality would surely have sounded especially horrendous to the young artist, engaged as he was in an exploration of the somewhat more traditional musical vocabulary of

Moreno Torroba or Turina. Moreover Segovia had now discovered a composer who appealed to him in every way, and the letters from Segovia to Ponce reveal a total delight in the music of his new ally in Mexico and in the possibilities of compositions yet to come.

It is to be regretted that *The Segovia-Ponce Letters* do not include any correspondence for the period between 1924 and 1925. Thus we do not tune in to Segovia's comments on some significant landmarks in his career during these years. One of the most important of these was the debut in Paris, 7 April, 1924, in the presence of Dukas, Falla, Madame Debussy, Roussel, Joaquín Nin, Miguel de Unamuno and others. In the same year Segovia played in Switzerland, Germany and Austria and made another tour of Latin America, including Argentina, Cuba (where he experienced his first recording session) and Mexico. Also during 1924 Segovia met a young American named George C. Krick, in Munich, who later helped persuade the impresario, Sol Hurok, to book Segovia for concerts in the USA.

The precise program of Segovia's Paris debut has unfortunately not come to light, as even the Segovia Museo of Linares is not in possession of a copy. But a recital given in Graz, Austria, on 3 October, 1924, offers an interesting update on Segovia's concert material at this time:

I

Sarabande, Gavotte, Menuet, Gigue	Robert de Visée
Theme with Variations	F. Sor
Two Folksongs	Llobet
Étude	Tárrega

II

Guitarra	G. Pedrell
Serenade a une Morte	F. de Lacerda
Sevillana	Turina
Sonatina *(Allegretto - Andante - Allegro)*	F. M. Torroba

III

Danza	Granados
Torre Bermeja - Sevilla - Leyenda	Albéniz

The performance of the music of Robert de Visée represents the beginning of the interest in this composer among concert guitarists. In recent times de Visée's writings have been taken over by the practitioners of Early Music, who prefer to restore the music to the original context of the Baroque guitar with its specific tunings and timbres. But between the early 1920's and the next half century, de Visée was fair game for classical guitarists and *Suite in D minor* became one of the most popular and frequently recorded works of the repertoire. As with several Renaissance and Baroque composers, Segovia's interest may have been stimulated by the pioneering scholarship of Emilio Pujol.

The inclusion of a piece by Francisco de Lacerda (1869-1934), the Portuguese conductor and musicologist, has something of a novelty value about it. Lacerda is mainly known for his compilation of *Cancioneiro musical portugues*, which contains some five hundred folksongs. The work which Segovia performed in 1924 seems to be lost to posterity, and the manuscript may have been destroyed in the events of 1936, along with many others.

Segovia did however produce his trump cards in this recital, namely the works of substance dedicated to him by Turina and Moreno Torroba. *Sevillana, Op. 29,* by Joaquín Turina was composed in 1923 and premiered by Segovia at the Sociedad Madrileña de Cultura Musical on 17 December of that year. This was Turina's first composition for solo guitar and in many ways his most inspired:

The title must be understood as a reflection of the spirit that inspired the composer but not in a formalistic sense, since the work is a small fantasia *which goes beyond the popular* seguidilla *of Seville. A section based on* rasgueos *(strumming) gives way to a more cantabile passage overwhelmingly Andalusian, which provides the* copla *section. There is a notable development before the cyclical return to the initial* rasgueos.[7]

The concert program for the Graz recital provided extracts from some of the reviews Segovia received for his concerts in Germany in 1924. They reveal the extent to which Segovia's remarkable performances and stage presence impressed the German critics:

Schwäbischer Merkur in Stuttgart, 2 May, 1924: Segovia - a technical genius... the Paganini of the guitar... The most wonderful thing is the sound, the soul of his playing... Words are inadequate to evoke this marvel of musical colors and deep inner knowledge.

Münchener Neueste Nachrichten, 11 May, 1924: Unbelievable ease in performance... A technique taken to the highest level. Everything earthly seems cast aside as Segovia plays... The line of beauty is always held firmly, the tone noble and delicate.

Elberfeld, Tägliche Anzeiger, 15 May, 1924: Andrés Segovia is presumably not only the greatest guitarist of Spain, but very likely altogether the most important artist of his kind.

Cassel, 18 May, 1924: One is allowed to call Segovia's playing, without exaggeration, a phenomenon of sound.

Stuttgart, 3 May, 1924: All superlatives in preliminary announcements proved valid, and actually insufficient.

The next few years of the decade were to see a complete consolidation of the movement towards a new guitar repertoire. What started as a trickle eventually became a flood, and it was this establishment of a new world of sound which distinguished Segovia from his competitors from now on. The compositions written for him were discreetly highlighted in the recitals, and at the same time Segovia, as with the music of de Visée, broadened the base of his offering of Renaissance and Baroque music. Meanwhile the core repertoire of Segovia's early years, the works of Sor, Tárrega (including selected revised transcriptions), Granados and Albéniz, etc. remained like giant pillars in the structure of his programs.

On 25 May, 1925, Manuel Ponce began his journey from Mexico to Europe to stay a while in Paris, the cultural heart of European music at this time.[8] In particular Ponce was to study with Paul Dukas, an association which would yield profound artistic benefits for the development of Mexican music. The move also enabled Ponce to lay the foundations of his close friendship with Segovia.[9]

The effects on Segovia of this relationship were enormous as the Segovia-Ponce letters reveal. The advantages of the friendship were obvious as Manuel Ponce continued to write works for the guitar for the rest of his life, providing Segovia with an extended repertoire of sonatas, variations, preludes, etc. and, in the fullness of time, a Guitar Concerto. The possible disadvantages are rarely, if ever, mentioned or discussed. But it is likely, because of the strength of the friendship, that Manuel Ponce's innate traditionalism and conservatism of harmonic language reinforced Segovia's own preferences for a musical vocabulary rooted in tonality and removed from any kind of experimentation.

As time went by Segovia judged many of his contemporaries by the example and principles of Ponce, and sometimes this may have gone too far. If Segovia had managed a friendship of a similar depth with Stravinsky (or even Villa-Lobos), the history of the guitar in the twentieth century would perhaps have been quite different. Historically however Segovia's relationship with Manuel Ponce was almost certainly the strongest musical inspiration of his life. For Segovia, Ponce was the best of all composers who had written for him, a view which he sustained over the years, as is evident by the moving testimony written as an epitaph for the composer in 1948:

It would be an unpardonable omission to finish these notes without making very clear the incomparably important place which Ponce occupies in the current revival of the guitar. Anyone who loves the instrument — let alone those who have professed its religion — unless he be hard-hearted and empty-headed, must reverence the memory of Ponce. He lifted the guitar from the low artistic state in which it had fallen. Along with Turina, Falla, Manén, Castelnuovo, Tansman, Villa-Lobos, Torroba, etc, but with a more abundant yield than all of them put together, he undertook the crusade full of eagerness to liberate the beautiful prisoner. Thanks to him — as to the others I have named — the guitar was saved from the music written exclusively by guitarists.[10]

With Heitor Villa-Lobos, Segovia had a less intimate relationship than with Manuel Ponce. But it was during the early years of the 1920's that the two were destined to meet in Paris, and from their friendship, tempestuous though it may have been, much of the most popular guitar music of the twentieth century would be forthcoming. Hermínio Bello de Carvalho took down the words of Villa-Lobos which described the first meeting with Segovia:

I first met Segovia in 1923 or 1924 (I can't remember exactly which year) at the home of Olga Moraes Sarmento Nobre in Paris. There were several distinguished people there. I saw a young man, with long hair, surrounded by women. I thought he was rather crass and arrogant, but at the same time, likeable. Costa, the Portuguese violinist, asked Segovia, if he knew Villa-Lobos, but without telling him that I was there. Segovia replied that Miguel Llobet, the Spanish guitarist, had told him about me and had shown him some of my works. I had written a Valsa-Concerto *for Llobet (unfortunately the score is lost). Segovia remarked that he found my compositions unsuitable for the guitar and that I had used some elements which were alien to the instrument. Costa replied, "Well, Segovia, Villa-Lobos is here." So I went straight up to him and said, "Why do you find my compositions unsuitable on the guitar?" Segovia, rather surprised — after all he couldn't have imagined that I was there — explained that the little finger on the right hand, for example, was not used on the classical guitar. I replied, "Is that so? Then we'll see about that!" Segovia still tried to protest, but I came up closer and said, "Give me your guitar, give it to me!" Segovia would not lend his guitar to anyone so he put up some resistance to my request, but without success. I sat down and played till the party finished. Segovia came to ask me afterwards where I had learned to play. I told him that I was not a guitarist but that I knew all the technicalities of Carulli, Sor, Aguado, Carcassi and the others. Segovia put on his coat, placed the guitar in its case and rushed out.*[11]

Many years later Segovia gave his own account of the meeting:

Of all the guests of that night, Villa-Lobos was the one who on arrival caused the greatest impression...
When I finished my introduction, Villa-Lobos came towards me and said in a confident tone: "I also play the guitar." "Marvellous," I replied. Stretching out his hands, he asked me for the guitar. He sat down, he laid it across his knees, holding it firmly against his chest, as if he were afraid it might escape... Then when least expected, he struck a chord with such force that I gave a scream, thinking that the guitar had broken... After several attempts to start playing, he finally gave up.[12]

The following day Segovia visited Villa-Lobos in the company of Tomás Teran, a Spanish pianist. According to one story Villa-Lobos pretended to be busy and Segovia was forced to return later in the day:

He went away, but returned later and we took turns playing the guitar until 4 a.m... He asked me to write a Study *for the guitar — the friendship that was born between us was so great that instead of there being one study, there were twelve.*[13]

The first meeting between Segovia and Villa-Lobos had been arranged with the help of Teran:

When Segovia arrived in Paris, he requested the Countess of Boisrouvray to take the pianist under her wing at the outset of his Parisian career. With her help, Olga de Moraes Sarmento Nobre organised a musical soirée for the purpose of introducing Segovia to contemporary musicians and personalities. The outcome of the meeting between Segovia and Villa-Lobos was also inadvertently aided by Tomás Teran, in 1925 through the guitar belonging to Maria Teresa, his wife. While the two friends were on holiday in Lussac-les-Chateaux, the composer discovered the instrument among his friend's luggage and spent many hours composing the studies.[14]

Villa-Lobos was clearly stimulated into composing by the presence of Segovia, and during this decade wrote the remarkable set of *Douze Études,* their completion apparently dating from 1929. Unfortunately Segovia did not champion these twelve studies with the same zest as inspired him with the works of Manuel Ponce, and played (and recorded) no more than three of the set. Moreover there was a long hiatus between the end of composition in 1929, and the date of publication. Segovia showed little or no interest in performing virtuosic studies of this kind and consequently it was left to a later generation of guitarists after 1960 to place the studies (in their entirety as a set) at the heart of the twentieth century repertoire where they belong as truly revolutionary and wholly unprecedented examples of creative guitar writing.[15]

Composers soon discovered that Segovia was not easy to please in terms of compositions presented to him. Joaquín Turina, for example, labored in vain to provide suitable material for Segovia but was destined not to satisfy, as a conversation with Segovia in 1983 revealed:

W. And what about Joaquín Turina — you knew him well?
S. Turina? Oh yes, he was a very good friend. But Turina had no idea how to write for the guitar. Sevillana *was the first piece he wrote for me. I had to keep sending it back and every three days he wrote it all out again. Everything he wrote included the theme of the* Sevillana. *When he came to write* Fandanguillo, *he wanted to put the same in again, and I had to say no! And of course* Fandanguillo *is a most beautiful composition. But with the* Sevillana *I had to work*

very hard; I had to make many modifications so that it could be more fluent over the fingerboard. And he was a perfectionist himself in every way. And every day came another version if there was anything I disliked. And one day he gave me a whole *sonata.*

W. *But you didn't play the* Sonata *by Turina very much, did you?*

S. *I played the* Sonata *on one tour and no more. That was because the themes are not really those of a sonata at all. Look at the sonatas of Ponce — all the themes are appropriate to the form of a sonata.* [sings themes from Ponce, then from Turina]. *Turina's themes are like a very robust lady doing the movements of a dance — they are not defined.*

W. *And Turina's* Homage to Tárrega? *I can't remember that you ever played that one either? But it's popular with a lot of recitalists.*

S. *No, I do not like it.* Homage to Tárrega *has nothing whatever to do with Tárrega. It has a* Garrotín *and a* Soleares, *and is very Andalusian. Tárrega was from a little place in Valencia, from Villarreal and lived in Burriana.*

W. *And* Ráfaga — *you didn't do that one!*

S. *No, not that either. The* Sevillana *and* Fandanguillo *are the pieces that remain throughout my career.*[16]

Turina's seminal works for solo guitar, each dedicated to Segovia, were composed and premiered in the following order:

Sevillana, Op. 29, composed 1923, premiered by Segovia in the Sociedad Madrileña de Cultura Musical on 17 December of that year, and published in 1927 by Sociedad Musical Daniel, Los Madrazo, 14, Madrid (republished by Columbia Music Co, Washington in 1964).

Fandanguillo, Op. 36, composed in a few days and finished 4 June, 1925, was published by Schott in 1926. J. L. García del Busto suggests it was premiered in the Teatro de la Comedia, Madrid, possibly as late as February, 1932.

Ráfaga, Op. 53, published by Schott in 1930.

Sonata, Op. 61, premiered by Segovia in the Academia Santa Cecilia in Rome on 29 January, 1932, was given its first Spanish performance at the Asociación de Cultura Musical, Madrid, in April of that year, and published by Schott in 1932.[17]

Homenaje a Tárrega. Op. 69 (Garrotín y Soleares), published by Schott in 1935.

From 1923 onwards some of the finest of Manuel Ponce's works appeared in rapid succession:

Sonatina Mexicana, (Sonata No.1), 1923. This has been described as the first "true guitar work by Ponce," growing out of a short piece, a serenade based on the theme of *Jarabe tapatío,* "termed as the national dance of Mexico."[18] Published in 1967, revised and fingered by Manuel López Ramos, Peer International Corporation, New York.

La Valentina, arrangement 1924.

La Pajara and *Por ti mi Corazón*, (from *Tres canciones populares mexicanas)*, 1925. Published 1928 by Schott in Segovia's Guitar Archive Series.

Estrellita, arrangement, 1925.

Prelude, 1925. This piece was intended to be played with a *cejilla* or *capotasto* on the second fret. Published by Schott, 1928.

Sonatina for Guitar and Harpsichord, 1926. Published in 1973 by Peer International Corporation.

Thème varié et Finale, 1926. Published by Schott in 1928.

Sonata III, 1927. This composition along with *Thème varié et Finale* and *Tres canciones populares mexicanas*, was among the first of Ponce's guitar compositions to be published by Schott in 1928.

Sonata Romántica (Homage to Schubert), 1928. Published by Schott in 1929.

24 Preludes, 1929. Segovia edited twelve of these for publication by Schott in 1930, the remaining *Preludes* having to wait until 1981 when the entire set was issued by Tecla Editions, edited by Miguel Alcázar.

Suite in A (Preludio, Allemande, Sarabande, Gavotte, Gigue), (in the style of the Baroque), 1929. This composition had a strange history, being performed (and recorded) for many years by Segovia as if it were an original work by Sylvius Leopold Weiss, the great German lutenist of the eighteenth century. The suite was eventually published fifty-three years after its composition under Ponce's name in 1983 by Editions Transatlantiques, edited by José Luis González.

Various editions appeared prompting questions on occasion of scholarly integrity on the part of editors who sometimes (but not always) claimed to have transcribed the movements from lute sources. Many guitarists recorded all or part of this suite over the next fifty years, commenting on the sleeve notes that this was authentic Weiss. (This kind of musical hoax, beloved also by the great violinist Fritz Kreisler, who passed off his own compositions as masterpieces from luminaries of the past, may inadvertently in the long run have aroused interest in the life and real music of Weiss.)

Such a remarkable catalogue of notable innovation in the guitar repertoire was also augmented by the composer who first rallied to Segovia's request for new compositions, Federico Moreno Torroba. His works were published from the outset in Segovia's Guitar Archive Editions inaugurated by Schott's Söhne, of Mainz, Germany in 1926. This series proved to be one of the most important publishing developments in the guitar's history and one of the foundation stones of the twentieth century guitar. At first sales were sparse but in time to come the financial returns would be remarkable as items from the series began to be performed by recitalists throughout the world and studied in academies by generations of students. Royalties for recording alone would ultimately prove phenomenal.

The following compositions of Moreno Torroba were published by Schott during the 1920's:[19]

Suite Castellana (Fandanguillo, Arada, Danza), Nocturno, (1926): *Burgalesa, Preludio, Serenata Burlesca,* (1928).

The piece that Segovia probably played most and which achieved the greatest fame of Moreno Torroba's compositions for guitar was *Sonatina in A,* (dating from c.1924),[20] published by Edición Musical Daniel of Madrid,1924,[21] (revised and republished, Columbia Music Co, Washington D.C., 1953).

Other composers surfaced during the 1920's and contributed to Segovia's repertoire. One immediate result of the Paris debut of 1924 was a work by the French composer Albert Roussel (1869 - 1937), entitled *Segovia, Op. 29,* premiered in Madrid, 25 April, 1925, followed by a first Parisian performance on 13 May. The composition was published by A. Durand et Fils, Paris (1925) and a piano transcription of the piece by the composer was issued at the same time.

Also in 1925 Segovia met the Polish composer, Alexander Tansman (1897-1986), who had settled in Paris. The result of their friendship was the publication in 1928 of *Mazurka.* Tansman then, for reasons unknown, produced little for the guitar until the 1950's when he was to achieve great success with further compositions for Segovia. Of *Mazurka,* Domingo Prat commented that "it reminds us at some moments of the sonorities of Ravel's compositions."[22]

In the same eventful year, Gustave Samazeuilh (1877 -1967), a French composer who had studied with Chausson, d'Indy and Dukas, wrote a most Spanish sounding piece entitled *Sérénade* (published Durand, 1926). Segovia performed this in Bueno Aires on 23 July, 1928, during his South American tour.[23] Samazeuilh also wrote for the violinist Eugène Ysaÿe, as well as for the violin-piano duo of Jacques Thibaud and Alfred Cortot. His little *Sérénade,* though not frequently performed, weathered the storms of time to be immortalized in a Segovia recording as late as 1976.

A neglected but interesting work of the 1920's was *Fantasía-Sonata, Op. A-22,* by Joan Manén (1883-1971), (published by Schott, 1930). Domingo Prat observes that this work is dedicated affectionately, *Por y para Andrés Segovia,* and describes it as "a glorious prize presented to the guitar".[24] Despite such accolades the composition never achieved the highest profile though Segovia recorded it in the 1950's. Its ten pages constitute a determined attempt to provide the guitar with a work of some magnitude but the lack of performances overall, by either Segovia or other leading guitarists, suggests that various aspects fail to satisfy.

Even more obscure was a small piece by the English composer, Cyril Scott (1879 -1970), for Segovia named *Reverie,* which according to Domingo Prat was performed at the Teatro Odeón, Buenos Aires on 23 July, 1928. Segovia in a letter of 20 July, 1927, refers to a Sonatina of Cyril Scott [25] (All attempts to locate the manuscripts of either of these pieces have failed.)

Apart from this territory of commissioning new works for the guitar, some of which were to fall by the wayside quite soon while others prospered, the decade of the 1920's revealed Segovia in a further act of reclamation — the transcription of suitable works by J. S. Bach. The background to this is integrated with the complex history of Bach scholarship dating from the nineteenth century.

On the centenary of the death of Bach in 1850, the *Bach Gesellschaft* (Bach Society), was founded, dedicated to the task of publishing the complete works. Over the next fifty years, forty-six volumes were steadily produced between 1851 and 1899. In January,1900, the *Neue Bach Gesellschaft* replaced the original *Bach Gesellschaft,* with the intention of presenting Bach's music in practical editions.

The *Bach Gesellschaft* was reprinted in miniature score in 116 volumes by Kalmus. Volume No. 903 offers: I. *Praeludium and Fugue* (for lute), II. *Suite* (for lute) and III. *Suite* (for lute). These works are now usually known as *Prelude, Fugue and Allegro* (BWV 998), *Suite in E minor* (BWV 996), and *Partita in C minor* (BWV 997). Each was printed in usual keyboard notation in two clefs.

The process of resurrection of the whole of Bach's output, so long neglected, was taken a significant stage further by the publication of *Johann Sebastian Bach, Kompositionen für die Laute,* edited by Hans Dagobert Bruger, published by Möseler Verlag in 1921, and being issued with a further preface and more editorial material in 1925. Segovia purchased a copy of the first edition. Interviewed on the *Woman's Hour* programme on BBC radio in 1981, Segovia talked about his first encounter with the treasure of Bruger's edition, and exclaimed, "I was in Heaven when I discovered that!"

The Bruger edition paved the way for Segovia's own transcriptions of selected compositions of Bach. (He had already been influenced by Tárrega's arrangements of a few of Bach's works.) In 1928 Segovia published his edition of *Prelude in C minor* (arranged in D minor for the guitar), (BWV 999), *Allemande* (from BWV 996), and *Gavotte* (from BWV 1006a), as well as *Courante* from the *Third Cello Suite* (BWV 1009).

His subsequent recordings on 78 r.p.m's of several Bach pieces would accustom many people throughout the world to hearing this composer on the guitar. Segovia became famous for his inimitable playing of Bach, quite unlike the playing of cellists, violinists, and pianists, yet performed with a tremendous vitality which delighted a public for whom the principles of the Early Music revolution were many decades distant.

A check list of Segovia's Guitar Archives Series, published by Schott, with the appropriate Guitar Archive number and date of publication, (plus one other publication for a different company), reveals the amazing amount of editorial work he achieved during the period between 1926 and 1930.

102. Turina, *Fandanguillo,* 1926.
103. Moreno Torroba, *Nocturno,* 1926.
104. Moreno Torroba, *Suite castellana (Fandanguillo - Arada - Danza),* 1926.
 (Turina, *Sevillana,* publ. Sociedad Musical Daniel, 1927).
106. J. S. Bach, Vol. I, *Prelude - Allemande - Minuetto I - Minuetto II,* 1928.
107. J. S. Bach, Vol. II, *Courante - Gavotte,*1928.
108. J. S. Bach, Vol. III, *Andante - Bourrée - Double,* 1928.
109. Ponce, *Thème varié et Finale,* 1928.
110. Ponce, *Sonata III,* 1928.
111. Ponce, *Tres canciones populares mexicanas,* 1928.
112. Ponce, *Preludio,* 1928.
113. Moreno Torroba, *Burgalesa,* 1928.
114. Moreno Torroba, *Preludio,* 1928.
115. Moreno Torroba, *Serenata Burlesca,* 1928.
116. Tansman, *Mazurka,* 1928.
117. Mozart, *Menuet,* 1928.
118. Franck, *Four Short Pieces,* 1928.
119. Pedrell, (*Three Pieces*), I. *Lamento,* 1928.
120. Pedrell, II. *Página romántica,* 1928.
121. Pedrell, III. *Guitarreo,* 1928.
122. Ponce, *Sonata clásica,* 1929.
123. Ponce, *Sonata romántica,* 1929.
124. Ponce, *Preludes I, Nos 1 - 6,* 1930.
125. Ponce, *Preludes II, Nos 7 - 12,* 1930.
128. Turina, *Ráfaga,* 1930.
129. Manén, *Fantasía-Sonata, Op. A-22,* 1930.

Thus the 1920's, following the apprenticeship period between 1910 and 1919, can be seen as a crucial decade in the evolution of Segovia's international reputation. The explosive power of his editorial work, moving to the future with the new composers and to the past with a range of transcriptions from J. S. Bach and others, was truly remarkable. So many of these works have remained central to the guitar repertoire of the concert platform and the recording studios. However, the development of the repertoire during this decade, as the next chapter will show, was against a backcloth of widening geographical horizons and the advent of recording. It was at this time that Segovia began to outstrip his possible rivals on various fronts and establish for himself the unique qualities which enabled him to be regarded as the most influential guitarist of the twentieth century.

7. INTERLUDE

By the mid 1920's, even before his publications and the debut recording sessions, Andrés Segovia had achieved critical recognition and acclaim. In Fritz Buek's *Die Gitarre und ihre Meister*, published in 1926, there is one of the first in-depth accounts of Segovia's early biography, his rise to success and his reputation at this time, (as well as an evaluation of other guitarists including Llobet, Pujol, and Sainz de la Maza):

Llobet's greatest rival was his compatriot, the Andalusian, Andrés Segovia, whose successes over recent years became well known and led to competition between these two great exponents of guitar playing. Llobet is the foremost representative of the Spanish school and above all of the Tárrega method. Segovia found his identity and his way by himself. The remarkable thing is that there is no essential difference between them. An explanation of this phenomenon might be in our assumption that both artists were products of the same school. We may suppose that the underlying elements of an art contain principles which the genuinely talented understand intuitively, so that it would seem that "schools" and "methods" were written and invented for the benefit of untalented pupils.

How Segovia came to the guitar appears best in his saying, "The guitar sought me and I sought the guitar, and so we met each other halfway." His career shows us that he was vocational by nature and art, and that music was his supreme law. Without guidance, by his feeling for what was right, he learnt to play the guitar. Like his famous compatriot, Sor, he obtained his education in a seminary, and also his first music lessons. He came to the guitar by accident. He saw a guitar at the house of a friend and was so fascinated by its sound, that he decided to master the art of playing the guitar. In his native town there were at that time no teachers and no guitarists. He had to rely on his own resources.[1]

Buek tells us that the first piece of music Segovia discovered was Tárrega's *Spanish Serenade* which the young man deciphered painstakingly, though as yet he could not read music or understand the system of guitar fingering:

This very difficult beginning has its advantages. He understood at once that the guitar was an instrument with its own values, that it was an instrument on which one could play everything, and that it required serious study. Now hard work began. Because there was a lack of study material, he made his own exercises... He was quite advanced in his playing when he heard of a guitarist in Granada, who was, however, paralysed. He sought him out and so came to know everything worth knowing about the guitar and its literature. Though the guitarist could not demonstrate anything to Segovia, as his left hand was paralysed, he told him about the required studies and gave him some explanation about techniques. Segovia acquired all the available material and, helped by these sources and also by the exercises of Aguado and the works of Sor, Tárrega and others, continued to study tirelessly until he acquired a high degree of skill.[2]

This account of Segovia's early learning of the guitar includes several aspects not included in the autobiography twenty years later as well as some points that were to be expanded. Segovia's education "in a seminary," the fact that he first "saw a guitar at the house of a friend," and the episode of the guitarist with the paralysed hand were not to be included in the definitive testimony.

Tárrega's *Spanish Serenade* provides a small mystery. What is presumably intended is *Capricho Arabe* (subtitled *Serenata)*, and mentioned in the autobiography not as the first piece he ever tackled but as "at that time the *pièce de résistance* of my repertoire and one especially suited to reach the sensitive chords of a feminine heart."[3]

Buek suggests that Segovia's age when he gave his first recital was eighteen not sixteen:

Aged eighteen, he decided to play his first concert. When it was advertised he met a young acquaintance, who addressed him, saying, "I hear there's a young guitarist around who intends to give a concert - we ought to hear him." To the great astonishment of his friend Segovia replied, "Yes, that's me!" The concert was a success, other concerts followed, and so began the artistic career of Segovia. Only after several recitals did he have occasion to meet other professional colleagues. It was Llobet who first introduced him to other colleagues in Barcelona. The influence of this great artist can be traced in Segovia's playing though Segovia retained his own personal style. But both these artists share certain qualities, above all the characteristic Spanish style.[4]

Segovia's anecdote about the friend at the first recital emerges over the years in one or two forms. There is one about an old man intending to go to the concert who is informed by Segovia that the recitalist, a close friend of his, is not a very good player. The man is then astonished to see none other than Segovia appear on the platform. In this story Segovia is first accused of disloyalty to his friend, the mythical bad performer, and then, after the concert, congratulated on his modesty. From the early years Segovia saw the value of the relevant parable in dealing with writers and journalists, though often creating a trail of confusion in the process, as well as deflecting more probing analyses of his life and personality.

Buek eloquently defines some elements of the "characteristic Spanish style," as well as attempting a comparison between Segovia and Llobet:

Segovia's guitar tells us much. It knows how to sing and how to sigh, it fills our ears with harmony and the magic of sound; it has many registers. It leads us from the old classics of guitar literature to Handel, Bach, Mozart, and Mendelssohn, from Llobet and Tárrega to modern composers. It was able to engage composers who were strangers to the guitar to compose works. It will, in Segovia's hands, lose every trace of vulgarity and move into a higher sphere, ennobled and made the equal of other instruments.

It would be pointless to compare Segovia with Llobet, as both represent the highest achievement of modern guitar playing. The difference only lies in temperament and expression of feeling. Segovia is more lyrical, he is stirred by the beauty of guitar tone, and loves the instrument for its own sake, while for Llobet it is a means to an end, to express the feelings of his own soul.[5]

There is also some useful information about Segovia's itineraries. Buek's account has the virtue of relative proximity to the events described:

After Segovia had played with great success in most towns of Spain, he also went to South America and played concerts there for two years in all. In 1923 he undertook a tour in the West Indies and Central America. First he played on the Canadian group of islands, then in Cuba. After a stay of six weeks in Cuba, he continued with a trip to Mexico. Here too the artist was received everywhere with enthusiasm. In 1924 he made his way for the first time to Germany. Like his compatriot, Llobet, he received unlimited admiration and his keen interest in the development of the guitar in Germany was fruitful and led on to further activity.[6]

Fritz Buek's book also offers an interesting comparison between contemporary guitarists of the day. Llobet is described, for example, as "an artist of the first rank."[7] He certainly possessed a definite advantage in that he was a former pupil of Francisco Tárrega, a qualification which carried enormous weight.

Some of Buek's descriptions of Llobet may seem remarkably similar to evocations of Segovia by other writers:

In Llobet's hands the guitar became a new instrument, whose power of expression forced other guitarists into the shadows. Colours and beauty of pure tone arose under his hands, whose mobility seemed almost unbelievable. But these technical skills, refined to the highest point of perfection, were not what baffled and overwhelmed the musical experts. Nature had put music into the heart of this artist and taught him to understand and shape, so that everything that arose from under his hands became music. Whether he played Bach or Mozart, the classics of guitar literature or whether he interpreted a modern composer, he always knew how to immerse himself within the style and spiritual content of every composition. His interpretation was able to draw out the musical worth of every piece. His unerring, assured technique and the vitality of his temperament roused the public to unprecedented outbursts of enthusiasm, packing his concerts and offering him the same kind of reception as the most famous violinists and other instrumentalists would receive.[8]

There is an acceptance here that the concept of the guitar recital was very much alive and that an international audience was ready to accept virtuosic playing without prejudice or condescension. Buek comments that Llobet's immense success in Germany and Austria in 1921, 1922, and 1924 "helped to strengthen his fame abroad."[9] Thus it could be argued that Llobet had already prepared the way for other guitarists to follow and Segovia's mission to spread the gospel of the guitar was not exactly the single-handed adventure that later generations often thought it was.

Buek devotes some space to "another artist whose star is in the ascendancy," Regino Sainz de la Maza, a guitarist whose influence in the history of the twentieth century guitar is often underestimated outside Spain:[10]

Critics praised his great musical insights and his brilliant technique. Of great merit also are his studies in the realm of old Spanish literature, whose tablatures he made intelligible to modern guitarists.[11]

Emilio Pujol receives half a paragraph at this comparatively early stage of a long career:

Emilio Pujol, whose cultivated playing was much admired by his colleagues, chose Paris to be his home, where he became the centre of guitar activities. Contrary to the others mentioned before, he is a fingertip player. He belonged to that period when Tárrega examined the different methods of playing the guitar and decided in favour of the fingertip.[12]

This account was published only a short time before the establishment of Pujol's *Bibliothèque de Musique Ancienne et Moderne* series, published by Editions Max Eschig, Paris, from the late 1920's onwards, which in its scope and influence, especially in the area of the "auteurs anciens," rivals Segovia's Guitar Archives Series. If Buek had been writing a few years later he would have had to revise this and acknowledge Pujol's central role among the guitar's great scholars of the twentieth century.

Buek's work helps us to gauge the mood and direction of the guitar in the 1920's in a unique way. We find there not an isolated or neglected art, but a culture that has plenty of vitality, with young players and editors, moving towards its own kind of golden age.

8. The Expanding Universe

The significance of the developing repertoire of the 1920's has already been examined. During this decade Segovia laid the foundation for a massive range of music which could not only be performed on the concert platform by the virtuoso but would also be published and available to guitarists the world over. At the same time, as mentioned at the end of the last chapter, Emilio Pujol was continuing his researches into the old repertoire and editing new pieces. His series for Editions Max Eschig introduced *Pavanas* by Luis Milán, selected pieces by Gaspar Sanz, *Suites* by Robert de Visée, and music by Corbetta, Mudarra, Pisador, Fuenllana, Santiago de Murcia, Roncalli, J. S. Bach, Narváez, Valderrábano, Besard (among others from 1926 onwards).

Pujol also brought forward new music including his own compositions such as *Tonadilla, Tango espagnol,* and *Guajira (Evocación cubana),* (publ. No. 1204, Auteurs Modernes, Bibliothèque de Musique Ancienne et Moderne, Editions Max Eschig, 1926), *Three Studies* (publ. 1929, Nos 1200 - 1203, the first items published in the series), seven *Evocaciones criollas* (publ. 1929, Nos 1209 - 1215) by Alfonso Broqua, and *Corranda* by Agusti Grau (publ. 1929, No. 1216, edited by Llobet). Also on its list in due course would appear Falla's *Homenaje, pour le tombeau de Claude Debussy* (No. 1219), Rodrigo's *Sarabanda lontana,* (No. 1226, publ. 1934), and *Suite populaire brésilienne* by Heitor Villa-Lobos (No. 1220, republished in 1955).

In retrospect this output, both prolific and of great musical worth, must have presented a formidable challenge to Segovia. He responded by recording only one item, Rodrigo's *Sarabanda lontana,* from the modern list, and also delved deeply into the *auteurs anciens* by taking into his repertoire, in the fullness of time, pieces by Milán, Sanz, de Visée, Santiago de Murcia, Roncalli, Corbetta, and many others, often using his own edition.

At the time, and for years afterwards, it was presumed by many guitarists that performances of these pieces provided a close rendering from the tablature of the great treasure house of the Renaissance and Baroque performers. It later became clear that various published editions were transcriptions generally faithful to the spirit of the urtext but purpose-built for the requirements of the modern guitarist. The Baroque literature of de Visée, Corbetta, Sanz, and Santiago de Murcia was written for types of guitar very different in stringing, structure, technique and tradition, from Segovia's Ramírez of the early twentieth century. Transcriptions from the Baroque guitar on behalf of the post-Torres guitar now often appear to leave an unacceptably wide imaginative gap between the notes on the page and their performance on authentic instruments. Players seriously interested in Baroque guitar music are usually strongly advised, following the researches of the Early Music scholars of the second half of the century, to go back to copies of instruments of the seventeenth and eighteenth centuries, while lovers of the Renaissance come on to the platform equipped with vihuelas and four course guitars. The lute repertoire has been re-discovered in its entirety and historically appropriate types of lute from the sixteenth to the mid-eighteenth century are nowadays mandatory for those who wish to give public recitals.

Anxieties about "authenticity," the composer's original intentions, and the actual physical sound of early music were never part of Segovia's advocacy of Renaissance and Baroque music. He was inspired by the sheer excitement of liberating great areas of repertoire left unperformed for centuries. The 1920's saw the establishment of his fascination with various historical epochs and the extension of the Baroque repertoire to include not only J. S. Bach, but a wider range of composers later to become extremely familiar to both recitalists and students of the guitar.

Many of the roots of this revival of interest in the Spanish guitar tradition can be traced to the work of Felipe Pedrell (1841-1922), composer and musicologist, whose pupils included Albéniz, Granados, Falla and Gerhard. Gilbert Chase summed up Pedrell's achievements as follows:

Throughout his long life Pedrell laboured indefatigably, not only as composer, but also as writer, lecturer, editor, historian, and teacher, for the elevation of Spanish music. From his earliest years, when as a boy he sang the music of Victoria in the cathedral of his native Tortosa, or listened to the songs of the blind beggars as he played in the streets, he was fascinated by the richness of Spanish music in its double aspect of folksong and artistic tradition. Delving into the priceless store of Spain's musical treasure he rescued from semiobscurity the works of Cabezón, Victoria, Morales, Guerrero, and the other great Hispanic masters of polyphony whose compositions are included in the eight volumes of his Hispaniae Schola Musica Sacra. *And in the third and fourth volumes of his* Cancionero Musical Popular Español *he included compositions of such men as Encina, Milán, Vázquez, Romero, Hidalgo, and Marín, to show how the classical Spanish school affirmed its national character by the technical procedure of composing nearly always on the basis of the popular melody.* [1]

Pedrell's *Cancionero musical popular español,* published in four volumes between 1918 and 1922, drew the reader's attention to the central significance of the vihuela of sixteenth century Spain in Volume I:

Segovia in the 1920's.

All these adaptations of the popular song applied to the sixteenth century vocal polyphony, perfected themselves in adaptations of the same kind to monody accompanied by the vihuela, a polystring instrument before it merged with the guitar of the people, which is to the musical literature of Spain what the lute, the theorbo, etc, are to the French, Italian and German musical literatures. The foundations of education of the perfect courtier of the sixteenth century concerned here, as everywhere, the art of knowing how to handle arms, the art of falconry, etc... and above all, the noble art of being able to sing and accompany with the vihuela according to the system of its own notation, called cifra *(tablature). The origin of modern instrumental forms, whether of music pure or symphonic, the same as accompanied monodies, has been found in these careful treatises of cifra. In these treatises is presented the process of transformation of the old art and the old modes into modern tonality, a curious process when one considers the folksong as the true origin and agent of this evolution.* [2]

For the guitarists of the 1920's this must have been an exciting discovery, drawing together the Spanish traditions of the guitar with the education of the "perfect courtier" and the later development of the instrument. Pedrell goes further for he saw in the work of the *vihuelistas* the opening up of European music:

These unconscious folklorists, precursors of modern harmony and the orchestra of the future (which culminates in Beethoven), begin with the genial treatise of Luis Milán (1535) and conclude with the transformation of the vihuela into guitar, from the supremacy of the former to the ultimate instrument of the latter, which from the hands of the courtly musicians passes to those of the people... And the very short but glorious reign of the vihuela finishes at the end of the sixteenth century and begins the oligarchy of the guitar with the little treatise written by the famous Catalan doctor Juan Carlos Amat. But from the era of Luis Milán, chamber musician for the Duke of Calabria in the court of Valencia, translator of Castiglione's The Courtier, *to the genial populariser of the guitar, who had the honour of seeing some of his medical works published in France, how many precursors are there of the accompanying forms of the modern orchestra, how many songs on the texts of ancient romances, how many dances and* diferencias *(variations), on themes of popular and liturgical songs, in the treatises of the followers of Luis Milán, Luis de Narváez (1538), the canon Alfonso Mudarra, (1546), Enriquez de Valderrábano (1547), Pisador (1552), printer of his own treatise and* maestro de vihuela *of Philip II; Miguel de Fuenllana, blind from birth, one of the first who considered the simple chord as a genuine harmonic value.* [3]

In 1925, J. B. Trend published his monograph, *Luis Milán and the Vihuelistas* (Oxford University Press), citing in his bibliography the third volume of Pedrell's work, where songs of Milán, Mudarra, Narváez, and Valderrábano are published in notation. Trend followed this up the following year with *The Music of Spanish History to 1600* (Oxford, 1926), further proof that the history of Spanish music was now a living presence. J. B. Trend was a friend of Manuel de Falla and well connected with the Spanish musical movement centred in Granada and his book on Luis Milán is included in Emilio Pujol's bibliography to *Escuela Razonada de la Guitarra, Volume I.* Pujol in his turn was also immensely influenced by the work of Pedrell:

Following advice, faithful to the teaching received from Felipe Pedrell, and at the request of Lionel de la Laurencie of the Paris Conservatoire, in 1926, Emilio Pujol began the first investigations on the guitar's historical past...

The search began among the archives and libraries of the principle European centres, dedicated to music, and as a result he delivered a historical-didactic study of the guitar from its origin which appeared in volume XXIV of the Encyclopedia of Music of the Dictionary of the Paris Conservatoire, Delagrave, 1926. The task took him to the Pedrell archives and those of Dr. Scheeherer de la Haya, the National Libraries of Madrid, Paris, Brussels, and Munich, and the British Museum, London. He brought forward the first transcriptions of the work of the Spanish vihuelistas of the sixteenth century and guitarists of the seventeenth century, published later by Editions Max Eschig, Paris, in a series edited by Pujol under the title of "Library of Ancient and Modern Music for Guitar".

These activities were a revelation for guitarists because not only was an unknown past opened up for them but it enabled them to enlarge the content of their programmes in an unlimited way, and for our musicology it was the recovery of a historical area which had remained hidden for more than four centuries.

On 6 December, 1927, in the Salle Erard, Rue du Mail, Paris, Emilio Pujol devoted a concert which featured for the first time in France the music of the vihuelistas, including in the programme, for the first hearing, a Pavana of Luis Milán. In this recital, without precedent in contemporary history, a new era began: the glorious names of Milán, Corbetta, Visée and Gaspar Sanz, arose to recover the prestige lost in past centuries.[4]

Thus from the mid-1920's onwards guitarists in Spain began incorporating into their recitals the luminous names of the Iberian golden age of the Renaissance and Baroque epochs. As new compositions for the contemporary guitar were asked for and received, researchers explored and revived previously unknown areas of the past, and shifted the ground from the emphasis on nineteenth century repertoire and transcriptions that had formed the core of guitar recitals. It is not always clear how far Segovia was in the vanguard of the advance into early guitar and lute music and to what extent he was drawn into this music by the scholarly activities of the decade which impelled him to follow suit. The primary thrust of Segovia's efforts to increase the repertoire had been, as we have seen, concerned with his contemporary composers and a few selected works of J. S. Bach. Segovia has never been known for his delight in wandering round libraries or wrestling with the mysteries of ancient tablatures. Pujol, on the other hand, was avowedly discovering the sources and urtexts of past ages, and in this area threw down the gauntlet to all other guitarists of the era. Yet he too, as we have also observed, was bringing forward his own group of composers and his own original compositions.

The strength of Pujol's commitment can be seen in a concert he gave in the Landschaftlichen Redouten Saal, Linz on 7 October, 1927 during his first trip to Austria:

I

Minuet	Sor
Serenata	Malats
Granada	Albéniz
Étude	Tárrega
Theme and Variations	Sor-Llobet

II

Pavana	Luis Milán (1535)
Gavotte	F. Corbetta (1671)
Folias - Gallarda	Gaspar Sanz (1674)
Prélude, Sarabande, Gigue	Robert de Visée (1682)
Bourrée	J. S. Bach

Interval

III

Evocaciones Criollas	A. Broqua
Vidala - Ecos del paisaje -	
Ritmos camperos	
Spanish Suite	E. Pujol
Guajira - Danza gaditana -	
Sevilla (evocación)	

This is a superb example of a recital programme of the 1920's, structured in the traditional tripartite form, blending the old, the new and the traditional guitar repertoire. In a short time Pujol would be moving the early music to the front of the recital, but at this stage it was obviously considered too novel to be risked as an opening to the concert. Instead the traditional staple diet of Spanish pieces settled the audience in their seats before the experience of Renaissance and Baroque and the adventure of the new compositions.

In the same year Miguel Llobet also visited Austria, performing the following recital in the Zeremoniensaal der Hofburg, Vienna, on 1 December, 1927.

I

Minuet	Sor
Andante	Mozart
Prelude -Sarabande	J. S. Bach
Recuerdos de la Alhambra	Tárrega

II

Étude	Sor
Serenade	Samazeuilh
Danza española	Granados
Vidala	A. Broqua
Allegro	M. Torroba

Interval

III

Estudio brillante	N. Coste
Torre bermeja	Albéniz
Two Catalan Folksongs	arr. M. Llobet
Corranda (Catalan Dance)	Grau
Jota	M. Llobet

Compared with Pujol's recital, the structure of this concert may seem less distinct. Yet it is a good example of an early twentieth century program where the player keeps the audience's interest by interweaving a variety of styles and moods without ever touching on larger structures such as sonatas or a set of variations. The purpose here would be to offer definite aspects of the guitar's strengths, with some genuflection to the new in the form of Samazeuilh, Broqua, and the music of Llobet himself, but slipping in studies by Sor and Coste, a nod towards Bach and Mozart, but primarily accentuating the Spanish nationalist flavours of Tárrega, Granados, Torroba and Albéniz.

Another recitalist of the time was Luise Walker (b.1910, Vienna, Austria). She studied with Josef Zuth (1879 - 1932) and Jacob Ortner (1879 - 1959), and later with Heinrich Albert (1870 - 1950) and Miguel Llobet, and represents the second generation of guitarists after Segovia to frequent the concert platforms of a variety of countries. Her recital of 11, April, 1928, in the Landschaftlichen Redouten Saal, Linz, where Pujol had played a few months before, reveals the mixture of the traditional and the innovative for which guitarists were striving:

I

Preludium and Fugato	J. S. Bach
Andante con moto	F. Sor
Variations on a Theme of Mozart	

II

Sonatina in E minor	H. Albert
Allegretto - Adagio - Rondo	
Nocturne, Op. 9, No. 2	F. Chopin
Hungarian Fantasy, Op. 65	J. K. Mertz

III

Spanish Dance	E. Granados
Cradlesong	R. Schumann
Capricho Arabe (Serenata)	F. Tárrega
Two Catalan Folksongs	M. Llobet
(La Filla del Marxant -	
El Testament de n'Amelia)	
Álborada	F. Tárrega
Fantasía	J. Viñas

This was a formidable program for a young person of eighteen years of age but Luise Walker had been playing in public for several years by this time. In an earlier recital in Linz on 3 December, 1925 she had performed several of the same pieces but also *Sonatina* by Moreno Torroba (the only visible sign of Segovia's influence in the two concerts). During the same year in Linz on 3 March, 1928, Heinrich Albert presented the following:

Suite:	de Visée
Prelude	
Allemande	
Sarabande	
Gavotte	
Minuet	
Sonata:	F. Sor
Allegro moderato	
Andante con Variazioni	
Minuet	
Mozart Variations	

Interval

Minuet in G	Heinrich Albert
Waldesrauschen	
Maurische Scharwache	
Vorspiel Nr. 1	
Mondnacht	
Totentanz	
Capricho Arabe	F. Tárrega
Fantasía in E	J. Viñas

There is a distinct flavour here of the structure of concerts to come many decades later. There are fewer composers represented than is usual in concerts of the 1920's, an attempt at the appearance of a full sonata and an entire suite by de Visée.

The information points to the build-up of a lively and committed culture of the guitar, with its established traditions stretching back to the nineteenth century, and a sense of extension and evolution of the concepts of how a guitar recital might be constructed. The era of the 1920's can thus be seen as not quite the wasteland that was later depicted. Throughout Europe there were already centres of excellence, some fine teachers and some prolific recitalists.

9. Segovia's Recitals 1926-1929

The extension of Segovia's geographical horizons in the 1920's coincided with the formation of a worthwhile repertoire. Following the Paris debut on 7 April, 1924, Segovia continued with a debut in Berlin and further tours of South America, including Argentina, Cuba and Mexico. In 1925 he performed throughout Spain and again in Paris.

On 2 March, 1926, two years after the death of Lenin, Segovia encountered his first Russian audience, the recital being held in the hall of the Moscow Conservatory. This debut took place in the year that Trotsky was expelled from the Politburo and one year before the tenth anniversary of the Revolution.

On 7 December, 1926, Segovia gave his first recital in England, performing at the Aeolian Hall, London. On Saturday, 29 January, 1927, at 3 p.m. he returned to play his debut recital at the Wigmore Hall, where his program was as follows:

I

Andante and Rondo	Sor
Danza	Moreno Torroba
Improvisation	C. Pedrell
Tonadilla	Granados

II

Sarabande	Handel
Gavotte et Musette - Loure	J. S. Bach
Canzonetta	Mendelssohn

III

Thème varié et Finale	M. Ponce
Serenata	G. Samazeuilh
Granada - Cádiz	I. Albéniz

On 29 April, 1927, Segovia made his debut in Denmark collecting his usual enthusiastic reviews from an admiring press:

The young Spaniard is really a phenomenon, just as the rumors said. We have never heard anyone who even roughly compares with the way he plays his guitar. With his incredible virtuosity and his tastefulness which proves the high standard of his musical culture, he makes the guitar an instrument on which 'proper' music can be performed to a greater degree than one might suppose.[1]

In 1928, Segovia made his debut in the United States, his first public concert being on 8 January at the Town Hall, New York. The program for this momentous occasion in the history of the guitar was:

Andante and Allegretto - Variations on The Magic Flute	Sor
Serenata	Malats
Danza	Tárrega
Étude	Alard, arr. Tárrega
Prelude - Allemande - Fugue - Courante - Sarabande - Gavotte	J. S. Bach
Minuet	Haydn
Sonatina	Torroba
Danza	Granados
Leyenda	Albéniz

The critics responded warmly to Segovia's playing. Lawrence Gilman of *The New York Herald Tribune* commented that Segovia "has made the guitar a thing to be spoken of in the same breath with the harpsichord of Landowska, the cello of Casals, the violin of Heifetz." In *The New York Times*, Olin Downes wrote that Segovia "belongs to the very small group of musicians who by transcendent powers of execution and imagination create an art of their own that sometimes seems to transform the very nature of their medium." However, not for the first or last time, the guitar as a medium came under mild attack in the same review:

... it must be added that Mr Segovia did not and cannot succeed in removing the limitations which will always surround his instrument. He has stretched these limitations to the utmost. He has far outdistanced in his knowledge and in his musical conceptions the ordinary twanger of strings. Nevertheless the guitar remains the guitar, with limits of sonority, color, dynamics. These limitations make Bach less impressive through its medium than on the piano or harpsichord. They reach their utmost effect and their entire significance in music less sculpturesque and contrapuntal than Bach's and with warmer harmony and more elementary rhythms.

The function of the recitalist in the twentieth century has been to define the nature of the guitar and Segovia would have disagreed with the concept of the instrument which Olin Downes perpetrated. The struggle for the serious ground of Bach would continue relentlessly in the 1930's and onwards. However, following the 8 January debut Segovia gave four more concerts in New York.

On 11 January he performed *Sonata* (Giuliani), *Folias d'Espagne* (Sor), *Suite* (Moreno Torroba), *Five Pieces* (Bach), *Moment Musical* (Schubert), *Thème Varié et Finale* (Ponce), *Danza española* (Granados), and *Torre Bermeja* and *Sevilla* (Albéniz). On 19 January the third Town Hall recital included *Prelude* (Sor), *Danza* (Tárrega), *Sonatina* (Moreno Torroba), *Suite* (de Visée), *Prelude* and *Gavotte avec Musette* (Bach), *Romance et Canzonetta* (Mendelssohn), *Sonata* (Ponce), *Danza española in G* (Granados), and *Zambra granadina* and *Cadiz* (Albéniz). On 29 January Segovia played at the Gallo Theater on West 54th Street and gave a final "Farewell Request Program" at Town Hall, New York on 4 February.[2]

A few months later in 1928 Segovia returned to Argentina, where he had not played since 1921. In the month of July he performed nine concerts at the Teatro Odeón to capacity audiences. The first of these concerts, on 3 July, 1928, was as follows:[3]

I

Minuet	Sor
Mozart Variations	
Fandanguillo	Turina
Estudio	Tárrega

II

Prelude - Allemande - Fugue - Courante - Gavotte	Bach
Minuet	Haydn
Sonatina	Torroba
Leyenda	Albéniz

Towards the end of the 1920's Europe was also the arena of Segovia's conquests as he completed his grand tour till there were few countries unvisited. At the Mozarteum, Prague, on 25 October, 1928, he performed the following recital program:

I

Andante and Rondo	Sor
Theme and Variations	
Fandanguillo	Turina
Guitarreo	Pedrell
Étude	Tárrega

II

Prelude - Allemande - Fugue - J. S. Bach
Courante - Gavotte
Minuet   Haydn

III

Sonatina   Torroba
  Allegretto - Andante -
  Allegro
Danse   Granados
Sevilla   Albéniz

There are several significant correlations between this program and the others performed by guitarists, as discussed in the previous chapter. Transcriptions from Bach and Haydn, the obligatory inclusion of Sor and Tárrega, the new works brought forward by Turina, Pedrell, and Torroba, and the Spanish romanticism of Granados and Albéniz, are aspects of the repertoire familiar in one form or another to the guitar public of the 1920's. What is also interesting is how Segovia's recitals were by this time exploring and consolidating fundamental patterns that he would preserve for the rest of his life. Thus he provides a liberal offering of Bach, ends the concert with Spanish composers, and keeps the tripartite structure of the recital followed by players of the early twentieth century.

In 1929 Segovia returned to the United States. A letter to Manuel Ponce dated 27 February, 1929, comments that he had already given twenty concerts, with more to follow, 23 March being his last New York recital of the tour.[4] He was then scheduled to move on to England where he intended to record some movements from Ponce's *Sonata in D*.[5]

A further letter of December, 1929, relates how Segovia had visited China and Japan. In Tokyo *Sonata Romántica* had been played, and in Shanghai, *Theme with Variations*, the encores being *Sarabande* and *Gavotte* from Ponce's *Suite Clásica*. Segovia had travelled back to Europe on the trans-Siberian railway, a journey covering eighteen days, apparently without sleep, and now required a period of recuperation before facing the demands of the new decade.[6]

In the same letter Segovia mentions two new pieces by Joaquín Turina, a little piece, possibly *Ráfaga, Op. 53,* and also *Sonata, Op. 61,* now in preparation, which would ultimately be premiered in Rome, Italy, on 29 January, 1932.

In September, 1929, Segovia's transcription of J. S. Bach's *Gavotte* (from *Suite in E, BWV 1006a),* was published in *Keynotes,* the leading British fretted instrument magazine of the time, by permission of Schott. Nowadays it would seem unusual for a published work of this kind to appear in a monthly magazine but it seems to have been part of a publicity competition between rival firms to publicise their wares. In October, 1929, Manuel de Falla's *Homenaje,* (published J.& W. Chester, London), appeared, followed in November by Llobet's edition of Carcassi's *Study No. 7* (published by J. Rowies, Paris, and later by Henry Lemoine, Paris and Ricordi Americana, Buenos Aires), and in December by Emilio Pujol's *Tonadilla* (published Max Eschig, Paris).

Not to be outdone, Daniel Fortea's *Canción de Cuna* (published Biblioteca Fortea, Madrid), had appeared in the periodical in August, 1929. *Keynotes,* edited by Louis A. Unger, was a house magazine for John Alvey Turner's, a store at 68, New Oxford Street, London, which sold banjos, guitars, sheet music and accessories. Like most journals of the era, its readers seemed mainly interested in the performance of banjo music, with articles concerned with the classic guitar making far fewer appearances. *Keynotes* eventually gave way to its long-established competitor, *B.M.G.* (Banjo, Mandolin, Guitar), which in 1929 had already reached its twenty-sixth year of publication. Such journals would continue to reflect the rise of interest among the grass-root amateurs who steadily over the next two decades switched their allegiance from banjo and mandolin to the classic or plectrum guitar.

In another letter of December, 1929,[7] Segovia mentions an evening spent with Pablo Casals, who had requested the premiere of Ponce's *Guitar Concerto*, when it appeared, for his orchestra in Barcelona. Unfortunately the felicitous juxtaposition of Segovia as soloist in a concerto with Casals conducting was never to happen. The political events in Spain of the 1930's were to prove disastrous to any creative relationship between these two outstanding artists.

10. SEGOVIA'S RECORDINGS OF THE 1920'S

A number of guitarists made recordings in the early part of the twentieth century, a fact which has only comparatively recently come to critical attention. Thanks in particular to the researches of Richard D. Stover, the contribution of Agustín Barrios to the early history of the guitar in this respect can now be understood, for the erstwhile obscure Paraguayan guitarist appears to have been the first recitalist to make 78 r.p.m. commercial phonograph recordings. His early recordings were made in 1913 in Montevideo for the Atlanta/Artigas labels and a later series of sessions between 1921 and 1929 were on the Odeon label of Buenos Aires. Stover mentions also a further recording of two discs in San Salvador in 1943. There may be others yet to be discovered but at the time of writing Richard D. Stover had established the survival of at least thirty-one recordings by Barrios.[1]

In 1982 a double long-playing record of the early discs of Miguel Llobet was issued with liner notes by Ronald Purcell.[2] In a subsequent issue of a compact disc, Purcell establishes through a comment by Vahdah Olcott-Bickford (1885 - 1980), the eminent American guitarist, that around 1910 Llobet "tried to make a recording at the Bell Lab. in Brunswick, New Jersey, but was dissatisfied with the sound."[3] His later solo recording sessions took place around 1925 in Spain, and in 1929 he recorded several discs of duo music with María Luisa Anido. Purcell lists some fifteen discs appearing on a variety of labels including Parlophon Electric/Parlophon S.A. España (Barcelona), Odeon, Decca, and Decca/Odeon-Parlophone.

Segovia's first experience of recording was possibly during a trip to Havana, Cuba, in 1923, though he may well have encountered some of the same problems with the quality of sound reproduced at that time as Llobet. His actual entry into the world of commercial recording seems to have begun on 2 May, 1927, with his rendering of Sor's *Thème varié, Op. 9,* coupled with Bach's *Gavotte en Rondeau (Partita No. 3 for solo violin in E major,* BWV 1006) (on HMV D.1255/Victor Red Seal 6766).[4] He recorded a further piece by Bach on the same day, this time *Courante (Suite for Cello,* BWV 1009) to be backed by *Allegretto* (from *Sonatina in A*) by Moreno Torroba (recorded 20 May, 1927) and issued on HMV E.475 (also Victrola 1298).

In Britain the prestigious journal, *The Gramophone,* reviewed a Segovia recording for the first time in August, 1927:[5]

Andrés Segovia *(H.M.V., D.1255, 12in., 6s.6d.) provides us with some truly astonishing playing on the guitar, an instrument which, by the way, appears to record excellently. His rendering of a Bach* Gavotte *is pleasantly rhythmic and the* rubato, *though meretricious, is effective. But the result, interesting as it is, is hardly Bach, and the guitar seems more naturally suited to the pleasant, childish prattling of a* Thème Varié *by Sor, which is most successful. The playing is, of course, the main thing, and this no one should miss. (P.L.)*

The critic noted the essential eccentricities of Segovia's Bach, and also commented on the slim substance of the traditional guitar repertoire. The latter became a characteristic observation of many critical accounts of Segovia's recording and concerts in the press and elsewhere down through the years with the proviso, stated or implicit, that "the playing is, of course, the main thing." This was not a firm intellectual basis on which to found a new musical empire but it would have to do. On countless occasions from now on critics would observe that Segovia's playing was superb but the repertoire was often less inspiring to the point of being unworthy of a great instrumentalist. Undaunted by such comment Segovia remained adamant in pursuit of the guitar's expressive values, and endeavoured to make up the deficit by recruiting contemporary composers to his cause whenever possible. In the meantime his recordings began to consolidate his fame internationally.

A list of his recordings during the last years of the 1920's thus reads as follows:

2 May, 1927:	J. S. Bach:	*Gavotte en Rondeau, (Partita No. 3 for solo violin in E major,* BWV 1006)
		Courante (Cello Suite in C major, BWV 1009)
	F. Sor:	*Thème varié, Op. 9*
20 May, 1927:	Torroba:	*Allegretto (Sonatina in A major)*
	Tárrega:	*Recuerdos de la Alhambra*

15 May, 1928: J. S. Bach: *Prelude in C minor* (BWV 999)

Allemande (Lute Suite, BWV 996)

Fugue in G minor (Sonata No.1 for solo violin, BWV 1001)

Torroba: *Fandanguillo (Suite Castellana)*

Turina: *Fandanguillo*

These were issued on 78 rpm, 12 inch recordings:

HMV D.1255, England, (also Victor Red Seal 6766)

J. S. Bach: *Gavotte en Rondeau*

F. Sor: *Thème Varié, Op. 9.*

HMV D. 1395, England (also Victor Red Seal 6767)

Tárrega: *Tremolo Study*

Turina: *Fandanguillo.*

Others were 78 rpm, 10 inch recordings:

HMV D. 1536, England (also Victor Red Seal 1824)

J. S. Bach: *Prelude & Allemande, Fugue.*

HMV E. 475, England, (also Victrola 1298)

Torroba: *Allegretto*

J. S. Bach: *Courante*

HMV D.1395 was ecstatically reviewed in *The Gramophone* :

...This seems to me to be the most perfect recording of any instrument I have ever heard. It feels like sitting next to the artist and, encouraged by the perfect impression on my ears, I visualised the performance more clearly than I ever have done before. Segovia is an uncanny player. His rhythm, and above all, variety of tone colour are as unusual as his musicianship is excellent.[6]

Useful publicity was provided by a short article on Segovia in *The Gramophone* in December, 1928. The first part of the article, accompanied by a photograph of the artist, praised his recording art:

Andrés Segovia: *To most people the guitar is but a glorified banjo with a monotonous, if jolly, twang. To hear Segovia is to be at once disillusioned. No effect seems impossible to him, and all shades of tone colour are at his command. At one time it is the sharp, staccato tones of the clavecin that one hears, at another the quality of the harp intrudes; he is even able to suggest the modern pianoforte.*

This is followed by an anecdote presenting a very different image of Segovia from that which he wished to cultivate in later decades. The article also provides what must be the first statement of some misleading information continuing down the years, that Manuel de Falla wrote for Segovia:

Segovia was born in Jaén in 1894. At first he studied composition and singing at several conservatoires, but turned to the guitar and the flamenco as an escape from the crabbedness and rutted traditions of the schools. His art attracted the attention of the leading Spanish composers, particularly Esplá, de Falla and Turina, who wrote special pieces for him. Segovia is a master of improvisation. One evening he wandered into the garden of de Falla's house near the Alhambra. With him were two gipsy singers he had collected from the Albaicín (the gipsy quarter of Granada) and Otaña, a noted church dignitary. A popular merrymaking was commenced, de Falla giving out themes which were sung by the gipsies, while Segovia improvised marvellous accompaniments. Suddenly, two of the party, neither of whom could sing a note, began a great argument on the form in which the cante was being sung. De Falla slyly egged them on and in the heat of the moment they challenged each other to a Cante Jondo (singing competition), Segovia to be the judge. One can imagine the startling transition from the romantic music of Segovia and the gipsies to the hideous cacophony which suddenly filled the orange-scented garden![7]

At this point Segovia was clearly not worried about being associated with either flamenco or gipsies, and the description of him as a "master of improvisation" is contrary to later impressions of the fastidious nature of his playing. A very human and convivial artist is pictured here, a man who collects two singers from the slightly disreputable area of the Albaicín before making his way to Falla's house, and who is willing to be the mock judge of the cacophonous singing competition. (Such incidents were not to be used very much in the autobiography written two decades later.)

HMV E.475 was reviewed in *The Gramophone* :

His phrasing by inflexion is a likeable bit of sprightliness with the Spanish tincture and a lightly cosmopolitan background. Here the player's varieties of tone are especially to be admired. I find his records uncommonly attractive.[8]

The editor of *The Gramophone* commented briefly on the existence of HMV E.475 in September, 1929, but after this mention there was to be no further publicity in this periodical until November, 1931.[9]

There were interesting historical aspects behind the bare facts of Segovia's entry into commercial recording. The development of electrical recording throughout the 1920's had enhanced recording technology by leaps and bounds, displacing the cruder techniques and intensifying the competitiveness of the music industry. Ernest Newman, the esteemed critic of the *Sunday Times*, London, wrote glowingly about a new recording by Columbia of *Symphonie Fantastique* by Berlioz (Weingartner and the London Symphony), and HMV's offering of Wagner's *Siegfried's Rhine Journey* (conducted by Albert Coates):

Until lately it was a little difficult to take even a good orchestral record quite seriously... All at once, however, as it seems, gramophone recording has taken an enormous step forward.

Those who have heard these records for themselves will have probably felt, as I did at my first hearing of them, that at last it is possible for the musician to sit at home and get the thrill of the real thing as he knows it in the concert hall.... At last the orchestra really sounds like an orchestra... We do not merely hear the melodies going this, that or the other way in a sort of limbo of tonal abstractions; they come to us with the sensuous excitement of actuality.[10]

In the mid-1920's profits for recording companies were healthy and Victor's sales in 1926 amounted to $48,000,000. In 1927 a million phonographs were manufactured and well over a hundred million records.[11] In Europe also the recording industry expanded in the late 1920's on the part of the two major English companies, HMV and Columbia. The crash of 1929 was to change this prosperity into a swift decline and provide a grimmer climate where profits toppled. Segovia entered the market at the point when the economic graph was healthy and reasonably optimistic and was well on his journey before the tide turned. By 1932 the picture had changed dramatically. In that year only six million records were sold in the United States, appoximately six per cent of the total record sales in 1927. The figures moved from 104,000,000 discs sold in 1927 to 6,000,000 in 1932.[12]

But even in the progressive situation of 1927, when Segovia made his first recordings, one can sense an element of caution. Three recording sessions on 2 and 20 May, 1927 and one on 15 May, 1928, produced a total of four 78 rpm saleable records. A recording debut in the 1990's for a young artist (though Segovia was thirty-four when he made his first records) would now involve the issue of a whole compact disc. For Segovia, almost twenty years after his professional debut, with hundreds of concerts behind him, his first recording sessions would produce little more than twenty minutes of music.

But despite Segovia's burgeoning reputation, recording companies were as conservative and cautious then as they are now with new artists. What was produced in these early days are classic recordings, essential to the history of guitar discography, albeit few in number. As a consequence one can but surmise at the processes of selection which went on between Segovia and the record company. The thrust of the offering was the music of J. S. Bach, with the rest of the composers, Sor, Tárrega, Turina and Torroba being Spanish musicians who wrote directly for the guitar. After many years in the business of giving recitals, these pieces represented the hard core of Segovia's best offering at that time, a microcosm of the structure of his concerts, divided between transcriptions, original works and pieces dedicated to him.

What perhaps should be remembered is that although these pieces are now totally familiar to the point of fatigue to guitarists and audiences, such repertoire, with the exception of the music of J. S. Bach, was unknown to both critics and public. Segovia surely believed, with the pioneering work still to be done and the experience in the recording studios to be faced, that these pieces would best project the nature of the guitar's sonorities and tone colours. His judgement was ringingly endorsed by the critics, and the early recordings have been praised throughout the years, being re-issued for the present generation first on long playing record and later on compact disc.[13]

The historic significance of the 1920's 78 rpm's remains supreme. The conditions of recording music at that time meant that each side had to be done in one take. Other takes were of course possible, though many musicians at the time seem to have favoured the first take:

Musicians knew that they had to play at their very best, and that any mistakes would be preserved for ever, unless a side was repeated. Sides were indeed repeated, many times on occasions, but it comes as a surprise to a modern musician to find how many 78 rpm recordings consist of first or second takes. For example, of the nine sides of Rachmaninoff's recording of his Third Concerto, seven are first takes. Admittedly the division of a long movement into several sides made it impossible to play right through the movement; but in many other ways the atmosphere of the recording in the pre-tape period was much closer to that of a live performance than modern recording sessions.[14]

Thus from Segovia's performances of the late 1920's we can gain some awareness of the nature of his recital playing in the early years. Moreover he used his Manuel Ramírez guitar at this time, playing on gut strings in the time-honoured traditions of lute and guitar pending the introduction of nylon strings some years later.

11. THE 1930'S

The 1930's, one of the most crucial political decades of the twentieth century, began with several events which would soon develop a far wider significance. In January, 1930, the Spanish dictator, Primo de Rivera, resigned following some years of crisis. In Spain the collapse of the peseta had begun in 1928 and in the following year suffered a catastrophic fall. In April, 1931, King Alfonso XIII left Spain after reigning for forty-five years. Thus the seeds of the Spanish Civil War were already sown.

In June, 1930, the foreign troops occupying the Rhineland after the Treaty of Versailles made their departure five years ahead of the original terms of the agreement. In the German Reichstag elections in September the Nazi Party won over six million votes, (compared with eight million gained by the Socialists), but Adolf Hitler was unable to take his seat because of his Austrian citizenship. The ominous shape of a new political landscape in Europe was already becoming apparent.

For Segovia the work of consolidation of the enormous artistic gains of the 1920's continued with increased vigour. In December 1929, he was working on Manuel Ponce's *Variations on Folia de España and Fugue*,[1] putting other works to one side in an attempt to prepare it for a forthcoming New York recital. By the end of December he was labouring, equally avidly, on the Fugue.[2] In January, 1930, he set sail from Bremen, Germany, heading for the United States. His tour took him from Chicago and New York to Palm Beach, Florida. In the latter venue, a millionairess paid for his return trip from New York, as well as a fee, for a house concert for six of her friends.[3] Segovia returned to Europe to arrive in Paris around 20 March for a concert at the Salle Pleyel, before moving off south to perform in Rome on 14 April.

During these months Segovia was negotiating with Schott for the publication of Ponce's *Preludes*. The original proposition was to publish the 24 Preludes in four volumes of six pieces,[4] but later in 1930 only two books were published (Guitar Archives Nos 124 and 125). Segovia would eventually record six of the published *Preludes* on the album, *An Evening with Andrés Segovia*, (Brunswick AXTL 1070), in the 1950's, a few years after Ponce's death.

In the same year Emilio Pujol was also enjoying success. On 11 February, 1930 he performed at the Salle Erard, Paris, and between August and November the Cuervas-Pujol Duo toured South America with several recitals in Buenos Aires and Montevideo.[5] The ample selection of his editions and compositions published in 1929 had already established his credibility as one of the most important scholars of the guitar's repertoire. On 27 November,1930, Pujol delivered a lecture in Montevideo, Uruguay, on the theme of *La Guitarra y su Historia*, in which he presented his idea for a comprehensive method for the guitar. This concept had been first outlined in 1927 in an article for Lavignac's *Encylopédie de la Musique et Dictionnaire du Conservatoire*. The work on the method, the renowned *Escuela Razonada de la Guitarra* would be completed in Paris in December, 1933, and published in Buenos Aires in 1934.[6]

In 1931 the Cuervas-Pujol Duo visited England, the event being recorded in the periodical, B.M.G.:

Mr. Emilio Pujol, the famous Spanish guitarist, and his wife (also a clever exponent of the guitar) who is known professionally as Matilda Cuervas, gave a recital during their recent London visit in the private studio of Mrs. C. Gow, a member of the Philharmonic Society of Guitarists. I give the items that were played because they will probably interest those readers of B.M.G. who prefer to play the guitar in the classical style.

Duets by Mr. E. PUJOL and
Madam MATILDA CUERVAS

1. *Mélodie et Pastoral de l'Arlésienne*	Bizet
2. *Goyescas*	Granados
3. *Tango Espagnol*	Albéniz
4. *Pantomime de l'Amour Sorcier*	M. de Falla
5. *Danse du Meunier*	M. de Falla

SOLOS by MATILDA CUERVAS

6. *Granadinas*
7. *Soleares*
8. *Guajiras*
9. *Flamenco*

SOLOS by Mr. E. PUJOL

10. *Pavana*	Gaspar Sanz
11. *Menuet*	Sor
12. *Serenade Espagnol*	Malats
13. *Caprice Arabe*	Tárrega
14. *Jota*	Tárrega
15. *Barcarole*	Mendelssohn
16. *Tonadilla*	Pujol

DUETS by Mr. E. PUJOL and
Madam MATILDA CUERVAS

17. *Danse du vie brève*	M. de Falla
18. *Danse du Feu*	M. de Falla
19. *Le Cou-Cou*	Daquin

There was a large and enthusiastic audience present. All the items were well chosen, and the two artistes demonstrated, with admirable brilliancy, clarity, and expression that the guitar can hold its own with any other musical instrument when properly played.[7]

The Philharmonic Society of Guitarists would provide a useful function in the 1940's helping the young Julian Bream to begin his concert career. The Society was formed by Dr. Boris A. Perott, (1882-1957), a Russian ex-patriate living in England, "with the idea of bringing into contact and co-operation all professional and amateur players of the classical guitar, and by means of organised lectures and concerts, to win the interest of the general public, and thus place the guitar in its rightful place as one of the finest mediums for the expression of classical music."[8]

The objectives of the Society as expressed in 1931 are particularly interesting:

To teach the right method of playing the guitar, and to prepare teachers and concert performers.
To establish courses in all the Academies.
To start a library for guitar music.
To organise lectures on the history of the guitar, its literature, principles and methods of playing, etc.
To organise a symphonic orchestra, composed of sixty to eighty guitarists, and to arrange for the manufacture of suitable guitars.
To assist eminent guitarists here and from abroad to arrange concerts.
To open branches of the Society in the provinces and abroad.
To organise annually, or more frequently, dinners and dances, to further interest guitar enthusiasts, and help forward the movement.
To co-operate with other musical societies for mutual benefit.[8]

The second of these objectives was ultimately wholeheartedly endorsed by Segovia many years later, his purpose being "to place the guitar in the most important conservatories of the world for teaching the young lovers of it, and thus securing its future."[9] But the Philharmonic Society of Guitarists appear to have got there some time before him in a fascinating prophetic vision of the guitar's twentieth century development.

A further illustration of the rising star of the instrument was an article in April, 1931 by Alexis Chess, one of the members of the Philharmonic Society, entitled *The Revival of the Classical Guitar*. At a time when one might think there was comparatively little focus on the classical guitar as a concert instrument, Chess wrote optimistically and positively about the contemporary situation as he perceived it:

There can be no doubt that classical guitar music is again being keenly appreciated by music lovers, and that the guitar played in this way can take its place with the piano, violin and 'cello as one of the finest mediums of musical expression.

Many brilliant guitarists who were formerly closely associated with Francisco Tárrega, 1858-1909, and his new method of guitar technique, are mainly responsible for arousing public interest in the instrument. Audiences and musical critics in all countries have been astonished at hearing beautiful music which they had hitherto imagined as being impossible to play on the guitar. Moreover, during recent years, beautifully recorded gramophone records have been issued, and guitar recitals given by great artistes through the medium of the wireless.

Societies devoted exclusively to the interest of the classical guitar are nowadays to be found in almost every country; and of course, the number of efficient teachers increases as the desire to learn the instrument steadily grows.

The amount of really good music that has been published for the guitar is enormous and is still increasing. Original works by the old classical composers such as Sor, Carulli, and Giuliani, are being republished and fingered to suit the modern technique. This work, by the way, is being done by artists of the highest reputation. As an example of this, only a few days ago, I spent some very interesting hours with a very great artiste on the guitar, Emilio Pujol, who at the present time is in this country investigating old guitar music in the British Museum.[10]

Chess goes on to mention how Madame Pelzer, sister to the guitarist Madame Sidney Pratten (1824-1895) had recently sold all her large collections of old guitar classics to Japanese publishers. After mentioning the advance of guitar schools "in almost every European capital," and citing Luise Walker and Daniel Fortea, he moves on to the subject of Segovia:

Perhaps no one person has stirred the world's interest for the classical guitar more than Andrés Segovia, who has played in almost every country, including China and Japan, and left behind him enthusiastic crowds of admirers and wonderful press reports.

The leading musicians and composers in Britain are also beginning to think very highly of the guitar. I remember a conversation with the famous violinist De Groot in his dressing room at the Palladium about three years ago, where I had sought his advice on some question of guitar technique as compared with the violin.

"Guitar!" he said, "Can anyone really play Bach and Handel on the guitar?"

Shortly afterwards, Andrés Segovia gave a guitar recital at the Wigmore Hall. After an immensely successful performance, the public demanded more and more encores; half the hall lights were switched off in order to compel the audience to leave, but the audience wanted more and refused to go. Two enthusiasts immediately behind me were clapping most vigorously. I turned round and was delighted to find that they were De Groot and Cyril Scott.[10]

It should be remembered that this article, written in a spirit of missionary zeal, appeared in the context of a periodical dedicated in the main to players of the banjo. However, many of the comments seem almost to belong to a later decade in their optimistic assessment of the instrument's progress and reputation. What is also clear is that Segovia was by this time indubitably top of the guitar hierarchy, though other players were also referred to.

On 6 May, 1931, Segovia performed a recital at the Wigmore Hall, London, receiving the following critique in the *Daily Telegraph* the next day:

It has been reserved for Señor Segovia to unravel the mystery of Paganini's love for the guitar. The guitar, as we knew it before this Spanish artiste appeared on the scene, was so decidedly inferior an instrument that it seemed utterly unworthy of a violinist's affection. In the hands of Señor Segovia it becomes a rival to the harpsichord — and a very successful rival. For the harpsichord cannot sustain a note, while the guitar, or, at least, Señor Segovia's guitar can do it.

An admirable example of this was given yesterday in the Tárrega study — technically, perhaps, the most interesting item of the programme. Whether other performers can achieve so dainty a touch (the effect is obtained by a kind of tremolo pizzicato) remains to be seen. Most attractive of all, apart from Scarlatti's Suite, was the familiar Canzonetta of Mendelssohn, adapted we suspect by Señor Segovia himself. There was a large and enthusiastic audience.

B.M.G. reported a little anecdote from an (unnamed) interviewer who went to see Segovia, by appointment, at the Park Lane Hotel just before his Wigmore Hall recital:

When I arrived at the hotel, I waited for some considerable time and was then told that he could not be found, although he had not been seen to leave the hotel. He was eventually traced to his bedroom where he was busily practising rapid exercises with his left hand alone.

"Excuse me," he said in French, "I must practise for my concert tomorrow." He did practise all the time, using only his left hand, while he conversed with me for about half an hour.[11]

A few nights later, on 19 May, 1931, Segovia played at the Opéra, Paris. Once again he relied heavily on works by Ponce, whether directly attributed such as *Variations on Folia de España and Fugue* or the pastiche Weiss and Scarlatti pieces, with other works by Roussel, Moreno Torroba, Turina, and Albéniz.[12] Already that year he had played in Siena, Italy, Athens, Greece, and in the German capital, Berlin.

On 11 October, Segovia returned to England to give a recital at the Queen's Hall, London, performing after that in Holland on 27 and 28 October. Ponce's *Variations on Folia de España and Fugue* and his Suite in the style of Weiss, were items apparently enjoyed by Segovia and his public at this time.[13] Segovia's obsession with the music and spirit of Ponce continued unabated in a series of requests, injunctions, and encouragement from recitalist to composer.[14] In response Manuel Ponce provided Segovia with *Tremolo Study*, a re-written *Sonata of Paganini, Sonata Clásica* (1930), *Sonata for Guitar and Harpsichord, Suite Antigua* (under the name of Scarlatti), (1931) and *Four Pieces (Mazurka, Waltz, Tropico, Rumba),* and *Sonatina Meridional* (1932).[15] After this Ponce's guitar writing seems to have completed its finest work, though an acknowledged masterpiece, *Concierto del Sur* (for Guitar and Orchestra) followed some years later in 1941.

On 13th October, 1931, the Philharmonic Society of Guitarists gave a dinner in London for Segovia (following similar dinners for Emilio Pujol and Matilda Cuervas on 14 March, and for Luise Walker on 4 June). *B.M.G.* also gave further information on Segovia's response to the Society:

This Society will shortly celebrate its fourth anniversary and it is satisfactory to note that the membership has increased by forty per cent. High society has also shown a keen interest in the movement. H.H. Princess Galitzine, the Earl of Dumfries, Baron von Haeften, and many other well-known people having become members. During the past year, the celebrated guitarist, A. Segovia, became a member and practically all the world's most famous players have now joined.[16]

During the early 1930's Segovia's former mentor and inspiration, Miguel Llobet, was also pursuing his successful concert career. In 1930 he performed Manuel de Falla's *Seven Spanish Songs* with the celebrated soprano, Nina Kochitz, in the Library of Congress, Washington D.C. as part of a Spanish Arts Festival.[17] Between 1930 and 1931 he made extended European tours, playing concerts in London, Berlin, Munich, Budapest, Vienna, Bologna, etc.[18] Around 1929/1930 he recorded some duet arrangements with María Luisa Anido on the Odeon-Parlophone label, distributed by Decca, following a solo series recorded by Llobet on the Parlophon/Electric series in Barcelona about 1925.[19] On 26 January, 1931, he performed the following program at the Sala dell'Instituto Musicale, Adria, Italy:[20]

Minuet - Estudio	Fernando Sor
Andante (from *Don Giovanni*)	Wolfgang Amadeus Mozart
Prelude	J. S. Bach
Sueño	Francisco Tárrega
Echos du Paysage	Alfonso Broqua
Chanson de Léon	Rogelio Villar
Nocturno	Federico Moreno Torroba
Torre Bermeja (transcr. Llobet)	Isaac Albéniz
Danza (transcr. Llobet)	Enrique Granados
Barcarole (transcr. Llobet)	Felix Mendelssohn
Chanson gitane (transcr. Llobet)	Manuel de Falla
Three Catalan Folk Songs - Jota	Miguel Llobet

Bruno Tonazzi mentions that Llobet also performed Robert de Visée's *Suite in D minor* (edited Emilio Pujol, published Max Eschig, Paris), as well as works by Pedrell, Moreno Torroba, Ponce, Broqua, Manuel de Falla (*Homenaje, pour le Tombeau de Debussy* and others) and works by Villa-Lobos.

Thus the decade of the 1930's had begun with considerable movement and progression on the part of career guitarists of the era. Politically the ominous rumblings preceding the earthquake were becoming perceptible to sensitive seismographs. But artistically, especially in Spain, things were optimistic. Segovia's friend, the author, poet and diplomat, Salvador de Madariaga, summed up the potential cultural landscape in a book first published in English in 1930:

Finally, Spain is now in a period of high intellectual productivity. Her literature is richer than it has been since the Golden Century. Poems, novels, essays, the theatre are flourishing, and at the same time a strong movement is turning the attention of the nation back to the classics of the sixteenth century without in any way impairing the originality of the new men... Music is also better cultivated than ever since the days of the great Spanish masters of old, and Albéniz, Granados, Falla are familiar names, while Spanish music is influencing more and more that of foreign composers. In the plastic arts Spain maintains her pre-eminence. She has given in Zuloaga and Picasso two of the greatest names of contemporary painting. Sculpture is equally strong. A similar vigour is to be observed in the philosophical, mathematical, physical and biological sciences and in engineering. Popular arts of all kinds — always a strong point in Spain — still witness to the wonderful creative genius of the race.[21]

Prophetically, however, Madariaga observed in the following paragraph that "Spain is far stronger and more creative in her life than in her politics and that she counts, and always will count, far more as a people than as a nation and as a nation than as a State." For the Spanish people "the constitutional problem" was still unsolved:

... In a sense, therefore, the future of Spain depends also on the future of world ideas. Are we to remain in the present economic stage? Are we to transcend it and rise to higher forms of life? Spain will be an entirely different country according to the answer which time reserves to this question.[22]

Years later in his autobiography, Madariaga recalls his days as the Spanish ambassador in France:

... I did my best to associate the embassy with every Spanish cultural activity that happened to occur, and in particular, recitals by Spanish artists. They knew that they were welcome and that nearly always the prelude to or the epilogue of their recitals, or both, was a family reunion at the embassy with their friends.

Chief among them was the great Andrés Segovia, known to me from the days when he had risen on our horizon in Spain, before he became a musical star of the first magnitude for the whole world. He has achieved for the guitar what Casals has for the cello, a near revolution in the way of playing it and of drawing out of it the potential wealth of beauty it had so far concealed; but in at least one way Segovia's achievement was wider and more complex, not merely musical but sociological and psychological as well; for he received from tradition a popular instrument, fallen from the status the vihuela had enjoyed in centuries gone by... this instrument it was which by faith, science and will power, Segovia raised to the sovereign state it enjoys today among the best musicians.[23]

Madariaga concludes these comments with a delightful reminiscence of a lyrical episode on Lake Geneva:

As luck or ill-luck would have it, though we never coincided in Paris while I was at the embassy; but we met now and then in Geneva; and I remember one day — or rather night — when after some persuasion, and with a borrowed guitar, for he would not expose his instrument to the damp vapours of the lake, we took a boat, rowed out in the light of the moon and listened to him playing, it seemed to us, lighter and more liquid and luminous than ever, lapped by gentle waves.[24]

12. RECORDINGS AND ENCOUNTERS

At the beginning of the 1930's Segovia undertook more recordings, in particular redeeming his debt to Manuel Ponce. The recording sessions worked out as follows:

6 October, 1930:[1]	Manuel Ponce:	*Suite (in the style of Weiss) (Prelude - Allemande - Gavotte-Sarabande - Gigue)*
	Joaquín Malats:	*Serenata española*
	Federico Moreno Torroba:	*Nocturno*
6-7 October, 1930:	Manuel Ponce:	*Folies d'Espagne - Thème, Variations et Fugue*
7 October, 1930:	Manuel Ponce:	*Sonata No. 3 (lst Movement), Canción (2nd Movement), Postlude*

These were issued on 78 rpm, 10 inch recordings:

HMV E-569, England

	Joaquín Malats:	*Serenata española*
	Federico Moreno Torroba:	*Nocturno*

HMV DA-1225, England

	"S. L. Weiss" (M. Ponce):	*Sarabande, Gavotte*

Others were issued on 78 rpm, 12 inch recordings:

HMV DB 1565, England

	"S. L. Weiss" (M. Ponce):	*Prelude and Allemande*
		Gigue

HMV DB-1567, England -Volume I

	Manuel Ponce:	*Folies d'Espagne*

HMV DB -1568, England -Volume II

	Manuel Ponce:	*Folies d'Espagne*

The recordings of Ponce, and the earlier issue of music by J. S. Bach were well explored in a review in June, 1932, offering later generations a contemporary judgement on Segovia's reputation at this time and an estimation of the quality of the music he performed:

DB 1567-8. **Andrés Segovia: Folies d'Espagne** (Ponce).
DB 1536. **Andrés Segovia: Prelude, Allemande and Fugue** (Bach).
It would be a pity if Segovia's incomparable genius were too often wasted upon music of the level of this four-sided Folies d'Espagne. Here, indeed, is linked sweetness long drawn out. Segovia stands alone: he has made the guitar an instrument capable of such beauty and subtlety as we had never guessed: he can perform upon it incredible feats of delicacy and (what is apparently his danger) incredible feats of ingenuity. These variations enable him to show off to perfection the technical possibilities of his instrument, but in their musical and emotional ranges they are terribly dull. Needless to say, Segovia makes the utmost of the opportunities the piece offers: from the simple theme sensitively played to variations of pyrotechnic luxuriance, the whole gamut of guitar-playing is here exploited. And all the time, of course, there is the undercurrent of that indescribable heart-ache quality of which Segovia and his guitar are such masters. Listen, for instance, to some of the dying tones (like crying heard over evening waters) which he achieves; or to the rich guitar-chords, like some lovelier harpsichord than we have ever known. And Segovia never overdoes his slurring; he has no need for such naïve devices...[2]

Over the years there has been comparatively little qualitative evaluation of the guitar repertoire. Few guitarists would dare to castigate Ponce's *Folies d'Espagne* as "terribly dull," especially during Segovia's lifetime. Yet here we have a critic prepared to hazard such an opinion. Most writers have accepted the set of variations as a masterpiece for the guitar or subtly evaded the ultimate question. Allan Kozinn, writing some fifty years after the original recording, puts it this way:

...But the lion's share of these early recordings, and in many ways the most interesting, are the works of Manuel María Ponce, recorded in the 1930's. The Ponce contributions are colorful pieces made all the more vivid by the care Segovia lavishes on them. We have Ponce's Kreisleresque baroque fake - the so-called Weiss Suite; a couple of short, characteristic works (the Petite Valse *and* Mazurka*), as well as two of his more ambitious guitar works, the third* Sonata *and part of the* Variations and Fugue on Folias de España.*

The last is presented incomplete and in an early version that was later revised at Segovia's suggestion — the difference being most immediately noticeable in the statement of the Folías *theme at the start. But while many have assumed that this short version reflects Segovia's feeling that the full work was too sprawling, that is most likely not the case. At this time, Segovia was sending out copies of the* Folías *variations to other composers as a fine example of idiomatic guitar writing; and in the aforementioned 1978 interview, he singled out the work as one of the peaks of the literature composed for him. The culprit in the shortening of the work was probably the recording process itself. As it was Segovia had to take four sides for the ten variations he selected. Unfortunately this titanic set is one of the few works from this first period that Segovia did not re-record during the LP era.*[3]

Segovia's unwavering admiration of Ponce and his music ensured that the recording of the Variations was one of his greatest achievements of these early years of 78 rpm's. Many years later Segovia wrote of his journey in September, 1932, from Switzerland to Italy in the company of Manuel de Falla and his efforts to put over to the Spanish composer the excellence of Ponce's music:

During the unforgettable journey from Geneva to Venice which Falla, Pepe Segura — a friend of both — and I made in my automobile, we spoke much of Ponce. I tried to convey to them with a wealth of examples and details the lofty nobility of character of the Mexican composer, the purity and simplicity of his habits and the humility of his way of life... One day, in Cremona, Falla came into my room while I was practising the "Variations and Fugue on the Folias de España." He listened to them with profound attention and such was his interest that at times he interrupted me to ask, more with gesture than with words, who had composed them. Withholding my answer until I had finished, I said "Ponce." And from Falla's generous heart came the exclamation, "How glad I am that they are his!" He was happy that such a noble and beautiful work should have been born of so beautiful and noble a soul, that the creation should reflect its creator, that there should be no difference of level between the moral nature of the artist and his art. For once the miracle had happened. For once? No, Falla himself was an example of this exquisite duality.[4]

An account of the epic journey is contained in a biography of Manual de Falla:

After San Sebastián, Falla had to go to Venice in response to an invitation to conduct The Puppet Show *at the International Festival of Music. Knowing this, Andrés Segovia, who wanted a short rest after a strenuous series of concerts, sent Falla a telegram suggesting that they should travel together from Geneva, where he was then staying. He proposed that they should make the journey by car stopping at interesting places on their way. Falla gladly accepted, but asked whether he could also bring a friend, Dr. José Segura, a professor from Granada University. They took the train to Geneva and left for Venice in Segovia's car. They went by way of the Simplon, saw the North Italian lakes, drove through Milan, and stopped in such wonderful Italian cities as Verona, Vicenza, and Padua before arriving at Venice.*[5]

Despite various difficulties with the order of the program in the concert, whereby Falla's *Master Peter's Puppet Show* was scheduled to be put on first, Segovia's diplomacy apparently prevailed and the organisers were eventually persuaded to allow the work to appear at a more prestigious point in the proceedings (i.e. as the second item of three works performed). *Master Peter's Puppet Show* was widely acclaimed by all present and the reputation of Manuel de Falla's music was internationally enhanced with promises of future performances.[6]

As well as these significant developments for the well-being of Spanish music, the history of the guitar in the twentieth century was also considerably changed by this short sojourn in Venice. Mario Castelnuovo-Tedesco (1895-1968), one of Italy's most promising composers of the young generation, was also attending the International Festival of Music, where his *Piano Quintet* (1932), was to be performed. Castelnuovo-Tedesco met Segovia for the first time and naturally the conversation turned to the subject of the guitar.

On the last day of the Festival, Segovia encountered Castelnuovo-Tedesco's wife, Clara, on the *vaporetto*, (the ferry boat which transports the inhabitants of Venice in the same way as an omnibus in a normal city). Segovia communicated to her his profound wish that Mario should write a piece for the guitar, asking Clara to intercede on his behalf, and giving her his address in Geneva to underline the point. Sure enough, after going home to Usigliano, Castelnuovo-Tedesco replied to Segovia expressing that he had a great desire to write for the guitar. In return Segovia sent him two pieces as examples of good writing which demonstrated the guitar's technical difficulties – Sor's *Variations on a Theme of Mozart, Op. 9,* and, inevitably, Ponce's *Variations on Folia de España and Fugue.*[7] Thus began a most remarkable relationship between composer and artist which was to produce so many beautiful contributions for the contemporary repertoire.

Castelnuovo-Tedesco would continue to compose for the guitar from 1932 to 1967, providing a remarkable number of substantial works, including concertos and chamber music, as well as many solos. His first offering to Segovia was *Variations à travers les siècles* (written 1932, published by Schott in 1933). This work, divided into six variations (*Chaconne, Preludio, Walzer I, Walzer II, Tempo del Walzer I, Fox-Trot*), is very much an exploratory work, seeking an appropriate style. Its intentions to cover the centuries include a *Chaconne* and *Preludio* in the style of Bach, waltzes reminiscent of Schubert, and a fox-trot evoking the dance rhythms of the twentieth century with jazz implications. On receiving the work Segovia wrote back to tell Castelnuovo-Tedesco that it was the first time he had met a musician "who understands immediately how to write for the guitar."[8] Despite Segovia's apparent liking for the work, he never recorded it, though there is mention of it appearing in his recitals in the letters to Ponce.[9]

If the meeting with Castelnuovo-Tedesco was the most fruitful outcome of the trip to Venice, the return trip also proved eventful. The following account may not be entirely factually accurate but it is certainly colorful:

> *They returned in Segovia's car. Falla had a very unpleasant boil on his right temple, which he attributed to an infection contracted from having shaken hands with so many people who came to congratulate him and which he had transferred to his forehead when putting on his glasses. In fact, the condition affected his whole face and threatened to become very serious. On reaching San Remo, they had to stop to find a doctor. They were dressed in dusty travelling clothes, Segovia with long, unkempt hair, Falla with his face distorted by the swelling and his pain. His friend Dr. Segura was at least dressed with a tidiness which contrasted with the disorder of his companions. They went into the doctor's house, and Segovia introduced Falla with suitable eulogies as "the great composer, Manuel de Falla," and Falla likewise introduced the great guitarist with similar praise. The doctor regarded them distrustfully as though he feared they were lunatics. They introduced Dr. Segura, who presented a more correct appearance. "Here's a more likely-looking person," exclaimed the doctor, shaking hands with him. The upshot was that he treated Falla very successfully, so that by the same afternoon they were able to continue their journey to Arles.*[10]

After Arles the party split up, Segovia returning to Switzerland, while Manuel de Falla and Dr. Segura travelled back to Granada by train via Barcelona.

Already in 1932 Segovia had given recitals in a number of countries including a charity concert in Geneva (his place of residence at this time), a tour of Italy and Spain, four concerts in Bohemia with the promise of more to come in the fall, and a performance in the Salle Gaveau under the patronage of Ysaÿe, the great violinist. Following the trip to Venice, Segovia performed in France, and (on 18 November, 1932), in Oslo, having obtained a work permit for Norway from the Norwegian embassy in Berlin. (In Norway Segovia endured treatment for a stone in his left kidney.) In December there were plans for a concert in London in honour of the violinist, Fritz Kreisler.[11] Artistically, therefore, 1932 was a very progressive year for Segovia, with considerable travel, a greater knowledge of the personality of Manuel de Falla, and the further spread of his reputation by intense concertizing.

The American guitarist, Vahdah Olcott Bickford, published an interesting article on guitar transcriptions during 1932, at the same time offering contemporary perspectives of informed opinion on Segovia's growing stature:

> *Segovia, the famous Spanish guitarist who has toured all over Europe, Russia and North America in the past few years, has achieved more recognition for the guitar among musical critics (in America particularly) through his inclusion of Bach works in his programs, than through all his charming playing of the original Spanish works, which so suit his instrument, and which he plays with such native charm and esprit. Had Segovia played chiefly or solely these original Spanish works for the guitar (which are always included in his programs, and which always charm, his audiences) he would have perhaps gained much of the well-deserved recognition of his own art which he now has, and a general concept of the beauty and fascinating charm of the guitar as an instrument for the expression of the Spanish idioms*

and rhythms, etc, but it is certain that he would not have achieved for his instrument the same respect of the critics which he has brought it through his playing of Bach, Haydn, and other classic composers. Segovia's works are in much demand among modern guitarists, but they are nearly all transcriptions of works originally written for other instruments; he has published very few original works, and these are of a small character. [12]

From our historical perspective these comments may now seem to miss an essential point. Segovia's transcriptions were important from the 1920's onwards when his Guitar Archives Series for Schott began publication. The dissemination of records also added to his reputation for transcriptions. Yet nowadays we would perhaps consider Segovia's most important role in matters of repertoire to be in persuading the composers of the day to write for the guitar. However Bickford's judgement was implicitly endorsed by *The Gramophone's* review of the recording mentioned earlier in the chapter. After expressing an adverse opinion of the musical quality of Ponce's Variations, the critic went on to praise Segovia's playing of transcriptions of the music of J. S. Bach:

Nevertheless, I find more pleasure in his Bach Suite. I know that, speaking from the purist point of view, such arrangements are a sin against the light. Yet is there so very much that is wrong, for instance, in his playing of the arpeggio Prelude or of the appealing Allemande? Here is something so near the keyboard of Bach's own day (save for an occasional "scooping at the close") that I feel he is justified in spite of it all. Of course the Fugue, which some would say is the ultimate test of the rightness of such transcriptions, loses much: even Segovia is unable to sustain passages as they should be, unable to keep up a convincing "running commentary" on the main subject; unable, in fact to give proper emphasis to the architecture of the whole. Yet for me anyway, Segovia wins: I shall sink a good deal of my purist prejudice for the sake of enjoying such miraculous playing. [13]

The concept that "such arrangements are a sin against the light" may seem somewhat pompous nowadays. But the passage represents the kind of thinking which a guitarist would have to confront in the course of his recitals. For this critic to allow that "Segovia wins" is a good sign of victories already achieved in the battle for a guitar repertoire.

13. 1933-1934

One of the most eloquent contemporary accounts of Segovia comes from the pen of William L. Shirer, the eminent American journalist, who spent a large part of 1933 in Spain. By some chance he shared a house with Segovia that summer:

The occupant of the other half of our house that summer in Spain turned out to be Andrés Segovia. I had first heard the great guitarist play in Paris seven years before, and had marvelled that he could get such a rich and vibrant music, especially classical music, from a guitar. I had heard him again in Vienna and we had met casually at a reception after his concert.

Sharing the house in Lloret, we became good friends. He proved to be as fine a person as he was a musician, courtly and gracious, like most Spaniards, modest and simple in his manners and extremely considerate. When he learned that I was writing a book he went to the farthest corner of the house to practise, as he did daily from 7 a.m. till noon so as not to disturb me with the sound of his music. All my protests that this generous gesture was unnecessary, that my writing was quite unimportant compared to his playing, he waved aside.

Three or four evenings a week he joined us in our living room to listen to the recordings of the Asian equivalents of the guitar which I had picked up in Bombay, Kabul, Baghdad and Istanbul. He seemed fascinated by this music from the East and would ask me to play the records over and over. Sometimes he would take up his guitar and strum through some of the Asian melodies. Many of them, he remarked, were not so very different from those of the Spanish flamencos, which derived from the Moors and the gypsies of his native Andalusia and were part of his repertoire.

The evening invariably wound up with Segovia playing some of the works he had been practising. These could be compositions from Albéniz, Manuel de Falla and other Spanish composers, but more likely they were transcriptions from Bach and Mozart that he made for the guitar. Segovia was the first guitarist, I believe, to play Bach and Mozart. Until you heard him render them you could scarcely imagine them on a guitar, but on his instrument they were magnificent, full of tone colors and subtle nuances. [1]

Presumably Segovia did not tell Shirer that Francisco Tárrega had also transcribed works by Bach and Mozart many decades before and that other guitarists such as Miguel Llobet also performed these composers in recitals. At such moments the ultimate post-war legend of Segovia emerging miraculously from an empty past more or less devoid of any significant guitar traditions can be seen in its embryonic form. But far more interesting is Segovia's interest in the music of India and the East, linking such influences with Andalusian flamenco. This fascination may have been reinforced by Segovia's journey to India some time in April, 1933.[2]

Shirer also mentions Segovia's interest in literature:

Unlike many musicians I have known, Segovia had a deep interest in literature. From his conversation it was obvious that he had read a good deal of fiction, poetry, history and philosophy. He never tired of talking of the wonders of Cervantes. (His farewell present to me was a beautiful edition of Don Quixote *in Spanish). He introduced me to the works of Miguel de Unamuno — he was a personal friend and admirer of the philosopher — urging me to read Unamuno's great work* The Tragic Sense of Life, *which I did that summer and fall, as soon as I had learned Spanish.* [3]

Miguel de Unamuno (1864 -1936), philosopher, essayist, novelist and poet, was part of the "1898" generation of writers, who were deeply concerned with the identity and destiny of Spain. There was a storm of protest in 1924 when Unamuno was deported to the Canary Islands by the dictatorship of Primo de Rivera, but he later resumed his appointment at the University of Salamanca where he taught Greek and philosophy. Ian Gibson describes him as "a supreme egoist, specialized in a very personal brand of monologue which made it difficult for others to get a word in edgeways."[4] His philosophy has been summed up as follows:

Unamuno is concerned about live ideas and not the scientific method. Science is universal but culture is national. As with most of his generation, Castile was for him the great symbol of Spanish spirit. In determining this essence of Spain, language is important, and wherever one speaks Spanish, there one can find a part of Spain... The worth of others can be recognized without giving up one's own national characteristics. In this connection, Unamuno discusses a new and as yet unborn Spain, one of an eternal tradition that can be vitalized by foreign ideas. This tradition, however, must be sought in the present and not in the past, although the present too is depressed by the old reactionary Inquisition in attenuated form...[5]

It is not difficult to see why Segovia, quintessentially Spanish, yet more and more living in an international context, should, in his struggle to raise the culture of the guitar, and through such music the spiritual life of his country, have found various strands of Unamuno's philosophy of considerable interest. However, even within *The Segovia-Ponce Letters*, the most sustained collection of Segovia's writings within the public domain, he does not waste much time in discussion of his own attitudes and values outside the musical context, a tendency which probably became more marked as decades went by. But clearly with William L. Shirer, Segovia not only practised the guitar but also discussed literature and philosophy in terms that he did not find necessary to put into writing. (Accounts of his actual friendship with Miguel de Unamuno also seem, unfortunately, to be lacking from available known sources, and the philosopher received no mention in Segovia's *Autobiography.*)

The Segovia-Ponce Letters indicate, in a letter dated 29 May, 1933, the quickening disintegration of Segovia's marriage to Adelaida.[6] In a following undated letter Segovia moved on to musical matters, explaining that he was performing Joan Manén's *Fantasía-Sonata,* Op. A-22 (published 1930, Schott), and was in contact with Torroba and Turina. He was also working on Castelnuovo-Tedesco's *Variazioni a traverso i secoli*, Op. 7, and the first movement of *Sonata (Omaggio a Boccherini)*, Op. 77. At the same time he requested a mazurka from Manuel Ponce, to which the Mexican composer replied by producing his own *Mazurka* a few months later.[7]

Elsewhere in the guitar world in 1933 there was movement and progress. Agustín Barrios gave recitals in Columbia, Panama, Costa Rica, El Salvador, Honduras, Guatemala, and Mexico. During these years Barrios assumed the *persona* of Nitsuga Mangoré (Nitsuga being Agustín spelled backwards), and appeared on stage dressed as a Paraguayan Indian, the purpose being to lure larger audiences into the concert hall. On 1 July, 1933, Barrios performed the following program at the National Theatre in San Salvador:[8]

First Part

1. *Serenata Morisca*	Barrios
2. *Cueca*	Barrios
3. *Vals No. 3*	Barrios
4. *La Catedral*	Barrios

Second Part

1. *Gavotte*	Bach
2. *Minuet*	Beethoven
3. *Mozart Variations*	Sor
4. *Nocturne in Eb*	Chopin

Third Part

1. *Granada*	Albéniz
2. *Sonatina*	Tárrega
3. *Un Sueño en la Floresta*	Barrios
4. *Diana Guaraní*	Barrios

The program follows the pattern of the composer/guitarist, very much in the tradition of Tárrega, with a middle section dedicated to past luminaries before the return to the performer's own contemporary creative work as a finale to the recital.

In Europe the Austrian guitarist, Karl Scheit (1909-1994), was appointed at the age of twenty-four as Professor of Guitar at the Vienna State Academy. His destiny was to become a distinguished teacher of guitar with many outstanding students as well as one of the most prolific of all editors and transcribers for the guitar this century. His extended series with Universal Edition, Vienna, first appeared in 1940 with pieces by the Austrian Professor of Composition at the Vienna Academy, Alfred Uhl (b. 1909). On 5 April, 1933, he performed a Guitar Evening in Vienna consisting of works by J. S.

Bach, Sor, and Tárrega, with chamber works for flute, viola and cello by K. Kohaut (1753-1789), and *Sonata* for the same combination by Karl Scheit's teacher, J. N. David (1895-1977), another respected Austrian composer.

In Spain, Emilio Pujol was putting the final touches to the first volumes of his massive *Escuela Razonada de la Guitarra*, (Rational School of the Guitar), "based on the principles of technique of Tárrega," to be published in 1934 by Ricordi Americana, Buenos Aires. His major coup here was to receive a vivid endorsement from Manuel de Falla, dated December, 1933, from Granada.

> *...Since the distant times of Aguado, we lack a complete Method which would communicate to us the technical progress which Tárrega began. You have excellently provided this need, offering your own magnificent personal contribution, and thus of benefit not only to the performer but also to the composer of sensibility, who will find in your Method the stimulus to discover new instrumental possibilities.*[9]

In this way Pujol entered the grand tradition of the guitar with a blessing from Spain's foremost composer. But apart from work on his Method, Pujol was already adding to his reputation with his series *Bibliothèque de Musique Ancienne et Moderne pour Guitare* for Editions Max Eschig of Paris, France. It was mentioned in an earlier chapter how Pujol's initiative here coincided in the 1920's with Segovia's *Guitar Archives Series* for Schott. In 1931 Pujol published further items of his *ancienne* series (which began at No. 1001 and continued with consecutive numbering from there), featuring Milán's *Pavane IV* (No. 1045), *Pavane V* (No. 1046) and *Pavane VI* (No. 1047). In the same year he also published another of his own compositions, *Canción de Cuna (Berceuse)* (No. 1203). In 1934 Joaquín Rodrigo's *Sarabande lointaine* made a proud entry into the Eschig lists, destined to be ultimately included in Segovia's recorded repertoire in the 1950's. Thus it cannot be argued that it was Segovia alone who at this time contributed forwards and backwards to the repertoire by commissioning new works and researching the old.

The state of the repertoire in the 1930's can be assessed to some extent by a concert program Emilio Pujol performed (including some duo pieces with his wife, Matilde Cuervas) on 21 February, 1934, at the Sala Mozart, in Barcelona:

I

Two Pavanes	Luys Milán (1535)
Gavota (favorite of Duke of Monmouth)	Fr. Corbetta (1615)
Gallardas y Folias	Gaspar Sanz (1674)

II

Passe-Pied (from a manuscript in the National Library, Paris)	Anon.
Gigue (for lute)	S. Leopold Weiss (1686 -1750)
Minuet	Sor
Preludes and Studies	Tárrega

III

Homenaje a Debussy	M. de Falla
Estudis Criollos (first performance)	Alfonso Broqua
Faula (first performance)	Agustí Grau
Els Tres Tambors (harmonised for guitar) (first performance)	Emilio Pujol
Guajira Gitana	Emilio Pujol

IV

Minuet (from Symphony in B minor)	Mozart
Therezinha de Jesus (Ciranda)	Villa-Lobos
Danza española	Albéniz
Danza de La Vida Breve	M. de Falla
	Matilde Cuervas: Emilio Pujol[10]

In the same year, 1934, Pujol travelled to England to perform one of the six Quartets by Paganini for guitar and bowed instruments with the Classic Quartet of London.[11] This was presumably one of the first occasions that this work had been presented since the nineteenth century and, if so, was a further significant milestone in the history of the guitar.

On 3 April, 1934, Segovia travelled to Florence, to give the Italian premiere of Castelnuovo-Tedesco's *Variazioni attraverso i Secoli* and Manuel Ponce's *Sonatina Meridional,* composed in 1932. According to Corazón Otero, it was after this event that Segovia first requested the Italian composer to write a four-movement Sonata.[12] Castelnuovo-Tedesco then set about composing his *Sonata (Omaggio a Boccherini),* Op. 77.

In October, 1934, Segovia gave a recital in Mexico, staying with Ponce and no doubt catching up on many items of news between them. He played the Ponce pastiche pieces, *Preámbulo* and *Gavotte* of "Alessandro Scarlatti," the fake Weiss Suite, as well as *Valse* and *Variations and Fugue on Folia de España.* Even in Mexico Segovia's favorite musical joke was sprung on the audience, once again fooling the critics who praised his playing of the old lute music.[13]

In July, 1934, Domingo Prat's great encyclopedia of the guitar, *Diccionario de Guitarristas,* was published by Romero y Fernández, Buenos Aires. The book was in a limited edition of 1605 copies, each one of which carried the author's signature.[14] Prat offers a penetrating analysis of Segovia's art, a critique which remains of perennial interest as one of the considered contemporary judgements as the guitarist approached the frontiers of middle age.

After quoting from Segovia's birth certificate, Domingo Prat sets the context of his estimation of Segovia by admitting that he could add little or nothing to the "enormous bulk of eulogies about his exalted art," quoting instead the judgement of the violinist, Fritz Kreisler, who commented that, "Only two great musicians exist in the world, Casals and Segovia." Prat then proceeds to give a quick resumé of Segovia's early years and triumphs in "London, Paris, Boston, Mexico, Berlin, Brussels, Saint Petersburg, Stockholm, Budapest, Rome, Vienna, and wherever he presents himself he is the better artist." Then he devotes an interesting paragraph to the nature of Segovia's appeal to his audiences and his stage manner:

Segovia, is a psychologist, par excellence, in regard to the public: that is one of the secrets of his successes. In his recitals he comes on to the stage deliberately, gracefully, without a smile but correct. There is no coarseness in his movements, no affected presentation. Sitting now, before the audience, with careful preparation he invites them to silence. When this is total he begins to play, convinced that those present must keep quiet to listen, because that is what they are there for. During the recital he exacts a religious silence from the devotees, the least sound annoys him and he indicates with a gentle gesture that it should not be repeated, making it understood that whoever makes it should leave. He stops playing in any section of the work if the noise persists in irritating or distracting him. This moral force and abiding serenity dominates the crowd, predisposing the audience to feel all the beauty of what he plays. He is the true actor who, in full control of himself, "speaks" as if he is in his own house and in his turn questions the public with his gaze in order that, like him, they may fully share in the joy or sadness which possesses him, according to the theme which he is playing. The actor with fear of the public cannot detach himself and give the complete artistic feelings of that which he interprets. In the same way the guitarist who is troubled can never put himself forward as a complete recitalist. Segovia, exempt from these fears, secure within himself, yearns with all his soul for the coming of the date of his concerts and experiences beforehand the pleasure of entering into contact with the public. This quality, apart from its intrinsic value, has strengthened him in all his successes... Segovia never needs favors. By his own merit he conquers the applause, and almost demands it, because he knows that his guitar, his art and his personality have a dominant and fascinating value.[15]

Domingo Prat, somewhat surprisingly, ends his lengthy entry on Segovia with a list of errors to be found in various Segovia's editions. For our purposes it is of interest if only because it confirms the source and date of publication for various works. Thus Moreno Torroba's *Sonatina* was first published by Edición Musical Daniel, Madrid, (1924), Albert Roussel's *Segovia* by A. Durand, Paris (1925), Gustave Samazeuilh's *Sérénade* by A. Durand (1926), and Sor's *Variations on a Theme of Mozart* by Romero y Fernández, Buenos Aires (c.1921).

This testimony of Domingo Prat reveals the quite remarkable esteem in which Andrés Segovia was held by the guitar's cognoscenti by the mid-1930's. Moreover he had perceived the mysterious essence of a Segovia recital which elevated this artist above all others of his era. Throughout Segovia's life audiences responded to something irresistibly charismatic in his stage presence, and many attempts would be made over the years to define what precisely happened in a Segovia concert to achieve those remarkable effects which so entranced international audiences. Domingo Prat's diagnosis of Segovia's appeal remains perennial and meaningful.

14. THE DARKENING YEARS 1935-1936

The Segovia-Ponce Letters indicate that by February 1935, Segovia and Paquita Madriguera were preparing for marriage, negotiating the labyrinth of the new divorce laws in Spain.[1] Paquita would, some years later, be mentioned in his autobiography. Segovia had been introduced to her by her celebrated piano teacher, Frank Marshall (1883-1959). Paquita had studied composition with Enrique Granados, given concerts in Europe and the USA, and written for piano.[2] In the autobiography Segovia describes her as "a beautiful young girl of fifteen, enormous blue eyes, a delicate nose, fine smiling lips, a graceful slim figure, half-child, half-woman... a delightful vision":

I had heard of this budding brilliant pianist. The London press and public had raved about her. Although her talent was mature for her years, it seemed to have a solid quality that went beyond the fleeting flash often displayed by child prodigies. She had studied with Granados since the age of eight, and she was already an accomplished musician as well as a very promising pianist...

In a few months Paquita left with her mother for New York. For months I thought of her time and time again, although I knew well that my work required all my energies and concentration. Whenever I would open the shrine where I kept my memories of her, a mysterious inner voice seemed to tell me softly that she and I were destined to meet frequently in the future and form a close and lasting relationship. Indeed, we did. She became my wife some time later.[3]

If Segovia's memoirs are accurate, the early meeting with Paquita may have taken place about 1915. They were to marry in 1936.

Along with these momentous developments in Segovia's personal life, came immense advances in the public perception of his artistic stature. In particular, Segovia's recital in Paris on 4 June, 1935, presented to the public for the first time his transcription of J. S. Bach's mighty *Chaconne* (from *Partita in D minor,* BWV 1004). As early as a letter dated 20 July, 1927, Segovia mentioned that he was working "deliriously" on the *Chaconne*,[4] and his arrangement of the piece was published by Schott in 1934. The premiere of the *Chaconne* was one of the landmarks of the guitar, setting a standard against which all future aspirants to guitar greatness would need to measure their prowess.

To enable a sceptical audience to swallow such a large pill apparently needed persuasion, and the French musicologist, Marc Pincherle (1888-1974) was commissioned to write the requisite program notes. In the event Pincherle excelled himself, but at the expense of blunting his argument with an excess of enthusiasm. Pincherle intended that Segovia should not be accused of disrespect in playing Bach's masterpiece on the guitar but overstepped the mark by arguing that perhaps the piece sounded less than comfortable on the violin, and that there may have been some direct connection between the *Chaconne* and the guitar itself:

You ask, my dear Andrés, that I should present to the public your transcription of the Chaconne. It seems absurd, in reality, that a musician of your standing should be defended against a possible suspicion of disrespect to J. S. Bach. Grim zealots may rise to protest in the name of the old cantor — and seek to prohibit precisely what he, himself, would have been the first to approve.

I admire the Chaconne profoundly yet I have seldom heard it played without a sense of discomfort. This dissatisfaction was wholly unrelated to the musical splendour of the composition itself, to its nobility and pathetic content which reveals itself, to its rich variety, its marvellous balance as well as its ingenuity in the treatment of the violin. In spite of all this, it is rare that a performance corresponds to our expectations, so great is the contrast between the frail resources of those four strings and the intensity of the truth which they must express, between the monodic character of the violin — a pure soprano voice — and the orchestral fullness demanded by the composition...

Among the instruments to which Bach devoted particular attention was the lute, close relative to the guitar. Scholars (among them N. D. Bruger and H. Neeman) have listed the works that exist in several instrumental versions for violin solo with lute, for lute and violoncello, but in most cases these researches have failed to reveal which of these versions was the original and which the transcription. Is it inconceivable that the Chaconne, perhaps, might turn out to be among the compositions with a double version and that further research might bring this fact to our knowledge?

Who can say that a direct connection with the guitar may not be brought to light? The very key of D, in which the Chaconne is written, is the perfect tonality for the guitar; the entire harmonic "schema" is based on progressions that are typical of Andalusian popular music, a thing which is characteristic throughout the composition but most striking in the whole of the last page. This Andalusian music is expressed traditionally on the guitar.

It is not unlikely, moreover, that the Iberian origin of the Chaconne might have suggested to Bach the idea of assigning it to a Spanish instrument, one which his universal curiosity could not ignore, since it had become the fashion in every country of Europe.

Obviously it is not on so frail a hypothesis that we can form a conviction. What really counts in the balance, the sole argument of weight likely to influence our opinion as to whether or not the Chaconne was composed originally for the guitar, is the clear evidence that the composer wrote as though he had no other instrument in mind.[5]

Thus, delightfully, Pincherle leads us through a labyrinth of false logic. Sixty years later no research has led us to believe that J. S. Bach ever had anything to do with Andalusia or the guitar. More detailed research has cast significant question marks on the area of Bach and the lute, for it is possible that his so-called "lute suites" were actually written for the lute-harpsichord, a keyboard which had the mechanism of a harpsichord but sounded like a lute. More to the point is that Segovia was eager to attempt the conquest of large mountains and by 1935 he had the reputation and the experience to achieve such an ambition.

Support for Pincherle's special pleading was echoed in an interesting account of Segovia's playing of the *Chaconne* in a book by Bernard Gavoty published exactly twenty years later:

Among the many evenings which I have spent listening to Segovia there is one in particular which has left me with an unforgettable memory. The program on that occasion announced one work which made the violinists start and tremble: Bach's Chaconne. Horror of horrors! The Chaconne for solo violin, the sacred Chaconne — were we going to hear — nay endure — its profanation by a guitarist? They covered their faces, as Spanish ladies do when watching a bull-fight — that is with their fingers slightly parted so as to see through the spaces... Segovia, however, had taken precautions: he was being supported by the competent musicologist Marc Pincherle, who had said to him merely, "Go to it!" Besides, it is very likely that Bach first wrote his Chaconne for the lute and later transposed it for violin. Be that as it may the violinophiles arrived in profound gloom to witness the "murder." As for myself, my enjoyment of the performance was unclouded. How refreshing it was to hear at last natural, flowing arpeggios instead of those of the violin, mimicking the squeal of rending calico. Instead of double-stoppings, always a bit sickly and tottering, we were given clear chords arranged on distinct harmonic levels, a polyphony in which each voice preserved its individuality. Furthermore, the variations were connected: for once they deserved their name. No painter's palette was ever richer than Segovia's guitar in tones and nuances on that particular evening. I myself extolled the Spanish master's victory with enthusiasm, and for that I received two days later a letter from a jaundiced violin-addict, who cried shame! and advised me to hear the Chaconne played on his own violin for comparison. In order to preserve my correspondent's illusions, I did not accept the invitation.[6]

What is interesting here is the establishment of Segovia's *Chaconne* in the realm of legend and mythology. It would not be the first time nor the last that a writer's thoughts would be guided along channels inspired by Segovia himself. Whether the "violinophiles" were only at the concert to witness the "murder" of a great piece, seems curiously improbable. (Nowadays many guitarists would consider it quite a triumph to attract violinists to guitar recitals for any reason whatsoever.) Gavoty also repeats Pincherle's assertion that Bach may have written the *Chaconne* for the lute.[7] Whether preferring the guitar over the violin for its apparent ease of performance is in itself any kind of a persuasive argument is dubious. A rather more satisfactory approach might be that transcriptions allow us a multitude of perspectives on the music of J. S. Bach, whether it is Stokowski's orchestrated version of the *Chaconne,* Busoni's pianoforte arrangement or Segovia's advocacy of the work in terms of the guitar. Segovia was certainly not averse to stirring up, through his friend, Pincherle, a little controversy, on the grounds that debate engenders publicity and entices the public. But Segovia was at the time attracting good audiences throughout Europe and probably would have done so whether he played the *Chaconne* or not. But the inclusion of this spectacular piece in his repertoire was, of course, destined to change the landscape of the guitar.

Christopher Nupen, the producer of several famous films on Segovia, sheds further light on the transcription of the *Chaconne:*

... Segovia was reluctant to attempt the Chaconne *"because I love that piece beyond any imagination" and for years he studied the transcriptions by F. Herman for two violins, Brahms for the piano (left hand), Busoni and Raff for the piano (two hands and how!), and Jena de Hubay for orchestra. It was therefore not until 1935 in Paris that, with the support of the distinguished French musicologist, Marc Pincherle, he decided to make the transcription and to play it in public. The success was instant and after so long a wait Segovia may be forgiven his quip "the success I could measure by the rage of the violinists." It should be added, however, that he refers to the violinists of that time, not present at the recital.*[8]

In his Paris concert of June, 1935, Segovia also premiered Castelnuovo-Tedesco's *Sonata (Omaggio a Boccherini)*, Op. 77, another equally significant advance in the annals of the twentieth century guitar.[9] This work was followed up by Castelnuovo-Tedesco's presentation to him of *Capriccio Diabolico (Omaggio a Paganini)*, Op. 85, written in 1935, which subtly paid double homage, first to Paganini, as supreme legend of the violin, but implicitly also to Segovia, the contemporary Paganini of the guitar.[10] The composition quotes in its opening bars the famous theme of *La Campanella*, taken from Paganini's *Violin Concerto No. 2*.

Segovia also returned to the recording studios at this time after a four year absence. In April, 1935, he recorded the following:

2 April, 1935:	J. S. Bach:	*Prelude,* (from *Cello Suite in G major,* BWV 1009)
9 April, 1935:	Francisco Tárrega:	*Étude in A major*
	Manuel Ponce:	*Mazurka, Petite Valse*

These were issued on two 78 rpm, 10 inch recordings in 1937:

HMV DA-1552 England (also Victor Red Seal 1824)

Manuel Ponce:	*Petite Valse*
	Mazurka

HMV DA -1553, ENGLAND

J. S. Bach:	*Prelude*
Alard/Tárrega:	*Study in A major*

On 2 June, 1935, Segovia gave a recital on BBC radio. The *Radio Times* offered the following introduction to the broadcast:

Before Segovia gave his first recital in a London concert hall some years ago, few realised how dignified and beautiful an instrument the guitar can be in the hands of an expert player who is also an artist. That first recital was a revelation. Segovia has such a command over his instrument, his execution is so fertile in range and colour and his artistry so imaginative that his popularity is not difficult to understand.

That public opinion at this time did not always grasp or understand a golden opportunity was well illustrated by a review of the broadcast in the *Evening News*:

That one can get too much of a good thing is more than true in radio listening. From day to day and from year to year the BBC turns out altogether more programs than are good either for itself or for us; often, too, an otherwise excellent programme is marred by long windedness.

The guitar, for instance, is a charming instrument when expertly played, and Segovia, who broadcast a guitar recital last night, is a rare master of this instrument. But the guitar lacks the variety of tone and expression to hold the listener's interest for a solid 25 minutes — that, at any rate, was my feeling when listening to Segovia's recital.[11] *The Wireless Correspondent*

15. SEGOVIA'S EDITIONS 1930-1935

Just as the 1920's changed the face of guitar publications, so throughout the first half of the decade of the thirties the steady accumulation of Segovia's recital material continued. The following is a list of his editions published between 1930 and 1935:

1930:	J. S. Bach	*Siciliana* (from *Sonata in G minor*, BWV 1001), Union Musical Española, Madrid.
		Sarabande (from *Partita in B minor*, BWV 1002), UMP
	Franz Schubert	*Three Little Waltzes*, UMP
	Ludwig van Beethoven	*Minuetto*, UMP
	Manuel Ponce	*Preludes 1-6*, Schott's, Guitar Archive No. 124
		Preludes 7 -12, G.A. No. 125
	Joaquín Turina	*Ráfaga*, G.A. No. 128
	Joan Manén	*Fantasía-Sonata*, G.A. No. 129
1931:	Fernando Sor	*Variations on "Das klinget so herrlich" (The Magic Flute) by Mozart*, Op. 9. G.A. No. 130
	Manuel Ponce	*Estudio*, G.A. No. 131
	Federico Moreno Torroba	*Pièces caractéristiques, Vol. I*, G.A. No. 133
		Pièces caractéristiques, Vol. II, G.A. No. 134
	Manuel Ponce	*Variations on "Folia de España" and Fugue*, G.A. 135
	Felix Mendelssohn	*Romanza sin Palabras, Op. 31, No. 3* , Ricordi, Buenos Aires.
1932:	Joaquín Turina	*Sonatina*, G.A. No. 132
	Mario Castelnuovo-Tedesco	*Variations à travers les siècles*, G.A. No. 137
1933:	G. F. Handel	*Air (Suite X)*, UMP
	Robert Schumann	*Canción silvestre, Mayo, buen Mayo*, UMP
	Edvard Grieg	*Canto del Campesino*, UMP
	Joseph Haydn	*Minuetto*, UMP
	Felix Mendelssohn	*Romanza sin Palabras, Op. 19, No. 4*, UMP
1934:	J. S. Bach	*Chaconne*, G.A. No. 141
1935:	Joseph Haydn	*Minuet from G minor Quartet* (Hoboken III:75), G.A. No. 139
	Frédéric Chopin	*Mazurka, Op. 63, No. 3*, G.A. No. 140
	J. S.Bach	*3 Pieces from the Notebook of Anna Magdalena Bach*, G.A. 142
	Johann Kuhnau	*4 Petits Morceaux*, G.A. No. 143
	Domenico Scarlatti	*Sonata in A minor*, G.A. No. 144
	J. S. Bach	*Prelude and Fugue*, (BWV 998), G.A. No. 145
	C. P. E. Bach	*La Xénophone, La Sybille*, G.A. No. 146
	C. P. E. Bach	*Siciliana*, G.A. No. 147
	G. F. Handel	*8 Aylesford Pieces*, G.A. No. 148
	Mario Castelnuovo-Tedesco	*Sonata (Omaggio a Boccherini)*, G.A. No. 149

There are several observations that can be drawn from perusal of this list. In particular it can be seen that the time from the production of a new work to the moment that it is published is sometimes quite rapid, as with, for example, Castlenuovo-Tedesco's *Sonata,* written in 1934, and premiered and published the following year. As well as the new pieces being brought forward in all their diversity, Segovia was diligently arranging a wide variety of classical compositions, ranging from J. S. Bach and Haydn to the lesser known Kuhnau and C. P. E. Bach.

Most amazing is the sheer abundance of the flow of editions that found their way into publication against a background of constant travel and concertizing, marital upheaval and daily practice. Segovia's editing is extremely detailed, the precise position of each note on the fingerboard being indicated in the established tradition of Francisco Tárrega. Moreover the Guitar Archives Series of the 1930's are more accurate on the whole than those of the 1920's, with fewer misprints and misfingerings, perhaps because of greater attention to the necessities of proof-reading.

It is also astonishing how many of these, published over sixty years ago, have indeed stood the test of time. Some of the arrangements from the classical era may be less played nowadays, but such jewels as the *Chaconne* continue to shine brightly. The achievement of this half-decade alone bears witness to the amazing energy and vision of Segovia, the editor/performer, desperate now to expand his repertoire and to create a worthwhile literature for the instrument.

16. 1936 — THE FATEFUL YEAR

There is some evidence as Andrés Segovia approached 1936 that he was claiming to be slightly younger than he really was. Certainly Domingo Prat had the correct age in his *Diccionario de Guitarristas* as he had access to the facts recorded on the baptismal certificate, but this book received a relatively limited circulation, so few at the time would have been aware of a discrepancy here. In a letter dated February, 1936, Segovia tells Ponce that "at forty years of age" he was presented with serious problems.[1] In a review in *The Gramophone* of March, 1941, there is a reference to "this most distinguished of modern guitar-players (b. 1896)."[2] It is perhaps a useful thing for an artist on the frontiers of middle-age to be considered more youthful than chronological dates demand though why Manuel Ponce did not share the truth in this instance is a little puzzling when he knew so many other secrets about Segovia and his repertoire.

1936 was destined either way to be the great divide in Segovia's life. In a crucial letter of February, 1936, he informed Ponce that he had now married Paquita Madriguera. At the same time acute financial difficulties confronted him, including alimony for Adelaida and the children, and support for his mother and his Aunt Gertrudis. A recent tour of England had earned no more than £140, with a subtraction of £24 for tax and the usual expenses for travel and subsistence. At this time Segovia and his new wife were living in Barcelona.[3]

On 27 February, 1936, Manuel Ponce finished his wedding present for the happy couple, *Prelude for Guitar and Keyboard*, which was attributed to Sylvius Leopold Weiss. When over two decades later the work was recorded on *Segovia Golden Jubilee*, Vol. 2, AXTL 1089, (1959), with Rafael Puyana on harpsichord, the sleeve notes were as follows:

German composer and lutenist, Sylvius Leopold Weiss (1686 -1750) was one of the most famous musicians of his day. He was regarded as Europe's outstanding lute player, renowned for his tone and technique and his skill at improvisation. He served in the employment of several European courts, and was known personally to Handel and Bach. This Prelude *was transcribed by the Mexican composer Manuel Ponce, and is played here in Ponce's arrangement with harpsichord accompaniment by the noted South American harpsichordist, Rafael Puyana.*

Segovia gratefully accepted the *Prelude* as a superb wedding present.[4]

On 19 May, 1936, Segovia, in the company of various friends and, of course, his new wife, dispatched a letter to Manuel Ponce from Moscow.[5] This was to prove the last epistle to Ponce from the "old world" for in Spain things were changing so drastically that henceforth life could never be the same. The turning point was about to be reached.

In July 1936 the Spanish Civil War began. The Spanish army under its generals rebelled against the elected Government. Beginning in Morocco, the army in North Africa crossed the Straits of Gibraltar with the assistance of Hitler's *Luftwaffe*, and began to fight its way through Spain from the south.[6] One of the generals in command of the advance was Francisco Franco, destined to become *El Caudillo*, the dictator of Spain. As the Nationalist armies drove northwards spreading horror and slaughter, the perspective from Barcelona, where Segovia found himself trapped was of an equal misery. On 19 July elements of the army attempted an uprising in support of events in the south and were defeated in the streets.

After this rebuff to the insurgent army, Barcelona was in the grip of a number of conflicting forces. Among these were the *Anarqistas*, a political grouping which had arisen in Spain during the late nineteenth century. They began as followers of the philosophy of Michael Bakunin (1814-1876), whose concepts were introduced to Spain by the Italian, Giuseppe Fanelli, who arrived in Spain in 1868. By 1873 there were some 50,000 followers of Bakunin in Spain. First known as "Internationals," they later became the "Anarchists." As well as the Anarchists, there were a number of other political groupings including the Spanish Socialist Party and the Communists, the latter being relatively few in number and antagonistic to both Anarchists and Socialists. The political scene in Barcelona in July, 1936, after the defeat of the potential insurgency there, was thus one of complexity and confusion with a subsequent catastrophic breakdown of law and order which threatened citizens of all persuasions, even those who considered themselves anti-fascist. (The same chaos extended to Madrid where the military revolt had been even less well co-ordinated than in Barcelona, and had been put down with great loss of life.)

Revolution now broke out in those places in the north where the insurgency had been defeated, the resulting political effects being of a patchwork quilt of influences, with no central authority in control. The breakdown produced murder and mayhem, with a great deal of impromptu slaughter as militia units formed into gangs, each autonomously carrying out their own program of atrocities. On the nationalist side there were more organised atrocities and a deliberate policy of terror. Without some awareness of the complex background to the events in Spain in July 1936, it is impossible to comprehend in the least degree the processes by which Andrés Segovia and Pablo Casals, both living in Barcelona through this terrible time, arrived at contradictory political positions. It used to be assumed by many that Segovia was not involved in politics. In a companion to a boxed recording published when Segovia was eighty-nine, the text states quite bluntly that "Politics was and remains a matter of indifference to Segovia." It goes on to say that Pablo Casals' "long refusal to perform in public, as a protest against Franco's rule in Spain, used to draw from Segovia a sad shake of the head." Segovia's comment here is that as far as Casals was concerned "We disagree on many things." He then goes on to see "order and discipline" in his guitar, the precise opposite of politics.[7]

The publication of *The Segovia-Ponce Letters* in 1989, two years after his death, revealed a somewhat different image of Segovia. In February 1936, a letter suggested that Casals was actually composing something for him.[8] But by July the differences of opinion about political events in Spain would separate the two great instrumentalists. While Segovia occasionally would mention Casals in the years to come, the autobiography of Pablo Casals, and the subsequent biographies, carry not the slightest reference to Segovia. It is as if the guitarist had dropped into a vacuum without trace.

The experiences and political views of Andrés Segovia concerning the Spanish Civil War remained well concealed for most of his life following the Second World War. With the publication of *The Segovia-Ponce Letters* his strong feelings emerged into the public domain in explicit form. In an undated letter of 1936, written from 171 West, 71st Street, New York City, Segovia explained to Ponce the horror from which he had emerged. Despite being warned about the situation by Salvador de Madariaga, Segovia and his wife had returned to Spain from their trip to Russia.[9]

Segovia lists those who have already fled, including Ortega de Gasset, the philosopher and novelist and a number of diplomatic or political figures, as well as all kinds of creative artists.[10]

Segovia had himself been in great danger and forced to join the militia. His house in Barcelona had been pillaged, with all his belongings taken. Most painful was the disappearance from the house of all his precious manuscripts, including those of works written for him by a wide range of composers (including many of Ponce's compositions) and his own transcriptions. However, Segovia and Paquita eventually managed to escape by ship to Genoa while Adelaida and the children fled to Switzerland.[11]

Under the slogan of *la Patria, la Religión y la Autoridad,* Segovia seems to have made his stand at this time. In a letter which brings that out, he expresses his fear that in the United States it was dangerous for a person to object to the ruling government of Spain.[12] Thus he found it necessary to hide his beliefs. Unfortunately this letter is not dated so its position in the chronology of this fateful year is not altogether self-evident. But the commitment behind this letter reveals that Segovia was not, and could not be, indifferent to politics. His experiences in Barcelona were sufficient to make his mind up. Whereas Casals could forgive the anti-Franco groups their violence and mayhem as random acts of lawlessness contrasting with the military's planned scheme of atrocities on the other side, Segovia found himself unable to adopt any kind of broader view.

That Segovia should express unreserved support for Franco, his actions, and his creed, still comes as a shock to many even decades later. Pablo Casals's beliefs and his conduct were public, open and consistent. In contrast Segovia's support of Franco's cause was hidden and secret, with frequent admonitions to Ponce in case his letters should be seen by others.[13] His secret affiliation to the cause of a callous and arrogant dictator, revealed publicly for the first time in *The Segovia-Ponce Letters,* necessarily cast shadows on his posthumous reputation. Yet this whole area needs greater information than just the one-sided monologue of the letters.

But as Segovia was aware, even with secrecy people did get to know about his views.[14] Segovia's subsequent policy would attempt to make sure that any damage caused by such information would be limited by discreet behavior and a refusal to talk in public about anything except music. From that time onwards Segovia's persona would have to change. He became an elusive man to pin down in conversation with journalists and the media. In time the creation of the image, legend and mythology of Maestro Segovia would serve well both as a vehicle for the dissemination of his music and also for the concealment of virtually any disturbing elements.

17. ONWARDS

Following the summer of 1936, after which the life of all Spanish people would never be the same, Segovia returned to work, finding himself in some financial difficulty, his savings gone.[1] On 13 October, 1936, he returned to the studios to record Mendelssohn's *Canzonetta* (from *String Quartet No. 1 in Eb major, Op. 12*), originally transcribed by Francisco Tárrega, (his version being adapted by Segovia), and the third movement, *Vivo e energico* of Castelnuovo-Tedesco's *Sonata (Omaggio a Boccherini), Op. 77.* This was issued on HMV DB 3243 the following year.

On 27 November, he made his debut in Holland, performing the following program:

I

Canzone e saltarello	ed. Chilesotti
Pavane et Gaillarde	Sanz
Preámbulo et Gavotta	A. Scarlatti

II

Chaconne	J. S. Bach

III

Fantasía	Turina
Tarantella	Castelnuovo-Tedesco
Granada	Albéniz
Torre Bermeja	
Sevilla	

(As so often throughout these years, "A. Scarlatti" refers of course to a composition by Manuel Ponce.)

Castelnuovo-Tedesco's *Tarantella, Op. 87a,* was composed in 1936 (to be published by Ricordi, Milan in 1939).[2] Also that year he composed *Aranci in Fiori* (Orange Blossom), *Op. 87b.*, a work also published in 1939 by Ricordi, edited and fingered by Segovia, but not performed much by Segovia, (if at all), and one he did not record. The piece was dedicated not to Segovia but to Aldo Bruzzichelli, a close friend of the composer. When Bruzzichelli's son had a severe attack of influenza, it was Mario Castelnuovo-Tedesco who supplied a large consignment of oranges, at that time considered one of the best cures for the affliction, hence the hidden allusion within the title. Bruzzichelli later became a music publisher in Firenze (one of his publications being Reginald Smith Brindle's *El Polifemo de Oro,* 1963). He was also the dedicatee of Castelnuovo-Tedesco's *Platero y Yo, Op. 190,* for Narrator and Guitar, (1960).[3]

In January, 1937, an article in the magazine, *B.M.G.,* throws an interesting light on Segovia's standing at the time. As we look back from the end of the twentieth century it may seem that Segovia had a clear supremacy over most of his competitors, a fact critically acknowledged. But some comments by one of the contributors concerning the Uruguayan guitarist, Julio Martínez Oyanguren (1905-1973), suggests that comparisons between players were not always coming out in favour of Segovia:

Señor Oyanguren's name will no doubt be already familiar to guitarist readers of "B.M.G." as signifying superb finger-style guitar playing, and I can assure them it is superb.

It appears to be a habit to draw comparisons between any good player of the Spanish guitar and Segovia, which, to my mind, is a foolish thing to do, as, is the case with Señor Oyanguren, the spheres of the two artists are entirely different. Naturally, they occasionally encroach on each other's ground, but that is unavoidable.

If one must compare Oyanguren and Segovia, I would be inclined to say that they are equally good, although I have an idea that Oyanguren will have a rather greater appeal to the non-playing public, but I would not say that this means that he, as a rhythm "fan" might put it, is "miles ahead of Segovia".[4]

The writer then goes on to examine in detail a disc by Oyanguren of *La Cumparsita*, "the well-known tango," on Columbia X5476, arguing that there should be more guitar recordings of popular tangos and that finger style guitar need not confine itself to "heavy classical" music. (*La Cumparsitas* was backed by Vladimir Bobri's *Danza en la*.) The following month the same writer reviewed another recording by Oyanguren on Columbia 547-X of two compositions by the guitarist himself, *Arabia* and *Andalucia*.[5]

The two articles reveal that Oyanguren's appeal was pitched towards the popular end of the repertoire, a strategy which Segovia had dispensed with long ago. The tone of the writing reveals however that Segovia was not yet regarded with that reverence which accompanied his listeners after the Second World War, and that Segovia's intentions concerning repertoire had obviously not yet been fully grasped by the author of the article.

Later that year two new recordings of Oyanguren were announced.[6] These included *Jerezana, L'Hereu* and *Zapateado*, (details of composers not given), backed by *Preludio No. 5 in E major* and *Danza Mora*, by Tárrega on Am. Columbia 69003-D and *Preludio No. 12 in A minor, Preludio No. 11 in D major, Preludio No. 6 in B minor*, and *Tremolo Study*, all by Tárrega, on Am. Columbia 17100-D.

As mentioned previously, Segovia's recordings, made in 1935, of Ponce's *Petite Valse* and *Mazurka*, Bach's *Prelude* (from *Cello Suite in C major*, BWV 1009), and Alard's *Study in A*, were issued in 1937. The pieces by Ponce on HMV DA1552 would be reviewed in *The Gramophone* in 1938, in the following ecstatic tones:

Segovia in the 1930's.

> *A critic recently remarked of Kreisler that he could play Three Blind Mice and convince his audience that it was a masterpiece. This I take to be a compliment, and I would like to borrow it, and convey it to Segovia, who makes these two trivial pieces by Ponce sound both interesting and charming.*
>
> *The Petite Valse in particular is a joy to listen to, and the deftness that characterises this amazing artist's playing is here most conspicuous. He makes it difficult for us to believe that the guitar is really an extremely difficult instrument to play. This is a record that will delight the listener again and again.[7]*

Concerning the critic's comments on an artist's ability to "play Three Blind Mice and convince his audience it was a masterpiece," a similar thing happened to Segovia after a recital in Geneva. J. Guilloux, critic of *Journal de Genève*, after hearing a performance of Castelnuovo-Tedesco's *Sonata (Ommagio a Boccherini)*, wrote that Segovia would be a "great artist even if he played *J'ai du bon tabac*," the item in question being, more or less, the French equivalent of *Three Blind Mice*. Segovia wrote angrily to Castelnuovo-Tedesco on the subject of the shortcomings of critics. In reply to Guilloux, the composer wrote an intricate set of variations entitled *Variations plaisantes, sur un petit air populaire, Op. 95 (J'ai du bon tabac)*, (1937, published Bèrben), for guitar, and sent it to the critic. The movements were as follows:[8]

Introduction (en éternuant) (sneezing)
Thème - Grognan et saccade (Mouvement mesuré) (groaning and jerky) (Measured movement)
Variation I - Plus vif et léger (Fat et vaniteux) (More lively and light) (Smug and conceited)
Variation II - Plaintif et monotone (Plaintive and monotonous)
Variation III - A l'espagnole (Hommage à Granados)
Gai et dansant
Variation IV - Intermède romantique (Assez agité) (Romantic Interlude) (Quite agitated)
Variation V - L'inevitable Fugue

In a letter to Ponce dated 10 August, 1937, written from Montevideo, Uruguay,[9] Segovia mentioned that he was shortly leaving for Geneva, so it seems probable that Castelnuovo-Tedesco's *Variations plaisantes* were written in the fall of 1937. Earlier that year, in a letter dated 10 March, Segovia had politely fended off what appeared to be a request by Ponce to write the guitarist's biography. Such a prospect probably did not fill Segovia with delight, though it may have sown the seeds of an idea which would come to fruition in the 1940's. In return he raised again the idea of a Guitar Method, written jointly by Ponce and himself, containing a systematic analysis of the instrument with studies, both elementary and advanced, composed by Ponce with a commentary by Segovia.[10] Unfortunately such a book never saw the light of day, though it would have been a fascinating milestone in twentieth century guitar history.

In *B.M.G.* of October 1937, two "Spanish guitar recitals" by Andrés Segovia in London were advertised, for 17 and 22 October in the Hyde Park Hotel and the Wigmore Hall respectively. The concerts were reviewed in *B.M.G.* in December, 1937:

A large audience was present at the Segovia recital given at the Wigmore Hall on October 22nd, and, although the eminent Spanish guitarist had, that day, heard of the death of his son, his playing was everything that one expects from him. One critic wrote: "The fastidious artistry of his playing, which owes nothing to vulgar tricks of virtuosity, was as enchanting as ever. Mr. Segovia need never apologise for his boldness in adapting works written for other instruments. Most transcriptions produce a volume of sound, a thicker sonority, than the originals. These do the reverse; they create a new intimacy and in doing so actually make possible a more vivid understanding. Or is it simply the magic of the playing, which regards nothing as unimportant and seems lovingly to lead us to the very heart of music?"

At the end of the recital the applause continued for over ten minutes.[11]

According to the entry on Segovia in the reference book by Philip Bone, the London press also made the following comments concerning the Wigmore Hall concert:

Reporting his London concerts the press said: "Praise is superfluous, his is, in its way, one of the most astonishing displays of musical and technical mastery at the present time. Despite the fact that he had learned of the death of his thirteen year old son, only a few hours before, Segovia insisted on giving his recital — the boy had been electrocuted when crossing an aqueduct near Geneva."[12]

Segovia thus reached one of the most tragic nadirs of his life. His son, Leonardo, was now taken from him, so soon after the recent upheavals of the divorce and the devastating effects of the Spanish Civil War in 1936, with its consequence of financial hardship and involuntary exile. His insistence on performing this concert a few hours after hearing of the tragedy may seem to some the triumph of professionalism over human values. The iron discipline and the creed that the show must go on here take precedence over private grief. Despite the anguish, Segovia's playing appears from the reports to have been impeccable.

His programme at the Wigmore Hall, London on that tragic night was as follows:

I

Chaconne	J. Pachelbel
Allemande - Bourrée	J. S. Bach
Andante and Minuet	J. Haydn
Canzonetta	F. Mendelssohn

II

Prelude - Allemande -	S. L. Weiss
Capriccio - Ballet -	
Sarabande - Gavotte -	
Gigue	

III

Sonatina Meridional	M. Ponce
Tarantella	M. Castelnuovo-Tedesco
Serenata	J. Malats
Torre Bermeja	I. Albéniz

B.M.G. gave details of a further concert in England:

Again on October 27th, Segovia appeared at the Mechanics Lecture Hall, Nottingham, at a concert-recital held under the auspices of the Nottingham Music Club, where he repeated his London success. The local newspaper, reporting Segovia's appearance, said: "The warmth of his reception induced the great guitarist to give two extras. The guitar is capable of very delightful effects — of soft harmonics, delicate nuances and rich tones and its resources were brilliantly demonstrated by Segovia who held the audience in the hollow of his hand."[13]

18. 1938

In a letter to Ponce of 14 February, 1938, Segovia further mourns the loss of Leonardo. Amidst the devastation of his life at this moment, however, came the news that Paquita was expecting a child towards the end of May, 1938.[1]

In the event, the new baby, Beatriz, was born on 5 July, 1938. The birth and its aftermath appear to have been problematical, necessitating an operation for Paquita a month later.[2] But there is a gap in the Segovia-Ponce correspondence here between 14 February, 1938 and 26 August, 1939, with Ponce apparently not replying to Segovia's letters. According to Corazón Otero, Ponce at this time was involved in a mass of bureaucratic duties, including the role of Inspector of Personnel of Kindergartens. In 1938 he was given three months' leave of absence with salary, and completed the symphonic suite, *Merlin,* inspired by the operas of Albéniz.[3] For whatever reason Segovia did not hear directly from Ponce for over a year in the period preceding the former's letter of 26 August, 1938.[4]

An interesting source concerning 1938 surfaced comparatively recently in the pages of *Guitar Review.* This was a letter from Carl Sandburg, (1878-1967), the celebrated American writer, written on 3 May, 1938,[5] following his first meeting with Segovia, who was performing recitals in Chicago.

The letter begins unequivocally with a description of Segovia as "the world's greatest guitarist" who "holds his guitar like it was the world's greatest treasure." If there was a fire in the house, alleges Sandburg, Segovia "would carry the guitar out first, then the baby." This is an early and prime example of extravagant writing about Segovia which would in decades to come be a feature of many comments about him. In retrospect, the remark appears inordinately foolish. Would Segovia really have gone for his guitar and not his daughter, Beatriz, if a fire had broken out in his home in the second half of 1938? Would not such an act have been tantamount to criminality? And if so, why should an intelligent man write such nonsense, even in a private letter? The answer lies in the effect that Segovia had on certain members of his circle of friends, his charisma apparently expelling both a sense of proportion and reason from discussion of his perceived *persona.*

Segovia is said to have remarked that he had twenty-two engagements in Russia "last year... from Petrograd to Tiflis in the Caucasus." The information, biographically interesting in itself, must surely refer to 1936, not 1937, as Segovia did not return to Russia after the Spanish Civil War. Segovia also is quoted as practising "Two hours in the morning... two hours in the afternoon, and now sometimes two more hours in the evening." This figure for public consumption would eventually, over the years, be amended to four sessions of one hour and a quarter a day, making five hours in all.

Another quote attributed to Segovia during the course of that evening concerns Segovia's concept of the guitar as an orchestra seen through the wrong end of a pair of binoculars. Already Segovia was acquiring the public vocabulary which could be objectively fed to an admiring public, quoted and re-quoted. Many years later, on 23 March, 1983, the *Chicago Sun-Times* would offer the self-same quote in its ultimately polished form:

The guitar is like a tiny orchestra, seen through the wrong end of a pair of binoculars. It is polyphonic and contains many different timbres. It has all the colours of an orchestra. It can sound like a flute or an oboe or like strings.[6]

In his letter Sandburg gets the date of Leonardo's fatal accident wrong, dating it as two years before his meeting with Segovia, when in fact it was only a matter of some seven months. But Sandburg also manages to get onto the dangerous ground of discussing politics. Segovia is seen as "a republican, his family long anti-royalist," and Sandburg perceives that he "seems to lean towards the Loyalists." Segovia comments to him that "it is not merely true that only a Spaniard can understand Spain now but it must also be a Spaniard who is there in Spain now, and even for such a one the chaos in many cases is beyond understanding." This line of argument, that only a Spaniard can truly understand the Spanish Civil War, then or now, is an often repeated line, and especially favored. It successfully curtails any discussion and implicitly warns foreigners to keep out of such family matters, unless you want to offend the person with whom you are having the conversation. Segovia goes one step further here by claiming, as he was not in Spain at that time, of being incapable of understanding things himself, even though he was a Spaniard.

A book by Gregory d'Alessio, cartoonist and writer, sets the context of the meeting between Sandburg and Segovia. At the party after the concert on 2 May, 1938, held at the house of Dr. and Mrs Buchbinder, were several newspapermen and historians, (one good reason perhaps why Segovia's remarks about Spanish politics remained discreetly enigmatic). Mrs Buchbinder had entertained Segovia after all his Chicago recitals. Carl Sandburg was at first reluctant to attend the gathering but the prospect of meeting Segovia was sufficient to persuade him in the end.

Gregory d'Alessio writes that on the very day of the Chicago party there was tension in the air as in Europe the army of Adolf Hitler was marching into Vienna. (In fact the infamous *Anschluss* had taken place on 11, 12 and 13 March.[7]) Having met his hero, Sandburg was fascinated in every way by Segovia's mastery of the guitar, his ability to tune the instrument in the middle of a piece, and "Segovia's mannerisms on the concert stage." After the party Segovia and Sandburg promised they would keep the new friendship going while Segovia said that he would help Sandburg with his playing of chords. (Twelve years later in Havana, Cuba, in March, 1950, when he was there to perform with the Havana Philharmonic Orchestra, Segovia at last fulfilled this promise and wrote out some exercises for Sandburg.[8] Gregory d'Alessio comments that Sandburg's "knowledge of notation was negligible and his willing fingers were not able to articulate the notes, even if he could read them.")[9]

Carl Sandburg's letter, published in *Guitar Review*, reveals him as very much an amateur guitarist, a man hitherto blissfully unaware how much dedication and practise the study of a musical instrument demands and a player who had forgotten his chords and "where my fingers must go." He seemed a little surprised by the fact that "afterward he [Segovia] had no word about my handling of the guitar." Segovia, however (in private), tactfully and magnanimously praised Sandburg's "exquisite feeling for the guitar" to the hostess, Mrs Buchbinder. As far as Sandburg was concerned Segovia had given him by his presence in the concert and at the party "one of the hardest and most beautiful lessons of my life." In return Segovia was no doubt immensely gratified to be so wholeheartedly admired by one of the most distinguished poets and biographers of twentieth century American literature.

In July, 1938, *The Gramophone* reviewed the re-issue of HMV E-526, Moreno Torroba's *Fandanguillo* and *Preludio*, first released in 1929:

This composer, unknown to me, has provided Segovia with good vehicles for the display of his genius. The variety of effects he gets is quite remarkable and were it not for the depth of tone in the bass one might at times be listening to the clavichord. The music, beautifully recorded, exhales a sweet melancholy which, in the circumstances, is heart-breaking to listen to.[10]

The reference in the last line of the review to the Spanish Civil War shows a true spirit of involvement on the part of the critic. In the 1930's reviewers of records were not afraid to reveal their emotions or a measure of subjectivity in public, aspects which may come over to modern readers as refreshing and spontaneous.

Also in July 1938, a long article appeared in *B.M.G.* about Segovia. The tone of the article is one of reverence, evidence of Segovia's rapidly increasing authority, and one of the first articles in the author's possession in which he is referred to as "the Maestro," a title which eventually transcended even the customary Spanish and Italian usage and became practically synonymous with his name in a unique way. At this time Segovia was still no more than forty-five years of age, but the terms of the article suggest that he had actually arrived at a point of prestige which would continue to develop within these terms for the rest of his life:

...I have had the extreme pleasure of spending two delightful evenings with the Master of Masters, Andrés Segovia, One meeting, in particular, will be forever remembered when the Maestro, and two or three of my intimate friends (all guitarists) spent a long evening together, Segovia talking at length of things guitaristic. Needless to say, we poor mortals interrupted as little as possible so as not to miss any information he might feel inclined to give us and all you guitar enthusiasts who rightfully envy this little group, sitting in silent, almost awed, attention to the words of the great Master, can well imagine that what we learned was priceless...

However, let me see what I can tell you from my good fortune in being so close to the Maestro.

First, you can never know the gracious majesty of this great musician without actually being in his presence. I say 'gracious majesty' as an American would. You, in England, as I well know from my English forebears, respect and love your Gracious Majesties for all they mean to each subject of their great Empire and from my English mother, I have inherited a feeling of pride and love for the Great House of Windsor, so it is with no feeling of disrespect that I use a term peculiarly reserved for Their Majesties as a means of expressing a word picture of a great musician; perhaps inspired by a feeling of acknowledgement that Segovia is King of our little Empire of guitarists.

...mpresses me with a feeling of great respect. His personality is one of musicianly elegance. Aside from this ... man in every respect: good looking, tall, vigorous, striking in appearance; a type which fills a room on its ... inviting questions and elaborating on their answers with evident interest and with gentlemanly reserve, ... ue least of the company at ease and at times exhibiting a free sense of humour and rare bursts of exuberance ove. ... ue remark that particularly strikes the fancy.

He presents a picture of a great personage, conscious of his fair-won superiority over others in his sphere, but humour all the way through. However, with all his geniality, a false expression of anything musical strikes fire in this musical martinet. Temporising with the slightest variation from the best in music brings Segovia to his feet with a flashing eye; a decided flush of anger... To Segovia there is good music and bad music, or, to use his own words, "not good music."[11]

The writer of the article now tries something slightly different, his performance of two pieces by Ponce, allegedly by Weiss, which he has managed to absorb from the recordings:

I had the frightful experience of playing the Gigue and Sarabande (Weiss) for Segovia, at the insistence of friends present. This suite has never been published, but an excellent Segovia recording and long hours with a portable gramophone; my guitar; black coffee and innumerable cigarettes, closeted where no one would be able to reach me, to preserve the peace, and I managed, after a fashion, to put this beautiful music on my fingerboard. To give some idea of how gracious Segovia can be, instead of being incensed at my presumptuousness and telling me just what a mess I had really made of it, he was most enthusiastic and grasped my hand... On meeting him a second time he expressed his desire to hear me play it again, correcting me on a number of points when I complied. This shows the real good fellowship of Segovia, and explains why we, who have been so fortunate to meet him, love and respect this great Master.[12]

Segovia's advice to the group on improving their playing was summarised as follows:

...If you are a fairly advanced player concentrate on Giuliani and Segovia exercises for technical advancement. If you are not so advanced, Sor has given us a host of simple studies.
...Without good tone and clean fingering the playing of a guitar is nothing.
...Learn to play simple studies of real musical value, with expression and assurance...
...Find an easy "stance"; raise or lower both chair and footstool until an easy, comfortable, but correct, hold on your instrument is discovered.
...Learn to "bite" the notes out with a slightly aggressive snap of the first joint of the right-hand fingers; do not "rub" the fingers across the strings, pulling from the elbow, so prevalent among players.
...Try playing four-string chords by a clutching motion of the fingers, as though trying to catch a fly. Keep the wrist motionless. Crunch out crisp, brilliant chords.
A position an inch or two from the bridge (to give the most resistance) is best for exercise.
Trim the nails perfectly round about 1/32 in. above the finger tip. Do not use the tip of the nail, but employ the side more towards the thumb side of the finger, without allowing the hand to turn into awkward positions...
...Do not become timid, but do not waste time on music obviously far beyond your capabilities.[13]

It is a pity that the writer did not supply the dates and context of his sessions with Segovia. Despite the somewhat obsequious tone of the early paragraphs, the article has considerable historical interest. At the same time *B.M.G.* was showing signs of moving off its perpetual obsession with the banjo, and devoting more attention to Segovia's kind of playing. (In the same issue there was an authoritative article on the young Ida Presti's progress.)

19. 1938 (CONTINUED)

The two years preceding the Second World War, despite (or because of) the profound disturbances and premonitions of utter disaster, were full of a remarkable creativity among composers for guitar and several works written in those difficult months would prove to be of a lasting significance for the repertoire. In bleak contrast, the saddest loss for the guitar at that time was the death of Miguel Llobet early in 1938, at the relatively young age of fifty-nine. Some sources, such as Philip Bone,[1] attribute his death to an air raid in Barcelona (giving the date as May, 1937) but Bruno Tonazzi's monograph on Llobet, gives pleurisy as the cause of death on 22 February, 1938.[2] (As we can see from a letter to Ponce written on 14 February, 1938, Segovia was in New York just before that date.)

In Europe, also in 1938, Joaquín Rodrigo composed his second piece for solo guitar, *En los Trigales*, (his first piece was *Zarabanda lejana*, 1926), to be dedicated (some years later) to Narciso Yepes.[3] According to Vicente Vayá Pla, Rodrigo's biographer, the composer spoke for the first time in the summer of 1938 of a guitar concerto and was encouraged in this venture by the guitarist, Regino Sainz de la Maza, to whom the famous *Concierto de Aranjuez* would be dedicated.[4] Rodrigo's wife, Victoria Kamhi, gives a full account of how, on returning to Paris from summer courses in Santander, in northern Spain, they stopped overnight at San Sebastián, and dined with the Marqués de Bolarque, a music-lover, and Sainz de la Maza, where the topic of a guitar concerto was first raised.[5] Though the chronology of Kamhi's account is not entirely clear, what is certain is that the work was completed by the time they returned to Spain in September, 1939. (She also relates how the *Adagio* movement of the *Concierto de Aranjuez* was written during a dark and tragic time in the late 1930's following the still-birth of their first baby.)

On 2 May, 1938, Emilio Pujol gave a recital at the Salle Erard in Paris, concentrating on music for vihuela. He accompanied Madame Conchita Badia in various songs, and played some of the solo vihuela masterpieces including *Pavana del Quinto Tono* (Luys Milán), *Guárdame las Vacas*, *Soneto del primer grado* (Luys de Narváez), and *Fantasía que contrahace la harpa en la manera de Ludovico* (Alonso Mudarra). (This followed the concert in Barcelona on 23 April, 1936, when Pujol had introduced Milán's *Seis Pavanas* and the other vihuela pieces mentioned here on a reproduction instrument.)[6] In *B.M.G.* (July, 1939), Pujol presented a scholarly article about the vihuela which must have come as something of a surprise to the majority of readers at that time:

Practically speaking, there is but little difference between the guitar and the vihuela; they are about the same shape and have nearly the same tuning, although the vihuela, like the old guitar, has double strings instead of the single strings of the modern instrument. It is thus easy for a guitarist to play works written for the vihuela and for many years I have included vihuela music in my programmes for the modern guitar, but I have always hoped to one day be able to play this music on the instrument for which it was written, a hope that has now been fulfilled. The chief disadvantage of playing vihuela music on the guitar is that the tone colour of the two instruments is substantially different.[7]

Emilio Pujol goes on to relate how he had discovered the vihuela dated 1500 in the Jacquemart-André Museum in Paris and how the luthier, Simplicio, had made him a reproduction for his concert in Barcelona before the Third International Congress of Musicology in 1936:

This concert was a great success; it was, in fact, quite a historic event for Spaniards to hear vihuela music played on, and sung to, the vihuela once again after some 200 years of silence.

But although the new vihuela was a beautiful piece of work, with a clear and resonant tone, the sonority was not quite what we believe to have been that of the vihuela long ago...

It was that great artist Arnold Dolmetsch (who not only has a profound understanding of old music and the instruments upon which it is played but also an extensive practical knowledge of how to make them) who solved our difficulties. Mr. Dolmetsch had long been attracted to the problem of the vihuela and when in the summer of 1937, it was suggested to him that he should make his fancy a reality, he set to work immediately with his usual enthusiasm. Discussions about the shape and other details finally produced an instrument with a sonority which is probably the equal of that of the ancient vihuela.

Segovia eventually played several vihuela transcriptions on the modern guitar besides the Milán *Pavanas* for which he seems to have had a particular liking. Pujol's edition *Hispanae Citharae Ars Viva* (published Schott, 1956) ultimately encapsulated many of the favourite pieces which attracted guitarists to vihuela music. But it was Pujol's scholarly volumes of the complete works of Luys de Narváez (published Barcelona, 1945), Alonso Mudarra, (publ. 1949) and Enrique de Valderrábano (publ. 1965) which really advanced the world's knowledge of the vihuela treasure trove of the sixteenth century.

What is remarkable is that nowadays reproduction vihuelas are customary for performing this music of the golden age of Spain. What Segovia may well have regarded as a scholarly cul-de-sac, has now, through the revolution of the Early Music Movement, become an essential part of contemporary music making. Pujol's views that he was not happy with the sound of the modern guitar for recitals of vihuela music have now become generally accepted, a situation which nobody in the late 1930's could have foreseen or believed. Instead, there has been something of a reaction against performing vihuela music on the modern guitar and against Segovia's style of interpretation in that area.

But in 1938, of course, Segovia's guitar was supreme, and going from strength to strength. In December, 1938, he made what was to prove his last visit to London for nine years. His program at the Wigmore Hall showed fascinating developments of his repertoire over the course of the decade, and included a special tribute to Miguel Llobet:

I

Aria con Variazioni	G. Frescobaldi
Menuet	J. P. Rameau
Andante	W. A. Mozart

II

Prelude and Mazurka	F. Chopin
Choro No. 1	H. Villa-Lobos
Three Pieces	E. Granados

III

Variations on Folia de España and Fugue	M. Ponce
Six Catalan Folk Songs	arr. M. Llobet
Capriccio Diabolico	M. Castelnuovo-Tedesco

Frescobaldi's *Aria con Variazioni detta "La Frescobalda,"* seems to have been a comparatively recent transcription in Segovia's repertoire. This would be published by Schott in 1939 (Guitar Archive No. 157) at the same time as Rameau's *2 Minuetti* (G.A. No. 160). *Andante* by Mozart may have been another playing of *Menuett* (G.A. No. 117, publ. 1928), with Segovia preferring to avoid an apparent clash or duplication of Minuets on the program, (or it could have been some unknown piece later jettisoned and never recorded).

The playing of a Chopin *Prelude* goes back to a precedent set by Francisco Tárrega, who transcribed no less than six (*Op. 28, Nos 4, 6, 7, 11, 15,* and *20*). In Segovia's case, it was very likely to be *Op. 28, No. 7*, while *Mazurka, Op. 63, No. 3*, was his own arrangement (G.A. No. 140, publ. 1935).

Choro No. 1 (1920) by Heitor Villa-Lobos remained unpublished for many years till released by Editions Max Eschig of Paris in 1959 with a signed note by the composer on the cover in French that this was the "only edition correct and in accord to my original manuscript." Another edition, revised and fingered by Sophocles Papas was published in 1963 by Columbia Music Co. of Washington D.C. *Choro No. 1* is the first of a series of fourteen Choros, which have been described as follows:

Significantly, it was the sound of the guitar that Villa-Lobos chose as the starting-point for a series of works in which the Brazilian synthesis first attempted in the Nonet, and continued in various ways in these other works of the 1920's, became absolute. Although commenced before his departure for France, the series of works collectively and individually entitled Choros *was primarily conceived and executed during the years 1924 -1929. This series embodies completely Villa-Lobos's vision of Brazil as a vast, teeming landscape, immense in its inclusivity, variety and proportion. As predicted by Schloeza, no European musical form was adequate to contain this vision and so, like the* Ciranda, *the* Seresta, *and the* Poema, *in the* Choros *a new mould was born, in which the improvisations and instrumental groupings of the choroes were merely a basis, a convenient name and embryo for a form, which would eventually accommodate not only popular elements, but also stylizations of Indian and black music, and of natural sounds.*[9]

The evidence of the majority of recital programs suggests that unfortunately this particular item was not suitable for Segovia in the long term and was soon discarded. The piece languished therefore until its publication in 1959, when it quite soon became one of the most popular solos for both recitalists and amateurs.

Six Catalan Folk Songs were not usually offered by Segovia in concerts, his normal practice being to offer no more than two or three at one sitting. His favorites appear to be *El Mestre,* described in his autobiography as "the most beautiful of Catalan Songs... making it one of the priceless jewels of the guitar repertoire,"[10] *El Noi de la Mare* (frequently played as an encore), *El Testament d'Amelia* and *La Filla del Marxant,* recorded some years later.[11]

The Daily Telegraph and Morning Post of London, on 5 December, 1938, included the following review:

A large audience assembled at Wigmore Hall, on Saturday to pay tribute to Andrés Segovia's well-known virtuosity on the guitar. Nor were they disappointed, for his hands and fingers have lost nothing of their cunning.

The programme consisted of two main divisions — works written for the guitar and transcriptions. In the former category Mr. Segovia made a special success with Ponce's "Folias" in the classical manner and Llobet's attractive Catalonian songs. In the latter, Frescobaldi's Air and Variations and two little pieces by Mozart and Rameau may be singled out. The Chopin transcriptions, on the other hand, seemed like a fish out of water, despite all the artist's virtuosity.

Praise of this is at this time superfluous. His is in its way one of the most astonishing displays of musical and technical mastery at the present time. In Segovia's hands the guitar acquires all the attributes of the harpsichord with from time to time a mixture of clavichord and ukelele thrown in.

F.T.

20. 1939

In terms of his editions, 1939 could be viewed as the end of Segovia's first phase of offering a viable repertoire to the world.   In this year Schott published a number of the smaller works which Segovia used to fill out his programs with classical composers in a very similar style to that chosen by Francisco Tárrega decades before.   In the 1930's, and in the post-1945 era, audiences seemed very willing to accept the performance of small scale pieces in classical or Baroque mould, contrasted against the larger structures such as sets of variations or sonatas which brought the guitar more or less into line with other solo recital instruments.   There was also a demand among amateur guitarists for short, accessible pieces in a context where good guitar tuition at the grass-roots level was still difficult to come by (in most countries) outside the big cities.   Segovia was always mindful of the basis of his audience which might consist of a proportion of amateur guitarists, hungry for studies, easy melodic repertoire and the promise of a way forward in their own playing.

Thus in 1939, the following editions were published by B. Schott's Söhne, Mainz:

Manuel Ponce	*Sonatina meridional* (G.A. No. 151)
Isaac Albéniz	*Tango* (G.A. No. 154)
Georg Benda	*2 Sonatinas* (G.A. No. 155)
Louis Couperin	*Passacaglia* (G.A. No. 156)
Girolamo Frescobaldi	*Aria con Variazioni detta "La Frescobalda"* (G.A. No. 157)
	5 Pieces (G.A. No. 158)
	(1. Corrente, 2. Passacaglia, 3. Corrente,
	4. Gagliarda, 5. Corrente)
Alonso Mudarra	*Romanesca* (G.A. No. 159)
Jean-Philippe Rameau	*2 Minuetti* (G.A. No. 160)
Christian Friedrich Schale,	*2 Minuetti* (with J. F. Wenkel, *Musette* (G.A. No. 161)
Johann Baptiste Vanhall	*Cantabile* (G.A. 162), *Minuetto* (G.A. No. 163)

(In the interim between publications from the first half of the decade Schott published Ponce's *Valse* (G.A. No.153) in 1937.)

From this batch only Ponce's compositions, Frescobaldi's *Variazioni* and Albéniz's *Tango* (not often played as a solo), have preserved a full and healthy existence over the years in terms of recital performances and recordings, though they are still in print some six decades later.   The shift away from the programming of isolated *Minuetti* or tiny movements from some obscure suite, has been virtually complete.   Yet such is the whirligig of fashion that such transcriptions might one day be found of some interest to recitalists as well as to guitar historians.

In February, 1939, Dr. Boris A. Perott published an article about Segovia in *B.M.G.* which dared to be both informative and critical.   First he offered an opinion about Segovia's effect on the guitar in Russia:

*The finest tribute one can give **Torres Andrés Segovia** is an acknowledgement of the work he has done to popularise the classical guitar; work in which he has no rival in the whole history of guitar playing.   Apart from his many gramophone records and personal appearances all over the world I have an example by personal experience of what he did in Russia.   The seven-string guitar practically monopolised Russian guitarists, it being perhaps only one player in a hundred who played on the six-string instrument.   Professional players like Decker-Schenk and Lebedeff had no choice but to play on both instruments... I remember later the seven-string guitar was strongly opposed in St. Petersburg where all Lebedeff's pupils... and afterwards mine... played only on the six-string Spanish guitar; and this spread even to Siberia before I went there in 1910.*

Moscow, meanwhile, had no teacher of the six-string guitar; every player being 100 per cent seven-string... I would have thought that it would have taken another half a century for the cause of the six-string revolution.   Segovia visited Russia and gave numerous concerts and "like the movement of a magic hand" the six-string Spanish guitar conquered

both capitals of Russia. Even the government was impressed for the guitar was declared to be a "na...
and called a "portable grand piano" and Isakoff was appointed a government teacher and started...
having many hundreds of pupils in the course of a year.

The second visit of Segovia to Russia increased still more this movement and one must admi...
unprecedented success and certainly only possible in after-revolutionary Russia... I am quite sure th...
guitar was dealt a deadly blow by Segovia from which she will never recover for the advantages of the six-string guitar
are so evident.[1]

After praising Segovia's "superhuman determination and perseverance" in mastering the guitar Perott then moves to more controversial areas when he comments that "in spite of his unparalleled success," Segovia could not claim to be "the very best guitarist ever born." Perott launches himself into a frontal attack:

The reader may still be in doubt as to why I consider that Segovia cannot claim to be the best guitar-player. It is not a question of taste, sympathy or antipathy nor due to the fact that I heard so very many outstanding guitarists during my long association with the guitar. No! It is because such a great artist may still be better and because he possesses some weak points in his playing. The more I watch him play the more I can see that he sacrifices expression for the sake of technique; he reminds me of Sarasate on the violin, not Kreisler. Segovia's immaculate technique is overwhelming but it is inclined to become monotonously wearisome. I think the reason is because in his early days of struggle without the aid of a teacher he repeated the same passage a hundred times and little by little, became used to striving for execution only.[2]

Perott then seems to get slightly confused:

Another point, I consider his repertoire is too much of the same character. Although playing different compositions most of them are by typical Spanish authors: Ponce, Torroba, Juan Manén, Albéniz, Turina, Carlos Pedrell, Granados, Castelnuovo-Tedesco and many others. He also specialises in Bach transcriptions but the guitar is not the best instrument on which to play them. Italian composers are heard very little in his repertoire, although Italian literature for the guitar is immensely rich and of a high standard.

Due to the foregoing, Segovia is not giving himself the chance to develop tone and expression to the highest standard for human nature, always admiring digitorial skill, demands food for the soul; which calls one's spirits, composes one's thoughts, and delights the ear and the mind. Admiration is not enough. It is a very short-lived passion that dies on growing familiar with its object...[3]

The list given by Perott includes a Mexican and an Italian composer (could it be that Perott thought Castelnuovo-Tedesco was of Spanish nationality?). This criticism of the narrowness of Segovia's repertoire also comes just a few months after his recital at the Wigmore Hall, London, where he had included works by two Italian composers as well as pieces by French, Austrian, Polish, Brazilian and Mexican, and (only two) Spanish composers! Yet, despite the apparent diversity of composers it is possible that Segovia's interpretative methods, applied equally to all types of music, might have made his repertoire seem as "too much of the same character." But this is not quite what Perott says.

The criticisms about Segovia's technical perfection are interesting if only because they anticipate by some two decades similar comments directed at John Williams. What could also be argued is that after the introduction of long playing records in the early 1950's, Segovia's playing did enrich and develop itself with greater feeling than was revealed in the early recordings and recitals from 1929 onwards. This of course would be a consequence not of the introduction of new technology but rather of the maturing and ripening processes of an artist who lived through and survived triumphantly so many tragic and potentially destructive experiences.

The plea that Segovia could get even better than he was in 1938 and 1939, was taken up in the correspondence columns a month later in an interesting letter:

...I wish to offer my personal thanks to the author for his frank and honest criticisms on a point which has, for some time, caused me some concern; namely, the music of Andrés Segovia.

I feel this criticism is long overdue, a criticism that may be classified by over ardent admirers of Segovia as blasphemous, but is, in actual fact, Dr. Perott's unbiased, non-abusive and helpful opinion with which I heartily agree. I state "long overdue" because had this criticism found its way into print years ago we may have been listening to an even greater Segovia today.

...agree with the author when he states that Segovia "sacrifices expression for the sake of technique" and with his ...ws on the reason for this weak point as, after each playing of a Segovia recording, I am left with the impression of having listened to an almost soulless, yet flawlessly executed, piece of music, which is just that fraction too perfect.

I live in hope that the friendly words of Dr. Perott will be accepted in the spirit in which they are given and that they may be the means of a development towards an ever greater Segovia, who with boundless means at his finger-tips, can give the guitar-music-loving world the music that only he can give it; an emotional music that only he, with his passionate understanding of an instrument that is surely a part of himself could express... the music of Andrés Segovia.

In conclusion, I would venture to suggest that Segovia record his own compositions in future since his best means of expression would be through the medium of his own music.

Yours sincerely,

BILLY NEIL [4]

This raises questions about the nature of the expression an audience might expect to receive from an artist or from music. It would seem axiomatic that even the greatest of musicians in the classical sphere can only generate the emotional substance that a piece contains. Thus a great pianist performing major extended works by Mozart, Haydn, Beethoven, Schumann, Chopin, Brahms, Liszt, etc. will be able to generate more of an emotional and intellectual current than a guitarist with the best interpretative and technical equipment in the world playing variations by Frescobaldi, *Menuet* by Rameau, *Choro No. 1* by Villa-Lobos, and Llobet's *Catalan Folk Song* arrangements. The real problems about the post-romantic guitar repertoire would be faced by a later generation spearheaded by Julian Bream. Segovia, by demanding from the guitar only a certain type of tonal expressiveness projected through an immaculately polished technique, and rejecting any other type of material, would in the long run lay himself open to a number of questions about his artistic attitudes to many twentieth century forms of music.

Segovia had played his part already, as he understood it, in broadening the possibilities of the expressive powers of the guitar, both by stimulating new works to be written and by his herculean labours of transcription. But there is plenty of evidence that at this very stage Segovia was also eager to broaden the emotional canvas of the instrument. This he achieved by the inspiring of two Concertos for guitar, albeit from composers such as Castelnuovo-Tedesco and Ponce whose musical horizons remained tonally conservative in accordance with Segovia's own concepts of what good music should be.

In her book on Castelnuovo-Tedesco, Corazón Otero gives an account of the events which finally stimulated the composer towards getting down to the task of writing the Guitar Concerto which Segovia had asked for some time previously. Worried by Mussolini's closer ties with Germany and increasing anti-Semitism in Italy, Castelnuovo-Tedesco considered the possibilities of leaving Europe to live in the United States. To avoid censorship with his mail, he visited Switzerland in 1938 to write letters to Toscanini and Heifetz, among others, who were already in the U.S.A. The reports that came back were promising about his opportunities in a new country and Heifetz even pledged that he could find him work in the film industry.

Segovia visited Castelnuovo-Tedesco in Florence for the Christmas festivities of 1938, speaking optimistically about a "better future," and assuring him that with his talents he would find a new life in America. Segovia's "words and solidarity comforted him enormously." Castelnuovo-Tedesco sketched out the themes of the first movement of the Concerto, and together they worked on the music. Segovia, satisfied with the progress achieved, departed for Uruguay.[5]

In the summer of 1939, the composer completed the last two movements and sent them off to Segovia.[6] The result was a refreshing and congenial work which has proved quite popular since then, especially in terms of recording. The vocabulary of the three movements is traditional as one would expect from this composer, yet its attempts to balance the guitar with the orchestra are innovative and imaginative. Of special interest are the expressive cadenzas, tailor-made for Segovia to impress the audience with the guitar's innate lyricism.

The Concerto opens *allegro giusto* with full orchestral *tutti* into which the guitar edges politely with little splashes of fourths and fifths, until embarking on a *tremolo* solo reminiscent of *Capriccio Diabolico*. A later solo passage in flowing arpeggios recalls the last movement of *Sonata (Omaggio a Boccherini)*. A particularly felicitous touch is the guitar's conversation with the cello shortly before the recapitulation, with its skilled deployment of instrumental textures.

The second movement, *Andantino - alla romanza,* which has been seen as a valediction to the Tuscan countryside,[7] is very characteristic of Castelnuovo-Tedesco's music, being poignant, lyrical and wistful, and a fine example of his ability to create a gentle but evocative atmosphere. The last movement, *ritmico e cavalleresco* is vivid and delightfully animated with a most attractive use of melodic themes and *con bravura* guitar passages.

In a letter to Ponce, Segovia praised Castelnuovo-Tedesco's *Guitar Concerto, Op. 99*, though he was not without reservations about some of the guitar writing.[8] As yet the date was not known to Segovia but the new Concerto would be premiered in Montevideo, Uruguay, on 28 October, 1939.[9]

Writing to Ponce on 26 August, 1939, Segovia complained that early in the year, he had been threatened by Jewish influence with a loss of recitals in the United States unless he retracted his support for the nationalists in Spain. Because of these circumstances he had returned, after seeing Castelnuovo-Tedesco in Florence, to Montevideo, and after that played in Argentina. If war did not break out, he planned an extensive tour throughout Europe followed by a visit to the Caribbean and several South American countries. He encouraged Manuel Ponce to continue with the composition of his Guitar Concerto. As far as the world situation was concerned Segovia anticipated the worst and believed that there would indeed be a war in Europe.[10]

In the latter he was proved tragically correct and, following the invasion of Poland by the Nazis on 1 September, 1939, Britain, France, India, Australia and New Zealand declared war on Germany on 3 September.[11]

Earlier that year, on 28 March, Madrid had surrendered to General Franco. The death toll during the Spanish Civil War had amounted to an estimated 750,000 people. The Italians had supplied some 75,000 "volunteers" for the Nationalist cause and Germany another 19,000.[12] After Britain declared war on Germany, Spain made a statement of its neutrality on 4 September, 1939, though at the same time secretly pledging support for Hitler and the Axis powers.[12]

21. THE SECOND HALF OF LIFE

In February 1940 Segovia celebrated the age of forty-seven, in fact, the mid-way point of his life. Although so much had already been achieved, far from reaching the summit, the bulk of his recording and performing triumphs, as well as considerable editing and publication of new music for the guitar, were in the future.

For Segovia, the decade of the 1930's had involved him in disastrous bad fortune in his personal life. Divorce after the lingering painful demise of his first marriage, the tragic death of a young son, the loss of home, possessions and political innocence in the Spanish Civil War, confrontation with elements he believed hostile to him, involuntary exile from Europe in Montevideo, and the spectacle of a world at war, were the fruits of the previous ten years. Yet in the same period, by his own efforts, Segovia had expanded his horizons and visited many countries, seen his recordings well received and popular throughout the world, extended his repertoire and those of other guitarists through many publications, and gone most of the way towards being universally acknowledged as the world's greatest guitarist.

On 4 March, 1940, Segovia's letter to Ponce tells us that he had seen the composer in Mexico, then travelled to Costa Rica, and on 5 March was departing for Lima, Peru, travelling by air, (at that time a rather risky proposition).[1] From Peru, Segovia took the long haul south to Chile but apparently (according to a letter of 15 March), came home to Montevideo early, as the recital season did not start for a further month. (Segovia's agent, Quesada had actually arranged the performances too early.) Back in Uruguay Segovia busied himself with plans for Manuel Ponce to visit Montevideo to receive an offical Homage.[2]

On 15 April, according to yet another letter, Segovia and Paquita were again in Santiago, Chile, and a performance of Castelnuovo-Tedesco's *Concerto* was scheduled for that evening. The concert proved a success in that Segovia was required by the audience to play the last movement once more. Meanwhile Ponce's health was improving, a fact that would result in the completion of his own *Guitar Concerto*, spurred on as he was by the success of Castelnuovo-Tedesco in this field.[3] A letter of 5 October announced that part of the promised work had indeed arrived, occasioning a burst of enthusiasm and encouragement for the new composition in a further letter of 8 October.[4]

In an important letter dated 22 October, 1940, Segovia had a few more harsh words about Heitor Villa-Lobos, at that time in Montevideo with a Cultural Embassy from Brazil. His presentation as a lecturer in the university had not been very satisfactory.[5] Segovia urged Ponce to acquire similar funding from the Mexican government to visit Uruguay as Villa-Lobos had achieved with the Brazilian government, a concept which would come to fruition.

According to this letter, Villa-Lobos had just visited Segovia's house with the present of six *Preludes* (dedicated to Segovia). Segovia was most scornful of the one which attempted to imitate Bach, considering it laughable. (This, of course, was none other than *Prelude No. 3* of Villa-Lobos which Segovia was to record beautifully in the 1950's on Brunswick AXTL 1069, on the same LP which contains Bach's *Chaconne.) Prelude No. 3* may seem now less like an imitation of the music of J. S. Bach than Homage to Bach. Segovia, however, took this opportunity to play Ponce's "Weiss" Suite to Villa-Lobos (following a performance with Paquita Madriguera at the pianoforte of Castelnuovo-Tedesco's *Guitar Concerto).*

Villa-Lobos was apparently taken in by the deception (as many others were), until Segovia told him the truth about the composer of the work. Segovia then followed up with a recital of several of the works of Ponce, including part of the Concerto. Segovia's description of the *Preludes* as "vulgar" and his assertion that of all the works of Villa-Lobos for solo guitar only the *Study* in E major (presumably *Study No. 7*, also recorded by Segovia in the 1950's) was worthwhile, shed new light on his relationship with both the Brazilian composer and his music.[6] It may be because of the ill concealment of these attitudes and some obvious measure of hostility, that Villa-Lobos changed the dedication of the *Preludes* from Segovia to Mindinha, (the composer's wife) by the time they were published by Max Eschig in 1954. Segovia had also neglected to tell Ponce that Villa-Lobos's *Choro No. 1* had been played at the Wigmore Hall recital in December, 1938, but this work also was not to be sustained as a permanent feature of his repertoire.

It seems very likely that Heitor Villa-Lobos modelled his *Douze Études* on the example of Chopin's *Études Op. 310* and *Op. 25,* perhaps the finest fusion of technical virtuosity and musical insight ever achieved in the history of any solo instrument as far as the genre of étude is concerned. If this were so, Villa-Lobos may have envisaged that the set would be played in recitals in its entirety. Such an ambition, if this is true, did not come to fruition in the lifetime of the composer because of Segovia's very selective habits. Segovia set a trend by playing (and recording) only a few of the *Études* (usually Nos 1, 7, and 8). In this he missed not only the glorious chance of playing No. 11 (which could well have been a most sonorous piece for Segovia), but also the opportunity to take the guitar many steps forward. It was not until after the death of Villa-Lobos, that Turibio Santos in Rio de Janeiro in 1963, at the invitation of the Villa-Lobos Museum, gave the first performance of the complete set. His historic recording of the *Douze Études* was released in 1969 (Erato ST1007). Narciso Yepes issued a recording of the whole set in 1971 on an album (DG 2530 140) that also included the complete set of five *Preludes*.

On 21 and 23 January, 1977, Julian Bream offered his performance of all twelve studies at the Wigmore Hall, London. The critic of *The Times*, London, Max Harrison commented:

Villa-Lobos's Etudes are usually scattered miscellaneously through programmes of the conventional sort and, considering how central to the repertoire that cycle of a dozen substantial movements is, one is surprised at how rarely they are played together.

However there is considerable internal and external evidence to show that is what the composer intended, and certainly Mr. Bream's performance justified the procedure once and for all.

At least initially the Etudes are less overtly poetic than Villa-Lobos's later Preludes. Yet they follow a coherent progression as the journey from the material for arpeggio practice found in the Bachian No. 1 through say the rhapsodic No. 8 to the ambitious concert pieces that make up the final Etudes.

There is plenty of Brazilian local colour on the way, some of it rather Frenchified, for Villa-Lobos composed the works in Paris during 1929, but here didacticism and fantasy meet.[7]

Thus decisions taken by Segovia in the 1940's and earlier about the performance of these works had interesting repercussions on the historical development of the guitar. Not for the first or last time, Segovia seems to have been slightly out of step with the judgement of posterity. After the 1970's it became customary for guitarists of merit to record and perform the *Douze Études* as an entity and not pull out the most seductive ones like plums from a cake to be devoured separately. Segovia's lack of activity in the field of Villa-Lobos had the beneficial result of leaving the gate open for another generation of players to do what had not previously been done.

Strangely enough, the same principles apply to the establishment of the *Preludes* among the most popular of all twentieth century solo works for the guitar. It was Abel Carlevaro (b.1916) who premiered *Preludes, Nos 3 & 4* on 11 November, 1943.[8] From Montevideo, Carlevaro developed a very positive relationship with Villa-Lobos while still a young man, so much so that the composer apparently gave him the original manuscript copies of *Prelude No. 1* and the first five *Studies*.[9]

I was lucky to become acquainted with Heitor Villa-Lobos during my youth: first in Montevideo where I played the guitar in his presence, later in Rio de Janeiro during a concert tour of Brazil, and finally in Paris. He told me that music should head towards a different goal, that musical education at the beginning of the century had been far from ideal. Private conservatories, badly oriented and deficient, he quipped, were in charge of raising "household" pianists...

He chose the human voice to educate his people: Brazilians know how to sing, they have it in their blood, it is part of their sonorous world; this is why he worked for so long towards educating the masses through choir singing. Today perhaps he would have chosen the guitar as it synthesises the drive of that great country while being as popular a manifestation as the human voice. In Rio he assembled choral concentrations aimed to prove the enormous socialising power of music. These united the voices of tens of thousands of schoolchildren in a single event. He invited me to the "Conservatorio de Canto Orfeonic," which he directed, where I attended a rhythm class that employed a large number of instruments (some of African heritage) brought by him from Indian villages throughout the country. These instruments were used to develop certain aspects of music while deepening the understanding of the Brazilian soul.[10]

The government of Getúlio Vargas in Brazil, described its own administration as "O Estado Nôvo" (The New State), and one of its supreme aims was the "promotion and propagation of all things Brazilian, to the detriment of any foreign influence or object be it physical or emotional, economic or artistic."[11] Villa-Lobos was caught up in this movement in his role as director of the Superintendentcia de Educaçao Musical e Artistica from 1932 onwards.[12] Huge choral events were organised to further the nationalistic needs of the government:

The numerous civic holidays and celebrations decreed during the Estado Nôvo period afforded Villa-Lobos in Rio de Janeiro ample opportunity to compose and perform works specifically designed to raise the patriotic temperature and to be accessible to mass audiences and amateur musicians. The celebrations for Independence Day (7 September) were always the grandest, with ranks of children assembled in Rio's football stadiums singing hymns to the glory of the nation (from Villa-Lobos anthologies) before the President (who disliked music) under a tropical sun. Twenty-three items were heard at the 1939 celebrations, three of them being the national anthem, sung by 30,000 children.[13]

Apart from a definite measure of personal antagonism towards Villa-Lobos, was there in Segovia something that disapproved of the sheer flamboyance of a conductor of a choir of 30,000? Contrasted against the reticent persona of Manuel Ponce, Villa-Lobos always appeared larger than life with an immense public profile in Brazil and an ability to grab the headlines. It was a long way from Segovia's more intimate artistic world. Segovia certainly disliked the dissonance of some of Villa-Lobos's music,[14] and it is to be wondered whether Villa-Lobos had not tailored his guitar music specifically towards the conservatism of his dedicatee. But even if he had deliberately written in a tonal language for the guitar, especially in his gentle and melodic *Preludes,* it was not to save him from Segovia's disdain. The roots of Segovia's antipathy towards the Brazilian composer seems according to *The Segovia-Ponce Letters* to have run deep, (perhaps going back to their first encounters in the 1920's).

In a letter of 9 November Segovia thanked Ponce for further parts of the Concerto. Another disaster had struck when the Bank of France went down, and Segovia's account with it.[14] Segovia might have been even more disgruntled if he had known that several thousand miles away Joaquín Rodrigo's *Concierto de Aranjuez* was to have its premiere in Barcelona that day, the guitarist being Regino Sainz de la Maza. This event was followed by performances in Bilbao and Madrid. The Spanish press of December, 1940, greeted the new Concerto with enthusiasm and in Madrid the composer was carried through the streets of the old city on the shoulders of his admirers.[15]

Several years would pass before the *Concierto de Aranjuez* achieved its clear supremacy over other Guitar Concertos. At this point in the guitar's contemporary evolution the idea of a Concerto for such a quiet instrument was something of a novelty. But in itself Rodrigo's new work was revolutionary, exploiting the guitar with an unprecedented intensity and complexity in an orchestral context. On the technical level alone it set new challenges and its interpretative demands as guitar and orchestra blend in remarkable union necessitate a virtuoso who is also an artist.

It is ironic that Segovia, at the centre of the stage with so many twentieth century developments had nothing to do with the genesis or establishment of Rodrigo's new work and was never to be associated with it. However, Segovia's deliberate lack of involvement and his subsequent failure to pick up this particular gauntlet was to create a magnificent opportunity for another young Spanish guitarist to make a name for himself:

The torch would be passed into Narciso Yepes' hands, after only ten years. When he played the work in the Théâtre des Champs Elysées in Paris, with the Spanish National Orchestra, directed by Argenta, it was the start of his long triumphal international career.[16]

For at least the immediate future, Segovia would remain blissfully unaware of the launching of the *Concierto de Aranjuez,* absorbed with important new developments of his own. For by 10 December, Ponce had sent him the slow movement to the *Concierto del Sur,* and by the beginning of January, 1941, the new work had been completed and earlier, unsatisfactory passages corrected.[17] With the help of Paquita, Segovia began preparations for the premiere, absorbing this new work into his fingers.[18]

In a letter to Ponce of 23 February, Segovia announced himself once more to be in trouble. The President of the Young Hebrew Association in New York had asked him to sign a manifesto against Nationalist Spain in view of Franco's anti-Semitisim. Segovia refused to sign any such thing, considering, somewhat illogically, that this request was somewhat more dictatorial than the activities of Germany, Italy and Russia.[19]

In March, 1941, *The Gramophone* reviewed several Segovia recordings at length, proving that he was not forgotten in wartime Europe, and that in the British Isles at least his reputation as a musician was continuing to grow. The first discs reviewed had been recorded on 6 and 7 October, 1930 and consisted of HMV DB1565 (Weiss, *Prelude, Allemande, Gigue*) and HMV DA1225 (Weiss, *Sarabande, Gavotte).* The critic refers to "this most distinguished of guitar-players (b.1896)," before launching into an analysis of the music of Weiss who reveals, in the *Sarabande,* "a gently, languishing female spirit, a clear aspiration perhaps, certainly nothing weakening." The *Gavotte* is "more sententious" but Weiss "had all the safe phrase-building plans well in mind." The *Gigue,* the "star-piece in both technique and style" is "an unusually developed piece, with some capital bits of declamation, and that improvisatory spirit that reminds one of Bach in fantasia-mood." Thus the Weiss suite, actually composed by Ponce, endlessly deceived the seemingly innocent critics.

Also reviewed was HMV DB3243, recorded in October 1936, and released in 1937 with Mendelssohn's *Canzonetta* and the third movement, *Vivo ed energico* from Castelnuovo-Tedesco's *Sonata (Omaggio a Boccherini), Op. 77*. The latter is seen as "a gay bit of salon music, with some toccata-like elements and good butter-spreading of melody-and-accompaniment." For the Mendelssohn, "its staccato and plucked effects make it good meat for the guitar" and "an admirable medium for the player's skill... a first-rate study of what the guitar can do."

The review concludes with HMV DA1553, recorded in 1935, with *Study in A major* by Alard (arr. Tárrega) and *Prelude (Cello Suite in G,* BWV 1009). As Tárrega is inaccurately attributed with the composition of the study, he is judged as being "more like minor Hummel, or the small-change thoughts of dozens of little German mid-nineteenth century composers." The music of J. S. Bach, though considered by "present standards" as also "small change" (being just part of a suite), is welcomed, and the "string-transference" admired.[20]

By 8 July, 1941, Segovia was even more desperate about the state of affairs with regard to his recitals because of agitation against his pro-Franco views.[21] Segovia's agent, Ernesto de Quesada (who had guided Segovia's career in Spain since his first foreign tour), was at this point tending to allow the organization of the South American concerts to fall by the wayside because of the tumult about Segovia in North America.[22]

The necessity for further letters to Manuel Ponce that year ended when the composer arrived in Uruguay at the end of August, 1941 for a working visit, with concerts, lectures on the history of Mexican music and receptions, all organized by Segovia. During the period of his stay, Ponce also visited Buenos Aires and later Chile. In Segovia's home there was ample opportunity to work with Ponce on the Concerto, the premiere of *Concierto del Sur* taking place in Montevideo on 4 October, 1941, with the composer conducting. The press reports were favorable, and the critic of the newspaper, *El Debate*, observing that the third movement had to be repeated as an encore, commented on the "magnificently inspired" music of Ponce and its "extraordinary quality."[23]

Ponce's *Concierto del Sur* is in three movements, *Allegro moderato, Andante*, and *Allegro moderato e festivo*. The sleeve notes for Segovia's recording of the work (*Segovia, Golden Jubilee, Vol. 1*, Brunswick AXTL 1088, 1959) describe the work as "a brilliant evocation of the South":

"A blend of native inspiration and impressionist harmonies," Nicolas Slonimsky has called the work, and this applies particularly to the Allegretto {First Movement}*the main movement of the concerto, in which native and original melodies are worked into a richly orchestrated fabric, to which the guitar contributes its own individual color. In the* Andante, *the romantic ardor and mystery of the South are contrasted with glowing effect and in more concentrated form. A sprightly festival mood prevails in the Finale.*

In liner notes for a recording made in 1987 by Eduardo Fernández (Decca 421 108-2), Simon Wright comments that the work "combines a delightfully lightweight neo-Classicism with a popular Mexican ethos derived mainly from typical melody and rhythm, rather than any deeper integration of materials." This comment catches the tone of ambiguity with which *Concierto del Sur* is often approached. The work remains an acknowledged masterpiece of its genre but is too rarely performed and not recorded as often as it deserves, its potential thunder stolen for posterity by the success of Rodrigo's *Concierto de Aranjuez*.

In the heady days of the 1940's, armed with two Guitar Concertos, Segovia was now able to advance the cause of the guitar in a new way, and this he did wholeheartedly. With the composer conducting Segovia performed Ponce's work in Buenos Aires (October 20th), Santiago de Chile and Lima.[24] Manuel Ponce returned to Mexico at the end of 1941. Though he would continue to write a few more pieces of real quality for the guitar, his finest output for Segovia was now completed. Work on his *Concerto for Violin and Orchestra* would be his most extensive project for 1942, to be orchestrated in June the following year.[25]

After Ponce's departure, Segovia continued his round of South American cities. He returned to Buenos Aires on 18 April, 1942, where he performed Castelnuovo-Tedesco's *Concerto* in an interestingly varied programme conducted by Juan José Castro:

I

Preludio y Fuga en mi bemol para organo   Bach
(Orquestación de Arnold Schönberg)

Pastoral del Oratorio de Navidad   Bach

II

Concierto para guitarra y pequeña orquesta   Castelnuovo-Tedesco
    a.) Allegretto giusto e un poco pomposa
    b.) Andantino alla romanza
    c.) Ritmico e cavalleresco

Soloist: Andrés Segovia

Iberia   Debussy
    I. Por calles y caminos
    II. Los perfumes de la noche
    III. Mañana de un día de fiesta

III

Sinfonia "Matias el pintor"   Hindemith
    I. Concierto de ángeles
    II. Entierro
    III. Las tentaciones de San Antonio

Director: Juan José Castro

22. SITTING OUT THE WAR

By 16 January, 1943, Segovia had received two movements of an ambitious work for guitar and orchestra from Mario Castelnuovo-Tedesco, *Serenade, Op.118,* scored for guitar, flute, oboe, 2 clarinets, bassoon, horn, tympani, percussion and strings. Unfortunately this work has been distinctly neglected, and at the time of writing possibly never recorded.[1] In a letter written in May, Segovia commented that he was planning to premiere the work in 1944.[2]

By this time Segovia's fortunes were picking up and in 1943 he planned to perform in Chile (playing both Ponce's and Castelnuovo-Tedesco's Concertos), Peru, Ecuador, Costa Rica, Columbia, and other places. Quesada was meanwhile promising fifteen concerts in the USA in the near future.[1] By December, 1943, Segovia had performed several concerts in New York, and was planning a USA premiere of Ponce's Guitar Concerto.[3] When the premiere took place, it was, according to an undated letter, very successful.[4] Segovia's solicitous care for Manuel Ponce and his music continued unabated throughout this time of the composer's illness and the guitarist's efforts to restore both his career and his financial stability.

In any event Ponce's tide of success was running high and on 20 August, 1943, his *Concerto* for violin and orchestra was premiered in Mexico City by Henryk Szeryng (1918-1988) with the Orquesta Sinfónica de Mexico conducted by Carlos Chávez.[5] (The work incorporates his famous theme, Estrellita, in the second movement.) However, in a letter of 13 December, 1943, Segovia (who spells the violinist's name as "Zsering"), roundly criticised the young man's musicality.

Szeryng, born in Warsaw, Poland, had been a child prodigy who studied with the great teacher, Carl Flesch. When World War II broke out, he enlisted with the Polish army in exile, and became involved with the placement of four thousand Polish refugees in Mexico. While giving concerts in 1943, he was asked to join the string department of the University of Mexico and stayed there for the next ten years, becoming a Mexican citizen. He was quite accidentally discovered by the pianist, Arthur Rubinstein, in the mid-1950's, and returned to the international concert scene, making a phenomenal New York debut in 1956.[6] Segovia's judgement of the young virtuoso was thus at variance with the kind of stature Szeryng would ultimately achieve. But he may, as the senior concert artist, have actually given some much needed counsel to the young violinist by urging more serious study.[3] An appraisal decades later on Szeryng commented that his playing "was characterised by a creamy smoothness and an infallible technical control."[7]

On 21 February, 1944, Segovia gave Ponce's *Concierto del Sur* its premiere at the Palacio de Bellas Artes in Mexico City with the Orquesta Filarmonica, under its director, Erich Kleiber. This was under the auspices of the Asociación Musical Daniel A.C., which ran subscription concerts as a non-profitmaking cultural institution. Erich Kleiber (1890-1956) was an Austrian from Vienna, who had studied at the Prague Conservatoire. In 1923 he became General Music Director of the Berlin State Opera, conducting the world premiere of Berg's *Wozzeck* on 14 December, 1925. In the mid 1930's Kleiber emigrated to South America in protest against the Nazi regime. Between 1937 and 1949 he conducted German opera at the Teatro Colón in Buenos Aires, conducted the Havana Philharmonic Orchestra from 1944 to 1947, and was guest conductor of the NBC Symphony Orchestra between 1945 and 1946. A year before his death he was appointed chief conductor of the Berlin State Opera but never took up the post, resigning on political grounds.[8]

The programme that evening was as follows:

I

Obertura "Tancredi"	Rossini
Sinfonia en mi bemol mayor, Op. 39	Mozart
Adagio - Allegro -	
Andante con moto -	
Menuetto (Allegro) -	
Finale (Allegro)	
El encantamiento del Viernes Santo,	Wagner
de Parsifal	

II

Concierto del Sur, para guitarra   Ponce
y orquesta
(Dedicado a Andrés Segovia)
A. *Allegro moderato e espressivo*
   Tu eres almas que dice su armonía
   solitaria a las almas pasajeras.
   ("Guitarra," Antonio Machado)
B. *Andante*
   Vuelve a Granada los ojos
   y el alma a su Felisarda
   ("Romance de Abemuneya")
C. *Final: Allegro moderato y festivo*
   (Rumores de Fiesta Lejana)

Solista: Andrés Segovia
(Primera audición de esta obra en Mexico)

Two days later on 23 February, 1944, Segovia performed this solo recital at the same venue:

I

Tres Piezas Cortas   H. Purcell
Sarabande   Handel
Sonata   D. Scarlatti
Minueto   Haydn

II

Sonata en re menor   Ponce
Tarantella   Castelnuovo-Tedesco
Madroños   Moreno Torroba

III

Danza en sol   Granados
Mallorca - Torre Bermeja - Sevilla   Albéniz

This appears as a deliberately short concert for Segovia, perhaps following intensive rehearsals of Ponce's Concerto in the same week. The tripartite pattern of the recital, with classical works, compositions written for Segovia, and the habitual signing off with Albéniz and Granados, provides however a neat symmetrical structure, no doubt topped up with several encores.

It was probably about this time that Segovia had a memorable encounter with the formidable English conductor, Sir Thomas Beecham.[9] A potential performance of Ponce's Concerto in Detroit was forfeited when Segovia refused to perform if what he considered adequate rehearsal time was not given to the work. Unfortunately, not one of the biographies of Beecham published so far mentions what must have been a clash of giant personalities, though the incident may well have pointed the way to the end of another possible musical relationship for Segovia.[10]

A musician who endorsed Segovia's adverse opinion of Beecham was the great English composer, Benjamin Britten (1913-1976), for whom Sir Thomas and Sir Adrian Boult were his "two least favorite conductors."[11] Emmanuel Hurwitz, one of the most distinguished orchestral leaders in Europe, commenting on the precision of Britten's conducting, remarked how incredibly different it was from that of "Beecham who enjoyed doing things that looked like sword-fighting — and we had to decide which of his ninety-three movements was the actual beat!"[12]

Segovia's incessant journeys through South America continued during this difficult period when his beloved Europe was not accessible to him. In 1944, he visited El Salvador, giving a recital there in San Salvador on 22 March. This was his last chance to meet and talk to Agustín Barrios, who suffered a major heart attack in 1939 and had been ailing ever since. Barrios had settled in El Salvador to teach, compose, and give recitals.[13] Barrios spoke to Segovia about an operation he had endured to make his mouth less big in order to make him more attractive to women and introduced his wife, Gloria, who Segovia decided was definitely not the kind of woman he liked. Segovia described Barrios as "an instinctive musician," a term in his phraseology which was not a commendation.[14] Segovia's ideal in musicianship was undoubtedly Ponce, in many ways the opposite of Barrios, with a more intellectual and reflective, view of art, his works being somewhat removed in spririt from the passionate immediacy of so many of the Paraguayan's compositions.

Barrios was, of course, at that time a very ill man and died a few months later on 7 August, 1944. Another opportunity open to Segovia to influence the guitar world for good was thus deferred for several decades as the music of Barrios, one of the great spiritual heirs of Francisco Tárrega, passed into temporary eclipse. His art would emerge in proper ripeness only in the 1970's when a protégé of Segovia's, John Williams, launched an enthusiastic revival, the effects of which still reverberate in the history of the twentieth century recital repertoire. Segovia did nothing to incorporate any of the music of Barrios into his repertoire, an omission which many critics find to be a grave error. Richard D. Stover claims that he heard Segovia publicly declare in 1982 that "Barrios was not a good composer for the guitar."[15] If this was indeed Segovia's belief throughout his life, his failure to perform a single work of Barrios in public would suggest that either he kept to his belief or was insufficiently aware of the wide range of the composer's output to develop a broader opinion. Certainly there were pieces among the collected works of Barrios which would have suited Segovia's style and ethos extremely well. But Segovia's strict code of selectivity as in the case of the works of Villa-Lobos, J. S. Bach, Rodrigo, Castelnuovo-Tedesco, and Frank Martin, was a filtering barrier which blocked off various worthwhile works at the same time as it brought other (sometimes less significant) pieces into prominence.

23. SEGOVIA'S EDITION OF SOR'S STUDIES

Segovia emerged from the war years and self-imposed exile in Uruguay as a stronger personality than ever and with a renewed vision of his possibilities. The blueprint of his new image is contained in one of the most successful publications in the history of the guitar. In 1945 Edward B. Marks Music Corporation published Segovia's edition of *Studies for the Guitar by Fernando Sor.* In a recent analysis of the pieces selected by Segovia, David Tanenbaum makes the following comment:

On the cover of Studies for the Guitar by Fernando Sor, *Segovia's name dwarfs Sor's, and his picture dominates everything. This is symbolic of the fact that the music inside is Segovia's version of what Sor wrote and intended. When the edition was first published in 1945, it became* the *version. Generations of students played the 20 studies without knowing that there were any changes from the original score.*[1]

But more interesting than the layout of Segovia's original edition (which may have been no more than a publisher's imaginative marketing concept), was the biographical note which encapsulates the legend of Segovia as would henceforth become familiar to the public:

Andrés Segovia was born in Andalucia, a region of Spain eminently suited for artistic contemplation. He spent his childhood in Granada. In this marvel of cities, the guitar is a daily element in the emotional life of the populace. Andrés Segovia felt vehemently attracted to the guitar ever since his infancy. Despite the limited aid that the easy-going imagination of the populace could contribute he imposed upon himself the duty of discovering the musical roots of the instrument, and consecrated all his youthful energies to the dual task of investigating the remote past of this beautiful instrument and to prepare the technique which one day he would reveal to the world. As he himself says he "was his own teacher and pupil, and thanks to the efforts of both, they were not discontented with each other."[2]

The phrase about being "his own teacher and pupil" would emerge in a thousand interviews for ever after. It was true in as much as Segovia had never taken a course of lessons with an established teacher. But it was some distance from Buek's account in 1926 when Segovia "obtained his education in a seminary and his first music lessons," and when he sought out a paralysed guitarist in Granada who gave him information "about the required studies and gave him some explanation about techniques." The biographical note of 1945 also omits all mention of Miguel Llobet's help for the young artist. In the next sentence Segovia gives his age when he gave his first recital as fourteen. (In Buek's account this had been eighteen.) Thus he becomes established as a child prodigy, which he may not have been in the accustomed use of the term. The biographical note then mentions his trip to South America in 1920, which took place slightly earlier, and his Paris debut "three years later," (this was in 1924). Segovia's use of dates and figures tended to be an obscuring rather than an enlightening experience:

From that moment on, his name remains within the group of highest international significance. Until 1939, he annually toured the major capitals of Europe, Russia, the Far East, United States, Central and South America. Thanks to him, the guitar of which Debussy said, "C'est un clavecin... mais expressif" won its place in the concert halls of the entire world.[2]

Segovia conveniently smudges an element of guitar history here, neglecting to mention that Miguel Llobet, Emilio Pujol, Luise Walker, Regino Sainz de la Maza, Julio Martínez Oyanguren, and Agustín Barrios, also toured widely winning a public which often Segovia could draw on for support. The comment by Debussy, "It is a harpsichord... but expressive" has been quoted ever since but it is difficult to find evidence outside this biographical note that the French composer ever actually said it.

The next paragraph states that "Andrés Segovia has endowed the guitar with a vast heritage, together with the happy results of his investigations in the field of history starting with the "vihuela" (original guitar). Segovia has "brought out beautiful musical pages by Alonso de Mudarra, Luis Milán, Robert de Viseo [sic]," and others from the "French, English, German and Italian 'lute,' and a prodigious volume of transcriptions of classical works." Thus in one bold statement Segovia pre-empts the massive researches undertaken by Emilio Pujol into the music and instrumentation of the vihuela. (In actuality Segovia published just one edition of a work by Alonso Mudarra (*Romanesca,* Schott's, G.A. No. 159, 1939), and no editions of the works of Milán or de Visée, though he played their compositions often.) This would have been particularly galling to Pujol, who gave many recitals and lectures on the vihuela from the late 1920's onwards and from 1945 was teaching a course at Barcelona University on *Vihuela history and literature.* Pujol's monumental edition of Luys de Narváez's *Los Seys libros del Delphin,* the first of several such volumes, was also published in 1945 by El Instituto Español de Musicología.

Finally the biographical note gives a list of "composers of high artistic standing" who collaborated "in the creation of a modern repertoire for the guitar." These are "Turina, Torroba, Manuel Ponce, Albert Roussel, Cyril Scott, Alexander Tansman, Castelnuovo-Tedesco, etc." The inclusion of an English composer is intriguing for Cyril Scott wrote only one work for guitar, *Reverie,* which Segovia did not play very much[3] and which disappeared, possibly stolen from Segovia's house in Barcelona in 1936. Another anomaly is the absence from the list of the name of Heitor Villa-Lobos who surely deserved better than being among the "etc."

The biographical note to the edition of Sor's *Twenty Studies* presents a credible picture which would be accepted by his eager public. Segovia was now preparing to raise the stakes. The new world after the war would not be a rose garden for artists, and following bitter experiences in the USA, Segovia was aware that careful marketing and presentation were essential. Like Paganini or Liszt a century before, Segovia began to capitalise on his inherent charisma, creating his own powerful legend and putting himself over to his public on his own terms. From this time onwards he would be aware of the importance of giving out only information essential to the legend-building processes. Like a film star he would grow into that *persona* more and more. (It is perhaps no coincidence that the appearance of his guitar shaped autograph in the edition, was signed and dated from Los Angeles, the city of stars and legends.)

Segovia's remarks on the twenty studies themselves indicate the more advanced techniques that he found the most valuable both musically and technically. The studies have been chosen to achieve "the right balance between the pedagogical purpose and the natural musical beauty." His preface to the selected studies provides a virtual checklist for competence, and acknowledgement of those skills which the guitarist, like any other instrumentalist, most urgently needs to master:

The studies of Sor which are published here can be used not only for the development of the technique of the student, but as well for the preservation of it at its height for the masters. They contain the exercises of the arpeggios, chords, repeated notes, legatos, thirds, sixths, melodies in the higher register and in the bass, interwoven polyphonic structures, stretching exercises for the fingers of the left hand, for the prolonged holding of the "cejilla" and many other formulas, which if practised with assiduity and intelligence, will develop vigor and flexibility in both hands and will finally lead to the better command of the instrument.[4]

Also in the preface Segovia cites the work of Scarlatti and Chopin as being representative of composers who unite technical development with musical quality. His preface to the *Douze Études* of Heitor Villa-Lobos in 1953 would voice the same preoccupations, when the studies of the Brazilian composer would be seen "as strong and delightful as those of Scarlatti and Chopin."

Over five decades after its publication Segovia's edition of Sor's *Twenty Studies for the Guitar* is still in print and has achieved enormous sales worldwide. The book is a fascinating demonstration of Segovia's performance practice, his methods of fingering, and his system of editing. Its influence on all kinds of players from virtuoso recitalists to students preparing for guitar examinations has been immense. In the 1950's many concert guitarists, such as Julian Bream or John Williams, would include a group of these studies inspired directly by Segovia's edition. John Williams, at an early stage of his career, recorded them on *John Williams plays 20 Studies for Guitar by Fernando Sor* (HMV CLP1702, issued 1963). Various other artists over the years followed this example, including David Tanenbaum (GSP 1000C, released 1989), whose intention was "to honor both Sor and Segovia's work while seeking a modern approach to these studies."[5] In his liner notes to the recording he intends restoring Sor's "notes and tempo indications" while maintaining "many of Segovia's ideas, particularly his modernization of various technical issues."

For many years Segovia's edition was accepted uncritically as one of the seminal texts of twentieth century guitar pedagogy, an essential part of any self-respecting guitarist's scheme of progressive work in pursuit of mastery of the instrument. With the rise of the Early Music movement reaching its peak from the 1960's onwards, the subsequent demand for Urtexts and scholarly editions, and the decline of the cult of the great personalities in musical studies (with instead an emphasis on objectivity in interpretation), it was inevitable that Segovia's work on Sor would eventually come under attack. Thus in 1981 the barrage began with an article by Dr. Brian Jeffery.[6] He regarded Segovia's standard of work in his editorial capacity as "not adequate for the editing of a book which affects the lives and studies of so many people," and proceeded to demonstrate "the very considerable differences between Sor's text and Segovia's version of it."

Examples of Segovia's alleged unscholarly peccadillos given by Dr. Jeffery include the changing of *andantino* to *lento* (Study No. 1), and *allegretto* to *moderato* (Study No. 5), putting a different system of right hand fingering in Study No. 6, altering notes and adding rests, changing the focus of a study from one aspect to another, and providing incorrect arpeggios. The writer's conclusion at the end of the article is that "to use this edition in teaching, in examinations, and in competitions, is to place something very dubious at the heart of the teaching process, and it is time to think very seriously about whether such use should continue."

This wholesale attack on Segovia's scholarly integrity was however thrown into doubt by further investigations by Erik Stenstadvold. These researches centered on the simple fact that Segovia may possibly (but not conclusively) have based his edition of Sor's Studies on a musical text originating from Napoléon Coste:

The purpose of this article is twofold: first to reveal the extent to which Coste has changed Sor's original compositions, and second to show that Coste was responsible for many of the 'wrong' notes in the Segovia edition.[7]

Of the twenty studies selected by Segovia, it was discovered that sixteen were in a guitar method published by Coste about 1845, six years after Sor's death. Thus it became clear "that Segovia's text is based on Coste's version of the studies, not Sor's original, as many of the alterations done by Coste are repeated by Segovia." The 1945 edition, unlike the early nineteenth century works, included right hand fingering, and introduced "radically new fingerings for the left hand." Segovia also added dynamic markings. In the light of Stenstadvold's research Segovia thus appears in a more creative role, adding certain elements but not corrupting his original text wilfully, and presenting a performer's edition rather as Coste did himself.

David Tanenbaum's judgement on Segovia's edition of the Sor *Studies* is both fair and thought-provoking:

The classical guitar is no longer dominated by a single figure, but Segovia's edition is perhaps the clearest technical legacy of the last great dominant personality. It shows a truly Romantic figure editing a Classical one. Segovia was not a pedagogue or a scholar, and he reveals his technical principles indirectly. This edition and Segovia's recordings are living performance practice. And although he altered Sor's work without telling us, many of Segovia's changes make the studies more relevant to contemporary technical needs.[8]

Thus some half a century after publication Segovia's edition of Sor not only retains a central significance in pedagogic development but manages to survive quite destructive analytic scholarly critiques. Its links with the vintage past of Napoléon Coste, and its undoubted ability to compel us as players to focus on Sor's music in a technically relevant way establish Segovia's role in the great traditions of the guitar which unite the virtuoso performers with the role of teacher. In the post-war years Segovia's active teaching would become an integral part of his own contribution to the guitar's development.

24. THE GUITAR IN 1945

The immediate post-war era would see the emergence of a number of young guitarists, though Segovia at the age of fifty-two had few if any potential challengers at his level for the affections of the general public. Miguel Llobet and Agustín Barrios had died and Emilio Pujol was concentrating on the vihuela.

Julio Martínez Oyanguren was winning a good public in the USA, but some of his recordings tended towards the more popular images of the guitar. In the *B.M.G.* of August, 1940, mention had been made of Oyanguren's recent releases, *La Paloma* (Yradier) and *Ay-Ay-Ay* (Freire) (23145, Decca Album No. 118), *Waltz in A major, Op. 39, No. 15* (Brahms) and *Kujawiak in A minor, Op. 3* (Wieniawski) (23146), and *Élégie, Op. 10* (Massenet) and *Serenade* (Schubert) (23147). The accompanying article commented:

Señor Oyanguren brings forth a wonderful variety of tones and musical expressiveness from his Spanish guitar and his records are a joy to listen to. The older school of players may have preferred Señor Oyanguren to play original music for the guitar (I know he himself would have preferred to play it) but to educate the non-playing public to the beauties of a sadly neglected instrument it is necessary to give them melodies with which they are familiar.[1]

Such a critique would no doubt have indicated to interested parties that Segovia was claiming the high ground while others set out to pander to the public by giving them "melodies with which they are familiar." Segovia had succeeded in both recordings and concerts to stamp his own mark on a specific repertoire which soared high above any possible insinuation that he was playing to the crowd.

The public image of Vicente Gomez (b. 1911), a pupil of Quintin Esquembre, (a student of Francisco Tárrega) was also that of the popular guitarist.[2] He had recorded *Romance de Amor* (on Brunswick 02866) and considerably advanced his career by a performance in the film *Blood and Sand (1941*, starring Tyrone Power and Rita Hayworth).[3] Such a *persona*, that of the itinerant wandering Spanish troubadour ever ready with a song below a maiden's balcony, was perhaps part of the reason why Segovia was to turn so violently against flamenco in the post-war years. The Hollywood image of "the guitarist" was primarily that of a subservient entertainer, a crude caricature of a Spaniard with flashing teeth and an immediate song, where the guitar was clearly secondary to a number of other considerations.

This entire aura of obsequious familiarity was deeply repulsive to Segovia who saw in it the most unfortunate stereotypes with which he did not want to be associated. Ironically this kind of exposure of the guitar in film and on record may have helped to raise the level of interest in guitar playing but at some cost to the instrument's credibility as a serious expressive medium. Some of the area which Segovia was to react against very strongly was contained in the notes of a long playing record Vicente Gomez made in the late 1940's:

Vicente Gomez is today one of the world's outstanding guitar virtuosos. He was born in 1911 in Madrid, in a tavern owned by his father. Learning the guitar from the wandering gypsies who came in to hoist tankards and improvise verses, he took to the instrument so naturally that by the time he was ten, he already entertained the visitors at his father's tavern... He received lessons from Quintin Esquembre, and when he was 13, gave his first concert at the Teatro Espagnol in Madrid.

In 1931, at the age of 20, Gomez undertook his first concert tour, playing through Spain, Italy and Morocco. This started him on a series of concerts that took him to all corners of the earth — to North Africa and through Russia, Poland, Austria, Cuba, Mexico, South America and eventually to the United States. He made his debut at New York's Town Hall in 1938, and soon had his own programme on NBC. He appeared, always with overwhelming success, at such theatres as the Roxy in New York and the Capitol in Washington, and at such nightclubs as the Versailles, Blue Angel and the Rainbow Room.

Gomez is not only one of the great interpreters of both classical and flamenco music, he is also a composer of fine distinction. In 1940 he was called to Hollywood where he wrote, composed and played most of the music for "Blood and Sand". He also composed and played the music of the motion pictures "Captain from Castile," "The Kissing Bandit," and "The Fighter," and interpreted the score of "Crisis" from music written by Miklos Roza. More recently he wrote and played the score of the magnificent documentary motion picture, "Goya." In addition to writing innumerable short pieces for his instrument, Gomez has composed a concerto for guitar and orchestra in three movements, "Concerto Flamenco."[4]

The recording included popular melodies such as *La Cumparsita, Malagueña, La Golondrina,* and even Ponce's *Estrellita,* arranged for guitar with an orchestral backing. As popular entertainment this was better than most and worse than some. But Segovia might have found a number of items in the notes that would have worried him. Mention of the guitar and the tavern in the same sentence was never a good union in Segovia's estimation and his autobiography would quote his aunt's dismissive comment, "What guitarist ever became famous outside of a tavern?"[5] The concept of being taught by "wandering gypsies" was also anathema to Segovia, and this kind of presentation may have persuaded him in the biographical note to the edition of Sor's *Twenty Studies,* to decry the "limited aid that the easy-going imagination of the populace could contribute."

The statements that Vicente Gomez "is today one of the world's outstanding guitar virtuosos" and "not only one of the great interpreters of both classical and flamenco" but "also a composer of fine distinction," invited direct challenging comparison with Segovia, which nowadays may seem absurd. But how would the public sift these competing claims and how would they be able to provide a distinction between true "greatness," which indicates the process on the part of a guitarist of changing the landscape of the instrument for all time, and the debasement of that word into meaningless ciphers. Moreover, how could the Concerto for guitar by Gomez be considered in any context of seriousness compared with those by Castelnuovo-Tedesco and Ponce?

Another performer through whom images of the guitar were focused in a way that would have been displeasing to Segovia was the flamenco artist, Carlos Montoya. His portrait was featured on the front cover of *B.M.G.* in July, 1945, with the following short biographical note appended inside:

Carlos Montoya's playing of the Spanish guitar is one of the major attractions of La Argentinita's touring company; his flamenco playing to the dancing in this show earning him unstinted praise from musical critics.

Señor Montoya is a Spanish gipsy, born in Madrid, who spent the early years of his life in the land of the flamencos. He has had more than twenty years of experience playing flamenco guitar and has accompanied most of Spain's famous gipsy dancers.

His playing of the Spanish guitar is not, however, confined to flamenco style. Señor Montoya has accompanied such famous soloists as Pilar López, Juan Martínez and Vicente Escudero.

He has toured the world and enjoys special popularity among his fellow gipsies and has earned fresh laurels everywhere for his solo recitals. At the present time he is touring America with La Argentinita's company while his album of recordings for the American Decca Co. — in which the fiery music of the Spanish gipsy is faithfully and skilfully recorded — has made the name of Montoya one to be coupled with other world-famous artists of the guitar.[6]

The repetition of "gipsy" four times in this passage carries its own value judgements. The general public apparently believed as far as Spanish music is concerned (having been well indoctrinated by Bizet's *Carmen*), that "gipsy," "flamenco," and "guitar," provided a magic formula for mysterious and beautiful music. It was to be a matter of some concern for Segovia in the post-1945 era to dispel some of this mythology where possible. In the early pages of his own autobiography he would try to portray the "strolling flamenco guitar player" (i.e. a gipsy) as both insensitive (making an "explosion of sounds") and incompetent ("In a month and a half I had learned everything the poor man knew — that is to say, very little.").[7] (This was a long way from the story of a Segovia who in 1927 brought two gipsies from the Albaicín of Granada round to Falla's house.[8]) The problem, from Segovia's perspective, of a proper public regard for the guitar, against all odds, was constantly renewed. The strength of the images of Hollywood and the spread of the recording industry was a double-edged weapon for Segovia, militating against his art at times in a very obvious way.

In February, 1945, *B.M.G.* featured a picture of Ida Presti on their front cover. At this point in the Second World War they were not sure of her whereabouts or progress, but it was the image of a classical player that was being projected here:

Ida Presti was born at Suresnes (just outside Paris) in 1924, and her first introduction to the Spanish guitar was when her father used to play the instrument to induce his little infant daughter to go to sleep. At a very early age her father commenced to give her lessons, and before she had reached the age of six her playing on the concert platforms of Paris was causing music critics to hail her as the "Female Mozart."

While still only thirteen she was made Membre d'Honneur of "Les amis de la Guitare" and ranked with the most celebrated guitarists. On February 13th, 1938, she was accorded the honour of being the first player of the guitar to be invited to appear before the Société des Concerts du Conservatoire de Paris. The Conservatoire was founded in 1828 and never before had a guitarist appeared in Paris who was considered worthy of playing before this austere gathering of renowned virtuosi — and most of the world's famous guitarists have visited Paris.

In 1937 she recorded eight sides for the French H.M.V. label which proved that the young Ida Presti was an outstanding performer on the Spanish guitar and that the Press notices eulogising her talents were not influenced by her sex or youth.

For three years prior to the outbreak of the war she was heard regularly broadcasting from the Paris P.T.T. station, and in 1938 took the leading part in a French film. [9]

The inadvertent insult to Segovia in the second paragraph that no guitarist "was considered worthy of playing" in front of the eminent Conservatoire before the advent of Ida Presti would not have impressed an older artist whose Paris debut in 1924 had been one of the most glittering of occasions with many eminent musicians in the audience. But at least in Presti there was a serious contender for fame on the guitar in a way fully acceptable to Segovia. Already between 1934 and 1936 Presti had recorded several pieces (on the Gramophon label) from the repertoire of Segovia including *Sonatina in A* (Torroba), *Serenata* (Malats), *Two Popular Mexican Folk Songs* (Ponce), and *Courante* (Bach), as well as pieces by Robert de Visée, *Spanish Dance No. 5* (Granados), *Rumores de la Caleta* (Albéniz), and works by Paganini and Fortea. She had also won high critical praise:

...After her debut concert Bernard Gavoty wrote: 'At ten she has a secure technique... her dull sound and the variety of her timbres are of the most beguiling.' (Le Figaro, 10 May 1935). And the reviewer of Aux Écoutes: 'An inborn feeling, an extraordinary sense of rhythm...' (4 May, 1935). On 26 January, 1938, L'Époque commented on her 'impeccable style'; and nine days before, on the 17th, A. Dandelot wrote that he had 'marvelled'. And La Presse said: 'Ida Presti is at the moment the youngest, the most astonishing and the most prodigious guitar virtuoso.' Emilio Pujol called her 'a miracle of facility and grace' in 1935 and Segovia himself said, when she was 13, 'I have nothing to teach her... she should not accept the advice of any other guitarist'. [10]

Despite this early promise as a solo performer, Ida Presti was destined ultimately to leave her mark on guitar history as a partner to Alexandre Lagoya in the Presti-Lagoya Duo rather than as a possible rival to Segovia's esteem as a soloist. Presti, of all the guitarists of her generation, was most suitably gifted to carry on his work as a recitalist. But in the event the full thrust of such a challenge would be left to the era of Julian Bream and John Williams, with Presti content to reign as monarch in an area uncontested by Segovia, that of the art of the duo.

Another solo recitalist of merit facing the post-war era was Rey de la Torre. Of Cuban origin, he had been sent at the age of fourteen in 1932 to study with Llobet in Barcelona. His first concert was at the Academia Marshall on 9 May, 1934 (in company with a pianist) followed by a solo debut on 4 July, 1934. In 1937 Rey de la Torre emigrated to the USA. In 1944-5, Joaquín Nin-Culmell, composer and pianist, was writing a piece (*Six Variations on a Theme by Milán*) for Segovia, who promised to 'fix' the work for him. Annoyed by this, Nin-Culmell dedicated the composition instead to Rey de la Torre, whose playing, according to the composer, was "aristocratic and exact, quite different from the romantic, improvisational school of Segovia." (The work was premiered in New York on 19 November, 1947.) [11]

Around the end of the Second World War, Rey de la Torre began his recording career with a contract from the Spanish Music Center, on 48th Street in New York. He recorded an all-Tárrega album, a number of Sor Studies (Nos 1 - 4, 6, 8 - 11, 14, 16 and 20, from the Segovia edition), and a reading from Juan Ramón Jiménez's *Platero y Yo*, with interludes from the music of Tárrega. [12] Thus the future in 1945 looked promising for a gifted guitarist in the line of Llobet.

In July, 1946, as a portent of things to come, a tiny picture appeared in *B.M.G.* of Julian Bream, aged thirteen years of age, whose repertoire, according to the caption, "includes several far-from-easy solos," and he also played "plectrum and electric Hawaiian guitar." His performance "at a recent meeting of the Philharmonic Society of Guitarists was acclaimed by experts." [13]

This then was the background to the guitar situation in 1945. Some of this information would undoubtedly have filtered through to Segovia in one form or another as he travelled widely and intensively, corresponded and conversed. He remained always singularly well-informed about developments, rivals, and possible opportunities. In the meantime he was building up a formidable technique and a most impressive repertoire. Just how impressive can be estimated by perusal of three concert programmes performed on 16, 19 and 21 of November, 1945, at the Palacio de Bellas Artes, Mexico City, copied here from the publicity for the events:

Primer Concierto

I

Aria "La Frescobalda"	G. Frescobaldi (1583-1644)
Preludio	J. S. Bach (1685-1750)
Sarabande	
Bourrée	
Double	
Allegretto grazioso	J. Haydn (1732-1809)

II

Sonata (homenaje a Schubert que amaba la guitarra) (dedicada a Segovia) a) Allegro moderato b) Andante espressivo c) Allegretto vivo d) Allegro ma non troppo e serioso	M. Ponce(1886-)
Capriccio (omaggio a Paganini) (dedicada a Segovia)	M. Castelnuovo-Tedesco (1895-)

III

Mazurca (dedicada a Segovia)	A. Tansman (1897-)
Vidala (dedicada a Segovia)	G. Crespo
Oriental	I. Albéniz (1861-1909)
Torre Bermeja	
Sevilla	

Segundo Concierto

I

Siciliana - Preámbulo - Allemande - Alegramento	C. Ph. Em. Bach (1714-1788)
Ballet - Sarabande - Gavotte - Gigue	S. L. Weiss (1680-1750)

II

Tres Estudios - Variaciones sobre un Tema de Paisiello, y Rondo	F. Sor (1778-1839)
Preludio, Canción y Danza (dedicada a Segovia)	F. Moreno Torroba(1891-)
Tarantella (dedicada a Segovia)	M. Castelnuovo-Tedesco(1895-)

III

Tema variado y Final (dedicada a Segovia)	M. Ponce (1886-)
La Maja de Goya	E. Granados (1867-1916)
Danza en sol	
Leyenda	I. Albéniz (1861-1909)

ULTIMO CONCIERTO

I

Pavana y Galliard	Don Luis Milán (c. 1500-1561)
Aria variada	G. F. Handel (1685-1759)
Preludio	
Fuga - Gavotte y Musette	J. S. Bach (1685-1750)

II

Largo assai y Allegretto	J. Haydn (1732-1809)
Andante	W. A. Mozart (1756-1791)
Minuetto	F. Schubert (1797-1828)
Canzonetta	Mendelssohn (1809-1847)

III

Mazurca (dedicada a Segovia)	M. Ponce (1886-)
Fantasía (dedicada a Segovia)	Turina (1881-)
Mallorca-Granada	Albéniz (1861-1909)

Between the last concert as originally advertised and the programme issued on the day, there were some interesting changes. Segovia seems at first to have intended to play Ponce's *Variations and Fugue on Folia de España* but changed it to the very much shorter *Mazurca.* Instead of Torroba's *Madroños,* he included *Granada* by Albéniz. The first piece in the third recital was originally advertised as *Pavana y Gallarda* by John Dowland, before being changed to Milán.

The program included a small admonitory footnote, the style of which seems close to Segovia's own poetic preferences:

La sonoridad de la guitarra es infinitamente más blanda y ténue que la del piano: menos penetrante que del violín; mas emotiva y suave que la del arpa.

Para percibir plenamente estas vivas qualidades espirituales del más bello de los instrumentos, se requiere un ABSOLUTO SILENCIO.

(The sonority of the guitar is infinitely softer and weaker than that of the piano; less penetrating than that of the violin; more emotional and sweet than that of the harp.

To receive fully the true spiritual qualities of the most beautiful of instruments demands an ABSOLUTE SILENCE.)

25. The Post-War Years

One of the most significant events of the immediate post-war period as far as the long-term health of the guitar was concerned, was the founding of *The Guitar Review,* in 1946, brought about by a small group of New York enthusiasts. The editor was Alfred N. Wesler, the managing editor Albert Valdés Blain, and the art editor, George Gusti, with moral support and artistic assistance from Vladimir Bobri, a confidante of Segovia for several years. The intention was to reclaim "the classic guitar from obscurity and disparagement so that it may regain its full measure of dignity in the musical world."[1]

The first issue mentions a recital given under the auspices of The Society of the Classic Guitar on 14 May, 1946, at the Steinway Hall, New York.[2] The artists included Suzanne Bloch (lute and virginal), Paul Smith (recorder), José Rey de la Torre. Ending the concert was Olga Coelho (b.1909, guitar and voice) who began a close friendship with Segovia about this time. (*B.M.G.,* March, 1946, commented on her "superb performance" of Segovia's arrangement of *Canción de Andalusia* on a Children's Hour radio programme and in *B.M.G.,* July 1946, she is described as "one of Segovia's pupils.")

The most grievous musical loss of 1946 was the death of Manuel de Falla on 14 November, in Argentina. Falla had left Spain on 2 October, 1939 following an invitation from the Institución Cultural Española of Buenos Aires to present some concerts of Spanish music to celebrate its twenty-fifth anniversary. His doctors in Argentina advised him to find a healthy climate and thus he had settled, with his sister, María del Carmen, in the town of Alta Gracia, in the Sierra de Córdoba. After his death Falla's body was taken back to Spain where he was buried in the crypt of Cadiz cathedral.[3]

In May, 1946, *The Gramophone* began to review Segovia recordings again, the works being *Granada* (Albéniz) (recorded 17 January 1939) and *Tonadilla* (Granados, arr. Segovia) (on Brunswick 1059, also issued on Decca Album 384/29.154, USA, 1945).[4]

Brunswick deserves much praise for bringing Segovia into the recording studio again, for he has been lost to us for many years. He is at his astonishing best in these two pieces and by some magic makes his instrument sound like a clavichord married to the genius of the guitar. The recording, which is very fine, must be listened to in the right company, or in solitude. You have been warned.[5]

The guitar was not yet a natural part of the milieu fostered by a magazine such as *The Gramophone.* Few guitarists other than Segovia were ever reviewed in its august pages. Yet the quiet, unobtrusive and occasional presence of a guitarist of his stature was now an accepted, if small, feature of the visible landscape. The onslaught would of course begin in earnest with the coming of the long-playing record. For now, a small reminder of things to come would keep whoever was interested in the Segovia phenomenon at least reasonably content for the time being.

The same recording was reviewed in *B.M.G.* in August, 1946:

The new gramophone record by Andrés Segovia (Brunswick 1059) has already been obtained by many readers, and several have written expressing their delight with it. Compared with some of Segovia's earlier recordings, tone and expression are better than ever. Undoubtedly Segovia is right on top of his form in this recording.

On one side is the Serenata "Granada" from Suite Española No. 1 by Isaac Albéniz, and on the reverse is the Tonadilla from the Suite "La Maja de Goya" by Enrique Granados.

These compositions are particularly well-chosen and would serve as an introduction to Spanish music...

The Tonadilla has more variety than the Serenata; harmonics and brilliant arpeggios being especially noticeable.

These recordings are easy to listen to and ideal to play to anyone who has not previously heard the Spanish guitar. I hope the Brunswick Co. will issue the remaining records from the album from which the recording is taken.[6]

In Mexico throughout 1946, Ponce's ill health did not improve. The periodical, *Excelsior,* of Mexico City announced on 9 January, 1946, that Segovia had spoken of his intention of "coming back from South America to give three concerts in the Hall of Fine Arts for the great Mexican musician's benefit."[7] The May issue of *B.M.G.* gave details of Segovia's North American premiere of Ponce's *Concierto del Sur* on 13 January, 1946, at Carnegie Hall, New York, in his first appearance with an orchestra in the U.S.A., when the audience were treated to a spectacular double:

Two concertos for guitar were performed, one in D major by the famous Italian composer, Castelnuovo-Tedesco, and the other "Del Sur" by the Mexican composer, Manuel Ponce. No extra effort was required by the soloist to make himself heard and Segovia's brilliant performance has established once and for all the suitability of the Spanish guitar for Concerto playing with full Symphony Orchestra.

In addition Segovia played solos (without the orchestra) by Bach, Handel, Sor and Albéniz with unsurpassed technique and musicianship.[8]

The writer was presumably not using the *Herald Tribune* of New York as the source for his comments on a concert he had obviously not attended himself. For that newspaper reviewing the event, "played in the vast auditorium of Carnegie Hall with an accompaniment of twenty players from the Philharmonic Orchestra, conducted by Ignatius Strasvogel," commented that "the guitar seemed rather overcome by the tonal weight of the orchestra," in Castelnuovo-Tedesco's Concerto:

Segovia in the 1940's.

...On the other hand the last concerto, that of M. Ponce, was a marvellous success and a true musical experience, a work so perfectly conceived for guitar and orchestra that it recreated the Andalusian ambience with variety and subtlety, by the amplification and development of Andalusian themes on which it was based, so appropriate to the guitar. The guitar has perhaps never reached a higher level than was enjoyed by Carnegie Hall listening to Segovia in this admirable Concerto.[9]

The years in Montevideo had thus provided a kind of apprenticeship for Segovia. Richard Pinnell charts this development from the premiere of Ponce's *Concerto* in 1941:

The manner in which Segovia dealt with the Ponce Concerto exposed the aggressive strategy of his career at midpoint. He developed an interpretation at Montevideo by playing to one of the large halls. If successful, he would engrain his approach in more concert-hall performances in Latin-America; then finally he was ready for any hall of Europe or the United States.[10]

Pinnell then quotes a review from Havana from the Cuban Guitar Society which explains how Segovia had performed Ponce's *Concierto del Sur* in Montevideo, Santiago de Chile, Columbia, Peru, the Teatro Colón of Buenos Aires, and later Mexico City:

Segovia was thus preparing and performing the repertoire he would later publish and record, the music that would perpetuate his fame for many years to come. After the war, however, he needed a change of scene. The investment of countless creative hours in his professional work over the course of nearly a decade of residence in Montevideo enabled him to launch the next phase of his career. Segovia moved directly to New York.[10]

Segovia's extraordinary capacity for both continuity of purpose and renewal of artistic aspiration meant that in the long perspectives of his life all transitions and shifts, the ups and the downs, could ultimately be seen as periods of creative development. In this way nothing was lost or thrown away. What might have daunted a lesser man, enabled Segovia to emerge with his experience and his ambitions enhanced, his muscles strengthened, in his own phrase, for the continued climb to the summit.

As the world began to recover its sense of balance and culture after the calamities of war, there were signs in various countries of increasing opportunities for the guitar as part of the musical scene. In England the Philharmonic Society of Guitarists, founded in 1929, had gained ground sufficiently to open a library of guitar music, and build up membership in towns away from the capital where it had originated.[11] (It was this organization which enabled Julian Bream to achieve "his first real triumph," in October, 1946, at "the largest and most successful (meeting) since the post-war revival of the Society.")[12]

In similar vein, Vladimir Bobri had founded the New York Society of the Classic Guitar, "of which Segovia is the Honorary President and whose members include Vicente Gomez, Olga Coelho, Rey de la Torre and other famous guitarists."[13] On the west coast of the United States, Vahdah Olcott Bickford had helped to found the American Guitar Society in 1923, another Society dedicated to the preservation and propagation of the guitar mentioned about this time in the pages of *B.M.G.*.[14] In October, 1946, a Segovia Society was formed in Washington D.C. under its secretary, Sophocles Papas. This organization sought "to widen the circle of those who appreciate the guitar as a serious instrument and a vehicle of the finest music." Its intentions were to publish a quarterly bulletin and assist in the arranging of concerts, as well as making possible "the recording and publication of serious guitar music on a wider scale, encouraging the study of the guitar and interesting contemporary composers in writing for the instrument."[15] Such coteries provided important centres of focus for sustained interest in the instrument's values and philosophy around 1946 and helped to popularize the guitar by putting on recitals, circulating literature, and making repertoire available to amateurs in their ranks.

It was also in 1946 that Vladimir Bobri introduced Segovia to Albert Augustine (1900-1967), a guitar-maker of Danish origin, who emigrated to the United States in the mid-1920's.[16] Before the 1940's guitarists had traditionally used gut treble strings for their instruments (despite the problems of correct intonation, constant breakages and other difficulties associated with the use of gut), and metal-wound spun silk strings for the bass. But in the 1940's experiments were made with nylon guitar strings. According to Alexander Bellow these were first tried on stage by Olga Coelho in New York in January, 1944.[17] In 1946, when nylon was still not always an easy commodity to obtain, Segovia asked Albert Augustine to research the possibilities of developing a nylon string. The Du Pont Chemical Company agreed to supply monofilament nylon (used in the manufacture of fishing lines) for the purpose, though they did not wish to produce strings themselves for the guitar trade.[18]

There were problems with the bass strings, even though the use of nylon treble strings was very successful and certainly impressed Segovia. The new bass strings however were "either unstable, toneless, or their windings would loosen," and they "also squeaked."

It took Augustine four hours to wind the first bass string and eventually after changing the metal thread many times (using successively copper, silver, 14-carat gold, aluminium and stainless steel) and smoothing and polishing the silver strings until his hands literally bled, he produced his first successful nylon-wound strings.[19]

Augustine copyrighted his nylon strings in 1947. The packaging included a small prose-poem in Spanish by Segovia which affirmed that as far as composers, ancient or modern, played on the guitar were concerned, "all sing out and sound more beautifully on the new AUGUSTINE strings than on any other which have come to my knowledge":

> *Por eso, el público filarmónico escucha esas obras con*
> *más intenso placer y sin esfuerzo fatigoso*
> *de atención.*
> *Líbrenos el cielo de la deshonesta imitación de estas*
> *cuerdas, per mercaderes sin escrúpulos!*

> (Thus, conveyed to the audience more precisely,
> the performance of these works is received
> with enhanced satisfaction.
> May the Lord deliver us from the bad merchants who
> imitate these strings!) [20]

This break-through in the use of nylon had the hidden effect of enabling recitalists to have a less anxious life and helped immeasurably in the spread of the classical guitar as a popular instrument easily tuned and kept in order by amateurs. From this invention a number of modifications to technique would follow, but the clock would not be put back. The benefits of nylon over gut were so demonstrable that no misplaced sense of conservatism, authenticity or nostalgia appear to have prevented guitarists in the 1940's from immediately joining the ranks of those keen to use the new technology.

The good news about the advent of nylon strings seems to have taken its time to cross the Atlantic. Wilfrid Appleby eventually commented on the discovery:

A correspondent in the U.S.A. tells me that Segovia and many other guitarists are now using nylon strings instead of gut. These strings are absolutely true and wear almost indefinitely. In reality they are Dupont nylon fishing line, and if bought as such are reasonable in price. One firm evidently saw the chance of making a "few" dollars out of guitarists and was actually charging twelve dollars (£3 sterling) for a set of three! - and they are now even wrapped in pure gold paper.

It has been one of the weak points of the Spanish guitar that gut first strings wore out so quickly and were often unsatisfactory in other ways. If a really satisfactory substitute has been found for gut it will help the guitar to become even more played than it is at present.[21]

Also in 1946 Schott reprinted sixteen items of their Segovia Guitar Archives series, which had presumably sold out in their original editions.[22] The re-issued works were as follows:

No. 102, *Fandanguillo,* Turina.
No. 103, *Nocturno,* Moreno Torroba.
Nos. 106, 107, 108, *Selected Pieces,* J. S. Bach.
No. 111, *Three Popular Mexican Songs,* Ponce.
No. 117, *Menuet,* Mozart.
No. 119, *Lamento,* Pedrell.
No. 130, *Variations from The Magic Flute, Op. 9,* Sor.
No. 133, *Pièces caractéristiques, Vol. 1,* Moreno Torroba.
No. 138, *Bittendes Kind,* Schumann.
No. 139, *Menuet,* Haydn.
No. 140, *Mazurka, Op. 63, No. 3,* Chopin.
No. 144, *Sonata in A minor,* Scarlatti.
No. 146, *La Xenophone,* Phil. Em. Bach.
No. 147, *Siciliana,* Phil. Em. Bach.

In 1946 Mario Castelnuovo-Tedesco wrote a composition for Segovia entitled *Rondo, Op. 129,* destined to be published in the Guitar Archives Series No. 168 in 1958. It was to be neglected by its dedicatee and most other guitarists, perhaps the most distinguished of its few recordings being that by Jorge Oraison (on Etcetera ETC1001) released in 1982. Manuel Ponce's only guitar works of that year were two miniatures, *Vespertina* and *Rondino,* first published respectively in *Guitar Review, Vol. 1, Nos 5 & 6,* in 1948. (Later published in 1989 by Fomento Cultural, ed. Corazón Otero, Mexico, 1989 under the title of *Vespertina y Matinal*). These were dedicated to Jesús Silva, described as "a pupil of Andrés Segovia," and later Director of the Escuela Superior Nocturna de Guitarra in Mexico.[23] The two pieces were published in *Guitar Review* fingered by Silva, but revised and approved by Segovia.

26. 1947

A crucial moment in *The Segovia-Ponce Letters* is one of the last letters that Segovia wrote to Ponce. Here a number of significant facts are laid bare. His marriage to Paquita was deteriorating and a conductor named Schiawitch was making overtures to her (much to Segovia's disgust). Moreover, communication between Segovia and his friend, Olga Coelho, had broken down.[1]

Segovia's personal life may indeed have been looking somewhat bleak by mid-1947, yet his artistic career was once again in full swing. His recitals for the early months of the year in the United States were as follows:

16 January:	Esconcido, California.
19 January:	Los Angeles.
3 February:	Aberdeen, South Dakota.
6 February:	Columbus, Ohio.
11 February:	Detroit, Michigan.
19 February:	Washington, D.C.
26 February:	Philadelphia, PA.
5 March:	Wellesley, Massachussetts.
15 March:	Toronto, Canada.
18 March:	Rochester, New York.

A New York recital had taken place on 2 March, 1947.[2] The program included *Chaconne* by J. S. Bach, *Prelude, Fugue, Courante, Sarabande, Bourrée and Gavotte* (J. S. Bach), *Sonata Romántica* (Ponce), *Antaño* (Esplá), *Norteña* (Crespo) and *Leyenda* (Albéniz).[3] On 12 May, Segovia returned to Canada performing at the Hermitage Concert Hall, Montreal, in a recital broadcast to Latin America by the Latin American section of CBS International service. According to *B.M.G.,* the audience "broke into prolonged cheering at the conclusion of the recital."[4]

In the third issue of *Guitar Review,* Segovia contributed an article on transcriptions, a topic which remains of perennial interest among guitarists as players constantly seek to broaden the instrument's range of expressiveness:

...If one examines the transcriptions of Tárrega one is struck by his ingenious ability to find the same equivalents as would a great poet in translating from one language to another the poesy of another great poet. Transcribing is not merely passing literally from one instrument to another. It means to find equivalents which change neither the aesthetic spirit nor the harmonic structure of the work being transcribed.[5]

Segovia's playing had from his youth been founded on the precedents of Tárrega. He was indebted to Tárrega for transcriptions of Albéniz (*Granada, Sevilla*), J. S. Bach (*Bourrée* from *Partita I* for solo violin, BWV 1002, *Bourrée* from *Suite No. 3* for cello solo, BWV 1009, and *Fugue* from *Sonata 1* for solo violin, BWV 1001), some pieces by Chopin, Handel's *Corale* and *Minuetto,* and Haydn's *Andante, Largo assai* and *Minuet.* Other pieces central to Segovia's repertoire inherited from Tárrega include *Serenata española* by Joaquín Malats, Mendelssohn's *Songs without Words, Op. 30, Nos 3 & 6,* and *Canzonetta* (from *String Quartet No. 1 in E flat major*), and Schubert's *Minuet* from *Sonata Op. 78.*

There were significant transcriptions by Tárrega that Segovia did not touch but he explains that, "Artists were not so critical of themselves in those days," and that "if Tárrega himself had lived in our days he would have thrown out many of his own transcriptions." He also makes the somewhat extravagant claim that "only the pianistic talents of Liszt, with his defects and qualities, are comparable to the works of Tárrega."

In the same article Segovia acknowledged his indebtedness to Miguel Llobet for "his transcriptions of the danzas and the Tonadilla of Granados," as well for the "popular Catalonian songs, above all the one known as El Mestre." Segovia wrote how compositions written for him by composers without "full knowledge of the guitar's resources," needed the assistance of his "translations in the idiom of the guitar" and commented how "that too is a way of transcribing."

The fourth issue of *The Guitar Review* was dedicated almost entirely to Segovia. In the editorial column, Paul Carlton, expressed his admiration:

...Segovia does not "interpret" music to us — what we hear is the music itself. Segovia is Bach — he is Albéniz, Weiss, Tárrega, Sor — Segovia is them, reincarnated in the works they perhaps hoped a Segovia might someday play.
Perhaps the most universal compliment that is ever paid to Segovia is, strangely enough, one that is never spoken. No one ever mentions Segovia's "technique." This is indeed high praise, for it means that so great is Segovia's Art that all art is concealed... which is what the definition of true Art calls for. There is no "technique" in Segovia's playing, which to be paradoxical again, is because of his technical perfection. It is all Music.
It is all Segovia.[6]

Nowadays such a judgement seems curiously misplaced. Segovia's concept of interpretation was indeed a total system which covered all his repertoire. But by the criteria of subsequent decades, Segovia's concept of interpretation, arrived at within the accepted tenets of early twentieth century principles, tended to reduce each piece, whatever its historical context, to similar artistic formulae. This approach, of course, was characteristic also of most of the great instrumentalists of the early decades of the twentieth century, including Paderewski, Casals, and Kreisler, as well as Segovia, one of the last survivors ultimately of that generation. Segovia, or any other instrumentalist for that matter, is demonstrably *not* Bach, Albéniz, Weiss, etc., but an interpreter working within a specific framework to perform music of the past for his contemporaries.

Carlton's comments emerge from a musical context where no other living guitarist could be regarded as being in the same league of performance as Segovia. This very fact is referred to in the same issue by Theodorus M. Hofmeester, Jnr., the Associate Editor:

There are other guitarists of concert merit but their influence has been either local or so limited in scope through circumstances beyond their control, that upon Segovia has fallen the whole task of impressing the guitar on the world as an instrument worthy of the name "musical." This constitutes the uniqueness of Segovia in the musical world today.[7]

Hofmeester goes on to make an impassioned plea for "the training, guiding, development and bringing before the public new talent," to ensure that "the great tradition created by him {Segovia} shall not die out." Unknown to Hofmeester, developments even in 1947 were under way which would indeed serve to continue and extend the tradition of Segovia's music.

Beginning therefore with this issue of *Guitar Review*, a specific definition and understanding of the Segovia phenomenon was thus formulated from 1947 onwards. Usually the acknowledgement of Segovia as supremo would not be accompanied by any particularly vigorous analytic or comparative critique of his playing. But *Guitar Review, Vol. 1, No. 4*, established a tone of reverence and respect which would set a pattern for future discussion. Segovia had done the playing, recording, and proselytizing on behalf of the guitar for many years and now it seemed an appropriate time for his supporters to set in place an ideological approach to his work. At the age of fifty-four, Segovia had achieved a remarkable eminence. The next twenty years would see that esteem disseminated among the widest possible public, his reputation being now in the post-war years firmly established among a small but highly motivated group of guitarists in a multitude of countries. The opposition, whatever it was and whatever its strength, had now been confronted by a massive wall of information and propaganda. From this point onwards Segovia could progress only to the level of "legend," a word mentioned in Carlos Vega's article, *The Miracle which is Segovia*:

When a man bursts through the limitations of human capabilities, his is the recompense of exaggeration, and from this — legend is born.[8]

But more important than the praise of his admirers in the formation of the legend were the excerpts of Segovia's autobiography, *La Guitarra y Yo* first published in Spanish and English in this issue of *Guitar Review*. The 1947 episodes, slightly different in various ways from the publication in book form of an autobiography in 1976, concentrated primarily on Segovia's acquisition of musical knowledge and his early guitar repertoire. His style of writing, slightly whimsical and overtly poetic, creates resonating anecdotes which somehow dissipate disturbances and inner probings, and, by their charm, deflect questions of a more basic kind about the actual nature of his early life, relatives and formative influences. The very title of the autobiography, *The Guitar and I*, puts the emphasis where Segovia wanted it, onto a consideration of his musical life alone, with little hard information about his family or his innermost thoughts.

Comparison of this approach with revelatory autobiographies by other great instrumentalists such as Pablo Casals (*Joys and Sorrows*, 1970, Macdonald, London), Arthur Rubinstein (*My Young Years*, 1973, and *My Many Years*, 1980, Jonathan Cape, London), and Yehudi Menuhin (*Unfinished Journey*, 1976, Macdonald and Jane's, London) show the disappointing evasiveness of *La Guitarra y Yo*. The *Segovia-Ponce Letters* reveal Segovia as a different kind of writer, perceptive, thrusting, analytical, and with a biting edge to his satire. Yet Segovia's chosen method of autobiography, as well as veiling whatever he wished to hide beneath a cloud of poetic anecdotes, can be regarded as typically Iberian. In his fascinating examination of the national character of the Spaniard, Fernando Diaz-Plaja regards such reticence as being of great significance in understanding the nature of the Spanish people:

The Englishman says that his home is his castle. He is referring to his individual rights as against the Government. The Spaniard also considers his home his castle — but as against everybody — a castle bristling with cannon surrounded by deep moats. He does not give his name or his address, easily...

And if the Spaniard does not like giving his name, how is he going to give something intimate, his personality? This is the reason for the lack of autobiographies or of love letters in Spanish literature. The man who has worn a cloak for many years to hide the patches in his trousers is not going to undress spiritually before people he does not know.[9]

Thus Segovia chose in 1947, at a time of particular adulation from American friends, to foster his public image in this way. The formulation of a *persona* or personal mythology became part of a public man's armour, defending his privacy and fending off awkward questions which seemingly explained certain things to satisfy public curiosity. What is more important is that this received portrait of Segovia became the stereotype accepted by journalists and other writers. Yet the presented caricature of a complex and profound character is in itself substantially less interesting than the real man behind the mask. The art of Segovia emerged from a richly enigmatic and deeply thinking artist, the product of a remarkable cultural background. To simplify the phenomenon of a great musician is to sell us all short.

Curiously enough it was left to Carlos Vega to cast a useful question or two in the direction of the mysteries of Segovia's growth as a musician and person, having established his position as "an artist dedicated to the guitar... a guitarist without whom the history of the guitar today would lack meaning," an "adaptor," and an "able creator of original compositions":

But in Segovia, with all these gifts, there is something more, his moral sense, his concept of the morality of the man and the artist. And still further there is the orbit of his development, an orbit that might be represented by the image of a bow in permanent tension and an arrow tracing an uninterrupted flight from the child-nonentity to the supremely-fulfilled adult. How can one know what must have been that time of incubation and aspiration, the exquisitely sensitive soul springing like a flower among the brambles, taming the rough material and every year striving to recreate a new and more profound spirit which developed the year before, accumulating ever greater knowledge and dexterity, ever greater power with each new conquest, and with each new satisfaction feeling itself tormented by a new thirst? What powerful and long-enduring ambition! His plans were brought to fulfilment with effort it is true, but they were conceived without violence, for the development of this natural spirit, this spirit laden with the message of millenniums, has been constantly watched over by fate.[10]

It was therefore in 1947 that Segovia's past was in the process of analysis and evaluation, both by himself and others. *The Guitar Review* was an excellent forum for such a debate. Yet it is clear that the self-defining autobiographical aspect by Segovia himself was the most crucial focus of any such operation. With this *persona* captured and established, Segovia could face the future secure in the cocoon of a specific public identity, which on account of its innocence and simplicity could not be challenged or penetrated. This is not to say that the autobiography did not convey elements of the life as lived and experienced. But a deep or prolonged reading of the episodes as published in 1947 may perhaps persuade many readers that there was more to it all than this, and that a number of more intimate aspects were charmingly, unobtrusively and adroitly side-stepped.

As part of the process of evaluating Segovia's life and work and preparing for further developments, *The Guitar Review* offered a list, verified by Segovia, of his recordings issued up to 1947. This was as follows:

Sonatina in A major, F. Moreno Torroba: *Courante*, J. S. Bach	Victor Red Seal 1298
Petite Valse, Mazurka, M. Ponce.	Victor Red Seal 1824
Fandanguillo, Preludio, F. Moreno Torroba	Victor Red Seal 1487
Tremolo Estudio, Francisco Tárrega: *Fandanguillo*, J. Turina	Victor Red Seal 6767

Prelude and Allemande, Fugue, J. S. Bach	Victor Red Seal 7176
Thème Varié, Fernando Sor: *Gavotte,* J. S. Bach	Victor Red Seal 6766
Prelude and Allemande, Gigue, 'S. L. Weiss'	His Master's Voice DB 1565
Sarabande - Gavotte, 'S. L. Weiss'	His Master's Voice DB1225
Study in A major, Alard (arr. Tárrega): *Prelude,* J. S. Bach	His Master's Voice 1553
Folies d'Espagne (Tema y Variaciones), M. Ponce	Gramófono SAE
Parte 1, Parte 2,	Barcelona DB 1567
Parte 3, Parte 4,	Barcelona DB 1568
Canzonetta, Mendelssohn: *Vivo y energico,* M. Castelnuovo-Tedesco	His Master's Voice DB 3243
Allegro from Sonata III, Canción y Postlude, M. Ponce	His Master's Voice AB 656
Nocturno, F. Moreno Torroba: *Serenata española,* J. Malats	His Master's Voice HMVE569
Music of Albéniz and Granados	Decca Album 384 -29 M (Personality Series)
Granada, Albéniz: *Tonadilla,* Granados	Decca 29154
Danza española No. 10, Granados: *Torre bermeja,* Albéniz	Decca 29155
Danza española No. 5, Granados: *Sevilla,* Albéniz	Decca 29156

Recordings made but not at this time released included, *Estudios* by Sor (Decca), Album 1 of music by J. S. Bach (*Prelude, Courante, Sarabande, Bourrée, Fugue, Gavotte*) and Album 2 (*Chaconne*), (Musicraft).[11]

By the standards of recording output of the 1940's this was a remarkable achievement. The contributions of any other guitarists of his day were already well eclipsed by Segovia's tenacious advocacy of the recording technology of the time. Yet in historical terms they may be seen as merely the first fruits of Segovia's discography, a foretaste of remarkable things to come. They stand now as monuments to the art of the guitar before the invention of nylon strings, representing the embodiment of early twentieth century techniques and interpretive practices.

While *The Guitar Review* roared forth its cannon in praise of Segovia and all his works, the man himself continued to triumph. After his tour of the United States at the beginning of the year he visited Mexico City where he played *Prelude* and *Chaconne* (J. S. Bach), *Allegretto* (Rameau), *Andante* and *Minuet* (Haydn), *Variations on a Theme by Mozart* (Sor), *Tremolo Study* (Tárrrega), *Sonatina* (Torroba), *Impresiones Ibéricas* (M. Ponce), and *Mallorca* and *Sevilla* (Albéniz).[12] In the fall Segovia presented three concerts at the Teatro Colón, Buenos Aires. The programs for these may be usefully compared with the three previous recitals at the same venue in 1945:[13]

FIRST CONCERT

I

Preámbulo, Sarabanda, Gavota	A. Scarlatti
Sonata	D. Scarlatti
Aria Variada	G. F. Handel
Allegretto	Rameau
Minuetto	Haydn

II

Sonata (Omaggio a Boccherini)	Castelnuovo-Tedesco
Fandanguillo	Turina

III

Tonadilla	Granados
Danza	
Torre bermeja	Albéniz
Sevilla	

SECOND CONCERT

I

Aria con Variazioni	Frescobaldi
Sonata romántica	Ponce

II

Dos Estudios	Villa-Lobos
Tarantella	Castelnuovo-Tedesco
Fantasía	Turina

III

Antaño	Esplá
Danza en Sol	Granados
Estudio	Tárrega

THIRD CONCERT

I

Andante y Allegretto	Sor
Tres Estudios	
Tema Variado	
Sonatina	Torroba

II

Chaconne	J. S. Bach
Capriccio	Castelnuovo-Tedesco
(Omaggio a Paganini)	

III

Mazurka	Tansman
Impresiones Ibéricas	Ponce
Granada - Leyenda	Albéniz

On 28 October, 1947, Segovia performed in Holland. The Dutch newspaper *Goois Dagblad* commented as follows:

Segovia puts the music under a microscope and each little sound, each nuance shines forth in its full beauty and significance against the background of silence of the spellbound audience. [14]

B.M.G. welcomed the return of Segovia in their November issue:

Here is news that will accelerate the heartbeats of every British enthusiast of the Spanish guitar.
SEGOVIA IS COMING
Yes, this is official. Andrés Segovia will be in Holland during the early part of this month and will arrive in London in time to broadcast on November 25th.
Other engagements which have been made up to the time of writing are:
    Dec. 3. Harpenden Music Club
    7. Cambridge Theatre
    9. Bradford Music Club
    12. Welwyn Music Club
No doubt other recitals will be arranged also.
It is just ten years since Segovia last visited this country and in that decade many people have become interested in the Spanish guitar and it can be asserted that a large proportion of these owe their enthusiasm to having heard a recording of Segovia's wonderful playing. Now we are to hear a direct broadcast by him and the fortunate few may even see and hear him at one of his recitals. [15]

A leaflet issued by the Philharmonic Guitar Society of Great Britain gave the date of the live broadcast from London as 25 November.[16] At the Cambridge Theatre, London, Segovia performed Castelnuovo-Tedesco's *Concerto in D, Op. 99*, with the New London Orchestra under Alec Sherman.

During 1947 the career of the young Julian Bream (b.1933) had begun to reach the attention of guitarists and the wider public. He had performed a debut recital at the Cheltenham Art Gallery on 17 February, 1947, and on 5 January, 1948, was scheduled to give another including Sor's *Mozart Variations, Op. 9,* Ponce's *Sonata clásica, Tonadilla* by Granados, and Segovia's *Anecdote No. 5.* By now he had received frequent mentions in *B.M.G.* and was establishing a formidable reputation. It was during the 1947 tour of England at this time that Bream first heard Segovia in person. Speaking in a broadcast on BBC Radio in August, 1974, he described this experience:

I was simply riveted by his playing. I had never heard such beautiful articulation, such a wealth of tone color, and such wonderfully integral interpretation. His technique really is formidable. There's never been a technique of such precision and control before Segovia and it would be remarkable if there would be in the future a superior technique.

I think the most remarkable thing on hearing Segovia would be the effect of the sound that he produces and the effect of the sound upon one's sensibilities. It is very clear, it is extremely fine, and if one may use the word, aristocratic.

Julian Bream was introduced to Segovia by Dr. Boris Perott, President of the Philharmonic Society of Guitarists, some time during this tour. Bream also received two or three lessons from the master, performing the *B minor Study* of Sor "very nervously," and on another occasion, was so tense that he left his guitar on the train on his way to the lesson.[17]

On 8 December, 1947, the Philharmonic Society gave a reception for Segovia at the Alliance Hall, London, an occasion reported for *B.M.G.* by Wilfrid M. Appleby:

...the maestro received a tremendous ovation when he entered. Dr. Perott in the name of the P.S.G., and its seven branches, welcomed Segovia, who replied in English, revealing a genial personality and a keen sense of humour.

Then Madame Olga Coelho, the famous Brazilian singer-guitarist, was introduced and enthusiastically welcomed...

After the interval Julian Bream played at Segovia's request. His solos received great applause and Segovia declared that in Julian we have a young guitarist of great promise.

W. Glover played his arrangement of Greensleeves and then Olga Coelho sang a Segovia arrangement of a Scarlatti song and a Brazilian folk song, The Little Frog, the speed of which left everyone breathless except the singer-guitarist.

After some flamenco, the audience joined in singing, For He's a Jolly Good Fellow, and cheers for Segovia.[18]

A review by the same writer of Segovia's recital in London duly arrived the following month in *B.M.G.*:

So many readers have asked for reports of Segovia's recitals that I give my impressions of the one I attended.

The dress-circle of London's Cambridge Theatre seemed to be full of P.S.G. members at the Sunday afternoon concert on December 7. In the dim light I recognised friend after friend. Conversation was short for most of us were anticipating seeing Andrés Segovia for the first time; wondering whether his playing would sound as we imagined it from hearing his records and broadcasts.

The orchestra played a Ballet suite and it is a tribute to the conductor, Alec Sherman and the New London orchestra that the music held my attention. In fact it was with something of a shock that I realised the placing of a chair and footstool to the left of the conductor signalled the appearance of Segovia with his guitar.

He was not so heavily built nor so serious as I had imagined.

There was some wiping of strings and hands with a cloth; the conductor's baton was poised; and the Concerto for Guitar and Orchestra began.

It was a new experience for most of us to hear the Spanish guitar in combination with the varied tones of the orchestra. I found it almost bewilderingly exhilarating but there was so much to apprehend that I should have liked to hear it played right through again so I might better absorb and appreciate such a feast of blended sound.

Among my chief impressions was the charm of the more melodious parts of the Concerto. Mario Castelnuovo-Tedesco has the Italian gift for melody and he knows how to combine it with interesting harmonies and rhythm. Nowhere was the voice of the guitar drowned, though the section of the orchestra used was quite considerable.

There were solo passages for the guitar and it was during these that I watched, through opera-glasses, Segovia's hands doing difficult things so easily that I almost forgot about the music.[19]

After a performance of Schubert's *Fifth Symphony*, Segovia returned to the platform (as was his custom for many years when playing Concertos), to provide some solos:

> ...*Segovia returned to play a group of solos. We had heard these in his recent broadcasts, or from his recordings, but few of us had seen him play them. Handel's lovely Aria and Bach's music for lute delighted the audience but in spite of the fact that Sor's "Thème Varié" is one of the all-too-few Segovia recordings the BBC frequently plays, this solo evoked the warmest applause. Segovia's rendering was superlatively beautiful — do not wish to hear it played better. Anyhow it could not be!*
>
> *There was no difficulty in hearing the maestro and no microphone was used. The tones of his guitar were full of life and he drew on a wide range of tone-colour.*
>
> ...*Andrés Segovia's popularity is greater than ever and with our appetites whetted by this short visit I hope a much larger number of concerts and recitals will be arranged for him when he again comes to Britain.*[19]

Appleby's use of the term 'maestro' is interesting here. The title had not yet become an inseparable part of Segovia's status as an artist and would not be so for a few years to come.

The actual solos played by Segovia according to the printed program were *Aria* (Handel), *Prelude, Sarabande and Gavotte* (J. S. Bach), *Thème Varié* (Sor) and *Sevilla* (Albéniz). The overall tone of the article suggests that Segovia's actual presence was until the post-war period an unknown quantity, and this short tour was for the British public a means of discovering exactly what kind of stage personality Segovia presented.

This process of establishing a connection between Segovia the man and his public also emerges in a letter the same month from John W. Duarte (b.1919). With a group from the Manchester Guitar Circle, the young Duarte, a fledgling and unpublished composer at that time, had driven across the Pennine moors to hear Segovia's concert in Bradford on 9 December, 1947, and afterwards they were invited to have coffee with him. Duarte had taken one of his compositions with him and Segovia's response to his creative efforts was distinctly encouraging. But it is clear from the following letter that though his playing skills were known to be immaculate, people were not always quite sure what kind of person Segovia really was. Such doubts were now resolved once and for all:

> *Dear Sir,*
>
> *We have long been aware that Andrés Segovia is a player of superlative ability and considerable musicianship; in fact, it was these qualities which drew us over the moors to Bradford to hear him give a recital at the Music Club there. We had some reserve in our judgment in respect of the flattering effects of recording conditions and were prepared for some measure of disappointment. Reports from certain sources had represented Segovia to us as an unapproachable and even disagreeable man.*
>
> *Without further delay we should like to disabuse anyone of these notions who is so misinformed as to hold them. In Segovia we found a guitarist of almost unbelievable ability to produce and to control both volume and tonal variety...*
>
> *The mastery of Segovia over the guitar is as complete as may be expected of mortal man and the depth of his musicianship and sincerity is beyond sensible doubt. We do not always agree with his readings but our disagreements are matters of interpretative preference and were we the composers themselves we could not question the musicianship and authority which Segovia brings to everything he touches.*
>
> *After the recital we spent some time with Segovia and found him to be a most friendly, helpful and charming human being — more than that, he displayed an ease of manner and a gentlemanliness which are all too seldom found in this country today. He showed, moreover, a remarkable and sincere interest in the activities and affairs of ourselves whom he had never before met and of whom he knew, at the most, little.*
>
> *Segovia, we would declare to all who read this letter, is a supremely masterful guitarist; a musician of the highest order; and a gentleman in the finest sense of the word. It is our loss that he is not more often and for longer among us — a loss which we in this country cannot afford.*
>
> *JACK DUARTE*
>
> *(Pres. Manchester Guitar Circle, on whose behalf this is written.).*[20]

Thus Segovia's first tour in Britain for ten years produced the best possible impression musically and personally on his potential supporters, providing a solid basis which would be nurtured carefully for the rest of his life.

The climax of his British tour was a recital at the Wigmore Hall on 11 December, 1947. The recital notes included Marc Pincherle's notes on Bach's *Chaconne* first written for the Paris concert in 1935. The program itself was as follows:

I
(Groups of pieces whose spirit and technique are adaptable to the guitar)

Three Little Pieces	H. Purcell
A New Irish Tune -	
Menuet - Jig	
Aria with Variations	Handel
Two Sonatas	D. Scarlatti
Allegretto	J. Ph. Rameau
Andante et Menuet	J. Haydn

II

Chaconne	J. S. Bach

(INTERVAL)

III
(Works composed for the guitar and dedicated to Andrés Segovia).

Sonata, omaggio a Boccherini	Castelnuovo-Tedesco
Allegretto con spirito	
Andantino quasi canzone	
Tempo di Minuetto	
Vivo ed energico	

IV
(Transcriptions of works inspired by the Spanish guitar).

La Maja de Goya	Granados
Torre Bermeja - Sevilla	Albéniz

Segovia's repertoire as a recitalist was now essentially complete. Further items would of course be added over the next twenty years, but the main guidelines were established. In a sense, compared with the world of the concert artist today, Segovia arrived at this point quite late in his life. But whereas guitarists of subsequent generations were able to take his work as a role model, Segovia's task had been to innovate and explore, steering the traditional recital format established by Tárrega and Llobet into new and challenging structures. With very few modifications he was able from the 1940's onwards to capitalise on the strengths and flexibility of his own recital designs for the next forty years.

27. THE DEATH OF MANUEL PONCE

Manuel Ponce, Segovia's close friend and Mexico's foremost composer, died on 24 April, 1948 at the age of sixty-six. His last work, *Variations on a Theme of Antonio de Cabezón,* was dedicated to his friend and confessor, Father Antonio Brambila. These variations were finished on 8 February, 1948, and are actually composed around the theme of the Easter hymn, *O Filii et Filiae,* the origin of which remains obscure.[1] Because of its proximity to the composer's death, the work has a special poignancy though unfortunately it did not enter Segovia's repertoire.

In a letter to Clema, the composer's widow, Segovia not only expressed his abiding admiration for Ponce,[2] but also promised to take steps to see that the *Concierto del Sur* was published.[3]

The Guitar Review, No. 7, 1948, provided a commemorative issue dedicated to Ponce. Segovia's epitaph to the composer, offers the most heart-felt tribute. Having spoken of "the incomparably important place which Ponce occupies in the current revival of the guitar," Segovia went on to evaluate Ponce's contribution to the repertoire as being the finest of all of his contemporaries:

He lifted the guitar from the low artistic state in which it had lain. Along with Turina, Falla, Manén, Castelnuovo-Tedesco, Tansman, Villa-Lobos, Torroba, etc., but with a more abundant yield than all of them put together, he undertook the crusade full of eagerness to liberate the beautiful prisoner. Thanks to him — as to the others I have named — the guitar was saved from the music written exclusively by guitarists...

...he composed more than eighty works for the guitar; large or small, they are all of them pure and beautiful, because he did not have the cunning to write while turning his face, like the sunflower, towards worldly success.[4]

Olga Coelho also wrote a tribute, having met Manuel Ponce and been welcomed in his house twice in 1947:

There were three decisive reasons which served as the basis for a sound friendship between us: his brotherly affection for my great friend and teacher, Andrés Segovia, his boundless love for the folk music of his country, and his equally great love for the guitar.

Mexican music, so extraordinarily rich in melody and rhythm, is closely linked to the guitar, and this is one more factor that must have induced Ponce to write some of the most beautiful pages for that noble instrument.

Ponce was a true pioneer in two senses: in creating a new literature for the guitar (outstanding examples are his magnificent Concierto del Sur *and the several sonatas, variations and many other works dedicated to Segovia), and in turning to the inexhaustible spring of Mexican folk music for themes for his symphonic works and other high forms of musical creation.[5]*

Further tributes to Manuel Ponce in *The Guitar Review* included contributions from Heitor Villa-Lobos, Jesús Silva, Carlos Chavez, and Marc Pincherle, with an editorial by Rose Augustine.

For Segovia the death of Ponce implied not only the tragic loss of a friend but also the end of an era, that remarkable period from the 1920's onwards when the repertoire expanded so rapidly over a comparatively short period of time. In the space of a few years the guitar had lost several personalities closely associated with its development, including Llobet, Barrios, Falla, and now Ponce. In his mid-fifties Segovia was not only the supreme player in the world but was assuming a further significance as a representative of the earlier twentieth century traditions of the guitar at the same time as younger players in Europe and the United States were establishing their careers.

Segovia's year followed its characteristic scenario throughout 1948. In the early part of the year he played two concerts in New York, on 4 January and 7 March. The two programs were respectively:

I

Two Pieces	Milán
Passacaglia	Couperin
Lento e Allegretto	Sor

II

Sonata, omaggio a Boccherini	Castelnuovo-Tedesco

III

Siciliana - Fuga - Courante	J. S. Bach
Gavotte et Musette -	
Sarabande - Bourrée -	
Menuet - Gavotte en Rondeau	
Sonatina	Ponce
Leyenda - Torre Bermeja -	
Sevilla	Albéniz

I

Aria con Variazioni	Frescobaldi
Two Sonatas	D. Scarlatti
Four Pieces for the Lute	S. L. Weiss

II

(Works written for guitar and dedicated to Segovia)

Mazurka	Tansman
Segovia	Roussel
Norteña	Crespo
Tarantella	Castelnuovo-Tedesco
Impromptu	Pedrell
Sevillana - Fandanguillo	Turina

III

Danza	Granados
Granada - Mallorca	Albéniz

The Guitar Review reported that Segovia gave six encores before being "permitted to pack away his guitar."[6] By this time the structure of his recitals deliberately allowed for a protracted session of extra pieces. Yet on this occasion, after his suite-like recitation of various pieces dedicated to him, this must have been a concert involving considerable stamina on the part of both performer and audience.

In between these New York recitals Rey de la Torre (1917-1994) performed at the same venue on 28 January, 1948, (having played there a few months previously on 19 November, 1947). Segovia was thus not without direct comparisons in terms of repertoire and style from a guitarist almost a quarter of a century younger. Rey de la Torre's program on 28 January was as follows:

Six Pieces	de Visée
Allemande - Bourrée -	J. S. Bach
Courante	
Fantasia	Dowland
Grande Sonate	Sor
Ecos de Paisaje - Vidala	Broqua
Three Mexican Songs	Ponce
Cádiz	Albéniz
Recuerdos de la Alhambra	Tárrega

Thus there was an alternative voice for the New York public to ponder. Rey de la Torre's repertoire at this time included music, such as the pieces by Dowland and Broqua which Segovia did not play, as well as other compositions clearly absorbed from the Segovian tradition including those by J. S. Bach and Ponce.

In Europe the decade of the 1940's encouraged the development of careers held back by the war. Foremost among recitalists was Ida Presti, whose concerts were now meriting attention in almost every issue of *The Guitar Review.* Apart from playing Paganini's *Grand Sonata* with violinist, Michel Chauveton, her solo contributions at a recital at the Salle Gaveau, Paris, were *Prelude et Allemande, Chaconne* (J. S. Bach), *Sevilla, Guajira* (Pujol), *Ecos de la Parada, Danza No.5* (Granados), and *Rumores de la Caleta* and *Asturias* (Albéniz).[7] On 16 September, 1948, Presti performed Rodrigo's *Concierto de Aranjuez* with the orchestra of Radio France.[8] This was a further indication of the independence from Segovia's precedents which young artists were now usefully exploring.

Meanwhile the Segovia juggernaut moved on relentlessly through 1948, extending his triumphs ever wider and achieving distinguished firsts. *The Gramophone,* for example in June, 1948, announced that Segovia had recorded an all-Bach album for Musicraft, "a few months previously," and had also recorded the Bach *Chaconne.*[9] (But it was not until July, 1955, that these Bach recordings would be reviewed in *The Gramophone.*[10]).

In September that year, after tours of Mexico and Holland, Segovia appeared for the first time at the prestigious Edinburgh International Festival, Scotland, giving no fewer than three recitals on 7, 8, and 10 September, and offering the following programs:

7 SEPTEMBER, 1948

I

Preámbulo, Sarabande, Gavotte	A. Scarlatti
Sonata	D. Scarlatti
Allegretto	Rameau
Andante and Minuet	Haydn
Prelude - Fugue - Courante - Sarabande - Bourrée - Minuet - Gavotte en Rondeau	J. S. Bach

II

Norteña	Crespo
Mazurka	Tansman
Fandanguillo	Turina
Danza in E minor	Granados
Sevilla	Albéniz

[Encores were *El Mestre* and *La Filla del Marxant* (Llobet) and *Recuerdos de la Alhambra* (Tárrega).]

8 SEPTEMBER 1948

I

Two Pavanas	Milán
Prelude - Allemande - Gavotte - Gigue	Weiss
Passacaille	Couperin
Variations Op. 9.	Sor
Chaconne	J. S. Bach

II

Madroños	Torroba
Impresiones Ibéricas	Ponce
Tarantella	Castelnuovo-Tedesco
La Maja de Goya	Granados
Leyenda	Albéniz

[Encores were *Study No. 9* (Sor) and *Fandanguillo* (Torroba).]

10 SEPTEMBER 1948

I

Two Galliards	Dowland
Three Little Pieces	Purcell
Aria with Variations	Handel
Menuet	Haydn

II

Sonata in D	Castelnuovo-Tedesco
(*Omaggio a Boccherini*)	

III

Two Studies	Villa-Lobos
Antaño	Esplá
Mazurka	Ponce
Danza No. 5	Granados
Mallorca - Torre Bermeja	Albéniz

[Encores were *Recuerdos de la Alhambra* (Tárrega) and *Norteña* (Crespo)]

On 26 and 27 October, Segovia was guest soloist with the Halle Concert Society, performing Castelnuovo-Tedesco's *Concerto* the first evening, with solos, *Aria* (Handel), *Thème Varié* (Sor) and *Sevilla* (Albéniz). The following evening at the Albert Hall, London, he played Ponce's *Concierto del Sur* (with Sir John Barbirolli conducting), and included the following solos — *Andante and Allegretto* (Sor), *Fugue, Bourrée* (J. S. Bach), and *Torre bermeja* (Albéniz).

On 2 November, he gave a solo recital in London, the first half being *Four Pavanas* (Milán), *Aria con Variazioni* (Frescobaldi), *Siciliana* (C. P. E. Bach), *Sonata* (Scarlatti) and *Gigue* ("Weiss"/Ponce). The second half included the seven Bach pieces played in Edinburgh in his first recital there, the compositions by Crespo, Tansman and Ponce, and finally *La Maja de Goya* (Granados) and *Leyenda* (Albéniz).

Also in 1948 Julian Bream gained a scholarship to the Royal College of Music, London, and in Spain, "the guitar soloist Narciso García Yepes played recently Joaquín Rodrigo's *Concierto de Aranjuez* with the Corunna Municipal Orchestra".[11] On 21 October, Olga Coelho gave birth to a son, Miguel, but by 13 January, 1949, was back at the Town Hall, New York, providing concerts with "her usual authoritative style and beauty."[12]

In a letter to *The Guitar Review,* Segovia explained that for the moment his autobiographical articles would have to be missed for one issue. From 5 September, 1948, until his concert in Genoa, Italy, on 26 December, he had given forty concerts in Europe, covering Switzerland, Holland, France and Italy. This was followed by "a series of thirty concerts in the vast area of the United States and neighbouring countries," before departing for his spring tour of Europe.[13]

28. 1949

On 15 January, 1949, Joaquín Turina died. He was not only one of the foremost Spanish composers of the twentieth century but his guitar works dedicated to Segovia provided some of the instrument's best loved repertoire. *The Gramophone* duly commented:

By the recent death of Turina, Spain has lost one of her remaining senior composers. Of the same generation as Falla, Turina differed widely in style from his greater contemporary, but like him based much of his work on Spanish national idioms... It is less than fair to call his music "picture-postcard Spanish," though it is true that the picturesque always made an appeal to him; and it should be remembered that at the time when he emerged as a composer Spain was virtually a musical terra incognita, *and national traits of melody and harmony had not yet been turned into the clichés we now know too well.*[1]

The Gramophone listed Turina's best known orchestral works as *Danzas fantásticas*, *Procesión del Rocío*, and *Rapsodia sinfónica* for piano and orchestra, mentioning also "what some judges consider his best work," *Oración del Torero*, as an example of his chamber music as well as Segovia's recording of *Fandanguillo*. Despite his remarkable contribution to the repertoire, Turina did not receive the kind of celebratory response in *The Guitar Review* offered in tribute to Manuel Ponce only a few months earlier. Yet since his death his reputation has continued to grow, especially in terms of his guitar works.

While Segovia pursued his annual recital tour of the United States in the early months of 1949, interesting developments in Europe offered indications of the direction the guitar might take:

The "Concierto de Aranjuez" was broadcast from France on September 16 last, with Ida Presti and the French National Radio Orchestra. Those of us who heard this broadcast will never forget the thrill of that superb music so brilliantly played. It was a studio performance, but the music lovers of Paris heard Ida Presti repeat her performance on March 24 at the Salle Pleyel, with the Orchestre des Jeunes Universitaires.

Earlier in March — on the 2nd — a special two-hour programme of Spanish music was broadcast by the Swiss Radio. It included orchestral works by Falla, Turina and other Spaniards as well as the "Concierto de Aranjuez" by Rodrigo.

The guitarist was Narciso García Yepes and the Orchestre de la Suisse Romande was conducted by Ataulfo Argenta, director of the National Orchestra of Madrid.

A friend, now living in Switzerland, wrote of this broadcast: "Not since Segovia's visit to England have I heard such an outstanding and masterly performance as the Rodrigo 'Concerto' played by Narciso Yepes. He interpreted this ultra Spanish music with a fiery musicality I have seldom heard equalled.

"His technique is so effortless that one does not notice it; his tone mellow and crystal clear. He made us live the very spirit of this remarkable modern work.

"The Adagio movement was particularly beautiful, full of restrained and dignified feeling, and the last movement was playfully sparkling. Altogether a remarkable performance by a remarkable young man."

I hope the B.B.C. will soon arrange for us to hear Rodrigo's "Concierto de Aranjuez".[2]

The guitarists of the younger generation were managing to break free of Segovia's gravitational pull, to create reputations of their own with works the master had not touched and to reach their own public. In particular Rodrigo's *Concierto de Aranjuez* was steadily gaining ground and presenting a unique challenge to aspiring soloists, as it has continued to do ever since.

But however much reputation the younger players gained, it was still Segovia who made the running and who set the standards. In the summer of 1949 he went back to the studios and recorded Castelnuovo-Tedesco's *Guitar Concerto No. 1 in D major, Op. 99*, and a number of very significant solos, thereby once again extending the discographical horizons of the guitar. The sessions in the studio produced these 78 rpm/12" records:[3]

Two Studies: Villa-Lobos (recorded 27 June)	COLUMBIA CAX 10567, LX 1248
Arada, Fandanguillo: Torroba (recorded 27 June)	COLUMBIA CAX 10568, LX 1248
Fandanguillo: Turina (recorded 27 June)	COLUMBIA CAX 10569, LX 1248
Norteña: Crespo (recorded 22 June)	COLUMBIA CAX 10569, LX 1248 England
Tarantella in A minor: Castelnuovo-Tedesco (recorded 30 June)	COLUMBIA CAX 10570, LX 1404-6
Sonatina Meridional: Ponce I. *Campo* II. *Copla* III. *Fiesta* (recorded 29/30 June)	COLUMBIA CAX 10574-5, LX 1275
Allegro (Rondo) (from *Sonata Clásica):* Ponce	COLUMBIA 21151, LB 130
Guitar Concerto No. 1 in D major, Op. 99 (with the New London Orchestra conducted by Alec Sherman): Castelnuovo-Tedesco (recorded 11/12 July, 1949)	COLUMBIA CAX 10582-87, LX 1404-6

In 1994 a compact disc entitled *Andrés Segovia, The Complete 1949 London Recordings* (Testament SBT 1043), revealed that further, hitherto unreleased, recordings were made during the sessions. These were *Six Divertimentos, Op. 2,* (Sor), recorded 21 June, *Estudio sin luz* (Segovia), recorded 22 June, and *Bourrée, Double* (from *Partita No.1 in B minor,* BWV 1002), (J. S. Bach), recorded 27 June, 1949.

Segovia's recording of Castelnuovo-Tedesco's *Guitar Concerto,* completed in the space of two days on 11 and 12 July, was conducted by Alec Sherman (b. 1907). Born in London, Sherman had spent the early part of his life as a violinist. He had joined the BBC Symphony Orchestra when it was formed in 1930 and from that vantage point worked with a wide variety of distinguished guest conductors, observing their art and learning from them the technique of conducting.[4]

Sherman left the BBC Symphony Orchestra in 1938 to make a career as a conductor, and in 1941 founded his own group, the New London Orchestra, an ensemble of some forty players, with a good contingent of musicians specializing in chamber and solo work. When the celebrated pianist, Dame Myra Hess, arranged to play the complete series of Mozart's Piano Concertos at the National Gallery, London, Sherman and his orchestra were chosen to accompany her. Later he conducted the BBC Symphony Orchestra himself, and made guest appearances with other leading British orchestras such as the London Philharmonic and the Hallé. In July, 1943 he became a conductor at the Sadlers Wells Ballet Company, working among others with the composer, Constant Lambert. Later, Sherman married the pianist, Gina Bachauer (1913-1976).[5]

Thus the choice of the New London Orchestra under Alec Sherman, with their wide experience of performing both concertos and a range of more intimate ensemble music, was ideal for Segovia's premiere recording of Castelnuovo-Tedesco's work. In Britain this album was reviewed in *The Gramophone* in August, 1951:

Castelnuovo-Tedesco. Concerto for Guitar and Orchestra. Andrés Segovia (guitar), **New London Orchestra** (*Alec Sherman*). *Columbia LX 1404-6 (12 in., 29s 1¹/2d.) Auto LX8807-9.*

This novel concerto opens with a most fascinating tune which is the best part of the work. The rest is very slight, easy going and melodious but it is pleasant to have this romantic vehicle to display Segovia's magical art. He begins the slow movement alone, with a tune of Neopolitan flavour, and plays it so beautifully that I resented the intrusion of the orchestra.

Try this light wine: it is well bottled and suitable for a summer's evening.[6]

Whether this is quite the kind of publicity Segovia enjoyed is not known. Despite its outwardly benevolent tone, the "light wine" of the guitar repertoire is something of a back-handed compliment. The same review was repeated in *The Gramophone,* December, 1952, when the performance was merged with *Sonatina Meridional,* (Ponce), *Arada and Fandanguillo* (Torroba), and *Fandanguillo* (Turina) to become a long-playing record on Columbia 33CX1020 (12 inch, selling at just under £2).

According to *B.M.G.,* "an album of three 12-inch records of the Castelnuovo-Tedesco Concerto for Guitar" was released around December 1950.[7] A review by Jack Duarte appeared in October, 1951:

There have been many recordings of guitar music of all kinds in the past but the recording of which I am about to write is the first to be released here or in the U.S.A. (unless I am misinformed) of a Concerto or other major work for guitar and orchestra...

...This concerto may be summed up as a delightful, tuneful piece of music for solo guitar and a small, lightly-constituted orchestra... The balance of guitar and orchestra is perfectly kept and in a way which can never be realised in a concert hall...

In every movement Castelnuovo-Tedesco shows himself to be a master of orchestral effect and tone-painting and he always contrives to show the guitar part in effective settings. All his themes are easily recognisable, tuneful and well-suited to the guitar. It is almost pompous to burden them with the correct technical term "subjects." Nevertheless they are musical subjects; developed with elegance and distinction in such a way that the development is easily followed by the least technical of listeners.

The union of Castelnuovo-Tedesco (the composer of delightful music) and Andrés Segovia (the perfect interpreter of such gifts and almost certainly the extender and adviser where the solo part was concerned) adds one more to the list of historic partnerships that already glistens with names such as Brahms/Joachim and Elgar/Menuhin.[8]

The review achieved a balance between the composer's mastery of "orchestral effects and tone-painting," and the "delightful, tuneful" aspect, which may associate such a concerto with "light wine" rather than with more substantial beverage. This attempt to square the circle would no doubt have pleased Segovia rather more than the comment in *The Gramophone* that the work is "very slight, easy going and melodious," which perhaps sells short the *Concerto's* resonance and appeal.

Shortly after these recording triumphs, Segovia played a recital at the Music Festival at Aix-en-Provence, France, on 29 July, 1949. Isaiah Berlin gave a radio talk about the Festival setting the context:

The Musical Festival at Aix is not a vast ambitious undertaking like the magnificent festivals of Salzburg or Edinburgh or Lucerne. During the performances which took place in Aix during the last two weeks in July, apart from Señor Segovia and Mr. Robert Casadesus, no celebrated virtuosi came to delight the public from the distant corners of the earth. The orchestras were those of the Baden-Baden Radio and of the Paris Conservatoire. The conductor was Herr Hans Rosbaud, from Baden-Baden, a good, experienced, scrupulous, honourable devoted musician, but not a man of towering genius.

Yet it was not only a most attractive but a remarkable occasion more attractive and more remarkable in one respect at least than the great rival summer festivals of Europe — it was fresh, spontaneous and endowed with a degree of natural charm which these more splendid occasions seldom possess...

Performances began late in the evening; at half past nine, in the cool night which succeeds the hot Provençal July day, under a dim and usually cloudless sky.[9]

Segovia's concert, like the opera performances which Berlin is describing, also began at 9.30 p.m., his program being as follows:

I

Andante et Allegretto	Sor
Cinq Études	
en si bémol - en do	
en sol - en si - en la	
Thème varié	

II

Sarabande et Gavotte	Scarlatti
Passacaille	Couperin
Prélude - Courante-	J. S. Bach
Sarabande - Bourrée -	
Gavotte	

III

Fantasía	Turina
Norteña	Crespo
Tarantella	Castelnuovo-Tedesco
Granada - Torre bermeja	Albéniz

In October, 1949, *The Gramophone* did its first review of a Segovia recording since May, 1946, though from this time on such a famine would change to a feast. The compositions on the recording were *Two Studies, Nos 1 & 7* (Villa-Lobos) and *Tarantella* (Castelnuovo-Tedesco) on Columbia LX 1229:

Castelnuovo-Tedesco's Tarantella *is a most seductive piece, played too, with all the skill and charm for which Segovia is so justly famous. His admirers will love this. The first of Villa-Lobos's studies needs knowing. At first it seemed to me vague and fumbling. Two or three playings, however, showed the piece to be coherent and also of considerable attractiveness. The second study is rather like a curious and rather fast version of the first of a certain 48 — doubtless very difficult to play but not, I think, much more to it.*[10]

Once again a reviewer presents a friendly face to Segovia's art, appearing slightly bemused and a little dissatisfied with the musical substance while being pleased enough with the "skill and charm" of the playing.

Later in 1949, Segovia visited Britain again where his itinerary was as follows:

26 and 27 October,	Hallé Orchestra, Manchester
30 October,	New London Symphony Orchestra, Tunbridge Wells
2 November,	Recital, Wigmore Hall, London
4 November,	Recital, Houldsworth Hall, Manchester (organised by Hallé Club)
6 November,	Philharmonic Orchestra, Liverpool
8 November,	Recital, Newcastle under Lyme
9 November,	Recital, Birmingham

At Manchester, Segovia performed his *Concertos* under the conducting of Sir John Barbirolli, thus repeating some of the pattern of his 1948 tour. A letter in *B.M.G.* provided useful information about the Tunbridge Wells concert:

On Sunday, October 30th, Segovia appeared at the Assembly Hall, Tunbridge Wells, with the New London Symphony Orchestra and although the hall was not full he was given an enthusiastic reception.

Segovia's contribution to the first half of the programme was the Concerto by Ponce, which he played with a chamber orchestra of seventeen players conducted by Alec Sherman. The second half of the programme opened with a recital by Segovia in which he played: Andante and Allegretto (Sor), Fugue and Bourrée (Bach) and Torre Bermeja (Albéniz). In response to further requests he played Allegretto (Rameau).

What are the main impressions felt after seeing and hearing the virtuoso? First, his complete mastery of the instrument, demonstrated by the effortless dexterity of both hands; then the varied range of tone colour obtained by exploiting the instrument's possibilities to the full; thirdly - and particularly noticeable in the large hall — the clarity of pp and harmonic passages.

Above all Segovia endeared himself to the audience by his genial appearance and charming manner.[11]

Segovia's solo recital at the Wigmore Hall, London on Wednesday, 2 November, 1949, divided the program once more into three categorised parts:

Works written for the Guitar

Suite in D	R. de Visée
Prelude, Allemande,	
Gavotte (Guitariste de la	
Cour de Louis XIV)	
Sarabande, Bourrée, Gigue,	
Menuet, Courante	

Romanza	Paganini
Four Studies	F. Sor
Andante and Allegretto	

Compositions whose spirit and technique are adaptable to the Guitar

Passacaille	L. Couperin
Prelude, Sarabande and Bourrée	J. Sebastian Bach
Menuet	J. Haydn
Romanza and Canzonetta	F. Mendelssohn

Pieces dedicated to Andrés Segovia or inspired in the Spanish Folklore

Sonata (dedicated to Segovia) *Allegretto - Andante - Allegro*	M. Ponce
Tarantella (dedicated to Andrés Segovia)	M. Castelnuovo-Tedesco
Danza in G	E. Granados
Torre Bermeja	I. Albéniz

Thus another truly remarkable decade drew to a close. In the 1940's Segovia had manoeuvred his career from comparative recession into new levels of fame and esteem. The years of exile in Montevideo had produced an unexpected harvest. His technique and his repertoire had been perfected, two concertos had been received and thoroughly performed and the solo repertoire fully structured for recitals in an unmistakable format. An image had been projected through the autobiographical chapters published in *The Guitar Review*. Nylon strings had revolutionised the voice of the guitar. Despite myriad personal problems Segovia had come through. He was now ready to confront the challenges of perhaps the most satisfactory decade of his life. In the 1950's recitals, recording, further publications and a teaching role would establish him as the truly greatest phenomenon in the history of the guitar at a time when he was the unchallenged master of the instrument and his competitors were still making their way up the immense mountain to international fame.

29. THE 1950'S

On 6 February, 1950, Segovia wrote a letter to Mario Castelnuovo-Tedesco from New York, expressing qualified admiration of the composer's *Suite, Op. 133.*[1] (This work, written in 1947, would eventually be published by Schott as Guitar Archive No. 169 in 1954.) While he was in the process of absorbing the first two movements, *Preludio — quasi un improvasione* and *Ballata Scozzese,* he expressed some apprehension about the third movement, *Capriccio,* which he believed to be unsuited to the character of the guitar. At the end Segovia commented that he had not been able to reach a final decision yet on the work.[2] (A choice was made quite soon however, and by the end of 1950 he appeared to have a desire to play the first two movements but not the last, as is made evident by one of his Wigmore Hall recitals on 8 November, 1950.)

But such discrimination did not apparently deter the composer who went on in 1950 to write *Quintetto Op. 143* for guitar and strings, in four movements (*Allegro, vivo e schietto, Andante mesto, Scherzi: Allegro con spirito, alla Marcia,* and *Finale: Allegro con fuoco*) and *Fantasia, Op. 145,* for guitar and piano.[3] Alfred Leonard, a German musicologist, asked Segovia to participate in a chamber music concert, and this was agreed providing that Castelnuovo-Tedesco could supply the modern part of the program.[4] (This work was recorded by Segovia some years later on Brunswick AXTL1092 and reviewed in *The Gramophone* in May, 1961. The critic, while complaining of the bad quality of the recorded tone from the strings, commented favourably that "through the course of four lightweight movements, of only an occasional Spanish tinge, the sonorities of guitar and string quartet are explored with obvious affection and skill."[5])

In notes for the recording by Manuel López Ramos of *Quintetto, Op. 143,* (RCA VICS 1367, issued 1968), Robert Offergeld makes an interesting observation about the retrospective mood of the work:

Although its language is concise enough, the Guitar Quintet refers insistently and with the special nostalgic concentration of the neo-romantic viewpoint, to matters of sentiment. The faculty of retrospection is necessarily implicit in such references, and given the stylistic timetable of modern music, the Guitar Quintet seems in consequence to be a somewhat earlier work than it actually is. Without exactly sounding like the irrepressibly lyrical, neo-romantic chamber works of the 1920's and '30's — for one thing, its posture betrays greater sobriety and its textures are in general less silky — the Quintet nevertheless belongs to the same moody family.

These aspects of nostalgic recall of a bygone age of tonality were of course the very attributes that Segovia admired in Castelnuovo-Tedesco's music. The work also filled a significant empty space in that very little chamber music for guitar and strings was available at this time and once again the Italian composer was, as Offergeld puts it in his sleeve notes, "expanding the accepted notions of the guitar's idiomatic resources."

Fantasia, Op. 145, for guitar and piano, dedicated *Pour Andrés et Paquita,* was not a piece that Segovia became closely associated with in terms of performance. But he seems to have done his duty by the work and ensured that it was published by Schott in 1954, Guitar Archive No. 170, whence it has acquired some limited popularity among later generations of players. It has two movements, *Andantino (Quiet and Dreamy)* and *Vivacissimo (leggero e volante),* described by Corazón Otero as *Nocturne* and *Danza.* Otero also comments that the composition "has, in general, a Spanish character."[6]

The *Fantasia* demonstrates many of Castelnuovo-Tedesco's essential imaginative qualities. The Debussy-like opening, evoking the atmosphere of a dream, broadens out to suggest fiestas, trumpets, drums and crowds. The final section of the two movements employs a theme similar to that used later in *Platero y Yo,* a motif akin to *Primavera,* expressing joy on waking one morning in spring. In the repertoire written for Segovia, Castelnuovo-Tedesco frequently seems to associate his dedicatee with specific thematic material, to be used in modified form in a number of otherwise unrelated works.

On 24 April, 1950, Segovia gave a benefit concert for the New York Society of the Classic Guitar, the proceeds going to the funds of *The Guitar Review.* The audience consisted of 120 subscribers to the periodical and took place in the mansion of S. L. M. Barlow, "composer, musician, and patron of the arts." The program included Milán, Sanz, de Visée, Bach, Sor, Ponce, Castelnuovo-Tedesco, Torroba and Albéniz.[7] The occasion is mentioned by Gregory d'Alessio:

Andrés Segovia was our honorary president. No mere letterhead honorary president. He worked for us, contributing pedagogical pieces to The Guitar Review, *advising us as to the choice of music, even beginning to write his autobiography for first publication in our fledgling magazine. Unfortunately, as his career burgeoned, he picked up the scrivener's pen less and less, and his guitar more and more, carrying it to every corner of the world that eagerly awaited his unique and precious art.*

Busy as he was, though, he found time not only to help with material for The Guitar Review, *but also to keep it from actually going under.*

In 1950, we were facing financial disaster. A big printer's bill was staring us in the face. Our money, much of it made up of donations from our own pockets to get the magazine started, had run out. Sadly, we realized that after only a few years, the promise of an American classic guitar magazine – the only American classic guitar magazine — would end up as a wistful dream.

But Maestro Andrés Segovia came to our rescue with a benefit concert. It netted us a thousand dollars. We were back on our feet, to flourish for many more years.[8]

Thus Segovia saved an important journal of the guitar, which is still flourishing. Its significance in the development of scholarship and critical opinion on all aspects of the guitar, at a time when the instrument was desperately in need of such a forum, cannot be overstated. *The Guitar Review* in itself became part of the guitar's post-war history as well as being a significant vehicle for the propagation of images of Segovia and a confident advocate on his behalf in all respects.

In May, 1950, Segovia's profile was further promoted in Europe by a lengthy article in *The Gramophone* by W. S. Meadmore, who acknowledged "how the possibilities of the instrument in the hands of such a consummate artist as Segovia was a revelation to me." Meadmore had visited the Wigmore Hall, London, in a somewhat sceptical mood to hear a guitar recital, but in the event "remained until the end of the recital, enthralled by every piece which Segovia played."

At this time Segovia appears to be giving his date of birth as 1894. In the details of his early life as related here there is evidence of a somewhat changing scenario for the roles of Uncle Eduardo and Aunt María:

1.) *The Guitar Review (Vol. 1, No. 4, 1947).*
Time went by, and my aunt and uncle, who had brought me up almost since the day of my birth died. The guitar then began seriously to occupy the greater part of my time...
I lived at that time with my grandmother... It was in the Albaicín...
The small legacy left by my aunt and uncle was soon exhausted and my grandmother and I had to separate. She went to Málaga to live near her daughter Gertrudis, a sister in the Order of St. Bernard. I joined my mother in Córdoba.
My character had been moulded by my uncle, Don Eduardo, a noble cultivated and upright gentleman, whose memory I hold in reverence. I found it difficult to accustom myself to my own family's way of living, and to put up with my brother was extremely trying, so after a few months I rented a small room...
(The Guitar and Myself) [9]

2.) *The Gramophone* (May, 1950)
Segovia was born in Linares in 1894. As he told me this he waved his hands deprecatingly... The deprecatory gesture was to emphasis that Segovia had nothing to do with Linares, he had spent the smallest possible time there: as soon as his mother was well enough to travel she had taken Andrés, the rest of the family and the train to Granada. That, said Segovia, was his town, his home. It was there and as a child that the conviction had first come to him that his vocation was music, music and nothing else. There was no tradition of music in his family, he vaguely remembers his mother singing the popular songs of Granada and Andalusia. His father, even if he had wished to, had no time to devote to or care for music. He was a lawyer. It was he who decided Andrés was also to be a lawyer. With this before him he "drudged" Segovia said, "for a time at the High School." At home there was a large family, it was not easy for his mother, on her husband's moderate income, to provide all that was necessary for her growing family. An uncle offered to take care of Andrés and more or less adopt him. The mother parted with her boy with reluctance but also with some relief.[10]

3.) *Segovia: An Autobiography Of The Years 1893-1920* (published 1976)
I was born in Linares, Andalusia.
A few weeks after my birth in 1893, my parents returned to their native city, Jaén...
I spent the first years of my life in Jaén, years which I can no longer remember, but I do recall the sad day when my parents left me in the care of Uncle Eduardo and my Aunt María... I was being taken from the living cradle of my mother's arms and I wept bitterly.[11]

Clearly through these years Segovia was working on a presentable story concerning his early childhood, though the constant revisions in the minutiae of the details remain both fascinating and confusing. It could be suggested that W. S. Meadmore misunderstood the story and managed to get parts of it wrong. Yet his account contains its own kind of coherence.

According to Meadmore's article, Segovia acquired a guitar at the age of ten and studied at the Granada Musical Institute for a time. He gave his first recital at the age of fourteen in Granada before going to Seville, where he gave fifteen concerts in the space of two months. This success was repeated at Madrid, followed a few years later by world tours.

The article traces Segovia's growing awareness of the guitar's literature, though he did not like "the repertory as it then existed" as this mainly consisted of "compositions of illiterates." The icon of Tárrega is also neatly disposed of:

Tárrega had realised the possibilities of the guitar, but he had not been able to develop his theories fully. Segovia remained bewildered that such a beautiful instrument had no serious music created for it. That was the starting point of an ambition that one day he would persuade serious composers to write for it, as in time, he did. Torroba was the first, after him de Falla composed his Homage for Le Tombeau de Debussy *for the guitar: a serious and deeply impressive work. De Falla was followed by Turina, Salazar, Halffter, Roussel, Samazeuilh and Tansman.*[10]

This may have been one of the first hints of an error repeated in musical dictionaries ever after — that Falla composed his only solo guitar work for Segovia. The list of composers is also interesting in its omissions of Manuel Ponce, Mario Castelnuovo-Tedesco, and Heitor Villa-Lobos, while at the same time mysteriously including Adolfo Salazar (1890 -1958) and Ernesto Halffter (1905 -1989).

Meadmore is in clear error elsewhere in the article when he affirms that Miguel Llobet, pupil of Tárrega was "still living." Whether the other errors are due to inaccurate journalism or distortion of the facts by Segovia cannot be resolved. What can be affirmed is that this article certainly raised Segovia's prestige to a new level, and its concentration on the theme of rescuing the guitar from neglect was always foremost in his preoccupations. Segovia might have admired one particular assertion:

...He has created an entirely new technique of guitar playing, and in doing so completely broken away from the tradition of the classical Spanish instrumentalists. He has succeeded in utilising all the contrapuntal resources of the guitar.[10]

(In *Grove's Dictionary of Music and Musicians*, published 1954, a similar comment was made that Segovia "may be said to have created an entirely new technique of guitar playing which broke in many respects with the classical Spanish tradition.")[12]

Between 10 August and 15 September that year, Segovia began a new adventure, the Summer School at L'Accademia Musicale Chigiana, in Siena, Italy. This was something that would resonate in the memory of all who attended the classes and through this context a younger generation of players became the virtual pupils of Segovia. Wilfrid M. Appleby reported the ground rules for attendance at Siena:

Students will be permitted to enrol for the course if they are successful in passing an examination which includes an elementary knowledge of musical theory, the ability to plays scales in all keys, all the studies in the first part of Aguado's Method, a Prelude by Tárrega or Ponce (own choice), Andantino in D minor (Sor), a solo (own choice) by Sor, Giuliani, Llobet, Torroba, Turina or Ponce, etc, and to play at sight an easy study or prelude selected by the examiner.

The guitarists and music-lovers responsible for organising this course are to be congratulated on their enterprise. The result will certainly be a raising of the standard of musicianship in Italy.[13]

Segovia's tour of Britain that year included engagements at Chelsea (2 October), Elgin (27 October), Oxford (2 November) and Whitchurch, near Cardiff, Wales (3 November) as well as two Wigmore Hall, London, recitals on 21 October and 8 November, where the programs were:

SATURDAY, OCTOBER 21ST AT 3 P.M.

Aria con variazioni	G. Frescobaldi
Suite in D major	R. de Visée
Prelude, Allemande,	
Bourrée, Sarabande,	
Gigue, Gavotte,	
Menuet, Courante	
Sonatina	Giuliani
Fantasía	J. Turina
Passacaille	L. Couperin
Siciliana	C. P. E. Bach
Andante and Allegretto	Haydn
Canzonetta	Mendelssohn
Preludio quasi	Castelnuovo-Tedesco
un'improvvisazione	
Ballata Scozzese	
(1st performance. Dedicated	
to Andrés Segovia)	
Tarantella	
Mallorca	Albéniz
Sevilla	

WEDNESDAY, NOVEMBER 8TH AT 7:30 P.M.

Two Gaillardes	Dowland
Three Pieces	Purcell
Aria	Handel
Fuga, Siciliana, Bourrée	J. S. Bach
Prelude and Gigue	S. L. Weiss
Six Études	F. Sor
1 in C, 2 in D, 3 in B, 4 in G, 5 in B minor, 6 in A.	
Allegretto	
*Norteña*J. G. Crespo	
Hommage à Debussy	M. de Falla
Improvisation	C. Pedrell
(Dedicated to Segovia)	
Petite Valse	M. Ponce
(Dedicated to Segovia)	
La Maja de Goya	Granados
Torre Bermeja	Albéniz
Leyenda	

Wilfrid M. Appleby attended the concert given at Oxford, and in a round-up of comments taken from critics, remarked on the inclusion of a *Sonatina* by Giuliani. Presumably, as was his custom, Segovia performed here the first movement of Giuliani's Op. 15, which had been published in Karl Scheit's Universal Edition in 1943:

The inclusion of a Sonatina by Giuliani in Segovia's repertoire was, I believe, an innovation and it was interesting to read what the critics thought of this music. A.F. Leighton Thomas, writing in The Isis *(Oxford), voted it "the most enjoyable item," and searched Grove and three other standard works of reference in vain for information about the composer. Other remarks were: "This demure Sonatina,"*
"Might have been early Beethoven," "In Giuliani's Sonatina a hauntingly bell-like note recurred. "[14]

The critics found praise for "the charming de Visée Suite and especially for *La Maja de Goya,*" though there was a hint of dissatisfaction here and there:

The Suite by Castelnuovo-Tedesco failed to impress some of the critics who thought this composer "capable of better things." All agreed however in praising Segovia's supreme artistry and superb mastery of the guitar.
I should like to add a word of appreciation of Segovia's kindliness and chivalry. The genial manner with which he received students of the guitar and even autograph hunters, after an arduous recital, portrayed a lovable personality. [14]

Perhaps because of adverse criticism Castelnuovo-Tedesco's *Suite* soon seems to have disappeared from Segovia's repertoire, but at least it was tried. Appleby quotes also from C.T. of the Oxford *Mail,* who not only remarked that the *Chaconne* "gained in depth of tone on the low D string what it lost in sostenuto," but commented:

In the polyphonic sections of this and other works the clarity of the parts was breathtaking.[14]

In the report by *The Times* of the second Wigmore Hall recital, the critic was equally enthusiastic:

Segovia — in best form — triumphed in that he made his large audience aware not of the instrument's limitations but of its scope; a Fugue, Sicilienne and Bourrée by Bach could scarcely have been more eloquent, however transcribed.[14]

A final accolade for 1950, was the announcement in December of an international guitar music contest by L'Accademia Musicale Chigiana of Siena, Italy, for a Concertino for Guitar with Chamber Music Ensemble, a Quintet for Guitar with String Quartet, and a composition for Guitar Solo (a Sonata, Suite or Fantasy). A total of 500,000 Italian liras was offered in prizes. With such enlightened patronage, and the promise of performances by Segovia, composers throughout Europe took up their pens. The results in August, 1951, showed that twenty-five compositions were submitted. Hans Haug (1900-1967) of Switzerland won the chamber music award with *Concertino for Guitar* and Alexandre Tansman was awarded the prize for a solo work with *Cavatina.* The judges included Georges Enesco (Chairman), Gaspar Cassadó, and Andrés Segovia, as well as Guido Agosti, Richard Brengola and Angelo Lavaginino.[15]

Also at Siena that year, as if to encourage the development of chamber music for the guitar, Segovia performed Castelnuovo-Tedesco's *Quintet, Op. 143* for guitar and strings. In a letter to the composer, Segovia commented that the work was "listened to with delight by a packed and enthusiastic hall," and he had asked the patron of the Summer School, Count Guido Chigi Saracini, to invite Castelnuovo-Tedesco to lecture the following year. In the letter Segovia names the prizewinners of the competition, including Haug, (whom he had not met) and his friend Tansman, mentioning that the second category of prize, for Quintet for Guitar with String Quartet was declared void. Segovia promised to play the *Quintet, Op. 143,* in London that year and to begin work on the poems of García Lorca.[16]

The latter was a reference to Castelnuovo-Tedesco's large scale work for 1951, *Romancero Gitano, Op. 152,* for guitar and vocal quartet, a setting of various Lorca poems. But the first performance of this work was eventually presented by Siegfried Behrend, several years later and the composition would be published by Bote & Bock of Berlin, not by Schott. Though during the next seventeen years Castelnuovo-Tedesco was to write over forty more works for guitar, many of them substantial in both length and quality, only *Tonadilla on the name of Andrés Segovia, Op. 191,* (1954) and parts of *Platero y Yo, Op. 190,* (1960) entered Segovia's repertoire. The composer somehow departed from Segovia's camp, seeking the allegiance of a multiplicity of other guitarists as dedicatees for his music. The great collaborative adventure with Segovia was subtly waning though without ever being totally extinguished.

Segovia's visit to England in the fall of 1951 provoked a strange little news item:

SEGOVIA IN TROUBLE
Segovia's recital in Sheffield, arranged for October 25th, but cancelled because of the General Election, took place on November 1st. The day before the recital, Segovia's agent telephoned the Sheffield Philharmonic Society and said: "Segovia must have a footstool. It MUST be seven inches high and eight inches wide. He cannot play without a stool."

Unable to beg, borrow or buy a stool of the exact measurement — despite visiting most of the Sheffield furniture shops — K. E. Crickmore, the "Phil" director made an appeal in The Star *to see if a member of the public could help.*

The newspaper, commenting on the matter, said: "Segovia has travelled more widely than any other player to exhibit the capabilities of the guitar. So the "Phil" is wondering: 'Why not a stool of his own?'"

This reminds us of the guitarist who has given some important recitals in London. On one occasion he used a Kelly's "Directory" as a footstool and on another was seated with his left foot on a dilapidated wooden guitar case!

Recitalists should be aware that footstools can be purchased and surely it is not asking too much of them to include such an important accessory in their equipment.[17]

Despite this storm in a tea-cup, Segovia continued on his triumphant way, performing a programme of Milán, Sor, Paganini, Purcell, Handel, Bach, Turina and Albéniz at the Wigmore Hall, London on 31 October, 1951. A few weeks later on 26 November, Julian Bream, aged eighteen, made his debut at the same prestigious hall, (having given his first broadcast of Rodrigo's *Concierto de Aranjuez* on the BBC earlier that year.) On 1 December, Ida Presti, made her first appearance in England at the R. B. A. Galleries in London under the auspices of the Philharmonic Society of Guitarists. The golden age of the guitar recitalist was now truly under way.

30. SEGOVIA AND THE RECORDING REVOLUTION

In January, 1950, Lionel Salter, reviewed Segovia's recording of *Arada* and *Danza* (usually entitled *Fandanguillo*), from *Suite Castellana* by Torroba and *Fandanguillo* by Turina on Columbia LX1248, issued on a 12 inch recording:

Segovia-fans and the still-unconverted alike should flock to hear this record, which contains three attractive pieces played with all this great artist's mastery. The Arada *(which according to Scholes is a ploughing song) is a slow tune with expressive harmonies, and both in this and the melancholy* Fandanguillo *the beauty and variety of tone-colour, the perfection of phrasing and the rhythmic vitality are exemplary. My only reservation about these two admirable sides concerns the distracting squeak of Segovia's hand sliding along the neck, which has been picked up very clearly by the mike.[1]*

Thus in Europe Segovia was capturing the attention of the wider music public and the specialist guitar audience. By the standards of the late twentieth century with its avalanches of recordings and videos, the issue of a few pieces may not seem an extraordinary event. But in 1950 the guitar repertoire was unfamiliar and as recordings slowly emerged they were eagerly anticipated and snapped up by enthusiastic fans.[2]

In March, 1950, Wilfrid M. Appleby wrote about the recording reviewed in *The Gramophone* the previous January:

The second of the new Columbia records by Andrés Segovia (LX1248) is now issued. It is a masterpiece in two senses. First the superb playing of the soloist, and secondly, the perfect recording.

Segovia's playing makes the listener realise that here is a musician who knows exactly what he wishes to express in whatever music he plays.

Torroba's Arada *and* Danza *are based on Spanish folk themes; the former being a ploughing song. Segovia's arrangement of them for the guitar enhances their natural beauty and gives them an atmosphere of idyllic charm.*

On the reverse side is a new interpretation of an old favourite and those who have the H.M.V. record of Turina's Fandanguillo *(which Segovia made in April, 1928) will find it interesting to compare with this new Columbia. This disc has attained a new high level in the art of recording the guitar. Never have I heard such extraordinary clarity and perfection of tone...*

This record demonstrates that the guitar is a suitable instrument for modern recording skill.[3]

In the May issue of *The Gramophone,* Segovia's recording (Columbia LX1275) of *Sonatina Meridional* by Ponce was reviewed. That the recording covered a sonatina and not just "short and detached" works like most guitar pieces, prompted admiring comments including a description of Segovia as the instrument's "completely-equipped sympathetic exponent."[4]

The same recording was reviewed by *Discus* in *B.M.G.* a few months later:

As of right Andrés Segovia takes pride of place this month with two sides on Columbia's LX1275 (12")both of which are occupied by the three movements of Manuel Ponce's Sonatina Meridional. This is the most atmospheric and nationalist of Ponce's guitar sonatas but its first movement in particular is organised on familiar European lines.

The structural lightness and brief development section of this movement justifies the term Sonatina as opposed to Sonata. During the brief development, it seems, to your reviewer, that Segovia could have pointed the antiphonal passages with more tonal variety — but we are in the face of formidable authority.

The second movement — Copla — is a brief song-like passage of great beauty which serves the usual purpose of pieces so titled, viz. to link the more energetic flanking movements.

The quality of the recording is variable and at its best in the opening movement. On the whole it shares the faults of the previous Columbia issues — lack of definition, slight echo, and lack of "top" which results in a "boxy" tone on the upper notes. Segovia compensates, however, freely for these shortcomings and we mention them only in the hope that Columbia Co. will bear them in mind when next Segovia visits them. [5]

Thus an effort was being made to evaluate the contemporary recording technology as well as Segovia's actual playing. Listeners today would of course detect even more flaws in the recording quality. But a new era was beginning as gramophone enthusiasts began to appreciate not only the sound of Segovia's playing but also the means by which his art was brought to them.

In July, 1950, *The Gramophone* announced the arrival in Britain of the "Long-Playing Record," an event which was to have a revolutionary effect on all areas of music technology and to boost the career and reputation of Segovia. As with all such inventions displacing previous developments, the LP was greeted with satisfaction and a few reservations:

Well, we have had to wait what some people thought was an unreasonably long time for the Long-Playing Record in this country, but at last here it is, and it is really gratifying to be able to affirm with conviction that it is worth waiting for. To Decca belongs the honour of being the first to issue it in this country, and if future records are as well chosen and as well made as the first few I have heard, and of course they will be, then without doubt a new era for the gramophone has opened.

This does not mean that the old 78's will at once become obsolete, though I suppose we may expect a slow but progressive decrease in the number of 78's as the L.P. repertory increases, for I assume that the necessary mechanical equipment to supplement existing gramophones will become available. [6]

Another advance mentioned in the same editorial, was the release of the "first electrically recorded disc... a 10-inch plum-coloured H.M.V. disc by Paul Whiteman and his band playing *Ah-Ha* on one side and *Just a Little Drink* on the other." With the new LP technology came recordings with as much as seventeen and a half minutes of music on one side of a 12 inch disc, though usually the preferred amount was about fifteen minutes at this point of development. A 10-inch recording could range comfortably on either side of ten minutes.

The first long-playing guitar record reviewed in *The Gramophone* was an anthology of Spanish pieces recorded by Felix Argüelles, in an album published by the Spanish Music Center, 1291, 6th Avenue, New York, 19. This received a short sharp rebuff from Lionel Salter:

To put over four LP sides of guitar music would require either far less empty and repetitious stuff than most of this, or the technical and interpretative mastery of a Segovia. Mr. Argüelles is clearly no Segovia: he is distressingly careless about damping (evidence of a faulty harmonic sense) and wrong notes and chords (e.g. the Alard Study); and some of his rapid passage-work (as in the Tárrega Alborada) is down-right bad. He is, however, an erratic player, and is considerably better in the Albéniz Leyenda and the Orlandi Nocturno. The Bach Courante is played without much conviction and its lack of ease reminded me of Dr. Johnson's dictum about performing dogs. [7]

(Dr. Johnson's dictum is in Boswell's *Life of Johnson* under 31 July, 1763: "Sir, a woman's preaching is like a dog's walking on his hind legs. It is not done well: but you are surprised to find it done at all."[8] This quote tends to find its way over the years into a variety of guitar critiques and is not always applied to indifferent performances.)

Ronald Purcell's *Andrés Segovia: Contributions to the World of Guitar* lists four LP's which featured Segovia, appearing in the USA between 1947 and 1950. (Segovia discography, even at this early stage, is something of a labyrinth with numerous duplications). The four LP's were:

1) *Magic Strings, A Treasury of Immortal Performances, RCA LCT 1002.* A 1950 LP compilation reprint which included other artists, Segovia being represented by Alard's *Study in A.*
2) Decca A384 (also DU 707, unbreakable, issued 1949, as well as under DL 8022). The compositions are *Granada, Torre Bermeja, Sevilla* (Albéniz) and *Tonadilla (La Maja de Goya), Danzas españolas Nos 5 & 10* (Granados).
3) Decca A596, including tracks used on 45 rpm's. The program consists of *Sonata* (Scarlatti), *Romanza* (Paganini, arr. Ponce), *Minuet* (Rameau), *Three Pieces* (Purcell), *Galliard* (Dowland), *Gavotte, Sarabande* ("Scarlatti"/Ponce) and *Minuet & Andante* (Haydn).

4) Decca DL8022, *Andrés Segovia — Guitar Solos.* This collection, later re-issued on MCA 24.018 in 1969, offered the following:

Side A: *Granada (Serenata)* (Albéniz), *Tonadilla, Danza española No. 10* (Granados), *Sevilla* (Albéniz).

Side B: *Tres Pavanas* (Milán), *Canzone e Saltarello* (Anon), *Dos Canciones Catalanas (El Noi de la Mare, El Testamento de Amelia)* (arr. Llobet), *Danza Mora y Minuetto* (Tárrega), *Entrada y Giga, Bourrée y Minuetto* (Robert de Visée).

These early LP's are essentially compilations from 78 rpm's and contained works which would later be re-recorded for the new format in their own right. The process of re-issuing old material could only be extended so far at this time without running into qualitative difficulties. Record companies, in a highly competitive and expanding market, would ultimately be eager to forge ahead, explicitly demonstrating in their products the distinctions between pre-war and post-war technology. At first the long playing record, a novelty to the public, was often subjected to the compilation syndrome, offering old wine in new bottles.

Thus when, for example, Segovia's recording of Castelnuovo-Tedesco's *Concerto for Guitar and Orchestra* was released in Europe (reviewed in *The Gramophone* in August, 1951), it was issued on 78 rpm, 12 inch records, the long-playing revolution being rather too late for Columbia to bring out this album in the new technology.

This was remedied in December, 1952 with the release of a long-playing record on Columbia 33CX1020 (mentioned in *The Gramophone*, December 1952, with a reprint of the review of August, 1951). On Side One were the three movements of the *Concerto* (originally from LX1404-6) and on Side Two, were *Sonatina Meridional* (Ponce) (from LX1275), *Arada, Fandanguillo* (Torroba) (from LX1248) and *Fandanguillo* (Turina) (also from LX1248). Although Segovia's first long-playing album was a compilation of masters originally put out on 78's, his joy on receiving a disc where a whole Concerto could be put on one side can surely be imagined.

In the USA the LP phenomenon was launched earlier than in Europe. In *The Guitar Review, No. 13* (1952) recordings by Rey de la Torre were advertised by the Spanish Music Center, New York. Their titles were *The Music of Francisco Tárrega* (SMC Pro-Arte 516) and *The Music of Fernando Sor* (SMC517), priced at three dollars each and "recorded on high fidelity unbreakable Vinylite plastic material."

The Guitar Review, No. 14 (also 1952) carried a whole page advertisement by the same company of "Long Playing (33rpm) GUITAR RECORDINGS featuring the finest music ever recorded by world-famous concert guitarists in high fidelity unbreakable records." These included another album (AL76, priced at $5.72) by Rey de la Torre, entitled *Grand Sonata, Op. 22 by Fernando Sor* with further pieces from the Sor repertoire including the inevitable *Op. 9, Variations on a Theme of Mozart.* Other guitarists with advertised LP's were Felix Argüelles (Two LP's in the *Spanish Composers Series, Vols. 1 & 2,* SMC512), Carlos Montoya *(Flamenco Inventions,* SMC 512), Vicente Gomez *(Vicente Gomez Plays a Guitar Recital,* DL8017) and Julio Martínez Oyanguren *(Latin-American Folk Music,* DL8018).

On the same page of advertisement were five recordings in the series *An Andrés Segovia Recital.* In a lecture at the University of Southern California, on the Segovia Masterclass Course in 1986, Ronald Purcell spoke of his researches in the archives of the Decca Company relating to the recording sessions for the albums. Tracks recorded were logged on file cards according to the number of takes for each. In 1949 Segovia had recorded over fifty tracks and file cards were still available to check the titles laid down during these sessions. Ronald Purcell reported that there was no evidence of any second takes being recorded by Segovia, whose method of recording was a preference for playing the entire piece from beginning to end rather than dropping in corrected notes and phrases. In these instances apparently no re-takes were considered necessary at any time, a remarkable achievement.

A further twist in technological development during these years was the introduction of HMV's new 45 rpm disc, following several years of research by RCA Victor in the USA. The reason for this speed of disc was that for technical reasons "a higher speed disc can be made to give reasonable quality on a smaller diameter than is possible at 33." If the 45 rpm discs had been released a few months earlier, the majority of record producers might well have followed RCA's lead instead of American Columbia's and concentrated on the higher speed for all LP's.[9]

Several Segovia recordings were issued on 45 rpm discs and these today are collectors' items. They included the following:

Decca ED 3503 Vol. 1.   *Sonata* (D. Scarlatti), *Romanza* (Paganini)
                          Spanish Dance No. 5 (Granados), *Sevilla* (Albéniz)
Decca ED 3510 Vol. 2.   *Gavotte, Sarabande* ("Alessandro Scarlatti" by Ponce)
                          Spanish Dance No. 10 (Granados), *Granada* (Albéniz)

| Deutsche Grammophon | *Recuerdos de la Alhambra, Marieta, Mazurca* (Tárrega) |
| 30 360 EPL | *Capricho Arabe, María, Gavota,* (Tárrega) |

Following the long-playing version of Castelnuovo-Tedesco's *Guitar Concerto, The Gramophone* next reviewed, in March 1953, *An Andrés Segovia Recital* (Brunswick AXTL 1005) (12 inch selling at thirty-nine shillings and sixpence, or about five dollars at that time). The program was *Romanesca* (Mudarra), *Prelude, Ballet and Gigue* ("Weiss," alias Ponce), *Prelude and Gavotte* (Bach), *Allegro* (Sor), *Song without Words, Op. 19, No. 6* (Mendelssohn), *Minuet* (Schubert), *Sonatina* (Moreno Torroba), and *Leyenda* (Albéniz). *The Gramophone* endorsed the recording wholeheartedly:

This is an enjoyable recital, extremely well recorded. All the music comes through and very little of the clicking, whirring or ghostly glissandi *that have marred some earlier recordings of the guitar...*

...Segovia plays all this music with consummate skill. Wide-ranging tone-colour and delicately controlled phrasing ensure that one does not tire of the sound of the instrument, and a better cross-section of the guitar repertory could hardly be devised. [10]

The significance of this program was enormous in historical perspective. For the first time Segovia could offer a total recital on a recording which followed the profile of a normal concert, starting with the sixteenth century and progressing through the ages, ending with Albéniz. This was also his first complete recording of Moreno Torroba's *Sonatina* (to be recorded by a multiplicity of players at least thirty times between 1952 and 1995), and of Segovia's transcription, completed many years before (according to his autobiography), of Albéniz's *Leyenda*. [11]

The Gramophone, in its review, observed how Segovia had moved from EMI to Brunswick (a branch of the Decca Recording Company), along with the great violinist, Heifetz. Segovia "at first an HMV performer, but latterly established on Columbia," was now represented on Brunswick by "one of the four recitals he has recorded for American Decca." [10]

The sleeve notes on the LP reinforce the new post-war images of Segovia. They mention how "as a result of the innumerable recitals of serious music given by Andrés Segovia, the guitar has attained new and prominent stature in the concert world," citing no guitarist before Segovia later than Sor. Thus the many concerts by early 20th century contemporaries which provided Segovia with a framework and precedents are ignored as if they never existed, an assumption which both guitarists and public henceforth largely accepted quite uncritically. The notes also emphasise that the "phenomenal technique at his command is all the more remarkable in view of the fact that he was entirely self-taught." In the post-war period Segovia wished to acknowledge artistic debts to no person but himself.

The work of scholars such as Pujol was also neatly obscured here by the statement that Segovia not only created his own technique, "but he further extended his preoccupation with his instrument into a thorough and painstaking musicological exploration of the art, history and literature of the guitar":

From the works of the renowned vihuelistas *such as Milán, Alonso de Mudarra, Gaspar Sanz, and others, Segovia has gone on to examine the various periods of English, Italian, French and German music and has rediscovered many neglected masterpieces.*

That these comments appear just a few years after the publication of Emilio Pujol's monumental editions of the complete works of Luys de Narváez and Mudarra indicates that a certain distortion of historical perspective is present here. From sleeve notes of this era one cannot always expect a great deal of enlightenment but here a definite process of claiming territory is signalled and guitar history is being simplified.

In a brief biographical note Segovia's debut in Granada, "his first public appearance as a serious artist," is said to have taken place when he was fourteen years old. In a book many years later Segovia wrote himself that he was "sixteen years old," when "I gave my first concert, pushed on to the stage by my kind friends in the Centro Artístico of Granada." [12] (But the year of his birth is given correctly as 1893.) These notes were to be particularly influential as they are repeated, either in total or in part, on various recordings during the 1950's, and for many people provided their first introduction to Segovia's art. It was this kind of writing which helped to promote Segovia's post-war image at the same time as it deliberately diminished the potency of the guitar traditions by which he was nourished in his early career.

In September, 1953, *The Gramophone* came to the second solo LP in the series, *An Andrés Segovia Recital* (Brunswick, AXTL 1005) now being followed by *An Andrés Segovia Concert* (Brunswick, AXTL 1010), endowed with the same introductory sleeve notes. The program was as follows:

Fantasía	(Milán)
Suite	(de Visée)
Prelude - Allemande -	
Bourrée - Sarabande -	
Gavotte - Gigue	
Variations on a Theme	(Sor)
by Mozart, Op. 9	
Allegretto grazioso	(Handel)
Gavotte	(Handel)
Bourrée	(Bach)
Courante	(Bach)
Sonata	(Giuliani)
Homenaje, "Pour le	(Falla)
Tombeau de Debussy"	
Étude No. 7	(Villa-Lobos)

The Gramophone review praised the recording quality as "full, clear and beautifully surfaced," and described the record as "wholly enchanting."[13] In Bach and Handel there was a slight reservation that "the changes of tone-colour that can be so ravishing don't seem here always to occur at the right moment." With regard to Falla's music, (that "moving memorial to Debussy," which "shows off all these colour changes ideally,") the critic refers to the "less colourful but perhaps more elegiac performance by Albert Harris," available in the Columbia History of Music series (COL. DB1789).

Suite by Robert de Visée is actually the *Suite in D minor,* to be recorded numerous times in the future in more or less the same arrangement. With a few strategic alterations here and there, Segovia seems to follow the contours of Karl Scheit's 1944 arrangement (Universal Editions, No. 11322). Here the editor commented in his Preface that, "As far as I can ascertain the Suite is published herewith for the first time with the original print as its basis." This is rather provocative if only because Scheit's version had some distinct similarities of voicing with Emilio Pujol's 1928 transcription (Max Eschig, Nos 1007, 1007 bis), who also must have consulted the "original print." On the recording Segovia offers no indication that he might have consulted other editions, the implication being in the sleeve notes that this is his own transcription, presumably from the original manuscript. From any available evidence it seems most improbable that Segovia ever consulted many sixteenth or seventeenth century tablatures in their raw authenticity, and it is likely that he preferred to amend existing publications for performance purposes. Of all the pieces on this recording, the Renaissance and Baroque music have worn least well, the Early Music Movement having decisively changed public concepts of how this music should be performed. But Segovia's rendering of the *Suite in D minor* would prove remarkably influential and this became, in Pujol/Scheit orientated arrangements, a favorite in concerts and on record for many years.

The critic, like much of the public at this time, was deceived by the recording to conclude that Giuliani had written "an effective one-movement Sonata, of classical keyboard derivation." It would be several years before Giuliani's music could be properly rehabilitated, but before then a number of guitarists would implicitly confirm this perception by only recording or playing in concert just one part of Giuliani's Op. 15, originally in three movements.

An Andrés Segovia Programme (Brunswick AXTL 1060) was the next in the series, and duly reviewed in *The Gramophone* in November, 1954. The program was as follows:

Side No. 1

Pavana	(Luis Milán)
Sarabande, Minuet	(G. F. Handel)
Ballet Music from "Orfeo"	(C. W. Gluck)
Sicilienne, Bourrée	(J. S. Bach)

Side No. 2

Minuet	(Fernando Sor)
Prelude in A major	(Frédéric Chopin)
Romanza	(Robert Schumann)
Andantino variato	(Paganini - Ponce)
Waltz in B flat	(Johannes Brahms)
Madroños	(F. M. Torroba)
Prelude	(Heitor Villa-Lobos)

The Gramophone critic commented that "the whole recital" was "both played and recorded with utter perfection." But there was a complaint about the "long succession of tiny pieces," and a plea that if a Sor *Minuet* is acceptable, "surely its parent *Sonata* would be?"[14] But the inexorable build-up and stockpiling of Segovia's repertoire was continuing, and to a fundamental critical acclaim despite the obvious reservations.

Next in line was *An Evening with Segovia* (Brunswick, AXTL 1070/DL 9633) reviewed in *The Gramophone* in May, 1955. On this recording it seemed that the critical warning about a string of tiny pieces had been taken to heart. Instead of thirteen small separate compositions, spaced in chronology but otherwise not apparently linked, Segovia now played some larger works, thus leaving far behind the concept of the LP being merely a collection of items as if selected from the old 78 rpm's. In other words the medium was now being used in the guitar sphere (as with other music), to allow expansion and space, revelation through compositional structure, and a sense of recital shape. Thus the program comprised:

Side 1

Aria and Corrente	(Frescobaldi — transcr. Segovia)
Capriccio Diabolico	(Castelnuovo-Tedesco)
Six Preludes	(Ponce)

Side 2

Minuet	(Rameau — transcr. Segovia)
Cavatina - Suite	(Tansman)
(Preludio - Sarabande -	
Scherzino - Barcarola -	
Danza pomposa)	
Nocturno	(Torroba)

Though the policy behind the recording may have changed, the critic remained unconvinced, stating that he couldn't help feeling "that the musical interest of this disc is less than that of some other Segovias," and that the "twelve-inch omnibus is carrying too many passengers."[15] Certainly in terms of the guitar repertoire in 1955, the only obvious "passenger" on this recording might be the tiny *Minuet* of Rameau. Segovia's transcription of *La Frescobalda Variations*, included here under the title of *Aria*, was to prove a most durable runner over the next forty years and a wonderfully imaginative addition to the recital repertoire. The other pieces were also front-line compositions written by Segovia's distinguished and sympathetic friends, and were destined for many excursions in concert hall and recording studio.

Two months later *The Gramophone* reviewed another Segovia record of enormous historical importance for the instrument, *Andrés Segovia, Guitar* (Brunswick, AXTL 1069), though it was variously released with other titles:

Bach: *Prelude; Gavotte; Chaconne; Loure*
Sor: *Minuet in C; Andantino; Minuet in D*
Mendelssohn: *Canzonetta*
Villa-Lobos: *Prelude*
Rodrigo: *Sarabanda*

In July, 1955, the critic of *The Gramophone* provided a mixed bag of approval. It was suggested that "not even Segovia's skill" could make the *Chaconne* "fully effective" and needed "a firmer tread to sustain interest over its long span." Rodrigo's *Sarabanda* was considered to be "of curiously thin consequence" especially when compared with the slow movement of his *Concierto de Aranjuez,* released only a few months previously by London International. The most effective piece on the disc, "instrumentally," was the *Prelude* by Villa-Lobos.[16]

Narciso Yepes's recording of Rodrigo's *Concierto de Aranjuez,* (London International TW91019, with the Madrid Chamber Orchestra, conducted by Ataulfo Argenta, with Falla's *Nights in the Gardens of Spain,* (soloist, Gonzalo Soriano), had been reviewed by *The Gramophone* in March, 1955, with an enthusiasm which might have slightly disturbed Segovia's peace of mind:

I must tell you that Rodrigo's Guitar Concerto is a charmer. The outside movements are witty, especially in the orchestra, and the middle movement is most evocative. The problem of balance between orchestra and guitar is brilliantly solved. My only disappointment is that the last movement is just too slight to be an adequate Finale - I felt let down by it. I hope any reader who buys this record will not feel let down after reading what I have written.[17]

Thus in 1955 Segovia could safely assume an authoritative supremacy in the quality and quantity of his solo recordings. But other elements were entering the arena and Segovia's was clearly not the only voice of the guitar reverberating round the world by means of the new technology. A few alternative possibilities were making themselves heard and would continue to do so in increasingly significant terms. Yet the recordings listed in this chapter surely can be perceived as the immortal part of a golden age for Segovia's art, released when he was at the top of his powers and with much experience of music and life behind him. They represent in both virtuosity and technology, a considerable advance on the pre-war recordings, played on nylon strings, and exemplifying an elevation of the guitar which would be a great inspiration to younger players. Historically these recordings throughout the 1950's may in themselves signify the climax of Segovia's contribution to twentieth century music and the complete fulfilment of his characteristic repertoire.

31. 1952-1954

In June, 1952, after an absence of some sixteen years, Segovia returned to Spain to play in the Festival of Music and Dance held in Granada. The concert, performed in the Teatro Isabel la Católica, was brought about by the efforts of his childhood friend, Antonio Gallego Burín,[1] described in Segovia's autobiography as "the most loyal, fine and intelligent," of his classmates at the local Instituto, where they enrolled at about the age of ten to be provided with a formal education.[2] From 1952 onwards Segovia played occasional concerts at selected venues in Spain, mainly for charity, though he did not undertake major extended tours of the Iberian peninsula.

It was during 1952 and 1953 that American foreign policy, whether under Truman or Eisenhower (who succeeded to the Presidency after elections in November, 1952), was intent on closer ties with Franco's regime, including the establishment of military bases and port facilities in Spain. The Defence Pact was eventually signed on 26 September, 1953, bringing $226 million in military and technological support from the United States.[3] Thus in the period that Segovia returned home, Spain, despite Franco's continuing repressive dictatorship, was in the process of becoming part of the western defences in the age of the Cold War, and the political *rapprochement* between the USA and Francoist Spain was secure.

The cultural dilemma of Spain in the post-war years has merited much discussion, a considerable amount of it focused on artists such as Casals, who throughout his life set his face against all that Franco represented. One of Casal's biographers saw the problem in these terms:

The Nationalist victory deprived Spain of an entire generation of writers, musicians and artists, and the country declined, as a result, into a cultural wasteland. Franco himself was astoundingly uncultured. He had no appreciation of literature or classical music — the zarzuela *being the upper level of his musical taste — and could dismiss their exponents without any sense of loss. Within Spain Casals had always been the property of a cultured elite: Bach was not a mass preoccupation. After a decade of exile, he like many others, had been largely forgotten, except by a Catalan few. Spain was deprived of a quality musical culture for almost forty years.*[4]

John Hooper expressed a similar message:

The scars left by the civil war healed at different rates according to where they were inflicted. The economy regained its pre-war level in 1954. Politics returned to their normal course in 1977. But the arts have still not recovered from the Civil War and until quite recently there was a widespread feeling that they never would.

In 1936 Spain was what you might call a creative superpower. She had given the world three of its greatest contemporary painters - Picasso, Dali and Miró. She could lay claim to one of the finest established composers — Manuel de Falla — and to several of the more promising younger ones like the Catalan, Roberto Gerhard, and the Valencian, Joaquín Rodrigo. Her fledgling film industry had already managed to produce a director of the calibre of Buñuel. In literature the leading figures of the celebrated "Generation of '98"... were all still alive, able to advise and influence younger writers...

The vast majority of Spain's artists and intellectuals took the side of the Republic against the nationalists. Some, like Lorca, were killed. Of those who survived, most fled into exile. Once the fiercest period of retribution was over they faced a grim choice. Returning home offered an opportunity to re-establish contact with the cultural traditions of their homeland, but it also meant handing the regime a propaganda victory and resigning themselves to a lifetime of censorship. Staying abroad meant losing touch with their roots, but it did guarantee them their creative integrity. Seen as a set of individual decisions it was understandable. Seen as a development in the nation's cultural history it was catastrophic. Most of what the exiles wrote, painted, sculpted and filmed went completely unnoticed within Spain until the sixties when Fraga at the Ministry of Information and Tourism eased the restrictions on imported works.[5]

What may be depressing to some is how the name of Segovia is rarely, if ever, included in this kind of discussion. His art being conservative and traditional would never need censorship and advanced no avant-garde concepts. But on the basis of the above arguments, Segovia's return to Spain was a positive advantage for Spanish culture. While the country was wounded, repressed, bereft of its former creativity, Segovia's guitar provided a focus of national pride and a reminder of the Spanish capacity for international artistic greatness.

Many Spaniards retain a reverence for the guitar, their national instrument, and in the grim, lean years, the return of Segovia to his roots surely provided a degree of hope and re-birth. Segovia's reticence since he left Spain, his determination to talk in public only about music, and his total identification with the cause of the composers he favored, as well as his world status as a recitalist, now became unusual strengths. At this point Segovia's presence in Spain was an enormous benefit for the cultural life of the country. In return he experienced the joy of performing for the first time for many years to his own people. Thus he returned not as an overt supporter of Franco, intent on making a political point, but as an artist wishing to live in the land of his birth, whose language was that of music only. For Segovia it was a symbolic return both to the city of Granada and to the source of his true Spanish identity.

A few months later, back in New York, Segovia wrote his famous Preface to the set of *Douze Études* by Heitor Villa-Lobos. Though composed in 1929, it was only in the 1950's that these pieces, so central to the advanced development of technique on the guitar, were finally prepared for publication.

Segovia described the studies as consisting of "formulas of surprising efficiency for the technical development of each hand," which have, at the same time, "a disinterested musical beauty." The studies brought to mind masters such as Scarlatti and Chopin of those few in the history of instrumental music who "achieved their didactic aims without a trace of aridness or monotony." Segovia admired their "nobility, ingenuity, the charm, and the poetic emotion that emanates from them." [6]

On the technical side Segovia mentioned that he would not wish to "change any of the fingering which Villa-Lobos has indicated for the execution of his pieces." This comment may seem enigmatic for looking through the published text of the *Douze Études* the reader will find comparatively little in the way of fingering. However, a copy of the composer's hand-written manuscript of the Studies, dated variously 1947 and 1948, shows a considerable amount of fingering which did not survive to the final printing. It seems very possible that Segovia was using one of these manuscripts as a basis for the Preface, though there is no explanation why the composer's editing was not ultimately carried over to the published edition.

Until quite recently it was usually assumed that the *Douze Études* were published in 1953. But an article by Matanya Ophee, the American publisher and scholar, establishes that this publication date was erroneously based on the dating of Segovia's Preface to the edition and on the 1953 copyright date of *Étude No. 1*. On a first edition copy of the Studies which is in the possession of Ophee, at the bottom of the last page, is the note: "Paris, Imp. MOUNOT Janv. 1957."[7] This delay in the publication probably accounts for the relatively slow absorption within the repertoire of these Studies. Though Segovia, in possession of the manuscript, recorded his chosen few in the 1950's, further recordings by other artists were slow in coming. One of the first was Laurindo Almeida's interpretations of *Studies Nos 11 & 5* (along with *Preludes Nos 4 & 2*) on *Guitar Music of Latin America* (Capitol, P8321), undated but released about 1958.

Segovia's triumphant progress through the 1950's, in terms of an ever widening series of recital engagements and the release of more and more recordings, was severely threatened later in 1953 by a serious problem with his eyes. This was reported in *B.M.G.*:

Late in July, Andrés Segovia entered a Madrid hospital in danger of losing his sight. Both his eyes were affected. We hear that he was operated on to rectify a displacement of the retina of the right eye — an operation the House Surgeon told us was one of the most delicate in eye surgery.

This major operation on the fine network of the optic nerves is such that results cannot be assessed until some weeks have passed — but as we go to press we learn that Segovia is on the road to recovery, the bandages being removed on August 7.

His first public recital after the operation is scheduled for October 1 in Europe.[8]

It was probably during this time that Segovia composed his poignant *Estudio sin luz* (*Study without Light*), published by Schott in 1954, as G.A. No. 179. In this piece Segovia's compositional abilities reached new heights. The key of B minor sets the mood for a plaintive little melody over arpeggiated chords. The middle section of the piece, with an adroit use of pedal notes, modulates enharmonically into a *legero e con grazia* section and passing momentarily through unusual keys before returning, once more by means of a Sor-like pedal note, to its home tonality. It remains a remarkable miniature, quite distinct from other compositions by Segovia, and, in its urgent intensity, never to be repeated.

Because of the eye operation, Segovia was unable to attend the Summer School at Siena and Emilio Pujol was recommended to take the class instead.[9] John Williams and Alirio Diaz both attended the Course that year, studying with Pujol.

Despite the setback, Segovia was soon on the road again, being fit enough to undertake strenuous engagements in England that fall. On 25 October, 1953, he performed Castelnuovo-Tedesco's *Concerto for Guitar and Orchestra* at the Town Hall, Birmingham, with the City of Birmingham Symphony Orchestra, under the conductor, Harold Gray. He also played his usual selection of solos including *Prélude et Loure* (J. S. Bach), *Menuet* (Rameau), *Tonadilla* (Granados), and *Leyenda* (Albéniz). On 28 and 29 October, Segovia played the same programme at the Free Trade Hall Manchester, with the Hallé Orchestra under Sir John Barbirolli.

On 10 November, 1953, Segovia played a solo recital in the cavernous Royal Festival Hall, London, a venue he was to continue to use for many years as the climactic point of his British tours in the fall. The program was as follows:

I

Aria con Variazioni	Frescobaldi (1583-1643)
Suite in A (for lute)	S. L. Weiss (1686-1750)
Prelude - Ballet -	
Sarabande - Gigue	
Andante et Allegretto	Sor (1778-1839)

II

Prelude et Loure	J. S. Bach (1685-1750)
Sonata	D. Scarlatti (1685-1757)
Allegretto - Menuet	Rameau (1683-1764)
Canzonetta	F. Mendelssohn (1809-1847)

III

Capriccio	M. Castelnuovo-Tedesco (b.1895)
(Homage to Paganini)	
(dedicated to Segovia)	
La Maja de Goya	Granados (1867-1916)
Mallorca - Torre Bermeja	I. Albéniz (1860-1909)

Guitar News, published in Cheltenham, England, by Wilfrid M. Appleby, reported that "the masterly performance" lasted nearly two hours and the program was repeated at the Winter Gardens, Bournemouth, on the south coast, on 12 November.[10] From England Segovia proceeded to the Salle Gaveau, Paris, where he gave a recital to a capacity audience of 2,000 people on 19 December, playing Bach's *Chaconne* and Tansman's *Cavatina,* as well as music by Couperin, Rameau, Albéniz and Granados.[11]

Information had circulated earlier in the year that Segovia's engagements with orchestras would include *Concerto for Guitar and Orchestra* by Heitor Villa-Lobos. In December, B.M.G. printed the following note:

Happily recovered from his major eye operation in Madrid earlier this year, Andrés Segovia returned to this country in October to fulfil the many engagements scheduled for him.

Because of his operations and subsequent convalescence, Segovia was unable to include the concerto by Villa-Lobos in his programmes. In its place the maestro performed the concerto by Castelnuovo-Tedesco.[12]

Behind these simple statements lie many complexities. *Concerto for Guitar* was completed by Villa-Lobos in 1951, yet by the end of 1953 it had still not been premiered. It would eventually be given its first performance in 1956. The hiatus between composition and realization in public is explained to some extent by Simon Wright:

After Villa-Lobos's long association with Segovia, it is not surprising that the Spaniard eventually commissioned a concerto. Villa-Lobos responded in 1951 with a Fantasía concertante, which disappointed the guitarist because it contained no cadenza. Segovia refused to play the work for several years, his agitation coming to a head when he heard Villa-Lobos's Harp Concerto, complete with cadenza. Villa-Lobos was persuaded that he had no option but to provide a cadenza (a separate unit between second and third movements), and re-title his work 'Concerto.' The delighted Segovia gave the work's premiere on 6 February 1956 in Houston under the baton of the composer. Traces of this genesis can be seen in the fact that the cadenza is published even today as an 'insert' in Eschig's printed score. It is difficult, however, to imagine the work without it.[13]

Relationships in 1953/1954 between guitarist and composer appear however to have been congenial because Villa-Lobos attended a recital by Segovia in New York on 7 March, 1954, when three of his solos were performed. But it seems likely that Segovia's failure to play the Concerto in 1953 was not entirely due to his medical problems and that, not being entirely satisfied, he preferred procrastination.

The *Concerto for Harp and Orchestra* was written in 1953,[14] and Nicanor Zabaleta, the dedicatee, and a close friend of Segovia, could well have informed the guitarist of this *Concerto's* content during the year. Segovia's instinct that a cadenza was essential seems in retrospect to be absolutely right, and the postponement of the premiere, though frustrating to the composer, served in the end to provide a more coherent and exciting structure.

In the early months of 1954 Segovia celebrated his 61st birthday with his customary tour of the United States. The itinerary covered thousands of miles and many states:

January: 23, Independence, MO, 24, Kansas City, 29, Boulder, CO, 31, New York (Television, Toast of the Town program). February: 1, Rapid City, SD, 6, Boston, MA, 9, Meridian, MS, 11, Louisville, KY, 12, Nashville, TN, 17, Lexington, VA., 20, New York (Town Hall), 23, Racine, WI., 25, Houston, TX. March: 1, London, Canada, 7, New York (Town Hall), 10, Pittsburg, PA, 13, Williamsburg, VA, 16, Sarasota, FL, 18, Midland, MI, 21, Chicago, IL, 23, San Francisco, CA, 25, Watsonville, CA, 27, Arlington, WV, 29., Los Angeles, CA, 31, Victoria, Canada, April: 3, Vancouver, Canada, 4, Seattle, WA.[15]

As *Guitar News* commented, "The great guitarist must be very fit to stand up to all this travelling and playing." As the years to come would reveal, not only was Segovia gifted with a robust constitution, but he delighted in his life on the road as a touring artist. For him, after so many years, this was his natural and normal existence. One of Segovia's favourite, oft-repeated comments was, "Like the poet, I can say, 'I have felt the roundness of the world beneath my feet.'"[16]

Though Segovia was clearly on the summit of Parnassus, there is evidence that his predominance was not always clearly understood by those who wrote the musical history books. In 1954's Fifth Edition of *Grove's Dictionary of Music and Musicians* he received the following entry:

Segovia, Andrés *(b. Linares, 17 Feb. 1893).*
Spanish guitarist. In his youth he came under the influence of Manuel de Falla and those other Spanish composers who at the beginning of the 20th century were working to enlarge and make more universal the somewhat limited and local idiom of Spanish music. Segovia gave his first concert at Granada in 1909 and a few years later started on a series of tours which have led him all over the world. He has proved conclusively that the guitar has its place as a solo concert instrument and achieves on it an intensity of expression and depth in which can be seen clearly that impressionistic influence which he encountered in his youth. He may be said to have created an entirely new technique of guitar playing which broke in many respects with the classical Spanish tradition. Many contemporary composers have written works for Segovia — there is even a Concerto with small orchestra by Castelnuovo-Tedesco — and he has also discovered or edited for his own purposes works by great composers of the past. S.K.[17]

Segovia's entry in the Dictionary is twenty-four lines long. At the time of publication he was 61 years old and the great man of the concert platform with a multiplicity of works dedicated to him, most of which had been edited and published in his own series, and he had made many recordings, distributed world-wide. In comparison, Julian Bream, then aged 21, and the rising star of both lute and guitar, receives an entry twenty-two lines long. Emilio Pujol, however, receives the longest entry, no less than sixty-five lines, also written by S. K. where he is described not just as "Spanish guitarist," but as "Spanish guitar and vihuela player, musicologist and composer." Most remarkably, Pujol's playing is given more detailed attention:

(Pujol) studied at Barcelona, where in 1902 he became a pupil of the famous guitar virtuoso Francisco Tárrega. He still further perfected Tárrega's method of playing the guitar, paying special attention to the problems of tone-production. While the technique of so many guitarists is based mainly upon the method of plucking the strings with the fingernails, the Pujol school uses this for special colouring effects only, preferring the strings to be plucked normally by the flesh of the fingers, which makes the tone much more beautiful and increases the expressiveness of the instrument. Thanks to Pujol's teaching the quality of tone-production on the guitar, considered as a concert instrument for classical music has been considerably improved. He has given recitals in Austria, Belgium, Czechoslovakia, England, France, Germany, Holland, Portugal, Spain and South America.[18]

That Pujol's playing technique "makes the tone much more beautiful" (than presumably the tone of Segovia) may have surprised many at the time. The entry goes on to catalogue Pujol's scholarly achievements in some detail. A comparison between the respective entries of Segovia and Pujol in 1954 might logically lead to the conclusion that Pujol was the more historically significant player of the two contenders, three times the space being allocated to the recitation of his achievements, praise for his playing certainly being more fulsome.

Though Segovia must have been disappointed by the subtle selling short of his own life's work in such an authoritative dictionary of music, the episode reveals the nature of the struggle he was engaged in for much of his life. Some undoubtedly wished to denigrate his achievement, or damn it, as here, with faint praise.

Meanwhile a higher creative activity on Segovia's behalf was being undertaken by Joaquín Rodrigo, who wrote *Fantasía para un Gentilhombre (Fantasia for a Gentleman)* in 1954. This full-length work for guitar and orchestra, dedicated to Segovia, is based on themes taken from the seventeenth century composer, Gaspar Sanz, whose book, *Instrucción de Música sobre la Guitarra española* (Instruction in Music on the Spanish Guitar) first appeared in 1674. Rodrigo's re-working of Sanz's themes is scored for strings and wind (one each of trumpet, piccolo, flute, oboe and bassoon). The Concerto has the following movements: *Villano y Ricercar, Españoleta y Fanfare de la Caballería de Nápoles, Danza de las Hachas* and *Canario*. The original themes by Sanz are quite short and Rodrigo expands each dance considerably by delicate interplay of guitar and orchestral statements of themes, or passages in partnership.

Segovia had first asked Rodrigo to write a new Concerto for guitar and chamber orchestra in 1951, and visited the composer in his chalet in Torrelodones, Spain, to discuss the possibilities:

After the triumph of Concierto de Aranjuez in Paris, Joaquín felt no great desire to compose another concerto and he postponed the work. One day, however, he told me that he had thought it over and that he would write a "Suite" on themes collected by Gaspar Sanz... he would also dedicate it to Andrés Segovia, whom, he greatly admired, as a tribute.[19]

In a letter from Chicago, dated 7 November, 1954, the third letter Segovia had written since hearing Rodrigo's announcement of the *Fantasía para un Gentilhombre* (the previous two being lost in the post), Segovia set out his immediate plans. He would be concertizing and travelling until 17 December, when he would take a twelve day rest in New York. From 1 January to 23 March he would be giving forty-eight concerts, not counting the Town Hall recital in New York or television appearances. Meanwhile he was "thrilled about the news you sent and burning with desire to get a look at the work."

Segovia admitted that when he first heard about the composition he had felt that "the foundation *(el fundamento)* for the work you were starting was very weak." But fortunately Rodrigo, like the spider, produced "the thread you need to weave your own work." He asked the composer to prepare a reduction for guitar and piano. In the last paragraph of his letter, Segovia mentions *Zarabanda lejana* to be "heard during my current tour in concerts, radio, television, and also on records." Segovia makes reference to the "Suite," presumably referring to the work *Tres piezas españolas (Fandango, Passacaglia, Zapateado)* also written in 1954.[20] This would be published by Schott in 1963 (Guitar Archive No. 212) and Segovia would record *Fandango* in 1959.

Thus 1954 was a remarkable year for Segovia. Moreover Schott published some more pieces in Segovia's Guitar Archives Series. These were J. S. Bach's *Sarabande* (from *Suite in C minor,* BWV 997, usually played in A minor on guitar but here in B minor, G.A. No. 171), *Gavotte* (from *Cello Suite VI,* BWV 1012, G.A. No. 172), *Prelude* (from *Suite in C minor,* BWV 997, G.A. 173), Brahms's *Valse, Op. 39, No. 8* (G.A. No. 174), Scarlatti's *Sonata in E minor,* K. 11, (G.A. No. 177) and Bellini's *Dolente immagine di fille mia* for voice and guitar (G.A. No. 152).

It was also the year Segovia first visited Iceland, performing a recital in Reykjavik.

32. 1955

In 1955 the image of Segovia received a particular boost by the publication of a book about him by Bernard Gavoty, musicologist and music critic of *Le Figaro*. With the title of *Segovia* and issued in the *Great Concert Artists* Series (published by René Kister of Geneva), it was one of a line of such books commemorating luminaries of the musical world such as Arthur Rubinstein, Wanda Landowska, Wilhelm Kempff, Yehudi Menuhin, Maria Callas, Isaac Stern, etc. (It ran parallel with another series, *Great Painters*, which included Picasso, Miró, Chagall, and Braque.) That Gavoty now chose to publish a book about Segovia was in itself an acknowledgement that a guitarist had achieved eminence in the pantheon of great twentieth century instrumentalists.

The prose style of the book was quite purple and deeply respectful, with a touch of sincere awe but memorable and perceptive also. As the first complete book published about Segovia, it set a tone which would influence many writers in later years. A description of a recital by Segovia in the castle of La Brede, near Bordeaux, France, in June, 1954, gives a good indication of the style and content:

And here he is: he comes forward carrying his guitar. His prelate-like gravity and natural grandeur accord perfectly with the throne on which he takes his seat. With his left foot on the stool, like a needlewoman, he sets the guitar on his thigh and turns it towards his breast. With his forearm resting on the edge of the sound-board and his right hand between sound-hole and bridge, Segovia contemplates his guitar before beginning to play. She is an elderly queen whom he has unceremoniously laid across his knees: the gleaming light varnish disguises like greasepaint the face of a centenarian coquette who won't admit to her age, a much-travelled woman no longer capable of surprise...

But has he really begun? That arpeggio sketched by the ball of his thumb has not really stirred the guitar. But he has quietly opened the door to a secret world where everything is caresses, murmurs and silences, a miniature world of which Segovia is the magician.[1]

The atmosphere of the opening of a Segovia recital is well evoked here and Gavoty digs deep to express that mysterious division when words cease and music takes over:

...Where Segovia leaves the tale the music takes it up, leading us in a dream to a place where human words cannot attain. What adjectives can ever bring Granada before us? But let those wise fingers be employed on the six taut strings: they will call up the chirping of the grasshopper, wing-shells rubbing together, the rasping saw of the cricket, the toad's golden blisters, the nocturnal fairyland of the slumbering gardens — and Granada, like a rose in the night, rises, swaying under the silvery moon.[2]

This tone of writing has long gone out of fashion. Yet for many readers at the time Gavoty's introduction to the atmospherics of the solo guitar would have been something of a revelation as the instrument was not invariably associated with such expressiveness. Today the evocation of a quiet, mysterious world has largely been displaced by reliance on amplified sound, even in many instances in classic guitar recitals, let alone in the noisy environment of pop culture.

Gavoty's book was also significant in its presentation of a letter by Segovia in which he sets out an artistic credo. The letter, written on 20 December 1954, is printed in its original Spanish in Segovia's hand and in translation:

...Few people suspect what the study of an instrument demands. The public watch the music-miracle in comfort, never dreaming of the ascesis and sacrifices which the musician must perform in order to make himself capable of accomplishing it...

Don't you agree with me that there is in the world of Art today a great crisis which threatens the love of work, and that we musicians might set an example of morality in this field? It is impossible to feign mastery of an instrument, however skilful the imposter may be; and it is impossible to achieve mastery unless he who undertakes that adventure supplements the generous gift of the gods by the stern discipline of lifelong practice.[3]

Segovia in the 1950's.

Segovia then launches into an attack on "creative artists in our time" who "make a show of taking more trouble with their work than they do in reality." These include "painters of great repute who wield their brushes carelessly on the canvas," sculptors with "comically 'synthetic' apparatus," and poets who string "together on paper disconnected words, because the creation of beautiful imagery demands the care of gestation and the pains of childbirth."

Composers too then come under the lash, those "who hunt up parasitic dissonances with which they take all melody from music and turn it into a grievous punishment for the ear — because even if God has touched their foreheads with His fingers they slothfully refuse to seek originality through perseverance." Such a commentary now appears implicitly dismissive of the work of so many twentieth century composers as they struggled throughout their lives to create a truly contemporary musical language. But the next paragraph tells us that Segovia is thinking particularly in terms of the world of the instrumentalist and of himself as workhorse, archetype, and exemplar of unstinting labour:

But as for us pianists, violinists, cellists and guitarists — how many hours of pain and self-abnegation, how many weeks, months and years do we spend polishing a single passage, burnishing it and bringing out its sparkle? And when we consider it "done to a turn," we spend the rest of our life persevering so that our fingers shall not forget the lesson or get entangled again in a brambly thicket of arpeggios, scales, trills, chords, accents and grace notes! And if we climb from that region of technique to the more spiritual sphere of interpretation, what anguish we experience in trying to find the soul of a composition behind the inert notation, and how many scruples and repentings we have before we dare to discover what does not *lie hidden in the paper!*

Reading this we know what Segovia intended to communicate and his own virtuosity and technical perfection were clearly the result of a total dedication to his art. But his blinkered approach to the new developments in poetry, art, sculpture, and, indeed, music, of the twentieth century, had the effect of isolating him from some vital currents. Sooner or later the debt for such reactionary views would have to be paid, especially when the younger players came to full prominence and discovered and demonstrated the magnificence of the contemporary voice of the guitar. In the meantime, Gavoty's book provided a splendid picture of the maestro species complete with excellent photographs and a full statement of the philosophy which informed and nourished Segovia's art.

On the cover of *Guitar News, No. 22,* December 1954 - January 1955, was a picture of Emilia Corral, destined some years in the future to be Segovia's wife, with an article by Juan Riera entitled *The Art of Emilia Corral:*

...under the tutelage of Emilio Pujol, Emilia Corral has lived intensely through the formative period when an artist acquires the cast and seal of individual qualities. Her outstanding natural gifts, her pliancy, her enthusiasm for the guitar, have enabled the master to mould a new force for the world of art. Already, at the outset of her career, she allies a superb technique with a spiritual sensitivity which makes her one with the music she interprets.[4]

Underneath these words is a sonnet by G. Gonzalez de Zabala written in honour of Emilia Corral on the occasion of her performance on Radio Madrid on 19 January, 1954.

By coincidence, below the article itself, was a small news item concerning her future husband's two recitals at the Salle Gaveau on 14 and 16 October, 1954, reviewed in *Le Figaro* by Marc Pincherle:

One feels, when hearing Segovia, that the art of guitar playing achieves its highest point in him, and that it will be an extremely difficult task for the younger generation even to attempt to reach such heights.

Within a few years this kind of comment would be out of place as younger players, particularly Julian Bream and John Williams, became established recitalists and their recordings proliferated. But in the mid-fifties such a remark did not appear extravagant.

Segovia's triumphs continued with his tour of the United States in the early part of 1955, culminating in a recital in Boston, USA, on 20 March. 1,500 people packed the Jordan Hall, where the capacity under normal circumstances was only 1,000. Ten days later, he appeared at the Lyric Theatre, Milan, Italy, followed by a tour of Holland, with recitals at The Hague and Rotterdam, and a radio broadcast. He returned to the Chateau de la Brede, Bordeaux, France, (the setting for Gavoty's book), on 27 May.[5]

On 14 July, Segovia wrote to Castelnuovo-Tedesco from Milan, Italy, announcing that he had just recorded the *Quintet, Op. 143,* for guitar and strings with the Quintetto Chigiano. Segovia commented enthusiastically about the composer's latest work, *Escarraman, Op. 177,* composed in 1955, a suite of Spanish dances from the sixteenth century, after Cervantes. The movements were as follows:

> *Gallarda, mosso e deciso*
> *El Canario, semplice e gaio*
> *El Villano, un poco animato (ma goffo e pesante)*
> *Pésame dello, andantino malinconico*
> *El Rey Don Alonso el bueno, allegretto moderato*
> *Alla Marcia, Var. I, II, III, IV, Finale, Tempo I,*
> *La Guarda Cuydadosa, alla marcia.*

(This work was dedicated, not to Segovia, but to the composer's friend, Arturo Loria, a devotee of the writings of Cervantes.)[6]

Segovia's letter expressed interest in *Escarraman*, which he had already begun to practise, and would do his utmost to give the composition its premiere in New York. With so many recitals now in demand, three a year in New York, two in London, and so on, it was was necessary to renew his repertoire for recitals and recordings.

By now he had almost learned the *Gallarda* and was about to begin *El Canario*. He was also planning to allow a little time each day for study of Castelnuovo-Tedesco's second Guitar Concerto, Rodrigo's *Fantasía* and *Tres piezas españolas,* the *Guitar Concerto* of Villa-Lobos (in which he had to brush up the cadenza) and some new compositions by Tansman. Added to all this, Segovia had to maintain his current repertoire, go on journeys, and look after his family.

Despite Segovia's encouraging words, *Escarraman* did not achieve lasting status within his repertoire. Siegfried Behrend recorded the last movement of the suite, *La Guarda Cuydadosa* (The Soldier in Love) on *Chitarra Italiana,* DG 2530 561, released in 1975. Before that there was a recording by Laurindo Almeida (c. 1958) on *New World of the Guitar* (Capitol P8392, later released on Everest 3287).

On 25 July Segovia was scheduled to give a recital in Austria where he had not played since 1936. The program was to form part of the annual Bach Week in Ansbach, near Vienna, and it was intended that Bach's *Chaconne* should be part of the recital. Unfortunately he was forced to cancel the concert through illness.[7]

Just over a month later, on 28 August, Segovia was in fine form when he appeared at the prestigious Edinburgh Festival, Scotland. Other solo artists engaged for the Festival that year included Solomon, Géza Anda and Rosalyn Tureck (pianoforte), Ralph Kirkpatrick (harpsichord), and the great German baritone, Dietrich Fischer-Dieskau, accompanied by Gerald Moore, at that time the most famous accompanist in the world.

Segovia's program for his Edinburgh Festival solo recital was as follows:

Six Little Pieces for Lute	Vicenzo Galilei (1533-1591)
Suite in D	Robert de Visée (1650-1725)
Entrée - Allemande -	
Bourrée - Sarabande -	
Minuet - Courante	
Fugue and Gavotte	J. S. Bach (1685 - 1750) *(trans. Segovia)*
Minuet	Schubert (1797-1828) *(trans. Tárrega)*

Cavatina	Alexandre Tansman (b. 1897)
Prelude - Sarabande -	
Scherzino - Barcarolle -	
Danza Pomposa	
(dedicated to Segovia)	
Prelude and Étude	Villa-Lobos (b. 1887)
(dedicated to Segovia)	
a.) Tonadilla on the name	Castelnuovo -Tedesco (b. 1895)
of Andrés Segovia	
b.) Tarantella	
(dedicated to Segovia)	
Dance in G	Granados (1867-1916) *(trans. M.Llobet)*
Torre Bermeja	Albéniz (1860-1909) *(trans. Segovia)*

On Wednesday, 31 August at 8 p.m. in the Usher Hall, Edinburgh, Segovia performed *Concerto for Guitar and Orchestra, Op. 99,* by Castelnuovo-Tedesco with the BBC Symphony Orchestra under Sir Malcolm Sargent. (This was also televised.) The program gave the following biographical note about Segovia:

Andrés Segovia is, in his own lifetime, a historic figure — the man who has made the guitar an accepted concert instrument and who is responsible for much of its current repertoire, either through his own transcriptions or through works specially written for him by contemporary composers. In his nearly fifty years before the public he has built up a unique reputation in the musical world.

The notes by Arthur Hutchings on the *Concerto* included some interesting observations:

This concerto is dedicated to Segovia, whose artistry we are lucky to hear tonight. It should be specially evident in the romanza which evokes our associations of the guitar with the rich languor of warm nights south of Edinburgh. The guitar, like the concert harpsichord of the concerto galant, *is an admirable instrument to sound clearly through orchestral texture. The composer does not here use any classical complication of concerto structure; his first movement, for instance, is simply an orchestrally accompanied sonata with a prelude to enable us to know the main themes and enjoy their later translations. No quotations are necessary for music which is patent in form and detail. One can hardly think of a better foil than this attractive and skilful concerto to the two symphonies* {Symphony No. 3 in C major, Op. 52, Sibelius, Symphony No. 5 in C minor, Beethoven} *that flank it on this programme.*

On 28 November, 1955, Segovia gave an exclusive and private recital to the lawyers of the Middle Temple Hall, London. This was reviewed by Ivor Mairants:

...I have listened to Segovia at every concert possible in London since 1939. I have heard him play to me in his hotel room. But never have I heard him sound so calm and serene. What emanated from his guitar on this occasion were truly noble sounds...

To hear him playing the "Sarabande" by Bach is to understand how to achieve a perfect balance between melody and all the other parts. This work has always been one of my favourites and to hear Segovia play it again was a fresh inspiration.

One thing I cannot understand; Why does Segovia try so hard to give Tansman's "Cavatina" the place which, musically, it does not deserve? The "Tarantella" by Castelnuovo-Tedesco that followed proved this. The music was so much better and more enjoyable...

The third part of the recital, after an interval, made a happy ending and included "Madroños, Nocturnetto e Danse" (Torroba), "Mazurka" (Ponce), "Sarabande Lointaine" (Rodrigo), "Dance in G" (Granados) and "Légende" (Albéniz). As Segovia said, although some were written for the piano, he made them revert to the guitar from whence they originally came — that is, before they were composed...

Again I want to say that to me, it was Segovia's greatest recital. It is surely impossible to make the guitar sound more beautiful or to produce a wider range of tone colour. In the hands of Segovia I think the ultimate in guitar playing has been reached.[8]

If this may seem too enthusiastic in its assumption that "the ultimate in guitar playing has been reached," it should be remembered that Segovia was then at the very height of his powers, a point confirmed by reference to the recordings made during this period.[9]

In 1955 Segovia published a number of editions of relevance through to the present time. The most significant was *Concerto for Guitar and Small Orchestra* (reduction for guitar and pianoforte) by Heitor Villa-Lobos, published by Max Eschig, apparently released ahead of the premiere in February, 1956. Also published were *Estudios - Daily Studies,* composed by Segovia (Schott, G.A. No. 178). These *Études* comprise *Oración* (dedicated to the soul of Manuel Ponce), *Remembranza* (dedicated to Olga Coelho) and *Divertimento* (dedicated to Vladimir Bobri). *Oración* was recorded by John Williams in December, 1958, for his second album (Delyse ECB 3151, and later on Decca 42116-2).

33. 1956

Segovia began 1956 with a broadcast performance on 11 January from Hilversum, Holland of the *Quintet for Guitar and Strings* by Castelnuovo-Tedesco with the Röntgen Quartet.

He then travelled to the United States for the customary tour at this time of year. For one of these concerts Segovia played at the Pacific Lutheran College, in Tacoma, Washington on 27 January. In an interview with Karl Weiss of the *Tacoma News Tribune*, Segovia gave his reason for not wishing to give a talk to a student gathering, "An artist should remain a mystery. He should just play."[1]

One could argue that to remain a true mystery, an artist should perhaps not give interviews. Segovia was by this time considerably adept at manipulating interviews with an almost papal authority quite distinct from the more free and easy discussions in *The Gramophone* and elsewhere before 1936. For one who wished to remain "a mystery," Segovia always presented a comparatively high profile among recitalists.

Perhaps the most significant event of the tour was the long awaited premiere of Villa-Lobos's *Concerto for Guitar and Orchestra*, performed on 6 February, 1956, in Houston, Texas, with the composer conducting. Turibio Santos added a further comment (see Chapter 31) on the genesis of the work:

But it had not been a simple route to this premiere. Arminda Villa-Lobos, the composer's second wife, was the godmother for this Concerto, a work which Andrés Segovia had asked for many times. But the composer had been reluctant, either through lack of time or perhaps due to lack of enthusiasm about combining guitar and orchestra. But at last Segovia received the longed-for work, only to be disappointed — it turned out to be a Fantasia Concertante, without a cadenza. However, the champion of the guitar would not accept defeat without a struggle. He was on the point of taking a plane to fly across the United States to attend a rehearsal of the Concerto for Harp and Orchestra, dedicated to Nicanor Zabaleta. Surely if the harp deserved a cadenza, so did the guitar! Andrés Segovia argued his case with Mindinha, who pleaded on his behalf with Villa-Lobos. After various onslaughts (with flowers and champagne at the hotel), the cadenza was ready.

At the premiere it was Arminda herself who increased the number of piano markings on the orchestral parts — turning p into pp, and pp into ppp. After a while Villa-Lobos was no longer sure whether the work was really for guitar and orchestra or just for guitar solo![2]

On the same tour, Segovia performed two recitals at the Town Hall, New York. The second of these, on 25 February, was again honoured by the presence of Villa-Lobos, of whose works Segovia played *Prelude No. 1* and *Study No. 7*. The enormous popularity of this composer was acknowledged by the audience:

The great Brazilian composer was in the audience and was given a tremendous ovation when Segovia indicated him. ...surely no other composer has ever delved so deeply into the spirit of the guitar and displayed its musical wonders with such artistic resourcefulness.[3]

The bond between Villa-Lobos and the grass roots audiences of the guitar is perennial, even though in time a superfluity of performances of a restricted number of favoured pieces would grow tiresome to the *cognoscenti*. But in the 1950's, and for many years to come, there was pleasurable surprise, excitement and novelty in any guitar piece of Villa-Lobos in a recital, as none of his output had at that time become jaded by familiarity or reduced to the status of a tired concert warhorse.

On 6 and 7 April, Segovia gave two performances of Castelnuovo-Tedesco's *Concerto* with the Cincinnati Symphony Orchestra, sponsored by the Cincinnati Society of the Classic Guitar. To pay homage to Segovia on behalf of Guitar Societies in the United States, several composers were asked to participate by writing compositions for guitar, dedicated to Segovia and to be given to him during the course of the evening concert. A "Medal of Cincinnati" was designed, to be presented by the Mayor and and also awarded in future ceremonies to distinguished musicians in the realm of the guitar. An audience of 3,600 watched Mayor Charles P. Taft [son of William H. Taft (1857-1930), the 27th President of the United States (1909-1913)] hand over the medal and make a short address:

Andrés Segovia, as a token of their high esteem for your musicianship and for the respect they give your instrument, the following composers have written and dedicated a work as their tribute to you on this occasion: from Joaquín Rodrigo (Madrid), a Duet for guitar: from Richard Pick (Chicago), Twelve Preludes: from Jenö Takács (Cincinnati), Introduction and Fugue, and Ronde: from Mario Castelnuovo-Tedesco (Beverley Hills), a Second Concerto for Guitar and Orchestra and a solo Tonadilla.

Rodrigo's *Duet* does not always appear in the catalogues of his works. Castelnuovo-Tedesco's offering was *Tonadilla on the name of Andrés Segovia, Op. 170, No. 5,* composed in 1954, and ultimately published by Schott in 1956 (Guitar Archive No.191). This was to become a highly favored Segovia program item and was also recorded in due course. The pieces by Richard Pick (b. 1915), the American guitarist, composer and teacher, and Jenö Takács (b. 1902), Hungarian composer and pianist, were not taken up by Segovia.

The citation read, "In recognition of your superlative artistry the Cincinnati Society of the Classic Guitar on behalf of all the Societies of its kind in America, awards you the Medal of Cincinnati. This award inaugurates the first of such presentations in this field of music in America and will be awarded to musicians and composers, who in the future distinguish themselves on behalf of the guitar. It is only proper that the first award be yours." This was the first of some twenty medals that Segovia would be awarded throughout the next thirty years. At the same time he was granted the Key of Gold of the City of Cincinnati, Ohio, (four more cities would present similar honors to him between 1956 and 1983.)[4]

In July, en route for Siena, Italy, Segovia arrived in Gibraltar, where he played for the Society for Musical Culture. (He had made his debut there in 1923, re-visiting the famous Rock later in 1925.) *The Gibraltar Chronicle* commented:

This guitar had the still small voice of conscience, speaking to each man individually, which is still the only worthwhile way to address human beings. It is hard to capture, hard to record, but, believe me, it was memorable and unique.

Between 15 July and 15 September, 1956, Segovia's Classic Guitar Course was held again at the Chigiana Academy, Siena, Italy. The momentum achieved by this event was now considerable and those attending it would provide several of the leading players and teachers of the next generation. The guitarists enrolled on the Course for 1956 were as follows:

> John Williams (England)
> Dimitri Fampas, Pantelis Kilias (Greece)
> Peter van der Staak (Holland)
> Angelo Amato, Piero Domenico Amerio, Ruggero Chiesa, Carlo Ghersi, Giuseppe Luconi, Domenico
>   Marando, Aldo Minella, Paolo Muggia, Paolo Pilia, Antonietta Zaccaria (Italy)
> Gustavo López, Jesús Silva Valdes (Mexico)
> Emilia Corral Sancho, Manuel Cubedo Alicart, María del Carmen Manteca Pascual, Antonio Membrado
>   Fernández (Spain)
> Dan Grenholm (Sweden)
> Albert Valdes Blain, Anna Kotsarenko, James Yoghourtjian, Theodore Norman (USA)
> Livio Floris (Yugoslavia)

The program presented at the Siena Academy on 11 September, 1956, at the end of the Course, shows the characteristic repertoire at that time:

Pantelis Kilias	*Fughetta* (Handel), *Prelude No. 4* (Villa-Lobos)
Aldo Minella	*Allemande* (J. S. Bach), *Fandanguillo* (Torroba)
Emilia Corral	*Aria con variazioni* (Frescobaldi), *Valse* (Ponce)
Gustavo López	*Gavotte (6th Cello Suite)* (J. S. Bach), *Minuet* (Sor)
Antonio Membrado	*Andante* (Haydn), *Study No. 7* (Villa-Lobos)
Manuel Cubedo	*Passacaglia* (de Visée), *Sevilla* (Pujol)
Alirio Diaz	*Sarabande with Variations* (Handel), *Allegretto (Sonatina)* (Torroba)

An article by Albert Valdes Blain provides an interesting insight into Segovia's teaching method, which over recent years has sometimes come under attack:

It would be impossible to relate everything that happened during this particular session or during the four weeks I attended the Segovia classes. However, I will say, first of all, no one showed more interest or worked harder than Maestro Segovia himself. He was indefatigable. He was made of iron. The classes were held every day. The duration of each class was about two and a half hours and on Sundays when the Academy was closed, the Maestro would invite us to his rooming house and conduct the class in his rooms. The total number of students attending the course was about thirty and from this number Maestro Segovia chose nine as his pupils. The students who were not chosen attended the class conducted by the concert guitarist and pupil of Segovia, Alirio Diaz: and, of course, everyone who enrolled in the course was permitted to watch Maestro Segovia teach. What Maestro Segovia stressed was not technique, was not tone production, was not the position of the hands or any matter of this nature: the pupils he selected were supposed to be good instrumentalists and equipped with a sufficiency of technique.[5]

There are several significant points in this article. It seems to be one of the earliest articles in which the title *Maestro* was closely associated with Segovia's name. In pre-war writing Segovia was often referred to as "Señor" and sometimes post-war references were made, when speaking about Segovia, to the *maestro,* with a lower case "m."

The Collins Dictionary of the English Language refers to the eighteenth century use of the word in its meaning of "master" as in maestro de capella, "a person in charge of an orchestra" linked to the German term "Kapellmeister," the master of the chapel. Its definition of "maestro" is that of "1. a distinguished music teacher, conductor or musician," and "2. any man regarded as the master of an art, often used as a term of address." The Collins Spanish /English Dictionary gives the meaning of the word as firstly "master" and secondly that of "teacher."

In the world of conducting the use of the term "Maestro" is widespread, particularly with conductors from Italy and Spain. As far as great pianists are concerned it is rare to see in print combinations such as Maestro Paderewski, Maestro Schnabel, Maestro Rubinstein or Maestro Horowitz, let alone Maestro Richter. For violinists, Maestro Heifetz or Maestro Menuhin are equally uncommon. However Maestro Casals, for the master cellist, was frequent, and, in the world of the guitar, Maestro Pujol was often used, especially by his students.

With Segovia any casual employment of the appellation presumably stopped after the Siena Academy courses were into their stride. He was now into his sixties and with sufficient gravitas and authority to demand not only that he was known as Segovia on his billboard headings (possibly first used by itself in Argentina and continued after the Second World War), but that he should be addressed by the public, journalists, managers, critics, students, etc, in an appropriate manner. With the title becoming almost part of his name, as far as common usage was concerned, Segovia's presence both formalised and dignified the accolade, giving it a new significance.

With the title of Maestro, certain aspects of behavior could be allowed to become associated with the artist. In films of his teaching in the 1960's Segovia can be seen suddenly becoming angry because of a minor musical pecadillo on the part of the student. What appears as a carefully staged bout of fury put on for the benefit of very well-meaning students could reinforce the distance between the object of the anger and the perpetrator, and induce an appropriate sense of apprehension among the spectators, who awaited their turn to play with considerable trepidation.

Segovia's teaching, as Albert Valdes Blain comments, was a mixture of the precise and the nebulous. Its primary purpose was to communicate how the Maestro performed a particular piece, this being carried down to the slightest nuance in dynamics, tone color, slurs, and phrasing, as well as tempo and the eternally thorny problem of precise fingering. The ideal student for Segovia would be one who could not, by definition, exist, a guitarist who played exactly like himself in every respect. As nobody did play like Segovia, except in terms of a parody of his style, tone and sometimes idiosyncratic phrasing, the scene was set for rich conflicts in the teaching situation. The student was often put in the position of an army recruit desperately trying to scale a high smooth wall; the more that was attempted the more the conflict and abuse as the instructor criticised the improbable contemplating the impossible. No wonder then that the participants were nervous before playing to the Maestro. The question often seems to arise whether he was helping the students or projecting an image of his own fierce firepower.

It was thus not surprising that the most successful graduates of the Segovia Courses escaped to produce their own styles of playing, John Williams, being the prime example and a foremost rebel in the long run against Segovia's teaching methods. When Valdes Blain commented that Segovia was "indefatigable" and "made of iron," he was actually applauding the very qualities which prevented Segovia from achieving real flexibility as a teacher, trapped as he was in the Maestro syndrome.

At the time such dictatorial methods of instruction were usually openly tolerated and admired. It was unthinkable then that such a style should ultimately be criticised. But John Williams, speaking on a BBC *Talkback* program in 1993, commented as follows:

With Segovia it was a great inspiration for a young person. But Segovia as a teacher (I can say now but would have hated to say when he was alive), was not a good teacher — he was a rather bad teacher. He was very simplistic and authoritarian, and it was all done by inspiration which could be a great experience in a class, where you may be inspired by the example that was being set, but it doesn't help actually develop you as a musician.

In each of his pieces Segovia had arrived at an ultimate interpretation for himself by many thousands of hours of practice. His knowledge of the pieces was absolute in his own terms, and this provided problems for the students, who then had to follow Segovia's guideliness as if only one ideal interpretation existed:

Maestro Segovia's musical memory is excellent. He knew to the minutest detail every number played by his students and even in the pieces which he himself had not reviewed in years, he was able to recall without hesitation the notation and fingering of every passage. If a mistake was committed by the student, for example, a note omitted from a chord, or a wrong note due to faulty reading or memorization, the Maestro would stop the player, look for the passage in the music, and bring the fault to the student's attention.[6]

When the master's years of assurance and consolidation met the exploratory interpretative indecisiveness of the young player, a measure of criticism was inevitable. The answer to all problems was thus, "Play like me!" This imperative was implicit rather than stated and the further away from the Maestro's promptings, the more the student failed in the task.

On the positive side there was Williams's sense of inspiration, and the confidence which comes from passing through the fear barrier into a greater self-knowledge. Closeness to the presence would be a good card to hold for many of these young guitarists in their future careers, and many would not hesitate to produce their main ace throughout their professional lives. Others, such as Williams, moved in an opposite direction, distancing themselves as they grew older from too much association with the dominance and power of the Maestro.

There were also casualties of the system, young players who ran headlong into the machine and were chewed up in the process. Segovia particularly abominated the occasional student who played in the Pujol way, without fingernails, using instead the fleshy pads of the fingers. One of these was Manuel Cubedo, who attended in 1956:

When Cubedo came to Siena, and began to play, after a few bars Segovia stopped him and said: You can't be heard. Turning to those about, Segovia asked them. Some agreed, others kept their own counsel. Segovia called John Williams, and asked for the same piece.
That's the way, said Segovia.
Pujol, of course, was not present. Afterwards, P. noted that Cubedo was cast down. In the evening P. met Segovia crossing the square and asked what had caused Cubedo's depression. Said Segovia: Look, it's not a question of ruining his career for some little thing. But the fact is he can't be heard. Said P. You surprise me, for he has given three concerts in Lisbon with many encores; there was no question of him not being heard.[7]

Another rather unpleasant story from Siena is told by Oscar Ghiglia:

Gustavo López, then a student in Siena, had had rough treatment from Segovia during a lesson. "Your thumb has a terrible tone. I can't stand it any more! Do something about it! If necessary, cut it off, perhaps a better one will grow!" That afternoon, Gustavo was sitting at Fontegay drinking camparis, until the table could hold no more glasses. A friend sat down beside him. "Qué pasa, Manito?" "I'm waiting for the tower to open at three. Then I will climb up and throw myself down from the top." His voice was emotionless, his mind seemed made up. "But why?" asked the friend. "Because of my bad thumb," and he continued drinking and watching the clock at the top of the 300 foot tower. Segovia, warned of Gustavo's state, quickly walked to the Piazza and stopped Gustavo as he was leaving the café. "Wait, Gustavo, don't do it; don't cut that thumb off; perhaps a new one would be even worse."[8]

Segovia's lesson here seems peculiarly harsh, especially as López was a mature student who had come to the guitar rather late in life. The humor of Segovia could have the edge of a boy pulling the wings off a fly and not knowing where to stop. (Despite the criticisms of his ugly thumb tone, López went on to have some kind of a concert career, playing recitals in such venues as the Carnegie Hall, New York in 1960, and the Wigmore Hall, London.)

Less potentially harmful was Segovia's mild joke to Aldo Minella at Siena:

When my pupil, A. Minella had to play for Segovia for the first time, he took up his guitar and his own stool and went to sit in front of the Master: Segovia, at the sight of the stool which was a double X folding model, exclaimed: "Oh! what a funny big insect!" and then, when the pupil sat down and placed his foot on it, as the old stool with its used and unscrewed joints started producing noises at the slightest movements of the leg, Segovia in humorous mood pointed out: "Have I not told you? — this is a real grasshopper!"[9]

After a struggle with tone quality and certain problems of attitude, Ghiglia ultimately became one of Segovia's favourite students, but only after a ritual humiliation, which he apparently endured bravely and almost willingly:

It took another year before I could reach out past Segovia's indifference to me. He did notice me before this; he even spoke of me to his other pupils and friends at his table in the café, but only to tell them of a nightmare he had had: "a dark shape moving around... full of hair all over... was it a spider... a gorilla? No! It was Ghiglia I dreamed of. "As was the case some years before with Gustavo, this indirect lesson did have a disciplinary impact on me. I did not get a haircut or trim my beard, but that winter the "dark hairy shape" worked hard — so hard — back in Rome.[10]

Ultimately Ghiglia found the message in Segovia's teaching, that "nobody could or would stand by me; I had to find my own core, that part of myself which could alone provide inextinguishable inspiration, faith and wisdom." This, in essence, was "only following Segovia's first 'commandment' to himself, the one with which he begins all recollections of his life, 'Be your own teacher and your own pupil.'"[11] It was a hard lesson and those who discovered this secret were indeed fortunate.

In the fall of 1956, the guitar was placed upon the program of the 12th International Competition for Musical Performers, held 22 September to 6 October at the Conservatoire of Music, Geneva, Switzerland. The jury announced in May were nominated as follows:

Luise Walker (Austria), José de Azpiazu (Spain), Julian Bream (Great Britain), Hans Haug (Switzerland), Hermann Leeb (Switzerland), Andrés Segovia (Spain) and Alexandre Tansman (Poland).[12]

Mr. Henri Gagnebin, director of the Conservatoire and Chairman of the Organisation Committee commented that "this instrument is enjoying a remarkable renaissance due, for the most part, to the renown and talent of Segovia." The competition was open to young artists between the ages of fifteen and thirty.[13] *B.M.G.* provided a short report of the concert, which in the end narrowed down to two students, Manuel Cubedo and Antonio Membrado:

Although guitarists from many countries took part, only two — Manuel Cubedo Alicart and Antonio Membrado (both from Spain) — were successful in the eliminating rounds. Although both played in distinct styles — the former using finger tips and the latter preferring nails — it was difficult to judge between them.

Both contestants started with the set piece, Ponce's "Variations on Folia de España"; Sr. Cubedo followed this with "Suite in D minor" (de Visée) and "Capriccio Diabolico" (Castelnuovo-Tedesco). Sr. Membrado chose a "Fantasía" (Milán) and "Studies Nos 7 and 8" (Villa-Lobos). Both chose the 2nd and 3rd movements of Castelnuovo-Tedesco's Concerto as their work for guitar and orchestra.

Sr. Cubedo is reported as being a seasoned player who produces a very full and mellow tone which is perhaps not as varied as it might be. Sr. Membrado, on the other hand, makes full use of the larger tonal resources of nail playing and is generally a most sensitive guitarist. However, Sr. Cubedo was finally judged the better player and was awarded second prize (no first prize was awarded) and Sr. Membrado received a medal and 500 Swiss francs.

It seems a great pity that Great Britain was not represented among the finalists, particularly as there is at least one young British guitarist who could almost certainly have made a difference to the final results.

Prof. José de Azpiazu of Geneva is to be warmly congratulated for his successful efforts in introducing the guitar into the International Competition. This will undoubtedly raise the status of the instrument and the standard of guitar playing.

Incidentally, Julian Bream was one of the judges.

Guitar News from Overseas, Collected by Peter Sensier.[14]

Segovia was not able to attend for the final rounds of the competition because of prior recital engagements, and this had been understood some months before. Julian Bream was, however, not on the jury at first but came in during the last stages when crucial decisions were made.[15] (Bream at the time was only twenty-three and eligible to enter the competition, but it is a sign of his unique status that even at this early stage of his career he was recognised as one of the leading performers in the world.)

1956 was another important year for Segovia in terms of pieces published. Foremost among these was *Tonadilla on the Name of Andrés Segovia, Op. 170, No. 5,* by Castelnuovo-Tedesco (Schott, G.A. No. 191). This was his last piece to be dedicated to Segovia, though the composer's guitar works would ultimately extend as far as *Opus 210*. (But it was not the last composition by Castelnuovo-Tedesco to be played by Segovia who several years later recorded various movements of *Platero y Yo, Op. 190.)*

Also that year the Guitar Archives Series received a unique addition with a work dedicated to Segovia but not edited by him. This was *Sérénade, Op. 118,* for guitar and orchestra by Castelnuovo-Tedesco, in a guitar/piano reduction. The "transcription for guitar and piano" carries the name of Siegfried Behrend, as editor. Behrend (1933-1990), born in the same year as Julian Bream, was thus another promising guitarist gaining valuable editorial experience at a comparatively young age.

Segovia launched a new series with Ricordi Americana of Buenos Aires in 1956. A substantial work here was *Second Sonata, Op. 25,* by Fernando Sor, revised and fingered by Segovia. The *Allegro* from this work was recorded on *An Andrés Segovia Recital,* (Decca DL 9633) (reviewed in *The Gramophone,* March, 1953). This edition provides many indications of Segovia's approach, especially with regard to slurs, left and right hand fingerings, stretching, movement across or along the strings, phrasing, etc. If players nowadays perform this piece, they are unlikely to choose this publication to work from, but in historical context it was a significant contribution to guitar literature, revealing Segovia's editing of a composition he seems rarely to have performed in its entirety.

Another in the Ricordi Americana series was *Minuet* by Haydn, transcribed by Segovia, and recorded by him on *Andrés Segovia Plays* (Decca DL 9734). This was an original transcription and not a re-working of a Tárrega precedent. This kind of arrangement has tended to fall from favour with recitalists. Contemporary performers with a penchant for Haydn, such as Eliot Fisk, usually prefer to play an entire sonata rather than a single movement. Segovia, however, delighted his audiences by including these pieces as convenient encores.

Other small works published by Ricordi Americana included *Andante Largo* (Sor), *Triste No 4.* (Aguirre), *Canción del Norte, Op. 68, No. 41, Alegre Labrador, Op. 68. No. 10* (Schumann), *Song without Words, Op. 10, No. 3,* (Mendelssohn). This delightful selection featured a number of small classical transcriptions, several of which Segovia had recorded. Though they are essentially short encore pieces, they represent also transcriptions which have become less fashionable in recent years. But close attention to the detailed fingering makes clear many aspects of Segovia's concepts of tone colour, interpretation and the problems of phrasing on the guitar.

34. 1957

In 1957 a film was shown of Segovia performing *Thème Varié* (Sor) and *Tonadilla* (Granados). This enabled those lucky enough to see the film an opportunity to watch his technique in action. An article in *Guitar News*[1] commented that "in some ways he is not 'strictly Tárrega'," that he "knows the rules and breaks them to suit himself where necessary," and that he "did *not* flex the first joint of the thumb as advocated by Roch."[2] It was perhaps natural at the time that many amateur players and teachers understood only limited perspectives about Segovia's technique, having absorbed what they thought they knew about technical matters through the early twentieth century published Methods, almost invariably orientated to the point of view of pupils of Tárrega, such as Pujol or Roch.

In these methods a complex system of rules concerning guitar technique was certainly perpetrated, though many such concepts were never part of any great player's own equipment. Moreover, the post-Tárrega methods were specifically for flesh playing without nails, and Segovia's technique had demonstrated the inadequacy of much of this traditional kind of thinking. There were hardly any Guitar Methods written from a post-Segovia viewpoint until 1957 when Laurindo Almeida's *Guitar Tutor, An Up-to-Date Classic Guitar Method* was published (Criterion Music Corp. New York, Belwin-Mills, London). Almeida's book was very different from those by teachers under the influence of Tárrega. Other great teachers, such as Len Williams (father of John Williams), who founded the Spanish Guitar Centre, London, in the early 1950's, regrettably never formulated their pedagogy into a systematic method, preferring personal contact between teacher and taught.

The comments on the film printed in *Guitar News* are the inevitable mixture of surprise and awe, with a modicum of puzzlement as cherished notions about technique appeared to be contradicted by Segovia's actual performance:

LEFT HAND
The terrifically powerful, thick and fleshy hand is deceptive. It is unspectacular because the fingers seem to move so slightly. They rise and fall on the strings with so little superfluous movement that one has to watch them closely to see them moving in the fastest scale passages. The wrist is not curved out and away from the fingerboard in a marked manner. It just seems to drop away normally... The whole picture arises from the extraordinary economy of movement of every part of the hand. At times he seems to clamp the hand to the neck of the guitar while the powerful fingers move up and down like the parts of a machine...

RIGHT HAND
The finger-joint connected to the hand is very full, but the remaining two joints taper down to a normal well-shaped fingertip. The nails give you the impression of being thick and, of course, beautifully shaped and groomed... The attack on the strings to produce a loud ringing note seemed so effortless — just like a punch from a great boxer — the movement so slight but the impact so telling...

A very noticeable point is the resting of the thumb on a lower string to steady the hand and give leverage when the fingers are plucking the upper strings...

In the Tonadilla *when playing muted passages in the bass, the ball of the thumb was laid on the bridge and the strings struck with the side of the top joint. To procure this result the hand was turned upward from the wrist, producing a stance which the student might think all wrong, not realising that it is the only way to attain a certain tonal effect!*

Another observer comments at the foot of the article that "it could be said that to a certain extent Segovia's technique is determined by the particular anatomical characteristics of *his* hands and fingers — just as is the technique of all players." A further inference is drawn, quite wisely, that "one might conclude from this circumstance that an attempt to copy Segovia's technique (especially right hand) could lead one into a sort of trouble." Throughout the years guitarists, especially amateurs, would ponder the cosmic question of how far copying Segovia's hand positions, posture, and technical tricks would improve their playing.

Thus the old methods of the post-Tárrega books where a diagram, sketch, or photograph of the ideal right hand was included for students to imitate, were transferred to a younger generation who now had a new blueprint to imitate. Needless to say, mindless imitation of the configuration of a virtuoso's hand is quite useless without an understanding of the principles that motivate its activities. These principles are quite obviously linked to the actual physical size and formation of an individual's body and are not usually transferable or imitable.

During Segovia's tour of the United States in the early part of 1957, the *New York Times* observed that only three artists during the past ten years had given three recitals at New York Town Hall in a single season — Lotte Lehmann, Wanda Landowska and Segovia. The total attendance at Segovia's three concerts amounted to 4,650. In *The Chicago Daily News* that year, the critic, Don Henahan, divided Segovia's audiences into three sections, "the coughers, the programme rustlers and the glarers," the glarers apparently carrying the day, "though not by much." Henahan concluded his report with a mild attack on the rock and roll guitarists steadily gaining ground at that time:

All those who believe the guitar, to be well played, must be beaten with the fist or thumped against the pelvis, should have been there. Never was the master more masterful.[3]

At this point in the history of musical appreciation the critics naturally aligned themselves with classical music against the encroaching tide of the swinging pelvis and the vigorous vulgarity of popular music. Before many years had passed this would be reversed as younger journalists began to see popular music as the norm, and the unamplified guitar played by an old gentleman in a dress suit, seated, performing without excessive movement, as something slightly eccentric. But the day had not yet arrived (though it would soon) when journalists tumbled over themselves to acquire that central nugget of information for their readers — Segovia's opinion about rock music.

Occasionally there would be anecdotes through the years of Segovia's encounters with chiming clocks and bells. A classic of the genre is to be found in *B.M.G.:*

There was an amusing incident during the concert that has probably never happened before at a Segovia recital and may not happen again. During his playing of "Sarabande Lointaine" everyone was startled by the loud chiming of the clock placed above the centre of the Middle Temple Hall. Competing with the softer voice of the guitar it chimed One! Two! Three! Four! Five! in a different key to the soloist and, by this time the maestro could stand it no more. He stopped playing with a gesture of helplessness.

While Segovia waited for the clock to chime ten o'clock a relieved titter of understanding came from the select audience. It placed the seal of informality and friendliness on the gathering as he resumed the piece.[4]

The concept that in nearly fifty years of concertizing Segovia had never encountered a striking clock or bell before is touching in its innocence. He was adept at controlling the responses of an audience through long practice at this craft, and could subtly turn such interferences to his advantage. At the Phillips Exeter Academy, New Hampshire, the same thing happened in 1957, as had happened in 1955 (and no doubt on numerous other occasions throughout Segovia's career):

Ten minutes after the programme had commenced a nearby church started up its recorded chimes, forgetting that it was the first day of 'Daylight Saving Time' and that they should have been an hour earlier. Segovia stopped in the middle of a Sarabande by R. de Visée and disappeared from the platform until someone at the church realised their mistake and stopped the record.[5]

On this occasion Segovia seems to have over-reacted. But from the Maestro audiences not only came to expect imperious behaviour but actually enjoyed it, adding such incidents to the stock of anecdotes which endorsed Segovia's personal mythology. Like small children with irritable parents, audiences could be pleased when Segovia did not on some occasions become angry, and at other times were not surprised when he did. Either way he was in control. Whether similar incidents of a transient chime caused pianists such as Rubinstein or Horowitz to vacate the stage during the slow movement of a Mozart or Beethoven sonata, sometimes equally *pianissimo* as the guitar, but with a much more prolonged musical structure to sustain, seems unlikely. But the very smallness of the guitar sound caused Segovia to take special care to impress discipline on his audience, as well as a greater degree of personal idiosyncrasies which he perhaps found necessary as a self-defence.

Another anecdote related through the years concerns Segovia's use of a handkerchief to indicate to an audience how to stifle a cough:

Well, what I did in Madrid (and other places) was a very amusing thing. They were coughing just as I was playing a piece by Bach which was very delicate and very slow. I stopped playing and I looked up. Then I took my handkerchief and I put it like that [coughing gently]; *of course when you put the handkerchief in your mouth like that you have no noise, no disagreeable noise, and if you cough that way it is perfectly all right.*[6]

It was natural that Segovia should have amassed a deep knowledge of audience psychology and used a number of persuasive techniques throughout all the countries he visited. What is remarkable was that so many who wrote about his activities, believed they were witnessing a unique event. (This happened too with the incessant circulation of the same little stories often relayed by journalists as if they were newly minted but could be traced back to many recitations.) Segovia did not mind being enveloped in some of his familiar public clichés as this could inhibit writers from asking questions about his private life and opinions. Through the medium of anecdote, Segovia was always able to answer questions without committing himself to controversial intellectual positions beyond the boundaries of a strictly controlled musical context.

35. THE LATE 1950'S

In his United States tour of 1957, Segovia once again featured Castelnuovo-Tedesco's Concerto, performing with the Seattle Symphony Orchestra (reduced to twenty-five players) on 16 January, at the Temple, Tacoma. (The conductor was Milton Katims.) The orchestra was also booked for a Students' Matinée at which Segovia made a surprise appearance.

Nine days later Segovia moved over to the Wilshire Ebell Theatre, Los Angeles, performing on his Hauser guitar and appearing "healthy and vigorous."[1] The first program included *Canción del Emperador, Diferencias sobre Guárdame las Vacas* (Narváez), *Three Pieces* (Dowland), *Suite in D minor* (de Visée), along with works by J. S. Bach, Handel, "Alessandro Scarlatti," *Sonata* (Domenico Scarlatti), Paganini, Llobet, Ponce, Crespo, Lauro, Castelnuovo-Tedesco, Esplá and Albéniz. At the second concert in Los Angeles, Mario Castelnuovo-Tedesco was in the audience and was introduced from the platform for a performance of his *Tonadilla on the name of Andrés Segovia.*

On this occasion Segovia also played music by Milán, Purcell, Couperin, Sor, Granados and Albéniz, as well as Bach's *Chaconne* and *Sonatina* by Moreno Torroba. Five encores were provided, though the third was interrupted by an automobile horn outside the hall through which Segovia played on.

On 16 February, Segovia returned to the Town Hall, New York, including music by Schubert, *Canzonetta* (Mendelssohn) and *Little Waltz* (Grieg). *The New York Times* commented:

His performances adhered to his norm — amazing technical control, even more amazing variety of touch and a musical elegance that made all of the music interesting.

Towards the end of April, 1957, Segovia spent a few days with Joaquín Rodrigo and his wife in New York:

We saw Andrés Segovia almost every day. He invited us to dinner at his home, or he took us to lively parties where we were introduced to many celebrities in the world of the arts...

We devoted our last days in New York to socializing, under the aegis of Andrés Segovia. We went with him to a cocktail party given by the pianist Ania Dorfman, where we met a number of well-known artists, including Vladimir Nabokov.[2]

The Rodrigo family departed on 10 May to return to Madrid. After a few days Segovia became ill with a kidney stone, which kept him in agony for nearly two weeks. When this cleared up Segovia went to Buenos Aires, where he resumed his normal activities, "concerts, travel, people, studies, etc." He premiered Rodrigo's *Fandango* at the Colón Theatre, enjoying an enthusiastic audience response and left for Geneva in the second week of August.[3] Segovia then set out for an extended stay in Madrid until the beginning of October to study the *Fantasía para un Gentilhombre* in depth.[3] Because of this schedule Segovia was unable to attend the Siena Course that year, much to the disappointment of various students who had enrolled believing he would be there.[4] Alirio Diaz therefore took over the main guitar classes while Emilio Pujol ran a course in vihuela music of the sixteenth century.

Segovia toured Sweden before his annual British tour, giving a recital to 2,200 people in the Concert Hall, Stockholm on 1 October. His several encores included *Recuerdos de la Alhambra* (Tárrega) which according to one concert-goer, "left the audience completely spell-bound." Segovia played twice more in Sweden.[5]

He arrived in London on 19 October, 1957. His three engagements in London consisted of a recital at the Chelsea Music Club on 24 October, a broadcast on the BBC Home Service on 25 October and a recital at the Royal Festival Hall on 28 October where the program was as follows:

Diferencias	Narváez
Two Galliards	Dowland
Preámbulo - Gavotta	A. Scarlatti
Sonata	Domenico Scarlatti
Fugue in A minor	J. S. Bach

Six Italian Dances	arr. Chilesotti
Introduction and Allegro	Sor
Three Studies	Villa-Lobos

Fantasía-Sonata	Manén
Three Levantine Impressions	Esplá
Fandango	Rodrigo
Torre Bermeja	Albéniz

This is an interesting program by Segovia with a slight shift in structure from some of his recitals. In the second and third sections of the concert, after the somewhat trivial and questionable arrangements of Chilesotti, he gets into a virtuosic stride, with *Fandango* by Rodrigo offering the newest and technically most exciting material. A review in *Guitar News* described Manén's *Fantasía-Sonata* as "a brooding, sultry work, and its twenty minutes playing time was perhaps too long to maintain undivided attention."[6] This was a judgement possibly shared by posterity for Manén's well-intentioned work has never become popular among later generations of recitalists.

But as ever Segovia's artistry achieved a synthesis of music taken from many periods and provided a panoply of guitar playing that was satisfying and richly moving for audiences:

Little can be said, which has not already been said, about Segovia's consummate artistry, his wide-ranging tone colour, and delicately controlled phrasing. Here is a sincere, even a devout artist, imbued with ardour, not only for musicianship, but for the instrument which gives it voice.[6]

From London, Segovia travelled to the Wexford Music Festival, Ireland, and then on to a tour of Germany. On 16 December he returned to London where he performed in the London Philharmonic Orchestra's Spanish concert. According to one report so many encores were demanded of him that finally he had to announce, "Thank you very much, but I think the orchestra wants to play also."[7]

One event that might have given Segovia pause for thought that year was the issue of *A Bach Recital for the Guitar* (Westminster XWN 18428) by Julian Bream recorded on his 1947 Hauser guitar at the Mozart-Saal in Vienna, Austria. The program consisted of *Chaconne* (from *Partita II in D minor*, BWV 1004), *Little Prelude in C minor*, (BWV 999), *Sarabande, Bourrée* (from the *E minor Lute Suite, BWV* 996), *Prelude and Fugue* (from the *C minor Lute Suite*, BWV 997) and *Prelude, Fugue and Allegro.* (BWV 998). Thus an early gauntlet was flung down to challenge the hegemony of the Maestro in some of his own territory.

Already Julian Bream's albums had boldly confronted the shores of Segoviana, offering superb recordings of Sor's *Estudios Nos 5, 9 & 12* (in Segovia's edition), and other favorites of the older man such as Sor's *Minuet (Op. 22), Largo, Op. 7, Rondo (Op. 22)*, and *Andante Largo, Op. 5*, on *Sor, Turina and Falla* (Westminster XWN 18135) (1956). Also here were *Fandanguillo, Hommage a Tárrega, Andante (Sonata in D)* and *Ráfaga*, by Turina, as well as Falla's *Homenaje pour le Tombeau de Claude Debussy.* This was followed the same year by *Villa-Lobos and Torroba* (Westminster XWN 18137) featuring the *Five Preludes* of Villa-Lobos, and *Prelude in E, Sonatina in A, Nocturno* and *Burgalesa* by Moreno Torroba.

But Bream's approach to Bach's *Chaconne* was something different, an assault on Everest at the age of twenty-four, a feat which Segovia had only attempted when in his mid-forties, and had not recorded until he was approaching sixty. A younger generation was at last taking over and the sensitive antennae of Segovia would not have been oblivious to this challenge.

Moreover, Bream was now, with his diminution of the number of composers included on a long playing record, beginning to change the hitherto accepted format of a guitar album. When eventually the Bream recording of J. S. Bach became available in his native country, *The Gramophone* swooped gratefully on this fact:

Julian Bream uses a wide range of tone-colour, a superlative technique, and a good sense of eighteenth-century style to present an all-Bach programme — a welcome departure from the thirty-seven short pieces chosen from the five centuries that so often seems to make up the guitar's LP.[8]

In Bream's biographical note on *A Bach Recital for Guitar*, a carefully ambiguous phrase had been inserted:

Born in London in 1933, Julian Bream gave up the piano for the guitar when eleven years old. He studied with Perott, President of the Society of Guitarists, and at the Royal College of Music. In 1945 he came to the attention of Andrés Segovia, who was so much impressed with Bream's talent that he offered to teach him...

The last sentence of this passage could perhaps imply to the uninitiated that Segovia took the young Bream under his wing as a promising student. But a few months later Julian Bream made it quite clear in an interview what the true situation was.

It is often thought that I was a pupil of Segovia. Even after hearing my playing people have remarked to the effect that they can hear that I was a Segovia pupil! I am sure that Segovia would be the first to state that I was never his pupil for, although I had several "sessions" with the great Maestro between 1947 and 1950 during which he made general observations on my technique and fingering, I never actually studied with him. All he said then has been of invaluable assistance to me in my pursuit of the guitar. In fact, by and large, I have evolved my own technique. With my right hand I employ a different stroke to that of Segovia, for whereas he habitually plucks the string with the right hand fingers at right angles to the strings, I tend to use a less rigid position for reasons of tonal variety.[9]

Though impeccably polite to Segovia, this paragraph was an effective disclaimer from a young player about the significance of the Maestro's influence. It was also a statement of simple truth since his "sessions" with Segovia had not been extended periods of tuition planned and sustained. There was a further section which could be construed as critical of concepts of the guitar repertoire at that time:

It has often struck me that guitarists limit musical potential by being too concerned with the instrument and not enough concerned with the expression from it. Whilst I am obviously a firm advocate for the guitar and a great lover of the instrument, my ultimate aim is to project music by using the guitar as just another vehicle for musical expression, the one which I happened to develop in much the same way as a conductor "takes up" conducting. At times I feel exasperated with the instrument, especially its seeming lack of sustained sound and rather insignificant repertoire. But no sooner than that mood has arrived, in the next breath I find something which is completely beautiful and captivating. The only way in which the guitar, now lifted to a hitherto unknown point of respectability, can maintain its position in the realm of serious music, is for it to be cultivated by enthusiasts who make a thoroughly musical, as well as practical, approach to its technique and possibilities...

Even after Segovia's many years in the arena, persuading composers to write for the instrument, Bream believed the repertoire to be "insignificant." Throughout his subsequent career he was to correct this deficit, establishing what Segovia had not achieved — a truly contemporary repertoire for the guitar.

As if to demonstrate this very point, the French composer, Darius Milhaud, finished a solo guitar piece on 26 November, 1957, entitled *Segoviana, Op. 366* (published Heugel). The Maestro found the piece of little interest and the first performance was given by another guitarist in November, 1969, in Strasbourg. There is thus, regrettably, no mention of Segovia in Milhaud's autobiography, *My Happy Life*.

A further incident that year was the withdrawal by Schott of Ponce's *Mazurka*, at the request of the composer's widow. Very few copies had been printed and no re-publication was anticipated.[10] The work would eventually be published by Laurindo Almeida (Brazilliance Music Publishing Inc., 1967), and, decades later, by Schott (*Cuatro Piezas para Guitarra*, ed. Miguel Alcázar, G.A. No. 519, 1992). *Mazurka*, composed in Paris in 1933, had been written at Segovia's request for a Chopinesque piece to act as a companion to *Valse* (G.A. No. 153).[11] Thus a most imaginative item disappeared from the concert repertoire for several years.

Whatever set-backs or disappointments, Segovia's career moved on inexorably, pursuing what he often described as "an ascending line." At the age of 64 his illustrious flight was hardly yet at its zenith and unprecedented glories lay hidden in the future. Segovia wasted no years and no opportunities. His career at all times advanced tenaciously despite the obstacles fate put in his path. The courage and integrity of Segovia never flagged and his energies were single-minded. Local difficulties were ultimately submerged in the magnificence of the total patterns of his forward progress. At all stages he was indeed an astonishing and great representative of human endeavour and achievement, as he matched the intensity of his dreams and ambitions with fulfilment and realisation of his genius.

Notes to Part I

1. The Early Years

1. Andrés Segovia, *Segovia: An Autobiography of the Years, 1893-1920* (New York: Macmillan, 1976)

2. Domingo Prat, *Diccionario de Guitarristas* (Buenos Aires: Romero y Fernandez, 1934, reprinted Columbus, Ohio, Editions Orphée, 1986), pp. 289-290.

3. Andrés Segovia, George Mendoza, *Segovia, My Book of the Guitar* (Cleveland: Collins, 1979), p. 10.

4. *Segovia: An Autobiography of the Years,1893-1920,* p. VI and Vladimir Bobri, *Segovia Technique* (New York: Macmillan,1972), p. 27.

5. Segovia, op. cit., p. 3.

6. Ibid., p. 6.

7. Ibid., p. 6

8. Ibid., p. 9.

9. Ibid., p. 9.

10. J. B. Stone, *A Tour with Cook through Spain* (London: Sampson, Low, Marston, Low, & Searle, 1873), p. 99.

11. Ibid., p. 100.

12. Maud Howe, *Sun and Shadow in Spain* (Boston: Little, Brown and Company, 1908), p. 209.

13. Ibid., pp. 205-6.

2. Towards a Debut

1. Segovia, op. cit., pp. 7-8.

2. Ibid., p. 10.

3. Ibid., p. 12.

4. Ibid., p. 12.

5. Ibid., p. 13.

6. Ibid., p. 14.

7. Ibid., p. 17.

8. Eugèn d'Albert (1864-1932), born in Glasgow, Scotland, was a pupil of Liszt. His pupils included Wilhelm Backhaus and Ernst V. Dohnányi.

9. Segovia, op. cit., p. 19.

10. Miguel Cerón Rubio, a businessman, also became a close friend of Federico García Lorca and Manuel de Falla.

11. Ibid., p. 20.

12. Ibid., p. 22.

13. Ibid., p. 27.

14. Ibid., p. 28.

15 & 16. Ibid., p. 35.

17. Ibid., pp. 49-52.

18. Ibid., p. 51.

19. Manuel Ramírez (1864-1916).

20. Ibid., p. 52.

21. *Andrés Segovia: The Guitar and I (Vol. II)* (MCA Records, DL710182).

22. José Romanillos, *Antonio de Torres: Guitar Maker - His Life and Work,* (Shaftesbury: Element Books, 1987), p. 48.

23. José Ramírez III, *En Torno a la Guitarra* (Madrid: Soneto, 1993), p. 183.

24. Ibid., p. 184.

25. Andrés Segovia, "La Guitarra y Yo," *The Guitar Review* (No. 8, 1949), p. 33.

26. Gregor Piatigorsky, *Cellists* (New Jersey: Da Capo, 1965).

3. THE EARLY REPERTOIRE

1. Segovia, op. cit., p. 68.

2. Ibid., p. 69.

3. Ibid., p. 73.

4. Emilio Pujol, *Tárrega: Ensayo biográfico* (Lisbon, Lerida: 1960), p. 169.

5. Julian Bream's *Romantic Guitar* LP (RCA SB 6844, issued 1971), included *Song without Words, Op. 19, No. 6 (Venetian Boat Song)* and *Canzonetta, from Op. 12,* Mendelssohn, *Menuetto from Op. 78,* Schubert, and four pieces by Tárrega.

6. The music of Mozart still fascinates guitarists. Perhaps the most interesting recording in this field is Manuel Barrueco playing *Piano Sonata in D minor (K. 283)* and *Adagio, from Piano Sonata in D minor, K. 576* (EMI CDC 7 49368 2).

7. Bruno Tonazzi, *Miguel Llobet, Chitarrista dell'Impressionismo* (Ancona: Edizioni Bèrben, 1966), p. 17.

8. Ronald Purcell, ed., *Miguel Llobet, Guitar Works, Vol. 1, 11 Original Compositions* (Heidelburg: Chanterelle, 1989), p. 14. Some of Sor's Variations were included juxtaposed with new ones by Llobet.

9. Ibid., p. ix.

10. ed. Melchior Rodríguez, *J. Arcas, Obras Completas para Guitarra* (Madrid: Soneto, 1993).

11. Richard D. Stover, *Six Silver Moonbeams: The Life and Times of Augustín Barrios Mangoré* (Clovis, CA: Querico Publications, 1992), p. 49.

12. ed. Purcell, op. cit., p. iii.

13. Ibid., p. ii.

14. Segovia, op. cit., pp. 98-108.

15. Ibid., p. 108.

16. Juan Riera, *Emilio Pujol* (Lerida: Instituto de Estudios Ilerdenses, 1974), p. 81.

17. ed. Purcell, op. cit., p. ii.

18. Emilio Pujol, *El Dilema del Sonido en la Guitarra (The Dilemma of Timbre on the Guitar)* (Buenos Aires:Ricordi Americana, 1960).

19. Segovia, op. cit., p. 58.

20. Ibid., p. 59.

21. Philip J. Bone, *The Guitar and Mandolin* (London: Schott & Co Ltd, 1st Edition 1914, reprinted 1954, 1972), p. 121.

22. Segovia, op. cit., p. 89.

23. Prat, op. cit., p. 129.

4. THE WIDER HORIZONS

1. Segovia, op. cit., p. 198.

2. The conversation on this subject between Ian Gibson and Andrés Segovia took place in Madrid on 19 December, 1980.

3. Miguel Cerón is mentioned several times in Segovia's autobiography: pp. 3, 4, 20, 49, 184-5, 188-190.

4. Ian Gibson, *Federico García Lorca, A Life* (London: Faber & Faber, 1989), p. 71.

5. Segovia, op. cit., p. 199.

6. Julian Aguirre (1868-1924), Argentinian composer, who wrote many miniatures for pianoforte in popular Argentinian forms. Segovia recorded his *Canción* in the 1950's on Brunswick AXA 4504.

7. Prat, op. cit., pp. 146-147.

8. Ricardo Zavadivker, "Andrés Segovia, entrevista," *Notas* (Buenos Aires) XII, pp. 50-51, quoted in Richard Pinnell, *The Rioplatense Guitar: The Early Guitar and Its Context in Argentina and Uruguay* (Westport, Connecticut: The Bold Strummer, 1993), p. 39.

9. Richard Stover, *Six Silver Moonbeams, The Life and Times of Agustín Barrios Mangoré* (Clovis, California: Querico Publications), pp. 56-57.

10. Pinnell, op. cit., p. 39.

11. Stover, op. cit., p. 58.

12. Segovia, op. cit., p. 194.

13. Ibid., p. 195.

14. Ronald Crichton, *Manuel de Falla, Descriptive Catalogue of His Works* (London: J. & W. Chester / Edition William Hansen Ltd., 1976), p. 35.

15. Manuel Orozco, *Manuel de Falla, Historia de una derrota* (Barcelona: Ediciones Destines S.A.,1985), p. 152.

5. Concurso de Cante Jondo, Granada, 1922

1. Ian Gibson's *Federico García Lorca, A Life* has an excellent account of the Concurso, pp. 108-116.

2. Federico García Lorca, trans. and ed. Christopher Maurer, *Deep Song and Other Prose* (London: Marion Boyars, 1980), p. 23.

3. Orozco, op. cit., p. 148.

4. Gibson, op. cit., p. 114.

5. Federico Sopeña, ed., *Manuel de Falla, On Music and Musicians,* trans. David Urman and J. M. Thomson (London: Marion Boyars, 1979), p. 110.

6. Sopeña, ed., op. cit., p. 112

7. Eusebio Rioja, "Andrés Segovia y La Guitarra Flamenca," *La Cana, Revista de Flamenco,* No. 4 (Winter 1993): p. 37.

8. Felix Grande, *Memoria del Flamenco,* Vol. 2, (Madrid: Espasa-Calpe S.A., 1979), pp. 495-496.

9. *Farsetas* is Andalusian slang for *falsetas* (variations).

10. Andrés Segovia, "Segovia on Flamenco," *Guitar Review,* No. 42 (Fall, 1977): p. 8.

11. Ian Gibson, op. cit., p. 115.

12. Segovia, op. cit., pp. 8-9.

13. *Music and Musicians,* November, 1973.

14. Ian Gibson, op. cit. p. 115.

6. The New Repertoire

1. Miguel Alcázar, ed., *The Segovia-Ponce Letters,* trans. Peter Segal (Columbus: Editions Orphée, Inc., 1989).

2. Corazón Otero, *Manuel M. Ponce and the Guitar* (Shaftesbury: Musical New Services Ltd, 1963), p. 18.

3. Otero, op. cit., p. 19.

4. Alcázar, ed., op. cit., p. 2.

5. Ibid., p. 5.

6. H. H. Stuckenschmidt, *Arnold Schoenberg* (London: John Calder Ltd, 1959), pp. 87-88.

7. J. L. García del Busto, *Turina* (Madrid: Espasa-Calpe, S.A.,1981), p. 72.

8. Nicholas Slonimsky, *Music of Latin America* (London: Harrap & Co., 1946) p. 245.

9. Otero, op. cit., p. 22.

10. Andrés Segovia, "Manuel M. Ponce, Sketches from Heart and Memory," *Guitar Review* No. 7, (1948), p. 4.

11. Turibio Santos, *Heitor Villa-Lobos and the Guitar,* trans. Victoria Forde and Graham Wade, (Bantry: Wise Owl, 1985), p. 17.

12. *Guitar Review,* No. 22, (1958).

13. Santos, op. cit., p. 18.

14. Ibid., p. 19.

15. Some of the implications of this are dealt with in later chapters.

16. Graham Wade, ed., *Maestro Segovia* (London: Robson Books, 1986), pp. 97-98.

17. J. L. García del Busto, op. cit., for this and other information on dates of composition.

18. David J. Nystel, "Harmonic Practice in the Guitar Music of Manuel M. Ponce," *Guitar Review* (Spring 1991): p. 1.

19. See checklist of Moreno Torroba's published solo guitar music in *Soundboard,* Vol. X, No. 1, (1983), compiled by Peter Danner.

20. Danner, ibid.

21. Prat, op. cit., p. 291.

22. Ibid., p. 310.

23. Ibid., p. 280.

24. Ibid., p. 190.
25. Alcázar, ed., pp. 11 & 13.

7. INTERLUDE

1. Fritz Buek, *Die Gitarre und Ihre Meister* (Berlin-Lichterfelde: Robert Lienau, 1926), p. 59.
2. Ibid., p. 60.
3. Segovia, op. cit., p. 10.
4. Buek, op. cit., p. 60.
5. Ibid., pp. 60-61.
6. Ibid., p. 61.
7. Ibid., p. 56.
8. Ibid., p. 58.
9. Ibid., p. 58.
10. Ibid., p. 62.
11. Ibid., p. 62.
12. Ibid., p. 62.

8. THE EXPANDING UNIVERSE

1. Gilbert Chase, *The Music of Spain* (New York: W. W. Norton and Co.,1941) pp. 146-7.
2. Felipe Pedrell, *Cancionero musical popular español* (Valls, 1918-1922, reprinted, Barcelona: Casa Editorial Boileau, 1958), pp. 28-29.
3. Pedrell, op. cit., Vol. I, pp. 29-30.
4. Juan Riera, *Emilio Pujol* (Lerida: Instituto de Estudios Ilerdenses, 1974), pp. 41-42.

9. SEGOVIA'S RECITALS 1926-1929

1. *Politiken,* Copenhagen (29 April, 1927).
2. For further details of Segovia's debut in the USA see *Soundboard,* Vol. XX, No. 3 (Winter 1994).
3. Stover, op. cit., p. 103.
4. Alcázar, ed., op. cit. pp. 43-45.
5. *Sonata No. 3,* recorded 7 October, 1930, issued on *Andrés Segovia Recordings 1927-1929*, EMI CHS 7610472.
6. Alcázar, ed., pp. 46-51.
7. Ibid., pp.52-53.

10. SEGOVIA'S RECORDINGS OF THE 1920'S

1. Stover, op. cit., pp. 219-226.
2. *Miguel Llobet.* EM8003 (Winnetka, California: El Maestro Records, 1982).
3. Liner notes for *Miguel Llobet, The Guitar Recordings, 1925-9* (Heidelberg: Chanterelle Verlag, 1991).
4. Dates taken from liner notes for *Andrés Segovia Recordings, 1927-1939,* EMI CHS 7 610472.
5. *The Gramophone,* Vol. V, No. 3 (August 1927), p. 102.
6. Ibid., Vol. 5, No. 12 (May, 1928), p. 500.
7. Ibid., Vol. VI, No. 67, W. S. Meadmore, "More Gramophone Personalities,"(December, 1928), p. 337.
8. Ibid., Vol. VII, No. 75 (August, 1929), p. 117.
9. See Chapter 12 for resumption of Segovia reviews.
10. *The Sunday Times* (11 July, 1926).
11. Roland Gelatt, *The Fabulous Phonograph 1877 - 1977* (London: Cassell, 1977), p. 246.
12. Ibid., p. 255.
13. *The Art of Segovia, The HMV Recordings 1927-1939* on EMI RLS 745 (1980) and *Andrés Segovia, Recordings 1927-1939* on EMI 7 61047 2 (1988).
14. Robert Philips, *Early Recordings and Musical Style, Changing Tastes in Instrumental Performance 1900-1950* (Cambridge: Cambridge University Press, 1992), p. 231.

11. THE 1930'S

1. Alcázar, ed., op. cit., letter of 22 December, p. 57.
2. Ibid., letter of December, 1929, p. 58.
3. Ibid, letter of 26 February, 1930, p. 66.
4. Ibid., undated letter, p. 138.
5. Riera, op. cit., p. 138.
6. Ibid., p. 138, and Matanya Ophee, ed., *Emilio Pujol Guitar School, Books One and Two* (Boston: Editions Orphée, 1983), p. xvii.
7. Emile Grimshaw (editor), "Notes and Comments," *B.M.G. (A Monthly Magazine devoted to the Interests of the Banjo, Mandolin, Guitar, and Kindred Instruments)* Vol. XXVIII, No. 313 (May, 1931): p. 389.
8. *B.M.G.,* Vol. XXVIII, No. 311 (March, 1931): p. 349.
9. Andrés Segovia's Acceptance Speech on receiving the degree of Doctor of Music, Honoris Causa, Florida State University, Tallahassee, (27 February, 1969).
10. Alexis Chess, "The Revival of the Classical Guitar," *B.M.G,* Vol. XXVIII, No. 312 (April, 1931): p. 374.
11. *B.M.G.,* Vol. XXVIII, No. 312 (June, 1931): p. 423.
12. Alcázar, ed., op. cit., p. 90.
13. Ibid., p. 92.
14. Ibid., p. 102.
15. Otero, op. cit., p. 81.
16. *B.M.G.,* Vol. XXIX, No. 322 (February, 1932): p. 99.
17. Ronald Purcell, op. cit., Vol. 1, p. iv.
18. Bruno Tonazzi, *Miguel Llobet, Chitarrista dell'Impressionismo* (Ancona: Edizioni Bèrben, 1966), p. 17.
19. Purcell, op. cit., p. iv.
20. Tonazzi, op. cit., p. 48.
21. Salvador de Madariaga, *Spain* (London: Ernest Benn Ltd, 1930), p. 480.
22. Ibid, p. 481.
23. Salvador de Madariaga, *Morning without Noon, Memoirs* (Farnborough: Saxon House, 1974), pp. 234 -235.
24. Ibid., p. 235.

12. RECORDINGS AND ENCOUNTERS

1. Dates taken from liner notes for the compact disc reissue of *Andrés Segovia Recordings 1927-1939,* EMI CHS 7 61047 2 (released 1988).
2. C. Henry Warren, "Additions to the HMV Connoisseur Catalogue," *The Gramophone,* Vol. X, No. 109 (June, 1932): p. 15.
3. Allan Kozinn, "Andrés Segovia on Disc," *Guitar Review,* No. 52 (Winter 1983): p. 13.
4. Andrés Segovia, "Manuel M. Ponce, Sketches from Heart and Memory," *Guitar Review,* No. 7 (1948): p. 4.
5. Jaime Pahissa, *Manuel de Falla, His Life and Work* (London: Museum Press, 1954), pp. 123-124.
6. Ibid., p. 124.
7. Corazón Otero, *Mario Castelnuovo-Tedesco, su vida y su obra para guitarra* (Lomas de Bezares, Mexico: Ediciones Musicales Yolotl, 1987), p. 48.
8. Ibid., p. 49.
9. Alcázar, ed., op. cit., pp. 159-160.
10. Pahissa, op. cit., p. 125.
11. Alcázar, ed., op. cit., pp. 109-135.
12. Vahdah Olcott Bickford, "The Importance of Transcriptions in Guitar Literature," *B.M.G.,* Vol. XXIX, No. 328 (August, 1932): p. 226.
13. *The Gramophone,* Vol. X., No. 109 (June, 1932) referring to DB 1536, p. 15.

13. 1933-1934

1. William L. Shirer, *20th Century Journey, A Memoir of a Life and the Times, Vol. II, The Nightmare Years, 1930-40* (Boston: Little, Brown & Company, May, 1984, reprinted Bantam edition, April, 1985), pp. 69-70.

2. Alcázar, ed., op. cit. letter dated 19 April, 1933, in which Segovia announces he would be leaving for India within six days, p. 139.

3. William L. Shirer, op. cit., p. 70.

4. Gibson, op. cit., p. 328.

5. Richard E. Chandler and Kessel Schwartz, *A New History of Spanish Literature* (Louisiana State University Press, revised edition 1991), p. 355.

6. Alcázar, ed., p. 144.

7. Ibid, p. 148.

8. Stover, op. cit., pp. 139-150.

9. Emilio Pujol, *Escuela Razonada de la Guitarra, Libro Primero* (Buenos Aires: Ricordi Americana, reprinted 1956): extract translated by G W.

10. Riera, op. cit., p. 83.

11 Ibid., p. 45.

12. Otero, *Mario Castelnuovo-Tedesco,* p.51.

13. Otero, *Manuel M. Ponce and the Guitar,* p. 52.

14. The copy in the present author's possession is No. 674 and cost $100 in 1994.

15. Prat, op. cit., pp. 289-292. This extract translated by G.W.

14. THE DARKENING YEARS 1935-1936

1. Alcázar, ed., op. cit., p. 153.

2. Wilson Lyle, *A Dictionary of Pianists* (London: Robert Hale, 1985), p. 179.

3. Segovia, op. cit., pp. 118-119.

4. Alcázar, ed., p. 13.

5. Marc Pincherle, "Letter written by Marc Pincherle for a Recital in Paris, June, 1935, by Andrés Segovia," reprinted as sleeve notes on *Andrés Segovia, Guitar,* Brunswick AXTL 1069, a long playing record issued in the 1950's.

6. Bernard Gavoty, *Segovia (Great Concert Artists)* (Geneva: René Kister, 1955) pp. 12-13.

7. The first lutenist to record the *Chaconne* seems to be Nigel North who recorded Bach's *Sonatas and Partitas,* BWV 1001-1006, on 12, 13 and 14 July, 1993, for Linn Records CKD 013/CKD 029.

8. Christopher Nupen, sleeve notes for *Alirio Diaz plays Bach,* EMI HQS 1145 (London, 1968).

9. Alcázar, ed., op. cit., p. 159.

10. Edited by Segovia, copyrighted by G. Ricordi & Co, 1939, reprinted 1969.

11. Quoted in *B.M.G.,* Vol. XXXII, No. 363, p. 230.

16. 1936—THE FATEFUL YEAR

1. Alcázar, ed., op. cit., p. 157.

2. *The Gramophone,* Vol. XVIII, No. 214 (March, 1941), p. 222.

3. Alcázar, ed., op.cit., pp. 157-161.

4. Corazón Otero, ed., Manuel Ponce, *Preludio para guitarra y clavecin* (Lomas de Bezares: Ediciones Musicales Yolotl), Preface.

5. Alcázar, ed., pp. 160-163.

6. Paul Preston, *Franco, A Biography*, London, Harper Collins, 1993, pp.160-163.

7. Otto Friedrich, *Andrés Segovia (Great Performers)* (Alexandria, Virginia: Time-Life Records, 1982), p. 14.

8. Alcázar, ed., op. cit., p.160.

9. Ibid., p. 166.

10. Ibid., pp. 166-167.

11. Ibid., pp. 167 -168.

12. Ibid., loc. cit..
13. Ibid., Letter dated 27 February, 1937, p. 174.
14. Ibid., p. 173.

17. ONWARDS

1. Alcázar, ed., op. cit., p. 168.
2. Recorded by Segovia on Col. Cax 10570, LX 1229 (30 June, 1949). Reissued on *The HMV Treasury, Andrés Segovia*, HLM 7134 (1978).
3. This information was kindly supplied by Angelo Gilardino.
4. Geoff Sisley, "A Gallery of Guitarists 7: Julio Martínez Oyanguren," *B.M.G.,* Vol. XXXIV, No. 381 (January, 1937): p. 94.
5. *B.M.G.,* (February, 1937): pp. 125-6.
6. *B.M.G.,* (December, 1937): p. 82.
7. *The Gramophone,* Vol. XV, No. 178 (March, 1938): p. 436.
8. Corazón Otero, *Mario Castelnuovo-Tedesco,* p. 59.
9. Alcázar, ed., op. cit. p. 183.
10. Ibid., p. 179.
11. *B.M.G.,* Vol. XXXV, No. 392 (December, 1937): p. 81.
12. Philip Bone, *The Guitar and Mandolin, Biographies of Celebrated Players and Composers* (London: Schott & Co. Ltd., 1914, Second Edition enlarged, 1954, Reprint of Second Edition with new Preface, 1972), p. 325.
13. *B.M.G.,* (December, 1937): pp. 81-82.

18. 1938

1. Alcázar, ed., op. cit., p. 184.
2. Ibid., p. 189.
3. Corazón Otero, *Manuel M. Ponce and the Guitar,* pp. 53-55.
4. Ibid., p. 53, and Alcázar, ed., p. 189.
5. *Guitar Review,* No. 88 (Winter, 1992): pp. 2-3.
6. Graham Wade, *Maestro Segovia* (London: Robson Books, 1986), p. 39.
7. Robert Goralski, *World War II, Almanac, 1931-1945* (London: Hamish Hamilton, 1981), p. 64.
8. *Guitar Review,* No. 88 (Winter, 1992).
9. Gregory d'Alessio, *Old Troubadour: Carl Sandburg with his Guitar Friends* (New York: Walker & Co., 1987), pp.16-22.
10. *The Gramophone,* Vol. XVI, No. 183 (July, 1938), p. 60.
11, 12, 13. *Lawrence G. Villa,* "Andrés Segovia," *B.M.G.,* Vol. XXV, No. 399 (July, 1938): pp. 279-280.

19. 1938 (CONTINUED)

1. Bone, op. cit., p. 214.
2. Tonazzi, op. cit., p. 12.
3. *En los Trigales,* publ. Ediciones Musicales Madrid (1958).
4. Vicente Vayá Pla, *Joaquín Rodrigo, su vida y su obra* (Madrid: Real Musical, 1977), p. 55.
5. Victoria Kamhi de Rodrigo, *Hand in Hand with Joaquín Rodrigo: My Life at the Maestro's Side,* transl. Ellen Wilkerson (Pittsburgh: Latin American Literary Review Press, 1992), P. 109.
6. Riera, op. cit., pp. 84-85.
7. *B.M.G.,* Vol.XXXVI (July, 1939): pp. 237-8.
8. Ibid., loc.cit.
9. Simon Wright, *Villa-Lobos* (Oxford: Oxford University Press, 1992), pp. 59-61.
10. Segovia, op. cit., p. 100.
11. *El Noi de la Mare* and *El Testament de n'Amelia* are on MCAM-24018 (1969) and *El Mestre* and *La Filla del Marxant* can be found on Moviegraf 170511/0 (1973).

20. 1939

1. Boris A. Perott, "The Famous Guitarists in Spain," *B.M.G.,* Vol. XXVI, No. 406 (February 1939): pp. 123-4.
2. Ibid., loc. cit..
3. *B.M.G.,* Vol. XXXVI, No. 406 (February, 1939): p. 124.
4. *B.M.G.,* Vol. XXXVI, No. 407 (March, 1939): p. 154.
5. Otero, *Mario Castelnuovo-Tedesco,* pp. 63-67.
6. Ibid., p. 67.
7. Burnett James in liner notes for John Williams/ Sir Charles Groves recording of Castelnuovo-Tedesco's *Guitar Concerto Op. 99,* (CBS 76634), comments that "Segovia described it as a kind of valediction, a tender farewell to the hills of Tuscany," which the composer was about to leave.
8. Alcázar, ed., op. cit., pp. 189-192.
9. Nicolas Slonimsky, *Music since 1900* (New York: Schirmer, Fifth Edition, 1994), p. 442.
10. Alcázar, ed., op. cit., pp. 191-2.
11. Goralski, op. cit., pp. 81-82.
12. For a full account of Franco's attitudes and conduct with regard to his alleged neutrality, the latest and most extensive research is contained in Paul Preston's *Franco, A Biography* (London: Harper Collins, 1993), Chapter XIV, p. 343 onwards.

21. THE SECOND HALF OF LIFE

1. Alcázar, ed., op. cit., p. 193.
2. Ibid., pp. 195 - 197.
3. Ibid., pp. 200-202.
4. Ibid., pp. 209-210. Also in Otero's *Manuel M. Ponce and the Guitar,* pp. 61-63.
5. Alcázar, op. cit., pp. 212-213. Otero, loc. cit., p. 61.
6. Alcázar, ed., op. cit., p. 214.
7. *The Times,* London (24 January, 1977).
8. Andrade Muricy, *Villa-Lobos - Uma Interpretação* (Rio de Janeiro: Ministerio da Educação e Cultura,1961), p. 146.
9. Abel Carlevaro, *Abel Carlevaro Guitar Masterclass, Vol. II, The Guitar Works of Villa-Lobos* (Heidelberg: Chanterelle, 1987), p. 5.
10. Ibid., p. 4.
11. Wright, op. cit., p. 114.
12. David P. Appleby, *Heitor Villa-Lobos, A Bio-Bibliographyg*(New York: Greenwood Press, 1988), p. 6.
13. Wright, op. cit., p. 115.
14. Alcázar, ed., op. cit., p. 213.
15. Kamhi de Rodrigo, op. cit., p. 113.
16. Ibid., p. 114.
17. Otero, *Manuel M. Ponce and the Guitar,* p. 64.
18. Alcázar, ed., op. cit., letter dated 6 January, 1941, p. 234.
19. Ibid., pp. 243-246.
20. *The Gramophone,* Vol. XVIII, No. 214 (March, 1941), p. 22.
21. Alcázar, ed., pp. 253-255.
22. Segovia, op. cit., p. 131.
23. Otero, *Manuel M. Ponce and the Guitar,* pp. 65-69.
24. Ibid., loc. cit., and Nicolas Slonimsky, *Music of Latin America* (London: George G. Harrap, 1946), p. 246.
25. See next chapter for mention of its premiere.

22. SITTING OUT THE WAR

1. Alcázar, ed., op. cit., p. 256.
2. Ibid., p. 259.
3. Ibid., pp. 262-263.
4. Ibid., p. 265.
5. Slonimsky, op. cit., p. 486.
6. Boris Schwarz, *Great Masters of the Violin* (London: Robert Hale Ltd., 1983), pp. 348-349.
7. Robert Stowell, *The Cambridge Companion to the Violin* (Cambridge: Cambridge University Press, 1992), p. 88.
8. Nicolas Slonimsky, *Baker's Biographical Dictionary of Musicians,* 7th Edition (Oxford: Oxford University Press, 1984), p. 1206.
9. Alcázar, ed., from a letter placed between 13 December 1943, and 2 May, 1944, pp. 267-268.
10. At the time of writing, the most recent biography was Alan Blackwood, *Sir Thomas Beecham, The Man and the Music* (London: The Ebury Press, 1994).
11. Humphrey Carpenter, *Benjamin Britten, A Biography* (London: Faber & Faber, 1992), p. 62.
12. Ibid., p. 250
13. Stover, op. cit., p. 171.
14. Interview between Andrés Segovia and Graham Wade in Madrid in 1983.
15. Stover, op. cit., p. 248.

23. SEGOVIA'S EDITION OF SOR'S STUDIES

1. David Tanenbaum, *The Essential Studies, Fernando Sor's 20 Estudios* (Chester NY: Guitar Solo Publications, 1991), p. 5.
2. Andrés Segovia, *Studies for the Guitar by Fernando Sor* (New York: Edward B. Marks, 1945).
3. Philip Bone, op. cit., p. 323. (An erroneous date is given in this entry of an alleged concert by Segovia in England in 1918. A letter to *Classical Guitar,* Vol. 4, No. 7 (March, 1986) by Dr. Stuart Button gives the correct date of Segovia's concert as 11 May, 1928.)
4. Segovia, op. cit.,.p. 33.
5. David Tanenbaum, op. cit., p. 5.
6. Brian Jeffery, "Fernando Sor's 'Twenty Studies' edited by Segovia (Alfred Marks Co., copyright 1945): a reconsideration." *Newsletter* of the Boston Classical Guitar Society (February, 1981), reprinted in *Soundboard*, Vol. VIII, No. 4 (November, 1981): pp. 253-255.
7. Erik Stenstadvold, "Napoleon Coste's Contribution to the 'Twenty Studies' by Sor," *Soundboard,* Vol. XI, No. 2, (Summer,1984): pp. 136-140.
8. Tanenbaum, op. cit., p. 5.

24. THE GUITAR IN 1945

1. *B.M.G.,* Vol. XXXVII, No. 424 (August, 1940): p. 216.
2. Maurice Summerfield, *The Classical Guitar, Its Evolution, Players and Personalities since 1800* (Newcastle-upon-Tyne: Ashley Mark Publishing Co., 2nd Edition, 1991), p. 6.
3. Leslie Halliwell, ed John Walker, *Halliwell's Film Guide* (London: Harper Collins, 8th Edition, 1991), p. 129.
4. Notes on *The Romantic Guitar of Vicente Gomez,* Festival Records, FR12-1444.
5. Segovia, *An Autobiography of the Years 1893-1920,* p. 11.
6. *B.M.G.,* Vol. XLII, No. 483 (July, 1945): p. 206.
7. Segovia, op. cit., p. 3.
8. See Chapter 8 for the account of this incident in The Gramophone (August, 1927).
9. *B.M. G.,* Vol. XLII, No. 478 (February, 1945): p. 114.
10. Eleftheria Kotzia, "Wish You Were Here: Ida Presti 1924-1967," *Classical Guitar,* Vol. 19, No. 9 (May, 1992), p. 11.
11. Anthony Weller, "José Rey de la Torre," *Guitar Review,* No. 99, (Fall, 1994): p. 2.
12. Ibid., p. 6.
13. *B.M.G.,* Vol. XLII, No. 483 (July, 1945): p. 202.

25. THE POST-WAR YEARS

1. *Guitar Review,* Vol. 1, No. 1 (October-November, 1946): p. 3.
2. Ibid., p. 13.
3. Jaime Pahissa, *Manuel de Falla; His Life and Works,* trans. Jean Wagstaff (London: Museum Press, 1954), pp. 159-184.
4. Ronald Purcell, *Andrés Segovia, Contributions to the World of Guitar* (New York: Belwin Mills, 1975), p. 31.
5. *The Gramophone,* Vol. XXCIII, No. 276 (May, 1946): p.143.
6. Wilfrid M. Appleby, "The Spanish Guitar," *B.M.G.,*Vol. XLIII, No. 496 (August, 1946): p. 203.
7. Otero, *Manuel M. Ponce and the Guitar,* p. 71.
8. Wilfrid Appleby, *B.M.G.,* Vol. XLIII, No. 493 (May,1946): p. 145.
9. Otero, op. cit., pp. 71-2.
10. Pinnell, op. cit., p. 41.
11. *B.M.G.,* Vol. XLIV, No. 499 (November, 1946): p. 28.
12 & 13. *B.M.G.,* Vol. XLIV, No. 500 (December, 1946): p. 47.
14. *B.M.G.,* Vol. XLIV, No. 501, (January, 1947): p. 66.
15. *Guitar Review,* Vol. 1, No. 2 (1947): p. 38.
16. Ivor Mairants, *My Fifty Fretting Years* (Newcastle-upon-Tyne: Ashley Mark Publishing Co., 1980), p. 333.
17. Alexander Bellow, *The Illustrated History of the Guitar* (New York: Belwin Mills, 1970), p. 193.
18. Summerfield, op. cit., p. 296.
19. Mairants, op. cit., p. 334.
20. As printed inside the leaflet accompanying strings from Albert Augustine Ltd of New York City.
21. *B.M.G.,* Vol. XLIV, No. 507 (July, 1947): p. 188.
22. *B.M.G.,* Vol. XLIV, No. 498 (October, 1946): p. 6.
23. *Guitar Review,* Vol. 1, No. 5 (1948): p.113.

26. 1947

1. Alcázar, ed., pp. 275-279.
2. *Guitar Review,* Vol. 1, No. 2 (1947): p. 39.
3. *Guitar Review,* Vol. 1, No. 3 (1947): p. 63.
4. *B.M.G.,* Vol. XLIV, No. 508 (August, 1947): p. 213.
5. *Guitar Review,* Vol. 1, No. 3 (1947): p. 53.
6. *Guitar Review,* Vol. 1, No. 4 (1947). Published as *The Guitar Review, Vol. I, Issues 1-6, 1946-8* (New York: The Society of the Classic Guitar, 1974), p. 76.
7. Theodorus M. Hofmeester, Jr., "Segovia and the Guitar," *Guitar Review,* Vol. 1, No. 4 (1947): p. 89.
8. Ibid., p. 88.
9. Fernando Diaz-Plaja, *The Spaniard & The Seven Deadly Sins,* trans. John Inderwick Palmer (London: Victor Gollancz Ltd, 1968), p. 54. *El Español y Los Siete Pecados Capitales* (Madrid, Alianza Editorial, 1966), pp. 83-84.
10. Carlos Vega, "The Miracle which is Segovia," *The Guitar Review,* Vol. I, No. 4 (1947): p. 88.
11. *The Guitar Review,* Vol. I, No. 4 (1947): p. 94.
12. Ibid, Vol. 1, No. 5 (1948): p. 122.
13. See Chapter 24.
14. *The Guitar Review,* Vol. 1, No. 5, (1948): p. 122.
15. Wilfrid M. Appleby, *B.M.G.,*Vol. XLV, No. 511, (November, 1947): p. 21.
16. *The Guitar Review,* Vol. 1, No. 5 (1948): p. 121.
17. George Clinton, ed., *Andrés Segovia, An Appreciation* (London: Musical New Services Ltd, 1978), p. 49.
18. Wilfrid M. Appleby, "Homage to Segovia," *B.M.G.,*Vol. XLV, No. 513 (January, 1948): p. 73.
19. Wilfrid M. Appleby, "The Spanish Guitar". *B.M.G.,* Vol. XLV, No. 514 (February, 1948): p. 87.
20. Jack Duarte, in "Correspondence," *B.M.G.,*Vol. XLV, No. 514 (February, 1948): pp.100-101.

27. THE DEATH OF MANUEL PONCE

1. Miguel Alcázar, ed.,*Variations on a Theme of Cabezón,* Manuel Ponce, (London: Tecla Editions, 1982), Preface.

2. Alcázar, ed., *The Segovia-Ponce Letters,* pp. 281-2.

3. *Concierto del Sur,* ed. Segovia, was published by Peer International Corporation, New York and Hamburg, 1970.

4. Segovia, "Manuel M. Ponce, Sketches from Heart and Memory," trans. Olga Coelho and Eithne Golden, *The Guitar Review,* No. 7 (1948): pp. 3-4.

5. Ibid., Olga Coelho, "Ponce, Lover of Mexican Folklore," pp. 8-9.

6. *The Guitar Review,* Vol. 1., No. 6 (1948): p. 147.

7. Ibid., p. 149.

8. *The Guitar Review,* No. 7 (1948): p. 21.

9. *The Gramophone,* Vol. XXVI, No. 301 (June, 1948): p. 8.

10. *The Gramophone,* Vol. XXXIII, No. 386 (July, 1955): p. 62.

11. *The Guitar Review,* No. 8 (1949): p. 50.

12. Ibid., pp. 48-49.

13. *The Guitar Review,* No. 9 (1949): p. 98.

28. 1949

1. Lionel Salter, *The Gramophone,* Vol. XXVI, No. 308 (January, 1949): p. 141.

2. Wilfrid M. Appleby, "The Spanish Guitar," *B.M.G.,* Vol. XLVI, No. 529 (May, 1949): pp. 166 -167.

3. These recordings were issued on LP (1978) by EMI Records Ltd on *The HMV Treasury,* HMV 7134.

4. Donald Brook, *Conductors' Gallery* (London: Rockcliff, 3rd Edition, 1945), pp. 135-136.

5. Abram Chasins, *Speaking of Pianists* (New York: Da Capo, 3rd Edition, 1985), p. 252.

6. *The Gramophone,* Vol. XXIX, No. 339 (August, 1951):p. 53.

7. *B.M.G.* Vol. XLVII, No. 537 (January, 1950): p. 95.

8. Jack Duarte, "Historic Recordings," *B.M.G.,* Vol. XLIX, No. 558 (October, 1951): pp. 18-19.

9. Isaiah Berlin, *Don Giovanni at Aix-en-Provence,* recorded 30 August, 1949, BBC Third Program, London.

10. *The Gramophone,* Vol. XXVII, No. 317 (October, 1949): p. 82.

11. C. B. Hodges, *B.M.G.,* Vol. XLVII, No. 536 (December, 1949): p. 77.

29. THE 1950'S

1. Otero, *Mario Castelnuovo-Tedesco,* pp. 103.

2. Ibid., loc. cit..

3. Ibid., p. 104.

4. Ibid., loc. cit.

5. *The Gramophone,* Vol. XXXVIII, No. 456 (May, 1961): p. 593.

6. Otero, op. cit., p.104.

7. Vladimir Bobri, "Introduction." *The Guitar Review,* Vol. I, Issue 1-6, 1946-1948, (New York: The Society of the Classic Guitar, 1975): p. x.

8. d'Alessio, op. cit., p. 25.

9. *The Guitar Review,* Vol. 1., No. 4 (1947).

10. W. S. Meadmore, "Andrés Segovia," *The Gramophone,* Vol. XXVII, No. 324, (May, 1950): p. 219.

11. Andrés Segovia, op. cit., pp. 1-11.

12. Eric Blom, ed., *Grove's Dictionary of Music and Musicians,* Vol. VII, R-So, 5th Edition (London: Macmillan, 1955): p. 685.

13. Wilfrid M. Appleby, "The Spanish Guitar," *B.M.G.,* Vol. XLVII, No. 544 (August, 1950): p. 253.

14. *B.M.G.,* Vol. XLVIII, No. 549 (January, 1951): p.71.

15. *The Guitar Review,* No. 13 (1952), p. 15.

16. Otero, op. cit., pp. 105-6.

17. *B.M.G.,* Vol. XLIX, No. 560 (December, 1951): p. 82.

30. Segovia and the Recording Revolution

1. *The Gramophone,* Vol. XXVII, No. 320 (January, 1950): p. 145.
2. *B.M.G.,* Vol. XLVIII, No. 537 (January 1950): p. 95.
3. *B.M.G.,* Vol. XLVII, No. 539 (March, 1950): p. 130.
4. *The Gramophone,* Vol. XXVII, No. 324 (May, 1950): p. 224.
5. "Discus," "The Guitar on Wax," *B.M.G.,* Vol. XLVII, No. 544 (August, 1950): p. 254.
6. Compton Mackenzie, "Editorial," *The Gramophone,* Vol. XXVIII, No. 326 (July, 1950): p. 21.
7. *The Gramophone,* Vol. XXVIII, No .335 (April, 1950): p. 251.
8. J. M. and M. J. Cohen, *The Penguin Dictionary of Quotations* (London: Penguin Books, 1960): p. 208.
9. G. Howard-Sorrell, "Technical Report," *The Gramophone,* Vol. XXX, No. 354 (November, 1952): p. 151.
10. *The Gramophone,* Vol. XXX, No. 358 (March, 1953): p. 261.
11. Segovia, op. cit., p. 182.
12. Andrés Segovia and George Mendoza, *Segovia, My Book of the Guitar* (Cleveland/New York/London: Collins): p. 1.
13. *The Gramophone,* Vol. XXXI, No. 374 (September, 1953): p. 104.
14. *The Gramophone,* Vol. XXXII, No. 378 (November, 1954): p. 260.
15. *The Gramophone,* Vol. XXXII, No. 384 (May, 1955): p. 531.
16. *The Gramophone,* Vol. XXXIII, No. 386 (July, 1955): p. 62.
17. *The Gramophone,* Vol. XXXII, No. 382, (March, 1955): p. 437.

31. 1952-1954

1. Alberto López Poveda, *Andrés Segovia, Sintesis Biográfica* (Linares: Poveda, 1986), p. 12. Juan Antonio Pérez-Bustamante de Monasterio, *Tras la Huella de Andrés Segovia* (Cadiz: University of Cadiz, 1990): pp. 24 & 237.
2. Segovia, *Autobiography,* p. 3.
3. Preston, op. cit., pp. 594-624.
4. Robert Baldock, *Pablo Casals* (London: Victor Gollancz, 1992): pp. 174 -5.
5. John Hooper, *The Spaniards, A Portrait of the New Spain* (London: Viking Press, 1986): pp. 144-145.
6. Heitor Villa-Lobos, *Douze Études* (Paris: Max Eschig, 1953): p. 1.
7. Matanya Ophee, "How Does it End?" *Classical Guitar,* Vol. 13, No. 9 (May, 1995): p. 22.
8. *B.M.G.,* Vol. L, No. 581 (September, 1953): p. 286.
9. Clinton, ed., op. cit., p. 59.
10. *Guitar News,* No. 17 (February-March, 1954): p. 8.
11. Ibid., p. 4.
12. *B.M.G.,* Vol. LI, No. 584 (December, 1953): p. 57.
13. Simon Wright, *Villa-Lobos* (Oxford: Oxford University Press, 1992), p. 106.
14. Andrade Muricy, op. cit., p. 156.
15. *Guitar News,* No. 18 (April-May, 1954), p. 9.
16. *The Guitar and I* (MCA 3965), sleeve notes.
17. Eric Blom,. ed., op. cit., Vol. VII, p. 685.
18. Ibid., Vol. VI, p. 993.
19. Kamhi de Rodrigo, op. cit., p. 174.
20. Ibid., pp. 186-187.

32. 1955

1. Bernard Gavoty, *Segovia* (Geneva: René Kister, 1955), pp. 3-6.
2. Ibid., p. 22.
3. Gavoty, op. cit., pp. 24-25 & p. 28.
4. Juan Riera, "The Art of Emilia Corral," trans. Mrs. A. Korwin-Rodziszewski from the cultural periodical *Ciudad,* Lerida (1954), *Guitar News,* No. 22 (Dec. 1954-Jan. 1955): pp. 1-3.
5. *Guitar News,* No. 25 (June-July, 1955): p. 17.
6. Otero, *Mario Castelnuovo-Tedesco,* op. cit., p. 118-119.

7. *Guitar News,* Ibid., loc. cit..

8. Ivor Mairants, "Segovia at the Bar Musical Society," *B.M.G.,* Vol. LIII, No. 609 (January, 1956): p. 97.

9. In conversation with Ivor Mairants at the West Dean International Guitar Festival, England, on 20 August, 1995, the present author was told that Mr. Mairants still believes this was Segovia's greatest recital.

33. 1956

1. *Guitar News,* No. 31 (June -July, 1956): p. 24.

2. Santos, op. cit., p. 36.

3. *Guitar News,* No. 31 (June-July, 1956): p. 24.

4. Poveda, op. cit., pp. 23-25.

5. Information relating to the 1956 Siena Course is taken from *Guitar News,* No. 35 (Feb-March, 1957): pp. 5-7.

6. *Guitar News,* No. 35 (Feb-March, 1957): p. 6.

7. J. D. Roberts, *Guitar Travels* (Valencia: Spain, 1977): p. 245.

8. Oscar Ghiglia, "A Decade near the Maestro,1958-1968," *Segovia and the Guitar Review*, No. 52 (Winter, 1983): p. 36.

9. Miguel Ablóniz, "The Right Hand," *Guitar News,* No. 35 (Feb-March, 1957): p. 14.

10. Ghiglia, *Guitar Review,* op. cit., p. 33.

11. Ibid., p. 35.

12. *Guitar News,* No. 31 (June-July, 1956): p. 8.

13. *The Guitar Review,* No.19 (1956): p. 32.

14. *B.M.G.,* Vol. LIV, No. 620 (December, 1956): p. 87.

15. Julian Bream kindly provided the present author with this information in a telephone conversation on 24 August, 1995.

34. 1957

1. "Impressions of Segovia on Film," (unnamed author), *Guitar News,* No. 37 (June-Aug. 1957): pp. 9-10.

2. Pascual Roch (1860-1921), *Método Moderno para Guitarra* (New York: G. Schirmer, 1921).

3. Quoted by Tim Verey in "Segovian Smiles," *Guitar News,* No. 37 (June-Aug. 1957): p. 18.

4. Ivor Mairants, "Segovia at the Bar Musical Society," *B.M.G.,* Vol. LIII, No. 609 (January, 1956): p. 97.

5. Tim Verey, loc cit.

6. Graham Wade, *Maestro Segovia,* op. cit., p. 64.

35. The Late 1950's

1. "Andrés Segovia in U.S.A." (unnamed author), *Guitar News,* No. 36 (April-May, 1957): pp. 30-31.

2. Kamhi de Rodrigo, op. cit., p. 170.

3. Ibid, letter from Segovia to Joaquín Rodrigo, from Buenos Aires (10 July, 1957): p. 189.

4. Victoria Kingsley, "The Siena Course in 1957," *Guitar News,* No. 39 (Nov.-Dec., 1957): pp. 17-18.

5. *B.M.G.,* Vol. LV, No. 632 (December, 1957): p. 86.

6. David Knapman, "Segovia in London," *Guitar News,* No. 40 (Jan.-Feb., 1958): pp. 11-12.

7. *B.M.G.,* Vol. LV, No. 634 (February, 1958): p. 134.

8. *The Gramophone,* Vol. XXXVIII, No. 446 (July, 1960): p. 74.

9. A. McIntosh Patrick, "Conversation with Julian Bream," *Guitar News,* No. 43 (July-Aug. 1958): p. 12.

10. *Guitar News,* No. 40 (Jan.-Feb. 1958): p. 23.

11. For details of the origins of *Mazurka* see *Preface* to Manuel M. Ponce, *Cuatro Piezas para Guitarra,* ed. Miguel Alcázar, (Schott, GA 519, 1992).

SELECT BIBLIOGRAPHY FOR PART I

BOOKS BY SEGOVIA

Segovia, Andrés. *Segovia, An Autobiography of the Years 1893-1920.* New York: Macmillan, 1976 & London: Marion Boyars, 1976.

Segovia, Andrés. *La Guitarra y Yo:* (Address read by Segovia, 8 January, 1978). Madrid: Real Academia de Bellas Artes de San Fernando.

Segovia, Andrés. *Segovia, My Book of the Guitar.* Cleveland and New York, Glasgow and London: Collins, 1979.

Segovia, Andrés. *Coplas del Pueblo Andaluz.* Madrid: Instituto de Cultura Andaluz, 1981.

Alcázar, Miguel, ed. *The Segovia-Ponce Letters.* Trans. Peter Segal. Columbus, Ohio: Editions Orphée, 1989.

BOOKS ABOUT SEGOVIA

Bobri, Vladimir. *The Segovia Technique.* New York: Macmillan, 1972.

Clinton, George, ed. *Andrés Segovia, An Appreciation.* London: Musical New Services, 1978.

Friedrich, Otto. *Andrés Segovia (Great Performers).* Alexandria, Virginia: Time-Life Records, 1982.

Gavoty, Bernard. *Segovia, Great Concert Artists.* Geneva: René Kister, 1955.

Pérez-Bustamante de Monasterio, Juan, Antonio. *Tras la Huella de Andrés Segovia.* Cadiz: University of Cadiz, 1990.

Poveda, Alberto López. *Síntesis Biográfica.* Linares: Poveda, 1986.

Purcell, Ronald C. *Andrés Segovia, Contributions to the World of Guitar.* New York: Belwin Mills, 1975.

Riera, Juan. *Emilio Pujol.* Lerida: Instituto de Estudio Ilerdenses, 1974.

Segal, Peter E. *The Role of Andrés Segovia in Re-Shaping the Repertoire of the Classical Guitar.* (A Monograph Submitted to the Temple University Graduate Board): 1994.

Usillo, Carlos. *Andrés Segovia, Artistas españolas contemporaneas.* Bilbao: Ministry of Education and Science, 1973.

Usillo, Carlos. *Acto de Investidura como Doctor Honoris Causa del Maestro Andrés Segovia Torres.* Cadiz: University of Cadiz, 1983.

Wade, Graham. *Segovia - A Celebration of the Man and his Music.* London: Allison & Busby, 1983.

Wade, Graham. *Maestro Segovia.* London: Robson Books, 1986.

BOOKS ABOUT THE CLASSICAL GUITAR AND GUITARISTS

d'Alessio, Gregory. *Old Troubadour: Carl Sandburg with his Guitar Friends.* New York: Walker & Company, 1987.

Bellow, Alexander. *The Illustrated History of the Guitar.* New York: Franco Colombo, 1970.

Bone, Philip J. *The Guitar and Mandolin,* reprint of 2nd edition. London: Schott, 1972.

Buek, Fritz. *Die Gitarre und ihre Meister.* Vienna: Schlesinger, 1926.

Chaîné, Jacques, compiled by, Matanya Ophee, ed. *The Orphée Data-Base of Guitar Records.* Columbus, Ohio: Editions Orphée, 1990.

Grunfeld, Frederic V. *The Art and Times of the Guitar.* New York: Macmillan, 1969.

Jeffery, Brian. *Fernando Sor, Composer and Guitarist.* London: Tecla Editions, 1977.

Liepins, Andrew. *The Guitarist's Repertoire Guide,* 2nd Edition. Nottingham: Spanish Guitar Centre, 1994.

Mairants, Ivor. *My Fifty Fretting Years.* Gateshead: Ashley Mark, 1980.

Otero, Corazón. *Manuel M. Ponce and the Guitar.* Trans. J. D. Roberts. Shaftesbury: Musical New Services Ltd, 1980.

Otero, Corazón. *Mario Castelnuovo-Tedesco, su vida y su obra para guitarra.* Lomas de Bezares, Mexico: Ediciones Musicales Yolotl, 1987.

Pinnell, Richard. *The Rioplatense Guitar: The Early Guitar and its Context in Argentina and Uruguay.* Westport, Connecticut: The Bold Strummer, 1993.

Prat, Domingo. *Diccionario de Guitarristas.* Buenos Aires: Romery Fernandez, 1934. Columbus: Editions Orphée, 1986.

Pujol, Emilio. *Tárrega: Ensayo Biográfico.* Lisbon, Lerida:1960.

Pujol, Emilio. *El Dilema del Sonido en la Guitarra.* Buenos Aires: Ricordi Americana, 1960.

Ramírez, José. *En Torno a la Guitarra.* Madrid : Soneto, 1993.

Roberts, J. D. *Guitar Travels.* Valencia, 1977.

Rodríguez, Melchior, ed. *J. Arcas, Obras Completas para Guitarra.* Madrid: Soneto, 1993.

Romanillos, José. *Antonio de Torres: Guitar Maker - His Life and Work.* Shaftesbury: Element Books, 1987.

Sainz de la Maza, Paloma. *Regino Sainz de la Maza: Semblanza de mi Padre.* Burgos: Ayuntamiento de Burgos, 1982.

Santos, Turibio. *Heitor Villa-Lobos and the Guitar.* Ed. G.Wade, trans. V. Forde & G. Wade. Bantry: Wise Owl, 1985.

Stover, Richard D. Stover. *Six Silver Moonbeams: The Life and Times of Agustín Barrios Mangoré.* Clovis, CA: Querioc Publications, 1992.

Summerfield, Maurice J. *The Classical Guitar, Its Evolution and its Players since 1800.* Gateshead: Ashley Mark, 1982 & 1991.

Tanenbaum, David. *The Essential Studies, Fernando Sor's 20 Estudios.* Chester NY: Guitar Solo Publications, 1991.

Tonazzi, Bruno. *Miguel Llobet, Chitarrista dell'Impressionismo.* Ancona/Milan: Edizioni Bèrben, 1966

Turnbull, Harvey. *The Guitar from the Renaissance to the Present Day.* London: Batsford, 1974. Westport, Connecticut: The Bold Strummer, 1991

Wade, Graham. *Traditions of the Classical Guitar.* London: John Calder, 1980.

BOOKS ABOUT IBERIAN AND SOUTH AMERICAN MUSIC, CULTURE AND POLITICS, AND SPANISH COMPOSERS

Appleby, David P. *Heitor Villa-Lobos, A Bio-Bibliography.* New York: Greenwood Press, 1988.

Baldock, Robert. *Pablo Casals.* London: Victor Gollancz, 1992.

del Busto, J. L. García. *Turina.* Madrid: Espasa-Calpe, 1981.

Casals, Pablo. *Joys and Sorrows, Reflections by Pablo Casals.* Ed. Albert E. Kahn. London: Macdonald, 1970.

Chandler, Richard E. & Schwartz, Kessel. *A New History of Spanish Literature.* Louisiana: Louisiana State University Press, rev. edition, 1991.

Chase, Gilbert. *The Music of Spain.* New York: Dover Publications, 1941.

Crichton, Ronald. *Manuel Falla: Descriptive Catalogue of His Works.* London/Frankfurt: Chester/Edition Wilhelm Hansen, 1976.

Gibson, Ian. *Federico García Lorca, A Life.* London: Faber & Faber, 1989.

Grande, Felix. *Memoria del Flamenco.* Madrid: Espasa-Calpe, 1979.

Hooper, John. *The Spaniards, A Portrait of the New Spain.* London: Viking Press, 1986.

Howe, Maud. *Sun and Shadow in Spain.* Boston: Little Brown, 1908.

Kamhi de Rodrigo, Victoria. *Hand in Hand with Joaquín Rodrigo: My Life at the Maestro's Side.* Trans. Ellen Wilkerson, Pittsburgh: Latin American Literary Review Press,1992.

Kirk, H. L. *Pablo Casals, A Biography.* London: Hutchinson, 1974.

Madariaga, Salvador de. *Spain.* London: Ernest Benn Ltd, 1930.

Madariaga, Salvador de. *Morning without Noon.* Farnborough: Saxon House, 1974.

Marco, Tomás. *Spanish Music in the Twentieth Century.* Trans. Cola Franzen. Cambridge, Mass.: Harvard University Press, 1993.

Muricy, Andrade. *Villa-Lobos-Uma Interpretação,* Rio de Janeiro: Ministry of Education & Culture/Servico de Documentaçao, 1969.

Orozco, Manuel. *Manuel de Falla, Historia de una derrota.* Barcelona, Ediciones Destino, 1985.

Pahissa, Jaime. *Manuel de Falla, His Life and Works.* Trans. Jean Wagstaff. New York: Belwin Mills, 1975.

Pedrell, Felipe. *Cancionero musical popular español.* Valls, 1918-1922 & Barcelona: Casa Editorial Boileau, 1958.

Pla, Vicente Vayá. *Joaquín Rodrigo, Su Vida y Su Obra.* Madrid: Real Musical, 1977.

Preston, Paul. *Franco, A Biography.* London: Harper Collins, 1993.

Slonimsky, Nicolas. *Music of Latin America.* London: George G. Harrap, 1946.

Sopeña Federico, ed. *Manuel de Falla: On Music and Musicians.* Trans. D. Urman and J. M. Thomson. London/Boston: Marion Boyars, 1970.

Stone, J. B. *A Tour with Cook through Spain.* London: Low & Searle, 1873.

Tarasti, Eero. *Heitor Villa-Lobos, The Life and Works 1887-1959.* Jefferson, North Carolina: Mcfarland, 1995.

Trend, J. B. *Manuel de Falla and Spanish Music.* New York: Alfred A. Knopf, 1934.

Wright, Simon. *Villa-Lobos.* Oxford: Oxford Univesity Press, 1992.

MISCELLANEOUS BACKGROUND MATERIAL

Brooks, Donald. *Conductors' Gallery,* 3rd Edition. London: Rockcliff, 1945.

Campbell, Margaret. *The Great Cellists.* London: Gollancz, 1988.

Carpenter, Humphrey. *Benjamin Britten, A Biography.* London: Faber & Faber, 1992.

Chasins, Abram. *Speaking of Pianists,* 3rd Edition. New York: Da Capo, 1985.

Cohen, J. M. & M. J. *The Penguin Dictionary of Quotations.* London: Penguin Books, 1960.

Diaz-Plaja, Fernando. *The Spaniard and the Seven Deadly Sins.* Trans. John Inderwick Palmer. London: Gollancz, 1968.

Gammond, Peter. *The Oxford Companion to Popular Music.* Oxford/New York: Oxford University Press, 1991.

Gelatt, Roland. *The Fabulous Phonograph,* 1877-1977. London: Cassell, 1977.

Goralski, Robert. *World War II, Almanac 1931-1945.* London: Hamish Hamilton, 1981.

Kirk, Elise, K. *Music at the White House, A History of the American Spirit.* Chicago: University of Illinois, 1986.

Lyle, Wilson. *A Dictionary of Pianists.* London: Robert Hale Ltd., 1985.

Melly, Georgeg. *Revolt into Style, The Pop Arts in Britain.* London: Allen Lane, The Penguin Press, 1970.

Philips, Robert. *Early Recordings and Musical Style, Changing Tastes in Instrumental Performance 1900-1950.*

Cambridge: Cambridge University Press, 1992.

Schonberg, Harold C. *Horowitz, His Life and Music.* London: Simon & Schuster, 1992.

Schwarz, Boris. *Great Masters of the Violin.* London: Robert Hale Ltd, 1983.

Shirer, William L. *20th Century Journey, A Memoir of a Life and the Times, Vol. II, The Nightmare Years, 1930-40.* Boston: Little Brown & Co., 1984, reprinted Boston: Bantam Books, 1985.

Slonimsky, Nicolas. *Baker's Biographical Dictionary of Musicians,* 7th Edition. Oxford: Oxford University Press, 1984.

Slonimsky, Nicolas. *Music Since 1900,* 5th Edition. New York: Schirmer, 1994.

Stowell, Robert. *The Cambridge Companion to the Violin.* Cambridge: Cambridge University Press, 1992.

PART II

*A New Look at the
Segovia Repertoire:
An Analysis of
Segovia's Classical Guitar
Masterpieces by
Narváez, Frescobaldi,
Bach, Scarlatti and Sor*

by Gerard Garno

LIST OF EDITIONS

The following is a list of Segovia editions, written and recorded, which includes all such materials used for the analysis presented here. Guitarists may find it helpful to utilize these when studying this repertoire:

> "...*take my record. Put the record in front of you and imitate it.*
> *That will be my lesson. Accept my lesson. Do not fail.*"
> — Andrés Segovia[1]

1.) Luys de Narváez

Canción del Emperador—written score: unpublished.[2] Recordings: Decca DL 9931; Decca DL 79931; Segovia and the Guitar, MCA 2521; The Legendary Andrés Segovia (1989 re-issues), MCA 42071.

Guárdame las Vacas—written score: unpublished.[3] Recordings: Decca DL 9931; Decca DL 79931; Segovia and the Guitar, MCA 2521; My Favorite Spanish Encores, RCA ARL 1-0485 (1974); The Legendary Andrés Segovia (1989 re-issues), MCA 42071.

2.) Girolamo Frescobaldi

Aria con Variazioni detta "La Frescobalda"—written score: Mainz, Schott, 1939. Recordings: Decca DL 9733; Guitar Recital (a recording of a 1968 live concert), Ermitage ERM119ADD.

3.) J. S. Bach

Prelude in D Minor, BWV 999—written score: Mainz, Schott, 1928. Recordings: Decca DL 9751; Saga 5248; The EMI Recordings 1927-39, Angel ZB 3896 (1980 re-issue); The Segovia Collection Vol. 1, MCA 42068 (1987 re-issue); A Centenary Celebration, MCA 11124 (1994 re-issue); Jan Peerce, Marian Anderson and Andrés Segovia, Long Branch, New Jersey, Kultur International Films (video re-release), 1977 (recorded c. 1955).

Fugue in A Minor, BWV 1001—written score: unpublished.[4] Recordings: Heliodor HS 25010; MGM E3015/M2306 (1953); MGM E123; Saga 5248; Decca DL 9795; The EMI Recordings 1927-39, Angel ZB 3896 (1980 re-issue).

Sarabande in B Minor, BWV 1002—written score: Madrid, Union Musical Española, 1930. Recordings: Decca DL 710140; MACS 1032; Segovia on Stage, MCA 2531 (1977); The Segovia Collection Vol. 1, MCA 42068 (1987 re-issue).

Bourrée in B Minor, BWV 1002—written score: Mainz, Schott, 1928. Recordings: Decca DL 710140; MACS 1032, AXTL 1069; Segovia on Stage, MCA 2531 (1977); The Segovia Collection Vol. 1, MCA 42068 (1987 re-issue).

Double in B Minor, BWV 1002—written score: Mainz, Schott, 1928. Recordings: Segovia on Stage, MCA 2531 (1977); The Segovia Collection Vol. 1, MCA 42068 (1987 re-issue).

4.) Domenico Scarlatti

Sonata in E Minor, K.11—written score: Mainz, Schott, 1954. Recordings: Decca DL A596 (1947); Decca ED 3501; MCA 3070; Segovia and the Guitar, MCA 2521; The Song of the Guitar, A Christopher Nupen film, Hamburg, Teldec Video, 1991 (recorded in 1976).

---

1. Constance McKenna, "A Segovia Masterclass," presented in *Guitar Review,* Fall 1986, p. 10.

2. Segovia based his edition on one by Pujol: *Hispanae Citharae Ars Viva, Anthologia de música selecta para guitarra transcrita de la tablatura antigua por Emilio Pujol,* Mainz, Schott, 1956.

3. *Idem.*

4. His edition was based on one by Francisco Tárrega. This may be found in a recent release: *Francisco Tárrega, The Collected Guitar Works,* edited by Rafael Andia & Javier Quevedo, Heidelberg, Chanterelle, 1992.

Sonata in A Major, K. 322—written score: unpublished.[5] Recordings: Decca DL 710140; RCA ARL1 0865; Segovia on Stage, MCA 2531 (1977); A Centenary Celebration, MCA 11124 (1994 re-issue).

5.) Fernando Sor

Variations on a Theme by Mozart, Op. 9—written score: Mainz, Schott, 1931. Recordings: HMV D 1255 (1927); Decca DL 9638; The EMI Recordings 1927-39, Angel ZB 3896 (1980 re-issue; The Legendary Andrés Segovia (1989 re-issues), MCA 42071; A Centenary Celebration, MCA 11124 (1994 re-issue); Jan Peerce, Marian Anderson and Andrés Segovia, Long Branch, New Jersey, Kultur International Films (video re-release), 1977 (recorded c. 1955).

Variations on La Folia, Op. 15a—written score: unpublished. Recordings: My Favorite Spanish Encores, RCA ARL1-0485 (1974).

---

5. Segovia based his edition on one by John Williams, but, to the best of our knowledge, this is also unpublished.

ANDRÉS SEGOVIA PLAYS

LUYS DE NARVÁEZ

Frontispieces from Los seys libros del Delphin de música de cifras para tañer Vihuela *by Luys de Narváez (c. 1500-1560).*

CHAPTER ONE

I n sixteenth century Spain, vihuela composers and performers were thriving.[1] Several outstanding writers for this close relative of the guitar emerged from this period. Luys de Narváez (c. 1500-1560) was one of Segovia's favorites.[2] Narváez was, and still is, one of the most respected vihuelistas of his day. He was a native of Granada, Spain, and the court vihuelista to King Philip II. Not only was he known as a great composer, he is said to have been a remarkable performer, capable of improvising polyphonically in four voices.[3]

While Narváez was a great performer, he differed from Segovia in that he did not occupy such an exclusive position with his instrument. Andrés Segovia is chiefly remembered for his unique achievement of rescuing an instrument from relative obscurity which was caused, in part, by the increasing popularity of the piano as it ascended in prominence to become the favored solo concert instrument in the 19th century. For these purposes, no such Andrés Segovia of the guitar or vihuela would have been necessary in sixteenth century Spain. The popularity of vihuela and guitar music remained strong for centuries to the extent that keyboard music remained relatively obscure.[4]

CANCIÓN DEL EMPERADOR

Several important collections of vihuela music remain from the sixteenth century. It is from the Narváez book, *Los seys libros del Delphin de música de cifras para tañer Vihuela* (Valladolid, 1538) that *Canción del Emperador* and *Guárdame Las Vacas* are drawn. *Canción del Emperador (The Emperor's Song)* is an example of the tradition of taking popular songs of the time and putting them into tablature so that they could be played on the vihuela.[5]

The song (*chanson*) used for this intabulation was *Mille Regretz* by Josquin:

MILLE REGRETZ
Josquin des Prés (c.1440-1521)

"Mille regretz de vous habandonner et deslonger, et deslonger vostre fache amoureuse,
jay si grand dueil et paine douloureuse, quon me verra brief mes jours deffiner,
quon me verra brief mes jours deffiner, brief mes jours deffiner, brief mes jours deffiner."[6]

---

1. Harvey Turnbull, *The Guitar from the Renaissance to the Present Day*, New York, Charles Scribner's Sons, 1974, pp. 5-23. The vihuela was strung with six double strings, or courses. A smaller instrument with only four courses existed alongside the vihuela. This instrument was called the "guitar" (*guitarra* in Spanish), while the vihuela was closer to being a guitar as we know it today (the guitar was used for folk and popular music while the vihuela was used for court and art music). The four-course guitar developed into the five-course guitar and then into the six string guitar which became the modern guitar that Segovia played. Segovia viewed the vihuela as being essentially the original guitar (in his preface remarks to his edition of *Studies for the Guitar by Fernando Sor*, New York, Edward B. Marks Music Corporation, 1945, Segovia called the vihuela the "original guitar"). Even though the vihuela is strongly related, this characterization can be confusing when considering the history of the instrument that was actually called "guitar."

2. George Clinton, editor, *Andrés Segovia, An Appreciation*, London, Musical New Services Ltd., 1978, p. 20. Out of all the vihuela composers, Segovia listed three as his favorites: Luys Milán, Alonso Mudarra and Luys de Narváez.

3. Rodrigo De Zayas, "The Vihuelists," presented in *Guitar Review*, No. 38, 1973. Zayas quotes a man named Luis Zapata, who apparently lived during Narváez's lifetime, as saying: "...There was in Valladolid when I was a boy, a musician of the vihuela called Narváez, of such extraordinary ability in music that he could improvise at first reading four voices on the vihuela from any four voice composition. This for those who didn't know music, seemed miraculous and for those who did understand it, very miraculous."

4. James Friskin and Irwin Freundlich, *Music for the Piano*, New York, Dover Publications, Inc., 1973, p. 44. "Spanish keyboard music of the seventeenth and eighteenth centuries is sporadic and limited. Music for the vihuela and guitar seems to have occupied first place in the attention of Spanish musicians."

5. Harvey Turnbull, *The Guitar from the Renaissance to the Present Day,* New York, Charles Scribner's Sons, 1974, p. 29. This process of rendering notation into tablature was called intabulation. This was not always done literally. Many times improvisational elements were added to the original, as is the case here.

6. Text source: Josquin des Prés, *Werke*, edited by Albert Smijers, Lepzig, Kistner und Siegel, 1925. For an excellent in-depth analysis and discussion of this piece see: Frances R. Poe, *Teaching and Performing Renaissance Choral Music*, London, The Scarecrow Press, 1994, pp. 11-15.

A THOUSAND REGRETS

"A thousand regrets in leaving you and going far from your loving face
I have great grief and grievous pain, so that soon people will see me end my days."[7]

This was said to be the favorite song of the Holy Roman Emperor, Charles V. For this reason, Narváez called it *The Emperor's Song*.

When approaching early music, some have gone so far as to use original instruments, contending that this is the way it was conceived and that this is the best way for the music to be heard today (the purist approach). Segovia took no such view, and preferred to hear early music played on modern instruments.[8] Because this approach involves the transfer of a type of music written specifically for a certain instrument with all of it's own peculiarities, strengths, and weaknesses to another, a literal rendition of the original is not only unnecessary but it could be accused of overlooking a fundamental principle. The principle is this: retain the essential elements and the spirit of the original while adapting it to the peculiarities, strengths, and weaknesses of the new instrument for which it is being edited. This is the approach Segovia took to Narváez and is the approach suggested here. This method does not absolve the editor from respecting the composer's intentions and the performance practices of the particular instrument and style period. It is possible to respect historical aspects while incorporating the excellent editing procedures used by Segovia.

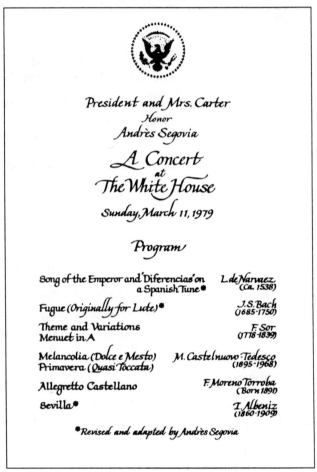

President and Mrs. Carter
Honor
Andrés Segovia
A Concert
at
The White House
Sunday, March 11, 1979

Program

Song of the Emperor and Diferencias on a Spanish Tune ●	L. de Narváez (Ca. 1538)
Fugue (Originally for Lute) ●	J.S. Bach (1685-1750)
Theme and Variations Menuet in A	F. Sor (1778-1839)
Melancolia (Dolce e Mesto) Primavera (Quasi Toccata)	M. Castelnuovo-Tedesco (1895-1968)
Allegretto Castellano	F. Moreno Torroba (Born 1891)
Sevilla ●	I. Albeniz (1860-1909)

● Revised and adapted by Andrés Segovia

Program from Segovia's historic recital at the White House, March 11, 1979.

The primary technical demands of this piece are in terms of its legato requirements. It is therefore a good piece to warm up on in concert. Segovia used it to start concerts, followed by *Guárdame Las Vacas*.

When doing an edition of this piece written for the vihuela, the first major decision that Segovia had to make was in regard to tuning. The vihuela tuning corresponds to the intervals of the guitar with the exception of the third string which would be tuned to F# if the vihuela were tuned to the same pitch level as the modern guitar. Retuning the guitar in order to play these pieces is a definite possibility.[9]

---

7. Translation Source: Dr. William Paden, Professor and Chair, Department of French and Italian, Northwestern University, Evanston, Illinois, 1995.

8. George Clinton, editor, *Andrés Segovia, An Appreciation*, London, Musical New Services Ltd., 1978, p. 20. Segovia said, "I prefer the pieces of the Renaissance and music of the seventeenth and eighteenth centuries to be played on a magnificent Steinway, or a Bechstein—by a great pianist, than on a harpsichord because they think they can remember it—you know, the old time. But it's not. We musicians sigh when the third or fourth piece is played by the harpsichord, because its always the same thing. I used to tease Wanda Landowska, I used to tell her that the harpsichord was like a guitar that had caught a cold... I heard the vihuela played of course... but all those instruments are dead, including the lute... Bream plays it and others also, but the vitality, you know, the guitar is another world." It is clear from these comments that Segovia viewed the expressive potential of the modern guitar as superior.

9. Some guitarists may feel the effort is worth it to retune if they can achieve more similarity to the sound of the original. If the decision is made to use the original tuning, concert performers may want to consider using this tuning for a whole set of pieces. After performing the set, the guitarist can legitimately take the time to go off the stage to concentrate on retuning so as to not burden the audience with this matter. Or, the guitarist can attempt a feat achieved by concert performer Eliot Fisk, who precisely retunes during a bow and the subsequent applause while keeping his attention focused on the audience!

It is also important to point out here that while we know the intervalic relationship between the strings of the vihuela, we do not know what exact pitches they were tuned to. There were different sizes of vihuelas and there can be no doubt that they had to be tuned to different pitches.

According to the liner notes on Segovia's recording, *Segovia and the Guitar* (MCA 2521), Segovia prepared his edition from a transcription by Emilio Pujol. Pujol used the vihuela tuning.[10] However, Segovia chose to leave the guitar in its standard tuning.

The first reason that probably compelled Segovia to do this was a practical one. Retuning the guitar in performance is troublesome. After retuning a string any significant amount it continues to stretch slightly, demanding the performer's attention (this was probably even more of a problem earlier in Segovia's life with the repertoire that he had to play on gut strings). It is hard enough to keep the guitar in tune, so whenever a significant retuning can be avoided, it is wise to do so. Unfortunately, this also means that these pieces cannot be played literally, with the fingerings that Narváez indicates in his tablature. But Segovia had no interest in playing these pieces with the original fingerings. Because of the inefficiency of early plucked chordophones in higher positions, vihuela composers used open strings and lower positions whenever possible. They felt that this way of playing showed off the instrument's best sounds and they were probably right, given the nature of Renaissance and Baroque plucked instruments.[11] These practices are exactly the opposite of Segovia's. He favored closed string fingerings and higher positions. Segovia would have greatly refingered these pieces anyway in order to exploit the type of expressiveness made possible by the modern guitar that he considered so beautiful.[12]

Sometimes the guitarist is forced to use an original tuning when the standard guitar tuning makes the piece too difficult to finger. That was not the case here, nor with the second piece in this set (*Guárdame las Vacas*). Both

---

Luys Milán said in his book *Libro de Música de Vihuela de Mano Intitulado El Maestro,* "If the vihuela is big, use the first string that is thicker than thin. And if the vihuela is small, have the first string thinner than thick. After doing this, raise (tune) the first string as high as it will go and after that you will tune the other strings to the tuning point of the first as will be later taught to you." (Quoted by Alexander Bellow in *The Illustrated History of the Guitar,* New York, Franco Colombo Publications, 1970, p. 57). So we see that vihuelistas simply tuned the highest string to whatever pitch it would hold and tuned the rest of the strings to the appropriate intervals. The gut strings in use at the time would obviously only be able to withstand a certain amount of tension and the tension varied according to the size of the vihuela. While we can say that the standard tuning of the modern guitar is, from the highest to the lowest strings, E B G D A E , we cannot say that the vihuela was tuned to any definite pitches with much consistency at all. This doesn't mean that vihuela composers never indicated any range for tuning. Some of the vihuelistas, including Narváez, did give markings to indicate the range (tessitura) for the vihuela to be tuned to when playing their compositions. In order to understand these markings we must keep in mind that the 16th century composers did not work with the modern tonal system based on diatonic major and minor scales that are used today. Rather, they were using the modal system inherited from the Middle Ages. The hexachord system developed by Guido of Arezzo, an interesting system which produced a scale without establishing a preference for tonality, was still in use. This can be seen by the fact that in his book *Los seys libros del Delphin* Narváez indicates his pieces to be played on vihuelas tuned to tones based on the hexachord system, for example "D sol re," which indicates that the tone belongs to two hexachords.

In the case of *Canción del Emperador,* Narváez indicated that the piece is to be played on a vihuela tuned to an A tuning, and specifically "A re." (For an in depth discussion of modes and the hexachord system see: Donald Jay Grout, *A History of Western Music,* New York, W. W. Norton & Co., Third Edition, 1960, pp. 55-63.) The problem is that we don't know exactly where the notes were fixed in relation to our modern concert pitch of A set at a frequency of 440 cycles per second. Frederick Noad, in the preface to his book *The Renaissance Guitar* (New York, Ariel Music Publications, 1974, p. 12) says: "The range of the top string appears to have been from the E of the modern guitar to an A a fourth higher, though the latter tuning was probably reserved to smaller instruments of shorter string length." What this means is that it would be legitimate to use a capo when playing this music if the performer so desires because the overall tuning level is somewhat arbitrary. Segovia obviously took no such approach. Why should he? To him, a capo would probably just be another hassle. Nevertheless, there are at least two good reasons to use a capo. The first is that it could allow this piece to be played literally by eliminating the sometimes difficult or even impossible stretches that are required, whether the performer decides to use the actual intervals of vihuela tuning or not. The second is that a sound can be achieved that some may feel is lighter and more delicate, producing a character that could be more consistent with sonorities that are in the original, especially if one pursues a purist approach, by playing the piece literally from the tablature. This is not the approach suggested here, but each guitarist is encouraged to experiment and find the approach that seems most favorable.

10. Emilio Pujol, *Hispanae Citharae Ars Viva, Antologia de música selecta para guitarra transcrita de la tablatura antigua,* Mainz, B. Schott's Söhne, 1956. Pujol's transcription is quite faithful to the original tablature.

11. Juan Bermudo, *Comienca el libro llamado declaratión de instrumentos musicales...* Osuna, 1555, p. 99. Bermudo says that the reason vihuelistas should not play on the higher frets is because the pitches are often inaccurate. This gives us reason to believe that they may have approved of using the higher frets and closed string fingerings if the instrument had been free of tuning imperfections. If they had the advantage of instruments like the modern guitar that were capable of good intonation in all positions, maybe they would have fingered things more like Segovia did.

12. Graham Wade, *Traditions of the Classical Guitar,* London, John Calder, 1980, p. 25. Graham Wade makes the point that the technique of exploiting the higher positions was established by Tárrega once the full string length of the modern guitar developed in the mid-nineteenth century. Segovia followed in Tárrega's footsteps.

pieces fit so well on the guitar in its normal tuning that it could be argued that the original tuning makes them more technically difficult. At any rate, Segovia felt that while some early music requires a change of tuning these particular pieces do not. His approach is a valid option.[13]

The next major editorial decision that Segovia made was regarding the use of left-hand slurs. There is no indication in the original score or in the vihuela performance of that time that slurs were used at any point except for select cadential trills.[14] This may have been because it was hard to do slurs on the double strings that were used on the vihuela (the vihuela was strung much like the modern twelve-string guitar).[15] On the modern guitar the use of slurs is much more feasible and they can greatly enhance this music in terms of articulation. They also break up the division of labor between the right and left hands.[16] Segovia's decision here was certainly appropriate. A number of slurs may be retained although some guitarists may prefer to dispense with them entirely as we have no definite evidence about Narváez's own preferences.

In m. 1-3 the "Canción" begins with a section that implies three voices:

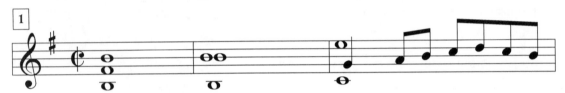

In his original score, Narváez achieved the compositional feat of maintaining a three voice presentation throughout most of the piece. While this creates intervallic sonorities that may sound impressive on the vihuela, the question we must ask (as Segovia probably did) is, does this texture work well on the modern guitar? Some sections may sound thin to modern guitarists, as they apparently did to Segovia. These sections are (in addition to m. 1-3):

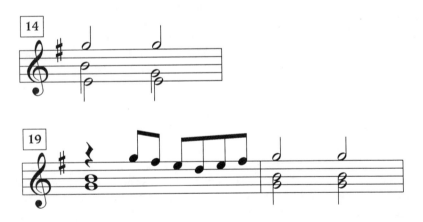

13. George Clinton, editor, *Andrés Segovia, An Appreciation*, London, Musical New Services Ltd., 1978, p. 20. Segovia commented, "Some of these [vihuela and lute] pieces require a change of tuning, it's true, but most of them—no it's not necessary."

14. Philip Pivovar, "Ornamenting Vihuela Music," Presented in *Guitar and Lute*, No. 18, July 1981, p. 35. The use of the trill is documented by Pivovar in a quote from Luys Venegas de Henestrosa's *Libro de cifra nueva para tecla harpa y vihuela* (Alcalá, 1557). Venegas says, "The quibro is to shake the finger on the string and the fret that you wish to play or keep it in place and shake with the second or the third finger one or two frets higher." Pivovar then makes the comment, "Clearly described is first the use of vibrato and second a trill." This does seem to indicate that a slur was at least used as a part of a trill. We are not told, however, if the right hand is plucking while the left hand is "shaking." If so, then the slur would obviously *not* have been used.

15. We do know that the technique of slurring did eventually develop on instruments that used double strings as we can see evidenced in the music of Baroque lutenist Silvius Leopold Weiss (1685-1750) and documented in Ernst G. Baron's *Study of the Lute* (1727, trans. by Douglas Smith in 1976. See also Smith's Ph.D diss., *Late Sonatas of Silvius Leopold Weiss*, 1977). My point here is that slurs are certainly not as natural to play on double strings. This technical reason may be why the use of slurs on double stringed instruments did not fully develop earlier in history, although we cannot rule out the possibility that vihuelistas did not like slurs for musical reasons.

16. Charles Duncan, *The Art of Classical Guitar Playing*, Princeton, New Jersey, Sunny-Birchard Music, 1980, pp. 87-90. Duncan gives a wonderful defense of the use of slurs in early music.

Since this piece is an improvisation on a four part vocal piece, Narváez probably wrote this way in order to show the moving voices, avoiding chordal structures as much as possible. Fuller vertical chordal structures were usually not a part of this trim polyphonic style (See the original setting, p. 397). While appreciating Narváez's efforts to follow this form in his writing, we can still appreciate why Segovia changed things to make what he felt was a better performance edition for the modern guitar. Segovia obviously felt that these sections involved a loss of fullness of sound, as well as projection in concert, so he changed them slightly:

Segovia's example may be legitimately followed by filling these sections out with more notes (although earlier in his life Segovia did play m. 19-20 as written). This approach is not totally heretical to the original version. In m. 36-37 and m. 71 to the end of the piece, Narváez expanded the music to four note chords. In order to keep the linear style of this music, the performer can play the fuller chords and bring out voices that Narváez originally gave. For example, when playing m. 1-3 with the fuller chords, be careful to bring out the inner voice which can so easily get lost (F#-B-G). Or the performer may decide to play these sections exactly as Narváez wrote them. It is possible to retain the spirit of the music either way and this aspect is an important point to consider.

In m. 5 Segovia dropped the note B, interrupting the three voice counterpoint. The original three notes may be retained. Some players may find the slur with the third finger from the first to the second bass notes too difficult, in which case Segovia's fingering may be the solution:

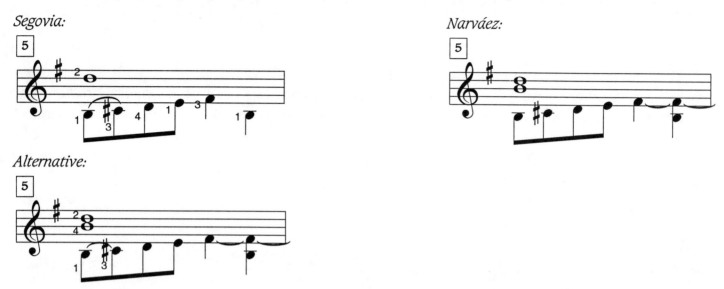

Segovia:

Narváez:

Alternative:

Strict attention should be paid to the counterpoint in m. 5-8. While the lines may not actually sustain that long, they are notated below in a way that shows maximum connection. Segovia achieved a real legato here, and considering the vocal style that generated this piece, we would do well to imitate his example:

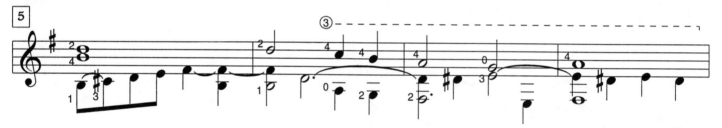

Measures 9-12 are fingered by Narváez in the first position (note: his third string would have been tuned to F♯):

Segovia elected to play these measures higher on the neck:

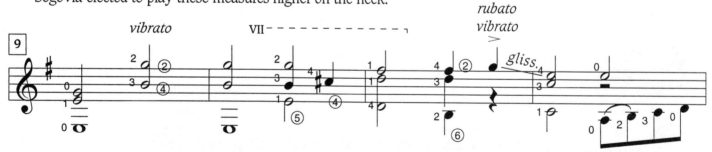

There is no doubt that Segovia thought the original sounded plain and thin compared to the full, rich sound the guitarist can achieve by playing this on the higher positions with a little vibrato. Still, we have little record of vihuelistas using vibrato.[17] The reason for this may be, in part, because of their manner of fingering in the lower

17. See footnote #14 above. The vibrato appears to have been used as a type of ornament (quiebro). It may have only been used in the higher positions where the greater flexibility of the strings would have permitted it. This means that it would have been used very infrequently, since vihuelistas favored lower positions and open strings.

positions and their use of double strings. Both of these characteristics would have made this effect difficult for them.

Segovia's fingering makes it impossible to sustain the note D, m. 11, which really should be sustained as a whole note as the original tablature implies.[18] A fingering is possible which preserves the original voice leading as well as the higher position approach used by Segovia:

In m. 11 Segovia accented the note G. He held it for a free rubato with vibrato and then slid down to the E in m. 12. The combination of these effects highlights the top voice but disrupts the steady rhythm as well as the legato between all three voices. Playing the music more in rhythm, while allowing the other voices to connect may be more faithful to historic performance practice.[19]

In m. 19, loud dynamics with metallic tone color are suggested to contrast with the similar notes just played. In order to achieve a sharp attack on each note, all slurs may be removed from m. 21, rather than playing it exactly the same as m. 15, as Segovia did.

To achieve a very smooth shift between m. 22 and m. 23, the guitarist may depress the bass note F# with the first finger (without playing it) at the same time as fretting the bass note B. Following this the rest of the finger may be laid down for a full bar right before playing the D♮ in the top line. All notes should be allowed to ring for full duration. The rest of the passage can be executed smoothly by sliding the first finger up from F# on the 6th string, where it has been resting through m. 23, to the bass note G for m. 24.

In m. 28, Segovia launched into the first of several ascending *glissandi* which he used throughout the piece:

---

18. Miguel de Fuenllana, *Libro de Música Para Vihuela, intitulado Silva de Sirenas...*, Valladolid, 1547. Fuenllana, as well as other great vihuelistas of the sixteenth century such as Mudarra and Bermudo, commented that the player should leave his left hand fingers down as long as possible to keep the counterpoint going. They also strongly urge the player to hold suspensions long enough so that the dissonances can be clearly heard.

19. Elizabeth V. Phillips and John-Paul Christopher Jackson, *Performing Medieval and Renaissance Music*, London, Collier Macmillan Publishers, 1986, pp. 39-42. While there are still many ambiguities regarding precise rhythmic practices in the Renaissance, one thing we are certain about is that they emphasized a definite and steady beat or pulse. This steady beat was called the "tactus" by Renaissance musicians. It was considered extremely important to maintain a steady tactus. Therefore, the kind of free rubato approach that Segovia used here was not predominate in this style. This is not to say that there was no flexibility at all in Renaissance rhythm but rather to say that the priorities were different from those of Segovia's Romantic style. Rhythmic discontinuities were probably emphasized to a much lesser degree. See also: Richard Hudson, *Stolen Time, The History of Tempo Rubato*, Oxford, Clarendon Press, 1994.

Some modern guitarists have a problem with this expressive device being used at all in this style of music, and rightly so, since this effect is foreign to the performance practices of the Renaissance.[20] Fingerings are given here that keep the closed strings and higher positions used by Segovia but eliminate the emphasis on the slide:

Vibrato along with free rubato was used by Segovia throughout these passages. How stylistic are these effects when compared to Renaissance performance practice? Regarding vibrato, we do have some evidence which suggests that this was used by vihuelistas, although we can't be certain to what degree.[21] Regarding rubato, Segovia tended to use the free or later rubato. This kind steals time from the pulse but does not pay it back. Only very slight amounts of this free rubato are appropriate in this style, and even then it is most stylistic to use it primarily at cadences.[22] Because of the steady "tactus" that was important here, any flexibility should probably be kept within the bar lines.[23] Non-free, or early rubato is the manner of stealing time from either a preceeding or following note so that the pulse is not disrupted. Ornamentation is a form of this non-free rubato, and is appropriate here[24] (to be discussed later).

The harmonics Segovia added in m. 29-30 were not indicated by Narváez. We have no knowledge of the use of harmonics in vihuela music. Segovia's imaginative orchestration techniques often included such modern guitar choices. While being out of character with the historical vihuela, the harmonics are not out

---

20. This technique appears to have been inspired by the vocal slide called *portamento*, which was first used by vocalists as an ornament in the early eighteenth century. The *blatant glissando* that Segovia uses here is certainly out of place. However, a *subtle glissando*, one that is almost imperceptible and used for purposes of legato, is desirable and may be used freely as a matter of articulation. See item #4 on the *glissando* under *The Segovia Style* in the introduction to this book.

21. See footnote #14.

22. Richard Hudson, *Stolen Time, The History of Tempo Rubato*, Oxford, Clarendon Press, 1994, pp. 1-8.

23. See footnote #19

24. Richard Hudson, *Stolen Time, The History of Tempo Rubato*, Oxford, Clarendon Press, 1994, pp. 18-40.

of character with the modern guitar and Segovia's approach to harmonics creates some interesting octave transpositions. The harmonics may be retained, although guitarists are free to omit them since they were not indicated by Narváez:[25]

Segovia:

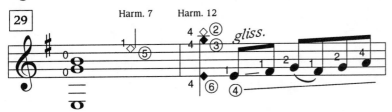

Narváez:

Alternative:

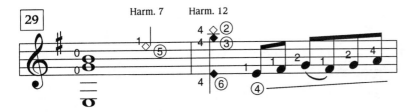

M. 31-34 can be fingered using an open B as presented in the original. Segovia used an open B in m. 31, then switched to a fretted B in m. 32, breaking the consistency. His fingering also requires a changing of note values and hinders the legato of some of the voices:

Segovia:

Narváez:

25. It should be noted that the tuning of the vihuela renders this particular harmonic passage impossible to play on the vihuela and makes natural harmonic sections in general less feasible. The intervallic relationship of the vihuela's open strings is rather dissonant whereas the standard tuning of the modern guitar produces more consonance. This brings to light the question of whether or not the reasons for not using natural harmonics on the vihuela were at least partly for technical reasons. Segovia's approach may be more legitimate on the modern guitar because of its more conducive tuning.

Segovia employed harmonics here as a *coloristic* effect. They may be justifiable on the same basis that some may see for other forms of tone color in early music. To be consistent, each guitarist may want to use the harmonics only if it is decided that tone color in general is to be used in the performance of these pieces.

Alternative:

Segovia fingered m. 48 all the way up the fourth string. A similar fingering can be used which allows for the same subtle sliding up the string effect, but leaves the third finger in place for the chord in m. 48:

Segovia:

Alternative:

M. 53 begins an interesting section of overlapping imitative melodic entries, with the first being the half note A in the second half of m. 53. The second entry begins with the half note E in the second half of m. 55 as the whole note G rings out. The third begins with the half note B in the second half of m. 57. Segovia's fingering emphasizes the moving, descending line. Another possibility is given below which allows for both vertical and horizontal sonorities to be maintained:

Segovia:

Alternative:

In m. 62 Segovia omitted the top melody note, A. This was obviously done for technical reasons because the stretch from F# to A is extremely difficult on the modern guitar whereas it may not have been on Narváez's vihuela.[26] It may be omitted, but those who can do the stretch may wish to include it:

Segovia:

Narváez:

Alternative:

Segovia typically fingered the bass line in m. 66 all the way up the fifth string, as a cellist might do, preserving the same voice:

Segovia:

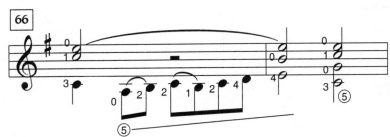

Narváez:

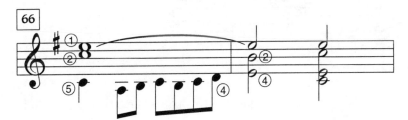

Alternative:

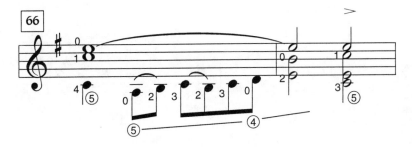

---

26. Vihuelas were made in various sizes (see footnote #9). The stretch seems to indicate that this piece was written for a small vihuela. A way to make such stretches more playable on the modern guitar is to use a capo. The capo can be put at whatever fret the music becomes comfortable, and this may vary depending upon the individual.

However, this means that the whole note C (1st beat of m. 66) cannot be sustained and connected into the B of the next measure, as the alternative fingering presented here allows for. But Segovia didn't seem to be thinking about connecting that line at all. Segovia quite often did not even play the chord at the beginning of m. 67:

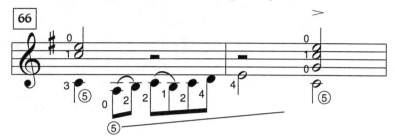

Segovia didn't sustain the whole note D in m. 65 either, but the D can be sustained if the third finger is left down throughout the entire m. 65, and the fourth finger reaches over to start the first note, C, of the bass run in m. 66:

Probably the most significant passage that shows how Segovia was thinking of this piece is m. 67-71, which is immediately repeated:

Segovia gave his concert debut at the age of sixteen. His goal was to raise the status of the guitar, an instrument that he considered to be "the most beautiful."

Segovia changed the voicing of the first C chord in m. 67. He played these chords with a sharp attack. Landing on the G chord, he held it longer than indicated, changing the rhythm.[27] Then he jumped to the third string for the run, ending the passage with a big *glissando* and lots of vibrato and some free rubato. Segovia's fingering preserves the good sound of the prominent line but shows vertical rather than horizontal priorities. These kinds of priorities are different from those of this Renaissance style.[28] The fingering given here for m. 67-71 is a bit more difficult. But, it allows for more legato in the voicing, and is very close to what Narváez indicated. (The passage in m. 70, repeated in m. 74, can be fingered up the third string as Segovia did, but without the blatant *glissando*):

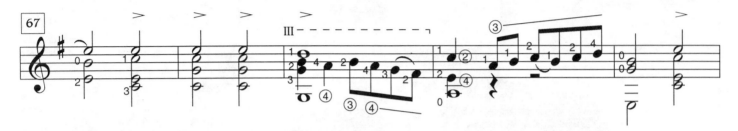

Segovia changed the next to the last measure (m. 78) by putting the bass note E on the second half of the measure. The original tablature may be followed more literally:

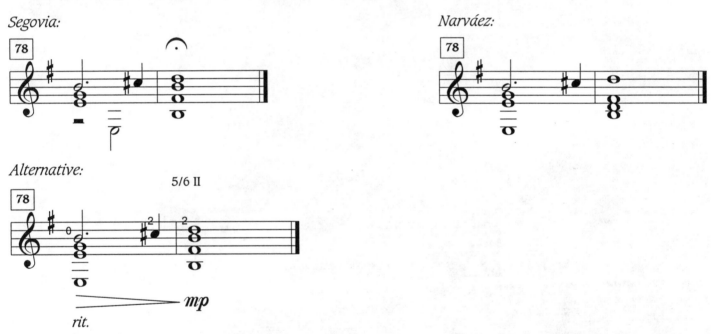

Segovia may have done this to carry the sound through the already slow tempo combined with the closing ritardando. However, if one thinks of this as the four voice Renaissance chanson that this piece is based on, it may make more sense to play it as written. When checking the original *Mille Regretz* by Josquin (see pp. 395-396) one will find that Narváez followed Josquin pretty faithfully in this ending section (Segovia also changed the voicing of the last chord, but this is necessitated by the slightly different tuning).

---

27. Richard Hudson, *Stolen Time, The History of Tempo Rubato*, Oxford, Clarendon Press, 1994, pp. 18-40. In m. 69 we see that Segovia held the chord of arrival for longer than indicated for expressive purposes (compare his version on p. 212 to that of Narváez). He did, however, pay the time back to the pulse by shortening the value of the note on the second beat of the measure. This is an excellent example of non-free rubato, and much more of this would also be stylistically appropriate.

28. Graham Wade, *Traditions of the Classical Guitar*, London, John Calder, 1980, pp. 25-26. Wade quotes the book by J. B. Trend, *Luys Milán and the Vihuelistas*, London, Oxford University Press, 1925: "Luis Milán and the earlier lutanists thought entirely in terms of counterpoint, and not in terms of harmony. They regarded music as made by a number of voices moving horizontally; they did not think of it vertically as a succession of chords." He then adds the comment: "This contrapuntal emphasis, then as now, demands a concentration on the linear flow of the music rather than on the interruptions of a rubato kind associated with Segovia's lavish display of instrumental tone colours. Renaissance timbres in keyboard, viol and other fretted instruments were quite different from modern concepts of what makes a good sound; even the principles of voice production of the sixteenth century could well have been in very different directions from the art of Caruso and Callas."

What about ornamentation? Segovia used no ornamentation in these pieces by Narváez. Ornamentation in general was practised in the Renaissance, although it was usually optional rather than obligatory, as it was in the Baroque. Renaissance composers generally did not use signs to indicate ornaments as Baroque composers often did. Another difference in the ornamenting practice of this period as opposed to the Baroque can be explained by the statement, "In Baroque music you ornament the note, in Renaissance music you ornament the line."[29] There were basically two types of ornamentation in the vihuela music of the Renaissance. The first type is that of diminutions, which is the substitution of faster moving melodic formulas known as "divisions" in place of some of the longer note values in the composition. It is a form that could be applied throughout a *whole piece*. The second type is called "graces." These are short quick ornaments applied to *specific notes*. This piece already incorporates a written out diminution type of ornamentation by Narváez of the original song *Mille Regretz*. Additional ornamentation of this type is not really necessary, although some may still be added. The second type, "graces," were not always written out and may also be applied here, although either type should be inserted with much caution.[30] Ornamentation of the line at cadences was a definite tradition,[31] and it is certainly appropriate to add some here at the final cadence.[32] One of the cadencial graces that was in use throughout the entire 16th century is the *groppo*.[33]

Here is an example of how the *groppo* can be applied to the final cadence of this piece (this ornament may be applied to other cadences as well):

The other most popular grace was the *tremolo*, and this may be tastefully applied throughout:

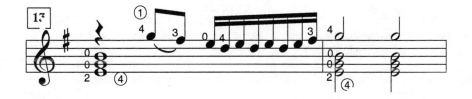

---

29. Noah Greenberg, quoted in "An Introduction to Renaissance Ornamentation," presented in *The American Recorder,* Fall 1967, p. 107.

30. Philip Piovovar, "Ornamenting Vihuela Music," presented in *Guitar and Lute*, Issue No. 18, July 1981, p. 33-35. Piovovar laments the fact that 16th century Spanish vihuela music is consistently performed on the modern guitar without ornamentation. He also acknowledges the fact that Bermudo and Fuenllana and other leading vihuelistas discourage the practice of performers adding their own ornaments: "Ornaments became a mania of over use and many of these writers made strong outcrys against their use, or at least encouraged that taste be exercised in their application."

31. *Idem.*, Piovovar quotes Fuenllana as saying that cadences are one of the few places where ornamentation is appropriate.

32. Diego Ortiz, *Tradado de glosas...* Rome, 1553. Modern edition, Kassel, 1936. This book is devoted to the subject of ornamentation, specifically for the viol. It stresses ornamentation at cadences.

33. Howard Mayer Brown, *Embellishing 16th Century Music*, Oxford, Oxford University Press, 1976, pp. 2-3. Two of the main graces in use throughout the 16th century were the *tremolo* and the *groppo*. The *tremolo* is a rapid alternation between a main note and its upper or lower neighbor. Brown says: "At least one sixteenth-century musician, the Spaniard Juan Bermudo, would tolerate no others." A *groppo* is a cadential trill that takes place between the tonic and the note a half step below. It starts on the tonic and ends by passing to the third below the tonic and returning stepwise.

Guitarists should feel free to experiment with ornamentation in this style. Remembering that extreme caution was urged by the vihuela authorities of the day, the guitarist would probably be very enlightened by reading the applicable treatises as well as listening to and studying the music of this period. Even then, a fairly conservative application is all that could be said to be appropriate.

One final point should be emphasized regarding Renaissance ornamentation. This is that it is impossible to be dogmatic about this issue. There is much that is still unknown. In addition, the ornamenting practices of the vihuelistas were constantly changing.[34] This led sixteenth century music theorists such as Juan Bermudo to say that, even at that time, it was impossible to set down specifics although he eventually did give some guidelines.[35] For modern guitarists that play vihuela music, some general postulations can be made after reviewing the applicable treatises:

1. Sixteenth century vihuela music should be ornamented, at least slightly.[36]

2. The ornaments should almost always begin and end on the main note so as to not disturb the consonances.[37]

3. Stealing time from some notes and adding it to others which results in *unequal* or *dotted* notes is a legitimate form of ornamentation here.[38]

4. Divisions of long note valves (diminutions) may be used, especially when the piece does not already contain them. They should leave the composer's original notes intact on the strong beat, and vary the material in between. Patterns should be based on those in use during the time of the composition.[39]

5. Ornaments applied to individual notes (graces) should be based on the "tremolo" or the "groppo."[40]

An alternate version of *Canción Del Emperador* is presented in Appendix B as an example of one possible way that a piece of sixteenth century vihuela music may be ornamented.

---

34. Philip Pivovar, "Ornamenting Vihuela Music," presented in *Guitar and Lute,* Issue No. 18, July 1981, p. 35. "It is apparent that ornamentation was in a constant state of flux and the variety differed not only from day to day but from musician to musician."

35. *Ibid.*, p. 34. Juan Bermudo in his *Declaratión de Instrumentos,* 1549, said he could not instruct the use of ornaments specifically because "...The fashion of playing them changes every day..." In his expanded version of the *Declaratión* (1555) he included a limited discussion of this practice.

36. Ben Bechtel, "Improvisation in Early Music," presented in *Music Educator's Journal,* January 1980, p. 111. "Most sixteenth century writers specified that each performer was to make up his or her own improvisations according to facility and the particular acoustic and technical difficulties of a given instrument."

37. The conclusion regarding consonances *and* the conclusion that vihuela music *does require* ornamentation were both made after reviewing the following treatises: Luys Milán, *Libro de música de vihuela de mano intitulado El Maestro,* (Valencia), 1536; Luis de Narvaez, *Los seys Libro del Delphin de música...* (Valladolid), 1538; Alfonso de Mudarra, *Tres libros de música en cifras para vihuela,* (Sevilla), 1546; Enriquez de Valderrábano, *Libro de música de vihuela intitulado Silva de Sirenas,* (Valladolid), 1547; Diego Pisador, *Libro de Música de vihuela...* (Salmanca), 1552; Miguel de Fuenllana, *Libro de música para vihuela intitulado Orf'nica Lira,* (Sevilla), 1554; Juan Bermudo, *Declaración de instrumentos musicales,* (Osuna), 1555; Luys Venegas de Henestrosa, *Libro de cifra nueva para tecla, harpa y vihuela,* (Alcalá), 1557; Tomás de Santa María, *Libro llamado Arte de tañer fantasía, assi para tecla como vihuela,* (Valladolid), 1565; Esteban Daza, *Libro de música en cifras para vihuela intitulado el Parnaso,* (Valladolid), 1576; Antonio de Cabezón, *Obras de música para tecla, arpa, y vihuela... recopiladas y puestas en cifra por Fernando a Cabezón, su hijo,* (Madrid), 1578.

38. This is discussed in Santa María's treatise. It is a form of early or non-free rubato. See also: Richard Hudson, *Stolen Time, The History of Tempo Rubato,* Oxford, Clarendon Press, 1994, p. 26-29.

39. For an excellent list of these see: Sylvestro Ganassi, *Opera Intitulata,* Venice, 1535, modern edition by Robert Lienau, Berlin, 1956. See also: Diego Ortiz, *Tretado de Glosas...*, Rome, 1553. Modern edition, Kassel, 1936.

40. Howard Mayer Brown, *Embellishing Sixteenth Century Music,* Oxford, Oxford University Press, 1976. This book gives excellent documentation and many examples.

Andrés Segovia was a master editor and interpreter, and offers an example of how to play this music on the guitar. Obviously, his goal was not to give an academically perfect reproduction of the original but to emphasize elements that he felt would communicate to his audiences on the modern classical guitar, and they loved him for this. For our purposes, however, it is good to point out the original style and intention of the composer for each performer to use as a reference point.

This piece is polyphonic, with the runs simply being divisions of larger notes with some improvisatory elements.[41] While Segovia was certainly aware of and sensitive to the moving lines, he did at times seem to be thinking vertically as if the piece were a series of chords and runs, like a fantasia. Music of this kind must be fingered so that voice leading is well served, sustained notes are held as long as possible, and all suspension figures are observed.[42] The Renaissance emphasis was on a steady beat (tactus) so rubato should be used carefully, within bar lines and not across them.[43] *Ritenutos* are always appropriate at cadences.[44] The music should be ornamented.

The goal sought after and suggested here is this: follow historical guidelines as much as possible without losing the intensity of feeling and expression that Segovia has achieved through his unique performance style on the modern classical guitar.

---

41. Juan Bermudo, *Comiença el libro llamado declaratión de instrumentos musicales,* Osuna, 1555, Barenreiter facsimile, 1957. The sixteenth century vihuelistas called this kind of treatment of a piece a "glosa," and the rules of Renaissance ornamentation applied when such a piece was being composed or improvised. Apparently these glosas were not done well very often. Bermudo says, "He who wishes to take advantage of this book should take as principle advice: that he not make glosas in music. The worst corruption in music is importune glosas." (f. 29v) Fortunately for us, Narváez did do this glosa, producing for us a timeless, charming masterpiece.

42. *Ibid.,* f. 28. Also, Miguel de Fuenllana, *Libro de Música Para Vihuela, intitulado Orphénica Lyra...* Seville,1554, (f. 6v) and Alonso Mudarra, *Tres Libros de Música en cifras para vihuela...* Seville, 1546.

43. Frederick Neumann, *Performance Practices of the Seventeenth and Eighteenth Centuries,* New York, Schirmer Books, 1993, p. 16. "In the sixteenth century, with its measural notation, the tempo was *theoretically* regulated by a standard beat, the tactus, its length referred to as *integer valor* (meaning the untouched, unchanged, and by implication, unchangeable valve). Theorists linked it with such natural rhythyms as the heartbeat or a leisurely walk or defined it by the pronunciation of certain words in a simple manner... For the better part of the sixteenth century the tactus referred to a semibreve but then gradually descended to smaller units; in the early part of the seventeenth century it was often the minum..." The semibreve was equivalent in time value to a whole note. This is the unit of time used for the standard measure length in this piece by Narváez. The tactus would fall on the barlines, and therefore should not be arbitrarily interrupted. Appropriate times to interrupt it would be at cadences. Most scholars agree with this, although Neumann makes the following point: "Though valuable as a rough reference point, the tactus was variable in practice and far from stable as some believe it to have been." (p. 16) It should be pointed out that he is *not* saying that we should apply an arbitrary Romantic *rubato ad libitum* in all sixteenth century music! He points out later that sixteenth century vocal music *did* keep an extremely strict tempo since "tempo fluctuations prompted by the expressive needs of one voice are bound to conflict with similar needs of the simultaneous, independent voices." (p. 21) Music that was not bound in this way could be more flexible. Hence, the original setting of *Mille Regretz* was probably performed with very strict tempo. Narvaéz's instrumental arrangement, *Canción del Emperador,* could have more flexibility. The tactus is still the reference point, and using rubato between barlines would leave it intact (early or non-free rubato). Any unevenness of the tactus itself (late or free rubato) would have probably been very slight when compared to Romantic practices. For an excellent discussion of this see: Richard Hudson, *Stolen Time, The History of Tempo Rubato,* Oxford, Clarendon Press, 1994, pp. 1-12. Regarding rhythmic irregularity that disrupts the steady pulse he says: "...music in general—from any period in history—is not to be performed mechanically and without regard for a sense of the sounds. On the other hand, flexibility of a somewhat higher degree has been recognized at particular times in history..." (p. 11).

Other respected authorities confirm the steadiness of the sixteenth century tactus with rubato in between. In speaking about the performance of sixteenth century lute music ("The Performance of Passaggi," presented in the *Lute Society of America Newsletter,* April 1977, p. 4), lutenist Paul O'Dette has said: "...therefore a fairly strict pulse should be adhered to, normally in whole notes, reflecting the original structure, with considerable freedom between these pulses (The tactus spoken of by Renaissance theorists refers to the semibreve or whole note in most modern transcriptions...)" O'Dette explains his points even further in "Renaissance Performance Techniques with Paul O'Dette" (a report by Christopher Morrongiello presented in the *Lute Society of America Quarterly,* Nov. 1990, pp. 24-26): "We need to develop individual interpretations with more personality... fifteen years ago it was fashionable not to bend any rhythms at any time. Bending rhythms was thought to be something unhistorical... There is, however, a lot of evidence for the use of rubato in Renaissance music, and in general, the contrast of tempo within the same piece... If you stretch in one place you have to make up the time in order to get to the next downbeat in time. This is quite different from the nineteenth century concept of *rubato* where you could take time wherever you want to and you don't have to make it up."

44. Diego Ortiz, *Tratado de Glosas...* Rome, 1553. Modern edition, Kassel, 1936.

Segovia in his dressing room at the Village Theater, East Kilbride, 1984.

GUARDAME LAS VACAS

When Luys de Narváez published his book of vihuela music, *Los seys libros del Delphin de Música* (Valladolid, 1538) it was significant in music history for two reasons. First, it was the book that brought into the realm of notated music the art of *intabulation*. *Canción del Emperador* is an example of a non-literal form of this art.[45] Secondly, and even more importantly, his book contains the first known printed examples of instrumental themes with variations.[46] Segovia was very much aware of this fact.[47]

Guárdame Las Vacas (Look After the Cows for Me) is one of the first examples of theme and variations and is the most popular of those that Narváez wrote. The theme is also called the *romanesca* theme.[48] This is because it was traditionally used as the instrumental accompaniment of an epic song called a *romance*. Variation form appears to have arisen in Spain through the necessity of varying the accompaniment during the singing of these *romances,* which could sometimes include many verses.[49] This practice led to the development of a purely instrumental variation form by the sixteenth century. It is this form that was used by Narváez.

The *romanesca* theme was known in Spain by the name *Guárdame Las Vacas*[50] and was also used by Mudarra, Valderrábano and Pisador.[51] The romantic element of this *romanesca* can be seen in its text:

GUARDAME LAS VACAS
text by court poet Cristóbal de Castillejo (d. 1550)

Guárdame las vacas carillejo y besarte he;
si no, bésame tú a mí, que yo te las guardaré.[52]

(Look after the cows for me, sweet boy, and I shall kiss you,
if not, you can kiss me and I will look after the cows for you.)[53]

The vihuelista's variations on the *romanesca* theme (or bass) were not so much contrapuntal as they were harmonic. The chord progression and its bass line are the fundamental elements. The bass line continues explicitly or implicitly throughout. The harmonic progression Narváez used for his "first part" variations is: III VII i V III, VII i V i. The progression for the "second part" variations is: i VII iv V i VII iv V i.[54]

---

45. Harvey Turnbull, *The Guitar from the Renaissance to the Present Day*, New York, Charles Scribner's Sons, 1974, p. 29. Narváez did not use the notation methods that are in use today. He and the other vihuelistas of his day exclusively used tablature. Therefore, someone had to translate music that was originally written in notation into tablature form (intabulation) as well as adapt the music to fit on the vihuela.

46. Alexander Bellow, *The Illustrated History of the Guitar*, New York, Franco Columbo Publications, 1970, p. 62.

47. George Clinton, editor, *Andrés Segovia, An Appreciation*, London, Musical New Services, Ltd., 1978, p. 20. Segovia said: "Narváez is supposed to be the first to arrange music into variations—in any form of instrumentation—he called them differences." [Ed. note: The Spanish term for variations is *diferencias* and this is without a doubt what Segovia was saying.]

48. The bassline of this theme is known as the *romanesca bass*. It is this ground bass pattern which became the foundation for numerous pieces throughout the Renaissance. Harmonies are implied but were not always included. The bass line is the constant element.

49. J. B. Trend, *The Music of Spanish History*, New York, Kraus Reprint Corporation, 1965 (original printing 1926), p. 105.

50. On his *My Favorite Spanish Encores* album (RCA-ARL1-0485) Segovia called this piece by Narváez, *Variations on a Spanish Folk Tune*.

51. Harvey Turnbull, *The Guitar from the Renaissance to the Present Day*, New York, Charles Scribner's Sons, 1974, p. 31.

52. Text source: Diana Poulton, *The Consort*, July, 1959.

53. Translation source: Diana Poulton, *The Consort*, July, 1959.

54. It is important to point out that the second part variations are *not* built upon the very common *romanesca bass* line, only the first part variations are. The bass line for the second part is similar, but it is really a different pattern called a *passamezzo antico*. See: John Ward, *The Vihuela De Mano*, Yale Ph.D diss., 1953, pp. 206-207.

Narváez's theme is essentially an announcement of the bass line and an arpeggiation of the harmonies that will be the structure for the first three variations. Segovia filled out the G chord on the first beat of m. 2. He sometimes slurred the first notes of this piece but not always. Some guitarists may wish to slur the first notes for reasons of articulation. Because of the technical difficulties associated with this kind of fourth finger slur, some may wish to omit it:

Segovia: *Segovia:*

Narváez:

Some guitarists may be tempted to play m. 3 this way:

Even though this results in parallel sixths, it also produces parallel fifths, which are not favorably regarded in this style, and should be avoided.[55]

M. 4 is a figure that appears in the first variation as well. Segovia fingered this with a totally closed string fingering. The resulting consistency of sound that Segovia was after may not be worth the added burden. The open B sounds clear and consistent enough and is a fine option:

Segovia: *Alternative:*

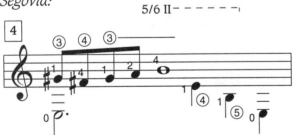

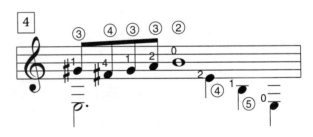

55. Timothy McGee, *Medieval and Renaissance Music*, Toronto, University of Toronto Press, 1985, p. 191.

In m. 7 Segovia used the fourth finger to slur the first eighth note C to the second eighth note D. This is a good solution if the performer finds that it is too difficult to produce significant sound with the third finger. Because the third finger is more consistent with the first position it is suggested here (the slur itself is a downbeat articulation that probably was not used):

Segovia: *Alternative:*

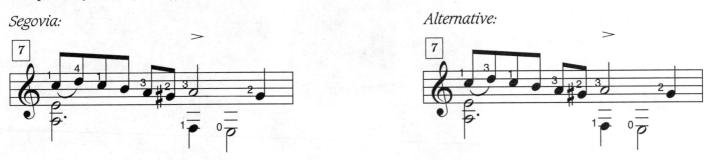

M. 7 brings us to the first cadence of the piece. Segovia sometimes added an extra bass note, playing it like this:

This half step cadence does not occur in the original, except at the end of the second variation. The other sections use the common i-V-i cadence:

Segovia rejected the i-V-i cadence throughout his edition by using the half step cadence instead. At first glance, it may seem that Segovia made this change without a significant reason. This appearance can be deceptive, and after closer examination a very strong reason for making this change can be seen.

Narváez wrote *Guárdame las Vacas* with a theme and three variations. He then composed *Three Variations on the Other Part* which are presented immediately thereafter in Narváez's book, *Los Seys Libros del Delphin.* The other part he is referring to is a slightly different bass line and harmonies, with a short coda added to each variation. Both parts apparently make up an extended version of the original Spanish folk song called *Guárdame las Vacas.*[56] Segovia showed his editorial brilliance by combining these two parts, making a performance edition that could be said to be much stronger and more inclusive than playing each of the parts separately.

In the Second Part, Narváez ended each variation with a half step cadence. Because Segovia combined both parts, he maintained consistency by using the half step cadence throughout the piece, except at the very end. His approach is certainly valid. For the guitarist who is playing only the First Part variations, the cadence should be left as Narváez

---

56. John Ward. *The Vihuela De Mano*, Yale Ph.D diss., 1953, pp. 206-207. The bass line for the First Part is that which is commonly known as the *romanesca bass.* By calling them the First Part and Second Part, Narváez seems to indicate that they are both part of a whole. However, he wrote them as seperate pieces for vihuelas with different tunings. The conclusion here needs to take several factors into account. First of all, *Guárdame Las Vacas* is the name given to the *romanesca bass* as it appeared in Spain. Its place of origin is Italy however (romanesca is Italian). In Italy another popular bass pattern was the *passamezzo antico* (old passamezzo. See: *Harper's Dictionary of Music*, New York, Barnes & Noble Books, 1972, pp. 256-257.) *Guárdame Las Vacas* most often included only the use of the *romanesca bass*, as we can see by the compositions called *Guárdame Las Vacas* by other composers (for example, those by Mudarra). However, the Narváez settings suggest that the *romanesca bass* could be paired with the *passamezzo antico* to form an extended version of *Guárdame Las Vacas*, and this is an excellent way of making the piece more substantial.

wrote it, since there is no need to make the change.

The Second Part variations may be included in an edition a little differently than they were in Segovia's. He inserted the first variation of the Second Part right after the first variation of the First Part (m. 17). He then repeated it down an octave (m. 27), and moved right into the second variation of the First Part (m. 57). He totally omitted the second and third variations of the Second Part. Why did he do this? Three possible reasons are suggested: 1.

Segovia fingered early music in a way that he felt exploited the expressive potential of the modern guitar.

Emilio Pujol did it this way. If, as one of Segovia's recordings suggests (MCA-2521, *Segovia and the Guitar*), Pujol did the transcription into modern notation, and Segovia never saw the original score, then the question becomes, "Why did Emilio Pujol do this?" However, Schott's transcription by Pujol does include all three variations.[57] 2. The piece was too long with all three variations added. This is a good reason. While the original indicates no repeats, Segovia's edition may be followed by repeating most variations, except for these two. Many nineteenth century variation pieces take a short excursion into a minor mode for one variation. But having three variations on this "Second Part" that starts with a minor chord and emphasizes minor harmonies is like having three minor variations in a variation piece, which is almost unheard of, especially in Segovia's time and this consideration may have affected his decision. 3. He didn't like the other two variations. Segovia was well known for his likes and dislikes (including music, guitars, students, and noisy audiences!) But this is not really a bad reason. Vihuelistas at this time were free to pick and choose from different sets of variations.[58]

When looking at the tablature, it appears that the First Part variations are in A minor and the Second Part variations are in D minor. What must be taken into consideration is the fact that Narváez wrote the First Part variations for a vihuela tuned to an A tuning, and the Second Part tuned to an E tuning. That means that even though it doesn't look like it in the tablature, both sets of variations are intended to be in the same tonal area. In the case of the standard guitar tuning, this means A minor. One famous publishing company has published a transcription with the First Part variations in A minor and the Second Part variations in D minor. It has been recorded that way as well.[59]

57. Emilio Pujol, *Hispanae Citharae Ars Viva, Antologia de música selecta para guitarra transcrita de la tablatura antigua* (Anthology of Guitar Music from old Tablatures), New York, Schott Music Corp., 1956, p. 16.

58. J. B. Trend, *Luis Milán and the Vihuelistas*, Oxford, Oxford University Press, 1925, p. 55-56. It should also be pointed out that the variation form developed out of a tradition of varying the accompaniment during recitation of a long romance in order to relieve the monotony of repetition. Apparently many different romances were sung to the same tune. Therefore, vihuelistas were certainly free to repeat variations at will depending on how long a particular romance was. The point is that deciding which variations to play, their order and how much each variation was repeated all seem to have been flexible rather than rigid determinations. See also: J. B. Trend, *The Music of Spanish History,* New York, Kraus Reprint Corporation, 1965 (original printing 1926), pp. 105-109.

59. Thomas E. Greene, "The Hexachord System as it Applies to the Spanish Vihuelists," presented in *Chelys* magazine, Vol. 1, No. 3, Sept. 1976, p. 16. Mr. Greene wrote some criticism as a response to modern vihuelistas who had recently recorded this music but apparently overlooked the original tonal relationships. He has a valid point in criticizing those who would overlook the original vihuela tunings, thereby playing the "second part" variations in a different tonality. This is not necessarily a problem except when doing an edition that combines the two parts. The ground bass for part one is not the same as that for part two, so these could be considered to be two different pieces. Editors are free to transpose whole compositions when they feel it is appropriate.

Fortunately, Segovia did not make this mistake. The consistency and strength of the Segovia edition would never have been possible if he had not been discerning of these details.

Probably the most dynamic section in the entire piece is the first variation beginning in m. 9. Segovia took it at a brilliant tempo. He achieved this, in part, by adding quite a few slurs:

Narváez indicated no slurs in the original, but slurs do help to achieve speed and give shape to the line. Trying to play this variation fast with little or no slurs can be hard on the right hand, causing tension and a loss of accuracy. Some of the string crossings (in m. 10, for example) can make this variation particularly difficult. Segovia's example of adding slurs to some of these fast passages has the technical benefit of helping to produce relaxation in both hands thereby increasing speed and clarity. His approach appears to be an excellent one.[60]

M. 17 begins the set of three variations from the Second Part. Segovia played the first of these with great feeling, using vibrato and some free rubato.

While Segovia usually fingered in a way that would maintain a same string kind of consistency, in m. 19 and 25 he did not. Alternative fingerings are possible, and are suggested here:

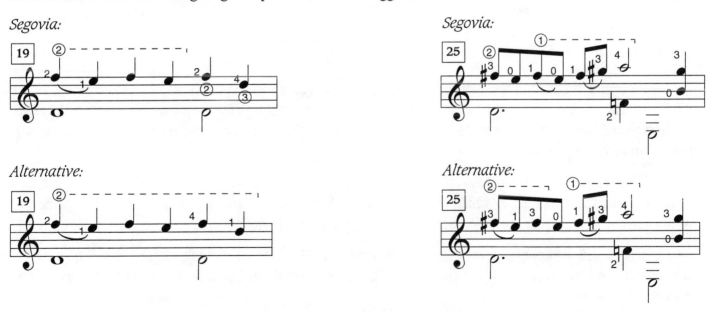

---

60. Segovia took this variation at the speed of about 208 (or faster) set to the quarter note. It is doubtful that many guitarists could achieve this kind of tempo without the use of slurs, since the amount of work required of the right hand at this speed is excessive. While Segovia's use of slurs was certainly not all for technical reasons (they also give shape to the line by articulating it), it is easy to see why he would have added them for those reasons. Segovia's fingerings are tried and proven by the master in performance, so even though one may feel that another fingering is just as good, this is inconsequential if the fingering doesn't prove to be technically secure at the proper tempo in performance. We know that Segovia spent a considerable amount of time working out the technical problems of his fingerings, so they can be trusted for these reasons to a great degree. If one decides to take this variation at Segovia's faster tempo, the chances are that the slurs will be found to be helpful.

Later in his life, Segovia sometimes combined this first presentation of the first variation of the Second Part (m. 17) with the octave lower presentation he played in m. 27. This is achieved by leaping from m. 20 to m. 31. Segovia then repeated the whole section. Guitarists may wish to play this section instead of variations 2 and 3 of Segovia's early edition:

M. 37 begins the second variation of the Second Part section which was omitted by Segovia along with the third variation. Some may choose to incorporate these, and this is a legitimate option. They can be fingered in keeping with Segovia's previous stylistic choices. We will number measures from here on assuming that these have been included (see the score on p. 423).

As if in response to the flowing, continuous line of the preceding variation, in m. 47 the bass line builds fluently in a continuous manner to a high point with the thirds in m. 52. Either a rest stroke or a strong free stroke with a leftward emphasis or "slice" on the *a* finger can help to sustain the top line.

Obviously, a high priority in these last two variations of the Second Part should be legato. It will take considerable practice and listening to achieve smoothness and connection throughout the two lines that weave through both of these variations.

The sixth variation, in m. 57 announces a totally different character. Segovia emphasized staccato in the top line and legato in the bottom. A strong forte approach is also required.

M. 61 may require some extra practice to hold the bar and play this run cleanly. Barring only five strings for m. 61 helps to play the run while holding down the bar. Segovia sometimes used an alternative fingering for m. 61-62 (the right hand fingering for the following two examples is editorial).

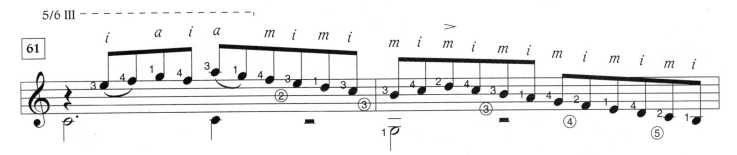

He also used this fingering later in his life:

Because these fingerings don't demand the bar to be held as long they are easier on the left hand. Guitarists who have a problem with the bar may find this helpful. They do, however, require a clipping of the bass notes, and for this reason some may prefer the original fingering shown on p. 425.

The last variation works well as a slur variation, although Narváez didn't indicate that it should be played that way. Segovia obviously felt the need for some additional variety here, and his approach may be maintained. However, a more consistent hammer-on approach is suggested in m. 67 where Segovia used the one blatant *glissando* in his entire edition of this piece:

Segovia:

Alternative:

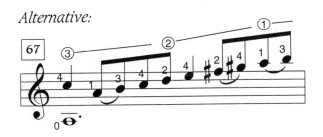

Segovia used a slightly different fingering than the alternative one presented below for m. 69-70, although his slurring pattern has been retained.[61] An interesting way to create variety would be to play this ascending run with only rest strokes and no slurs on the repeat, achieving louder dynamics and a crescendo (Segovia played everything the same on the repeats):

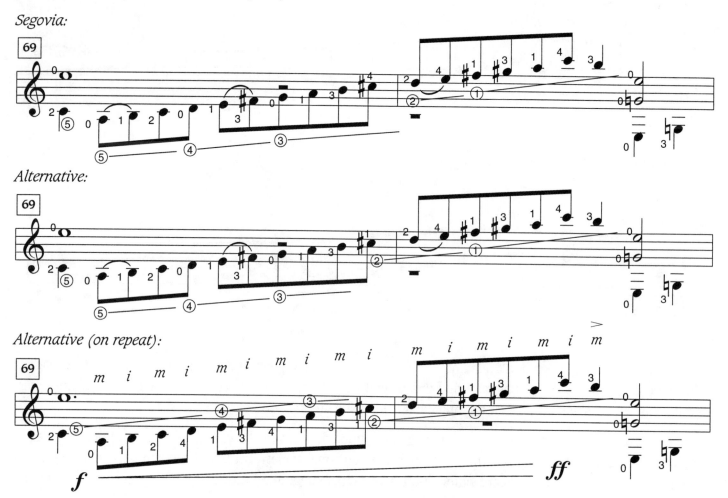

This last variation presents two occasions for Segovia-style free rubatos. Segovia took advantage of the first example, but not the second. They are:

61. Later in his life Segovia played this run with only one slur. He played the slur on the second beat of m. 69, from A to B. He then played the rest of the run in a way similar to that suggested here on the repeat, by making a crescendo to the quarter note B at the end of the run.

The word *rubato* literally means to rob or steal. Rubato can be played in two ways, one in which the stolen time is paid back, the other in which it is not.[62] Especially considering the Renaissance emphasis on the steady beat (tactus),[63] it may be more historically faithful to do the former. When holding the note D in m. 66, one can pay back the stolen time by rushing the next several bass notes slightly. In m. 70, one can speed up while playing the ascending run that starts in m. 69, then pay the time back by holding the quarter note B. Or, the quarter note B can be held for the length of a half note and the remaining notes in the measure may be shortened. Adding a little vibrato to these slightly held notes, as Segovia did to the note D, m. 66, and with a very subtle descending *glissando,* gives the passages more life:[64]

Unpredictably, Segovia didn't use the following closed string fingering for the beginning of the coda in m. 73-74:

---

62. Richard Hudson, *Stolen Time, The History of Tempo Rubato*, Oxford, Clarendon Press, 1994.

63. Elizabeth V. Phillips and John-Paul Christopher Jackson, *Performing Medieval and Renaissance Music*, London, Collier Macmillan Publishers, 1986, pp. 39-42.

64. Vihuelistas did use vibrato, so we really can't say that its use in this music is unstylistic. See footnote #14 under *Canción del Emperador.*

Instead he used a first position fingering:

He achieved a good musical contrast by using the first position fingering for these thirds, and then switching to a second string closed string fingering for the last note, E, of m. 75, continuing down the second string to the cadence.

Segovia had a habit of pausing a significant amount on the last bass note, A of m. 73. He obviously thought of this as an area for a big breath after the phrase and before starting the section in thirds:

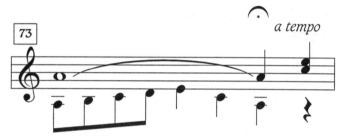

Narváez ended this piece very simply by cadencing to an octave:

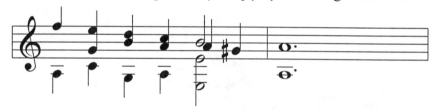

Because Narváez gave no dynamic marking, we don't know whether he intended the piece to end fortissimo or piano. Segovia decided to build through the coda and end strongly with a full chord and his approach is a good alternative. It is interesting to note however, that Segovia sometimes played a minor chord and sometimes a major chord, employing the Picardy third.[65] Rather than ending just with a Picardy third it may be more stylistic to end with some ornamentation at the cadence. Here is a suggested ornamented ending which employs the ornament called a *groppo*:[66]

---

65. Christine Ammer, *Harper's Dictionary of Music*, New York, Harper and Row Publishers, 1972, p. 268. Harper's dictionary defines this as "a major third appearing at the end of a composition that is otherwise in a minor key." The origin of the title is not known. It was in use from about 1550 to 1750, so for Segovia to use it on this piece that was written in 1538 is probably not unstylistic. It is an editorial change since Narváez did not indicate it, but performers at this time may have considered the Picardy third to be an optional performer's choice at the cadence.

66. Howard Mayer Brown, *Embellishing 16th Century Music*, London, Oxford University Press, 1976. For a detailed explanation of how and when to ornament 16th century music, consult this excellent book.

An ending that applies a *groppo* and a *tremolo* may also be used:

One fascinating aspect of this piece that is so vital for the guitarist to hear and understand is the rhythmic aspect. Narváez is continually alternating the division of the 6/4 measures between groupings of two beats per measure and groupings of three per measure, producing a *hemiola*. For example, notice the first three measures from the first variation:

Segovia played these rhythms with great clarity. The bass notes are a helpful guide. Narváez arranged them within the two or three beat measures to create interesting accents:

When preparing an edition it is wise to use notation which connects the beams of the bass notes, as much as possible, in a way which indicates their proper rhythmic groupings. This will show whether two or three beats occur per measure.

Segovia was a great colorist, and he achieved his colors by articulation, voicing and his unique method of fingering up and down the fingerboard as well as by making right hand position changes, from *dolce* to *ponticello*. Interestingly enough, Segovia did not use color or dynamics on the repeats here to achieve variety. Some guitarists may wish to vary the tone colors on the repeats by moving up towards the fret board or back closer to the bridge (Segovia played *ponticello* on the top line of the sixth variation, m. 57-59). The dynamics may also be varied by playing louder or softer on the repeats. Some may think this is too predictable but there are many shades of dynamic and tonal colors that can be employed to keep things interesting.[67]

Segovia achieved some interesting articulations by putting accents on notes or chords throughout this entire composition. For example:

---

67. It should perhaps be mentioned here that Segovia's color in 16th century music was similar to his coloring of other music. Many now consider such coloring to be inappropriate in vihuela and lute music. Still, this does not prohibit us from following Segovia's example, especially since color on the vihuela and lute may be limited by technical considerations that do not apply to the modern guitar.

One great technical benefit that can be found in this piece is that it presents plenty of opportunities for the right hand to arrive at strings ahead of time and be waiting there in preparation to play. For example, m. 1:

As *p* and *a* play the first two notes, *m* arrives ahead of time and is waiting and ready to play, and likewise for each successive note. In m. 3, a rest provides plenty of opportunity to be planted on the notes in preparation for the second beat:

Even in fast passages such as variation one, m. 10, there are opportunities to apply this method of preparation:

After *m* plays the last note, A, of m. 9, *i* travels to and arrives at F# before *a* is done playing the first note, B, of m. 10. In all the staccato passages of the second to the last variation, starting in m. 57, there is wonderful opportunity to have the fingers planted and ready to play ahead of time thus ensuring clarity and tone. Obviously, the amount of time we are discussing is very small, but a metronome can be used to slow the piece down while learning to take advantage of early arrival of the fingers. This control can be maintained by gradually increasing the speed of the piece (by moving the metronome speed up one or two settings at a time) until performance tempo is achieved. Great rewards in terms of control and confidence reminiscent of Segovia, as well as speed and clarity, await the patient guitarist who is willing to study this piece, or any piece, in this way.[68]

Segovia pauses after playing a piece during a recital in the 1980's.

As we have seen, Andrés Segovia took certain liberties when editing this music. He rejected a purist approach. While we can say that some of his interpretive decisions were unstylistic and dated, we can certainly applaud his commitment to excellence in creating a concert edition. Here he applied his lifetime of experience and wealth of knowledge about fingering. To those who would reject his examples totally rather than building upon them with the new scholarship available, we might ask, why re-invent the wheel? If nothing else, Segovia's approach to fingering can be said to have exploited the strengths of the modern guitar. This was one of his great contributions, and to prepare an edition for the modern guitar without considering Segovia's approach is to overlook the work of a great master.

---

68. Charles Duncan, *The Art of Classical Guitar Playing*, Princeton, N.J., Summy-Birchard Music, 1980. See the section on "The Value of Preparation," p. 48-49, and "Homophonic and Contrapuntal Textures," p. 82-86.

ANDRÉS SEGOVIA PLAYS

GIROLAMO FRESCOBALDI

Girolamo Frescobaldi (1583-1643). Drawing by Claude Mellan.

CHAPTER TWO

The most celebrated organist/composer of 17th century Italy was Girolamo Frescobaldi (1583-1643).[1] While remembered today primarily for his compositions, during his lifetime he enjoyed great fame as a performer. Indeed, it is said that at his first concert in Rome in 1608, some 30,000 people came to hear him play![2] This same year Frescobaldi was appointed organist at St. Peter's, and he held this post until his death. It was during this time that Frescobaldi composed his most important works for keyboard. Though he also wrote madrigals and motets, he is chiefly remembered today for his organ and harpsichord works. His publications for keyboard exhibit much diversity of style and tremendous innovation.[3]

In 1637, just a few years before his death, Frescobaldi published final versions of his two main books of keyboard pieces, calling them *The First Book of Toccatas* and *The Second Book of Toccatas*. It is these books that contain the music that was to become Segovia's Frescobaldi repertoire (published by Schott): three *Correnti*, one *Passacaglia*, one *Gagliarda*, and the piece called *Aria detta la Frescobalda (Air called "La Frescobalda")*. This last work is the most substantial of them all, and is the Frescobaldi piece that Segovia was most known for. He often used it as the first piece he would play in concert, and sometimes combined it with other shorter Frescobaldi pieces.

ARIA DETTA LA FRESCOBALDA

On March 18, 1987, I had the privilege of being at one of the last concerts that Andrés Segovia gave before he died. Segovia began the concert that evening with this charming piece by Frescobaldi, which he called "Aria con Variazioni." Segovia's performance of this piece was described as one of the most cherished moments of the concert.[4]

Looking back over concert programs from famous guitarists, it is clear that not only did Segovia open his concerts with *La Frescobalda*, but other famous concert guitarists did so as well. All this shows this composition to be a great piece of music as well as a great piece to warm-up on in concert. Full of variety, yet never overly technically demanding even to an intermediate level performer, *La Frescobalda* provides a good foundation for building a concert program by giving much opportunity for control and expression, thereby giving the performer confidence before he moves on to perform more technically demanding material.

Much of the charm and beauty, and certainly uniqueness, that is contained in this composition springs from the fact that it is one of the earliest systematic attempts to integrate two compositional principles: a cycle of dances and the variation form.[5]

Being originally written for keyboard,[6] *La Frescobalda* presents more difficulties when being edited for the

---

1. Frederick Hammond, *Girolamo Frescobaldi*, Cambridge, Mass., Harvard University Press, 1983.

2. *Grove's Dictionary of Music and Musicians*, Eric Blom, editor, Fifth Edition, New York, St. Martin Press, 1954, vol. 3, p. 494.

3. Alexander Silbiger, editor, *Frescobaldi Studies*, Durham, Duke University Press, 1987, pp. 2-5. "In 1615, Frescobaldi issued two new publications of keyboard music, the *Recercari et canzoni* and the *Toccate e partite d'intavolatura di cimbalo*. On the surface these two collections appear to be a compendium of the varieties of genre in the keyboard music of the time. In truth, he redefined these genres, and introduced new norms that would be observed by many future generations... In 1626 Frescobaldi prepared an edition which combined the *Recercari et canzoni* and the *Capricci* in a single volume... The following year saw the publication of the *Secondo libro de toccate*. Although this volume includes some of the same genres as the first book, the conception of most of these genres is considerably broadened."

4. John Guinn, "A Stellar Performance by Segovia," a review presented in the *Detroit Free Press*, Friday, March 20, 1987. See Appendix E.

5. Frederick Hammond, *Girolamo Frescobaldi*, Cambridge, Mass., Harvard University Press, 1983, p. 185. "A growing interest in dance rhythm is apparent in the collection's five *gagliarde*, six *correnti*, and variations on *Aria detta Balletto* (More Palatino) and *Aria detta la Frescobalda*... The combination of dance and variation procedures is carried a step further in the two variation-sets, which include dancelike sections. These are identified as Gagliarda and Corrente in the *Frescobalda*, which is the first variation suite..."

6. During this period, a tocatta could be played on either the harpsichord (cembalo) or organ. Frescobaldi did specifically designate some of his pieces for organ, but most of his keyboard pieces have no such designation. *La Frescobalda* is no exception. The amount of tied and long sustained notes, however, suggest that this piece was probably written for the organ.

guitar than pieces that were written for a related instrument such as the lute or the vihuela.

Segovia's published edition of this piece[7] shows that he went beyond the point of just adding notes to actually change the original melodic content. His more radical editorial decisions can be re-examined in the light of contemporary scholarship.

The first question we must ask is, "What manuscript did Segovia work from when preparing his edition?" I have found no one who seems to know the answer to this question for certain. He may not have had access to the original. The Bärenreiter edition, a faithful reproduction of the original manuscript, came out in 1948,[8] but this was years after Segovia did his edition. Some of the more severe editorial changes in Segovia's edition may not be his at all, but may have been present in the edition that he was working from.

Segovia may have made changes based on his own preferences. This is a definite possi-

Program from one of Segovia's last concerts.

bility, especially in view of the fact that we find such changes throughout his editions, and he himself has stated his own intention to edit things that he didn't like in the compositions he played.[9] For our purposes, since we do not know otherwise, let's assume that Segovia did work from the original score.[10]

---

7. Andrés Segovia, *Girolamo Frescobaldi, Aria con Variazioni detta "La Frescobalda,"* Mainz, B. Schott's Söhne, 1939.

8. Pierre Pidoux, *Girolamo Frescobaldi, Organ and Keyboard Works*, Paris, Bärenreiter 2204, 1948.

9. Clare Callahan, my professor of guitar at the Cincinnati Conservatory, studied with Segovia for several years at Santiago de Compostela, Spain. She told me that Segovia strongly disliked the minor second dissonances that Joaquin Rodrigo uses throughout his music as a unique aspect of his compositional style. Therefore, he promised to edit those out of the music after Rodrigo died. Fortunately for Rodrigo, he outlived Segovia!

Jim Ferguson has prepared an edition of F. Moreno-Torroba's *Castles of Spain* (published by Guitar Solo Publications, San Francisco, 1993) which documents Segovia's many editorial revisions of those pieces. In his preface remarks, Ferguson gives a concise summary of Segovia's methodology: "A dynamic, opinionated artist, Segovia showed little reluctance to revise, or recompose, a composition—by a guitarist or not—when he saw need for improvement." For more documentation and discussion of this issue, see: *A New Look at Segovia,* Volume Two, pp. 118 and 313.

10. Girolamo Frescobaldi, *Il Secondo Libro Di Toccate* (The Second Book of Toccatas), Rome, 1637. Frescobaldi wrote *Aria Detta La Frescobalda* as one composition among the many that he included in this book. See the original on p. 400. Be aware that this manuscript was engraved in a form of tablature that can be very deceiving at first. Frescobaldi used six and eight line staves which was the common practice with Renaissance keyboard music and, as seen here, was still in use during the early Baroque Period. The staves correspond to the modern and universally accepted five note staves when starting from the bottom line.

At first glance, Segovia may have thought that this piece was in the key of D minor, but that the B flat was not included in the key signature. The truth of the matter is that, as it was originally written, this piece is not clearly in a minor key. It is a piece of early Baroque music that exemplifies the transition from the medieval church modes that were employed through the Renaissance to the standard major-minor tonality that is predominantly used today.[11] This composition was written in the Dorian mode and the accidentals are part of the early Baroque movement to experiment with inflections of the line by chromatic alteration. Therefore, this piece is to be included with those toccatas that Frescobaldi wrote which are neither clearly tonal nor clearly modal.[12]

Modern scholarship does indicate that the inclusion of accidentals in the Baroque period was at times left up to the performer's own discretion. However, this principle does not apply to early Baroque music where the context was unmistakably modal.[13]

What Segovia did with this piece was to raise the seventh and lower the sixth degrees of the scale that provides the basis for this entire composition in many instances when Frescobaldi did not indicate to do so. Also, when Segovia did his edition, he put it in a standard minor key (he chose E minor, one sharp). When this piece is put in a minor key, it appears that Frescobaldi was raising the sixth and seventh scale degrees and just forgot to do so at certain times. But when the key signature is left to correspond to the Dorian mode (two sharps in E, no sharps or flats in original key at D) the sixth degree is naturally always raised (except when modulating) and we can see that Frescobaldi raised the seventh only occasionally as a chromatic alteration. When the piece is left in Dorian, it makes sense to have the sixth raised and not the seventh. Without an understanding of the historic modal context, any editor would naturally think it would be a mistake to raise the sixth degree of a minor scale and not the seventh, since this does not in any way conform to the commonly accepted standards of using the natural, harmonic or melodic minor scales.

What Segovia presents us with is an edition that fairly consistently employs the melodic minor scale (T=tone or whole step, S=semi-tone or half step):

Original tonal center, D:

Guitar edition tonal center, E:

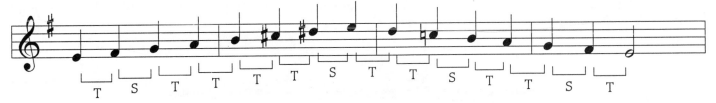

11. Donald Jay Grout, *A History of Western Music*, New York, W. W. Norton & Company, 1960, pp. 302-303.

12. Frederick Hammond, *Girolamo Frescobaldi*, Cambridge, Massachusetts, Harvard University Press, 1983, pp. 152-153.

13. Robert Donington, *Baroque Music: Style and Performance*, London, Faber Music Ltd., 1982, pp. 70-73. Donington says, "Except where modal tonality intervenes, it may be regarded as almost certain that the seventh of the scale as leading note, and the sixth of the scale in support of it, are to be taken sharp..."

as opposed to the Dorian mode:

Original tonal center, D:

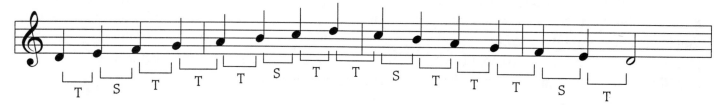

Guitar edition tonal center, E:

When looking at the original it becomes obvious that Frescobaldi was employing the raised seventh mostly within harmonic structures and at cadences. He almost always changes the dominant (v) to a major dominant (V). In addition, he almost always raised the third of the final chord (Picardy Third) to end each section, which was common practice at that time.[14]

All in all, there are indications that, in the Baroque period, different interpretations of where accidentals are to be applied are acceptable, but only when there are no ambiguities as to the composer's intentions.[15] How do we know, then, that Frescobaldi did not leave the treatment of accidentals in this piece ambiguous and up to the performer's discretion, thereby justifying the kind of editorial treatment that Segovia applies here? We have a definite confirmation of Frescobaldi's intention in regard to accidentals shown to us by a manuscript tablature at Turin, which was probably written about 1637, right after Frescobaldi finished the original. This manuscript is known for giving precise notation of the composer's intention for accidentals.[16]

Changing this piece from the Dorian mode to a minor key is a radical change in the sense that what is changed is the melodic content and the sound of the whole composition. Guitarists who have always played the Segovia edition may be a bit surprised when first playing this piece as Frescobaldi wrote it. The Segovia edition has caused many to become used to the sound of the strict minor tonality that he put it in. Early music may sound somewhat foreign to us, but part of the beauty of historic music is its representation of the melodic and harmonic style of the period that it was written in. The musical creativity that comes to us through history provides concert performers with a rich and colorful musical palette to choose from and the variety of historic styles keeps concert programs interesting. Therefore, it is preferable to leave the melodic content of this piece just as Frescobaldi wrote it.

---

14. *Idem.*

15. *Idem.*

16. In the preface of a modern transcription for keyboard by Etienne Darbellay the following footnote describing the manuscript at Turin is given: "Frescobaldi's two toccata books were almost entirely copied in this sizeable manuscript collection written in German organ tablature notation: cf. O. Mischiati, L'intavolatura d'organo tedesca della Biblioteca Nazionale de Torino, in <L'Organo> IV (1963), pp. 1-154. This type of notation, as it is known, does not allow, at least in principle, any accidental to be left ambiguous."

Segovia changed many notes by adding accidentals or just by virtue of the fact that he changed the key signature. The following is a list of some sections where Segovia changed notes as compared with the original (transposed to the same tonal center as the guitar edition for the sake of comparison.):[17]

Segovia:*

Frescobaldi:

Alternative:

Segovia:*

Frescobaldi:

Alternative:

---

17. Because Segovia divided measures up differently at cadences, the measure numbers for his edition and this edition do not correspond exactly. For the sake of convenience, we will label Segovia's measures so that they correspond to the modern edition presented in Appendix B.

Segovia:

Frescobaldi:

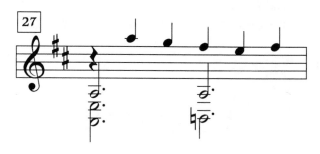

Alternative:

hinge bar II

Segovia:

Frescobaldi:

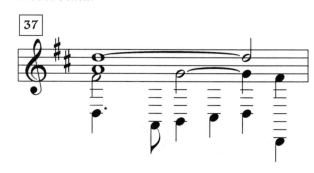

Alternative:

Segovia:

Frescobaldi:

Alternative:

*Segovia:**

Frescobaldi:

Alternative:

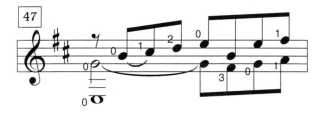

*Segovia:**

Frescobaldi:

Alternative:

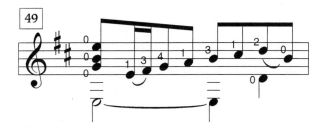

*Segovia:**

Frescobaldi:

Alternative:

*Segovia:**

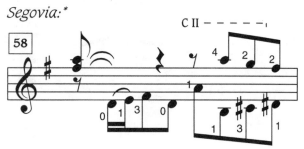

Frescobaldi:

Alternative:

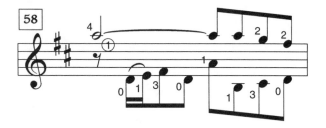

*Segovia:**

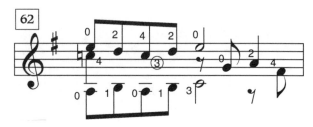

Frescobaldi:

Alternative:

Another major consideration Segovia had to make when preparing this edition was the question of what key this piece should be transcribed into in order to make it playable on the guitar. The original being in D, it was very possible to use that key for the guitar version. It would therefore have started like this:

The melody sounds very low in D. Keeping in mind that the guitar sounds an octave lower than written, we must realize that this is drastically low. A higher key would probably work better. Segovia chose to transpose the piece to E, which is a good key for this piece. It allows for the use of the open bass strings without taking the music too far from the original key.

Segovia started his edition by indicating that the melody is to be played on the second string. He played this melody with lots of heavy vibrato and rubato. His musical marking is "pp, dolce y bien cantado" (very soft, sweet and very singing). He also indicated that the first chord is to be rolled:*

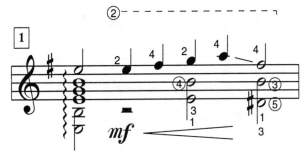

Segovia obviously had a musical concept in mind here. But does this concept line up with the intentions of the composer? It is helpful to read the instructions that Frescobaldi himself wrote in the preface to the collection of pieces from which this composition is taken.[18] The things he said that are relevant to the performance practice of these compositions as played on the guitar are:

1. This music should not be played strictly. The performer should take the beat sometimes slowly, sometimes quickly, or even pausing depending on the performer's sense of expression.

2. Individual sections may be played separately (We can probably assume that Frescobaldi means here that individual movements can be played separately).

3. The opening chords should be played slowly. They should also be arpeggiated. Chords in the middle of the piece, as well as suspensions and dissonances, should not be arpeggiated.

4. The tempo should be strongly retarded at cadences, and especially at the ending cadence.

5. One should observe a broad tempo, but movements where there is no passage work should be played fairly quickly.

6. It is left to the good taste and judgment of the player to select the right tempo and style of playing which are best suited to the spirit of each movement.

As we can see, Frescobaldi allows for much liberty to be taken with his music. Segovia's approach seems very consistent with Frescobaldi's guidelines in regard to musical interpretation. Throughout the piece we find Segovia observing *ritardandos* and taking the kind of liberties granted by the composer. The performer should follow in Segovia's footsteps and make this piece as full of life, variety and expression as possible.

But what about vibrato? Contrary to what some may have thought, this expressive device was freely in use throughout the Baroque period.[19] Even in the early Baroque period, musicians were describing vibrato. They said that this was produced by a "trembling" of the left hand fingers on stringed instruments. Agricola says that "one shapes with free trembling the sweet sound of the melody." It is good to keep in mind that

18. Girolamo Frescobaldi, *Il Secondo Libro Di Toccate*, Rome, 1637.

19. Sylvestro di Ganassi, *Regola Rubertina*, Venice, 1542, Ch. 11, also: Martin Agricola, *Musica Instrumentalis Deudsch*, Wittenberg, 1645, pp. 42-43.

while the musicians during this period did use vibrato, it was a moderate vibrato.[20] Therefore it is wrong to exclude vibrato from Baroque music for any historical reason. It is also not historically accurate to use a very intense romantic vibrato either. Segovia certainly did seem to use the latter.

In m. 1 we see that Segovia played the note B on the third and fourth beats as two half notes when it was written in the original as two half notes tied together (a whole note):

Frescobaldi:

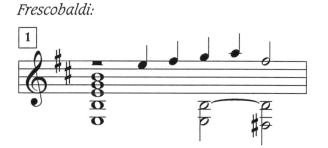

*Segovia:**

We must keep in mind that this piece was probably written for organ, an instrument of infinite sustain. By contrast, when a note is played on the guitar, it begins to decay immediately. In editing this piece for guitar, it is sometimes helpful to divide longer notes up into smaller ones, and especially if the notes concerned are only harmonic tones, rather than melodic. Segovia was very sensitive to this issue.

A quick analysis of this piece reveals that, while it is contrapuntal, the bass and the melody lines are prominent with inner voices serving to help create the harmonic framework that provides the basis for this composition. This shows the tendency in the Baroque period to fit compositions around a series of harmonic chord progressions.[21] The important parts in this style are the harmonies and the bass and treble lines. The harmonic structure for Frescobaldi's theme and variations is: i V i iv V III v VI VII III. This section is repeated, followed by: II i iv V IV VI V i (or I). This is helpful to know when preparing an edition so that we can make sure that these important elements are preserved.

Segovia's sensitivity to these facts can be seen even in the first measure of his edition. Here he preserves the harmonic and melodic elements even if the inner voice line had to be somewhat altered. However, if a guitarist wanted to play the first measure exactly as Frescobaldi wrote it, with the whole note B sustained, it would be easier to finger this section down in the second position:

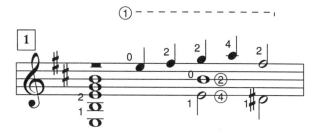

But to finger this measure this way means that the fingering of the melody on the second string in the higher positions cannot be done. The question is, what is more important, sustaining that inner voice whole note, or having the melody played on the second string in the higher positions where a fuller and richer sound can be obtained? Segovia was a master at making these types of editorial decisions.

---

20. Michael Praetorius, *Syntagma Musicum*, Wolfenbuttel, 1619, Vol. III, p. 231. Praetorius advised singers to use a "fine, pleasing trembling and shaking voice... but with moderation."

21. Donald Jay Grout, *A History of Western Music*, New York, W. W. Norton & Company, 1960, pp. 300-302. Grout says, "...the sound ideal of the Baroque was a firm bass and a florid treble, held together by unobtrusive harmony... The ideas that were new in the Baroque were the emphasis on the bass, the isolation of the bass and treble as the two essential lines of the texture, and the seeming indifference to the inner voice lines."

Segovia was the most celebrated classical guitarist in history.

He obviously knew that the inner voices were not as important in this style as the harmonies, melody and bass. Dividing inner notes up into shorter notes rather than sustaining them is also very appropriate when it helps to preserve the important elements. (Dividing long notes up achieves this by causing the notes to be heard longer rather than to have their sound die out due to the guitar's inability to sustain them for very long. Segovia also took the liberty of tying notes together at certain times when the decay factor was *not* an issue, as shown in m. 17 below.) It is also not destructive to the important musical elements to add notes that are a part of the harmonic structure, or to transpose notes up or down an octave to facilitate a more playable edition. Segovia edited many sections throughout this piece based on these important considerations:

*Segovia:**

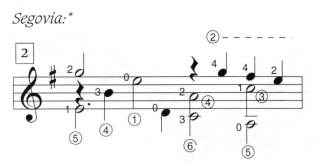

Frescobaldi:

Alternative:

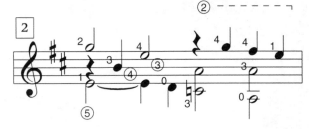

*Segovia:**

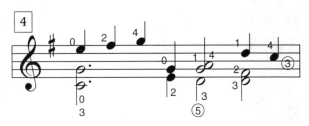

Frescobaldi:

Alternative:

*Segovia:**

Frescobaldi:

Alternative: hinge bar VII   hinge bar VII

Segovia:*

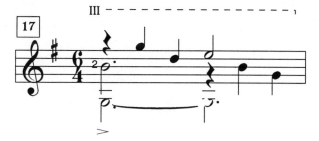

Frescobaldi:

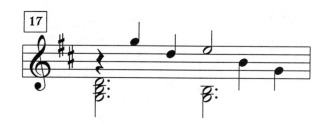

Alternative:

Segovia:*

Frescobaldi:

Alternative:

Segovia:

Frescobaldi:

Alternative:

We can see how Segovia masterfully edited sections of this piece to bring out the important elements with utmost expression. He created a playable edition by taking into consideration the unique qualities of his own instrument. There are, however, some editorial aspects of Segovia's work that are questionable. If we edit this piece with the premise that we are trying to preserve the original, then certainly melodic and harmonic content are primary. Segovia did make changes that go past the point where some may draw the line in this matter. For example, Segovia started the piece with a full E minor chord:*

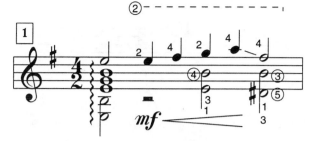

In the original, Frescobaldi did not include the note E on the top of this chord. This is an editorial decision that changes the melody which Frescobaldi obviously intended to start on the second beat of m. 1:

In m. 4-5, Segovia ended the first section and did not replay the E minor chord to start the repeat:*

He obviously agreed that it was better to play it as written, since later in his life he began to do so.

Segovia sometimes ended the first section of the theme and then began the repeat with a chromatic alteration of the melody:

Segovia was probably puzzled by Frescobaldi's cadence in m. 4-5 (see original score, p. 400) which is inconsistent with the time signature. Therefore, we may agree with Segovia in holding the G chord a little longer than Frescobaldi indicated at the end of the first time through the first section:

Frescobaldi:

Alternative:

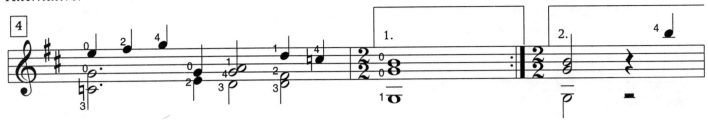

In m. 7 Segovia did a rhythmic and harmonic change:

Segovia:

Frescobaldi:

Alternative:

hinge bar 5/6 VII   hinge bar 5/6 VII

Earlier in his life, Segovia played this measure differently:

In m. 34 a restriking of the chord was introduced by Segovia, adding to the melody and rhythm:

Segovia:

Frescobaldi:

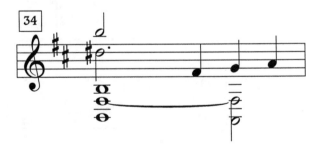

Alternative:

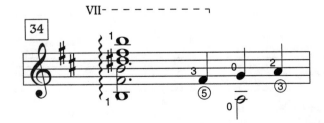

Earlier in his life, Segovia also played this measure differently:*

In m. 37 Segovia changed both bass and treble melodic elements, including playing a C natural in the bass line. While it is certain that he had a good reason to do so, we do not know what his reasoning was. A good guess is that he was trying to make this section cadence in a way similar to m. 4 and m. 19:

*Segovia:**

Frescobaldi:

Alternative:

In m. 60 Segovia added the notes E and F# to the top line. What he was really doing here is doubling the bass voice, but this does result in a significant change of Frescobaldi's melodic content.

*Segovia:**

Frescobaldi:

Alternative:

In all of these examples it seems preferable to stick as closely as possible to Frescobaldi's original in order to preserve the strong points of this style (the melodic and harmonic content). Segovia, for his own good reasons, chose to do otherwise.

At final cadences it was common to end with a Picardy Third in the Baroque period.[22] There were, however, certain exceptions.[23] As we see in the original, Frescobaldi raised the third in every section except for the opening theme. It is permissable to leave the opening theme in a minor cadence since Frescobaldi did not indicate a major cadence, and this does add a little variety (Segovia did all cadences in major).

Speaking of variety at cadences, Frescobaldi did some different things at cadences that are rather interesting. Segovia did not follow Frescobaldi in the cadence at m. 44. Guitarists may want to play the little variation cadence that Frescobaldi indicated. For example:

Segovia: *

Frescobaldi:

Alternative:

In accordance with a certain concept, a cross string fingering may be used at the cadences in m. 63 and 91. (Segovia did not play m. 91 since he omitted the fourth variation.) Segovia used a same string kind of trill that some guitarists may wish to use instead:

Segovia: *

Alternative:

The fourth variation *(Corrente)* has different possibilities for its cadential trills:

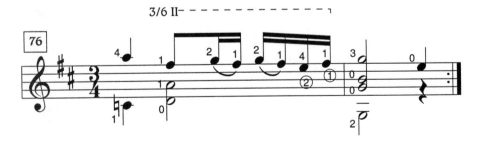

---

22. Francesco Bianciardi, *Breve regola per impar' a sonare sopra il basso con ogni sorte d'instrumento*, Siena, 1697, second of the nine rules.

23. Friedrich Erhard Niedt, *Musikalische Handleitung*, I, Hamburg, 1700, Ch. VIII, Rule 6.

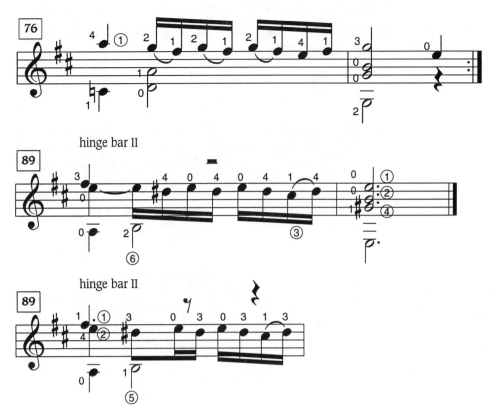

The performer who utilizes some of the above trills will have to adjust the tempo of the *Corrente* so that whatever trill is selected can be executed properly. This variation sounds good at a speed of about 152 (set to the quarter note), and at this tempo, some of the alternative trills are very difficult to execute. For this reason guitarists may wish to avoid complicated ornaments except at the very end of the variation in m. 91. Because of the closing *ritardando* the longer trill fits very comfortably in this section and also helps to keep musical intensity through the cadence.

In Frescobaldi's preface comments, he gave liberty to play whatever sections we desire. In Segovia's recorded version, he took Frescobaldi up on this. He changed the order to: theme, var. 1, var. 3, var. 2, recap. of theme. He omitted the last variation, var. 4, and after the recap played a *Corrente* taken from another place in Frescobaldi's book of Toccatas. In Segovia's published version he followed Frescobaldi more closely, only dropping the fourth variation and adding a repeat of the theme. While he may have the liberty to do this from the composer himself, one could make a case for unification of the piece as written so that the movements can show the diversity of the variations and yet have the common bond of the harmonic structure, as well as the interesting merger of the variation and dance suite form. (Frescobaldi marks var. 3 as "Gagliarda" and var. 5 as "Corrente.") For these reasons, it is suggested that editors leave this marvelous composition as written, with the same order and number of movements. However, some may wish to follow Segovia's example by repeating the theme, a procedure which Frescobaldi did not specifically indicate.

While suggested tempos are legitimate, Segovia gave us no exact metronome markings for the tempo of each section. What he did give us is some markings that are helpful: theme, not marked; var. 1, *mas animato;* var. 2, *allegro y vivaz,* var. 3, *assai sostenuto;* recap of theme, Tempo I. Frescobaldi gave no tempo markings in the original. This music, as with much Baroque music, leaves tempo up to the discretion of the performer.[24]

Segovia did not depart from his style of editing when it comes to the use of slurs in his edition of *La Frescobalda.* While the original keyboard score obviously does not employ this technique, we can infer from

---

24. Anton Bemetzrieder, *Lecons de clavecin et principels d'harmonie,* Paris, 1771, p. 68. Bemetzreider tells us that "taste is the true metronome." This sums up the attitude of Baroque composers that tempo was variable.

the medium (organ music) that the context was to be legato. Segovia used slurs throughout this piece to help the connection of the line, but also to give it shape by creating interesting accents. For example, notice what he did with the first half of the first variation (In Segovia's published edition he included a slur between the fourth and fifth notes of m. 12. In his recorded version he omitted the slur):[25]

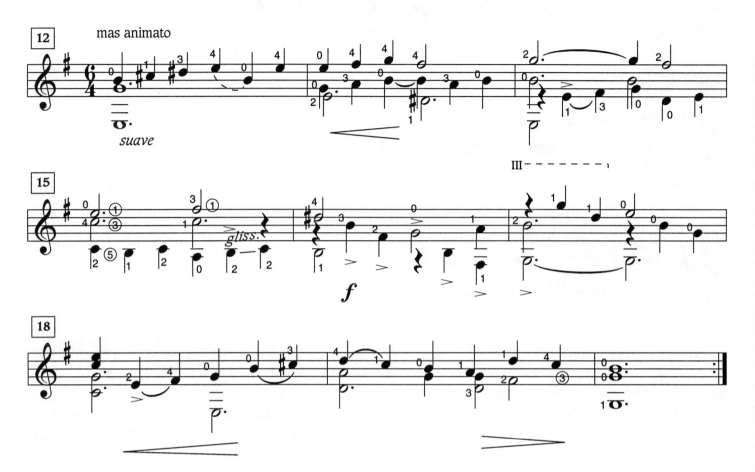

Surprisingly, Segovia decided to use an open E for the inner voice in m. 2 instead of playing this section all in the higher positions:*

The E sounds more consistent when played on the third string with some vibrato, and it is this approach that is suggested here:

Later in his life, Segovia omitted the second note of the inner line, G, in m. 3 (repeated in m. 95). He apparently wanted to emphasize the bass line instead:

Three interesting rubatos were achieved by Segovia in his performance of this composition. In m. 9 (which is also repeated in m. 100) he rolled the chord on the second beat and held it for a rubato. Segovia did pay the time back by shortening the notes that immediately follow:

A different kind of rubato was employed by Segovia in m. 12 where he held the fourth note of the melody, E. He did not pay back the stolen time:

In m. 22 Segovia also held the first note B for a free rubato where the stolen time is not paid back:

In m. 22 Frescobaldi used a musical motive which he also used in the third variation, m. 57. Consistency is achieved here by playing these on the first string:

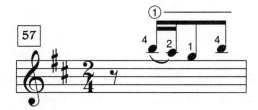

While Segovia usually took this kind of approach, in these cases he decided on an "in position" kind of approach:

Segovia played m. 31 in two different ways, neither of which was exactly as Frescobaldi wrote it:

Segovia: *

Segovia:

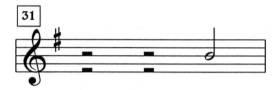

Frescobaldi:

Segovia also played m. 36 and m. 44 in two different ways:*

Throughout his edition Segovia gave many dynamic and expression markings, providing a definite concept of interpretation. Many additional interpretive ideas that guitarists may want to consider when performing this piece may be suggested. For example, when playing the second half of the theme the second time, it works well to use a brighter tone color from the beginning of m. 7 to the second note, B, of m. 8. In m. 9, instead of ritarding when playing this cadence on the first and second endings, it is quite effective not to do the *ritardando* the first time and to do a big *ritardando* with a crescendo the second time. The theme can then end on a big rolled chord played forte. This effectively leads into the first variation, which can be started fairly soft and then played louder on the repeat.

In m. 22, the second half of the first variation works well if it is played medium soft with no *ritardando* at the end. The second time through a nice contrast is achieved by playing loud and *ponticello,* then ending loud with a big *ritardando.*

Variation #2 has a strong and rhythmic character, and is effectively played loudly. The first time the nail of the thumb may be used to play the chords forcefully. The second time through, variety can be achieved by playing only medium loud and using the flesh of the thumb to achieve a different quality of sound on the chord rolls. The second half of Variation #2 could be treated with the same loud-softer dynamic contrast, although this can become redundant. Therefore, guitarists may wish to play this section strong and bright the first and second time.

Variation #3 is effective when played straight the first time. The second time a nice contrast is achieved by starting very *ponticello* and then building to the cadence in m. 48-49. The following phrase in m. 49 is striking to the ear when played with a very sweet *dolce.* In m. 51 vibrato with a descending *glissando* on the second time through can give much expression to this descending passage. (It is interesting to note that Segovia did not use any blatant *glissandi* in his performance of this piece, except for the one towards the end of m. 1 and one in m. 51.) A fairly big *ritardando* to close the first half helps to set the contrast to the more rhythmic second half. These ideas combined can create great interest:

The second half of Variation #3 seems most effective when played *dolce* the first time. On the repeat it is interesting to start *ponticello* and continue this way until the first beat of m. 60, and then switch back to a softer sound:

Frescobaldi, in his preface to the *Second Book of Toccatas*, gives liberty to slow down or even pause if the performer so desires. Does this mean that Segovia-style free rubatos are appropriate here?[26] If so, the repeat of m. 61 presents a wonderful opportunity to use such rubato:

For variety's sake rolled chords are not suggested at the end of Variation #3.

Variation #4 is effective when played straightforward with a steady, even rhythm. There is one spot that works well to hold a note a little on the repeat (it really seems that Segovia would have done so if he had played this variation):

A significant aspect of Baroque performance practice is ornamentation.[27] Segovia's use of ornamen-

---

26. Richard Hudson, *Stolen Time: The History of Tempo Rubato,* Oxford, Claredon Press, 1994, p. 10. This type of free rubato which robs the tempo of its regular beat is not usually thought to be appropriate in Baroque music, except at cadences. Nevertheless, Hudson confirms that free rubato was practiced in the early 17th century for expressive purposes in certain forms of music: "Early in the seventeenth century tempo changing in the keyboard toccata was compared to that in the madrigal; one should play slowly at the beginning and at cadences, and when performing syncopations, trills, runs, and *expressive passages*." (emphasis mine)

27. See the discussion in the introduction to this book for a description of how ornamentation is a form of non-free rubato.

tation was minimal.[28] He employed only the cadential trill in m. 63. One additional type of ornamentation guitarists may want to consider is that which can occur in the repeat (da capo) of the opening aria. In the Baroque period it was common (especially in the later Baroque period) to ornament the repeat of the first section, especially when the first section was an aria. They called this the "Da Capo Aria."[29] Here is an example of how the repeated aria may be ornamented:

Segovia indicated that the recapitulation (da capo) of the theme should be played "piú lontano" (more distant, as if from a distance). To play the repeat of this aria as a reminder of the opening theme as if being heard from afar is a fitting and beautiful conclusion to this graceful masterpiece.

With his edition of *La Frescobalda*, Segovia provides for us another example of masterfully editing a piece of music for the guitar which was originally written for another instrument. While respecting his contribution, we have examined his edition in light of historical and musicological considerations. It is strongly suggested that guitarists leave this composition closer to the original than Segovia did. There is a good chance that Segovia did not even have access to the original score. He obviously did not have the benefit of all the advances in modern musicology at his disposal to help him prepare his edition. The original mode is most certainly better left as it is.[30] However, there are different opinions regarding the use of accidentals.[31] Leaving the variations intact that Frescobaldi wrote, as well as his original order of movements, provides continuity that is pleasing to the listener.[32] What should never be abandoned is Segovia's emphasis on playing this piece with the utmost sensitivity to every expressive element that can touch the heart of the audience.

Segovia built his career on a repertoire of music from five centuries. The amount of information that was available to him about this music, however, was sometimes very limited.

---

30. Alexander Silbiger, editor, *Frescobaldi Studies*, Durham, Duke University Press, 1987, essay by Emilia Fadini, "The Rhetorical Aspect of Frescobaldi's Musical Language," p. 285. A good point is made by Emilia Fadini in showing us that composers of the Middle Ages followed aspects of Greek music theory in regard to modes and music in general. Being an early Baroque composer, Frescobaldi may have inherited these serious views regarding musical structure and may not have approved of changing the modal basis for his compositions. "Also from Greek culture derived the theory regarding the influence on the human soul of the various modes, which were capable of arousing moderate (ethos) as well as more violent (pathos) emotions. During the Middle Ages, music was similarly regarded as a force of nature, exerting its influences on man. As late as the end of the fifteenth century, Johannes Tinctoris listed twenty different effects that music could produce upon man: it could elevate the spirit, subdue sadness, put the devil to flight, enrapture, cure sickness, gladden, give relief to the laborer, excite sensuality and lust, soothe suffering, communicate astral influences, and so forth."

31. Robert Donington, *Baroque Music: Style and Performance*, London, Faber Music, 1982, p. 73. Donington says, "There are altogether more performer's options over Baroque accidentals than has been until recently appreciated. They do need, however, a practiced ear and considerable caution. We do not always have to assume that only one solution is acceptable."

32. The length of this whole piece (about six minutes in duration) should allow it to fit comfortably within the average person's attention span. Therefore, even though length is a significant consideration when deciding whether to perform some whole Baroque suites, it need not be an obstacle here. See footnote #65 on p. 299.

JOHANN SEBASTIAN BACH

J.S. Bach (1685-1750). Painting by Elias Gottlieb Haussmann.

CHAPTER THREE

Johann Sebastian Bach (1685-1750) is considered by many to be the greatest composer of all time. There is little doubt that Andrés Segovia shared this view.[1] In contrast to the tremendous worldwide fame J.S. Bach now enjoys, he was not well known during his lifetime. He had a relatively uneventful career and spent most of his life serving as an organist and music director at various churches in Lutheran Germany.[2] Bach was married twice and had twenty children.[3] Several of them achieved a high status as musicians, most notably Carl Philip Emmanuel Bach (1714-1788).[4]

It is Bach that music historians look to as the climax and end of the Baroque period. He wrote primarily in the styles that were in use in his day and in earlier periods and did not concentrate on innovations.[5] This is not to his discredit, however, for he took the forms that were available and created works within those parameters that are some of the finest of their kind. Of particular interest to guitarists are his works for solo lute. Understandably, these all fit well on the guitar and have become a part of the standard guitar repertoire.

Bach was an extremely prolific composer. Being the author of thousands of different instrumental and vocal compositions, one would have to wonder how Bach ever found time to practice! Nevertheless, he was known as a virtuoso keyboard player, being proficient on the harpsichord, clavichord and organ. His degree of involvement with other instruments is still somewhat a matter of dispute, the lute being no exception.[6]

It is well known that Andrés Segovia had profound respect for Bach's music. His affection was manifested in a strong attachment that assured Bach a spot on most of his concert programs. He was able to introduce this historic music to millions worldwide as it is heard in a unique medium. Interestingly enough, Segovia's status as an authoritative Bach interpreter has come into question in recent years.[7] The twentieth century has produced an approach to Bach that has rejected much of the freedom of Segovia's Romantic style.[8] Questions have arisen, however, as to whether or not this rejection has gone too far. Scholars are now saying that Segovia's example has much to offer, especially regarding his effort to express the *feelings* in Bach's music.[9]

1. Miguel Alcázar, editor, *The Segovia-Ponce Letters*, Columbus, Ohio, Editions Orphée, 1989. Segovia's belief that Bach was the greatest composer can be seen in his continual reference to Bach as the standard in music composition. He encouraged Ponce and others to follow this standard.

2. Donald J. Grout and Claude V. Palisca, *A History of Western Music*, Fourth Edition, New York, W.W. Norton & Company, 1988, p. 498. "He regarded himself as a conscientious craftsman doing his job to the best of his ability for the satisfaction of his superiors, for the pleasure and edification of his fellow man, and the glory of God. Doubtless he would have been astonished if he had been told that 200 years after his death his music would be performed and studied everywhere and his name more deeply venerated by musicians than that of any other composer."

3. Some died in infancy or at birth.

4. C.P.E. Bach is noteworthy because he wrote an important book, *Versuch über die wahre Art das Klavier zu spielen* (Treatise on the Correct Way to Play Keyboard Instruments) and because he is associated with the *gallant* style. This genre was a move away from the contrapuntal forms of J.S. Bach and a transitional one toward the Viennese Classic style of Haydn and Mozart.

5. Anthony Newman, *Bach and the Baroque*, Pendragon Press, 1985, pp. 6-9. Bach worked only within traditional styles while many others (including his own sons) were turning to new ones such as the *style galant* (gallant style). Musical evolution in the eighteenth century was such that composers and theorists began referring to the *old style* and the *new style*. Regarding the *old style* in Germany Newman says, "...a Baroque style which had not yet gone through transformation to become the later styles of Rococco (*galant*) and Empfindsamkeit." For more discussion of this issue, see also: Frederick Neumann, *Ornamentation in Baroque and Post Baroque Music, with Special Emphasis on J.S. Bach*, Princeton, Princeton University Press, 1978, pp. 41-43.

6. Phillip Spitta, *Johann Sebastian Bach*, translated by Clara Ball and J.A. Fuller-Maitland, 3 vols., New York, 1951, vol. 3, p. 167. Bach did possess a lute in his collection of instruments but we can't be sure that he actually played it. For an excellent discussion of this matter see: Alice Artzt, "The Third Lute Suite by Bach, Three Manuscripts and their Implications," presented in the *Journal of the Lute Society of America*, No. 1, 1968, pp. 9-14.

7. Allan Kozinn/Pete Welding/Dan Forte/Gene Santoro, *The Guitar: The History, The Music, The Players*, New York, William Morrow and Company, Inc., 1984, p. 35. In its discussion of Segovia's approach this book says, "In Baroque works, though, we must consider what now seems a lexicon of stylistic error as the fashion of the time, and accept it (as we do similar affectations in the performances of Kreisler, Mengelberg, and Horowitz) on its own terms."

8. See the introduction to Chapter One of Part II, Volume Two for an overview of the Romantic style and the introduction to this book for a review of the Segovia style in particular.

PRELUDE IN D MINOR

From Bach's many compositions, Segovia chose to play a segment of those that were written for the violin, lute and cello. He apparently felt that these types lent themselves to performance on the modern guitar. It is from the collection of lute works that Segovia derived the *Prelude in D Minor*.

When guitarists of our present day think of the *Prelude in D Minor*, BWV 999, it is most often perceived as the prelude to precede the *Fugue in A Minor*. Some feel that the harmonic conclusion suggests that it is to

be followed by another piece.[10] We do not have Bach's autographed handwritten score (the manuscript source we get this piece from is a copy by J.P. Kellner, one of Bach's students). Therefore, we may never know if he wrote the *Prelude* to go along with another piece. It is noteworthy, however, that the *Prelude in D Minor* and the *Fugue in A Minor* are both thought to be written at about the same time.[11] They fit together effectively, especially since the *Prelude* modulates to the dominant, preparing the way for the new key of the *Fugue*. This could suggest that Bach may have approved of the two pieces being played together.

This conclusion may never have occurred to Segovia, since his knowledge of the *Fugue* may have only been in the context of the *Violin Sonata #1*. (It is the sonata version that Segovia employed when making his edition of the *Fugue*. Bach originally wrote the *Fugue* as one of the four movements of the *Sonata*.) The lute version of the *Fugue* was not published in the first edition of the *Bach Gesellschaft* that was released in the late 1800's. It was not until the Bruger edition was published (by Dr. Hans Dagobert Bruger) in 1921 that most of the lute compositions

A youthful Segovia is portrayed here in a sketch by Muñoz Lucena, done in 1918.

---

9. John Schneider, composer and author of the book *Contemporary Guitar* (University of California Press), is quoted in *Guitar Review* (Fall 1986, p. 7) as saying, "I used to be critical because of his glaring inconsistencies with what I consider the truth to the printed page. Segovia's 19th century interpretations went against the grain of the music." He goes on to say that the early music movement made him aware that Baroque composers only intended to notate rhythm and pitch. Therefore, other important musical elements must be added by the performer, and this is what Segovia did, although not always stylistically: "The treatises tell us that Bach is emotional, romantic music; maybe it's not correct but at least he's been out there with his heart on his sleeve." The great concert guitarist, Eliot Fisk, spoke similar words in *Guitar Review*, Winter 1983, p. 6: "I have always found his masculine, serious Bach thoroughly convincing. I would go so far as to say that Segovia's sense of this music is consonant with modern scholarship... Indeed, Segovia's overall emotionalism is very much in line with what we know of the Baroque aesthetic with its emphasis on the expression of the *affetti*, while Bream's more controlled, tensile view of the music is more a reflection of 20th century life."

10. Graham Wade, *The Guitarist's Guide to Bach*, Ireland, Wise Owl Music, 1985, p. 63. "The unusual feature of ending in the dominant key has caused some scholars to suggest that another piece, probably a fugue, was intended to follow—as the title 'prelude' implies."

11. *Ibid.*, p. 62-64.

became available to the public. By this time Segovia was well into his career.[12] It is possible that Segovia may never have seen or had access to the solo lute version of the *Fugue* in the early part of his life. This may be the reason that he performed the *Prelude* as a separate piece throughout his career.[13]

Segovia's published version of the *Prelude in D Minor*[14] shows that he prepared an edition that is very consistent with the original. This is very much due to the fact that Bach wrote this piece for the lute and was writing it in a way as to be sensitive to the idioms of the instrument.[15] Since the lute and guitar are related, this type of writing, called "style brisé,"[16] fits very comfortably on the guitar as well.[17]

---

12. *Ibid.*, p. 10-11.

13. *Ibid.*, p. 27. It was Julian Bream who first started performing the *Prelude in D Minor* as a pair with the *Fugue in A Minor*.

14. Andrés Segovia, *Prelude*, Mainz, B. Schott's Söhne, 1928.

15. Donald Jay Grout, *A History of Western Music*, New York, W.W. Norton & Company, 1960, p. 298. An idiom is a figure or pattern that is written specifically to fit on a particular instrument. For example, the guitar music of Giuliani and Villa-Lobos is obviously "idiomatic" to the guitar, since it is written around the tuning, open strings, etc. of the guitar. Idiomatic writing did exist prior to the Baroque period, such as in the lute writing of Francesco da Milano (1497-1543), but the general trend was to write non-idiomatic music that could be sung or played by almost any combination of voices or instruments. It was in the Baroque period that the focus shifted to idiomatic writing.

16. Manfred F. Bukofzer, *Music in the Baroque Era*, New York, W.W. Norton & Company, 1947, p. 165, "...what was known as the style brisé. The quickly fading sound of the lute did not lend itself to polyphonic voice-leading and called for specific techniques that compensated for the technical limitations of the instrument. The "broken style" [style brisé] of lute music, a most ingenious and consistent application of such a technique may be called the glorification of the simplest lute figure: the arpeggio. The broken style is characterized by rapidly alternating notes in different registers that supply, in turn, melody and harmony."

17. *Ibid.*, p. 15, "With the discovery of idioms in the Baroque, new possibilities arose from the deliberate exchange of idioms between different instruments, or between instrument and voice. This transfer of idioms forms one of the most fascinating aspects of Baroque music." It should be pointed out here that some idioms fit remarkably well on more than one instrument, as we see here with the transfer of this lute music to the guitar. This arpeggio style (style brisé) is also idiomatic to the keyboard and is very reminiscent of Bach's keyboard works of the Cöthen years, especially the C Major Prelude of the *Well-Tempered Clavier*, Book I, BWV 846. This may explain why the *Prelude* was originally published in the Bach Gesellschaft edition and in numerous other editions since then as the third of 12 *Little Preludes for Harpsichord*. Still, it seems strange that this would be thought of as a keyboard piece since the source manuscript, by J.P. Kellner, identifies the piece as *Praelude in C Moll pour la Lute di Johann Sebastian Bach*. Since we do not have Bach's original autograph manuscript, it is possible to speculate that Bach originally wrote this piece for keyboard and later either he or someone else (maybe J.P. Kellner) transcribed it for lute. This leads me to my next point concerning the Baroque practice of "transcription."

Idem., paragraph 3, "Baroque composers went a step further in the exchange of idioms and transposed entire forms, with all their stylistic peculiarities, from one medium to another." It is entirely possible that this piece was written for another instrument, such as the harpsichord, and then "transcribed" by Bach himself to another instrument such as the lute. It was in the Baroque period that this common type of adaptation began to be called a "transcription," and Bach himself became a master at it. Some examples of Bach's works transcribed for other instruments are:

1. The *Suite V in C Minor* for violoncello (BWV 1011) was transcribed for lute in G minor (BWV 995).
2. The *Partita III in E Major* for violin (BWV 1006) was transcribed for lute in the original key of E major (BWV 1006a).
3. The *Fuga* from *Sonata I in G Minor* (known to guitarists as the *Fugue in A Minor* BWV 1001) was transcribed for organ in D minor (BWV 539) and for the lute in the original key of G minor (BWV 1000).
4. The *Sonata II in A Minor* (BWV 1003) was transcribed for harpsichord in D minor (BWV 964).
5. The *Adagio* from *Sonata III in C Major* (BWV 1005) was transcribed for harpsichord in G Major (BWV968).
6. The *Preludio* from *Partita III in E Major for Unaccompanied Violin* (BWV 1006) was transcribed as the Sinfonia to the Cantata BWV 29: *Wir danken dir, Gott, wir danken dir*. It was transposed to the key of D major and set for obbligato, three trumpets, timpani, two oboes, strings, and basso continuo. Bach also transcribed the *Preludio in E Major from Partita III* to be a part of Cantata BWV 120a: *Herr Gott Beherrscher aller Dinge*. Here he also transposed it to D major. He set it for organ obligato with three trumpets, timpani, two oboes, two oboes d'amore, strings and basso continuo. (For an excellent reference that shows how very extensive Bach's transcription practice was see: Norman Carrell, *Bach the Borrower*, Westport, Connecticut, 1967, reprinted by Greenwood Press, 1980. This book proves that not only did Bach very frequently adapt his own compositions for other instruments, but he also frequently adapted music composed by others for use as a part of his own. In fact, today he probably would have been sued for copyright violations!)

At any rate, what we can conclude is that Bach would have very much approved of Segovia adapting his works that were written for other instruments and making a guitar edition from them. We can also conclude that Bach would have approved of changing or adding notes (as

Segovia made three significant changes when adapting Bach's *Prelude* for the guitar. The first is the key. Bach originally wrote this piece in C minor. Segovia transposed it to D minor, which allowed the music to fall very comfortably on the fretboard while taking advantage of the guitar's open strings.

The second significant change Segovia made occurs in m. 23. Here Segovia followed Bach's original by raising the consistent pedal a half step for this measure.[18] Yet to follow Bach's bass line exactly, the measure would look like this:

Bach original (manuscript by J. P. Kellner):

Obviously, this stretch is impossible to play, so Segovia raised the bass note F up an octave to play the measure this way:

Moving the note up an octave does separate it a lot from the other notes of the pedal, and most editions solve this consistency problem by maintaining the low E throughout m. 23. This is the approach that Segovia took later in his life:

Segovia often did) to fit the technical parameters of a different instrument, or to fill out the original texture with bass notes (as Bach himself did when transcribing the *Suite V in C Minor,* BWV 1011 for lute in G Minor, BWV 995). Most scholars agree with my assertion here, but some may urge us to use caution: "Each writer of course fails to make the connection that because Bach did something does not necessarily justify the actions of lesser men some centuries later in altering the sonorities or notation of the master; on this basis an argument could be made out for performing Bach on moog synthesizers, banjo or harmonica, and probably has been!" (Graham Wade, *The Guitarist's Guide to Bach*, Ireland, Wise Owl Music, 1985, p. 26.)

Nevertheless, we can see that many of the source manuscripts for Bach's compositions show that it was common in Bach's time for other lesser people to copy or transcribe Bach's works. For example, we have examined the possibility that J.P. Kellner may have transcribed this *Prelude,* BWV 999, from an original by Bach for keyboard. The *Fugue in A Minor,* BWV 1001, exists in a lute version, BWV 1000, but that version is not by Bach. The manuscript is in French lute tablature by Johann Christian Weyrauch, and it is now believed that he did the transcription himself. This fugue also exists in an organ version. Researchers Ulrich Siegle and Dietrich Kilian of the Bach Institute believe the organ transcription of this fugue to be by someone other than Bach as well. (For an excellent examination of this subject, see the preface to *The Solo Lute Works of Johann Sebastian Bach*, edited for the guitar by Frank Koonce, San Diego, California, Neil A. Kjos Music Company, 1989.) Did Bach agree with all these people transcribing his compositions? If not, we have not discovered any record of his protest. The conclusion here seems to be that Bach humbly went with the very common practice of the time, that is, a liberal approach toward transcription. This is not to diminish our responsibility for integrity to this great master. Doing the best we can to discern his editorial procedures and respect for different sonorities should be our goal.

18. Please be aware that the original score does *not* use a standard treble clef. It uses a soprano clef where middle C is located on the bottom line. For the sake of comparison, the piece has been transposed and the standard treble clef is used here.

The third significant change Segovia made was in the closing measures, m. 42-43. His alteration is clear when compared with the original:

Segovia:

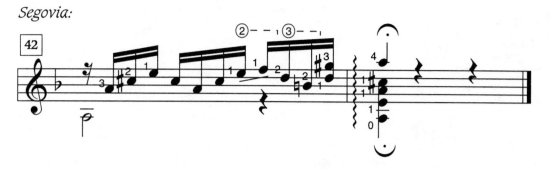

Bach:

Segovia added the note D below the last note, G♯, of m. 42. He then filled out the last chord, playing it as a rolled chord rather than a block chord. His change here seems to create more interesting voice leading and a fuller ending, but modern guitarists may wish to consider a different approach, especially since we now know that one of the outstanding characteristics of the Baroque period was ornamentation.[19] While this type of piece does not allow many opportunities for ornaments, a mordent works well on the final note of m. 42 before resolving to the tonic chord. It is, in fact, at cadences where ornaments were expected to be inserted by the Baroque performer,[20] in the form of cadential trills. There is certainly not much time for a trill at this cadence, but a mordent works just fine. This is the stylistic approach suggested here. The voicing of the final chord as it appears in the original manuscript causes poor voice leading from the dominant to the tonic (Bach probably did not do this transcription used for our original score) so a chord similar to Segovia's voicing can wisely be used:[21]

rit.   *mp*

---

19. Robert Donington, *Baroque Music: Style and Performance*, London, Faber Music, 1982, p. 91. Donington makes the seriousness of this matter clear when he says "Baroque ornamentation is more than a decoration. It is a necessity."

20. *Idem.*, paragraph 3.

21. It is also suggested here that the last chord *not* be rolled. This makes sense when we consider that the piece is essentially a series of arpeggiated chords *(style brisé)* played throughout. The last chord played without the roll provides a refreshing contrast.

Segovia began his edition by fingering the bass pattern on the same string:*

While this does require a stretch, the resulting consistency is the kind we find throughout Segovia's fingerings and it makes sense to follow his example. For those who have a problem with the stretch, the following may be the solution:

Segovia also retained the low bass note from the lute tablature in m. 15 which creates an even more difficult stretch:*

An acceptable option would be:

In his later years, Segovia employed the help of an assistant at his concerts.

Measures 31 through 33 present another difficult juncture when fingering this piece. Segovia fingered the section this way earlier in his life:*

This fingering, while preserving the three note ascending arpeggio pattern, requires a difficult stretch combined with a leap from the high to the lower positions. Segovia obviously decided that the effort was not worth the benefit involved, for later in his life he began to finger the passage this way:

The addition of the slur may seem to be an uncomfortable discontinuity with the original, but if articulated properly it presents the passage quite smoothly.

Segovia played m. 42-43 this way:

His approach to this ending cadence draws critical attention when consulting historical sources. First of all, Segovia broke the rhythm by accenting the E on the end of the second beat, creating a syncopation. He then slid to the next note F with his characteristic *glissando.* Holding the F for a significant free rubato with lots of vibrato, he continued to the end with a dramatically decreased tempo. The intensity of feeling he achieved is marvellous, but the rhythmic continuity was greatly disrupted. We must question this decision based on the fact that the Baroque period saw the development of two main types of rhythmic approaches. While everything in the Renaissance was based on a steady tactus, a Baroque rhythm that was free and at times divorced completely from the beat appeared in the affective recitative style. Another extreme developed in which the tactus was transformed into mechanically recurrent pulsations.[22] This piece most certainly is in the latter category. A dramatic interruption of the rhythm as Segovia did here is foreign to this style. This is not to imply, however, that no *rallentando* is appropriate, especially since this is a final cadence.[23] The solution is to maintain Segovia's sensitive fingering on the inner strings, but remove the *glissando* which causes a syncopation from the E to the F. The vibrato and abrupt rubato may be removed, and a very gradual *rallentando* used instead. If an accent is to be used, the F at the beginning of m. 3 may be accented to keep the rhythmic pulsation consistent with the rest of the piece, while creating some drama and variety.[24]

Although this piece is composed in the category of those with a regular rhythmic pulse, this does not mean that it should be played in an absolutely mechanical fashion.[25] We can take a lesson from Segovia as he so masterfully pulled the rhythm ever so slightly at times by holding the bass note at the beginning of the measure as it announces a new harmonic destination. For example (musical markings for pages 270-72 derived from Segovia's recorded performances):*

rubato

rubato

---

22. Manfred F. Bukofzer, *Music in the Baroque Era*, New York, W.W. Norton & Company, Inc., 1947, pp. 12-13.

23. Robert Donington, *Baroque Music: Style and Performance*, London, Faber Music, pp. 20-21. "Baroque music is constructed with many cadences. Most are so transitory that we take them in our stride... Yet other cadences are clearer still and require quite a perceptible rallentando..."

24. It is interesting to note that some professional guitarists have continued to play m. 42 as Segovia did, with the syncopated *glissando*. John Williams may have been the first to break with the Segovia tradition on his recording of all of Bach's lute music for Columbia Masterworks in 1975 (Columbia Masterworks, M2 33510).

25. Robert Donington, *Baroque Music: Style and Performance*, London, Faber Music, 1982, p. 20. "The listener is not aware of it, but nevertheless feels at ease, and does not get that monotonous sensation (which used to be more familiar at Baroque performances than it is at present) of being driven along with the depressing punctuality of a machine. The tempo is not arbitrary, but it is not ruthless either. The tempo is flexible." See also: Richard Hudson, *Stolen Time, The History of Tempo Rubato,* Oxford, Clarendon Press, 1994, p. 8-11. Hudson points out that "A motoristic sort of rhythm developed during the late Baroque period for almost all music..." He says that preludial forms are an exception because they were many times unmeasured or improvisational. This prelude does *not* fall in these categories. However, this doesn't mean that it should have no flexibility: "...music in general—from any period in history—is not to be performed mechanically and without regard for the sense of the sounds." (p. 11)

IV doigt au barré – – – – – ⌐C I – – – – – ⌐

1/2 C – – – – – – – – – – – ⌐

C VII – ⌐

In each of these cases, less is probably better than more. The resulting pull in rhythm is achieved from a slight emphasis of the bass note rather than from consciously holding it.

In two spots Segovia drove the rhythm ahead. This, combined with a subtle crescendo, creates a great interpretive effect:*

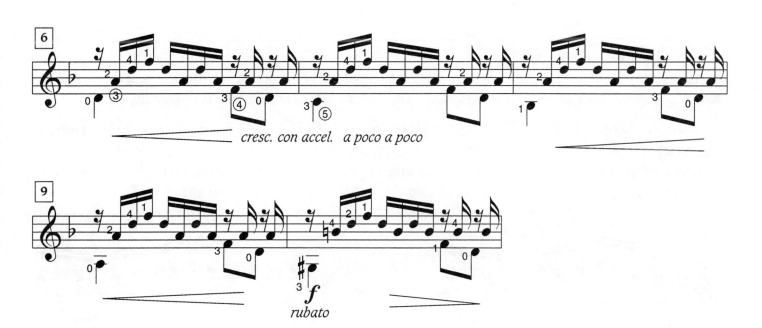

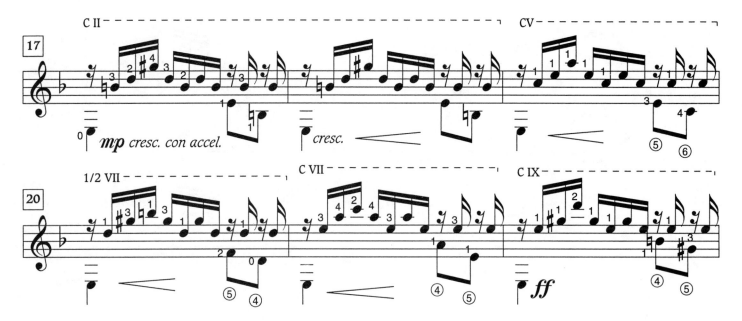

In the latter case, sensitivity to the pedal note, as the harmonies intensify and build to the climax at m. 22, is necessary to follow Segovia's example. He continued with a decrescendo and feeling of release from m. 22 to m. 31.

We can notice immediately from the original manuscript (p. 401) that the bass note rhythmic pattern throughout is one quarter note, followed by a quarter note rest, followed by two eighth notes. Some guitarists may want to observe the bass note patterns literally. The resulting articulation is quite interesting and effective. Segovia did not play these literally. He played the first note of each measure as a half note:

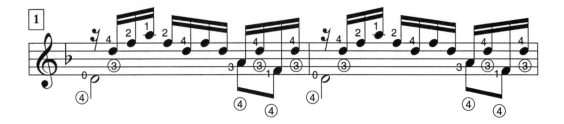

Most guitarists choose to follow Segovia's example here. If one does decide to play the bass rhythms literally, it may be wise to experiment with playing some of the bass notes as quarter notes and some as half notes. Some sections can sound a little clipped if the bass pattern is always observed literally.

Interestingly enough, Segovia's edition provides detailed left hand fingerings but no right hand fingerings.[26] This is not difficult to understand since one right hand pattern is used for most measures. Obviously, one of the keys to playing this piece well is selecting a very secure right hand fingering. Two helpful right hand fingerings are given below (Segovia appears to have favored the first of these. See footnote #28):

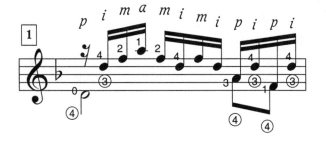 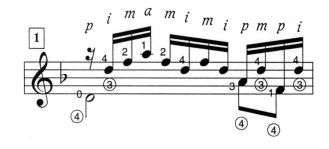

26. Andrés Segovia, *J. S. Bach, Prelude*, Mainz, B. Schott's Söhne, 1928.

Some guitarists may find, however, that the need to concentrate on the complex left hand fingerings may make it hard to achieve the necessary control and accuracy in the right hand. One of Segovia's most famous students has suggested an efficacious solution to such problems in arpeggio playing,[27] which is a technique called "planting." Simply put, it is planting the fingers on the ascending arpeggio pattern before they are played. In this case, the fingers could be planted at the beginning of the measure as the first bass note is played. Another

Segovia greets Christopher Parkening at the aspiring virtuoso's Spanish concert debut.

helpful option is to employ a pattern in which *p* and *i* follow the plant for the remainder of the measure. Since the greatest independence is in these fingers, maximum control can be achieved:

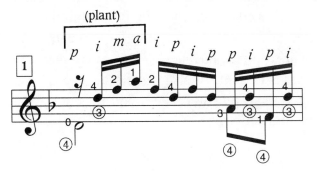

Measures 31 through 34 depart from this pattern, but the planting technique may still be used:

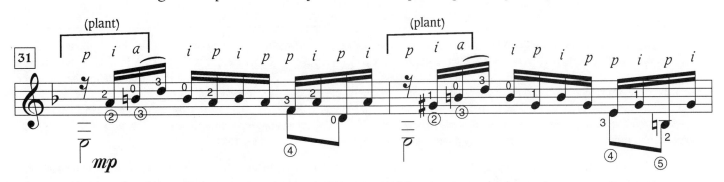

27. Christopher Parkening, *The Christopher Parkening Guitar Method*, Vol. I Chicago, Antiqua Casa Sherry-Brenner, 1972, p. 32.

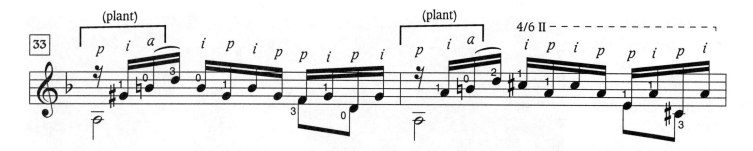

The only other measures that depart from the original pattern are m. 42-43. They may be fingered like this:

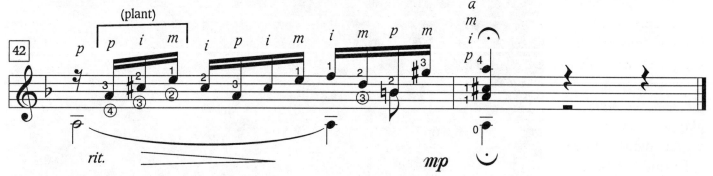

Segovia apparently used the planting technique, and it may be one of the surest ways of obtaining the tremendous control he exhibited.[28]

Ironically, Segovia did not use changes of tone color or dynamics in the many sections of this piece which present great opportunities for doing so. For example, there are many repeated sections throughout this piece. M. 1 is the same as m. 2; m. 3 is the same as m. 4; etc. Dynamic and color changes can be used effectively, for example, in m. 13 and 41, but certainly many other options are appropriate according to the desire of the performer.[29]

Segovia performed this prelude at a tempo of anywhere from the quarter note set to 100 to the quarter note set to 120. It seems to sound good anywhere in this range and each guitarist should feel free to select the tempo that feels comfortable.

Segovia's published version and spirited recordings of the beloved *Prelude in D Minor* have left a lasting mark on generations of guitarists. Except for a few stylistic considerations, his edition of this piece is as faithful to the original manuscripts as anything he did throughout his career. One can conclude that this springs, in part, from the characteristics of the piece itself, which is playable on the guitar with few alterations. This surely points to Segovia's keen ability to spot pieces that will perform well on his instrument. We can thank him, to a great extent, for the popularity of this piece, since he began to perform it in the early part of the twentieth century and sent it around the world through his recordings, published version and performances.

---

28. Christopher Parkening recommends the "planting" technique on p. 32 of the *Christopher Parkening Guitar Method.* I wrote to him and asked him if Segovia used this technique. He sent me a letter, dated February 29, 1996, which said: "I believe that Segovia did, in fact, use the 'planting' technique when he played an arpeggio. However, he never discussed technique with me, only interpretation." For more information about this procedure, see: David F. Marriot, "Some Notes on the Advantages of Planting," presented in GFA *Soundboard,* Spring 1982, pp. 52-53.

On a video re-release of an archival film (c. 1955), Segovia can be seen performing the *Prelude in D Minor.* Close up shots reveal that he is planting during the ascending arpeggios. It can also be seen clearly that he is using the first right hand fingering pattern given at the bottom of p. 272. See: *Jan Peerce, Marian Anderson and Andrés Segovia,* Long Branch, New Jersey, Kultur International Films, 1977.

29. Edith Borroff, *The Music of the Baroque,* New York, Da Capo Press, 1978, p. 55. The concept of tone color is one that would probably have been viewed very positively by Bach and other musicians in the Baroque: "...they shared a love of color, of tone quality. The Baroque era was one of diversity, and the musicians rejoiced in the diversity of sound which his great number of instruments permitted him."

FUGUE IN A MINOR

A careful look at the programs of most professional concert guitarists in the late 20th century will reveal an obvious difference with those of Andrés Segovia. One will notice that the contemporary performance practice, when it comes to J.S. Bach, is to program entire Bach suites, sonatas or partitas. Andrés Segovia rarely performed an entire Bach suite, and never performed an entire sonata or partita. While Bach wrote the *Fugue in A Minor* originally as part of the four movement *Sonata #1*, BWV 1001,[30] Segovia never performed the Sonata in its entirety. He either performed the *Fugue* as a separate piece or in conjunction with the *Siciliano*.

Segovia's practice of playing movements from Bach's multi-movement works rather than playing the work in its entirety seems to have historical precedence even in Bach's time. This fact is most certainly exemplified by an examination of the three historical versions of the Fugue that still exist:

1. Lute Version, BWV 1000, in French lute tablature by Johann Christian Weyrauch.

2. Violin Version (from *Sonata #1*, BWV 1001), by Bach himself.

3. Organ Version, BWV 539, by an anonymous arranger.

The lute version was transcribed as a single piece and the later organ version was transcribed as a separate piece with a short prelude added. Apparently eighteenth century lutanists and organists felt no particular obligation to play all the movements of the original Bach sonata.[31]

Segovia may have focused on playing individual movements by Bach throughout his career simply because he liked various movements in a particular suite, sonata or partita better than others. However, it is unlikely that Segovia ever *disliked* any of the movements by Bach. He proved his capacity to play whole Bach suites in 1961 when he broke with his normal practice and recorded the entire *Third Cello Suite*, BWV 1009, transcribed by John W. Duarte.

It is more probable that Segovia focused on programming only incomplete suites, sonatas and partitas because he followed the 19th century performance practice that began with Francisco Tárrega (1852-1909). Tárrega was one of the first guitarists to transcribe Bach. He focused on transcribing and performing individual movements from larger works, including the *Fugue* from the *Violin Sonata #1*, BWV 1001. These have recently been reprinted in a facsimile edition.[32]

An examination of the Tárrega edition of the *Fugue* shows much similarity to the Segovia transcription, especially when it is compared to Segovia's earliest recorded version.[33] It is possible that Segovia began by

---

30. The four movements that Bach wrote for this sonata are: 1. *Adagio* 2. *Fuga* 3. *Siciliano* 4. *Presto*. This work was called a "Sonata" by Bach because he wrote it in the tradition of the Italian church sonata called the *sonata da chiesa*. This title initially was given to those sonatas that were intended for use in church. Bach probably used the title because he was writing the piece with the characteristics of a church sonata rather than indicating that it was for church use. This seems evident from the fact that Bach's employer at this time, Prince Leopold of Anhalt-Cöthen, was a Calvinist who followed the teachings of the Reformed church and allowed no instrumental music in the service, but wanted plenty for secular use. By the seventeenth century the *sonata di chiesa* had the definitive characteristics of: a.) four movements, the first and third slow, the second and fourth fast. b.) movements headed by an indication of tempo—adagio, largo, allegro, presto, etc. c.) the use of imitative contrapuntal writing. d.) usually the melodic material was played by two instruments that were supported by the conventional continuo team of harpsichord/organ and gamba/cello. (See: Owain Edwards, *Baroque Instrumental Music*, the Open University Press, 1974, pp. 24-36, and Christian Ammer, *Harper's Dictionary of Music*, Barnes & Noble Books, New York, 1972, p. 332.) Bach shows his willingness to be flexible here by adapting the first three characteristics but not the fourth.

31. Donald Jay Grout, *A History of Western Music*, New York/London, W.W. Norton & Company, 1980, pp. 391-392. Baroque composers never intended for performers to *always* play all of the movements: "Performers in the Baroque thus had the liberty to add to the composer's written score; they were equally free to subtract from it or change it in various other ways... Composers of variations, suites, and sonatas took it for granted that players would omit movements ad libitum."

32. Rafael Andiá and Javier Quevedo, editors, *Francisco Tárrega, The Collected Guitar Works*, Heidelberg, Chanterelle Editions, Ltd., 1992.

33. Andrés Segovia, *The EMI Recordings*, 1927-39, Hollywood, California, Capital Records, 1980 (Angel ZB-3896).

playing Tárrega's edition of this *Fugue* and over the years developed many of his own fingerings.

It has become common among guitarists of the late twentieth century to use the lute version of the *Fugue in A minor* if playing the piece separately. The organ version has also been used. Modern scholarship has raised serious doubts that the slight differences in the lute and organ versions can be attributed to Bach.[34] Therefore, when comparing Segovia's edition with Bach's original, as well as in preparing a new modern edition, we will primarily use the violin version.

Segovia took the obvious step of transposing the *Fugue* into A minor. Bach originally wrote it in G minor, and it can be played as originally written.[35] If one is to follow Segovia's example by adding bass notes and filling out harmonies, the A minor key makes more sense, since it allows the open A and E strings, which correspond exactly to the tonic and dominant, to be used quite effectively.

Concerning the practice of adding notes, Segovia did a lot of this when adapting this music from the violin score. For example, m. 7-10, Bach original (transposed for the sake of comparison to A minor):

m. 7-10, Segovia edition:

---

34. Frank Koonce, *The Solo Lute Works of Johann Sebastian Bach*, San Diego, California, Neil A. Kjos Music Company, 1989, p. viii. "The autograph score for violin and the faithful copy by Anna Magdalena Bach are the only versions of the present Fugue which may be regarded as authentic. Researchers Ulrich Siegele and Dietrich Kilian of the Bach *Institut* have seriously questioned Bach's authorship of the organ version.

Segovia sometimes added an additional bass note to m. 6:

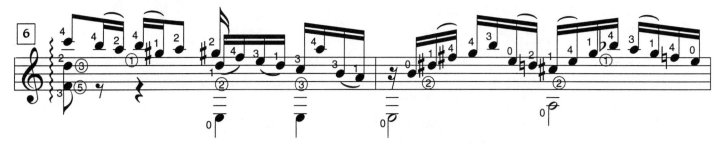

Some guitarists have taken the "purist" option when playing Bach's music written for the violin on the guitar, playing it exactly as written. Segovia's approach seems to make more sense, first of all, because the capabilities of the guitar do allow for a fuller texture. Segovia may have felt that by filling out the music he could make it sound better suited to the potentials of the guitar and bring a greater degree of listening pleasure to his audience. Certainly, Segovia's desire to please his audience does not give sufficient justification in the minds of most trained musicians for adding to the work of an undisputed master such as Bach. Segovia's ideas, however, cannot be said to be arbitrary when we look at Bach's own example. Bach arranged his own *Fifth Cello Suite*, BWV 1011, for the lute. This suite is known to guitarists as the *Third Lute Suite*, BWV 995. Bach, apparently realizing the greater harmonic and contrapuntal capabilities of the lute, filled in chords and added bass notes to a greater or lesser degree. He changed the *Prelude* just slightly by adding scattered bass notes. In other movements, such as the *Gavotte en Rondeau*, Bach went so far as to create a truly contrapuntal bass line. In the *Gigue* he changed it from a non-polyphonic piece to one that contains independent two part polyphony throughout.[36]

Bach probably would have felt that his violin music should have been filled out when played on the guitar in keeping with the expanded possibilities of the instrument. What we cannot safely say is that Bach would have agreed with each of Segovia's changes. A thorough study of Bach's example in pieces such as the *Fifth Cello Suite* to the *Third Lute Suite* would seem to be a necessary and wise precursor to any attempt to maintain integrity when making such adaptations. We can only guess if Segovia made such a study when making his Bach editions. His changes certainly do indicate a keen and thorough sense of maintaining the spirit of the original work, while adapting it to the particular textures and sonorities of the guitar that he knew so well. In doing so, he indisputably followed the clear example of J. S. Bach (considering the adaptation of the *Fifth Cello Suite* to the *Third Lute Suite* as Bach's model) when transcribing from a bowed to a plucked medium.

Segovia started his edition by fingering the fugal subject on the third string in the high positions with plenty of vibrato:

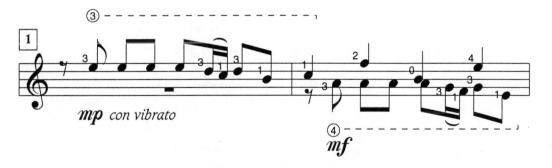

However, they considered the lute version likely to have been based upon an original Bach transcription because of its higher quality. It would seem, nevertheless, that some of the variants found in the tablature result from technical consideration for the lute and therefore must be attributed to the intabulator, J. C. Weyrauch."

35. I have heard Eliot Fisk perform this entire sonata in its original key of G minor.

36. Alice Artzt, "The Third Lute Suite by Bach, Three Manuscripts and Their Implications," presented in the *Journal of the Lute Society of America,* No. 1, 1968, pp. 9-14.

Especially earlier in his life, Segovia achieved a very romantic interpretation of Bach that definitely included vibrato. This effect should probably be used with moderation, since it was used very sparingly in the Baroque period in both violin and lute performance practice.[37]

Segovia's manner of fingering (designed to exploit the richness of the guitar's sound qualities) is fundamentally different from that employed by Baroque lutanists. Segovia avoided open strings when possible and favored high positions. The lute version of the *Fugue*, BWV 1000, did not employ Segovia's standards for fingering, as made evident by the tablature. Still, Segovia's approach to fingering is not in conflict with a stylistically correct rendering of Bach. It could be argued that since Bach himself did not do the lute transcription, BWV 1000, there is no indication that he favored the open string and lower position approach that is shown by that version and rejected by Segovia.

We can see from the first few measures of Segovia's edition that he included many slurs that were not indicated by the composer. Modern guitarists have to decide whether to follow Segovia's example in regard to slurring when playing Bach. One thing to keep in mind is that Segovia was greatly influenced by Tárrega's Bach editions, which included many slurs. Tárrega's slurring patterns may have been due to his use of gut strings. Segovia used gut also, until after World War II, when nylon strings began to be used. Apparently, as was explained at one of Segovia's last master classes,[38] Segovia's approach to slurs changed when he switched to nylon strings. His recordings of the *Fugue*, early and late in his life, indicate that he used fewer of them later. One must also keep in mind that the liberal use of slurs was a characteristic of the Romantic period, but not of the Baroque.[39] Does this mean that Bach should be played without slurs on the guitar, unless he indicates otherwise? No, absolutely not. Segovia used slurs in Bach as a matter of *articulation*.[40] While he may be accused of overdoing his use of slurs because of romantic tendencies, his excellent use of accent and articulation to bring Bach's music to life is not without historical precedence.[41] It seems doubtful that anyone would accuse Segovia of giving a flat performance. His use of slurs is one of the techniques that he used to shape the music and bring it to life. However, guitarists are wise to examine the exact usage of slurs in Bach.

As the *Fugue* announces its subject in the first measure, Segovia gave it crisp articulation:[42]

---

37. Manfred F. Bukofzer, *Music in the Baroque Era*, New York, W. W. Norton & Company, 1947, p. 377: "There is no place in Baroque music for the perpetual string vibrato that 'graces' modern violin playing. The references to vibrato which appeared first in the lute instructions of Mersenne and Mace, and later in Merck's violin tutor, bear unequivocal proof that vibrato was, like the crescendo, a special ornament, indicated by a symbol of its own and to be used with discretion only at proper places."

38. Constance McKenna, "A Segovia Masterclass," presented in *Guitar Review*, New York, Fall 1986, p. 5.

39. Jean-Claude Veilan, *The Rules of Musical Interpretation in the Baroque Era, Common to all Instruments*, Paris, 1979, p. 15. "...characteristic of the music of this period, the use of slurs is much more restricted than it was to be in the Classical and more especially the Romantic periods."

40. Dr. Mario Sicca, "Articulations in the Lute Music of J. S. Bach," presented in *Guitar Review*, New York, Fall 1985, p. 29. "The fact that in many works of Bach, particularly those for string instruments, articulation symbols are rarely found does not mean that the musical rendering may be flat!"

41. Leopold Mozart, *Versuch einer Gründlichen Violinschule*, 1756, Third printing 1787, XII chapter, Section 11, p. 263. "In precisely the sixth and seventh chapters one sees how much legato and staccato differentiate the melody. Therefore, one must not only observe the written slurs, but also bring in legato and staccato tastefully and at the proper moment even if there is nothing indicated in the composition itself."

42. This is especially true later in his life, as heard on Decca DL 9795.

Notice the pattern of legato and staccato articulations Segovia used to give clarity to the subject. Throughout his edition he was sensitive to employ this articulation whenever the subject appeared, bringing it clearly to the ear of his audience. Segovia maintained the subject's articulation, complete with slur, throughout the piece. In m. 20-21 the slur is difficult to maintain and an open string alternative may be used instead:

Segovia:

Alternative:

Segovia used *glissandi* in this piece, the first being the one in m. 10:

No stylistic defense can be given for the use of this effect in Bach in the blatant manner Segovia used.[43] An alternative fingering is possible:

---

43. There was a slide (*portamento*) used as a vocal ornament at this time in history, but the use of this effect in instrumental music is not certain. See the discussion of *glissando* in the introduction to this book.

In m. 11-14 Segovia employed a fingering which involves a prolonged bar with many slurs. Some guitarists may find this section extremely difficult, if not impossible, to perform. An alternative fingering using the lower positions is an acceptable solution:

Segovia:

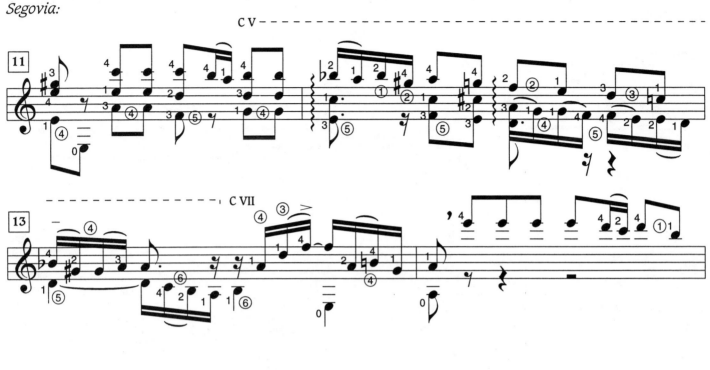

Alternative:

In m. 24 Segovia employed a trill at the cadence. His decision to include this trill is correct even though Bach gave no indication for it in his manuscript.[44] Segovia employed it in the nineteenth century fashion which may be less stylistic if we are trying to be faithful to Baroque performance practice.[45]

---

44. Robert Donington, *Baroque Music: Style and Performance*, London, Faber Music Ltd., 1982, p. 91. "...certain contexts implied a specific ornament so habitually that leaving it out is like making a wrong note. One is the cadential trill..."

45. *Ibid.*, p. 125. "Cadential trills have mainly a harmonic function, which they fulfill by behaving like appoggiaturas, accented from the upper (i.e. the auxiliary) note, to which the main note serves as a resolution." Christine Ammer, *Harper's Dictionary of Music*, Harper & Row Publishers, New York, 1972, p. 380: "In the seventeenth and eighteenth centuries the trill was usually begun on the upper note; since the early nineteenth century it generally has been begun on the lower note."

Recent scholarship has shown that the main-note trill was not completely excluded in the Baroque period, especially in Italy in the earlier Baroque.[46] Nevertheless, the main note trill probably became the exception, certainly not the rule, in Bach. Segovia used the main note trill as the rule.

A trill from the upper note is virtually impossible using Segovia's fingering. An alternative fingering makes the trill from the upper note more feasible:

Segovia:

The music of J.S. Bach was almost always included in Segovia's concert programs.

Segovia used a half step *glissando* in m. 28:

The fingering is suggested here because the *glissando* lies easily within the reach of the second finger, and essentially functions as a slur (half step slurs do not tend to sound like *glissandi*). Bach did indicate these slurs in the original:

---

46. Frederick Neumann, *Ornamentation in Baroque and Post-Baroque Music, With Special Emphasis on J. S. Bach*, Princeton, Princeton University Press, 1978, pp. 312-344. Also, see the introduction to *A New Look at Segovia*, Volume One, for a discussion of Baroque trill practices.

Instead of using 3 and 4 for the D# to E, they may be fingered with 1 and 2, to allow easy preparation for the three fourths bar on beat three:

In Bach's original he begins a slur section in m. 30-35:

Early in his career, Segovia followed Bach's slurring indications more literally:

In spite of Segovia's efforts, it is impossible to follow Bach's slurring indications in a totally literal way, and later in his life Segovia decided to play this section with fewer slurs. The passage seems to have more consistency this way, and Segovia's example is a good one to follow:

Measures 35-41 were changed by Segovia in terms of rhythm and by dividing longer notes into several shorter notes:

Bach:

Segovia:

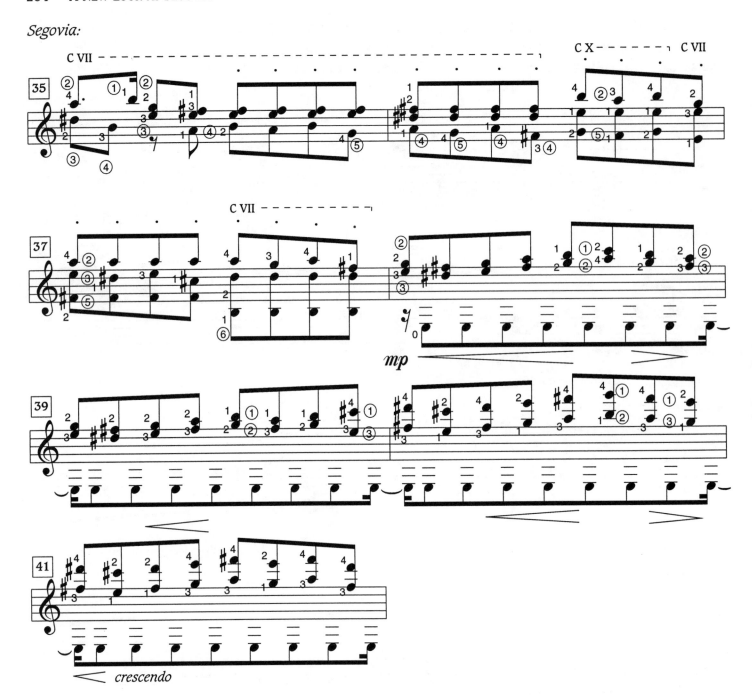

Segovia then changed Bach's original by transposing bass notes and even adding a note in m. 42-46:

Bach:

Segovia:

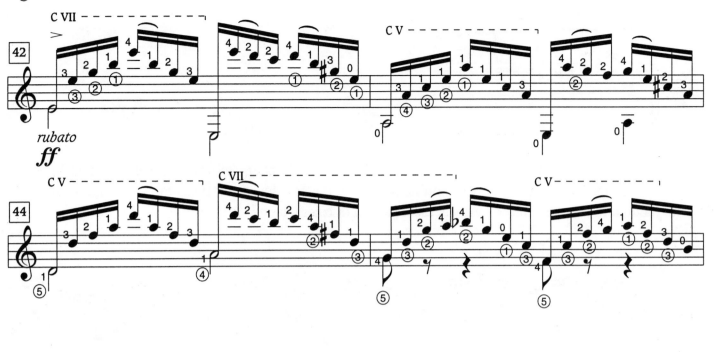

Are the kinds of changes Segovia made in m. 35-46 acceptable for modern guitarists? One thing we must consider is that the violin is an instrument of infinite sustain whereas the guitar is not, so Segovia obviously divided long notes into notes of smaller rhythm to help them ring longer. He transposed and added bass notes to make the texture more fitting to the guitar. These are not arbitrary changes, but ones that help adapt the music better to the medium it is being performed in. Bach himself commonly made these kinds of changes when arranging his music written for one instrument for a different one.[47]

Of course there are many different ways this music could be changed when being adapted for the guitar, and opinions vary among editors. One valid approach is to follow Segovia closely, except for m. 37. Here Bach's half note in the bass may be retained for the first half of the measure. This breaks the monotony of the persistent eighth note rhythms Segovia employed, yet achieves the sustain which is necessary (notice also the different articulations):

Bach:

Segovia:

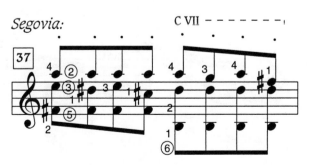

47. Nicholas Goluses, "J. S. Bach and the Transcription Process," presented in *Guitar Review*, New York, Spring 1989, p. 17. This article points out that another important transcription to study when trying to observe what changes Bach made is the *Violin Partita in E major,* BWV 1006, adapted as the *Fourth Lute Suite,* BWV 1006a. "...Bach's masterful setting of this work is characterized by at least six types of alteration: 1. Changes of note range, 2. Changes of notes or figures, 3. Changes in ornamentation, 4. Changes in rhythm, 5. Addition of notes, 6. Changes in the time-value of notes." We can see that Segovia was not deviating from Bach's own practices when it came to transcription.

Alternative:

In m. 47-50 Segovia incorporated a slur into this arpeggio pattern which was not indicated in Bach's original. He probably did this to give technical fluency to the passage, but it tends to cause an uncomfortable syncopation and may be omitted. An alternate pattern of color changes is suggested:

Bach:

Segovia:

Alternative:

mf *dolce*   f *ponticello*   mf *dolce*   f *ponticello*

mf *dolce*   f *ponticello*   mf *dolce*   f *ponticello*

The harmonics in m. 52 are not in the original. They are Segovia's excellent solution to sustaining those notes while shifting to the lower position in time to play the chord at the beginning of m. 53.[48] They may be the only way to play this passage smoothly:

Bach: *Segovia:*

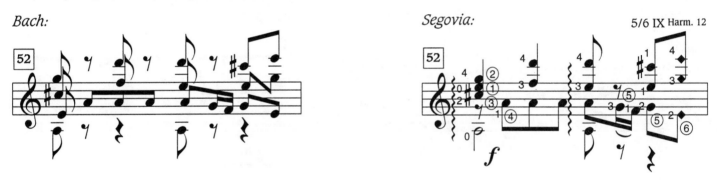

Segovia made a crescendo to the cadence in m. 54. He then arrived at the cadence loudly and started the next section softly:

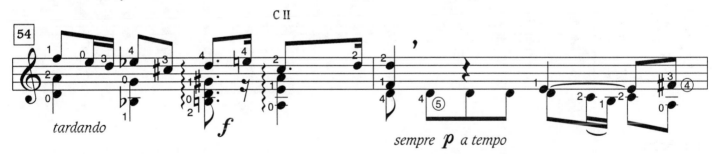

tardando   f   *sempre* p *a tempo*

The dynamics are quite effective and guitarists may want to follow Segovia's example. Segovia played no cadential trill at this spot[49] and the context certainly does call for one.[50] Either a main note or upper

---

48. Actually, this is probably Tárrega's idea, since the harmonics appear in his original transcription. See: *Francisco Tárrega, The Collected Guitar Works,* Heidelberg, Chanterelle Editions, Ltd., 1992.

49. I received a copy of Segovia's edition of the *Fugue in A Minor* (unpublished) from one of his most renowned students. There is an indication for a trill in this spot. However, on his recordings (reissue of old EMI records, Angel ZB-3896, 1927-39, and a much later one, Decca DL 9795, c. 1960) he did not play a trill here or at the huge cadence in m. 86.

50. Robert Donington, *Baroque Music: Style and Performance,* London, Faber Music Ltd., 1982, p. 91. See footnote #44.

note trill can be played, but most scholars have supported the use of the upper note:[51]

Alternative:

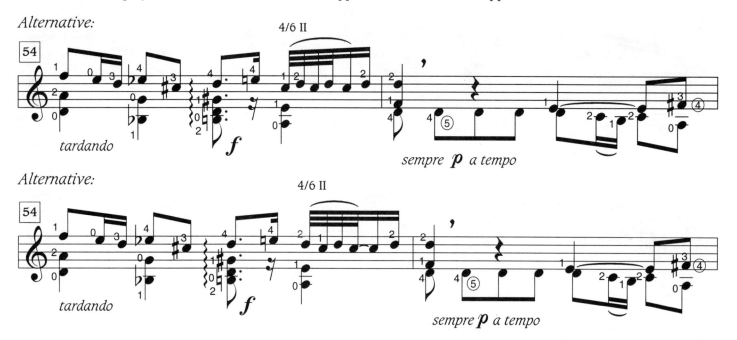

In m. 57-58 Segovia moved Bach's bass note on the last beat of m. 57 and the first note of m. 58 down an octave. While this achieves a deeper sonority, it makes the passage much more difficult technically (it requires a slur to be played over a bar). Following Bach's original is another option:

---

51. There has been almost universal agreement among scholars that the Baroque period favored the use of the upper note trill. There is one important scholar who has produced much evidence that main note trills were *always* an option to varying degrees depending on the factors of nationality and exact time of composition within the Baroque. See: Frederick Neumann, *Ornamentation in Baroque and Post-Baroque Music, With Special Emphasis on J.S. Bach*, Princeton, Princeton University Press, 1978.

Segovia shares his insights with some students at a master class.

Segovia's fingering of m. 61 is an excellent solution to the technical difficulty created by a long pattern of sixths. Playing the passage exactly as Bach wrote it is still an option. Or, only one note of the sixths on beat three may be dropped and the top notes can be played as a slur on the first string:

Bach:

Segovia:

Alternative:

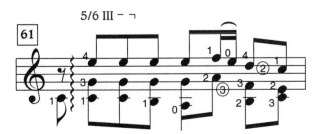

In m. 66-69, Segovia added some interesting bass notes:

Bach:

Segovia:

In m. 74, Segovia changed Bach's notes. Bach's original can be followed more closely here:

Bach:

Segovia:

Alternative:

M. 75-77 were indicated by Bach with a specific slurring pattern. Segovia omitted the slurs, which are awkward here on the guitar. He also may have sometimes added different bass notes.[52] Some may want to omit the slurs and make an effort to follow Bach's notes closely:

In m. 78-79, Bach indicated a specific slurring pattern which Segovia changed. He also played an A for a bass note at the beginning of m. 79 when Bach's original shows a B.[53] An alternative is given below which follows Bach more closely (Bach indicated some interesting syncopations by his slurs in m. 79):

Bach:

Segovia:

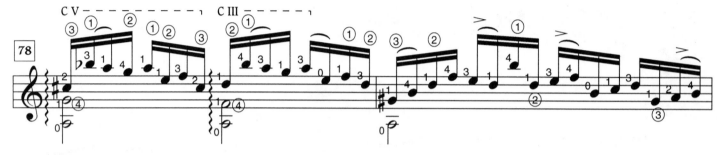

Alternative:

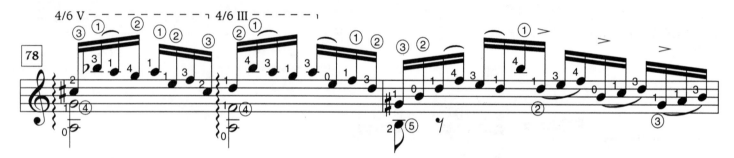

Segovia played m. 81 and m. 83 two different ways.[54] The version that is closer to Bach's original is suggested here:

Bach:

Segovia:

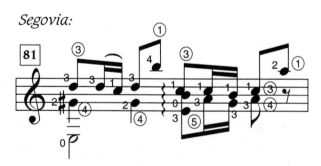

---

52. The bass notes were in Segovia's score that I obtained from one of his well known students. However, in two of his recordings that were used for this analysis (Angel ZB-3896 and Decca DL 9795) Segovia did not include the extra basses.

53. It really shows an A, but A in the original key of G minor is a B in this key of A minor.

54. Once again, this is according to his recordings and transcription manuscript.

Segovia:

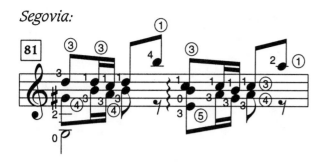

Bach:

Segovia:

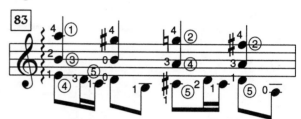

Segovia:

In m. 84 Segovia omitted some of Bach's notes, apparently for technical reasons. He sometimes thinned this section out less by including the final chord:[55]

Bach:

Segovia:

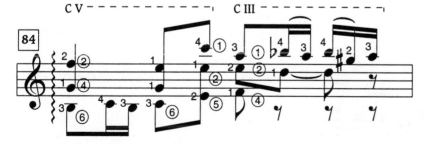

Segovia:

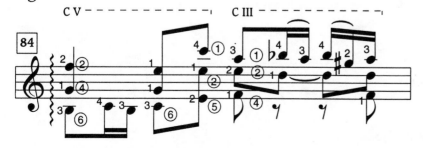

As we have seen, cadential trills are an absolute must in Baroque music.[56] For some unknown reason, Segovia omitted the cadential trill in m. 86:

Bach:

Segovia:

Alternative:

Segovia added a blatant *glissando* to the closing passage in m. 90. The *glissando* may be omitted by modern guitarists for stylistic reasons:[57]

Segovia:

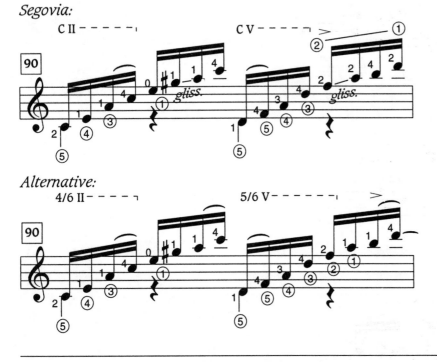

Alternative:

---

55. The final chord is indicated in his transcription manuscript.

56. See footnote #44.

57. See the discussion of *glissando* in the introduction to this book.

In the violin score, Bach indicated a tie from the top note of the dominant chord, m. 93, to the first note of the cadenza-like flourish. Segovia omitted the tie, and in so doing, followed the example of the lute version, BWV 1000. This is a most effective solution, since the tie cannot be sustained as it can on the violin:

Bach violin version, BWV 1001:

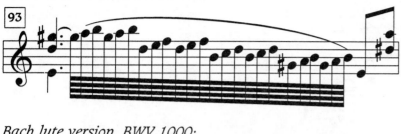

Bach lute version, BWV 1000:

Segovia:

Segovia filled out the chord on the first beat of m. 94. Earlier in his life he played the last trill from the bottom note, but later changed it to a cross string cadential trill from the top note which was *anticipated* by the main note. The main note was played on the beat as the final note of a roll of the dominant chord:[58]

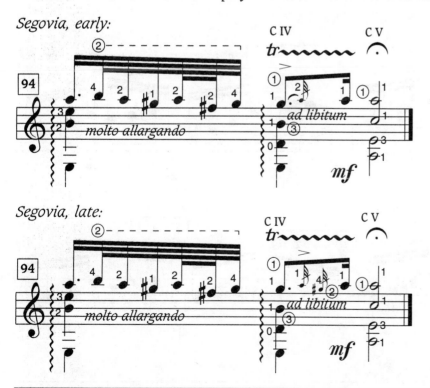

Segovia, early:

Segovia, late:

---

58. For an excellent discussion of the various types of trills that could be used here see: Frederick Neumann, *Ornamentation in Baroque and Post-Baroque Music, With Special Emphasis on J. S. Bach*, Princeton, Princeton University Press, 1978.

Segovia played the final chord as a four voice block chord, just as Bach wrote it. Some may want to use a full six note chord. The violin does not have the potential to do this (it only has four strings!). The fuller chord seems to add to the intensity of the *Fugue's* triumphant conclusion and its use is therefore suggested. An upper note cross string trill that starts on the beat is also suggested here:

Alternative:

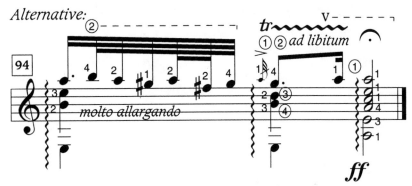

Segovia gave no indication for right hand fingering when playing this piece. Understandably, its complex nature opens the door to so many ambiguities that each guitarist must find what works individually. It may be helpful to observe, however, that quite a few opportunities present themselves for using the right hand technique of "planting"[59] throughout this very demanding composition. Control can certainly only be gained by those willing and able to study the piece to discover such opportunities. A few examples are:[60]

59. Christopher Parkening, *The Christopher Parkening Guitar Method, Vol. 1*, Chicago, Antiqua Casa Sherry-Brenner, 1972, p. 32.

60. The brackets indicate that all of the fingers contained therein are to "plant" on the strings during the first note of the figure.

Segovia's interpretation of this fugue was anything but lifeless and stoic. He took plenty of time to breathe after cadences and applied slight rhythmic flexibility, very appropriately, within the context of what is essentially a motor rhythm.[61] He employed subtle yet tasteful tonal colors, used dynamic contrast and was generous with articulation. His technique was much more than "just getting the notes," and future generations, no matter what their particular approach to Bach, can most certainly derive inspiration from his work. We can be sure that, because of his romantic approach, Segovia may be accused of over-expression. He cannot, however, be accused of performing Bach in the poor way in which all notes are played alike![62]

---

61. Richard Hudson, Stolen Time, *The History of Tempo Rubato*, Oxford, Clarendon Press, 1994, pp. 8-11. See footnote #25 in the section on *Prelude in D Minor.*

62. Carl Philipp Emanuel Bach, *Versuch über die wahre Art, das Clavier zu Spielen*, facsimile reproduction of the first edition, Berlin, 1753, Breitkopf & Härtel, Leipzig, 1957, p. 117. If anyone can be trusted to have learned from J. S. Bach what constitutes a good performance, his son surely can. He says: "What constitutes a good performance? Nothing other than proficiency, making musical thoughts sensible to the ear through singing or playing in accordance with their true context and affect. Through differentiation in the presentation of one musical thought, one can change it so much that it can hardly be perceived as having once been the same thought... The contents of a musical realization are the strength and weakness of the tones, their pressure, speed, push, pull, trembling, dimming, governing, dragging and moving on. One who employs these devices either improperly or not at all offers a poor realization." It seems that Segovia fits C.P.E. Bach's description of a good performer quite well.

Andrés Segovia always gave his utmost attention to the expression of the music he was performing.

SARABANDE IN B MINOR

Because of its elegance and charm, and most of all, its technical simplicity, the *Sarabande in B Minor* has become one of the most popular pieces in the Segovia repertoire.

Segovia excerpted this piece from the *Partita No. 1 in B Minor*, BWV 1002, which was originally written for solo violin. It is the fifth of eight movements (*Allemanda, Double, Corrente, Double, Sarabande, Double, Tempo di Bourrée, Double*).[63] Segovia, as was most often the case, decided not to perform the whole multi-movement work. He usually performed the *Sarabande, Bourrée* and its *Double* as a concert set. Segovia published his edition of the *Sarabande* in 1930.[64]

Certainly, when one considers the great length of this partita, we can guess that Segovia may have thought it was too long to be performed in concert. He had, of course, the special job of convincing the world that the guitar was and still is an instrument worthy of serious concert status. Because he had a limited time with each concert, he probably wanted to play only what he considered the best movements to allow plenty of time for an eclectic program. He could therefore make a more convincing presentation to his audiences of the guitar's diverse and comprehensive potential.[65]

The *Sarabande* lends itself extremely well to the guitar, and Segovia exercised his excellent abilities as an editor to make the piece more conducive to the nature of the instrument. He filled out and revoiced chords, added bass notes, and used octave transposition very effectively. For example:

Bach:

Segovia:

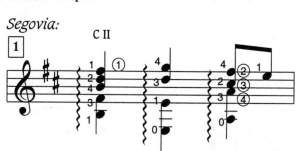

---

63. Owain Edwards, *Baroque Instrumental Music*, The Open University Press, 1974, pp. 24-26. We can see here that Bach followed the traditional German concept for a dance suite by building the composition around the basic slow-fast-slow-fast relationship of the Allemande-Courante-Sarabande-Gigue. His departure from tradition comes with his addition of the doubles, which are variation pieces in which note values have been halved. These were added after each movement. This piece is essentially a suite but Bach called it a partita. Owain Edwards tells us why: "A word about Bach's use of the terms 'suite' and 'partita' is necessary... when the collection of pieces was made up entirely of dances and an air, but no other movements which were not dances had been added, Bach referred to it as a suite or, if it were more similar to the conventional French model, an overture. When it comprised also other 'free' movements it (usually) constituted a partita."

64. Andrés Segovia, *J.S. Bach, Sarabande*, Union Musical Espanola, Madrid, 1930.

65. I am convinced that a whole Bach suite is too long to be played for average audiences. For example, on Thursday, October 12, 1995 I went to hear Eliot Fisk play a concert at Hillsdale College in Hillsdale, Michigan. The auditorium was filled to capacity with people, many of them students. To the end of the first half of the concert he played the entire *Sonata in C Major*, BWV 1005 (about 20 minutes long). After the intermission, only about two-thirds of the audience returned! Whether or not this had anything to do with the Bach *Sonata* is a matter of debate (it certainly had nothing to do with Fisk's phenomenal technique and musicianship). It seems evident that most people are conditioned by the popular media to hear only the four minute song or the short sound bite. A whole Bach suite may push the limits of the average person's attention span. The only audiences that may be accepting of the performance of whole suites which are quite lengthy are those in musicological settings, or where this practice is an understood part of the musical culture. Modern performers should not feel that they must always perform whole Baroque sonatas, suites or variation pieces in order to be "authentic" or "stylistic." Baroque composers did not expect this. Donald Jay Grout, *A History of Western Music*, New York/London, W.W. Norton & Company, 1980, pp. 391-392: "Performers in the Baroque thus had the liberty to add to the composer's written score; they were equally free to subtract from it or change it in various other ways... Composers of variations, suites, and sonatas took it for granted that players would omit movements ad libitum."

Bach:

6

Segovia:

6

Bach:

8

Segovia:

C II ------------

8
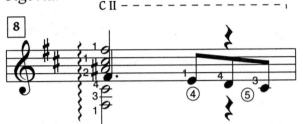

Bach:

10
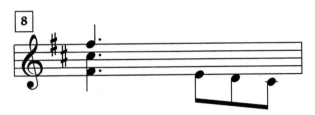

Segovia:

C VI ------------

10
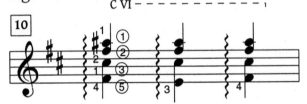

Bach:

13
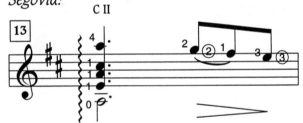

Segovia:

C II

13

Bach:

17
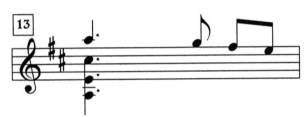

Segovia:

17
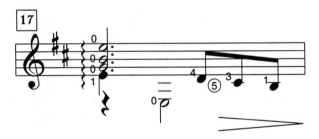

Bach:

18

Segovia:

18

Bach:

Segovia:

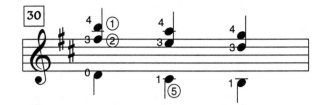

Bach:

Segovia:

Bach:

Segovia:

Most of Segovia's changes seem wise when using the guitar as the medium for performance of this music, and they are still a valid option.

Later in his career, for no obvious reason, Segovia played a B rather than a C as Bach originally indicated on the last eighth note of m. 21:

Bach:

Segovia:

Alternative:

Throughout the piece, Segovia consistently employed his standards of fingering in the higher positions while avoiding many open strings. A comparison of some passages from his early version[66] with those from

---

66. Andrés Segovia, *J. S. Bach, Sarabande*, Union Musical Espanola, Madrid, 1930.

his late one[67] proves that these standards were always a concern for Segovia. Over time he was able to achieve even greater consistency:

Segovia, early: *

Segovia, later:

Segovia, early: *

---

67. As played on the record called *Segovia on Stage*, MCA-2531, 1977.

Segovia's approach to the ending cadence in m. 32 may have been more stylistic if he would have started the cadential trill from the upper note played on the beat:[68]

Segovia filled out the last chord, whereas Bach indicated only a fifth and an octave. The Segovia approach seems to exploit the richness of the guitar more fully (especially since he uses a unison with the third string B and the second string open B):

68. Robert Donington, *Baroque Music: Style and Performance*, London, Faber Music Ltd., 1982, p. 125. "Cadential trills have mainly a harmonic function, which they fulfill by behaving like appoggiaturas, accented from the upper (i.e. the auxiliary) note, to which the main note serves as a resolution. Christine Ammer, *Harper's Dictionary of Music*, Harper & Row Publishers, New York, 1972, p. 380. "In the seventeenth and eighteenth centuries the trill was usually begun on the upper note; since the early nineteenth century it generally has been begun on the lower note."

Segovia's interpretation was very sensitive, and, as always, he employed rich expressive nuances. Uncharacteristically, he did not use any blatant *glissandi,* but he did use subtle ones frequently to shape the line.[69] The impression given to the listener is one where the melody is played in a way reminiscent of a skilled female vocalist singing an elegant aria. Rhythmic flexibility in the form of free rubato is appropriate in this slow movement, and Segovia used it throughout.[70]

For all of our appreciation of Segovia's melodic sensitivity, one aspect seems to be strikingly absent to those who are aware of and listening for the historical aspects of Baroque music. That aspect is ornamentation. Regarding this subject, one thing can be said for certain: it is a divisive issue on which scholars have not yet reached a consensus.[71] Attitudes and opinions have changed greatly over the 20th century as more research has been done. Segovia used very little, if any, ornamentation and his approach simply mirrors the beliefs and practices of the late 19th to mid 20th century. Even if musicians from Segovia's time believed in ornamenting, the general belief was that Bach's music was never to be ornamented because he was German. It was believed that the Germans wrote out ornaments when they wanted them; only the Italians did not.[72] Therefore, Bach's music was *not* to be ornamented.[73]

69. See the discussion of the *glissando* in the introduction to this book.

70. Richard Hudson, *Stolen Time, The History of Tempo Rubato,* Oxford, Clarendon Press, 1994, p. 11. "The violin, as the main solo instrument of the Baroque period, did, however, imitate the solo vocal form, and it was no doubt appropriate in certain sections or movements to employ the sort of rhythmic freedom used by singers..." Does this mean that a very romantic style approach is appropriate here? We do know that the Baroque doctrine of *affections* held that music was to convey feelings. However, the feeling was to be expressed by the composer through various compositional techniques rather than by imposition of individual performers, from without. See: Donald Jay Grout, *A History of Western Music,* New York/London, W. W. Norton & Company, 1980, pp. 298-299. Grout says, "The music of the Baroque was thus not primarily written to express the feelings of an individual artist, but to represent the *affections*; these were not communicated haphazardly or left to individual intuition, but were conveyed by means of a systematic, regulated vocabulary, a common repertory of musical figures or devices." Therefore the flexibility (as well as the overall interpretation) used here should convey the feelings suggested by the music but avoid individualistic romantic excess.

71. Don Michael Randel, editor, *The New Harvard Dictionary of Music,* London, England, Cambridge, Massachusetts, The Belknap Press of Harvard University Press, 1986, p. 598. "The most difficult problem for the modern interpreter of early music is to know where ornamentation is needed and what kind to add in the absence of any sign... Disagreements about the amount and kind of ornamentation to be added to the composer's product are documented from the time of Josquin on, and thus the performer should not imagine that there is only one 'right' solution for a given passage... The applicability of the treatises of C.P.E. Bach and Quantz to the music of J. S. Bach is, for example, a matter of vigorous dispute. The question of whether repeats should be ornamented has never had comprehensive treatment. The large incidence of varied repeats written out in English virginal music and early 17th century French lute music suggests that repeats indicated by sign also could be varied. The successive strophes of *airs de cour* were ornamented differently. A few instances of written *doubles* intercalated as varied repeats can be found in French 17th century lute music, but it is not true, as Margarete Reimann states (MGG 3:713), that *doubles* can be treated 'without further consideration' as varied repeats. In general, Baroque method books that explain repeat marks say nothing about varying the repeats. Some music, e.g. the harpsichord pieces of François Couperin, would seem to exclude additional ornamentation on repeats; indeed, the composer inveighs against any liberties with his notation. The preface to C.P.E. Bach's *Sonatas with Varied Reprises,* implies that such variation was a mid-18th century fashion, not a long standing tradition. On the other hand, Tosi (1723) suggests that the reprises of da capo arias had long been varied. Method books of the later 18th century recommend little or no ornamentation on the first appearance of a melody and ornamentation of increasing complexity on further appearances (as in reprises of rondos, sonatas, arias, and other solo music)."

72. Manfred F. Bukofzer, *Music in the Baroque Era,* New York, W. W. Norton & Company, Inc., 1947, p. 375. Bukofzer gives us the opinion of scholars in the 19th and the first half of the 20th century: "The French and German methods both curtailed the improvisatory additions of the performer, [which was] typical of Italian practice. Characteristically, Lully, Couperin, and Bach do not call for additional ornamentation..."

73. Victor Rangel-Ribeiro, *Baroque Music, A Practical Guide for the Performer,* New York, Schirmer Books, 1981, p. 87. "Through the decades Bach's music has become encrusted with a whole system of traditions and sacred myths. His high priests are legion: their followers fanatical. Witness the child who instinctively inserts a Baroque short mordent or half trill at a cadential point in a minuet and is promptly stopped by the teacher. 'Bach always set down all the notes,' the teacher says. 'You never, never, NEVER tamper with Bach!'"

There is no doubt that the musical climate has changed,[74] and modern scholarship has shown that Bach did write his music expecting it to be ornamented. Still this view is not universally accepted.[75]

The controversy over whether Baroque music, and in particular, that of J. S. Bach, can be ornamented seems to have shifted its emphasis in recent years. While it is increasingly accepted that it is *permissible* to ornament, the question has been raised by such authoritative figures as Ralph Kirkpatrick as to whether Bach *should* be ornamented.[76] There is legitimate concern that Bach's music could be ornamented in a way that he would not have approved of. However, Bach himself left strong evidence that he wanted the repeats of those simple movements that he did not already ornament to be ornamented. Bach wrote out ornamented repeats to the *Sarabandes* of his *English Suites*, #2 and #3, BWV 807 and BWV 808. This fact is particularly relevant to the *Sarabande in B Minor*. We can safely conclude that Bach may have been giving approval and even possibly encouragement for other Sarabandes to become vehicles for expressive ornamentation on the repeats, as long as he had not already done so.[77]

Some may argue that the *Sarabande in B Minor* should be left unornamented and simple because Bach put it in between two doubles, one of which is an ornamentation of the *Sarabande* itself. This is true only if the *Partita* is played together in its entirety. Baroque composers usually did not expect a rigid approach to be followed in regard to playing whole suites, and it may be better to avoid such a practice, except under certain circumstances.[78] If a case can be made for ornamenting any of the movements from the *Partita in B Minor*, BWV 1002, it seems that the *Sarabande* has the strongest one in its favor.

---

74. *Ibid.*, p. 1. Victor Rangel-Ribeiro relates the following true story to show how the tide is turning in favor of those who believe in ornamenting Baroque music: "In a recording studio in Europe, not too long ago, the big maned, big-named conductor sat in his high rehearsal chair, clothed in authority. The virtuoso recorder soloist, renowned in his own field, sat alert and waiting. The musicians leaned forward in their chairs, instruments at the ready, eyes on the conductor. The music began to flow, smooth and professional; the solo line soared—and within seconds the conductor stopped the orchestra, incredulous.

'Just what do you think you're doing?' he demanded.

'Why, I'm ornamenting the melodic line,' said the soloist, rather taken aback.

'And you'd better stop!' shouted the conductor, suddenly enraged. 'If Handel had wanted the solo line ornamented, he would have written in the ornaments himself! We'll play the music as written!'

'I'm sorry,' said the soloist, bristling, 'but to play this music as written would be barbaric. I must play it with the ornaments the style calls for.'

'I'll be damned if you do!' cried the conductor.

'God rest your soul!' retorted the soloist.

And the conductor stomped off in a rage, expecting that the recording company would have the soloist replaced. Instead, a new conductor took the chair half an hour later, and the recording proceeded without further incident."

75. *Ibid.*, p. 87. "Even quite knowledgeable musicians—eminent pianists among them—believe that Bach took care of the ornamentation at all times... It is rarely acknowledged that there are many pieces that the performer can ornament. For Bach wrote in the Italian style in two ways: sometimes he wrote out the florid passages as in the slow movement of the *Italian Concerto* for harpsichord, and sometimes he set down only enough notes to make a complete melody, leaving the elaboration to the performer."

76. Ralph Kirkpatrick, "Fifty Years of Harpsichord Playing," presented in *Early Music*, January 1983, p. 40. "I have always thought that the decoration of reprises was something that should be a privilege of a player, rather than a duty. I find that in the case of movements like those of the Bach partitas which are themselves already decorations of an unstated original, attempts to show one's originality inevitably run into conflict with the originality of Bach himself. One cuts a very sorry figure with one's poor little deposits of excremental ornaments on Bach's marvelous musical fabrics. One is reminded of bird droppings on the statues erected in the memory of great and illustrious men... what is there wrong about elegant simplicity? Why must one be fussy?"

77. Victor Rangel-Ribeiro, *Baroque Music, A Practical Guide for the Performer*, New York, Schirmer Books, 1981, p. 116. "In summary, one should not be afraid to ornament the music of Bach, but the project must be approached with extra care. A thorough study must be made of Bach's idiom so that the strong individuality of the music is maintained. The artist must determine the manner in which Bach was writing at that particular moment. If the melody is written out in the florid Italian style, then Bach has already done most of the ornamenting himself; the artist can however legitimately change some of the ornamentation the first time around and is at perfect liberty to make further changes on the repeats. If the writing is spare, is it deliberately spare to provide a contrast between two florid sections? If so, the line may be very discreetly ornamented, but the outline should be left alone. If the outline is spare because Bach was writing in true Italian style—with the ornamentation left to the will of the performer—the artist has the obligation to ornament. The only requirements are that the ornamentation should be so Bach-like in nature and grow so naturally out of the original that the listener accepts it with delight."

78. Donald Jay Grout, *A History of Western Music*, New York/London, W. W. Norton & Company, 1980, pp. 391-392. For an explanation of why it may be better to not program whole multi-movement works, see footnote #65 above.

Some careful study of Bach's own ornamentation is necessary to ornament this music with integrity. A look at Bach's *Sarabande* from the *English Suite #2* in its non-ornamented and ornamented versions will be helpful (we will look at the A section only):

Sarabande from English Suite #2:

Sarabande from English Suite #2, ornamented by the composer:

Treble clef part of non-ornamented and ornamented versions:

As we can see, Bach employed longer ornamentation (division, diminution or figuration) as well as smaller melodic formulas (trills, turns, appoggiaturas, etc.). Following his example, here is a way the repeats of the *Sarabande* could be ornamented:

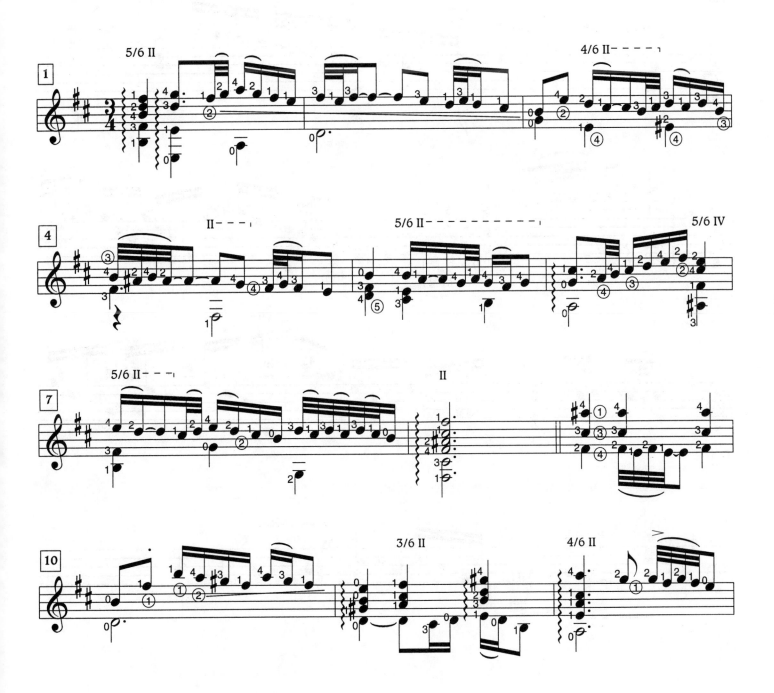

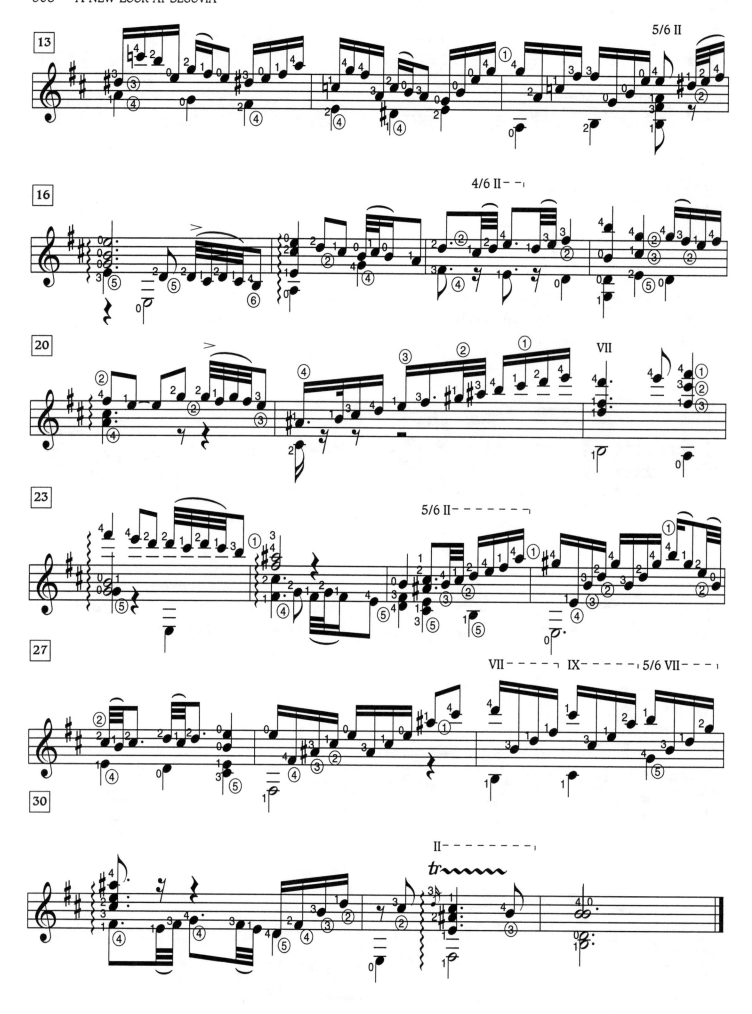

Of course, there are many possibilities when it comes to ornamenting the melodic line. If the decision is made to ornament, one is put in a place of taking a risk, however. It is certainly possible to fall short of doing a job that could be said by others to be worthy of a master such as J. S. Bach. This kind of risk taking calls to mind another master, namely, Andrés Segovia. After all, it was his adventurous spirit that brought Bach to the world on the guitar through his myriad concerts, drawing praise from some and criticism from others.[79] We must also remember that Segovia provided an audacious example for us to follow when he transcribed and performed the revered *Chaconne* from Bach's *Partita No. 2 in D Minor*.[80] In doing so he made a challenge to the musical establishment of his day, even causing some to recoil in horror![81] Segovia's example calls us to continue on, blazing the trail that he started, by pressing forward into the vast territories on the musical horizon—with the beauty of the classical guitar.

*J.S. Bach, *Sarabande*. Trans. para guitarra por A. Segovia. Copyright by union Musical Española, Madrid, 1930. All Rights Reserved. Reprinted by permission of Music Sales Corporation on behalf of Union Musical Ediciones.

---

79. Graham Wade, *The Guitarist's Guide to Bach*, Ireland, Wise Owl Music, 1985, p. 17. Wade quotes a translation that appeared in an article by Matanya Ophee in *Soundboard* magazine, Spring 1982, p. 75: "On 26 March, 1926, Segovia played a recital in Moscow, performing several Bach pieces. An article appeared in *Izvestia* praising Segovia's ability to play serious music on the guitar which is 'poor in resources and mainly destined for accompaniment.' The fact that Segovia brought Bach into recitals continued to astonish and delight the public, especially when it became apparent that the guitar was capable of dispatching a fugue with dexterity and clarity. The problem of whether it was appropriate or not to perform Bach on such an instrument continued to vex critics for some time to come."

80. *Ibid.*, pp. 7-8.

81. Bernard Gavoty, *Andrés Segovia*, Geneva, René Kistler, p. 13. Gavoty describes the reaction when Segovia began playing the respected Chaconne in Europe: "The program on that occasion announced one work that made the violinists start and tremble: Bach's *Chaconne*. Horror of horrors! The *Chaconne* for solo violin, the sacred *Chaconne*—we were going to hear—nay, endure—its profanation by a guitarist? They covered their faces, as Spanish ladies do when watching a bullfight—that is, with their fingers slightly parted so as to see through the spaces... Be that as it may, the violinophiles arrived to witness the 'murder.'" A review that appeared in the United States (*Chicago Maroon*, January 21, 1949. See also Appendix D) confirms that Segovia was raising controversy worldwide over this issue of Bach, yet we know that he remained undaunted: "...Segovia's transcriptions have engendered much discussion in musical circles. Particularly controversial is the transcription of the Bach *Chaconne* from the D Minor solo violin partita..."

BOURRÉE IN B MINOR

The *Bourrée in B Minor* takes on special significance in that it is probably the first Bach piece that Segovia played.[82] Francisco Tárrega (1852-1909), who was one of the first guitarists to play Bach on the guitar, was the first to transcribe the *Bourrée*.[83] It is very possible that Segovia first became aware of the *Bourrée* and its potential as a guitar solo through Tárrega's edition. While Segovia originally used Tárrega's edition as his source for performance,[84] a comparison of Segovia and Tárrega's published editions shows that the two eventually had few similarities.[85]

Segovia initially played the *Bourrée* as an individual solo, as Tárrega and his students apparently did also.[86] Later, Segovia played it in a set with its *Double* and the *Andante* from the *Violin Sonata No. 2 in A Minor*, BWV 1003. Finally, in the latter part of his life, he performed it in a set with its *Double* and the *Sarabande*, all from the *Partita No. 1*, BWV 1002. He made a splendid recording of it in this context.[87]

While the performance practice for playing Bach has shifted in the late 20th century to an emphasis on playing Bach suites in their entirety, Segovia cannot be criticized from a historical perspective for not doing so himself. Baroque composers did not expect all movements of their suites to be played at one time.[88]

Because this is one of the first pieces that Segovia played, he had quite a long period to work on it before recording it on his *Segovia on Stage* album in 1977. Comparing this recorded version with his published version[89] shows that Segovia, as an editor, was not static in his approach. The later arrangement is quite faithful to the original, while his early transcription reflects more of the 19th century attitude that the score was insufficient and therefore performers needed to add notes:

Bach:

---

82. Graham Wade, *The Guitarist's Guide to Bach*, Ireland, Wise Owl Music, 1986, p. 15.

83. Rafael Andiá and Javier Quevedo, *Francisco Tárrega, The Collected Guitar Works*, Heidelberg, Chanterelle Editions Ltd., 1992. In this valuable facsimile edition of scores from Tárrega's time, Rafael Andiá gives a description of Tárrega's highly 19th century style edition of the Bourrée: *"Tempo di Bourrée* from *Partita No. 1 in B Minor* BWV 1002. The original tone of B minor has been retained. Apart from the addition of some notes which give more clarity to the polyphony and make it more suitable for the guitar, the transcription is faithful. It is fingered true to the period of the transcription with an excessive amount of slurring, frequently without reason. There are also some stylistically inappropriate *glissandi* and too many barrés which hinder the musical discourse."

84. Andrés Segovia, *Segovia: An Autobiography of the Years 1893-1920*, New York, Macmillan Publishers, 1976, p. 19. Segovia describes himself playing the *Bourrée* as a very young man in Spain: "Trembling, barely able to control my fingers, I played Tárrega's transcription of the Bach Bourrée in B minor from the second sonata for solo violin."

85. Andrés Segovia, *J.S. Bach, Verschiedene Stücke: Vol III, Andante-Bourrée-Double*, Mainz, B. Schott's Söhne, 1928. It is interesting that Segovia chose to pair the *Bourrée* and its *Double* with the *Andante* from the *Violin Sonata No. 2 in A Minor*, BWV 1003, for publication. Segovia's edition of the *Bourrée* is not as literal as Tárrega's and the fingerings are very different.

86. Graham Wade, *The Guitarist's Guide to Bach*, Ireland, Wise Owl Music, 1985, p. 15.

87. Andrés Segovia, *Segovia on Stage*, MCA Records 2531, Universal City, CA, 1977. Segovia's recording of these pieces was reissued after his death in *The Andrés Segovia Collection*, Vol. 1, MCA Records 42066, 1987.

88. Donald Jay Grout, *A History of Western Music*, New York/London, W.W. Norton & Company, 1980, p. 392. See footnote #65.

89. Andrés Segovia, *J.S. Bach, Verschiedene Stücke: Vol III, Andante-Bourrée-Double*, Mainz, B. Schott's Söhne, 1928. The version recorded by Segovia in 1977 (*Segovia on Stage*, MCA-2531) is practically a different transcription.

Segovia, early:

Segovia, late:

Bach:

Segovia, early:

Segovia, late:

A certain amount of filling in or revoicing chords, adding or transposing bass notes and dividing longer notes into shorter ones in order to sustain notes for their intended duration is appropriate, as can be seen in Bach's own transcriptions. This kind of editing is necessary when adapting a piece of music to the peculiarities of a different instrument. Segovia often went beyond the necessary into the realm of adding new voices and harmonies, a truly Romantic approach.[90]

It is no longer considered acceptable to add to Bach's music beyond limited editorial modifications to adapt to the strengths and weaknesses of a particular instrument when transcribing.[91]

---

90. Michael Cedric Smith, "Fashions in Bach," presented in *Guitar Review*, Summer 1985, p. 2. "No one typified this approach more than Ferruccio Busoni (1866-1924). To him music was heroic—in it lay a grandeur and largeness, a dramatic passion with the power to ennoble mankind. He added new voices and harmonies, dynamic markings and pedallings in his transcriptions and editions... Andrés Segovia's of Bach and those he made in collaboration with Manuel Ponce are clearly written within this tradition."

Segovia practicing on his Ramirez guitar in his Madrid studio, 1982.

While approving of scholarship and the effort to be "correct" in playing Bach, some have lamented that this approach sometimes seems to lose expressive elements and makes the music seem more geared for the head than for the heart. The general trend has shifted away from Segovian romanticism and towards the scholarly and what is perceived as the historically correct way of playing Bach.[92]

Civilization has indeed developed into an age of abundant information and high technology in the late 20th century. Machines can be programmed to play Bach correctly in terms of speed, accuracy, ornamentation and fidelity to the original score.[93] Guitarists, while playing "correctly" can sometimes sound like

---

91. *Ibid.*, p. 3. "The *Bach Gesellschaft* brought out a complete edition of his works in their original form... This edition, together with the new science of musicology paved the way for a fashion favoring the accuracy of the score in the performance of Bach."

92. *Idem.* "Great thinkers and writers have contributed much in directing our thoughts about Bach... The result of their research has led to more knowledgeable and thoughtful performances which displace the emotional intensity of the 19th century approach."

93. For example, it is now possible for a Macintosh Power PC computer to play any of the pieces in this book. By hooking it up to a MIDI keyboard with synthesizer, it can digitally simulate the sound of almost any instrument. It can play anything perfectly and at dazzling speeds. This clearly emphasizes the fact that performers *must* offer their audiences something more than the mechanical aspects of music, for mechanical perfection can easily be heard elsewhere. What a performer does with the music interpretatively constitutes the human element that makes a concert unique and worth hearing. There is no better example of this than Segovia.

machines, regardless of pyro-technical display (a machine can still play faster and cleaner than a person). But a machine cannot yet provide the variety of inflection, dynamics, articulation, and tone color that we find in the work of Andrés Segovia. Most of all, it cannot produce the emotions that are unique to human beings.[94] Hopefully, guitarists, when searching for a more "thoughtful," "knowledgeable," and "correct" approach to Bach will not displace the emotion and expression that gives life and a human quality to a performance. Andrés Segovia, that pioneer who resisted those who said that Bach should not be played on the guitar, also resisted the approach to Bach that would sap much of the emotion and life out of music by one of the world's most spiritual composers.[95]

Segovia believed in playing Bach on the guitar, and he believed strongly in using all of the guitar's expressive potential when playing this music.[96]

Guitarists have moved away from the Romantic style in terms of its adding lines and harmonies not originally indicated as well as its overemphasis on techniques such as slurs, free rubato, vibrato and *glissandi.* The new movement in playing Bach tends towards virtuosity, power, showmanship, and scholarship, and the progress in those areas deserves to be applauded. Bach himself applauded changes in style and even admitted that old forms can be improved upon and made to sound more appealing.[97]

One of the strongest arguments in favor of maintaining the emotive and expressive aspects of the Segovia style when playing Bach is based on the spiritual quality of the music itself.[98]

Bach had tremendous dedication to and love for God. He also had a great love for his family, and was not content to be separated from them.[99] He expressed his love for God, family and all things of life in his

94. Since 1994 there is one machine that seems to come close to reproducing the human elements: the *Yamaha Disklavier Piano*. While browsing in a shopping mall in December of 1994, I kept hearing elegant Christmas music being played live on a piano, as I had heard many other years before. Only this time, as I joined the crowd of people to listen, it became obvious that the piano was playing by itself! These new digital pianos can be programmed to play with emotion. They can also record and reproduce the performance of a fine pianist. Needless to say, these pianos have put a lot of pianists out of work. Guitarists need not fear, however. Chances are that it will be a long time before we will be able to sit down and hear a classical guitar play a concert by itself. Besides, do people come just to hear the music, or do they come to see and hear the artist? In Segovia's case, it was definitely the latter.

95. Paul Hindemith, *Johann Sebastian Bach, Heritage and Obligation,* Yale University Press, 1959, p. 35. "And he [Bach] was also a God fearing man whose art was dedicated to the Lord."

96. Andrés Segovia, *Segovia on stage*, MCA Records 2531, Universal City, CA, 1977. On the back of this album, Alan Rich describes a conversation where Segovia gave his philosophy towards Bach on the guitar: "'Why,' I ask, 'do you feel it proper to play on the guitar music that may have been written for some other instrument?' I have my own answer, but I wait for his.

'The answer,' he replies, 'is very simple, and also very complex. First of all, Bach, Handel and other Baroque composers often made their own transcriptions, so that pieces written for one situation might be transferred to another. They were concerned more with the expression that is in the music itself, rather than with the particular sound. That is the simple part of the answer.

'Now to the more complex part. Many years ago I used to argue with other musicians and scholars about Baroque music, and especially about Bach. You know, there used to be an idea that Bach must be played very carefully, very stiffly, with all his dissonances very harsh and mathematical. It was almost as if Bach in his own lifetime, had merely been a statue of himself. I do not believe for one minute that Bach really meant his music to sound that way.

'I am a guitarist, but I also love Bach. So, I play him on the guitar so I can show the expressive side of his music, the noble, the serious and the dignified. And, also the beautiful.'"

97. Robert L. Marshall, *Bach the Progressive: Observations on his Later Works*, presented in the Journal of the American Musicological Society, Vol. LXII, No. 3, July 1976. Bach wrote a letter in 1730 which shows that he may have been happy with the changes of musical style and taste that he observed in his time: "The state of music is quite different from what it was, since our artistry has increased very much, and the gusto has changed astonishingly, and accordingly, the former style of music no longer seems to please our ears..."

98. Theodore Hoelty-Nickel, *The Little Bach Book*, Valparaiso, Indiana, Valparaiso University Press, 1952, p. 52. "...The musical inspiration of Bach does not, so to speak, 'come out of a vacuum.' We cannot ever take it for granted; we must find whence it comes and the way it is. We see in certain passages, for instance, the gesture of prayer, and we try to correlate the gesture of prayer and the direction of the musical theme. Imagery produces music in Bach, or to see it from a different angle, all his music is mainly the result of religious faith."

99. *Ibid.*, pp. 82-83.

music with various kinds and degrees of emotion.[100] Bach's music conveys those positive emotions and attributes mentioned in the Bible as those to be sought by the Christian open to God's Holy Spirit.[101] Therefore, any manner of playing Bach which does not emphasize the humanness, the emotion, and especially the holy, spiritual and therefore beautiful expressive qualities inherent in Bach's music could be said to be debasive.[102] While it should be readily apparent to all that the adjectives used here are subjective (beauty is in the eye of the beholder), it is easy to see that these are the very qualities Segovia strove for in his style. When it comes to acceptable concepts of feeling, tone and beautiful expressiveness, most agree that Segovia's playing was of the highest quality.[103]

Hopefully, the general aspects of expressiveness which were ever so present in Segovia's playing, without which music can become less moving and interesting, can be maintained when modern guitarists play Bach.

Segovia's recorded version of the *Bourrée in B Minor* (*Segovia on Stage*, MCA 2531)[104] is a good one to examine to hear him demonstrate the kinds of expressive possibilities available to the serious player. The following analysis is provided as a guide when considering some of the editorial and interpretive aspects of Bach's music that a guitarist may wish to employ when preparing for performance.

---

100. *Ibid.*, p. 79. The discussion here of Bach's organ work is revealing of his other instrumental works, and his music in general. "The expression of all these works ranges from jubilant joy to dejected sadness, from quiet meditation to majestic sublimity. His compositions share one thing in common, however; they express much more than human emotions and desires. Joy and sorrow are placed on a higher sphere, the sphere of prayer. It is not true that Bach was an abstract, methodical mathematician who dealt with sound. Every one of his measures breathes a human warmth, and all his organ works are vigorous and euphonious, even those of his later years. Yet, because of their strict ordered discipline and their humble submission to a higher Law, they place everything that is human under the surveillance of God."

101. *The Thompson Chain Reference Bible*, New International Version, Indianapolis, Indiana, the B. B. Kirkbride Bible Company, Inc., 1983, p. 1194, Galatians 5:22: "...but the fruit of the Spirit is love, joy, peace, patience, kindness, goodness, faithfulness and self-control." This is not to say that one has to be a Christian to play Bach's music. What is apparent is that Bach, as a dedicated Christian, probably did his best to model his music *compositionally* to express these qualities. This is completely consistent with the Baroque doctrine of *affections* (see footnote #70 under *Sarabande in B Minor*). Therefore, these Christian elements would be in the music to a certain degree regardless of whether a Christian or an atheist were performing it. A sensitive performer such as Segovia only aided in making explicit what was already implicit in the music.
It is fair to point out here that some have questioned this strong emphasis on the religious element in Bach's music. Pablo Casals has said (J.M.A. Corredor, *Conversations with Casals*, translated by André Mangeot, London, Hutchinson & Co. Ltd., 1956, p. 114): "In my opinion there has been much too much leaning on the exclusively religious side of Bach's music. The intensity of his faith is evident in a great many of his compositions. Bach was a sincere believer and a man whose occupation led him to serve the church. However, I cannot rally myself to this idea of exclusively religious feeling in his music. I find that very exaggerated. Religious inspiration is not everything. In Bach we find infinite gradations of musical allusion: the simple joy of the people, the popular dances, the elegance, the perfume, the loving contemplation of nature and the rest.
"We know that Bach had the most sincere religious feeling: in all the Passions and Chorales he has given expression to his faith in the most complete and the greatest way, but I insist this inspiration is far from being the only one in his work. I think that Bach was a poet who felt the necessity of translating all noble thoughts into music." Is this the correct view of Bach? Contrary to Casal's opinion, religious inspiration *must* have been everything for J. S. Bach since he adorned his scores with S.G.D. (*Soli Deo Gloria*, which means "to God alone be the glory"). This does not mean there aren't other elements, but it seems that the religious one was foundational.

102. Theodore Hoelty-Nickel, *The Little Bach Book*, Valparaiso, Indiana, Valparaiso University Press, 1952, p. 82. "Bach's music is never inherently bombastic, gaudy and theatrical; it is never cheap, puerile and debasive; but is invariably wholesome, ennobling, pure and beautiful."

103. *Guitar Review*, New York, Fall 1986. The following statement was made by the editor of *Guitar Review* magazine on the inside cover of this issue: "In recent months there has been a barrage of articles written by eminent critics appraising the current state of various art forms. With remarkable unanimity, they decry the trend away from quality, be it of tone, expressiveness or style, and towards virtuosity, power and sheer showmanship. As members of the often victimized audience, we tend to agree with the writers.
"It is refreshing, therefore, to read the account of Andrés Segovia... taking up the cudgels for a return to quality. Here is a man whose very name evokes memories of some of the most poignant and memorable moments in music history, battling vigorously to preserve the exalted position to which he has brought the guitar.
"In an interesting parallel, Will Crutchfield recently wrote of the malaise that has befallen operatic singers. He also suggests the cure by quoting Verdi, 'Let us return to the past, it would be progress.'
"When from the critics Verdi, Crutchfield and Segovia comes the same admonition, 'Let us return to quality,' its time to heed the call. Yes, let's return to quality."

104. This piece was reissued after Segovia's death on *The Andrés Segovia Collection*, Vol. 1, MCA Records 42066, 1987. This recording is widely available. Listening to Segovia's performance can be very helpful for those who want to grasp clearly the analysis presented here.

Segovia started the piece by filling out the opening harmonies. He started forte using a strong brush stroke across the first two chords. The tempo was kept somewhere in the area of half note=80. In m. 4 he articulated the first two beats with staccato. He played a trill, from the main note on beat 4 (the trills may be changed to upper note trills) while at the same time dividing the bass note F (which was a half note in the original) into two quarters while doing an octave transposition. He added slurs in m. 5 and filled out the two note figures to make chords in m. 6:

Segovia achieved a slightly contrasting tone color in m. 7-9 by using the third string in a higher position. He filled out the notes in m. 8 to make three note structures. He then continued down the stepwise pattern which starts in m. 9 and descends in thirds by emphasizing the lower notes. He arrived in m. 11 on the minor second dissonance and immediately started the following run with a *glissando* while making a crescendo up to the note A on the second string. He played this note with a slight emphasis and left it with a subtle *glissando* down to the lower position in preparation for the chords in m. 12. He filled out the chords in m. 12 and played them with a sharp attack. He then filled out the passage from m. 13 to m. 15, using subtle *glissandi* for the melody as well as staccato on some of the chords:

In m. 16 Segovia held the bass notes, achieving a feeling of legato throughout m. 16-17 (Bach wrote the bass notes as quarters in the original). In m. 18 Segovia arrived on the first note G. He played the next note C staccato and then leapt up on the second string to the half note, A. He played this note delicately with vibrato and a slight amount of free rubato.[105] Obviously trying to follow Bach's original, Segovia then played the descending run in m. 19-20 as two slurs. (Bach wrote the entire passage as one slur, which is fitting to the violin technique, but impossible on the guitar.) Segovia then achieved more sonority at the cadence by playing it on the inner strings. He articulated the cadence by playing the first chord, or the fourth beat of m. 20, with a short staccato and the next chord legato:

Segovia practiced for at least five hours every day.

---

105. Some rhythmic flexibility is appropriate here even though this is essentially a motor rhythm. See footnote #25 under *Prelude in D Minor.*

Segovia repeated the A section almost exactly as he played it the first time through.

M. 22 starts the B section with thirds which Segovia played staccato with a metallic sound. As if in answer, he gently emphasized the bass notes in m. 25 (he omitted Bach's bass note on the last beat of m. 24). More chords are filled out in m. 26-27, and Segovia built this pattern of sixths that started in m. 24 to the third beat of m. 28, which he accented and played staccato while adding a bass note. After a short breath he continued with the thirds on the second and third strings. The trill in m. 29 was played from the main note. M. 31 was played with contrasting staccato and legato articulations. In m. 33 the ascending chords were filled out and the bass line was continued by adding a bass note in m. 34. M. 34 begins a pattern in the treble that is answered by the bass, and Segovia made the most of this by emphasizing the bass response with the thumb. The run in m. 38 was rushed to the cadence, which Segovia arrived at forte:

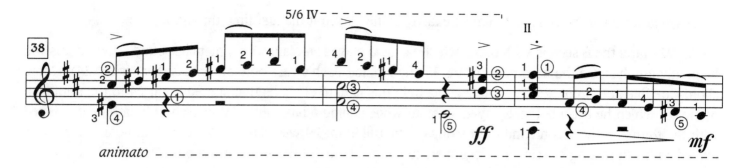

In m. 41, Segovia played the top note A on the second string while building toward a slight rubato with gentle vibrato on the first beat of m. 42 (the rubato emphasis here takes advantage of the time stolen from the pulse by the slight rushing that began in m. 38). He brought this top note out even more by playing the chord on the third beat of m. 41 staccato. When Bach repeats this pattern down a step in m. 43, Segovia gave it the same kind of treatment by emphasizing the top note G and playing the chord on the third beat of m. 43 staccato. However, this time he did not dwell on the notes by doing a rubato. He followed this by creating a passage in thirds (not in the original) and then playing the bass notes in m. 45 as half notes instead of the original quarters:

Segovia's sensitivity to the line was manifest in his treatment of the single line passage beginning in m. 46. He added generous amounts of slurs and *glissandi* which gave shape and created a heightened awareness of peaks, such as those in m. 50 and m. 52. The descent to the cadence which starts in m. 52 was woven skillfully by the maestro with a generous dose of slurs as well, and the cadence itself emphasized by adding additional notes:

Segovia continued by bringing out the bass response in m. 56-57. He filled out the three note chord on the first beat of m. 57 to a four note chord and emphasized it with a roll (arpeggiation). He added a bass note in m. 60 which seems to keep the texture from sounding too thin. Then, he built the line towards what is perhaps its most dramatic peak in the entire work in m. 64. Here he prepared our ear to hear the climax and arrival of the treble line by doing a heavy downstroke with the thumb on the A# and E on the first beat. The melodic line was then played on the second string with vibrato:

The descent to the final cadence was then rushed slightly and the last note of the run, A#, was played staccato. This was followed by a very slight pause, presumably to get set for the following chords at the seventh fret. Segovia played the recapitulation of the opening chordal section which closes the piece as he had begun it: strong and with full chordal strums with the thumb. He added a note to the last beat of m. 67 and continued to the ending fortissimo and with a *ritardando.* He repeated the B section, like the A section, almost exactly, but closed the piece with a more deliberate *ritardando* (he also let the bass note E in m. 60 ring for at least the duration of a whole note, when he played it as a quarter the first time):

Certainly when examining the editorial and interpretive aspects of Andrés Segovia's playing of Bach, one can see a rich and varied array of musical and guitaristic expression. The lesson here is twofold. First, in the sense that we can learn that an interesting performance of Bach consists of more than just mechanical playing of the notes. Furthermore, we can be certain that this level of instrumental art requires more than just innate musical intuition, although this is most certainly the foundation. Andrés Segovia bore testimony to the expression of Bach and any other music he chose to play. His music was given life through patient hard work, the results of which are shown through his success around the world in a career which spanned most of the 20th century.[106]

106. Charles Duncan, *The Art of Classical Guitar Playing*, Princeton, New Jersey, Summy-Birchard Music, 1980, p. 116. "The fact remains, however, that [Segovia's] recorded performance more than bears out the detailed explication, here and elsewhere. And, if during the actual performance, conscious awareness of such minutiae is impractical, in the preparation of the piece, it is not only practical but obligatory if real instrumental art is the object. The unglamorous truth, so difficult sometimes to accept, is that great artists are also thoughtful, painstaking workers. The achievement of any competence whatever requires a discipline; the higher the level, the more arduous the discipline. If the goal really matters, then it will seem to justify the effort."

DOUBLE IN B MINOR

Andrés Segovia successfully played the violin music of J. S. Bach on the guitar. Part of his success with this music is due to the advantages the guitar possesses as a natural result of its physical qualities.[107] For example, the guitar has the advantage over the violin of being able to play block chords, whereas the violin must roll them. The guitar can also play arpeggios in a truly flowing and legato manner, allowing the notes of the chord to ring out after being played. By performing this music on the guitar, Segovia has caused some to speculate that Bach's music actually sounds better on the guitar than on the violin.[108] Segovia's edition of the *Double* shows off some of the guitar's unique abilities when playing Bach's violin music. Because the Double is basically an ornamentation of the *Bourrée*,[109] plenty of arpeggiation of the *Bourrée's* harmonies are woven between the persistent running eighth notes. By allowing the harmonies to ring out, the guitar causes vertical sonorities to come alive more fully in the ear of the listener. Also, Segovia's unique method of finger-

Segovia at the Westbury Hotel in London, 1985.

ing by being sensitive to the various coloristic capacities of each string in all positions allows for gracious exploitation of the melodic potential inherent in the music.

Bach's violin music works well on the guitar technically, in general, because of its thinner texture. This texture can sound somewhat *too* thin on the guitar, however, and it is not surprising that Segovia chose to add bass notes to create a fuller texture for his guitar edition. He therefore followed in the footsteps of Bach himself, who altered his music in this way when transcribing.[110]

---

107. This is not to imply that the violin does not possess advantages over the qualities of the guitar. The violin can sustain notes indefinitely. It can also play fast scales with ease. The guitar is at a definite disadvantage in these areas.

108. Bernard Gavoty, *Andrés Segovia*, Geneva, René Kistler, 1955, p. 12. Mr. Gavoty gives us his impression of playing Bach's monumental *Chaconne* from the *Partita No. 2 in D Minor* for unaccompanied violin, BWV 1004. His comments are revealing of the difference in performing Bach's music on the guitar rather than on the violin: "How refreshing it was to hear at last natural flowing arpeggios instead of those of the violin mimicking the squeal of rending calico. Instead of double stoppings, always a bit sickly and tottering, we were given clear chords arranged on distinct harmonic levels, a polyphony in which each voice preserved it's individuality. Furthermore, the variations were connected: for once they deserved their name. No particular palette was ever richer in colours than Segovia's guitar in tones and nuances on that particular evening."

109. J. A. Westrup & F. L. Harrison, *The New College Encyclopedia of Music*, New York, W. W. Norton & Company, 1960, p. 202. "Double... (3) Fr. [dooble]. An 18th cent. term for a variation (of an air or dance movement), consisting primarily of ornamentation or new figuration."

110. Alice Artzt, "The Third Lute Suite by Bach, Three Manuscripts and their Implications," presented in the *Journal of the Lute Society of America*, No. 1, 1968.

Segovia's addition of bass notes was very tastefully done, even though they occasionally tread into the realm of composing a bass line that must be considered an addition to the work of Bach:

Bach:

Segovia:*

Bach:

Segovia:*

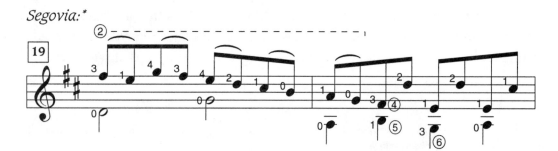

Bach:

*Segovia:**

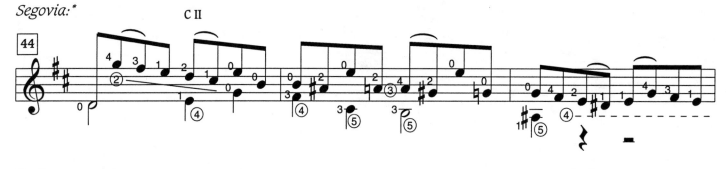

Bach:

*Segovia:**

Bach:

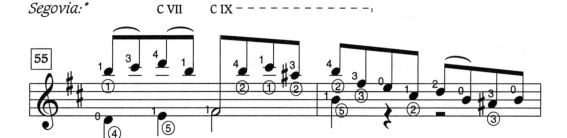

Segovia:

allargando

At the outset it is important to mention that this *Double*, as well as the *Bourrée* that it is an ornamenta-tion of, were both given a time signature by the composer of 2/4.[111] However, Bach clearly *barred* both pieces in 4/4. Most editors have taken this to mean that Bach was simply indicating cut time.[112] If this is the case, then why didn't he just indicate cut time as he often did throughout his sonatas and partitas?[113] It may be

---

111. The handwriting in the original score is somewhat unclear but it does appear to say 2/4.

112. Cut time is also known as *alla breve*. It indicates that there are to be two half note beats per measure. Segovia *did not* indicate cut time in his published version (Schott, 1928) of the *Bourrée* and *Double*. Instead he indicated common time (4/4).

113. There are many pieces that Bach clearly indicated in cut time, including the *Fugue in A Minor*, BWV 1001 (an interesting observation is that many editors, including Segovia, put this fugue in common time).

that Bach was showing that the pieces have a definite pulse of two beats per measure but not in all sections. For example, the opening of the *Bourrée* has a strong rhythmic feel of two, but the scale passages and thinner texture that occur later emphasize this less. Similarly, there are passages in the *Double* that are ambiguous. In fact, Segovia started this piece with a 6/8 triplet grouping, but his bass notes in m. 4 certainly bring out 4/4:

The pieces have been put in cut time here, but performers should be sensitive to the rhythmic ambiguities. Here is an alternate fingering[114] for the opening section that brings out the cut time rhythm clearly by bass note placement and accents:[115]

114. If one decides to use this alternate fingering then m. 68-69 should be adjusted to correspond to m. 3-4 for the sake of consistency.

115. It should be pointed out that since a strong feeling of two is present in the opening of the *Bourrée*, this same type of accent grouping for the opening of the *Double* may be more consistent. A similar tempo for the half note can also help to maintain continuity between the two movements.

Segovia used several of his characteristic *glissandi* throughout his edition. Alternative fingerings are suggested here:

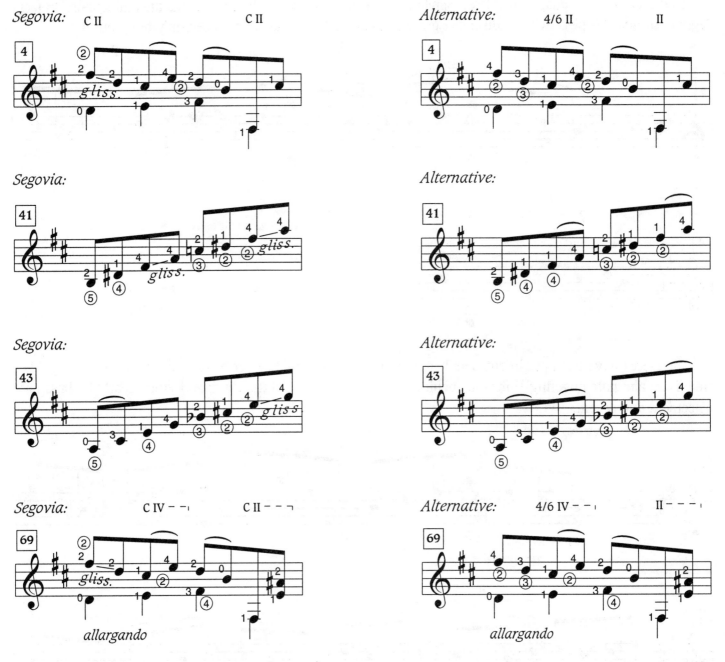

Segovia made a significant change in Bach's original in m. 22-25. He changed the three eighth notes that introduce the B section to make a slightly different figuration. He then changed Bach's pedal by placing it on the downbeat of the quarter note, rather than leaving it in its interesting placement on the upbeat of the quarter. It is certainly possible to follow Bach more closely:

Bach:

Segovia:

Alternative:

Segovia omitted the note B right after the cadence in m. 40. Performers may want to follow his example for technical reasons, since the cadence makes the continuation of the line difficult:

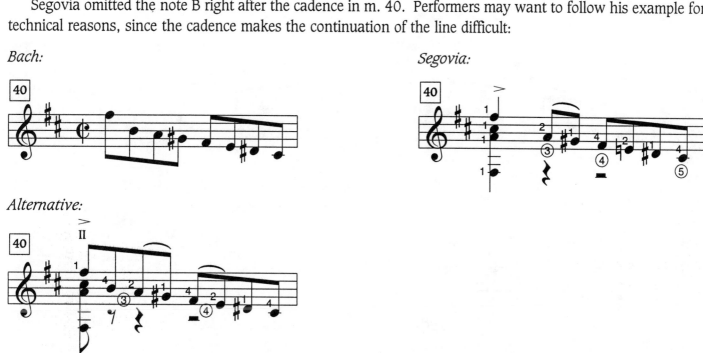

Bach:

Segovia:

Alternative:

Segovia fingered the *Double* in such a way as to be responsive to the rising and falling of the melodic line. His fingering also is sensitive to the lines and harmonies implied by the "style brisé."

One gets the sense from Segovia's playing that he has complete control of the rhythm. In a *moto perpetuo* piece such as the *Double*, a steady and even rhythm is foundational for a good performance. In addition, this piece requires subtle yet deliberate melodic and rhythmic shaping to keep it interesting. At this kind of expression, Segovia was a master.[116] Whenever Segovia did a rubato, it was done in a meaningful way that seemed to provide a unique point of interest, an unpredictable moment in the midst of a predictable rhythm.[117]

---

116. Robert Donington, *Baroque Music: Style and Performance*, London, Faber Music, 1982, p. 29. "The first stage in shaping the line is to sustain the flow of sound with no increasing, no diminishing and no interruption which is not meaningful. The second stage is to inflect the flow of the sound with phrasing, articulation, and dynamic, rhythmic or other modifications which would mould it into meaningful patterns. Some of this moulding is intuitive and some of it is deliberate, but all of it depends on the sound first just reliably being there, and not distorted by meaningless fluctuations." This could be said to be a fitting description of what made Segovia's artistry so great.

Segovia's practice of dwelling on notes almost always included vibrato as well, giving a natural *cantabile* quality to the line.[118] Some places where Segovia used free rubato are:[119]

A tempo of quarter note=184-200 was used by Segovia throughout this piece. This dynamic pace was relaxed only during rubatos and during *ritardandos* at final cadences. Segovia's *ritardando* at the very end was slight, and arguably, more could be made of it.

---

117. C.P.E. Bach, *Versuch über die wahre Art das Clavier zu spielen*, Berlin, 1753, III. C.P.E. Bach said that "certain deliberate disturbances of the beat are extremely beautiful" and that "certain notes and rests should be prolonged beyond their written length for reasons of expression."

118. Listen to Segovia play this piece on his *Segovia on Stage* album, MCA-2531, 1977. Or, his performance can be heard on *The Andrés Segovia Collection*, MCA-42068, 1987 (reissue).

119. Richard Hudson, *Stolen Time, The History of Tempo Rubato*, Oxford, Clarendon Press, 1994, pp. 8-11. This piece is *definitely* a perpetual motion type that uses a motor rhythm. Hudson reminds us that even this kind of music should not be performed mechanically, without any rhythmic sensitivity at all (see footnote #25 under *Prelude in D Minor*). Segovia cannot be accused of this! On the other hand, Segovia has been accused of going too far in the other direction with Bach's music: "It was also with the *Chaconne* that certain irregularities of rhythm and a tendency to sentimentalize manifested themselves." ("Guitarist's Skill Charms Critic," a concert review that appeared in the *Chicago Maroon*, January 24, 1949, see Appendix D). The conclusion here is that performers should strive for a balance that is somewhere between an absolutely strict rhythm and that which is obviously romantic excess. More emphasis on dynamics, articulation and tone color than rhythmic manipulation may be the best way to keep the performance interesting.

Segovia relaxes in his Madrid studio.

Segovia's playing of Bach is brilliantly virtuoso, but in a much more comprehensive way than mere accuracy. The expression of the notes is central to the work of the great maestro, and nowhere is this more clearly seen than in the music of the esteemed J. S. Bach.

Perhaps some of Segovia's affection for this music can be felt in a comment he made in one of his last interviews where he said that the music of Bach, "like the moon and the planets, will be forever."[120]

*J.S. Bach, *Andante-Bourée-Double*, Vol. III. Transcription by Andrés Segovia. Copyright B. Schott's Soehne, Mainze, 1928. Copyright renewed. All Rights Reserved. Used by permission of European American Music Distributors Corporation, sole U.S. and Canadian agent for B. Schott's Soehne, Mainz, 1928.

120. John Guinn, "A Stellar Performance by Segovia," a concert review and interview presented in the *Detroit Free Press,* Friday, March 20, 1987 (see Appendix E).

ANDRÉS SEGOVIA PLAYS

DOMENICO SCARLATTI

Domenico Scarlatti (1685-1757). Anonymous portrait.

CHAPTER FOUR

The guitar has often been compared to the plucked sound of the harpsichord. Indeed, this association naturally leads one to the conclusion that some of the music originally composed for the harpsichord may be adapted for the guitar. Therefore, one of the greatest sources of repertoire available to harpsichordists and guitarists is the music of Domenico Scarlatti (1685-1757).[1]

Domenico Scarlatti, an Italian, was the son of the famous Alessandro Scarlatti (it is also noteworthy that he was born in the same year as Bach and Handel). At the age of sixteen he became organist at the royal chapel in Naples. There he practiced the art of composition that he had learned from his father, and followed in Alessandro's footsteps by composing operas as well as sacred works.

In 1709 Scarlatti moved to Rome where he was eventually employed by the Vatican. In 1719 he resigned from his post there to enter the service of King Joao of Portugal. One of Scarlatti's responsibilities there was to instruct the King's daughter, Maria Barbara, in music. In 1729 the Princess married Prince Ferdinand of Spain. Scarlatti followed her to Madrid, where he remained for the rest of his life in the service of the Spanish courts.[2]

SONATA IN E MINOR

Segovia's interest in the music of Domenico Scarlatti is understandable when one considers the strong role the guitar played in inspiring this composer's music.[3] Scarlatti was heavily influenced by the guitar culture in Spain. It was under this influence that he wrote more than 550 sonatas for harpsichord.[4] Segovia became aware of Scarlatti's connection with Spain and the guitar at some point later in his career and began to perform some of Scarlatti's sonatas in concert.[5]

Despite Segovia's great love for and admiration of Scarlatti's sonatas,[6] he performed only a few of them throughout his career, and the two that he is most remembered for are K. 11 and K. 322. One reason that Segovia may not have played more Scarlatti sonatas is that this music was not a part of the repertoire of the guitarists from whom Segovia descended, namely, Tárrega and Llobet. Certainly one of the biggest reasons, however, is that much of Scarlatti's music, like keyboard music in general, does not fit on the guitar very well. We can only be thankful that Scarlatti wrote some of his sonatas with a texture that was thin and simple enough to be playable as a guitar transcription.

---

1. Donald J. Grout and Claude V. Palisca, *A History of Western Music*, Fourth Edition, New York, W.W. Norton & Co., 1988, p. 551. "The chief Italian keyboard composer of the eighteenth century, and one of the most original geniuses in the history of music was Domenico Scarlatti."

2. *Ibid.*, p. 552.

3. Ralph Kirkpatrick, *Domenico Scarlatti*, Princeton, New Jersey, Princeton University Press, 1953, p. 205. "As far as we know, Scarlatti never played the guitar, but surely no composer ever fell more deeply under its spell. In the Spanish dance pieces its strumming open strings form many an internal pedal point, and its arpeggiated figurations evoke a kind of intoxicating monotony. Some of Scarlatti's wildest dissonances seem to imitate the sound of the hand striking the belly of the guitar, or the savage chords that at times almost threaten to rip the strings from the instrument. The very harmonic structure of many such passages that imitate the guitar seems to be determined by the guitar's open strings and by its propensities for modal Spanish folk music."

4. Sacheverell Sitwell, *A Background for Domenico Scarlatti*, London, Faber and Faber Limited, 1945, pp. 117-119. "The harpsichord can suggest vividly the twanging effects of the guitar, and these sounds were probably as stimulating to Scarlatti as was the ripple of the modern piano to Chopin... It would appear that there has always been a body of serious composers for the guitar in Spain. This fact will become plain to anyone who has ever heard Señor Segovia play pieces by Sor, Torroba or Tárrega. They are conclusive evidence as to that. Now, no musician of the standing of Domenico Scarlatti could live for more than a few days in Madrid without meeting all of the contemporary talent, so that it is probable that his inspiration came alike from the professional players of that instrument, the sort of persons who would be employed in giving lessons to the young Spanish ladies, and, also from the street musicians."

5. MCA Records, *Segovia on Stage*, Universal City, California, 1977. Segovia made these comments on the back of this record: "Scarlatti, you know, spent most of his life in Spain, and that is where he wrote his great harpsichord sonatas, some of which I play on my guitar. But Scarlatti himself was fascinated with the guitar and with Spanish folk songs and dances. He did not actually use Spanish tunes, but he transcribed the spirit of these tunes."

Segovia sometimes enjoyed smoking his pipe while he practiced!

The first Scarlatti sonata that Segovia edited and performed was the *Sonata in C Minor*, K. 11.[7] As is most often the case, Segovia imbued this edition with the late 19th and early 20th century style. Part of the characteristics of Segovia's playing of Scarlatti may be attributed to the source he worked from. His sources were the editions of Alesandro Longo. These were the main sources for Scarlatti sonatas until 1972 when Ralph Kirkpatrick came out with his comprehensive publication of 550 sonatas. This historic work contains photographic facsimiles of the earliest existing manuscripts.[8]

---

6. Malcolm Boyd, *Domenico Scarlatti, Master of Music*, New York, Schirmer Books, 1985, pp. 166-167. The name "Sonata" was given to Scarlatti's harpsichord pieces, but this title can be misleading. These pieces are actually very related to the dance suite movements that were so common in the Baroque period: "It is perhaps unfortunate that Scarlatti chose the term 'sonata' for the single movement binary pieces that make up the bulk of his keyboard works. Obviously these have nothing to do with either the multi-movement structures for melody instrument and continuo that we normally associate with the Baroque sonata (the violin and flute sonatas of Bach, Handel and Telemann, for example) or the solo sonatas of Haydn, Mozart, and Beethoven and other Classical masters... the starting point for their binary structure was the dance movement familiar today from the suites of Bach and Handel..."

Ibid., p. 173. Scarlatti has been considered to be a transitional composer to the Classical period in that his sonatas move away from the traditional binary dance movements toward the Classical sonata by implementing a certain degree of exposition, development, and recapitulation. Boyd and others contest this view by saying that Scarlatti was not as transitional as he is commonly believed to have been. Still, much scholarly evidence has been put forth to support the transitional nature of Scarlatti's sonatas. For an excellent discussion of this subject see: Barbara Foster, *Dynamic Contrast in the Keyboard Sonatas of Domenico Scarlatti to 1746*, Champaign, Illinois, University of Illinois at Urbana, D. Mus. A., 1970.

7. Andrés Segovia, *Domenico Scarlatti, Sonata e-moll*, London, Schott & Co., 1954. This is one of only three Scarlatti sonatas that Segovia published.

8. Longo made all kinds of unstylistic editorial changes. It is now commonly acknowledged that the Kirkpatrick edition is the one to use to get the original intent of Scarlatti. For this reason, we will be using the Kirkpatrick facsimiles and therefore, his numbering system, when comparing Segovia's editions and referring to the sonatas in general. The Longo number that corresponds to this *Sonata in E Minor* is L. 352. For the *Sonata in A Major* it is L. 483.

Although Scarlatti wrote this piece in C minor, Segovia very appropriately transposed it to E minor where it fits well on the guitar. It is interesting to note that while Scarlatti was clearly writing in C minor, the key signature in the original was written with two flats.[9]

Segovia started this sonata by playing the first trill Scarlatti indicated as a main note trill or turn. Later in his life he used a different type of main note trill:

Segovia, early: *Segovia, late:*

   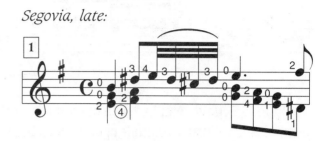

Scarlatti simply put a trill indication and did not write out the trill, except for its termination.

The question has to be asked, "How did Scarlatti want his trills played?" The great Scarlatti scholar, Ralph Kirkpatrick, assures us that Scarlatti wanted his trills to begin with the upper note.[10]

Segovia did not only play the first trill from the main note, he played *all* the trills in this piece from the main note (few instances have been found where Segovia played a trill from the upper note). Some may wonder if the matter of playing the trills from the main note or the upper note is really that big an issue. In response, we must first question the integrity of playing trills from the main note in Scarlatti's music when we know that the composer may not have approved of it being done that way. Furthermore, we must consider that composers such as Scarlatti who used the upper note trills were composing in a way as to rely on the certain sound effect that these trills created. Not using the upper note trills will create a certain flavor to this music that may have

---

9. To parallel what Scarlatti did we would have to use a key signature with C# and F# and write the appropriate accidentals in the score. This involves a certain amount of redundancy, however, and for the sake of ease of comparison the relative minor key signature is employed here.

10. Ralph Kirkpatrick, *Domenico Scarlatti*, Princeton, New Jersey, Princeton University Press, 1953, p. 379. "According to common eighteenth century practice as represented by the best contemporary instruction books, the trill began with the upper auxiliary note. (The few eighteenth century exceptions are so rare and so unimportant as to be almost negligible here.) The trill from the main note so frequently imposed on eighteenth century music by performers and editors (including Longo) is a nineteenth century tradition which has no foundation in the surviving evidence left by the most respectable performers and composers of the eighteenth century. An examination of the specious recommendations of editors for trills from below or for 'inverted mordents' will invariably prove that they are without genuine historical foundation. The all too frequently quoted 'rules' that permit choice between trills from below belong in the same category. They cannot be justified by eighteenth century evidence." In all fairness it should be pointed out that at least one important scholar has disagreed with Kirkpatrick about Scarlatti's trills always starting from the upper note. See: Frederick Neumann, *Ornamentation in Baroque and Post-Baroque Music, With Special Emphasis on J.S. Bach*, Princeton, New Jersey, Princeton University Press, 1978, pp. 361-364. "For many composers, among them Vivaldi, Domenico Scarlatti, Handel, and probably all other masters of their generation, the main note design was most likely the basic trill form." (p. 364) Neumann admits that the upper note trill was used frequently during the later part of Scarlatti's life (which is when he composed most of his sonatas): "That the plain appoggiatura trill was also used can be taken for granted, though it is probable that its use was more frequent toward the later part of the period under consideration [1710-1760]." (Idem.) Therefore, even if one accepts Neumann's view and allows for main note trills in Scarlatti it seems highly unlikely that Scarlatti would have always done *all* of his trills in this way, as Segovia did.

been foreign to its style.[11] For these reasons, upper note trills are suggested.

If an upper note trill is to be used in the first measure, the technical difficulty of playing this trill becomes greater. The solution used here is to drop the note A from the second chord and do the trill with a bar on the fourth fret:

In m. 8 Segovia employed an open string, probably for technical reasons. The inconsistency in sound, however, seems to justify another option. Keeping the notes on the inner strings is not much more difficult:

*Segovia:**   *Alternative:*

In m. 10-12, not only did Segovia employ main note trills, he changed the rhythm from 32nd notes on the trill terminations to 16th notes. This eliminates the dotted feel that Scarlatti created. Scarlatti's original rhythm in addition to upper note trills may used:

Scarlatti:

*Segovia:**

---

11. Ralph Kirkpatrick, *Domenico Scarlatti*, Princeton, New Jersey, Princeton University Press, 1953, p. 381. The unique flavor given to the

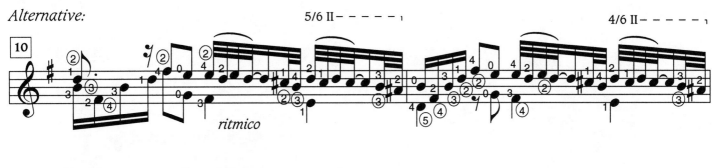

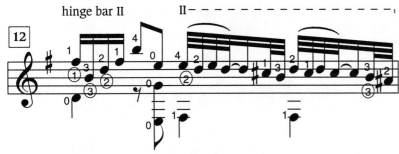

Segovia added notes throughout this piece, creating lines and chords that Scarlatti did not write. We know that Scarlatti did not approve of such procedures and modern guitarists may want to avoid such nineteenth century practices in favor of Scarlatti's original score.[12]

A significant spot where Segovia added notes is in m. 12 (seen above). Segovia filled out the chord on the second half of beat two and then added an extra voice on beats three and four. Scarlatti's original may be followed more closely.

In m. 14 Segovia edited out the chord Scarlatti had written to introduce the dominant harmony on the third beat of the measure. It is technically possible to play this measure as written, so Scarlatti's original writing is retained in the alternative presented here (Scarlatti may also be followed more closely where this material is repeated in m. 28 of the B section):

Scarlatti: *Segovia:**

---

music when using upper note trills is created by this type of trill's relation to the *appoggiatura*. This important Baroque ornament derives its name from the Italian *appoggiare,* which means to lean, and implies an auxiliary note which is stressed, dissonant, played on the beat and then resolves to the main note (see Donnington, *Baroque Music, Style and Performance*, pp. 110-111). Kirkpatrick tells us that Scarlatti was using upper note trills for this very reason: "For him, as for other eighteenth century composers, the trill was associated with the prepared and unprepared *appoggiatura,* to such a degree as to be interchangeable with them, or as to permit inconsistency in notation."

12. *Ibid.,* p. 397. "...Scarlatti has written for the most part exactly what he intended to be played... when Scarlatti leaves a chord empty, or a resolution hanging, or resorts to a bare unison, it is nearly always because he intended it that way. He almost never indulges in thickness of sound for its own sake. In fact, it would seem as if he had avoided the use of full chords except for certain specific effects... Nearly all of Longo's suggested fillings of chords are not only unnecessary, but undesirable."

Segovia practicing in Switzerland in the 1950's.

Alternative:

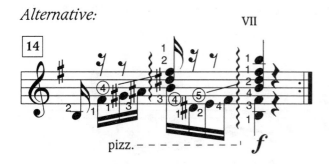

Occasionally, the Scarlatti manuscript does show some obvious errors. For example, notice the D# (B natural in the original key) in m. 9:

Scarlatti: *Scarlatti (transposed to guitar ed. tonality):*

On this basis we can conclude that inconsistencies in the notation may be errors.[13] Editors have to use discernment in this respect. Segovia shows his discretion by changing what, according to the original, should be an E on the second half of the second beat in m. 10 (C in the original key) to a G. He therefore preserved the consistency of this lower melodic line which is repeated in m. 11:

Scarlatti:

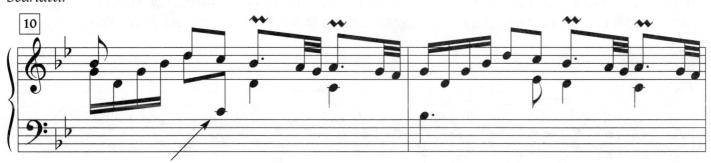

Segovia: *

Segovia's judgment also worked against him at times when trying to discern errors in the original manuscript. In his published version,[14] he shows that he must have concluded that the erroneous D# in m. 9

---

13. *Idem.*, "...apart from obvious slips, small inconsistencies, and certain conventional inaccuracies of rhythmic notation, Scarlatti has written for the most part exactly what he intended to be played."

14. Andrés Segovia, *Domenico Scarlatti, Sonata e-moll*, London, Schott & Co., 1954.

was an indication that the raised 7th degree of the scale was also an error in m. 13-14. Therefore, he indicated D naturals:*

This was obviously a mistake, since the piece was modulating to the dominant at this time, requiring the raised 7th to suggest a major dominant. Segovia did correct this section, and on his recordings he played the D#:

No matter how much we respect the fact that Scarlatti wrote exactly what he wanted to be played, at times certain additions and subtractions of notes *must* be done by an editor when adapting this harpsichord music for the guitar. Scarlatti's own choice of notes should be preserved when at all possible. When this is not possible, wise choices can be made that are consistent with Scarlatti's intent, taking care not to be so inflexible as to leave the listener dissatisfied.

The first six measures of the B section are an editorial challenge. Segovia added plenty of notes, filled out chords, dropped notes, changed rhythms, etc. Scarlatti's exact voicing of chords will not work on the guitar, so some editorial decisions are necessary. An alternative closer to Scarlatti's intent is suggested here:

Scarlatti:

Segovia:

Alternative:

In m. 22, Segovia again used an open string that, while intended to be a technical solution, obscures the consistency that he always strove for. (The open string used in the midst of notes played in the higher positions can be easily noticed on his recordings.) An inner string alternative is possible:

*Segovia:**

Alternative:

The ornaments and rhythms of their terminations[15] in m. 24-26 were altered by Segovia although they may be kept closer to the Scarlatti original:

Scarlatti:

Segovia:

Alternative:

15. In the original the trills terminate with 32nd notes. Segovia changed them to 16ths.

Segovia closed the piece in m. 28 by playing the last chord as a harmonic. This approach can be retained, but for the final chord the second time through an alternative is suggested that may allow for a stronger ending:

While Scarlatti gave no tempo marking, Segovia marked the piece *Allegretto*, and played it at a tempo of anywhere from eighth note=126 to 144. Performers should keep in mind that if the upper note trills are used, a minimum of four notes is required compared to the minimum three of a main note trill. This means that care should be taken that the tempo is not set too fast to be playable (Scarlatti tends to be played too fast in general).[16] It would be wise for each guitarist to determine the proper tempo from the fastest notes (which are the trills), for smooth melodic flow, technical ease, and harmonic rhythm.[17]

Throughout the original score (p. 408), a marking occurs several times that looks like a fermata over an "M." This is the way Scarlatti indicated *manca*, which means to do a crossing over of hands.[18] Obviously, this marking is irrelevant to guitarists.

Segovia repeated the A section almost exactly. Some suggested ideas for variety are: open strongly the first time, but softer the next. The second time through, some sections could be played *ponticello,* for example, to the last eighth of m. 4, then switch back to *dolce.*

Segovia rushed the descending sixteenth notes in m. 9. Upon arrival at m. 10, he gradually built the one measure motives that are repeated in m. 11 and m. 12 to the arrival in m. 13.[19]

M. 13 presents an opportunity to introduce interesting syncopations suggested by the line itself (this is also true when the material is repeated in the tonic, m. 27). Segovia did not play the scale this way, but used accents to emphasize the beats:

---

16. Ralph Kirkpatrick, *Domenico Scarlatti*, Princeton, New Jersey, Princeton University Press, 1953, p. 294. "All of us, especially the young, have been guilty of playing Scarlatti too fast."

17. *Idem.*, "The performer's choice of a tempo is affected in almost equal measure by the melodic declamation of the fastest notes and by the underlying harmony."

18. This has been verified by Eji Hashimoto, professor of harpsichord at the Cincinnati Conservatory of Music.

19. Ralph Kirkpatrick, *Domenico Scarlatti,* Princeton, New Jersey, Princeton University Press, 1953, pp. 299-300. Kirkpatrick says that a performer must be able to keep a regular pulse with Scarlatti, but must use this regularity as a point of departure for some rhythmic flexibility that is sensitive to the musical activity: "A steady inexorable beat can achieve enormous expressive power... Yet too great attachment to metrical regularity can render the player insensitive to momentary displacements of pulse or to declamations that move contrary to it. This does not mean for an instant a recommendation to play out of time. On the contrary, the basic proportions of movement must be strictly regarded at all times, even when transgressed, and an absolutely clear relationship of the fundamental note values maintained." For a detailed discussion on the subject of rubato, see Richard Hudson, *Stolen Time, The History of Tempo Rubato*, Oxford, Clarendon Press, 1994.

Alternative:

In m. 13 Segovia also paused for a breath before the descending scale. In m. 14 he used *pizzicato* for the last seven eighth notes. Modern guitarists may want to retain the *pizzicato* since this is a good harpsichord-like sound. To secure the rhythmic drive to the end, the breath is not suggested (the same goes for this material when it is repeated at the end of the B section).

Segovia repeated the B section almost exactly. Instead of opening this section strong, and then playing it soft on the repeat (this can become predictable), it is interesting to open this section strong the first time, and then strong and *ponticello* the second time. The switch back to *dolce* can begin with the melody note B, the last eighth of m. 16.

Measure 19 begins a section that Segovia played forte and *ponticello*. He made a *ritardando* to the end of m. 20, and held the last note of the trill for a fermata. He then did a *glissando* (not a heavy, romantic one, but one that was light and connected at both ends) from the G on the last eighth on m. 20 to the first notes of m. 21. From there he started softly and built the piece to a climax on the high E on the second beat of m. 26, aggressively driving to the end. He played the final run in that measure *pizzicato*.

Are performers at liberty to impose their own interpretations on Scarlatti's music to any significant extent? We must remember that Scarlatti himself gave very few expression markings in his sonatas, so his exact interpretive preferences cannot be determined. To follow in Segovia's footsteps would be to make the music as meaningful and interesting as possible.[20]

20. Ralph Kirkpatrick, *Domenico Scarlatti,* Princeton, New Jersey, Princeton University Press, 1953, pp. 282-283. "Scarlatti's text, as represented by the Venice and Parma manuscripts, gives little but the bare note picture... All [interpretation] is left to the implications of the musical context and to the taste and sensibility of the player."

SONATA IN A MAJOR

Of the two most famous Scarlatti sonatas that Segovia played, the *Sonata in A Major,* K. 322 is the most literally playable on the guitar. Segovia's version of this sonata shows that he avoided the 19th century practice of filling out chords and adding lines and notes that were not in the original score. Segovia never published his edition.[21] There are only five places in this entire piece where Segovia made changes that deviated from the original manuscript.[22]

Segovia:

Scarlatti:

Segovia:

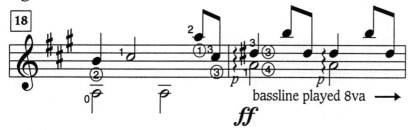

bassline played 8va ⟶

Scarlatti:

---

21. Segovia recorded this piece on MCA 2531. The liner notes indicate that he is playing a transcription by John Williams. This piece requires no key change or other major editorial revisions to make it playable on the guitar and a careful look at the John Williams transcription (unpublished, I have a copy of it) reveals that Segovia changed many fingerings to fit his own playing style. Therefore, the issue of who did the initial transcription is not really that relevant except to say that maybe Segovia remained faithful to the original score because Williams had done so to begin with.

22. Carolyn Maxwell, *Scarlatti Solo Piano Literature*, Boulder, Colorado, Maxwell Music Evaluation Books, 1985, p. 7. It needs to be emphasized that none of Scarlatti's autographed manuscript copies has been discovered. What we are working from is the earliest known non-autographed manuscript copies that have also been compiled by Kirkpatrick. He believed that all of Scarlatti's autographed manuscripts were probably kept in one place and destroyed by a fire. It is also possible that they still exist somewhere and are waiting to be discovered. If anyone does find them, they can plan on retiring early. These scores are priceless.

Segovia:

Scarlatti:

Segovia:

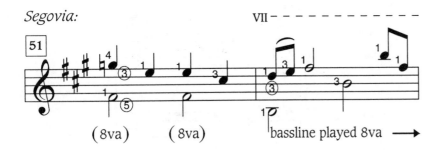

(8va)   (8va)   bassline played 8va ⟶

Scarlatti:

Segovia:

Scarlatti:[23]

As was most often the case, Segovia's approach to ornamentation was possibly unstylistic when examining what would have been considered appropriate by the composer. For example, in those places where Scarlatti indicated a trill, Segovia played the trill from the main note. We must remember that trills in Scarlatti's time were based on the *appoggiatura*, and Kirkpatrick felt that there is no strong evidence to support the use of main note trills in Scarlatti.[24] While the upper note trills can be more difficult, they have been

23. It should also be obvious after consulting the original score that while Scarlatti was, beyond a shadow of a doubt, writing this piece in the key of A major, he used a key signature of only two sharps. This may be because Baroque composers still had some tendency to associate pieces with modes, but in this case, any association is purely theoretical since there is no ambivalence about the A major key. Therefore, the A major key signature of three sharps will be used in the guitar examples presented here in order to make the standard tonal structure more clear.

24. Ralph Kirkpatrick, *Domenico Scarlatti*, Princeton, New Jersey, Princeton University Press, 1953, p. 381. See footnote #10.

considered necessary to maintain integrity in Scarlatti performance and are suggested here:

Scarlatti:

Segovia:

Scarlatti:

Throughout this piece Scarlatti gave indications for *appoggiaturas.* Modern scholarship shows that Segovia played these correctly:[25]

Scarlatti:

Segovia:

---

25. J. A. Westrup and F. L. Harrison, *The New College Encyclopedia of Music*, New York, W. W. Norton & Company, Inc., 1960, p. 27. We see from the original that Scarlatti indicated his appoggiaturas by a small note that looks like a grace note: "...In the 17th and 18th cent. it was a convention to allow the harmony note to occupy the whole of the time to be shared between it and the appoggiatura, and to indicate the appoggiatura by a stroke or a curve or a note of smaller size. The reason for this was that the appoggiatura was regarded as an ornament and hence subordinate to the main melodic line." This should not be interpreted to indicate that this ornament could be played quickly like a grace note. There were some that were played quickly in this way and they were appropriately called *short appoggiaturas.* In Robert Donington's book, *Baroque Music, Style and Performance*, p. 110 and 111, he tells us that during the Baroque period the notation of the appoggiatura did not indicate its literal length and, especially in the late Baroque, it was to take one half the length of the main note. Hence, Segovia is justified on this point: "When either the long or the short appoggiatura will fit the harmony, the choice rests with the performer, since the notation if any is very seldom intended to be literally indicative of length. In late Baroque music, with the partial exception of the French, there is a general presumption in favor of the long appoggiatura, with its characteristic intensification of the harmonic progression; if, however, the effect is to confuse or to weaken the harmony, a short appoggiatura may be desirable instead... But from the last years of the seventeenth century onwards we meet evidence to suggest that the standard appoggiatura now took half of the length of an undotted main note..." It might also be added here that even if a performer wanted to play Scarlatti's appoggiaturas as short ones, the melodic line would become quite disjointed, especially at this sonata's common tempo.

Probably one of the most remarkable aspects of Segovia's interpretation of this piece was his sensitive approach to *articulation*. Throughout the piece he used accents, slurs, and legato and staccato articulations of the line to shape its melody. Tastefully used vibrato and free rubato were used throughout, and as long as these do not cross into the area of the dramatically heavy and strongly emphasized Romantic style, these effects are legitimate:[26]

*Domenico Scarlatti lived in Spain for many years and his music was deeply influenced by the guitar.
Segovia returned the music to one of its greatest sources of inspiration.*

We turn now to examine Segovia's interpretation of this sonata. At the outset, it might be worthwhile to point out that Segovia had a certain advantage in his interpretations of Scarlatti. This is due to the fact that Scarlatti's sonatas were highly influenced by the music of Segovia's native Spain and the guitar in particular. Perhaps we can even say that Segovia, because of his Spanish background, was able to discern elements of expression inherent in the music that others could not.[27] Because Scarlatti began this piece with phrases that are separated by rests, breathing between the phrases is automatically built into the music. Towards the end of the A section, however, the melodic line becomes perpetual. Rather than perform this section like a run-on sentence, Segovia exhibited his sensitivity by separating the phrases with short breaths and subtle changes of

---

26. Francesco Geminiani, *The Art of Playing on the Violin*, London, 1751, p. 8. Geminiani sums up a positive attitude towards vibrato close to the time period when Scarlatti was writing his sonatas: "…it only contributes to make their sound more agreeable and for this reason [vibrato] should be made use of as often as possible."

Arnold Dolmetsch, *The Interpretation of the Music of the 17th and 18th Centuries Revealed by Contemporary Evidence*, London, Novello and Co., Ltd., 1946, p. 284. "By *Tempo Rubato* are meant the alterations of time introduced by the performer for the sake of expression. This device is as old as music itself. It is obvious that emotional feeling, if there be any, will cause the player to linger on particularly expressive notes and to hurry exciting passages. If there are people who think that the old music does not require the *Tempo Rubato*, it is because they do not perceive its meaning; and are, moreover, ignorant of the fact that it was as common formerly as it is now." Regarding free rubato see: Richard Hudson, *Stolen Time, The History of Tempo Rubato*, Oxford, Clarendon Press, 1994.

27. Ralph Kirkpatrick, *Domenico Scarlatti*, Princeton, New Jersey, Princeton University Press, 1953, p. 322. "After my visit to Spain and during the completion of the biographical part, I prepared performances of forty or fifty of the sonatas in light of what I had learned and was learning. The result was a discovery, no longer of virtuosity piled on virtuosity, of striking ephemeral 'happy freaks,' but instead of an inexhaustible variety of expression inherent in the music, running the gamut of a complete artistic personality."

tone color (he did the same when this passage is repeated in the tonic at the end of the B section):

Segovia used one blatant romantic *glissando* in this piece. While it was used at a time when a striking diminished harmony seems to call for added expression, little historical support has been found to justify such an effect in music from this period.[28] However, vibrato is certainly appropriate. An alternative fingering is suggested:

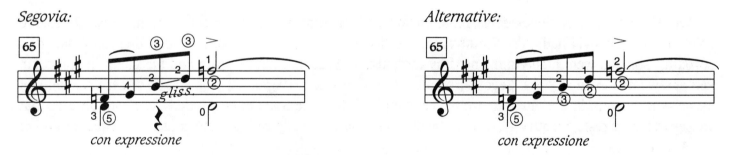

Segovia: *Alternative:*

One of the most interesting revelations about Scarlatti's sonatas that came as a result of modern scholarship is that Scarlatti is now believed to have composed many of his sonatas with the intent that they be performed in pairs.[29] If it is known that a composer wanted his music to be played in a certain way, then very significant justification must exist for an editor or performer to depart from the composer's intentions. When looking at the Scarlatti sonatas in regard to this matter, it must first be determined if the sonata was written as part of a pair (or possibly a triptych). If consecutive sonatas under the Kirkpatrick numbering system show that they are related in

---

28. See the discussion of *glissando* in the introduction to this book.

29. Ralph Kirkpatrick, *Domenico Scarlatti*, Princeton, New Jersey, Princeton University Press, 1953, p. 141. "Most of the sonatas after Venice XIV are copied out in pairs in both the Venice and Parma manuscripts. In a few cases the arrangement appears to be accidental, but for at least 388 of the sonatas, the pairwise arrangement is so consistent in the Venice, Parma and Münster manuscripts as to make it absolutely clear that it was intentional." Kirkpatrick goes on to say that at times there are blatant instructions in the manuscript that a sonata is to be followed by its pair. It is also interesting to note that Kirkpatrick discovered that at least twelve of the sonatas were intended to be played in groups of three.

terms of key (tonic or tonic and relative minor), range and character, then the basis for pairing is evident and simply must be followed to maintain integrity.[30] If no such relationship exists, then the composition may be one of the minority of sonatas that Scarlatti wrote to be performed as a single piece.[31]

Unfortunately, Segovia did not play Scarlatti's *Sonata in A Major*, K. 322 (L. 483), along with its pair, the *Sonata in A Major*, K. 323 (L. 95). He therefore joins the long list of editors and performers who have overlooked this important historical aspect of the Scarlatti sonatas.[32] The sad part about this is that the world was therefore deprived of hearing Segovia play Scarlatti in the way that the composer probably intended his music to be heard. Of course we can blame Longo to a certain extent for this, because Segovia was working from his editions. Kirkpatrick's book, however, came out in 1953 and has been one of the greatest authorities on Scarlatti ever since. Did Segovia keep up with modern scholarship? Maybe not, for he was an individualist, a product of the Romantic period.[33]

Segovia was probably unaware of the pairwise arrangement of Scarlatti's sonatas.

It is evident that performers have a responsibility to play Scarlatti in pairs as intended, thereby showing the real meaning of Scarlatti's music.[34] This is a meaning that Scarlatti may have had strong emotional, financial, and physical reasons for sustaining in his music.[35] There are some weak reasons why some may

---

30. *Ibid.*, p. 143. "...by and large the pairwise arrangement predominates and must be accepted as a requisite to any intelligent and adequate approach to the Scarlatti sonatas."

31. *Ibid.*, pp. 141-142. "There is no reason to suppose that single movements were not performed separately, as might be the case with an isolated prelude or fugue of Bach, or a single movement of a Beethoven or Mozart sonata, but the majority of the Scarlatti sonatas seem to have been conceived in pairs." The previous sonata that we have examined, K. 11, seems to have been written separately with no companion piece.

32. *Ibid.*, p. 143. "Almost without exception, the pairwise arrangement of the Scarlatti sonatas has been overlooked by modern editors. Only rarely have the two members of a pair not been separated."

33. See the discussion of the Romantic style in the introductory notes to Chapter One of Part II, Volume Two and the introduction to this book.

34. *Idem.*, "The real meaning of many a Scarlatti sonata becomes much clearer once it is reassociated with its mate."

35. Carolyn Maxwell, *Scarlatti Solo Piano Literature*, Boulder, Colorado, Maxwell Music Evaluation Books, 1985, p. 3. It is reported that the King of Spain, for whom Scarlatti was employed, suffered from melancholia almost to the point of insanity. Part of Scarlatti's job was to compose music for the King and Queen, who were both harpsichord players, that would help the King to regain his mental state. I say emotional reasons because if Scarlatti did not succeed in pleasing the King with his music, he may have suffered a rebuke; financial because he could have lost his job, and physical because if he irritated the King, he could have been burned at the stake!

feel justified in ignoring the pairing arrangement. One of these is that since we do not have Scarlatti's original autograph manuscripts, we do not know for certain that the pairing arrangements are always his. How do we know that they were not paired by an early editor? It is doubtful that the two earliest surviving manuscripts contain many editorial revisions.[36] This matter can only be completely settled with the discovery of the original autographed manuscripts. Until then, some may continue to cast doubts on the mandatory requirements for playing the sonatas in pairs.[37] In general, however, the consensus of scholars supports playing Scarlatti in pairs. It is no longer considered respectable to ignore the pairwise arrangements.[38]

While guitarists have no justifiable reason to *ignore* the pairwise arrangements, they do have a legitimate reason not to play the pair. The reason is that many of the Scarlatti sonatas are impossible to play on the guitar. Impossible to play *literally*, that is. Many of the sonatas could conceivably be edited significantly to retain the essential elements of the piece and yet be playable as a guitar transcription.[39] Still, there are many that just will not work. All of this even more raises the question, "Why didn't Segovia play the pair to the *Sonata in A Major*, K. 322, when it is one of the few sonata pairs that works so well on the guitar?" New generations of guitarists will have to make their own decisions based on available scholarship, which seems to point to playing the pair whenever possible. This is the approach taken here. K. 322 and K. 323 are both presented in Appendix B, and each fits on the guitar remarkably well with few alterations from the original.

It can certainly be said that Andrés Segovia made a significant contribution by introducing the sonatas of Scarlatti to the world as heard played on the guitar. Hopefully, it can also be said that future generations of guitarists continued his pioneering work by tapping into one of history's richest sources of instrumental music, exploring and presenting yet more of this master composer's great sonatas.

36. *Ibid.*, p. 4. "[Queen] Maria Barbara is remembered as the inspiration and instigator of the great copies of Scarlatti sonatas. The copying of them began in 1752 and continued for the next five years. The collection of thirteen volumes, each containing thirty sonatas, was prepared for use by the Queen. A parallel series containing more of Scarlatti's early and late sonatas, was collected at the same time and appears to be copied by the same hand."

37. Malcolm Boyd, *Domenico Scarlatti, Master of Music*, New York, Schirmer Books, 1986, p. 166. "The most powerful arguments against performance in pairs are, first, that the sonatas each have a separate title and number in the sources and, second, many of them are differently paired in different sources... Neither of these arguments, however, really affects the priority of the pairwise arrangement, although both can be taken to indicate an option for the player."

38. Eiji Hashimoto, "Domenico Scarlatti," presented in the *American Music Teacher,* June/July 1979, p. 13. Hashimoto protests the practice of ignoring the sonata pairs when programming: "While they [performers] may find their reasons for singling out sonatas of their choice and grouping four or five of them (most likely in different keys) together according to their facility and preference, they are likely to play preludes and fugues by composers like Bach together without any hesitation, because this is the way they find them in most editions, even though there exists manuscripts of some preludes which are separate from their respective fugues. Then, what is the basis for arbitrary choice of Scarlatti's sonatas? Is it a matter of habit, or is it simply a lack of understanding? Performers might well ask themselves these questions before they play Scarlatti sonatas."

39. Malcolm Boyd, *Domenico Scarlatti, Master of Music*, New York, Schirmer Books, 1986, p. 185. "Many of the technical difficulties in Scarlatti's keyboard works are not intrinsic to the substance of the music, and not even apparent to the listener except when wrong notes betray their presence. Numerous passages could be simplified to produce the same effect with little or no alterations to the actual notes."

FERNANDO SOR

Fernando Sor (1778-1839). Portrait by J. Goubaud.

CHAPTER FIVE

Though having written for different instruments while employing a variety of genres, it is primarily for his guitar compositions that the Spanish composer Fernando Sor (1778-1839) is remembered today. He is recognized as being one of the greatest composers for the guitar from the Classical period.

Some degree of confusion has been generated by the fact that by the composer's own choice he sometimes went by a variation on his first name, calling himself *Ferdinand*. He also used the common Catalan form of his last name, which is *Sors*.[1] The established usage of his name, Fernando Sor, is retained here.

Sor obtained his early education at the famous mountain monastery of Montserrat, located near Barcelona. Here he received a general education, including lessons in harmony and counterpoint as well as training in sacred music.

Besides being proficient on the violin, piano, and as a singer, Sor was an accomplished guitarist from an early age. He continued his studies on the guitar, remaining at the monastery from the ages of eleven to sixteen. During that time his skills as a guitarist were described as "amazing."[2]

One of the interesting aspects of Sor's life is that he spent a considerable amount of time in a military career, initially serving in the Spanish army. In spite of the obvious dangers to life that a military man such as Sor had to endure (including Napoleon's invasion of Spain),[3] Sor was still able to find time to perform and compose.

After the French occupied Spain, Sor accepted their occupation and joined in service to the French army. After the Spanish reconquered their country, Napoleon and the French were forced to leave Spain by 1813. Sor, probably fearing the consequences of being tried as a traitor, left Spain with the French, who had sought to impose the secular ideals of the French Revolution on this Catholic country. Sor never returned to Spain but spent the rest of his life in various European centers: Paris from 1813 to 1815, London from 1815 to 1823, Paris, Berlin, Warsaw, Moscow, and St. Petersburg from 1823 to 1827, Paris from 1827 to his death in 1839.

One of Sor's most significant contributions to the world of guitar, besides his many compositions, is his *Méthode pour la Guitare*, which was published in Paris in 1830.[4]

Sor, Catalan by birth, was raised in a Spanish and European musical culture saturated with Italian opera. This melodic style had a continuing and lasting impact on Sor's writing and the lyric quality of his works can be attributed to this operatic influence.[5]

Many in Sor's day viewed the guitar as mainly an instrument of chordal accompaniment. Sor, however, sought to raise the general expectations of guitarists to the ideal of not just playing chords but playing music with several parts. He himself was influenced in this direction earlier in his life by a fellow officer in the Spanish Army, Federico Moretti, an accomplished guitarist/composer.[6] In addition to his works for guitar, Sor composed operas, ballet music, piano solos and duets, music for harpolyre, chamber music, music for orchestra, music for military band, sacred vocal music, and many types of secular vocal music.

---

1. Brian Jeffery, *Fernando Sor, Composer and Guitarist*, London, Tecla Editions, 1977, p. 13.

2. *Ibid.*, p. 15. Brian Jeffery quotes a man named Baltasar Saldoni (the source given is the *Diccionario*, I, 1868, p. 264) as saying: "When he was at that school, [Sor] performed such prodigious things on the guitar that all his co-pupils and everyone who heard it were amazed. This was told to me on several occasions by the priest Marti, who was a co-pupil of his at Montserrat."

3. *Ibid.*, p. 21. "Invasion, bitter war, starvation, sieges, and the most outrageous horrors were the order of the day from 1808 to 1813."

4. The *Méthode* was translated into English, published by A. Merrick in London in 1832 and called *Method for the Spanish Guitar*. A modern version is available from Da Capo Press (Da Capo Reprint Series, Frederick Freedman, editor), 227 West 17th Street, New York, NY 10011.

5. *The New Grove Dictionary of Music and Musicians*, Stanley Sadie, editor, London, Macmillan Publishers Limited, 1980, Vol. 17, p. 534. "...vocal music influenced his [Sor's] guitar music, above all in its treatment of melody."

6. Brian Jeffery, *Fernando Sor, Composer and Guitarist*, London, Tecla Editions, 1977, p. 16. "Moretti's music inspired Sor to compose in several real parts or voices, something which he continued to do for the rest of his life: many years later, his concerts in Paris were reviewed in the *Revue Musicale*, and the reviewer, F.J. Fétis, praised him continually for doing just that."

Variations On A Theme By Mozart

Of the many pieces for guitar that flowed from the pen of this prolific composer, none have achieved the level of fame equal to his *Variations on a Theme by Mozart*, Opus 9. While this composition certainly ranks as one of Sor's best because of its capacity for being a brilliant concert showpiece, its fame can be directly attributed to the efforts of Andrés Segovia. He discovered this piece early in his life, and it was the first Sor piece that he recorded.[7] Segovia accepted it as one of the staples of his concert repertoire, performing it often throughout the span of his career.

While Sor was a Spaniard, he is more correctly thought of as a classical composer. This is because Sor largely followed the Viennese Classical style of Haydn and Mozart rather than basing his music on elements springing from native Spanish origin.[8] This is true in regard to Sor's *Mozart Variations*. Variation form was a favorite of classical composers. Most often the tune that was used was a well-known melody of the day. Doing variations on a popular melody was thought of as a way to add variety. Most 18th century pieces were sets of short variations with each divided into two sections and repeated, and the Sor's *Mozart Variations* are no exception.[9]

Sor was following the common practice of his day in selecting a famous theme to use when composing this variation piece. He picked one that was extremely famous at the time, taking it from Mozart's opera *The Magic Flute*.[10] Guitarists in Sor's day had an advantage over present day guitarists in that they probably all were well acquainted with the famous tune by Mozart that Sor used. Their great familiarity with the original tune would certainly have helped when discerning what was intended by Sor to be melodic and what was ornamental.

The theme chosen by Sor is *Das Klinget So Herrlich (This Jingles So Softly)* and is the music played by the character called Papageno to charm some wild beasts.[11] The section begins with Papageno playing his "magic bells" music. He is then joined by the singing of Monostatos and some slaves in m. 301 (during all this music the violins, violas, cellos and bass are slightly emphasizing the harmonies). By studying the original opera score and listening to a good performance of this piece guitarists can get a feeling for the real character of the music. The overall effect is that of a steady quick tempo. The soft, hushed voices sing as the bells play making the sound appear light and delicate.[12] This is certainly light and happy music, for as

---

7. Graham Wade, *Traditions of the Classical Guitar*, London, John Calder, Ltd., 1980, p. 103.

8. William Gray Sasser, *The Guitar Works of Fernando Sor*, University of North Carolina, Doctoral Dissertation, Chapel Hill, North Carolina, 1960, p. 118.

9. Leonard G. Ratner, *Classic Music, Expression, Form, and Style*, New York/London, Schirmer Books, 1980, pp. 255-256. "Many sets of variations were published in the later 18th century, as separate works or as movements of instrumental compositions. The appeal of this genre was twofold, namely: (1) The theme itself, generally very tuneful and often familiar through having been heard elsewhere—in opera, song, popular dance, and other works; (2) The embellishment, which added something fresh to the melody.

"Variation required both skill and taste on the part of the composer. Reicha says, 1814: 'It is very important that a composer know how to vary a melody well, and vary it so that one can easily recognize the original ideas.' Variation, which must retain recognizable features of the theme, makes use of simple forms—periods and two reprise plans—to achieve this purpose. The location of melodic, harmonic, and rhythmic events in a small two reprise form can easily be grasped by a listener, whatever elaborations or modifications may be incorporated upon the structural plan. Hence most 18th century variations are composed as a set of short two-reprise pieces."

10. Paul Nettl, *Mozart and Masonry*, New York, Philosophical Library, 1957, p. 5. *The Magic Flute* was extremely popular right after it was written, and still is. Many people, however, do not realize that it is a work based on ideas of the secret society called *Free Masonry*. "But most important for the intellectual history of Masonry is Mozart, because *The Magic Flute*, one of the greatest art works of all time, was the direct result of his Masonic associations." p. 88: "Many passages in *The Magic Flute* have either been taken directly from the Masonic ritual, or allude to it."

11. It can be found in bars 293-325 of the finale to Act I in the *Neue Mozart Ausgabe*, Serie II, Werkgruppe 5, vol. 19 (Kassel 1970).

12. Mozart specified that a Glockenspiel was to be used to perform the bell part. The delicate quality of this instrument also helps to create a light music-box type sound.

Papageno plays the bells, Monostatos and the slaves are dancing while singing[13] "This jingles so softly, this jingles so clear!"[14]

DAS KLINGET SO HERRLICH

W. A. Mozart (1756-1791)

13. In the libretto the following introduction is given for this section of the opera: *Papageno spielt auf seinem Glockenspiel. Sogleich tanzen und singen Monostatos und die Sklaven.* (Papageno plays on his chimes. Immediately Monostatos and the slaves dance and sing.) This statement confirms that this music is intended to be festive dance music.

14. It seems that this particular section of the opera was a favorite one, even for Mozart, because of the interesting effect created by the bells: "...Mozart attended performances at the Freihaustheater and spoke proudly of its great success in his last letters to his wife. And once he went to play the set of bells, 'because I had such a desire today to do it myself.' He took a childish delight in playing pranks on Schikaneder, who was singing Papageno..." (Hamburg State Opera, program notes translated by Eugene Hartzell)

Andrés Segovia was a performer from another era: the Romantic period.

THIS JINGLES SO SOFTLY
W.A. Mozart (1756-1791)

This jingles so softly, This jingles so clear!
La la ra, la la la la la ra, la la la la ra!
How gently it touches my heart and my ear,
La la ra, la la la la la ra, la la la la ra![15]

We can see from the opera score that Sor did not transcribe the music literally but was in reality paraphrasing this section from Mozart's opera.

Our look at the original music from the opera has relevance for various reasons. First, it gives us a clue as to the nature of Sor's variation piece, and we may gain insight when evaluating Sor's approach as opposed to Segovia's interpretation. As we have seen, this music is light, happy, and delicate. Sor probably had this character in mind for the theme as well. Yet Segovia's interpretation was heavier and more dramatic, punctuated by much free rubato[16] (notice that he also changed Sor's original rhythms):[17]

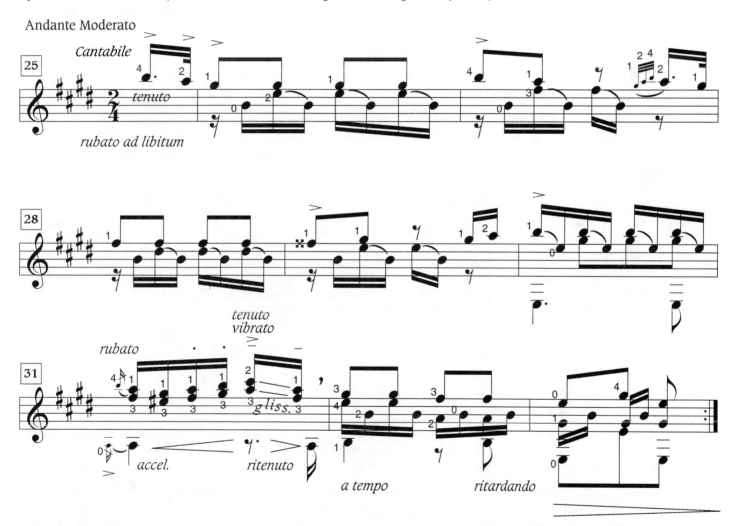

The use of *tempo rubato* in music from this period is not always out of the question because such an effect did, at times, characterize performances in the 18th century.[18] However, if one is to approach this particular

---

15. Translation source: from a translation of W. A. Mozart's *The Magic Flute* by Ruth and Thomas Martin, (as revised for the Metropolitan Opera) New York, G. Schirmer, 1951, pp. 69-70.

16. Segovia played this piece with a very Romantic style throughout his whole life. For confirmation of this, listen to his early recording (*The EMI Recordings*, 1927-29, Angel, ZB 3896) and a later one (currently available on *The Legendary Andrés Segovia*, (1989 reissue) MCAC-42071.

17. All measure numbers have been adjusted here to correspond to the modern edition presented in Appendix B.

Mozart theme with any concern for the style of its origin, the use of a romantic free rubato *ad libitum* must be completely ruled out. In the Classical period there was a relatively rigorous strictness of rhythm.[19] The original setting of the theme confirms that this is the intention here. If the theme is to resemble Mozart's original, it should be played as a light and happy *dance*, with a straight and steady pulse. The chances are that Sor intended his theme to resemble the character of the Mozart original. Segovia played it more like a beautiful aria marked *cantabile*.[20] Naturally, anyone who knows that this is an operatic theme would initially assume that it is a melodic aria rather than a graceful dance unless they heard the music in its original context. Segovia may not have checked the original. Indeed, from the standpoint of Segovia's romantic outlook, he may not have even *cared* that much about the original or the composer's intent. Segovia's *cantabile* and *free rubato* approach is attractive but most certainly inappropriate here when considering these elements, especially in regard to the Mozart theme.[21] It may not have found favor with the composer or the public in Sor's day.[22]

When considering that Sor was basing his music on a Mozart opera, another curious aspect of Segovia's edition of this major guitar work comes into question. That is the fact that Segovia, in his published and recorded versions, completely omitted Sor's introduction. This can be considered to be a serious matter, since the introduction serves as an overture to the work. Overtures are an important part of this operatic style. This omission may have been seen by the composer as taking a liberty which destroys the work's resemblance to the operatic style on which it is based. Of course, it is possible that this was not Segovia's intention. It may be that he only had an incomplete score to work from, and did not have access to Sor's original in a complete version. The question would then have to be asked, "Why didn't he include the introduction later in his life when the facsimile was made widely available?" The answer to this was that he was probably just being true to his approach. This approach was consistent with the nineteenth century performance practice which championed individualism, excluding sections and movements freely at the whim of the performer.[23] Sor himself has not been found to give such liberty and out of respect for the composer and historical sources the introduction is included by most modern editors.[24]

Segovia published his edition of the Sor-Mozart variations in 1931.[25] When comparing Segovia's edition with the original it becomes immediately apparent that Segovia inserted generous amounts of fingerings.

---

18. Leonard G. Ratner, *Classic Music, Expression, Form, and Style*, New York/London, Schirmer Books, 1980, p. 186. "...there remain special situations in which the expression can be heightened by *extraordinary* means. Among these I include especially (1) performance without measure (*ad libitum*), (2) quickening and holding back, (3) the so-called *tempo rubato*. These are three means which can have great effect when played *seldom and at the proper time... tempo rubato*, in the 18th century, signified specific disturbances of the normal *quantitas intrinseca*..."

19. Richard Hudson, *Stolen Time, The History of Tempo Rubato*, Oxford, Clarendon Press, 1994, p. 160: "In general, notated indications for tempo fluctuations as well as descriptions of flexibility added by the performers, all seems to point toward a relatively rigorous strictness of rhythm during the Classic period..."

20. Christine Ammer, *Harper's Dictionary of Music*, New York, Harper & Row Publishers, 1972, p. 55. "Cantabile: (kän tä´ be le) *Italian*. A direction to perform in a melodious, singing manner."

21. Richard Hudson, *Stolen Time, The History of Tempo Rubato*, Oxford, Clarendon Press, 1994, p. 174. "...we must keep in mind the restrained rhythmic control which generally prevailed [in Mozart's] time. Against this strict background, very slight alterations of tempo or note value—alterations that might be barely noticeable to later generations—would be conspicuous, and hence expressive, to the listener of this period."

22. Leonard G. Ratner, *Classic Music, Expression, Form, and Style*, New York/London, Schirmer Books, 1980, p. 185. Ratner describes the late 18th century view that seemed to look upon a frequent and heavy rubato interpretation like Segovia's as being inappropriate: "Irregularities of pace also drew the fire of critics. Koch in his *Journal*, 1795, complains that many soloists neglect a steady tempo, as a matter of fashion... The slight quickening or holding back of a strict tempo was regarded as an important expressive nuance, to be used when appropriate and only by the most accomplished performers."

23. For more discussion of this matter, see the translation of the Segovia entry in Domingo Prat's *Diccionario* in Appendix C.

24. Ferdinand Sor, *Method for the Spanish Guitar* (reprint of 1832 London edition), New York, Da Capo Press, 1971, p. 48. Segovia interpreted this work as a brilliant showpiece, but his omission of the introduction may have obscured (at least partly) the musical effect that Sor was trying to create. Segovia's approach could be contrary to the first of the twelve general maxims that Sor gave in his *Method*: "To regard the effect of the music more than the praise as to skill as a performer."

25. Andrés Segovia, *Fernando Sor, Variations sur l'air de La Flute enchantée (Mozart) "O Cara armonia,"* Mainz, B. Schott's Söhne, 1931.

Sor included very few fingerings, and because the guitar of
Sor's day was smaller, modern
guitarists may have had to
refinger the piece anyway to
make it consistent with the
larger modern guitar.[26]

Sor was a guitarist from a
different age, and his approach
to technique influenced the
way he wrote his music.
When editing a piece like this,
these considerations must be
taken into account. The modern editor is not necessarily
bound to a literal realization of
Sor's original score when it is
recognized that certain ele-

Segovia kept a demanding concert schedule throughout his life.

ments exist for a technical rather than a musical reason. For example, Sor did not generally use nails, and he
seems to indicate that he had a hard time playing fast scales.[27] He obviously made use of slurs to help him
perform fast sections. With modern technique, fast scales are much easier, and Segovia omitted slurs in fast
passages in favor of plucking each note:

Sor:

Segovia:

One legitimate way to edit this piece that Segovia did not take great advantage of here is regarding tone
color. Sor believed very highly in changing tone color on the guitar by moving toward or away from the bridge.
Also, he occasionally used different amounts of flesh with some nail to vary the sound. In his *Method* he

---

26. Ferdinand Sor, *Method for the Spanish Guitar* (reprint of 1832 London edition), New York, Da Capo Press, 1971, p. 48. This is consistent
with Sor's own principles as expressed in his *Method* as maxim number four: "To consider fingering as an art, having as its general object to make
me find the notes that I want, within reach of the fingers that are to produce them, without the continual necessity of making deviations for the
purpose of seeking them."

27. *Ibid.*, p. 21. "I have never aimed to play scales staccato, or detached, nor with great rapidity, because I have been of the opinion that I
could never make the guitar perform violin passages satisfactorily..."

specifically discusses trying to emulate the different kinds of sounds made by various instruments.[28] Unfortunately, he did not have the advantages of greater sonority and timbre that we have on the modern guitar. If he did, it is possible that he would have exploited the greater coloristic capacities of such an instrument by fingering things in the way that Segovia did.[29]

Because Sor was not radically concerned with differences in timbre between open and stopped notes,[30] he may have seen no problem with jumping to a different string in the middle of a melody. In m. 63 Sor took this approach, and more consistency may be achieved by staying on the same string:[31]

When looking at Sor's original it is immediately apparent that, while he does give some tempo indications, there are virtually no dynamic markings. This is not to be taken as an indication that Sor wanted the piece to be played blandly. Performers were expected at this time to edit the piece with interesting dynamic contrasts.[32]

In consideration of the points just mentioned, guitarists may want to vary the repeats with different fingerings, color changes, and dynamic markings. The repeats may be treated as an opportunity for contrast consistent with the composer's stated ideas and historical support. Segovia took none of these opportunities, choosing to play repeats exactly, or even skipping them altogether (as he did on an early recording, Angel 2B-3896).[33]

---

28. *Ibid.*, pp. 15-17.

29. Michael Decker, "Sor's Principles of Guitar Fingering," presented in *Guitar Review*, Spring 1986, p. 20. "Sor was not radically concerned about the difference in timbre and duration between open and stopped notes... There may have been less difference in timbre between open and closed notes on the early 19th century gut string guitar played without fingernails than on the modern nylon string guitar played with nails."

30. *Idem.*

31. Segovia may have included Sor's fingering in his edition (the Segovia fingering looks ambiguous) but on his recordings it appears that he used the same-string fingering shown above. In m. 65 Sor used a fingering similar to that which he used in m. 63. It may be wise to finger this measure exactly as Sor did because at this point the melody is moving twice as fast, making the consistency issue less obvious. Also, because of the speed, m. 65 is more technically secure when played as Sor wrote it.

32. Leonard G. Ratner, *Classic Music, Expression, Form, and Style*, New York/London, Schirmer Books, 1980, p. 187. "Dynamics in the classic era ranged from *pianissimo* to *fortissimo*... The absence of detailed dynamic signs in classic music placed the responsibility on the performer."

33. This may have been because of the short recording time on early 78 R.P.M. records (7 or 8 minutes, 3 1/2 to 4 minutes on each side) in which Segovia was sometimes forced to reduce the length of longer pieces. Incidentally, this may have also been an initial factor in Segovia's decision to omit the introduction to this piece.

We have a disadvantage when looking at Sor's original score in that it is impossible to discern consistently the duration of the notes as he intended. It is equally difficult to tell exactly which notes belong to melody, accompaniment, ornamentation, etc. This is because he wrote in what is called *intermediate* notation. This means that while a certain degree of voicing and duration of notes is indicated, rests, note duration, or stem directions to indicate voicings are not very precise.[34] Unfortunately, Segovia did not help us much in this respect. His edition makes it obvious that he simply published Sor's original with his own fingerings inserted. The modern edition presented in Appendix B is an effort to translate this masterpiece into more precise "advanced" notation.

Segovia changed or added notes throughout this piece:[35]

---

34. Thomas P. Heck, *The Birth of the Classic Guitar and its Cultivation in Vienna, Reflected in the Career and Compositions of Mauro Giuliani,* Chapter III, "Mensural Notation and the Guitar," Dissertation, Yale University, New Haven, Connecticut, 1970, pp. 149-170. Heck gives an excellent study by tracing guitar notation from the tablature in the eighteenth century to the "advanced" form of notation which developed by the time of Napoleon Coste (1806-1883). He reminds us that the intermediate notation used here by Sor contains many hidden implications (p. 170): "The foregoing discussion of the various stages of notation for the classic guitar leads us to an inevitable conclusion, namely, that one must thoroughly understand the nature of the instrument, and sensitize oneself to those notes which normally will resonate in specific situations, in order to have an accurate idea of the relationship between notation and actual sound."

35. The measure numbers used here correspond to the new modern edition presented in Appendix B.

Alternative:

Sor:

Segovia:

Alternative:

Sor:

Segovia:*

Alternative:

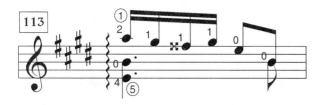

Sor:

Segovia:

Alternative:

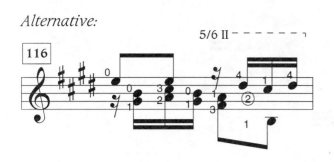

Sor:

Segovia:

Alternative:

Sor:

Segovia:

Alternative:

Sor:

Segovia:*

There really is no need to change Sor's music to the extent that Segovia did. It is certainly possible to make an edition that remains closer to Sor's original.

With fierce determination and a solid technique, Segovia sustained a concert career that spanned nearly a century.

Segovia not only played the theme with intense romantic feeling, he interpreted the variations in a similar way. In Variation I, he carried over his idea for doing a heavy rubato (although a straighter approach that reflects the character of the theme is another option that modern guitarists may want to consider):[36]

---

36. Richard Hudson, *Stolen Time, The History of Tempo Rubato*, Oxford, Clarendon Press, 1994. As we have seen in our previous discussion of rubato, a free romantic approach can be out of place here. There should be a tendency toward a strict rhythm. This doesn't mean that there should be no flexibility used at all. My point has been that the Mozart *theme* should definitely be in strict time. The rest of the piece is really original music by Sor (1778-1839) who lived at a later time than Mozart (1756-1791). During Sor's life, he probably tended towards more flexibility of rhythm than did Mozart, so we can probably use more rubato (especially at cadences and in slow sections), but avoiding obvious romantic excess. Richard Hudson confirms this: "terms relating to the changing of tempo, however, appear only in the 1780's—and even then rarely—in works of Haydn and Mozart. With Beethoven, finally, such terms become more frequent." (p. 154) "In general, notated indications for tempo fluctuations, as well as descriptions of flexibility added by performers, all seem to point toward a relatively rigorous strictness of rhythm during the Classic period, with increasing amounts of freedom slowly and gradually permitted for expressive purposes as one moves into the next century." (p. 160)

Segovia added grace notes at various places in this piece (such as m. 73, which he performed exactly as m. 64 seen above) that were not indicated in the original. These short *appoggiatura* type ornaments are stylistic, and therefore are still an option for modern guitarists. See footnote #53 under *Variations on Folias de España*.

He interpreted Variation II very freely. This minor variation certainly does seem to lend itself to a slower tempo, and in such cases rhythmic variety is more feasible.[37] He continued with this flexibility into the third variation, taking it moderately slow and gracefully. Segovia supplied these two expressive variations with an abundance of articulation, using slurs, staccato, and accents. This is very appropriate for this style.[38] Even the slight bit of vibrato combined with sensitive dynamics is stylistic, especially in imitation of a vocal operatic style.[39] But what about the times when he uses his characteristic *glissandi?* These types of effects did exist in the guitar literature of this time, but they were specifically indicated by the composer.[40] Sor did not indicate any such thing here, although *glissandi* can probably be justified based on the imitation of operatic vocal music. In that case, this effect would more appropriately be called a *portamento*:[41]

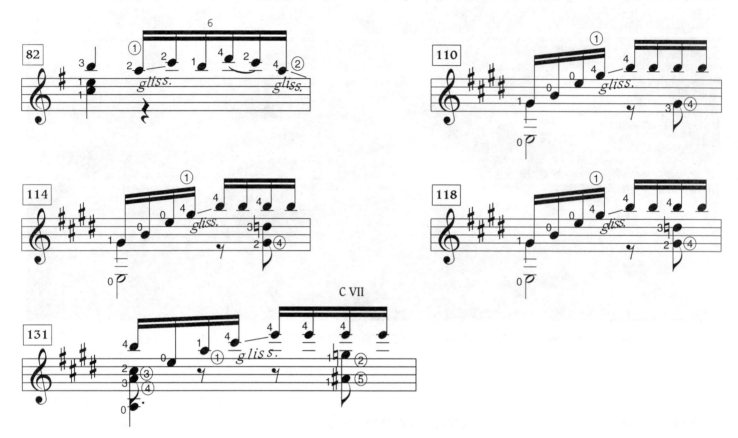

In three of the above instances a fingering in Sor's original precludes the use of Segovia's *glissandi*.

Sor facsimile:

---

37. H.C. Robbins Landon, *The Mozart Compendium*, London, Thames and Hudson Ltd., 1990, p. 373. "Four types of tempo rubato were applied in Mozart's time, the most common involving a natural flexibility of the prescribed melodic rhythm within a constant tempo, chiefly in slow movements."

38. *Ibid.*, pp. 374-376.

39. *Idem.*

40. Thomas P. Heck, *The Birth of the Classic Guitar and its Cultivation in Vienna, Reflected in the Career and Compositions of Mauro Giuliani*, Chapter III, "Mensural Notation and the Guitar," Dissertation, Yale University, New Haven, Connecticut, 1970, p. 172.

41. J.A. Westrup and F.L. Harrison, *The New College Encyclopedia of Music*, New York, W.W. Norton & Company, Inc., 1960, p. 510. "Portamento: An effect used in singing, obtained by carrying the sound in a continuous glide from one note to the next." The *portamento* is more of a vocal term, whereas *glissando* pertains to instrumental usage. See the discussion of *glissando* in the introduction to this book.

Before entering the virtuosic domain of the fourth and fifth variations and coda, a significant *ritardando* is appropriate at the end of the third variation.[42] To sustain the sound through the *ritardando,* the final chord may be filled:

molto ritardando

Sor indicated that the fourth variation was to be played faster (*Piú mosso*). Segovia made a *ritardando* the end of the A section followed by a pause for a breath after he returned to the original tempo. This type of interpretation seems a bit disjointed considering the rapid and aggressive character. He emphasized the bass notes in the B section with accents, making a *ritardando* the final time:

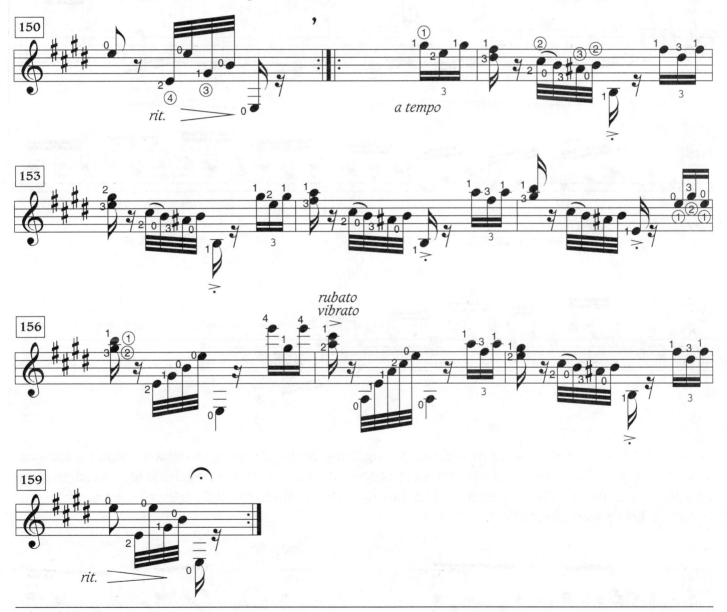

42. Richard Hudson, *Stolen Time, The History of Tempo Rubato*, Oxford, Clarendon Press, 1994, p. 154. It would be ridiculous to omit completely any slowing of the tempo *(ritardando)* at any of the cadences in this piece just because this type of music is more rhythmically strict. Rubato at a cadence is used for structural purposes, and this is appropriate in this style: "Both types of rubato occur in classic music to reinforce formal structure." However, it is suggested that the biggest *ritardando* be at the cadence before the start of the very fast ending variations (starting with Variation IV). During these last fast variations, a very subtle *ritardando,* if at all, is more appropriate. Segovia's continual fast-to-slow approach created by a *ritardando* at the end and a free rubato at the beginning of each section does not seem to help the strong forward drive.

The fifth variation is certainly one of the most virtuosic in the entire work. Sor again marked the opening *Piú mosso*, telling us that it is to be even faster than the preceding variation. Segovia began by emphasizing the opening reference to the theme at the beginning of the A and B section, using much free rubato. Each time, he accelerated through the ascending and descending passage to the end:

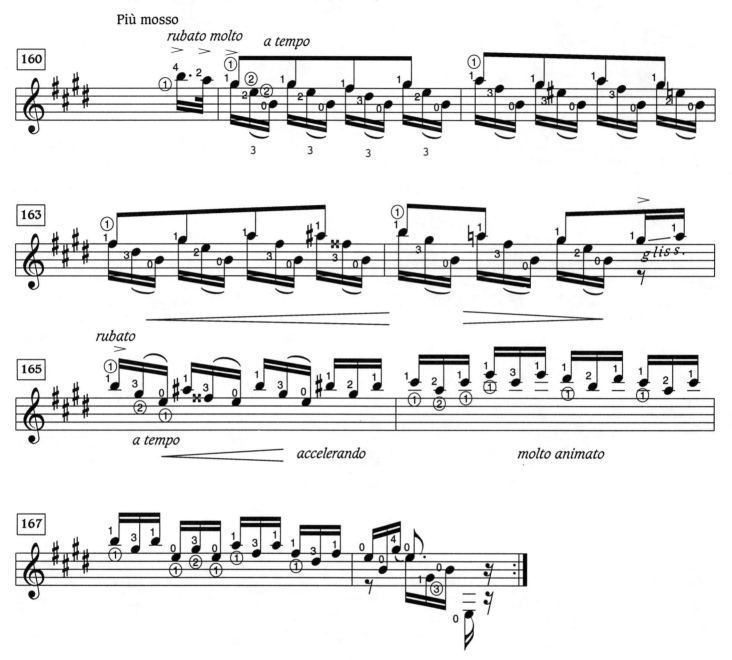

One spot in particular in Variation V is hard to finger in order to achieve its extremely virtuosic character. The last beat of m. 164 and m. 173 were altered by Segovia to make them more playable at high speed (Segovia also played this figure with a duple rather than the original triplet rhythm). If Sor's literal notes are followed, a slur can help achieve smoothness:

Sor: *Segovia:*

Alternative:

Alternative:

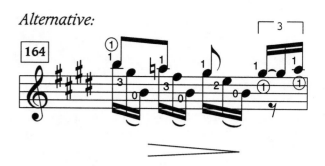

Sor gave no right hand fingering at all in this piece. Right hand fingering patterns are critical, especially in variation four and five. In Segovia's published edition he shows his solutions. An alternative fingering which includes the thumb is another possible solution (the use of planting is also helpful for ascending arpeggio figures):

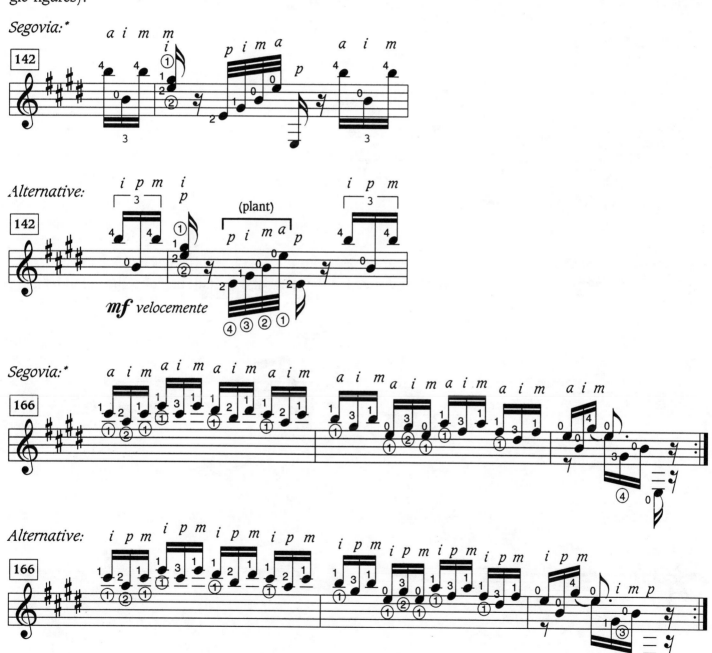

Segovia's addition of bass notes in the ending section can be justified since we see the tonic pedal prevailing through the entire coda, even in the first measure immediately preceding the first E major arpeggio.[43] The inconsistency could indicate an accidental omission. Such mistakes were common in manuscripts at this time.[44]

The E major arpeggio in m. 186 (repeated in m. 188 and 190) represents another technical difficulty in terms of fingering. Segovia's pattern is an option, but some may find a different right hand fingering to be helpful:

*Segovia:**

Alternative:

The triplet runs in m. 194 and m. 196 offer an opportunity for contrast that is not indicated by Sor, but is taken advantage of by Segovia. He plucked each note the first time and slurred the notes the second time. A slightly different option is given here:

Sor:

*Segovia:**

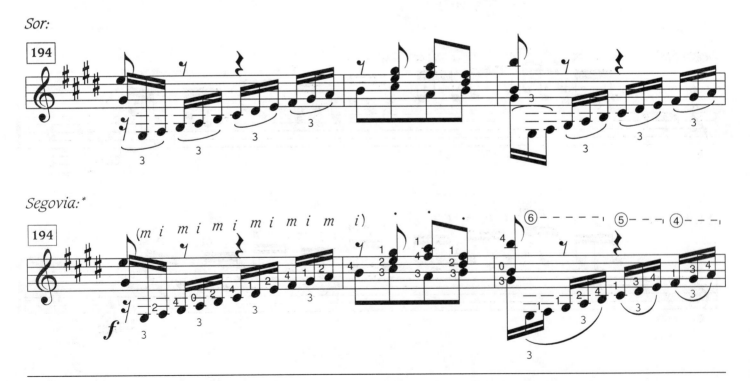

---

43. Segovia played the E bass note pedal throughout the coda on his recordings, but in his published edition he omitted the pedal in some spots.

44. Leonard G. Ratner, *Classic Music, Expression, Form, and Style*, New York/London, Schirmer Books, 1980, p. 183. "Musical notation [in the Classical period] suffered from countless errors and inconsistencies, both in manuscript copies and in published music. Rousseau's long article on 'Capiste' in his *Dictionnaire*, 1768, mentions many requirements faced by the copyist as he transcribes the composer's notation."

Alternative:

Segovia played a harmonic in m. 191 where Sor did not indicate one. The harmonic greatly helps to facilitate this passage:

Sor:

Segovia: *

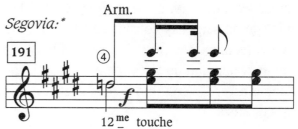

Alternative:

The voicing of the final chord may sound thin to many as originally written by Sor. It may be a mistake but chances are it is not, since this is typically a part of Sor's style.[45] Segovia filled this chord out to a six note harmony as opposed to the original three notes:

Sor:

Segovia: *

45. Michael Decker, "Sor's Principles of Guitar Fingerings," presented in *Guitar Review*, Spring 1986, p. 22. "Of course the fixed right-hand and three-finger technique had a significant influence on the density of Sor's textures. There are seldom more than three voices; even final cadential chords were not expanded."

Alternative:

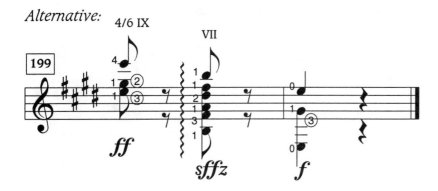

While continuing to respect historical sources, it is still possible to learn much from Segovia's edition of the great *Variations on a Theme by Mozart*. He made the piece famous and therefore has earned the right to have his edition seriously considered. Hopefully our study of his work has only helped to illuminate valid options when looking at a piece that, by the very scant nature of its "intermediate" notation, has left many questions unanswered and up to the performer. It is to Segovia that we continue to look for answers. Even if we can no longer accept everything he had to say, the study of his work can still most certainly benefit future generations of guitarists.

Segovia made Sor's music famous. He played Variations on a Theme by Mozart *throughout the world over the span of his long career.*

VARIATIONS ON FOLIAS DE ESPAÑA

If Segovia had a favorite theme, it was probably *Folias de España*. He showed his great affection for this theme in the letters he sent to Manuel Ponce, as he encouraged him to write a set of variations based on it.[46]

Sor's treatment of *La Folia* (opus 15a) is actually a set of four variations on the theme and a minuet. While Segovia passionately loved the *La Folia* theme, he did not develop much affection for Sor's treatment of it until later in his life.[47]

Segovia did not play Sor's work in its entirety, for he chose to omit the minuet that Sor included as a last variation. His reasons, judging from his remarks (in his letter to Ponce),[48] were probably that he did not like it. Of course, the minuet is not a native Spanish form and maybe Segovia thought that this was not an appropriate way to treat a theme that he called "Spanish to the core." Sor, on the other hand, was writing in the Viennese Classical style of Haydn, Mozart, and Beethoven. He appears to have had an affection for dance forms such as the minuet, and he made it a prominent form in his compositions.[49]

Sor may not have approved of Segovia's omission of the minuet and it is not certain that he gave performers the liberty to divide up his works. Out of respect for the composer and for historical sources, guitarists may want to play Sor's composition in its entirety.[50]

---

46. Ponce responded by writing his monumental *20 Variations and Fugue on Folia de Espana*. John Williams made some interesting comments about *La Folia* on a record jacket: "...this old, simple, and dignified tune. *La Folia*, as it is sometimes called, has its origins in Portugal and Spain and, like the *Sarabande*, was probably quite lively in its original dance form but settled to a slower pace as an instrumental piece with increasing ornamentation. Its simple eight bar melody make it ideal for variations and it is no surprise that, like the *Chaconne*—its companion from the Iberian Peninsula—it has been used by composers ever since its discovery in the sixteenth century, including Gaspar Sanz for guitar, Corelli for violin, Rachmaninoff for piano and Bach, Scarlatti, Liszt, etc." (John Williams, *John Williams Plays Manuel Ponce*, CBS Masterworks, M35820). For an in-depth discussion of the *Folia* theme, see: Richard Hudson, "The Folia Melodies," presented in *Acta Musicologica*, Vol. XLV, Jan. 1973, pp. 98-118. The folia originated as a pattern of bass harmonies. It was usually employed as a bass for continuous variations. Eventually the pattern came to be associated with a single melody. See: Christine Ammer, *Harper's Dictionary of Music*, New York, Barnes & Noble Books, 1972, p. 122.

47. Miguel Alcázar, editor, *The Segovia-Ponce Letters*, Columbus, Editions Orphée, 1989, p. 50. Statements such as these reveal Segovia's great love for *La Folia*: "I want you to write some *brilliant variations* for me on the theme of Folias de España... Do not refuse me now, and ask in exchange for whatever sacrifice: except for that of renouncing the variations!" Interestingly enough, in this same letter he expresses his disdain for the Sor *La Folia* variations: "Have them play the ones by Corelli on the grammaphone, if you do not remember them, and you will see how it is a great sin that this theme, which oldest version is in the Berlin manuscript, *for lute, Spanish*, moreover, to the core is exiled from the guitar, or *feebly treated by Sor* (last emphasis mine), which is worse." Later in his life he adopted Sor's piece as one of his favorites, even recording it on an album entitled *My Favorite Spanish Encores*, 1974 (RCA ARL1-0485).

48. *Idem.*

49. William Gray Sasser, *The Guitar Works of Fernando Sor*, University of North Carolina, Doctoral Dissertation, Chapel Hill, North Carolina, 1960, p. 118. "It is true that dance pieces and their traditional rhythmic schemes abound in Sor's works. Spanish dances, however, such as the jota, bolero, etc. have left little imprint on these works. It is the minuet and the newly popular waltz which figure most prominently." The waltz and minuet are common forms in the Viennese Classical style.

50. Thomas P. Heck, *The Birth of the Classic Guitar and its Cultivation in Vienna, Reflected in the Career and Compositions of Mauro Giuliani*, Chapter III, "Mensural Notation and the Guitar," Dissertation, Yale University, New Haven, Connecticut, 1970. Even though he didn't like everything that Sor composed, at least Segovia gave this great guitarist/composer a significant amount of attention. The other significant guitarist/composer of this period received no such attention, in spite of the fact that he is praised by Heck as "the most significant and gifted [guitarist] composer of his generation." (p. 227) This was Mauro Giuliani (1780-1829), and the only Giuliani piece Segovia ever played was the first movement of the *Sonata*, Op. 15. The question needs to be asked, "Why didn't Segovia play more of Giuliani's music?" The answer, I suspect, is that Segovia was a Spanish nationalist. Consider the statement he made when receiving an Honorary Doctorate from Florida State University (presented in *Guitar Review*, Fall 1969): "Allow me to say with pride that the guitar by being deeply Spanish is becoming universal. Spain took the guitar because the Spaniard has so rich an individuality that he is a society in himself, and the guitar by her rich polyphonies and tone colors is an orchestra in itself." This is a view that Heck refutes, showing that it was Italy, and specifically Italian guitarists like Giuliani that had a more central role in the history and development of the six-string guitar. Segovia's strong national pride and his view of the guitar as being so Spanish may have been some of the reasons that he favored a Spanish composer like Sor over the Italian Giuliani. (For more discussion of Segovia's Spanish nationalism, see: *A New Look at Segovia*, introduction to Chapter One of Part II, Volume Two.)

In studying Sor's original, it becomes apparent that the work of an editor is necessary when working with facsimiles of music published during the Classical era. Therefore Segovia's examples should be enthusiastically welcomed. Because the guitar used in Sor's day was significantly smaller, and because of the less than precise "intermediate" notation[50] that Sor used as well as the many mistakes and inconsistencies in this notation in general, great skill is needed when preparing a modern edition from these old scores. Segovia proved to be equal to the task, and a look at his arrangement reveals excellent answers to many of the problems encountered by an editor (Segovia did not publish his rendition but he recorded it on *My Favorite Spanish Encores*, RCA ARL-0485, 1974). This is not to say that all of his editorial procedures should be accepted. Indeed, there are times when we can question and even reject, on the basis of various considerations, some of the things Segovia did.

In Sor's original theme, an inconsistency becomes immediately apparent in m. 8 (as shown by the facsimile):

Each time this figure has appeared previously, it ends the measure with a major second interval:

Segovia edited this measure to match the others. Such a decision is warranted, since we can suspect such inconsistencies are mistakes in the original manuscript.[51]

In variation one Segovia changed the notes of the chord progression in m. 21:

Sor:

Segovia:

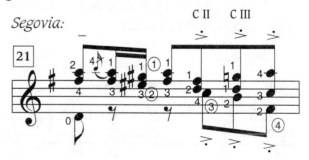

Maybe he thought the original writing was a mistake because of the dissonances. However, Sor does exactly the same thing in m. 29, indicating a strong case that the progression was intentional. Therefore, it may be better to retain the original writing.

---

50. *Ibid.*, For an excellent discussion of intermediate notation see pp. 149-170 of Heck's dissertation.

51. Leonard G. Ratner, *Classic Music, Expression, Form, and Style*, New York/London, Schirmer Books, 1980, p. 182. Ratner confirms these common manuscript errors in 18th and early 19th century music: "Musical notation [in the Classical period] suffered from countless errors and inconsistencies, both in manuscript copies and in published music."

While Sor decorated only m. 18 and m. 26 with *grace notes* (short *appoggiaturas*), Segovia, probably in an effort to achieve consistency, sprinkled them tastefully throughout the entire variation. Such kinds of light *appoggiatura* ornaments were permissible in the Classical period and Segovia's approach is a valid one.[53]

In variation two of the original score we can see a blatant example of the kind of errors which are so prevalent in these Classical period manuscripts. This variation is still in E minor, but the F# was mistakenly omitted from the key signature.[54]

Sor indicated a slur in m. 36 and m. 44. This is awkward on the larger modern guitar. It also results in an inconsistency with the predominant open string sound created by using the open first string, E, throughout this variation. Probably for the sake of technical ease and consistency, Segovia omitted the slur.[55]

In m. 39 Segovia added a melody note, G, probably based on comparison with similar measures such as m. 47:

Sor original:

Sor original:

Segovia:

A bass note, D, appears to be missing from m. 40, based on comparison to similar measures such as m. 38. Segovia added the bass note:

Sor original:

Sor original:

---

53. *Ibid.*, pp. 196-197. "Melodic ornaments added by the performer were confined to solo music or to the leading voice in an ensemble... The two most important melodic ornaments were the *trill* and the *appoggiatura*..."

54. The F# is also missing from variation three. I remember reading through this piece for the first time years ago, and how as an inexperienced player this error caused me great confusion. This all the more emphasizes the need for good modern editions.

55. Michael Decker, "Sor's Principles of Guitar Fingering," presented in *Guitar Review*, Spring 1986, p. 20. "Sor was not radically concerned about the difference in timbre and duration between open and stopped notes... There may have been less difference in timbre between open and closed notes on the early 19th century gut string guitar played without fingernails than on the modern nylon string guitar played with nails."

Segovia:

M. 45 is a repeat of m. 37. The error in the notes is obvious and Segovia corrected it:

Sor original:

Sor original:

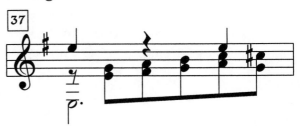

Segovia:

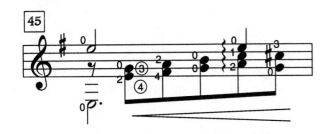

M. 47 appears to contain an error based on comparison with a similar measure, m. 39. Segovia's solution is workable:

Sor original:

Sor original:

Segovia:

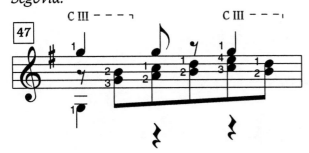

In the third variation, only one measure appears to be an error, m. 55. We can see the inconsistency by comparing it with m. 63, which is the same idea repeated:

Sor original:

Sor original:

The question is, which measure is the correct one? Clearly, m. 63 is consistent with the long *appoggiatura* so prevalent at this time, and that is the one followed here. Segovia changed the measure altogether, omitting the melody note D, on the last eighth note of the measure:

Segovia:

Alternative:

Segovia omitted the slurs indicated by Sor in m. 58. He then changed m. 59 slightly so that it could be fingered in the higher positions while emphasizing the descending top melodic line. His approach to these two measures is legitimate when considering that the guitar in Sor's time was much smaller, making it easier to play the slurred passage in m. 58. M. 59 works much better Segovia's way because the modern guitar is capable of much more sustain. Sor's gut string guitar probably lacked the timbre and resonance possessed by the modern guitar, so he may not have been as concerned about using higher positions based on coloristic considerations:[56]

Sor:

Segovia:

---

56. *Idem.*

Segovia began the brilliant fourth variation by omitting the octave indicated by Sor. He did the same thing to begin the first variation. The facsimile shows some variations starting with the octave B and others starting only with a single note B. This inconsistency does lead one to question whether they should all be the same. Segovia must have decided that this was an engraving error, since he changed these measures. For reasons of sonority and bass emphasis, guitarists may prefer to follow Sor's original:

Sor facsimile:

Segovia:

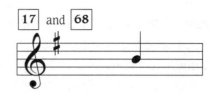

Segovia changed m. 70 to correspond to m. 78 and achieved consistency by emphasizing a chord on each beat in the similar passages in m. 72 and m. 80. Errors in the published score can safely be assumed from these inconsistencies. Segovia's solutions are worth considering:

Sor facsimile:

Sor facsimile:

Segovia:

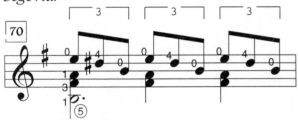

Segovia:

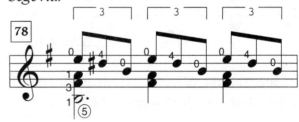

Segovia added additional slurs throughout the fourth variation to help achieve greater fluency.

One particularly difficult stretch is implied in the fourth variation, and this can probably be attributed to the fact that Sor was composing on the smaller guitar of his day.[57] For those guitarists who find the stretch impossible, Segovia's or another alternative fingering is suggested (Segovia's includes a revoicing of the initial chord):

Sor:

Sor, implied fingering:

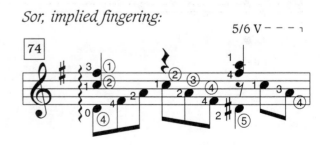

57. Frederick Noad, *The Classical Guitar,* New York, Ariel Music Publications, 1976, p. 8. "Perhaps the most important difference from the contemporary guitar lies in the shorter string length of the early nineteenth century instrument, the closer frets permitting a greater compass of notes by the left hand. This becomes significant when the composer called for a reach which is impossible on today's guitars, necessitating in some cases a change of fingering, in others simply abandonment of the piece. Fortunately, the problem is not insuperable in the case of most composers, the major exception being Dionisio Aguado who in a large number of his works makes demands on the left hand which are quite impossible to realize on a modern fingerboard."

Segovia:

Alternative: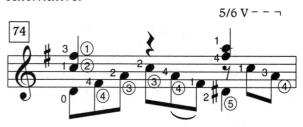

Segovia interpreted this piece in a *cantabile* style, bringing the most out of the lines. This is certainly appropriate, for Sor, being highly influenced by opera, does not depart from his lyric quality in this marvelous composition.[58] Some free rubato and subtle *glissandi* are, to a certain extent, appropriate here in as much as they emulate the singing voice.[59] Occasionally Segovia emphasized the line with these effects:

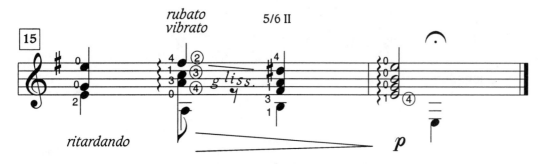

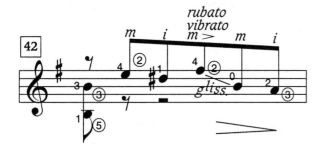

Segovia maintained a steady tempo of about quarter note=84 throughout the piece. Only in the fourth variation did he speed along the tempo to a brilliant quarter note=104.

One outstanding aspect of Segovia's interpretation in this piece was his sensitivity to articulation. For example:

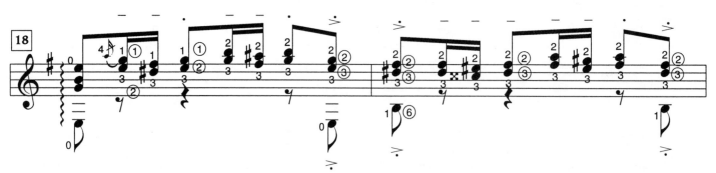

---

58. William Gray Sasser, *The Guitar Works of Fernando Sor*, University of North Carolina, Doctoral Dissertation, Chapel Hill, North Carolina, 1960, pp. 124-128. "The influence of Italian opera was particularly strong both during Sor's formative years and during his years in Paris. His almost daily contact with this art form left its imprint on his music most noticeably, of course, in his melodic lines, but also in a certain sense of rhythmic freedom which goes hand in hand with the melodies."

59. See the discussion of rubato and *glissando* in the introduction to this book.

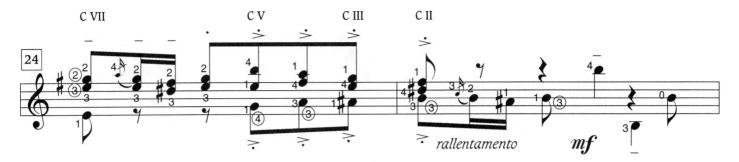

Segovia gave attention to dynamic contrasts but used only a minimal variety of tone colors. Guitarists are encouraged to experiment with their own ideas. Of course, the interpretive possiblilties are infinite.

By the later part of his life, Segovia was regarded as a living legend. He drew packed halls everywhere he went.

While Sor does not indicate to do so, Segovia repeated the theme at the end of the piece. Especially when the minuet is being included with the variations, this may be a good idea, since by that time the theme may tend to get obscured in the mind of the listener. This is the approach suggested here.[60]

Earlier in history, the repeat of a theme was expected to be ornamented by the performer (Da Capo Aria). In this particular style period, the Classical period, that kind of approach was no longer considered appropriate.[61] A good way to vary the theme on the repeat is with dynamic or tempo contrast, or even possibly with tone color.

While Sor was an expert guitarist and composer, his compositions come down to us through history with various technical and interpretive difficulties. They therefore require sensitive editing to bring out the intentions of the composer and the spirit of the music. Andrés Segovia has indeed provided us with fine editing. It is ever more clear after examining his editions of Sor's works that a more excellent and intelligent approach to editing is rarely found.

---

60. Douglas M. Green, *Form in Tonal Music*, New York, Holt, Reinhart and Winston, 1979, p. 106. Ending a set of variations by repeating the theme does have historic precedence: "The problem of finding a satisfactory means of concluding a set of variations is one which has admitted a great number of solutions. Handel, in his *Harmonious Blacksmith Variations*, provides no special finale, simply ending with the last and most brilliant variation. In the *Goldberg Variations*, Bach concludes by repeating the theme *da capo*."

61. Leonard G. Ratner, *Classic Music, Expression, Form, and Style*, New York/London, Schirmer Books, 1980, p. 197. "Improvised ornamentation no longer occupied the central position it had enjoyed in Baroque and mid-century music; in fact, it was openly frowned upon."

BIBLIOGRAPHY FOR PART II

BOOKS

Agricola, Martin. *Musica instrumentalis deudsch,* Wittenberg, 1645.

Alcázar, Miguel (editor). *The Segovia-Ponce Letters,* Columbus, Editions Orphée, 1989.

Ammer, Christine. *Harper's Dictionary of Music,* New York, Harper and Row Publishers, 1972.

Andiá, Rafael and Quevedo, Javier (editors). *Francisco Tárrega: The Collected Guitar Works,* Heidelberg, Chanterelle Verlag, 1992.

Bach, C.P.E. *Versuch über die wahre Art das Clavier zu spielen,* Berlin, 1753.

Bellow, Alexander. *The Illustrated History of the Guitar,* New York, Franco Columbo Publications, 1970.

Bemetzrieder, Anton. *Lecons de clavecin et principels d'harmonie,* Paris, 1771.

Bermudo, Juan. *Comienca el libro primero de la d' claratión de instrumentos musicales,* Osuna, 1949, 50, 55. Barenreiter facsimile, 1957.

Bianciardi, Francesco. *Breve regola per impar' a sonare sopra il basso con ogni sorte d'instrumento,* Siena, 1697.

Bobri, Vladimir. *The Segovia Technique,* New York, Macmillan Publishing Co., 1972.

Borroff, Edith. *The Music of the Baroque,* New York, Da Capo Press, 1978.

Brown, Howard Mayer. *Embellishing 16th Century Music,* Oxford Early Music Series 1, London, Oxford University Press, 1976.

Bukofzer, Manfred F. *Music in the Baroque Era,* New York, W. W. Norton & Company, Inc., 1947.

Cabezón, Antonio de. *Obras de música para tecla, arpa, y vihuela, de Antonio de Cabezon, Musico de la camara y capilla del Rey Don Felipe nuestro señor. Recopiladas y puestas en difra por Hernando de Cabezon, su hijo,* Madrid, 1578.

Clinton, George (editor). *Andrés Segovia, An Appreciation,* London, Musical New Services Ltd., 1978.

Corredor, J.M.A. *Conversations with Casals,* translated by André Mangeot, London, Hutchinson & Co. Ltd., 1956.

Daza, Esteban. *Libro de música en cifras para Vihuela intitulado el Parnasso,* Valladolid, 1576.

Dolmetsch, Arnold. *The Interpretation of the Music of the 17th and 18th Centuries Revealed by Contemporary Evidence,* London, Novello and Co. Ltd., 1946.

Donington, Robert. *Baroque Music: Style and Performance,* London, Faber Music Ltd., 1982.

Donington, Robert. *The Interpretation of Early Music,* London, Faber and Faber, 1979.

Duncan, Charles. *The Art of Classical Guitar Playing,* Princeton, NJ, Summy-Birchard Music, 1980.

Edwards, Owain. *Baroque Instrumental Music,* The Open University Press, 1974.

Fields, Victor Alexander. *Training the Singing Voice,* New York, King's Crown Press, 1947.

Frescobaldi, Girolamo. *Il Secondo Libro Di Toccate,* Rome, 1637.

Friskin, James and Freundlich, Irwin. *Music for the Piano,* New York, Dover Publications, Inc., 1973.

Fuenllana, Miguel de. *Libro de música para Vihuela, intitulado Orphenica lyra,* Seville, 1554.

Ganassi, Sylvestro. *Opera Intitulata,* Venice, 1535. Modern edition by Ganassi, Sylvestro. *Regola Rubertina,* Venice, 1542.

Robert Lienau, Berlin, 1956.

Gavoty, Bernard. *Andrés Segovia,* Geneva, René Kistler, 1955.

Geminiani, Francesco. *The Art of Playing on the Violin,* London, 1751.

Green, Douglas M. *Form in Tonal Music,* New York, Holt, Reinhart and Winston, 1979.

Grout, Donald Jay and Palisca, Claude V. *A History of Western Music,* Third Edition, New York/London, W.W. Norton & Company, 1980.

Grout, Donald J. and Palisca, Claude V. *A History of Western Music,* Fourth Edition, New York, W.W. Norton & Co., Inc., 1988.

Hammond, Frederick. *Girolamo Frescobaldi,* Cambridge, MA, Harvard University Press, 1983.

Heck, Thomas P. *The Birth of the Classic Guitar and its Cultivation in Vienna, Reflected in the Career and Compositions of Mauro Giuliani,* Dissertation, Yale University, New Haven, CT, 1970.

Henestrosa, Luys Venegas de. *Libro de cifra nueva para tecla, harpa, y vihuela,* Alcalá, 1557.

Hindemith, Paul. *Johann Sebastian Bach, Heritage and Obligation,* New Haven, CT, Yale University Press, 1959.

Hoelty-Nickel, Theodore. *The Little Bach Book,* Valparaiso, IN, Valparaiso University Press, 1952.

Hudson, Richard. *Stolen Time, The History of Tempo Rubato,* Oxford, Clarendon Press, 1994.

Jeffery, Brian. *Fernando Sor, Composer and Guitarist,* London, Tecla Editions, 1977.

Kenyon, Nicholas (editor). *Authenticity and Early Music, A Symposium,* Oxford, Oxford University Press, 1988.

Kirkpatrick, Ralph. *Domenico Scarlatti,* Princeton, NJ, Princeton University Press, 1953.

Koonce, Frank. *The Solo Lute Works of Johann Sebastian Bach,* San Diego, CA, Neil A. Kjos Music Company, 1989.

Kozinn, Allan. *Mischa Elman and the Romantic Style,* London/New York, Harwood Academic Publishers, 1990.

Kozinn, Allan/Welding, Pete/Forte, Dan/Santoro, Gene. *The Guitar: The History, The Music, The Players,* New York, William Morrow and Company, Inc., 1984.

Landon, H.C. Robbins. *The Mozart Compendium,* London, Thames and Hudson Ltd., 1990.

Leppard, Raymond. *Authenticity in Music,* Portland, OR, Amadeus Press, 1988.

Maxwell, Carolyn Scarlatti. *Solo Piano Literature,* Boulder, Colorado, Maxwell Music Evaluation Books, 1985.

McGee, Timothy. *Medieval and Renaissance Music,* Toronto, University of Toronto Press, 1985.

Milán, Luys. *Libro de Música de Vihuela de mano Intitulado El Maestro,* Valencia, 1536.

Monahan, Brent Jeffrey. *The Art of Singing,* Metuchen, NJ & London, The Scarecrow Press, Inc., 1978.

Mozart, Leopold. *Versuch einer Gründlichen Violinschule,* 1756. Third Printing, 1787.

Mudarra, Alfonso de. *Tres libros de Música en cifras para vihuela,* Sevilla, 1546.

Narvaez, Luys de. *Los seys Libro del Delphin de música de difras para tañer Vihuela,* Valladolid, 1538.

Nettl, Paul. *Mozart and Masonry,* New York, Philosophical Library, 1957.

Neumann, Frederick. *New Essays on Performance Practice,* Ann Arbor/London, UMI Research Press, 1989.

Neumann, Frederick. *Ornamentation in Baroque and Post-Baroque Music, With Special Emphasis on J.S. Bach,* Princeton, NJ, Princeton University Press, 1978.

Neumann, Frederick. *Performance Practices of the Seventeenth and Eighteenth Centuries,* New York, Schirmer Books, 1993.

Newman, Anthony. *Bach and the Baroque,* Pendragon Press, 1985.

Niedt, Friedrich Erhard. *Musikalische Handleitung,* Hamburg, 1700.

Noad, Frederick. *The Classical Guitar,* New York, Ariel Music Publications, 1976.

Ophee, Matanya. *Andrei Sychra, Four Concert Etudes, The Russian Collection Volume II,* Columbus, Editions Orpheé, 1992.

Ortiz, Diego. *Tradado de glosas...,* Rome, 1553. Modern edition, Kassel, 1936.

Parkening, Christopher. *The Christopher Parkening Guitar Method, Vol. 1,* Chicago, Antiqua Casa Sherry-Brenner, 1972.

Phillips, Elizabeth V. and Jackson, John-Paul Christopher. *Performing Medieval and Renaissance Music,* London, Collier Macmillan Publishers, 1986.

Pidoux, Pierre Girolamo Frescobaldi, *Organ and Keyboard Works,* Paris, Bärenreiter 2204, 1948.

Pisador, Diego. *Libro de Música de vihuela,* Salmanca, 1552.

Poe, Frances R. *Teaching and Performing Renaissance Choral Music,* London, The Scarecrow Press, 1994.

Poulton, Diana. *The Consort,* July, 1959.

Praetorius, Michael. *Syntagma Musicum,* Wolfenbuttel, 1619.

Prat, Domingo. *Diccionario De Guitarristas,* Buenos Aires, Romero y Fernandez, 1934. Reprint edition with an introduction by Matanya Ophee, Columbus, Editions Orphée, 1986.

Prés, Josquin des. *Werke,* edited by Albert Smijers, Lepzig, Kistner und Siegel, 1925.

Pujol, Emilio. *Hispanae Citharae Ars Viva, Antologia de música selecta para guitarra transcrita de la tablatura antigua,* Mainz, B. Schott's Söhne, 1956.

Randel, Don Michael (editor). *The New Harvard Dictionary of Music,* London, Cambridge, MA, The Belknap Press of Harvard University Press, 1986.

Rangel-Ribeiro, Victor. *Baroque Music, A Practical Guide for the Performer,* New York, Schirmer Books, 1981.

Ratner, Leonard G. *Classic Music, Expression, Form, and Style,* New York/London, Schirmer Books, 1980.

Reid, Cornelius L. *A Dictionary of Vocal Terminology,* New York, Music House Ltd., 1983.

Santa María, Tomás de. *Libro llamado Arte de tañer fantasía, assi para tecla como, vihuela y todo instrumento,* Valladolid, 1565.

Sasser, William Gray. *The Guitar Works of Fernando Sor,* Doctoral Dissertation, University of North Carolina, Chapel Hill, NC, 1960.

Scott, Charles Kennedy. *The Fundamentals of Singing,* London, Cassell and Company Ltd., 1954.

Segovia, Andrés and Mendoza, George. *Segovia, My Book of the Guitar,* Cleveland/New York, William Collier Publishers Inc., 1979.

Segovia, Andrés. *Segovia: An Autobiography of the Years 1893-1920,* New York, Macmillan Publishers, 1976.

Segovia, Andrés. *Studies for the Guitar by Fernando Sor,* New York, Edward B. Marks Music Corporation, 1945.

Silbiger, Alexander (editor). *Frescobaldi Studies,* Durham, Duke University Press, 1987.

Sitwell, Sacheverell. *A Background for Domenico Scarlatti,* London, Faber and Faber Limited, 1945.

Smith, Joseph. *Voice and Song, A Practical Method for the Study of Singing,* New York, G. Schirmer, 1907.

Sor, Fernando. *Méthode pour la Guitare,* Paris, 1830. Translated into English and published by A. Merrick in London, 1832. Modern edition, Da Capo Press, New York, 1971.

Spitta, Phillip. *Johann Sebastian Bach,* translated by Clara Ball and J. A. Fuller-Maitland, 3 vols., New York, 1951.

The Thompson Chain Reference Bible, New International Version, Indianapolis, Indiana, the B. B. Kirkbride Bible Company, Inc., 1983.

Trend, J. B. *Luis Milán and the Vihuelistas,* Oxford, Oxford University Press, 1925.

Trend, J. B. *The Music of Spanish History,* New York, Kraus Reprint Corporation, 1965 (original printing 1926).

Turnbull, Harvey. *The Guitar from the Renaissance to the Present Day,* New York, Charles Scribner's Sons, 1974.

Valderrábano, Enriquez de. *Libro de música de vihuela, intitulado silva de sirenas,* Valladolid, 1547.

Veilan, Jean-Claude. *The Rules of Musical Interpretation in the Baroque Era, Common to All Instruments,* Paris, 1979.

Wade, Graham. *Segovia, A Celebration of the Man and his Music,* London/New York, Allison & Busby, 1983.

Wade, Graham. *The Guitarist's Guide to Bach,* Ireland, Wise Owl Music, 1985.

Wade, Graham. *Traditions of the Classical Guitar,* London, John Calder, Ltd., 1980.

Ward, John. *The Vihuela De Mano,* Doctoral Dissertation, Yale University, New Haven, CT, 1953.

Westrup, J. A. & Harrison, F. L. *The New College Encyclopedia of Music,* New York, W. W. Norton & Co., Inc., 1960.

ARTICLES

Artz, Alice. "The Third Lute Suite by Bach, Three Manuscripts and their Implications," presented in the *Journal of the Lute Society of America,* No. 1, 1968.

Bechtel, Ben "Improvisation in Early Music," presented in *Music Educator's Journal,* January 1980.

Collins, Walter S. "What is a Good Edition?" presented in *The Choral Journal,* November 1971.

Decker, Michael. "Sor's Principles of Guitar Fingerings," presented in *Guitar Review,* Spring 1986.

Duncan, Charles "The Segovia Sound, What is it?," presented in *Guitar Review,* Fall 1977.

Fisk, Eliot. "A Problem in Perspective," presented in *Guitar Review,* Fall 1987.

Goldmon, James. "Guitarist's Skill Charms Critic," presented in *The Chicago Maroon,* January 24, 1949.

Goluses, Nicholas. "J. S. Bach and the Transcription Process," presented in *Guitar Review,* New York, Spring 1989.

Greene, Thomas E. "The Hexachord System as it Applies to the Spanish Vihuelists," presented in *Chelys*, Vol. 1, No. 3, September 1976.

Grove's Dictionary of Music and Musicians, Eric Blom, editor, Fifth Edition, New York, St. Martin Press, Vol. 3, 1954. Entry on "Frescobaldi, Girolamo."

Guinn, John "Guitar Master Segovia Dies in Spain at 94," presented in the *Detroit Free Press,* June 4, 1987.

Guinn, John. "A Stellar Performance by Segovia," presented in the *Detroit Free Press,* March 20, 1987.

Hashimoto, Eiji. "Domenico Scarlatti," presented in the *American Music Teacher,* June/July 1979.

Hudson, Richard. "The Folia Melodies," presented in *Acta Musicologica,* Vol. XLV, January 1973.

Jeffery, Brian. "Fernando Sor's 'Twenty Studies,' a Reconsideration," presented in GFA *Soundboard,* November 1981.

Kanengeiser, William. An interview presented in GFA *Soundboard,* Fall 1993.

Kirkpatrick, Ralph. "Fifty Years of Harpsichord Playing," presented in *Early Music,* January 1983.

Leonard, William. "Segovia's Guitar Ignores Own Land For Early Classicists," presented in the *Journal of Commerce,* January 24, 1949.

Marriott, David F. "Some Notes on the Advantages of Planting," presented in GFA *Soundboard,* Spring 1982.

Marshall, Robert L. "Bach the Progressive: Observations on his Later Works," presented in the *Journal of the American Musicological Society,* Vol. LXII, No. 3, July 1976.

McKenna, Constance. "A Segovia Masterclass," presented in *Guitar Review,* Fall 1986.

Morrongiello, Christopher. "Renaissance Performance Techniques with Paul O'Dette," presented in the *Lute Society of America Quarterly,* November 1990.

O'Dette, Paul. "The Performance of Passaggi," presented in the *Lute Society of America Newsletter,* April 1977.

Ophee, Matanya. "Some Considerations of 19th Century Guitar Music and its Performance Today," a multi part series presented in *Classical Guitar,* August, September, October and December 1986.

Ophee, Matanya. "Historical Research, A Guest Essay," presented in *Guitarra,* No. 39, July-August 1980.

Ophee, Matanya, "Response to the Offensive," presented in *Classical Guitar,* September 1987.

Ophee, Matanya. A review of the Russian biography "Andrés Segovia" by Miron Abramovitch, presented in GFA *Soundboard,* Spring 1982.

Parkening, Christopher. "Of Gift and Discipline," an interview by John Schroeter, presented in *Fingerstyle Guitar,* No. 11, September/October 1995.

Petschauer, Roy. "Denis Gaultier and the Unmeasured Prelude," presented in *Guitar Review,* No. 36, 1972.

Piovovar, Philip. "Ornamenting Vihuela Music," presented in *Guitar and Lute,* No. 18, July 1981.

Segovia, Andrés. *Segovia on Stage,* MCA Records 2531, Universal City, CA, 1977. Interview of Segovia by Alan Rich in the liner notes.

Sicca, Dr. Mario. "Articulations in the Lute Music of J. S. Bach," presented in *Guitar Review,* New York, Fall 1985.

Smith, Michael Cedric. "Fashions in Bach," presented in *Guitar Review,* Summer 1985.

Stenstadvold, Erik. "The Bother over Broken Chords, Another Historical Perspective," presented in *Classical Guitar,* May 1987.

Stenstadvold, Erik. "Napoleon Coste's Contribution to the 'Twenty Studies' by Sor," presented in GFA *Soundboard,* Summer 1984.

The New Grove Dictionary of Music and Musicians, Stanley Sadie, editor, London, Macmillan Publishers Limited, 1980, Vol. 15. Entry on "portamento."

The New Grove Dictionary of Music and Musicians, Stanley Sadie, editor, London, Macmillan Publishers Limited, Vol 8. Entry on "ornamentation" by Robert Donington.

The New Grove's Dictionary of Music and Musicians, Stanley Sadie, editor, London, Macmillan Publishers Limited, 1980, Vol. 17. Entry on "Sor, Fernando."

Williams, John. "A Conversation with John Williams," an interview by Gareth Walters, presented in *Guitar Review,* Winter 1992.

Zayas, Rodrigo de. "The Vihuelists," presented in *Guitar Review,* No. 38, 1973.

APPENDIX A:

Original Scores for the Pieces Included in the Segovia Analysis

MILLE REGRETZ *by Josquin des Prés.*

From: Josquin des Prés, *Werke,* edited by Albert Smijers (the original source did not use treble clefs, which are used here for the sake of convenience).

Table of Contents, CANCIÓN DEL EMPERADOR and GUÁRDAME LAS VACAS *by Luys de Narváez.*
From the book *Los seys libros del Delphin de música de cifras para tañer Vihuela.*

CANCIÓN DEL EMPERADOR

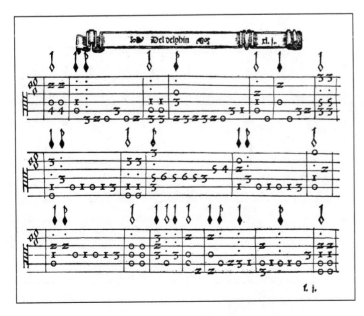

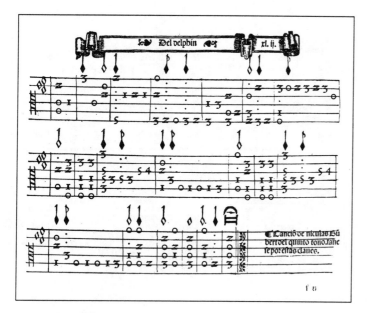

GUÁRDAME LAS VACAS

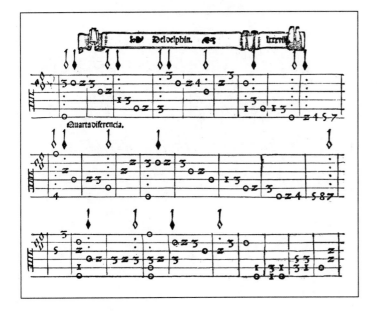

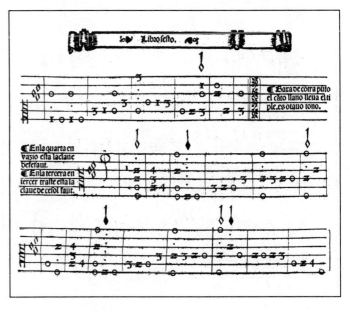

Frontispiece and **ARIA DETTA LA FRESCOBALDA** *by Girolamo Frescobaldi.*
From *Il Secondo Libro Di Toccate.*

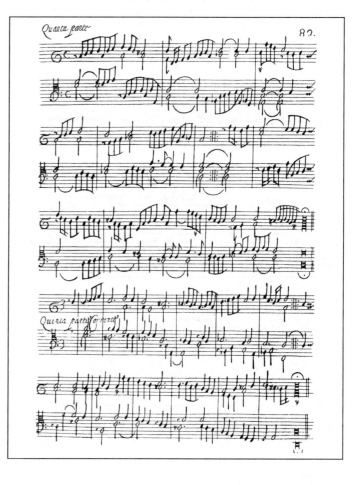

PRELUDE, BWV 999 *by J. S. Bach.*

Facsimile of the manuscript by J.P. Kellner.

FUGUE, BWV 1001 from *Violin Sonata I by J. S. Bach.*

Facsimile copy of the composer's autographed handwritten score.

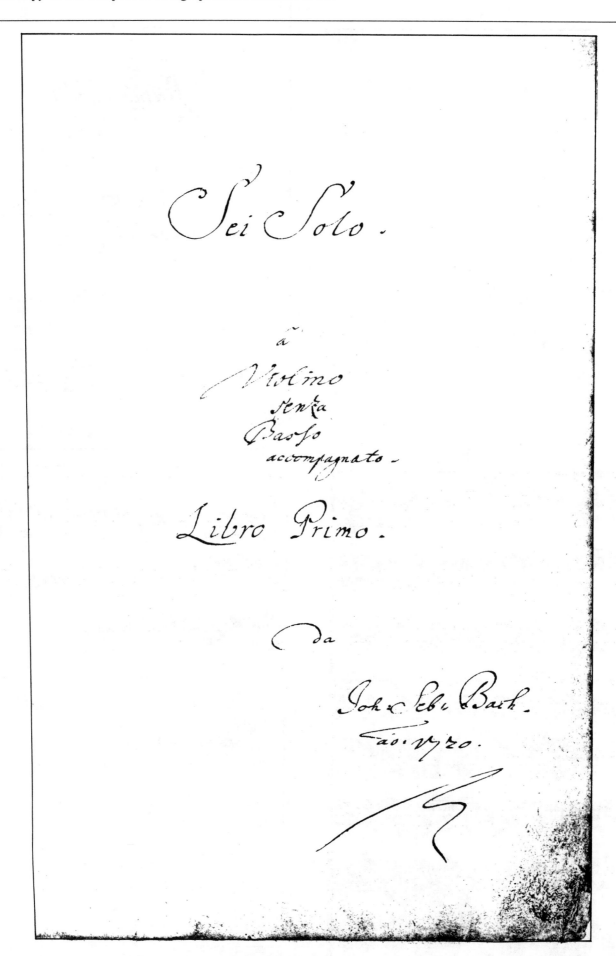

SARABANDE, BWV 1002 (and its *Double*) from *Partita No. 1 in B Minor by J. S. Bach.*

Facsimile copy of the composer's autographed handwritten score.

BOURRÉE, BWV 1002 from *Partita No. 1 in B Minor by J.S. Bach.*
Copy of the composer's autographed handwritten score.

DOUBLE, BWV 1002 from *Partita No. 1 in B Minor by J. S. Bach.*

Facsimile copy of the composer's autographed handwritten score.

SONATAS, K. 11, K. 322 AND K. 323 *by Domenico Scarlatti.*

Facsimiles from the Venice and Parma manuscripts.

VARIATIONS ON A THEME BY MOZART *by Fernando Sor*

Facsimile of a score published during the composer's lifetime.

Variations on Folias de España *by Fernando Sor.*

Facsimile of a score published during the composer's lifetime.

APPENDIX B:

Modern Editions of the Pieces Included in the Segovia Analysis

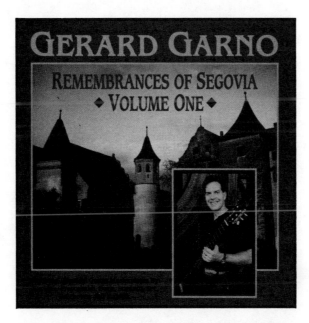

A CD recording is available which serves to demonstrate the modern editions presented in this appendix. The publisher strongly recommends the use of this recording along with the text to insure accuracy and ease of learning.

Canción del Emperador

Edited for the guitar
by Gerard Garno

Luys de Narváez
(c. 1500-1560)

(optional harmonics.
See p. 208-209)

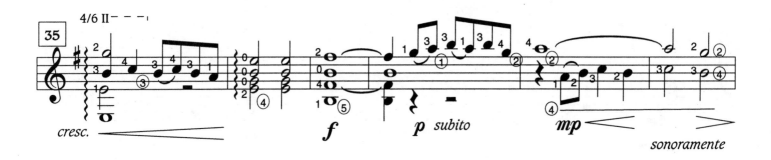

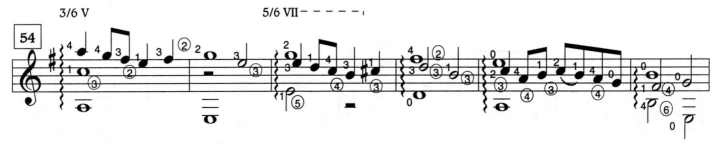

A Modern Edition
Canción del Emperador - 2

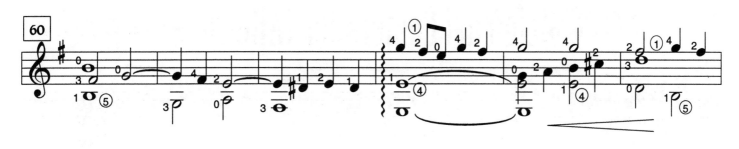

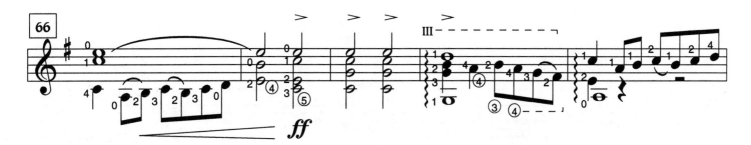

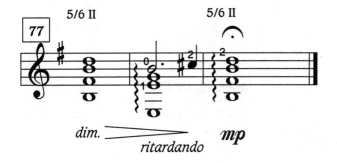

dim. _____ ritardando **mp**

Canción del Emperador (Alternate)

(Ornamental Version)

Edited for the guitar
by Gerard Garno

Luys de Narváez
(c. 1500-1560)

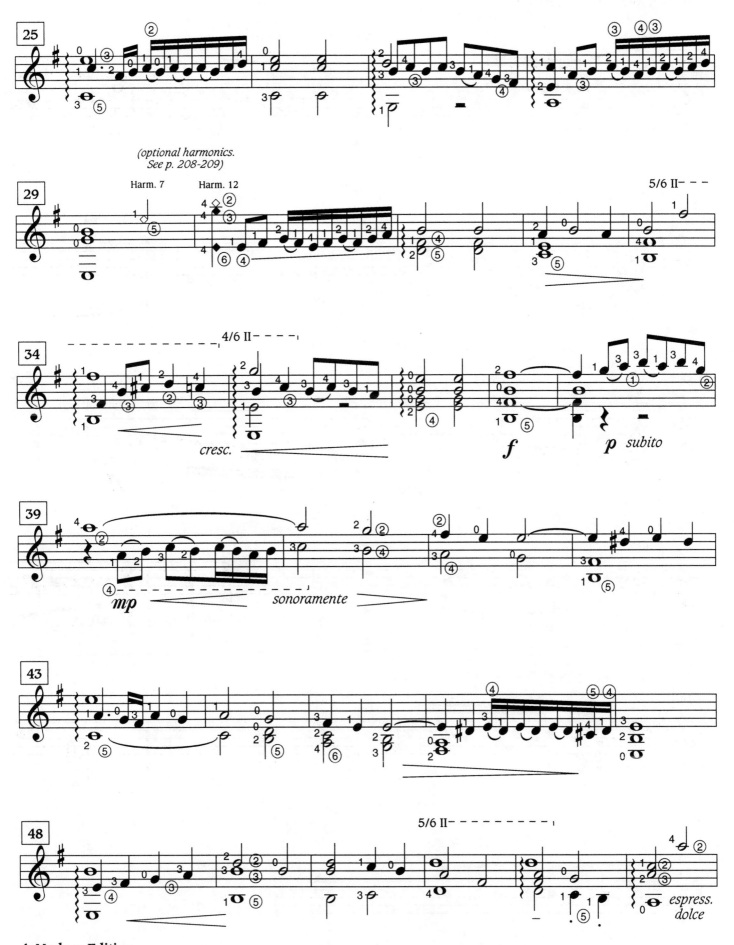

A Modern Edition
Canción del Emperador (Alternate) - 2

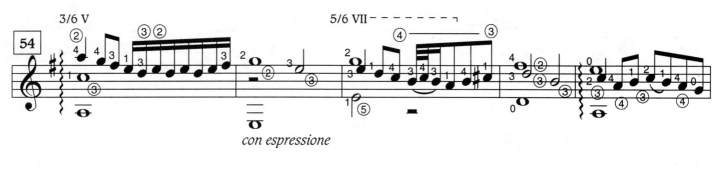

con espressione

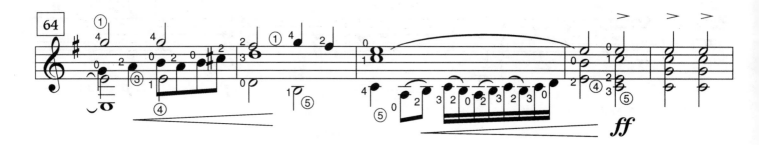

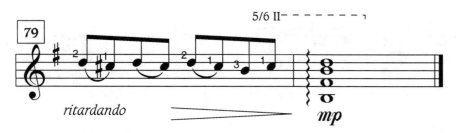

ritardando

A Modern Edition
Canción del Emperador (Alternate) - 3

Guárdame Las Vacas

*Edited for the guitar
by Gerard Garno*

*Luys de Narváez
(c. 1500-1560)*

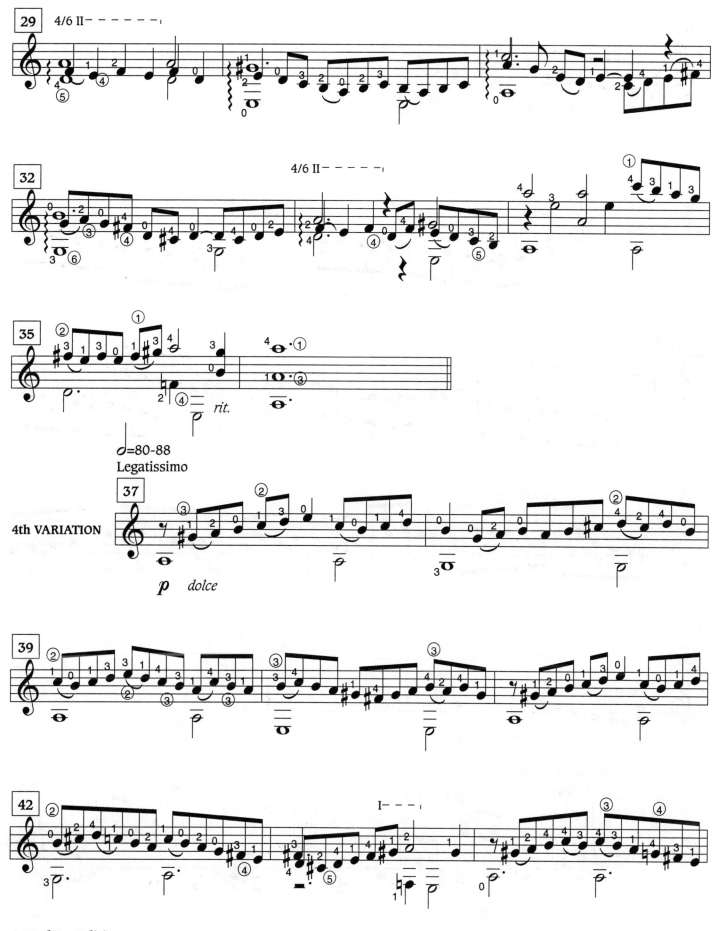

4th VARIATION

A Modern Edition
Guárdame Las Vacas - 3

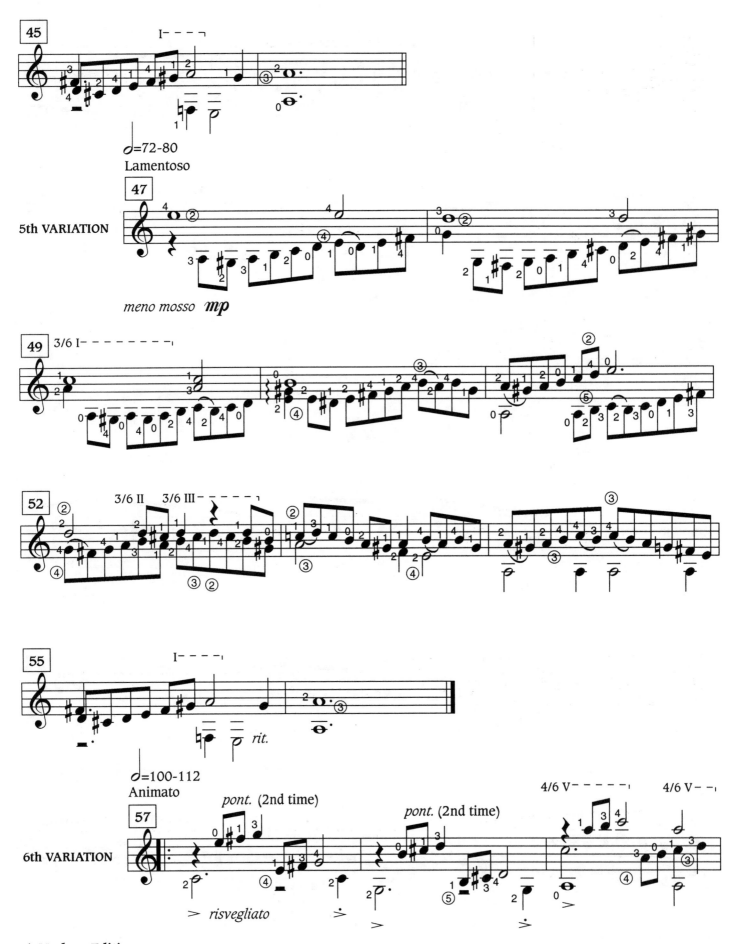

A Modern Edition
Guárdame Las Vacas - 5

Aria Detta La Frescobaldi

Edited for the guitar
by Gerard Garno

Girolamo Frescobaldi
(1583-1644)

A Modern Edition
Aria Detta La Frescobaldi - 1

A Modern Edition
Aria Detta La Frescobaldi - 2

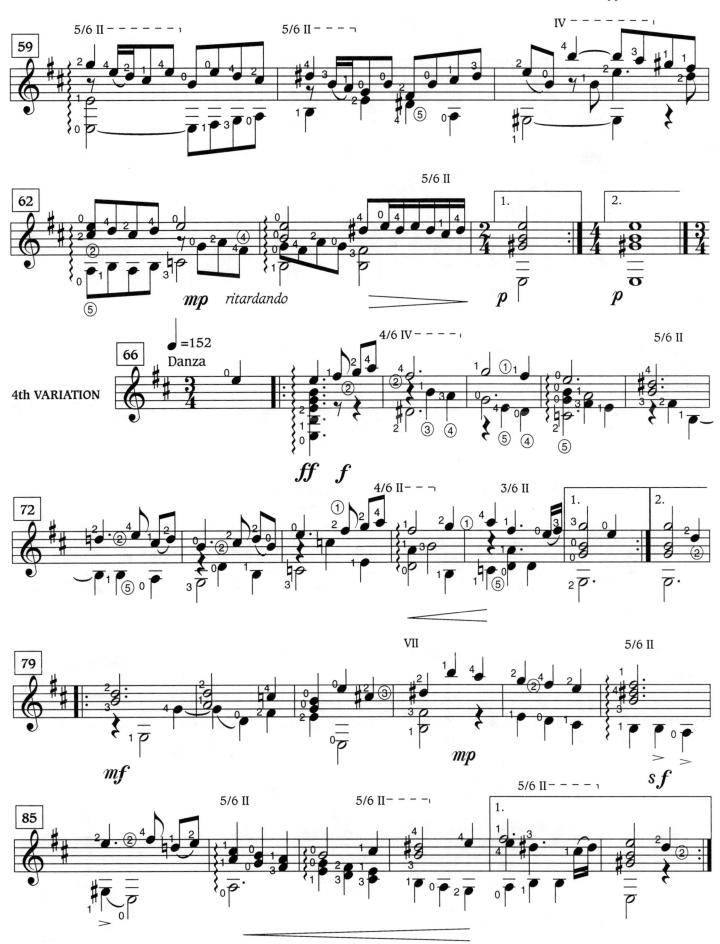

A Modern Edition
Aria Detta La Frescobaldi - 4

Prelude in D Minor

*Edited for the guitar
by Gerard Garno*

*Johann Sebastian Bach
(1685-1750)*

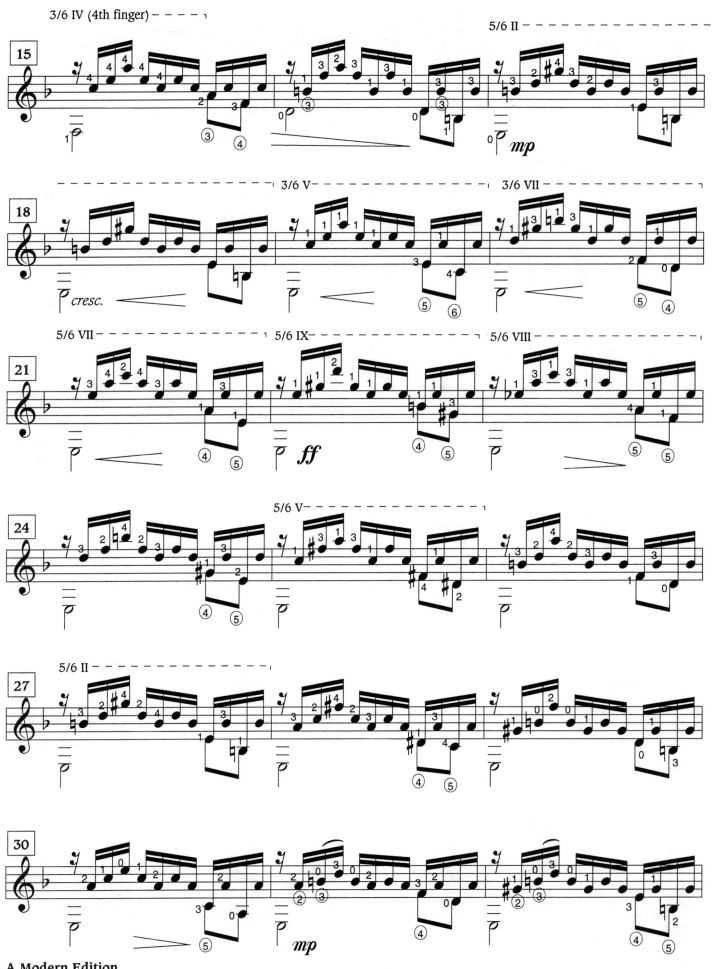

A Modern Edition
Prelude in D Minor - 2

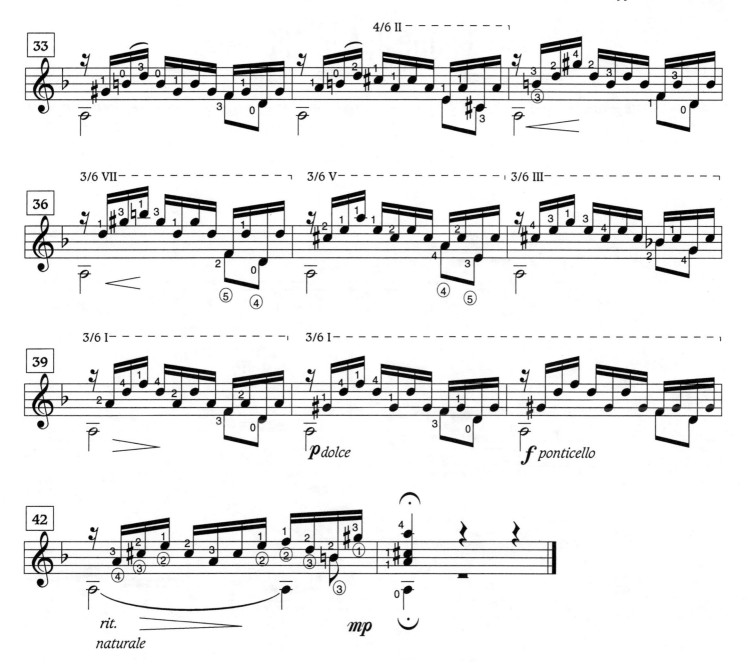

A Modern Edition
Prelude in D Minor - 3

Fugue in A Minor

Edited for the guitar
by Gerard Garno

Johann Sebastian Bach
(1685-1750)

A Modern Edition
Fugue in A Minor - 1

A Modern Edition
Fugue in A Minor - 2

A Modern Edition
Fugue in A Minor - 3

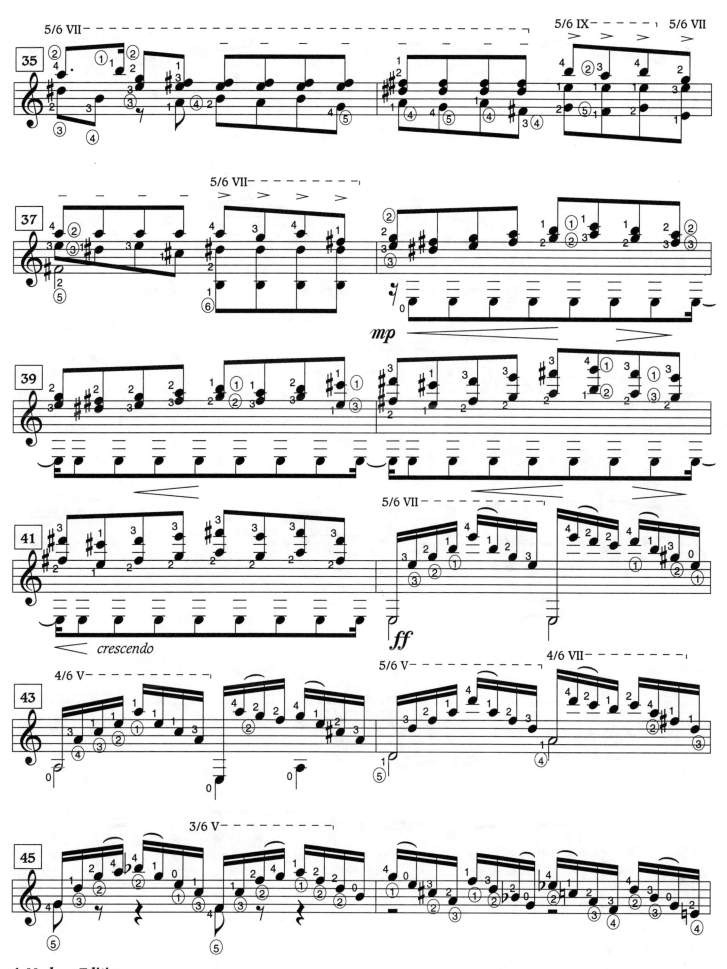

A Modern Edition
Fugue in A Minor - 4

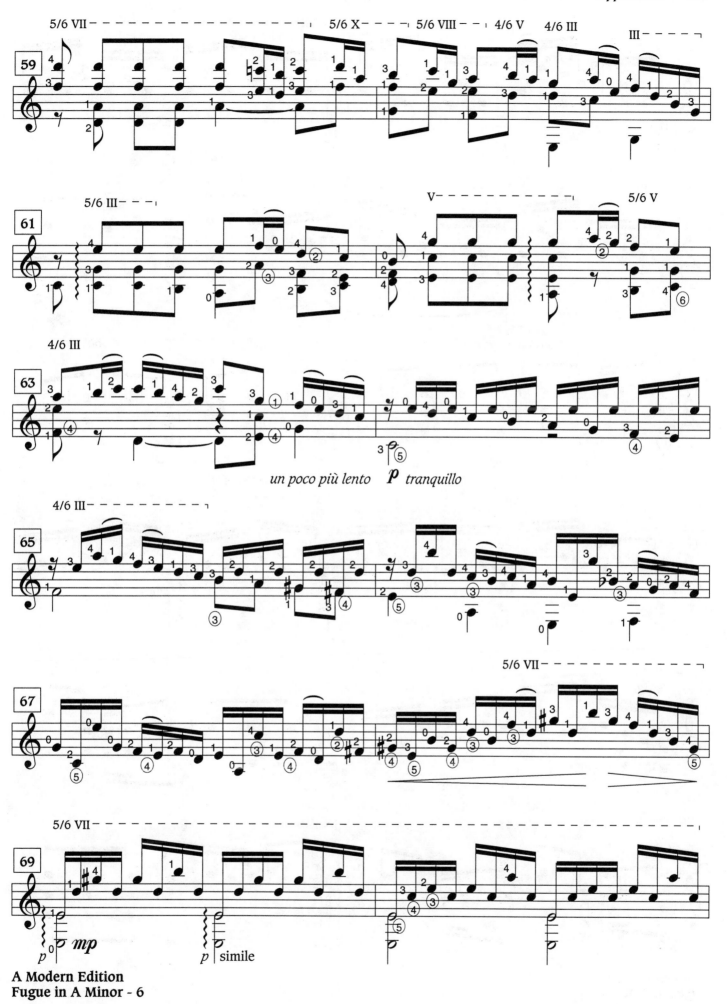

un poco più lento *p tranquillo*

A Modern Edition
Fugue in A Minor - 6

A Modern Edition
Fugue in A Minor - 7

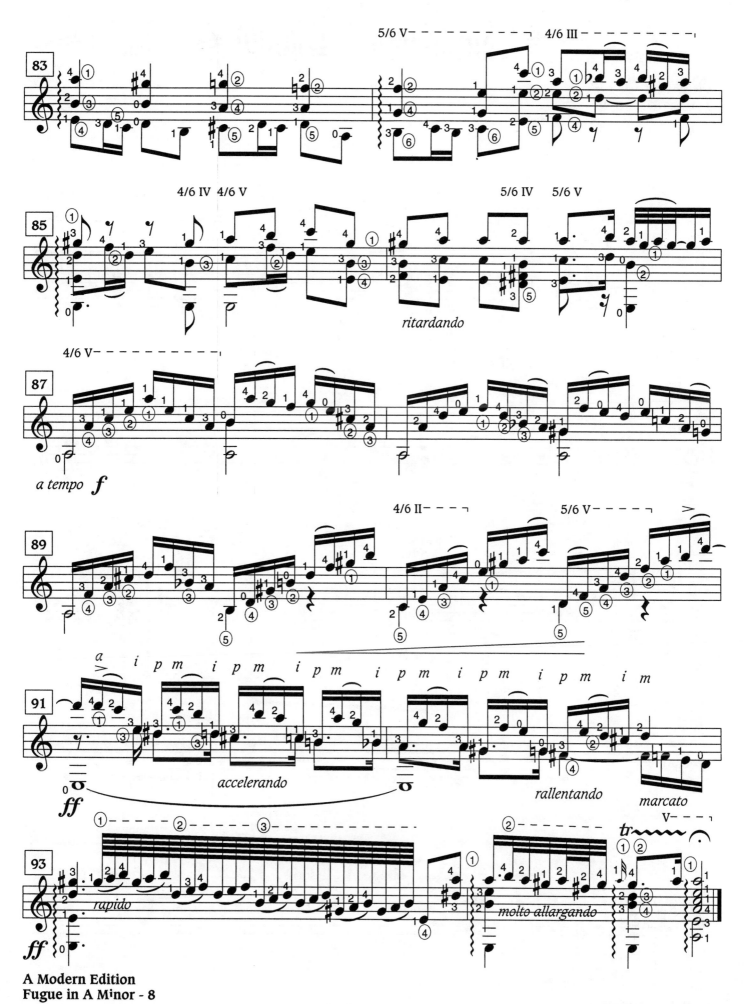

A Modern Edition
Fugue in A Minor - 8

Sarabande in B Minor

*Edited for the guitar
by Gerard Garno*

*Johann Sebastian Bach
(1685 - 1750)*

A Modern Edition
Sarabande in B Minor - 2

Bourrée in B Minor

*Edited for the guitar
by Gerard Garno*

*Johann Sebastian Bach
(1685 - 1750)*

**A Modern Edition
Bourree in B Minor - 1**

A Modern Edition
Bourree in B Minor - 2

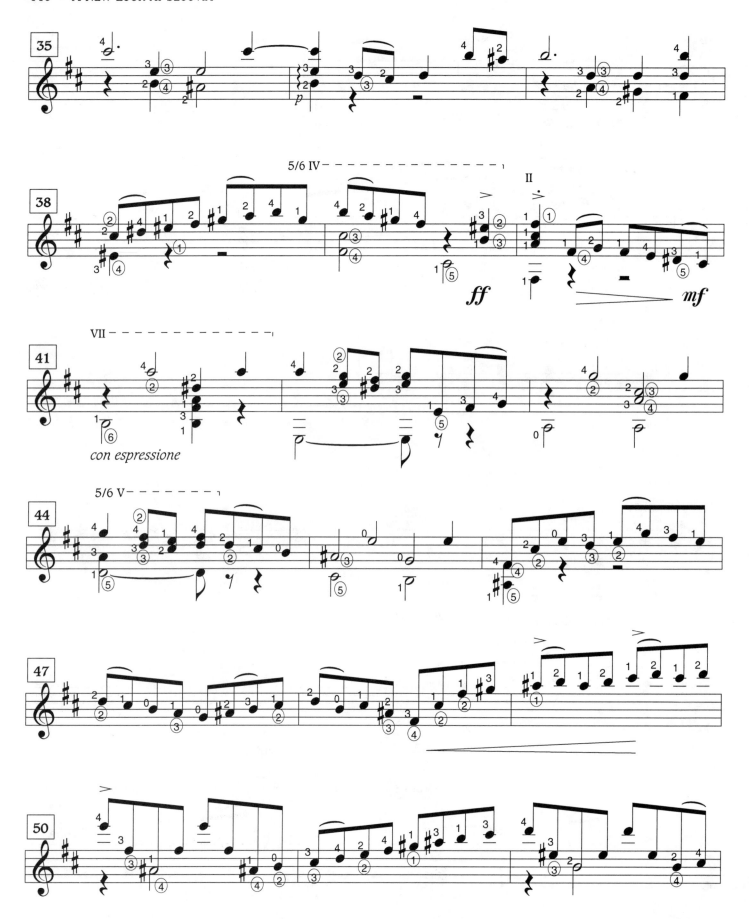

A Modern Edition
Bourree in B Minor - 4

Double in B Minor

*Edited for the guitar
by Gerard Garno*

Johann Sebastian Bach
(1685 - 1750)

**A Modern Edition
Double in B Minor - 1**

A Modern Edition
Double in B Minor - 2

A Modern Edition
Double in B Minor - 3

A Modern Edition
Double in B Minor - 4

Sonata in E Minor, K. 11

Edited for the guitar
by Gerard Garno

Domenico Scarlatti
(1685-1757)

A Modern Edition
Sonata in E Minor, K. 11 - 1

A Modern Edition
Sonata in E Minor, K. 11 - 2

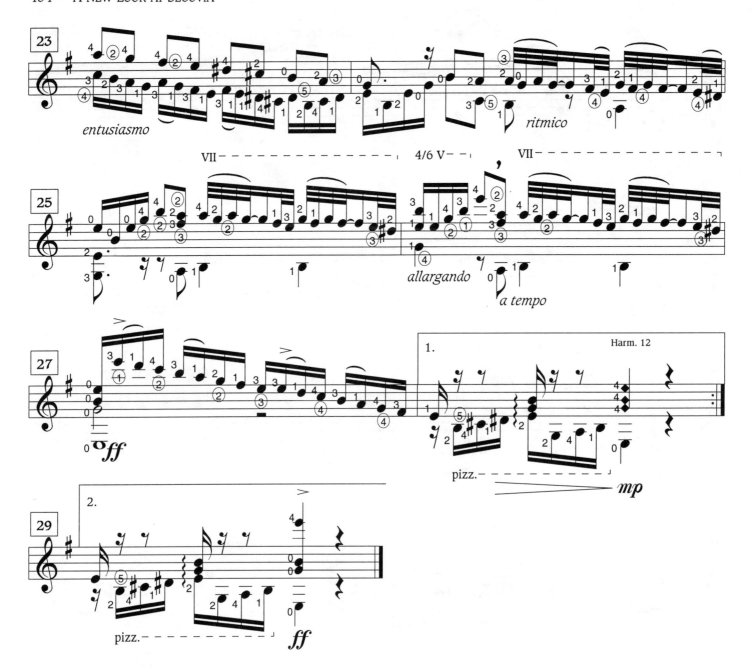

A Modern Edition
Sonata in E Minor, K. 11 - 3

Sonata in A Major, K. 322

*Edited for the guitar
by Gerard Garno*

*Domenico Scarlatti
(1685-1757)*

A Modern Edition
Sonata in A Major, K. 322 - 1

A Modern Edition
Sonata in A Major, K. 322 - 2

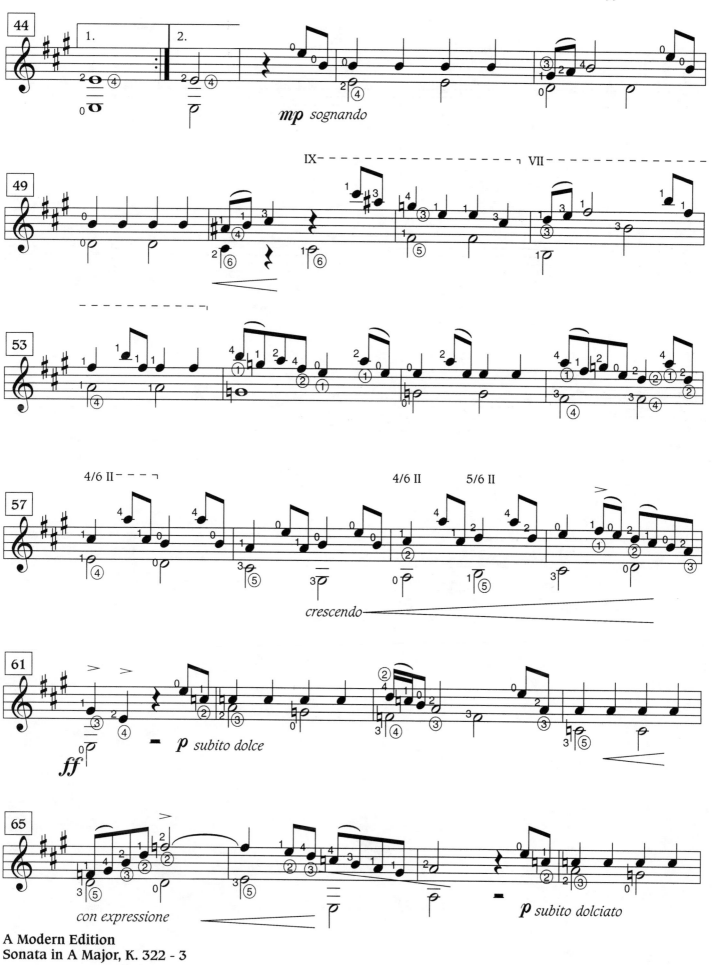

A Modern Edition
Sonata in A Major, K. 322 - 3

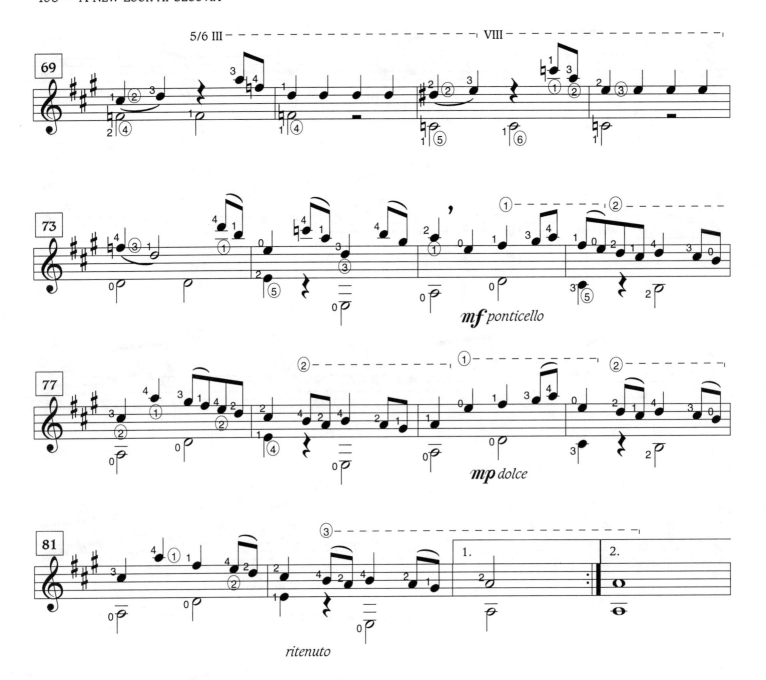

A Modern Edition
Sonata in A Major, K. 322 - 4

Sonata in A Major, K. 323

Edited for the guitar
by Gerard Garno

Domenico Scarlatti
(1685-1757)

A Modern Edition
Sonata in A Major, K. 323 - 1

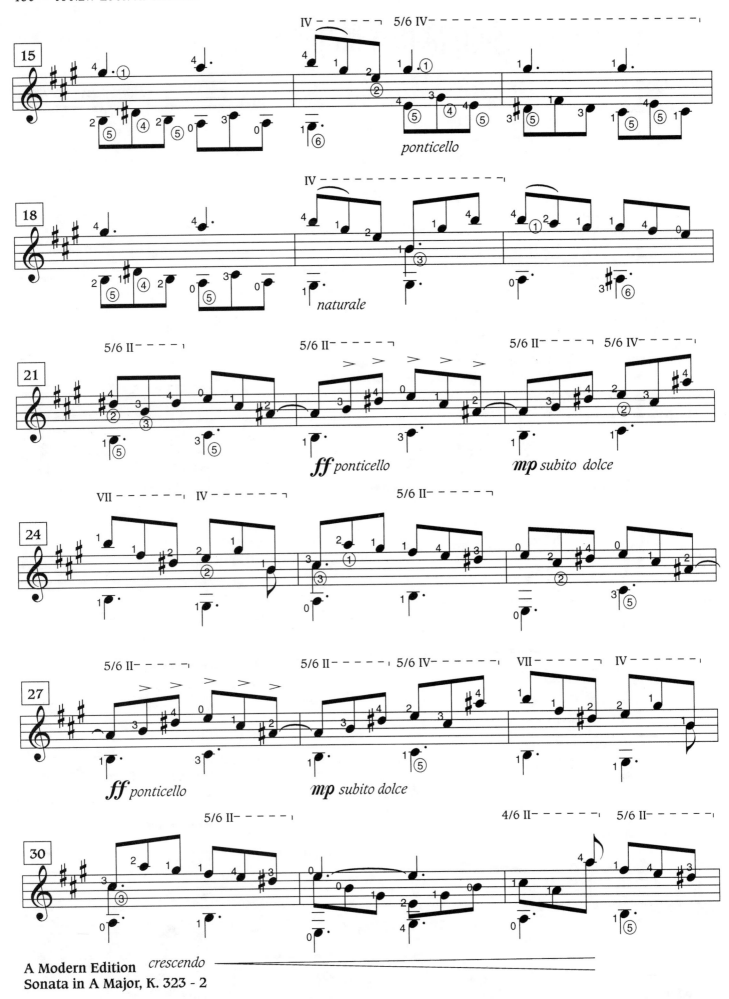

A Modern Edition
Sonata in A Major, K. 323 - 2

A Modern Edition
Sonata in A Major, K. 323 - 3

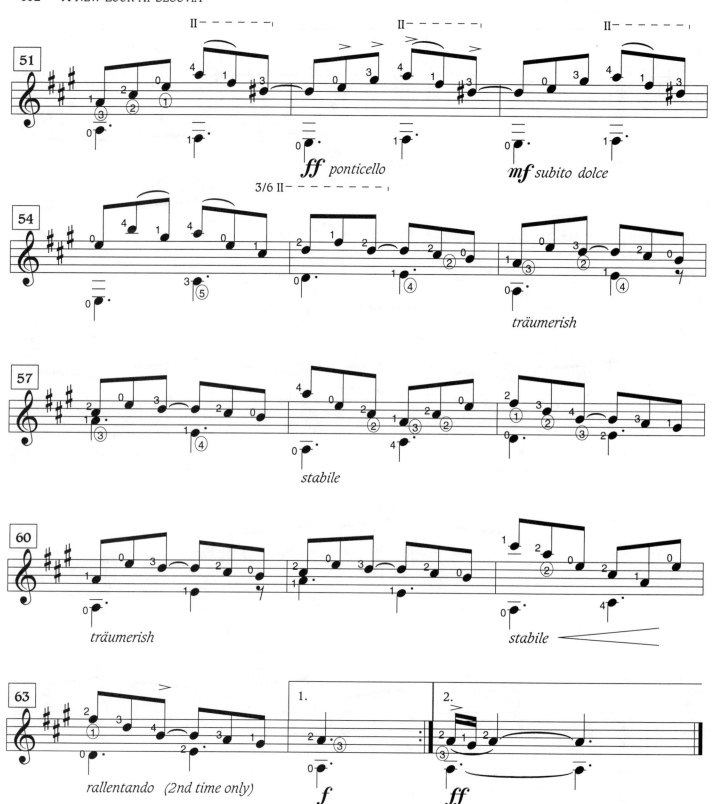

A Modern Edition
Sonata in A Major, K. 323 - 4

Variations on a Theme by Mozart

Edited for the guitar
by Gerard Garno

Fernando Sor
(1778-1839)

A Modern Edition
Variations on a Theme by Mozart - 2

A Modern Edition
Variations on a Theme by Mozart - 3

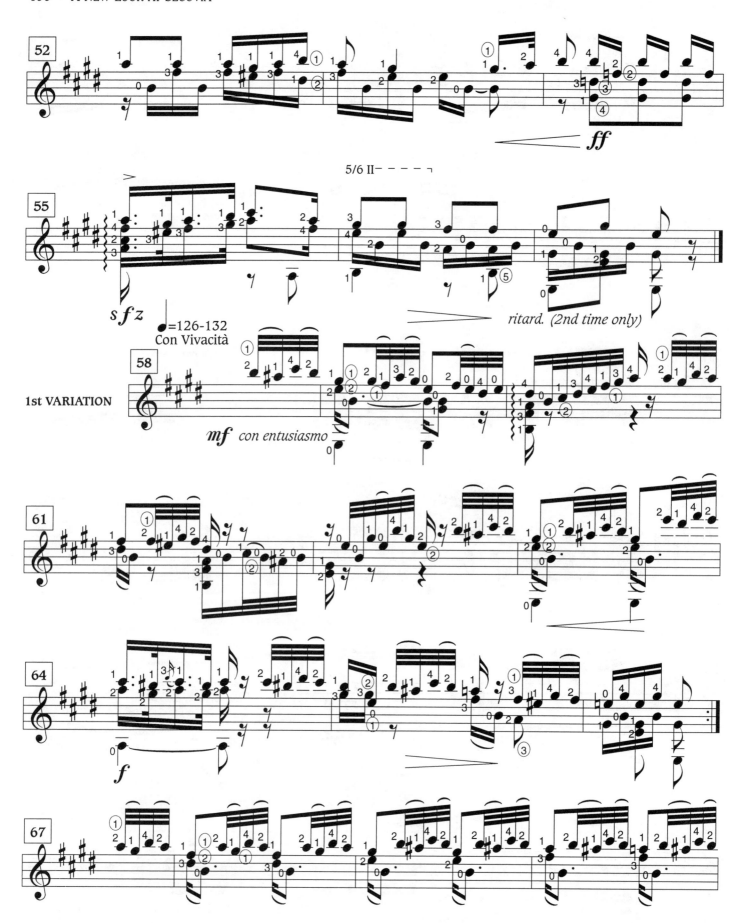

A Modern Edition
Variations on a Theme by Mozart - 4

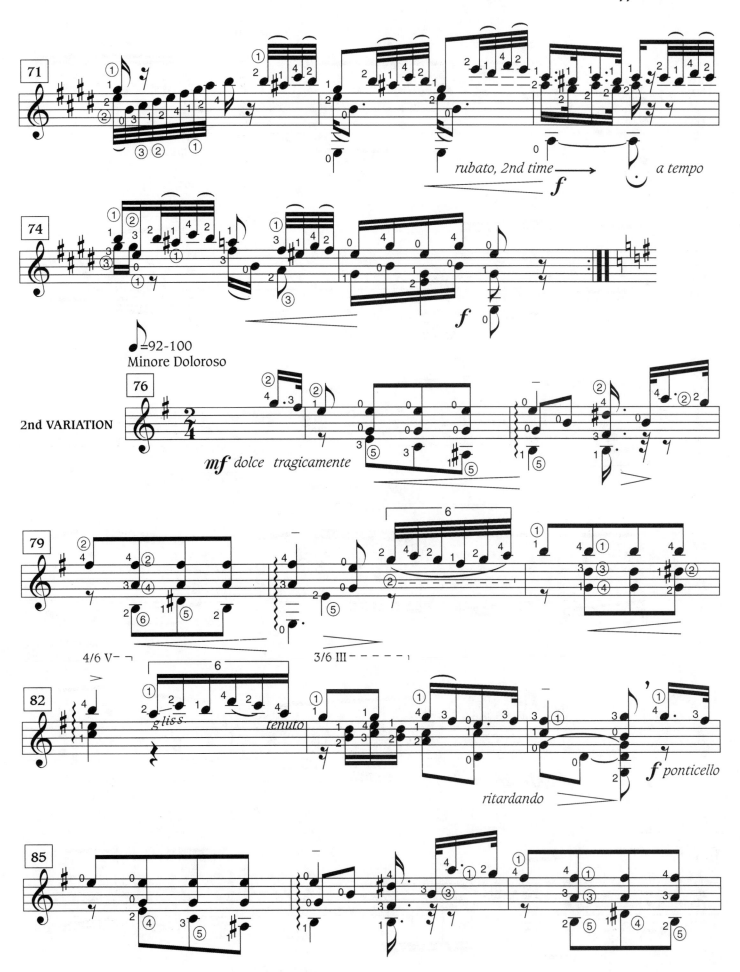

**A Modern Edition
Variations on a Theme by Mozart - 5**

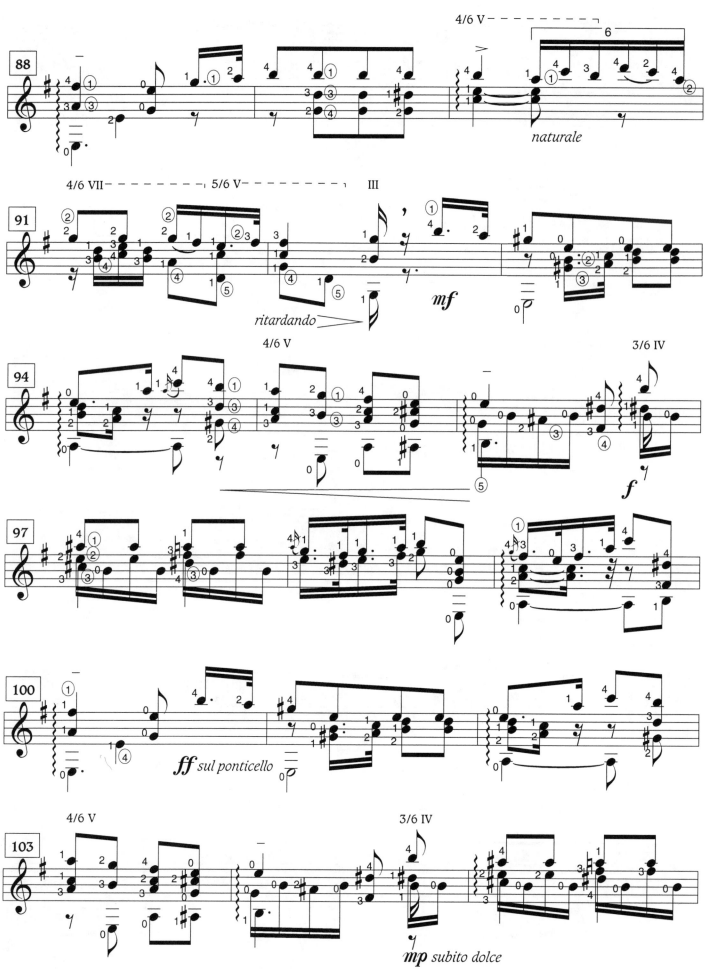

A Modern Edition
Variations on a Theme by Mozart - 6

A Modern Edition
Variations on a Theme by Mozart - 7

A Modern Edition
Variations on a Theme by Mozart - 8

A Modern Edition
Variations on a Theme by Mozart - 9

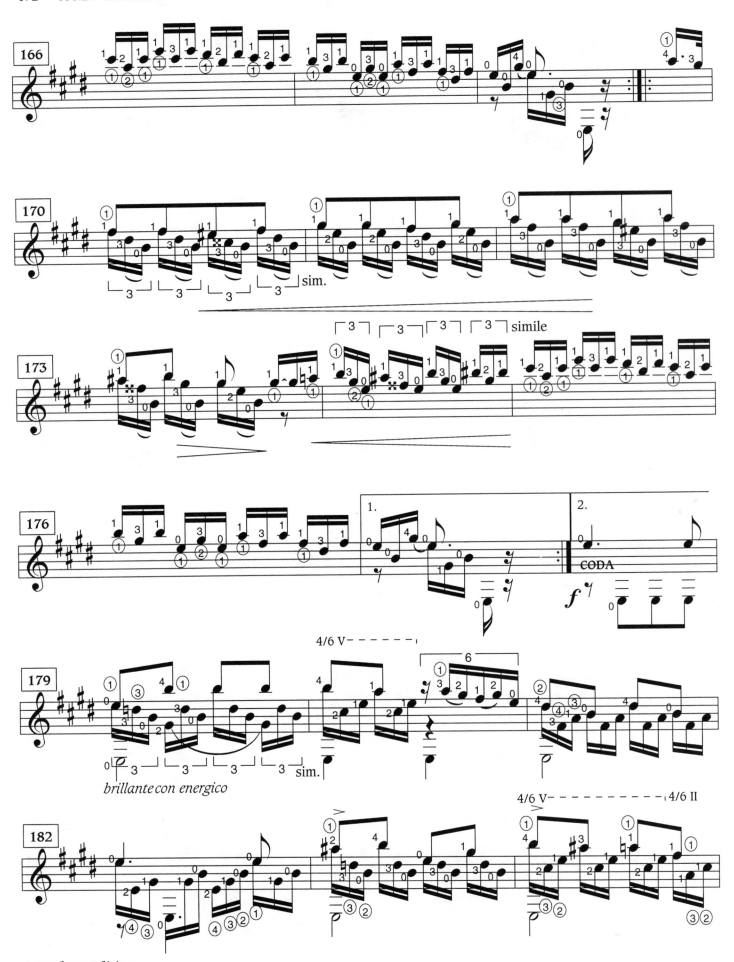

A Modern Edition
Variations on a Theme by Mozart - 10

A Modern Edition
Variations on a Theme by Mozart - 11

Variations on La Folia de España

Edited for the guitar
by Gerard Garno

Fernando Sor
(1778-1839)

A Modern Edition
Variations on La Folia de España - 1

A Modern Edition
Variations on La Folia de España - 2

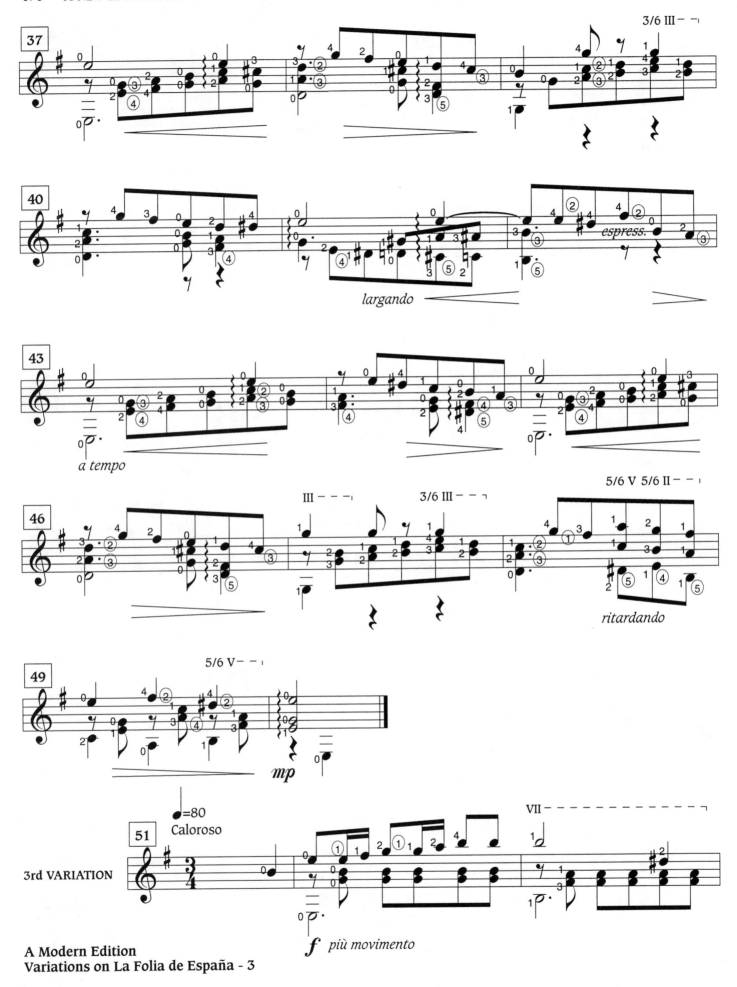

A Modern Edition
Variations on La Folia de España - 3

4th VARIATION

A Modern Edition
Variations on La Folia de España - 4

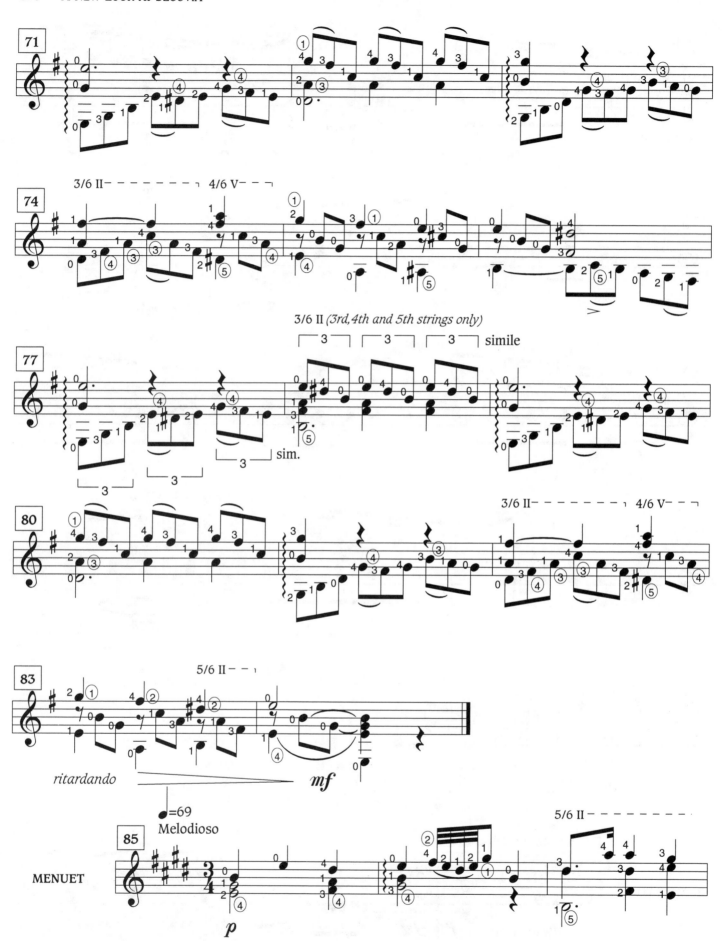

A Modern Edition
Variations on La Folia de España - 5

A Modern Edition
Variations on La Folia de España - 6

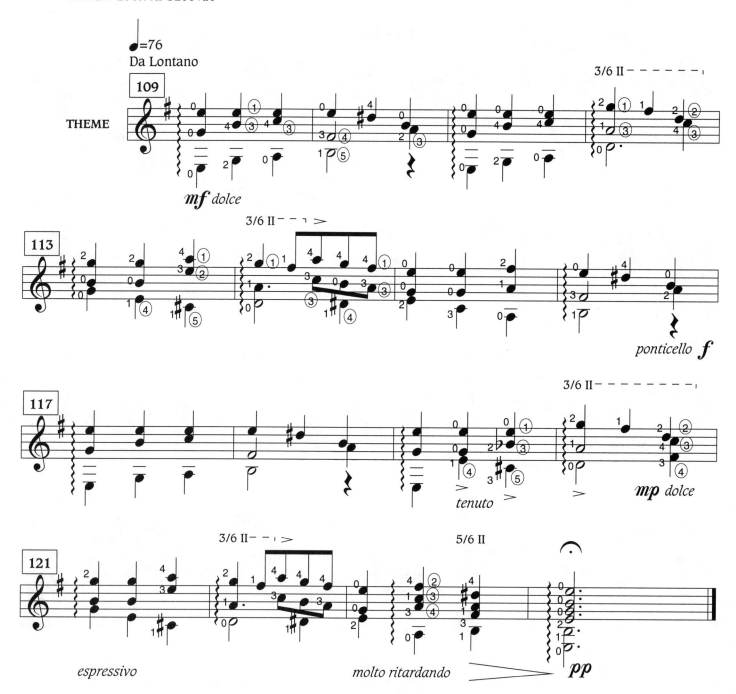

APPENDIX C

The following is an excerpt from the *Diccionario de Guitarristas* by Domingo Prat (1886-1944). The book was originally published in 1934.[1] This excerpt is important in that it presents significant information about Segovia. It proves that he was very well respected yet somewhat controversial even in the early part of his career.

Segovia Torres, Andrés. — Concert guitarist, distinguished in his artistic achievement, and a moderate composer. He was born in Linares on March 17, 1893; we refer to his baptismal certificate, which we quote: "Don Francisco Morales Aballes, parish priest of the church of St. Peter in this capital—Certified: that in volume 66, book 21 of the Baptismal records of the parish archives appears the following—Entry: in the city of Jaén, the 24 of March in the year 1893: I, Don Juan Garrido y Quesada, associate pastor of the same, solemnly baptized a baby boy, who, according to declarations given in appropriate form before me and the witnesses José Carpio and Miguel Moya, members of the parish, was born on the 17th of the present month at 6:30 in the afternoon at Corredera #94 in the city of Linares to Bonifacio Segobia y Montoro and Rosa Torres Cruz.—Paternal grandparents, Andrés and María Francisca: the father and paternal grandparents being natives of this city; the mother and maternal grandmother being from Málaga; the maternal grandfather being from Churriana. I christened him **Andrés;** Teresa Granadino, a single woman, was his godmother whom I advised of her spiritual relationship along with its obligations. In witness whereof I sign along with the reverend pastor. Signed—Juan Garrido. Signed—Don Romero. This is an exact copy of the original to which I refer. Jaén, the 31 of December, 1930. Given with the seal of the church of St. Peter of Jaén." I call attention to the fact that his baptism took place in the church at Jaén, and not in Linares where he was born, pointing out in the document that the paternal name is written with B, Segobia, even though he is known universally as SEGOVIA. A curious biographical detail and possibly an important one for the interested.

Even if we wanted to, we could add very little to all that has been written in praise of his exceptional artistry. Referring to Segovia, the famous violinist Kreisler declared: "Only two great musicians reside in the world, Casals and Segovia."

Not intending to stir up controversy in the musical world among its various branches but focusing only on the most accomplished instrumentalists, we can consider the name of Segovia as placed many steps higher in that temple of unending glory, together with others like Casals, Kreisler, etc.

Understanding the instrumental technique of the violin or cello can be a stepping stone to examining its place on the guitar. The union of three or more notes in a single sound (at the same time, that is a chord) creates a beauty similar to that obtained by the painter in the mixing of two or more colors; but it is reserved for the orchestra (the union of violin, cello, flute, etc.) or for the piano or for the guitar. The trills of the violin or the slides and vibrato of the cello, which by themselves seem quite incomplete, just as the emotional content is found in the totality of the work being listened to, would not create so perfect or so complete a sense of beauty if they did not have harmonic support upon which to play. The rose, bathed in the golden rays of a rising sun, is admired in the foreground of a beautiful scene. It contains within itself all the beauty of the scene, to such an extent that, when the scene is out of sight, we remember one thing only—the rose—such a thing of beauty! And thus we exclaim too when calling to mind a musical work, remembering the cadence of the violin or the vibrato of the cello. Yet rose, violin or cello, outside of its appropriate frame of reference, is like the sentence of a Shakespearean drama which, **without losing its intrinsic value,** has a very distinct emotional feel when considered apart from the drama to which it belongs.

Producing harmonic support or melody is what distinguishes the guitar from the violin or cello when taken as solo instruments. The guitar is a harmonically complete instrument on a plane of the highest delicacy, since in it converge the sounds of the harp, the chords of the piano, the basses of the orchestra, the slides of the violin, and the vibrato of the cello. The other instruments need support. The violin and the cello represent only the idea of the beauty of the rose, which in our case is the guitar—the rose, bathed in the morning sun and part of its beautiful surroundings. Such is the distinction between the guitar of Segovia and the cello of Casals or the violin of Kreisler. It should be noted that I make no pretense about establishing a model based on personal preference, but rather I do wish to set forth a working principle, the result of a fair analysis of instrumental values.

The personality of Segovia, known through the guitar and closely examined by the famous Kreisler, continues to intrigue us because of the process of his formation, his development, his evolution, and his performance which brought him to the pinnacle of success.

---

1. Domingo Prat, *Diccionario De Guitarristas,* Buenos Aires, Romero y Fernandez, 1934. This excerpt is taken from: Domingo Prat, *Dictionary of Guitarists, A Reprint Edition With an Introduction By Matanya Ophee,* Columbus, Editions Orphée, 1986. Reprinted with permission. English translation by Ken Hummer, 1995.

In Granada, even as a child, he played the guitar. But the revelation of the true musical possibilities of the instrument was given him by a friend and disciple of Tárrega, the ventriloquist and Valencian guitarist Paco Sanz, applauded in Buenos Aires in 1912. On one of Sanz's many tours through Spain, Segovia, finding himself in Andalusía, heard something of the repertoire of Tárrega through the person of the modest Sanz (according to facts reported by him); and so was produced the spark. Segovia questions, inquires, analyzes, studies, learns, and frees himself from a provincial attitude, distancing himself from the popular art forms of his region. And, as if under a spell, he begins to act in the manner that one newspaper article reported: "Segovia, that romantic concert artist, travels about from city to city and village to village bearing the pure light of art and poetry burning on the strings of his guitar, which our insensitive public does not appreciate." (Bulletin of the "Biblioteca Fortea" January, 1914).

He leaves for Madrid, passes through Valencia and arrives at Barcelona in 1915. He plays, struggles and triumphs. The guitar is unknown as a concert instrument for pay in Barcelona, but only in the salons of humble fans, full of their preferences, admirers of such and such a maestro. At the beginning everyone admires Segovia. They help him and applaud him; but, even though their appreciation banished the sorry state in which they lived, they neither recognized nor knew how to see in him an artist destined to belong to the world. With guitar in hand he conquered those who represented the fine arts and the sciences in that cultured city of Barcelona. Without fear of being misunderstood, we can assert that he won his "ticket" to fly through the musical universe in that city. In one of our visits to Barcelona in 1916, we met him, listened to him and befriended him. A group of admirers, among which there were many guitarists, offered him a supper at "Casa Juan," a type of modest Parisian tavern. There Segovia played. His resolve, self confidence, clarity and sonority in presenting his repertoire, well known to us, affirmed the predictions made of this prodigy: "This is the artist that the guitar needs."

He begins presenting one concert after another.

The impresarios, sharp-eyed as always, see in him a new means of making money. He travels to Argentina three times (always under contract), he passes through New York (the contractors dispute it), and he is applauded in London, Paris, Boston, Mexico, Berlin, Brussels, Saint Petersburg, Stockholm, Budapest, Rome, Vienna, and everywhere he is heralded as the greatest artist.

Segovia is the supreme psychologist when it comes to his public: that is one of the secrets of his success. In his concerts he enters deliberately, elegantly, without smiling: but rightly so. There is no stiffness in his movements, nor feigned presentation. Now seated, in front of his audience, right on schedule, he waits for total silence. When this is absolute, he begins to play, convinced that those present must sit quietly to listen, which after all, is why they came. During the performance, he demands a religious silence from his devoted listeners. The slightest noise disturbs him, and with a graceful gesture he asks that it not occur again, giving to understand that the one who caused it should leave. He ceases to play at whatever spot it occurs, if the noise continues to bother or distract him. This moral force and constant serenity dominate the masses, disposing them to feel all the beauty of his performance. He is the true actor who, trusting in himself, "speaks" as if he were in his own dwelling and at the appropriate time casts a questioning glance at the audience so that they, like he, may experience the joy or sadness that seizes him, according to the feeling of the piece he is interpreting. The fearful actor cannot bring these feelings to the public nor create the total artistic experience of that which he interprets; thus, the ill-at-ease guitarist will never succeed completely as a concert artist. Segovia, having freed himself from these fears, sure of himself, awaits with great longing the arrival of his concert dates and experiences even beforehand the joy of entering into contact with his public; a quality which, apart from its intrinsic value, has reaffirmed him time and again in all his successes. It is perfectly understandable that the nervousness of the guitarist who does not possess these qualities would cause many lapses of memory and a loss of technical control, which are indispensable for artistic success. And, if under these conditions one tries to redeem himself by sheer force of study or technical prowess, he will scarcely bring to the public the full satisfaction which comes from the joy of the conquest, receiving only half-hearted applause which is offered merely as alms. Segovia never needed such gifts; by his own merits he wins the applause which he demands. He knows that his guitar, his art and his personality have a fascination that wins an audience.

It is for this reason that, without schooling, without musical instruction, of humble birth and from unfavorable surroundings, but resolved and single-minded he moves on with a look of defiance, throwing up in the faces of those learned failures his celebrated statement: "I'm glad I never knew Tárrega; if I had known him, perhaps I would not be what I am today." It is this just and profound independence which reveals to us not only the concert artist, the musician, but also a man of confidence and strength of character. These exceptional qualities are what bewitched and attracted to the guitar many of the world's famous composers: Moreno-Torroba, C. Pedrell, Turina, Tansman, Cyril Scott, Samazueil, Ponce and others whose name is legion, obliging them to write for the guitar beautiful musical works, which shed light upon and honor both composer and performer, reaffirming the beauty of the instrument.

Segovia's recordings, while being of great value, lack the natural and positive beauty which is always impossible to record. In the sound, as well as in the color, there are subtleties which cannot be captured, just as in a photograph: since it is an approximation which establishes a way to approach something, emphasizing the imperfect and rendering the good unnatural. All the beauty of a lovely woman is incapable of being captured on film, just as the subtlety of Segovia's art exists on none of his recordings. A master in everything and continually surpassing himself, perhaps even he did not totally appreciate the great success achieved during his last visit to Buenos Aires in 1928. He arrived on June 30 and presented his first concert four days later. He offered nine more programs after that, two per week, performing likewise during the intervals in Montevideo and in some other province of the Republic. He departed for Europe on August 20, forgetting an announced concert which he had scheduled for that date with the largest musical society of Argentina.

Seven years separated his second from his last tour of Argentina. An almost total revision of his repertoire was an important factor in awakening the interest that produced the enthusiastic welcome he was accorded: as a beautiful and telling detail of his great success, we recall his seventh concert, which took place on August 8 (in the afternoon, just like all the others). At the same time and a short distance away, the distinguished pianist Rubinstein was presenting his fourth concert with a very appealing program. The six previous concerts of Segovia, even though they followed one another, gave rise to the following announcement at the ticket office: "Sold out." As regards the seventh concert, to which we are referring, which occurred on the same day and hour as that of Rubinstein, we expected that a guitar program would be at a distinct disadvantage. The piano concert, which took place at the Opera Theatre, played to a full house; but Segovia's was a success of unparalleled public response, a complete and total "sellout." The case in point, besides elevating the name of Segovia in a unique manner, speaks well of the high level of musical culture of the people of Buenos Aires and of the devotees of the guitar; even though others had presented like concerts with like instruments but did not achieve the success they dreamed of.

As regards Segovia the composer, we remember the following works: "Impromptu," "Three Preludes" and "Tonadilla" (Bib. Fortea). Their worth lies in the success they have achieved as didactic pieces, "Scales and Arpeggios." His fingering of the works which were written for him by the previously mentioned composers gives rise to an originality that deserves to be praised; also as regards special effects on the guitar if he does not surpass those already indicated that Juan Parga gave to us, he is at least on an equal plane. As regards those works, we consider it worthwhile to list the many errors he makes and the liberties he takes, not only when he fingers works of other composers but even in his own transcriptions. We will present various examples of these fingering errors, from the first to the most recent editions of the following publishers: "Orfeo Tracio," Madrid; "José B. Romero," Buenos Aires; "Sociedad Musical Daniel," Madrid; "Durand," Paris; and "Schott," Germany. These same errors, which we will now present, are found in his original works already cited, published before 1920. **"The Peasant's Song"** of Grieg. Edition "Orfeo Tracio." In the 5th measure, 4th beat, it is not possible to sustain the quarter note G of the chord, if one plays the portamento from E to C. The same error occurs in the 10th measure, 2nd beat, where it indicates to sustain a quarter note while one plays two eighth notes. From the transcriptions and fingerings which he left in Buenos Aires on his second visit, and which were published by Jóse B. Romero, in **"Vidalita,"** of J. Aguirre: 5th measure, it is not possible to sustain the half-note A for its written value.

"Leyenda," of Albéniz page 5, measures 3 and 4. C cannot be sustained for the value indicated.

"Sonatina," of Moreno Torroba, "Edición Musical Daniel," Madrid, 1924. The first chord cannot be quarter notes.

"Segovia," of Albert Roussel: Edition "A. Durand," 1925. In measure 9, we do not believe it necessary to indicate the 3rd beat in two ways, that is with the barre and without it.

"Serenade," of Gustave Samazeuilh, Editor "A. Durand," 1926. In the 9th staff, 2nd measure, it is not possible to sustain the G half-note of the first beat because of repeating the same G in the second half of the beat noted.

The following works apply to the publisher Schott:

"Nocturno," of Moreno Torroba, 1926: on the 5th staff, 2nd measure, the half-note E cannot be sustained. The 3rd measure of the same line is unplayable the way it is written.

"Prelude," of J. S. Bach, 1928: Measure 5; in other scores, the F, the last sixteenth note of the first beat, is G. The fingering of this measure is barely possible.

"Courante," of J. S. Bach, 1928: In the 2nd measure of the 5th staff, the fingering could be a printing error or fault of the transcriber.

"Sonata III," of Manuel M. Ponce: on page 3, 6th staff, 1st measure, it is impossible to make the barre 2. We admit this could be a printing error. But we find these same errors time and again in the works fingered by Segovia.

"Preludio," of Moreno Torroba, 1928: in measure 8 it is impossible to realize the B and E sixteenth notes, while sustaining the G# of the chord. On page 3, 4th staff, 2nd measure, the B cannot be dotted because of playing the F# at the 7th fret on the 2nd string.

"Mazurka," of Alexandre Tansman. Page 4, last line, 2nd measure. Impossible to play the initial chord with barre 9.

"Four Short Pieces," of César Franck. 6th measure: When playing the E on the 2nd string as indicated, it is impossible to sustain the quarter note B for its written value. 9th measure: playing the A on the first string as he indicates, the quarter notes B and E of the chord cannot be sustained.

"Lamento," of Carlos Pedrell: 8th measure. The dotted half-note A cannot be sustained, if the F is played on the 6th string. The following measure contains a similar mistake.

"Preludes" VII, of Manuel Ponce, 1930: 4th staff, 4th measure. This measure is a real disaster. It defies analysis.

"Fantasía-Sonata" of Juan Manén. This work consists of 87 lines. Nevertheless, in the 1st measure the 3rd half-note B cannot be sustained, because one must play the G#, the 3rd sixteenth note, with the 1st finger. There is a similar problem the last time in the same measure. We will go no further in reviewing this work because of its great length...

"Characteristic Pieces" of Moreno Torroba, 1931. **Preámbulo:** 4th staff, 1st measure. It is not possible to sustain the half-note A for its full value.

...**"Sonata,"** of Joaquín Turina, 1932: 4th staff, 2nd measure. This can only be played as written using barre 5. In the following measure the half-note E of the chord cannot be sustained because of having to slur the B flat.

"Variations on the 'Folias de España'" of Manuel Ponce. Variation I: The printing mistakes in the first eight measures are deplorable. Variation III: 4th measure. We believe that the second beat of the melody line ought to follow the same written form as the following two measures, referring to notes of the same name being tied.

"Variazioni (attraverso i secoli...)," of Mario Castelnuovo-Tedesco, 1933: 5th staff. The first two measures have a rather capricious fingering. And in the 2nd measure, in order to play the 2nd tied A, it is necessary to remove barre 2.

The **"Variations on a Theme of Mozart"** by Sor deserves its own paragraph. We know that they were published in Buenos Aires by the publisher Romero and Fernández in 1921(?). Years later, even though we don't know why, he had them published by Schott in Germany. There are some changes in these two editions; but the important thing is that in neither of the editions did Segovia let the **Introduction** of Fernando Sor appear. We don't know why Schott did this, especially since it had published the same work before, containing the **Introduction** but not revised by Segovia. In our personal archive we have "Variations on a Theme," printed by Hemgel, successor to Meissonnier, with the following title page: "Variations/Brillantes/sur un Air Favori de Mozart/de l'Opéra la Flute Enchantée/(O Cara Armonia)/Pour Guitarre Seule/ Executées par l'Auteur au Concert donné á l'Ecole Rte. de Musique/et dediées a son Frére/op. 9". Beyond a shadow of a doubt, it is the most complete of the editions. Another publication, also in our possession, from the publisher N. Simrock, was published in the cities of Bonn and Cologne with the number 2292 of the publishing house. These last three editions differ in the order and the tonality of the variations; but, nevertheless, all carry the **Introduction** of Sors, which should be respected, since we owe him this for giving us such a gem in the guitar repertoire.

Also, we deplore the lack of artistic integrity on Segovia's part, not only as regards the fingering of this work, but also as regards his execution on the recording. Besides the missing introduction, there are variations which he does not repeat; and this places a stain on the aura of Segovia the musician.

Never do we see in the recording of a Beethoven symphony or a work by Chopin this failure to repeat as indicated. We affirm that Beethoven, Chopin and Sor were equally great, and deserving of all consideration.

We will not continue with our analysis of this work, nor with listing his shortcomings. We have only made note of some errors, found by chance in some parts of the works transcribed or fingered by the great Segovia. We are doing this with him because we are analyzing the greatest guitarist. We would not do this with a mediocre talent, since there would be no interest in doing so.

Nevertheless, we give witness to the fact that in the humble works of Manjón, the blind guitarist, be they original works or transcriptions, there are no errors of this kind; possibly because he would have a competent musician review his music. We are of the opinion that Segovia would do well to do the same so as not to defraud the hopes of so many guitarists who look to the works that carry, for one reason or another, his name, for the respect it deserves, and for the good of the works of so many great composers, which are placed in his hands, because of his being considered rightly the guitar's greatest performer. Clearly if we dedicated ourselves to revising the works of Manjón or any other composer or transcriber, we would encounter problems of this type; but never with the frequency of the works on which Segovia has placed his personal seal.

Segovia Torres, Andrés—Concertista de guitarra, eximio en su más alta concepción y compositor modesto. Nació en Linares el 17 de Marzo de 1893; nos remitimos a su fe de bautismo, que copiamos: "Don Francisco Morales Aballes, Cura Párroco de la de San Pedro de esta capital—Certifica: Que al folio sesenta y seis, vuelta del libro veintiuno de Bautismos de este Archivo Parroquial aparece la siguiente—Partida: En la Ciudad de Jaén, a veinte y cuatro de Marzo del mil ochocientos noventa y tres: Yo Don Juan Garrido y Quesada, Cura Coadjutor de esta de San Pedro, con licencia del Párroco de la misma, bauticé solemnemente a un niño, que, según declaración prestada en debida forma ante mí y los testigos que tambien lo fueron en ésta José Carpio y Miguel Moya, dependiente de esta Iglesia; por la que dijo ser y llamarse Rosa Torres Cruz, madre del bautizado, nació el día diez y siete de los corrientes a las seis y media de la tarde en la Corredera No. 94 de la Ciudad de Linares, y residiendo en ésta accidentalmente, hijo—de Bonifacio Segobia y Montoro, y de Rosa Torres Cruz:—Abuelos paternos Andrés y María Francisca: naturales, el padre y abuelos paternos, de esta Ciudad; la madre y abuela materna, de Málaga; el materno, de Churriana. Le puse el nombre **Andrés**: fué su madrina Teresa Granadino, de estado soltera, a quien adverti el parentesco espiritual y sus obligaciones. Y para que conste lo firmo con el Rdo. Cura Párroco, Juan Garrido, rubricado, Dn. Romero—rubricado. Es copia literal del original a que me remito Jaén a treinta y uno de Diciembre de mil novecientos treinta. Hay un timbre de la Iglesia de San Pedro de Jaén." Llama la atención que esta su Fe de bautismo pertenezca a la iglesia de Jaén, y no a la de Linares donde ha nacido, haciendo presente que en el documento transcripto, en apellido paterno está escrito con B, o sea Segobia, siendo conocido para nosotros y universalmente por SEGOVIA. Curioso detalle de biografía y quizá dato importante para el interesado.

Poco o nada podriamos añadir, si lo pretendiéramos, al voluminoso tomo de albanzas de su arte excelso. El famoso violinista Kreisler, refiriéndose a Segovia, declaró: "Sólo existen dos grandes músicos en el mundo, Casals y Segovia".

Sin hurgar en el mundo musical por entre sus distintas ramas y enfocando solamente a instrumentalistas sublimes, el nombre de Segovia lo podemos considerar colocado muchos peldaños más arriba en ei templo de la gloria sin fin, junto a otros como Casals, Kreisler, etc.

A través del violoncello y del violín, repectivamente, el conocimiento de la técnica instrumental puede ser una plataforma donde se aquilate con exactitud el concepto de lo que se desarrolla en la guitarra. La reunión de tres o más notas en un solo sonido (en un solo tiempo, como es el acorde) da una belleza, equivalente a la que obtiene el pintor con la mezcla de dos o más colores, y que queda reservada para la orquesta (reunión de violín, violoncello, flauta, etc.), o para el piano y para la guitarra. Los trinos del violín o los arrastres y vibraciones del violoncello que, al destacarse, parecen por sí solos como el cuerpo emotivo en que radica el caudal de sentimiento de la partitura que se escucha, no darían una sensación de belleza tan acabada y tan perfecta, si no actuaran como sobre el telón de fondo que les forman los graves, y el resto de la parte armónica de la orquesta en que actúan como primeras figuras. La rosa que, iluminada por el dorado rayo de un sol naciente, admiramos en el primer plano de una verde frondosidad, concreta en si toda la emoción de la belleza del marco en que la vemos, hasta tal punto que, pasada la visión, de ella sólo recordamos una solo cosa—la flor— ¡¡qué hermosa!! Así exclamamos, recordando en la partitura, la cadencia del violín o el vibrar del violoncello; pero rosa, violín y violoncello, ya fuera de su marco propicio, son como la frase sacramental de una drama shakespearino, **que sin perder valor,** tiene muy distinta apreciación de sentimiento emotivo, según se la considere en relación al ambiente del drama a que pertenece.

Producir o ejecutar, en un grado sublime, ambiente y frase es la diferencia que existe entre la guitarra y el violín o el violoncello, considerados como instrumentos que actúen solos. La guitarra se basta a sí misma en un plano de suma delicadeza, ya que en ella convergen tonalidades de harpa, acordes de piano, graves de orquesta, arrastres de violín, vibraciones de violoncello. Los otros instrumentos necesitan de complementos. El violín y el violoncello representan sólo la concepción de la belleza de una flor, que en nuestro casa es la guitarra; la rosa, del dorado rayo de sol, y de la verde frondosidad. Tal es la apreciación entre la guitarra de Segovia, y el violoncello de Casals o el violín de Kreisler. Bien entendido que no he pretendido establecer parangón entre valores personales, sino dejar sentado un principio, producto de un equitativo análisis de los valores instrumentales.

Presentada la personalidad de Segovia a través de la guitarra y aquilatada por el famoso Kreisler no deja de ser altamente interesante el proceso de su formación, su gestación, su desenvolvimiento y su actuación hasta llegar al pináculo alcanzado.

Allá en Granada, desde muy niño, tocaba ya la guitarra del rasguido y las falcetas. La revelación del instrumento músico se la dió un amigo y discípulo de Tárrega, el ventrílocuo y guitarrista valenciano Paco Sanz, aplaudido en Buenos Aires por el año 1912. En una de las continuas giras por España de este ultimo artista, hallándose Segovia en Andalucia, oyó algo del repertorio de Tárrega a través del modesto Sanz (según datos aportados por éste): así se produjo la chispa. Segovia pregunta, indaga, analiza, estudia, aprende y se independiza de un ambiente provinciano, apartándose de un semiarte regional, y como por encanto empieza a actuar en la forma que nos dice un suelto de prensa que reproducimos: "Segovia, ese romántico concertista que, de ciudad en ciudad, de pueblo en pueblo, va llevando prendidas en las mágicas cuerdas de su guitarra ráfagas puras de arte y de poesía que este nuestro público insensibilizado, no aprecia en lo que vale" (Boletin de la "Biblioteca Fortea", Enero 1914).

Salta a Madrid, pasa a Valencia, llega a Barcelona en el año 1915. Se presenta, lucha y triunfa. La guitarra en concierto público y de pago no es conocida allí en Barcelona, y sí sólo en "capillitas" de aficionados humildes, cuajados de prejuicios, admiradores de tal o cual maestro. A Segovia al comienzo todos lo admiran, lo ayudan y lo aplauden; pero, aunque estas apreciaciones ahuyentaban el raquitismo en que vivían, no descubrieron o no supieron ver en él al artista que nacía para el mundo. Con la guitarra se conquistó lo más representativo de las bellas artes y de la ciencia en la culta ciudad barcelonesa; donde, sin miedo de equivocarnos, podríamos asegurar que ganó su "brevet" para volar por el universo musical. En una de nuestras visitas a Barcelona en al año 1916 conocimos, escuchamos y fuimos camaradas de Segovia. Un grupo de admiradores, etre los que había muchas guitarristas, le ofrecimos una cena en "Casa-Juan", especie de modesta taberna parisién. Allí Segovia tocó. Su decisión, seguridad, dicción, sonido y "posse", a medida que iba desgranando su repertorio, bien conocido por nosotros, afirmaban los felices augurios que el padre de quien suscribe había hecho de este portento: "Este es el artista que la guitarra necesita".

Empieza dando continuos conciertos.

Los empresarios, linces en la materia, ven en él un nuevo elemento para sus ganancias. Va a la Argentina tres veces (siempre con contrato), pasa a New York (los contratistas se lo disputan), es aplaudido en Londres, Paris, Boston, Méjico, Berlin, Bruselas, San Petersburgo, Estocolmo, Budapest, Roma, Viena y en donde quiera que se presenta es el mejor artista.

Segovia es psicólogo, por excelencia, respecto al público; tal es uno de los secretos de sus triunfos. En sus audiciones sale al proscenio pausado, gallardo, sin sonrisa; pero correcto. No hay dureza en sus movimientos, ni afectada presentación. Sentado ya, delante del auditorio, con tiempo prudencial lo invita al silencio; cuando éste es absoluto, da comienzo a su ejecución, convencido de que los presentes deben callar para oír, que es a lo que allí han ido. Dutante la audición, exige el religioso silencio de los devotos, el menor ruido le molesta, e invita con suave gesto a que no se repita, dando a entender que debe marcharse el que lo produce y deja de tocar en cualquier trozo de una obra, si el ruido insiste en molestar o distraer. Esta fuerza moral y continua serenidad dominan la masa, predisponiéndola a sentir toda la belleza de lo que ejecuta. Es el verdadero actor que, posesionado de si mismo, "habla" como en su propia casa y a su vez interroga al público con la mirada, para que, como él, se compenetre de la alegría o tristeza que le embarga, según el tema de lo que ejecuta. El actor con miedo al público no puede abstraerse y dar la completa sensación artistica de lo que interpreta: así el guitarrista intranquilo jamás puede presentarse como concertista completo. Segovia, exento de estos temores, seguro de sí mismo, anhela con toda el alma la llegada de la fecha de sus conciertos y experimenta de antemano el goce de entrar en contacto con el público: cualidad ésta que, aparte de todo su valor intrínseco, le ha reafirmado siempre en todos sus éxitos. Es perfectamente explicable que la nerviosidad del guitarrista que no posee estas condiciones, produzca en él turbación de memoria y ausencia de sutil tacto, tan indispensables para la conquista del triunfo. Y si en estas condiciones actúa salvándose por la fuerza de su entrañado estudio o capacidad ejecutoria, jamás brinda al público la satisfacción plena del placer de la conquista, obteniendo sólo complacientes aplausos que en el fondo son limosnas. Segovia jamás necesitó dádivas: por propio mérito conquista el aplauso, que casi exige; porque sabe que su guitarra, su arte y su personalidad tienen un valor dominante y fascinador.

Es por esto que, sin escuela, sin maestros músicos, de cuna muy humilde y de ambiente nada propicio, pero fuerte y único, se yergue con gesto de desafío, lanzando al rostro de los estudiosos fracasados su célebre frase: "Me silénto feliz de no haber conocido a Tárrega: pues, de haberlo conocido, quizá no sería lo que soy". Justo y profundo en esta independencia suya, que nos revela no sólo al concertista, al músico, sino al hombre certero y de viril carácter. Son sus condiciones excepcionales las que embrujaron y atrajeron a la guitarra a los sabios del pentagrama: Moreno Torroba, C. Pedrell, Turina, Tansman, Cyril Scott, Samazueil, Ponce y otros que forman legión, obligandoles a escribir para la guitarra bellas páginas musicales, en cuyas obras lucen y se honran compositor y ejecutante, reafirmándose con ello la belleza del instrumento.

Las impresiones en discos por Segovia, aun teniendo un alto valor, adolecen de la belleza natural y positiva que siempre escapa a la grabación. En el sonido, como en el color, hay sutilezas imposibles de encerrar en un disco como en una fotografía: ya que ésta es la copia aproximada de aquél, que establece siempre una plano de acercamiento que realza lo malo y desnaturaliza lo bueno. Toda la belleza de una mujer hermosa es de todo punto imposible condensarla en una fotografía como lo sutil del arte de Segovia no existe en ninguno de sus discos. Grande en todo y superándose a sí mismo continuamente, quizás él mismo, no apreció en todo su valor el gran éxito alcanzado en su última visita a Buenos Aires en 1928. Llega el 30 de Junio y da su primer concierto cuatro días después; ofrece nueve audiciones seguidas, dos por semana, actuando además en estos cortos intervalos en Montevideo y en alguna provincia de la República. Se embarca rumbo a Europa el 20 de Agosto, olvidando realizar un anunciado concierto que en esta fecha tenía con la asociación musical más grande de la República.

Siete años duró el intervalo de su segunda a la última turnée por la Argentina. Una renovación casi total de las obras de su repertorio fué factor de gran importancia para despertar el interés que produjo la entusiasta acogida que se le dispensó: como detalle hermoso y sugestivo de sus grandes éxitos, recordamos su séptimo concierto, realizado el 8 de Agosto (en la tarde, como todos los demás). A la misma hora y a unos metros de distancia, el eximio pianista Rubinstein daba su 4° concierto con programa atrayente. En los seis conciertos anteriores de Segovia, a pesar de ser seguidos, todos dieron ocasión a que en la boletería del teatro asomara el simpático cartelito "No hay más localidades"; en este 7.° a que nos referimos, que coincida en día y hora con el de Rubinstein, esperábamos como por duelo casual que la guitarra quedara en desventaja. El concierto del pianista, realizado en el teatro de la Opera, resultó un lleno completo; pero el de Segovia fué un éxito de público único, un "llenazo" completo y absoluto. El caso citado, además de realzar de una manera única la personalidad de Segovia, deja bien sentado el alto valor de la cultura musical del público de Buenos Aires y de los devotos que en él tiene la guitarra; suponiendo igualmente un sugestivo interrogante, para los que se presentaron tambiém con el mismo instrumento y no alcanzaron el éxito que soñaron.

A Segovia, como compositor, le recordamos las siguientes obras: "Impromptu", "Tres preludios" y "Tonadilla" (Bib. Fortea). El valor de éstas queda marcado con el éxito que ellas han alcanzado como didacta, "Escalas y Arpegios". El aporte personal de digitación en las obras que, para él escribieron los compositores anteriormente mencionados, da margen por su originalidad, a muy dignos elogios, así como también en los efectos de rasguido, tambora y otros más, que si no supera, a los ya marcados que nos legó Juan Parga, con ellos se equipara en un plano de valor. Creemos de conveniencia anotar, con respecto a estas obras, los muchos errores y distracciones en que incurre Segovia, no sólo cuando digita obras de otros compositores, sino también en sus transcripciones. Daremos varios ejemplos de estas faltas de digitación, desde las primeras a las últimas ediciones en las casas "Orfeo Tracio", Madrid; "José B. Romero", Buenos Aires; "Sociedad Musical Daniel", Madrid; "Durand", Paris y "Schott", Alemania. Estos mismos errores que presentaremos a continuación, se ven en la producción original ya citada de este concertista, publicada antes del año 1920. **"Canto del Campesino"**, de Grieg. Edición "Orfeo Tracio". En el 5.° compás, 4.° tiempo, no es posible sostener el SOL negra del acorde, si se hace el portamento del MI al DO. La misma falta se repite en el compás 10.°, segundo tiempo, que ordena sostener negra, mientras que se tocan dos corcheas. De la producción de transcripciones y digitaciones que dejó en Buenos Aires, en su segunda visita, y que publicó la casa José B. Romero, en **"Vidalita"**, de J. Aguirre: compás 5.° no es posible sostemer el LA, blanca, en todo su valor.

"Leyenda", de Albéniz pág. 5, compás 3.° y 4.° No se puede sostener el valor del DO, como está indicado.

"Sonatina", de Moreno Torroba, "Edición Musical Daniel". Madrid, año 1924. El ler. acorde inicial, no puede ser negra.

"Segovia", de Albert Roussel: Edición "A. Durand", año 1925. En el compás 9.° no creemos necesario indicar el 3er. tiempo de 2 formas, es decir, con cejilla y sin ella.

"Sérénade", de Gustave Samazeuilh. Editor "A. Durand", año 1926. En el pentagrama 9.°, compás 2.°, no es posible sostener el SOL blanca del ler. tiempo, por repetirse el mismo SOL, en la 2.ª mitad del tiempo citado.

Las obras que nombraremos a continuación pertenecen a la editorial Schott:

"Nocturno", de Moreno Torroba, año 1926: En el 5° pentagrama, 2° compás, no se puede sostenter el MI blanca. El 3er compás del mismo pentagrama es irrealizable como está escrito.

"Prelude", de J. S. Bach, año 1928: 5° compás. En otros textos, el FA, última semicorchea del 1 er. tiempo, es SOL. La digitación de este compás está al margen de lo posible.

"Courante", de J. S. Bach, año 1928: En el 2 ° compás del 5° pentagrama, la digitación de la mano izquierda, puede ser error de imprenta, o del transcriptor.

"Sonata III", de Manuel M. Ponce: en la página 3°, 6° pentagrama, 1 er. compás, imposible hacer cejilla 2. Admitimos que puede ser error de imprenta. Pero estos mismos errores los encontramos muchas veces en obras digitadas por Segovia.

"Preludio", de Moreno Torroba, año 1928: En el 8° compás es imposible realizer el SI y el MI semicorcheas, sosteniendo el SOL sostenido del acorde. En la página 3°, 4° pentagrama, 2° compás, el SI no puede llevar puntillo, por tener que hacer el FA sostenido en el 7° casillero de la 2ª cuerda.

"Mazurka", de Alexandre Tansman. Página 4ª, último pentagrama, 2° compás. Imposible efectuar el acorde inicial con ceja 9.

"Cuatro piezas breves", de César Frank. 6° compás: Haciendo el MI en la 2ª cuerda, como está indicado, imposible sostener un tiempo entero el SI negra. Compás 9°. Haciendo el LA en la prima, como indica, no puede sostenerse el SI MI negra del acorde.

"Lamento", de Carlos Pedrell: 8° compás. No se puede sostener el LA, blanca con puntillo, si se tiene que hacer el FA de la 6ª cuerda. El compás siguiente muestra un error semejante.

"Preludes" VII, de Manuel Ponce, año 1930: 4° pentagrama, 4° compás. Este compás es realmente desastroso. Imposible de analizar.

"Fantasía-Sonata", de Juan Manén. Esta obra consta de 87 pentagramas. Sin embargo, en el 1er. compás el 3er. SI blanca no puede sostenerse, porque hay que hacer el SOL sostenido, 3ª semicorchea, con dedo 1. Un defecto semejante hay en el último tiempo del mismo compás. No continuamos la revisación de esta fantasía por ser demasiado extensa...

"Piéces caracteristiques", de Moreno Torroba, año 1931. **Preámbulo:** 4° pentagrama, 1 er. compás. No es posible sostener el LA blanca durante todo su valor, como está indicado.

...**"Sonata"**, de Joaquín Turina, año 1932: 4° pentagrama, 2° compás. Solamente se podría ejecutar como está escrito, haciendo ceja 5ª. En el compás siguiente no puede sostenerse el MI blanca del acorde por tener que ligar el SI bemol.

"Variations sur "Folia de España", de Manuel Ponce. Variación I. Son deplorables las faltas de escritura en los ocho primeros compases. Variación III, 4° compás: Creemos que en el 2° tiempo, parte **cantábil**, debería seguir la misma forma de escritura de los dos compases siguientes, en lo que se refiere a las notas del mismo nombre ligadas.

"Variazioni (attraverso i secoli...)", de Mario Castelnuovo-Tedesco, año 1933: 5° pentagrama. Los dos primeros compases tienen una digitación un poco caprichosa. Y en el 2° compás, para poder efectuar el 2° LA ligado, es necesario quitar la cejilla II.

Las **"Variaciones sobre un tema"**, de Mozart-Sor, merecen un párrafo aparte. Sabemos que fueron publicados por Segovia en Buenos Aires, en la casa Romero y Fernández, en 1921(?). Años mas tarde, aunque no sabemos el porqué, las imprimió en la casa Schott, de Alemania. Hay algunos cambios en estas dos ediciones; pero lo importante es que en ninguna de las nombradas Segovia hizo constar la **Introducción** de Fernando Sor. No comprendemos porqué ha hecho ésto la casa Schott, cuando ella misma ha publicado antes la misma obra, con la **Introducción**, aunque no revisada por Segovia. En nuestro archivo particular tenemos las "Variaciones sobre un tema", impresas en la editorial Hengel, sucesor de Meissonnier, con la siguiente portada: "Variations/Brillantes/sur an Air Favori de Mozart/de l'Opera la Fl^ute Enchantée/(O Cara Armonia)/Pour Guitarre Seule/Execatées par l'Auteur au Concert donné á l'Ecole Rte. de Musique/et dediées a son Frére/op. 9°. Es, sin duda alguna, la más completa de las ediciones. Otra publicación, también en nuestro poder, de la casa N. Simrock, fué publicada en las ciudádes de Bonn y Cologne, con el número 2292 de la editorial. Estas tres últimas ediciones nombradas difieren en el orden de colocación y en la totalidad de las variaciones; pero, no obstante, todas llevan la **Introducción** de Sors, que se debe respetar, pues a él debemos esta belleza guitarrística.

También deploramos la falta de seriedad artística de Segovia, no sólo en lo que se refiere a la digitación de la obra que nos ocupa, sino también con respecto a su ejecución en el disco. Además de faltar en éste la introducción, hay variaciones que no se repiten, y ésto pone un borrón sobre la aureola del Segovia musico.

Nunca veremos en la impresión fonográfica de una Sinfonía de Beethoven o una obra de Chopin, la falta de repeticiones en alguna de sus partes, sino que se ejecutan tal cual fueron escritas originalmente. Nosotros afirmamos que Beethoven, Chopin y Sor fueron igualmente grandes y, por lo tanto, dignos de toda consideración.

No continuamos el análisis de esta obra, ni la enunciación de las fallas en sus trabajos. Solamente hemos hecho notar algunos errores, tomados al azar, de una parte de las obras, transcriptas o digitadas por el gran Segovia. Lo hacemos con él, por tratarse del guitarrista cumbre. No lo haríamos con una mediocridad guitarristica, porque no hay interés en ello.

No obstante, dejamos constancia de que en la humilde producción original o transcripta de Manjón, el guitarrista ciego, no hay errores de esa clase: tal vez porque haría revisar por una persona competente sus músicas. Opinamos que Segovia debería hacer lo mismo, para no defraudar las esperanzas de tantos guitarristas que acuden a las obras que llevan, por una u otra causa, su nombre, por el respeto que éste merece, y para bien de las obras de tantos grandes compositores, que a él se entregan, por considerarlo, con razón, el mejor ejecutante. Ciaro, que si nos dedicáramos con empeño a revisar a conciencia las obras de Manjón y las de cualquier otro compositor o transcriptor, encontraríamos faltas de esa clasa; pero nunca con la frecuencia de las que contienen las obras donde Segovia he puesto su sello personal.

APPENDIX D

The following are two reviews of a concert given by Segovia in Chicago, Illinois, in 1949.

GUITARIST'S SKILL CHARMS CRITIC[2]

By the end of his first selection, Andrés Segovia had won the admiration of the overflow audience in Mandel Hall Friday night. One cannot fail to be entranced by the amazing effects which the Spanish guitarist is able to draw from his instrument. Segovia affords an example of an extremely rare musical phenomenon, a musician who has attained complete mastery over his chosen instrument. The changes of tone color, delicacy of dynamics, almost vocal tone and remarkable finesse which characterize his playing have to be heard to be believed.

His program, by and large happily chosen, was invariably interesting. To no one's surprise, the music originally written for the guitar or for a similar instrument produced the best effect. The pavanes by Don Luis Milan which opened the program were almost too good to be true. The same can be said for the lute Gailliards by John Dowland, and the guitar suite by the obscure de Viseo.

Chaconne Better for Violin

The transcriptions, which made up the major portion of the program, were performed in such a persuasive manner that their occasional incompatibility with the guitar was all but obscured. It is granted that it is interesting to hear the famous solo violin *Chaconne* of Bach played on the guitar. Nonetheless, this writer does not wish to seem a purist when he says he vastly prefers to hear it played on the instrument for which it was written. It was also with the *Chaconne* that certain irregularities of rhythm and a tendency to sentimentalize manifested themselves.

Segovia is Legendary

One cannot, however avoid feeling petty about making unflattering comments on such a performance. Andrés Segovia is a performer of almost legendary quality. Take him for all in all, it may be years before we look upon his like again.

SEGOVIA'S GUITAR IGNORES OWN LAND FOR EARLY CLASSICISTS[3]

Andrés Segovia does not have to demonstrate, at this late date, that the Spanish guitar breathes the musical spirit of his people. But his use of the git-box as a contrapuntal instrument attuned to the classics still possesses some feeling of the miraculous to North American ears which seldom hear it as anything but an accompanist for voice.

At Mandel Hall Friday night, in the University of Chicago's subscription series, Segovia chose to ignore the Spanish composers and turn his amazing technique to music (very little of it originally written for guitar) by Sixteenth, Seventeenth and Eighteenth Century composers of Italy, Germany, England and France. There was none of the Albéniz, Granados and de Falla which gave a flavor of Spain to so many of his programs.

There were three pavanas written for the vihuela (the Spanish lute) four hundred years ago by Luis Milan, and there was a theme with flowing variations of wonderfully soft tone by Fernando Sor, great Spanish guitarist of the early Nineteenth Century.

Frequently, the music written especially for his instrument is the weakest part of a Segovia program, and the Milan may have been inferior, at that, but on this occasion the works transcribed for guitar did not, for all their merit, completely dominate the concert.

The harmonic variety to be found in Bach and Rameau, the two Scarlattis, Frescobaldi and Haydn, is not too much for the ingenuity or the artistry of this genius. His guitar is a small-voiced thing, delicate and intimate, that demands attention on the part of the listener, but it possesses such clarity, and at the same time with such incredible wealth of color, that despite its smallness of scale it speaks with a directness that is almost human. It's a pity more humans don't have the dignity and self respect and intelligence that guitar possesses.

2. James Goldmon, "Guitarist's Skill Charms Critic," presented in the *Chicago Maroon*, January 24, 1949. Reprinted with permission.

3. William Leonard, "Segovia's Guitar Ignores Own Land For Early Classicists," presented in the *Journal of Commerce*, January 24, 1949. Reprinted with permission.

APPENDIX E

A STELLAR PERFORMANCE BY SEGOVIA[4]

Does Andrés Segovia deserve a press card?

Wednesday night at Orchestra Hall, after performing a recital filled with dazzling examples of his unique artistry, the 94-year-old Adam of the classical guitar scooped the scribes by giving an extemporaneous, highly unfavorable review of his own performance.

"I do not deserve your applause," Segovia told the audience, "because of my difficulty of playing. I am sorry. But I will come back next year, if I am living, and give a benefit recital for any charity in this town."

Gail Rector, Orchestra Hall's artistic programming consultant, said that Segovia told him afterward he wants the benefit to be for Orchestra Hall.

So how does Segovia stack up as a music critic?

Not very well. Granted, there were times—the initial measures of the Bach Fugue that opened the program's second half, the second phrase of the Haydn Allegretto—where things went awry for a measure or two.

In fact, Rector said, Segovia was distracted by three irritants. A pesky cough interrupted his concentration several times. (When he first coughed, he apologized to the audience before resuming his performance.)

In addition, one of Segovia's fingernails had not grown back to the proper length for strumming and plucking his instrument. And he was also thrown off by a warp in the fingerboard of his Ramirez guitar.

Such distractions are not offered as excuses, because no excuses are needed. The 2,373 people who heard Segovia (which included, in addition to the 2,133 regular seats, 100 onstage seats, 60 pit seats, 30 extra seats set up in the loge and 50 standing room places) heard a stellar performance by a master artist.

In most of his playing, the variety of tonal colors, the clean separation of polyphonic lines and the logical spinning out of phrases emerged intact. Half of the pieces on the program were transcribed by Segovia for his instrument. One of them, Albéniz' Capricho Catalan, was so exquisitely played several audience members in divergent parts of the hall stood up spontaneously in tribute—a rare occurrence these days.

There were many moments to cherish. Among them: the simplicity of the set of variations by Frescobaldi, the impish quality of Tárrega's Little Study, and the eloquent elegance of the Gavotte by Bach, whose music, Segovia said at Tuesday's press conference, "like the moon and the planets, will be forever."

This concert marks the first under Gail Rector's aegis, and it bodes well for the hall's renaissance as a home not only for the Detroit Symphony but for the finest of the world's soloists and ensembles. Wednesday's audience included most of the luminaries of Detroit's classical crowd, and, according to Orchestra Hall box office spokespersons, a goodly number of first-time visitors.

Rector will announce next season's series in May. It will include visiting European orchestras as well as groups from the Orient, including Japan's famous Kodo Drummer. "Segovia showed us how effective pianissimos can be in Orchestra Hall," Rector quipped. "The Kodo Drummers will do the same for fortissimos."

As for Segovia, he showed up at the St. Regis Hotel for a post-concert reception. He ate, conversed and stayed until the party broke up at 12:30 a.m.

Segovia came to the reception a bit late, Rector said. Was he tired out? Discouraged? Vexed with his performance?

No. Rector said he had to call his wife in Madrid.

---

4. John Guinn, "A Stellar Performance by Segovia," presented in the *Detroit Free Press*, March 27, 1987. Reprinted with permission.

APPENDIX F

GUITAR MASTER SEGOVIA DIES IN SPAIN AT 94[5]

Andrés Segovia, the gentle Spanish maestro who single-handedly brought the classical guitar into the mainstream of the world's musical life, is dead at 94.

Segovia was a frequent visitor to Ann Arbor and Detroit in a career that spanned 71 years. He last played here in March, at Orchestra Hall.

It was during that recital that Segovia, troubled by a recurrent heavy cough that caused him to interrupt his playing several times, finally stopped and told the audience in a faint voice: "I do not deserve your applause because of my difficulty of playing. I am sorry. But I will come back next year, if I am living, and give a benefit recital for any charity in this town."

The audience responded with even more applause.

Several weeks after that appearance, Segovia was hospitalized in New York for cardiac irregularities, and had to cancel a Carnegie Hall recital. Upon his release from the hospital, he returned to Spain for what was to be the last time.

Dr. Angel Castillo said Wednesday that the renowned guitarist died Tuesday afternoon in his Madrid home while watching television with his third wife, Emilita, 50, and their son, Carlos Andrés, 16.

"He was sitting comfortably in an easy chair when he slumped over," Castillo said. "It was a quick and peaceful death."

Castillo, who said he arrived minutes after Segovia's death, said the cause was "a heart attack brought on by a lung edema."

Segovia often said he would continue playing "as long as the audiences come." At a press conference the day before his Orchestra Hall recital, he spoke out against forced retirement.

"If an older person is healthy and in full possession of his mind and feelings, he should not be forced to retire," he said. "He has something a young man doesn't have—experience. And he should be allowed to use it."

Segovia was born in the southern Spanish town of Linares on Feb. 21, 1893. He improvised on the guitar as a child and began violin lessons at the age of six. He abandoned the violin, he said, because his teacher had a terrible tone and a terrible sense of pitch and "pinched me whenever I played a bad note."

Soon afterward he turned to the guitar, which he taught himself. "I was my own pupil and my own maestro," he once told an interviewer. "We have traveled all through life without a single quarrel."

He gave his first public guitar recital in Granada at the age of 14.

He once compared the guitar to "a small orchestra seen through the wrong end of a pair of binoculars." He said he agreed with composer Igor Stravinsky's observation: "The guitar does not play loud, but far."

Segovia criss-crossed the world performing concerts. He already had spent four years touring South America when he gave his first Paris recital on April 7, 1924. That recital is considered to have spawned his international reputation.

He made his U.S. debut at a sold-out recital in New York's Town Hall on Jan. 13, 1928. It was the first recital given in this country by a classical guitarist.

Segovia transcribed for the guitar more than 200 works originally conceived for other instruments. He also commissioned compositions from most of the world's major composers.

Segovia made numerous recordings, many of them bestsellers.

He lived in New York during the 1936-39 Spanish Civil War and did not return to Spain until 1952. "I am interested in the welfare of my country," he said at the time, "but without mixing in politics."

When he reached his late 70's he limited his public appearances, but still performed about 60 concerts a year. In the spring of 1986 he toured the United States, followed by a tour of Japan in the Fall of the year. His final U.S. appearances took place this Spring.

In 1980, Segovia told an interviewer he felt he had fulfilled the four tasks he had set for himself at the beginning of his career: "to redeem the guitar from its flamenco associations, to develop a real musical repertoire for it, to travel to all civilized countries and play there in order to gain a following for it, and to influence conservatories to take the guitar into their curriculum at the same dignified level as the piano, the violin, the cello or the voice."

He kept a house in Andalusia and an apartment in Geneva, but spent most of his time at a apartment in Madrid with a studio where he practiced daily.

In 1961 he married his third wife, Emilia Corral, a former pupil. Nine years later, when he was 77, his son Carlos

---

5. John Guinn, "Guitar Master Segovia Dies in Spain at 94," presented in the *Detroit Free Press*, June 4, 1987. Reprinted with permission.

Andrés was born.

Segovia married Paquita Madriguera, a Spanish pianist, in 1920. They had two children, Andrés Segovia, 60, a painter who lives in Switzerland, and a second son, Leonardo, who died in a power line accident at age 13.

After Madriguera's death, he married Olga Coelho, of Portuguese-Brazilian background, in 1935. They had a daughter, Beatrice, who died in Guatemala at age 28 of a lung disease.[6]

Segovia's body will lie in state today in Spain's Royal Academy of Fine Arts. A mass will be said before burial in Madrid's San Isidro Cemetery.

---

6. Segovia had three wives: 1.) Adelaida Portillo, 2.) Paquita Madriguera, 3.) Emilia Corral. Beatriz was a daughter from his marriage to Paquita. Segovia never married Olga Coelho, but he did father a child with her and this is evidently the source of some confusion as seen above.